AF632997

French Poetry in the Nineteenth Century

THE ANCIENT THEATRE.

Miniature from the *Térence*, of CHARLES VI, M.S. executed at the beginning of the XVth century. No. 25. B.L.L. Arsenal Library, Paris.

French Poetry in the Nineteenth Century

Ferdinand Brunetiere

ANMOL PUBLICATIONS

Published by :

ANMOL PUBLICATIONS
4378/4B, Gali Murarilal
Ansari Road, New Delhi-110002
Phone 261597

French Poetry in the Nineteenth Century
Reprinted , *1990*
ISBN 81 7041 332 X

Printed at :
MEHRA OFFSET PRESS
1979, Chandni Mahal
DELHI-110006
Phone No. 268574

TABLE OF CONTENTS.

		PAGE
French Poetry in the Nineteenth Century	*F. Brunetière*	(Introduction)
Sonnets	*Richard Garnett*	1
The Dyer's Story	*William B. Hockley*	3
The Destruction of Sennacherib	*Lord Byron*	23
Hymn of Apollo	*Percy Bysshe Shelley*	24
Homer's Hymn to the Moon	*Trans. by P. B. Shelley*	25
Napoleon's Sangaree	*Richard Garnett*	26
To a Mouse	*Robert Burns*	29
Street Music	*Hugh Reginald Haweis*	31
The Wind in a Frolic	*William Howitt*	46
Charles Auchester	*Elizabeth Sara Sheppard*	48
The Cane-bottomed Chair	*Wm. Makepeace Thackeray*	72
The Fisher Lassie	*Björnstjerne Björnson*	74
Bingen on the Rhine	*Caroline Norton*	89
The Death of the Prince Imperial	*Archibald Forbes*	91
Death's Valley	*Walt Whitman*	104
From "Beauchamp's Career"	*George Meredith*	104
The Warfare of Life	*Owen Meredith*	124
From "The Stickit Minister"	*Samuel R. Crockett*	126
On Being Hard Up	*Jerome K. Jerome*	141
An Ancient Mariner	*Pierre Loti*	146
Died at Sea	*François Coppée*	165
Lotus Farm	*Frédéric Mistral*	167
Morality Independent of Utility	*Wm. Edward Hartpole Lecky*	174
The Last Journey to Jerusalem	*Ernest Renan*	184
Mother Country	*Christina G. Rossetti*	193
The Heart	*Jean Macé*	195
The Investigation of Life	*Thomas H. Huxley*	201
The Petrified Fern	*Mary L. B. Branch*	213
Checks to the Increase of Genius	*Francis Galton*	214
The Tombs of the Kings	*Mathilde Blind*	219
Jiujutsu	*Lafcadio Hearn*	223
Lines on Leaving Italy	*Adam Gottlob Oehlenschläger*	229
Canadian Absolutism	*Francis Parkman*	230
North and South	*Nora Perry*	235
Nihilist Circles in Russia	*Georg Brandes*	238
Liberty	*William Lloyd Garrison*	

		PAGE
Camille and Armand	*Alexandre Dumas, Fils*	248
Flowers of Evil	*Charles Baudelaire*	248
April Hopes	*William Dean Howells*	259
The Sightless	*Maurice Maeterlinck*	260
Light	*Francis W. Bourdillon*	271
How Brichanteau Almost Saved the Emperor	*Jules Claretie*	293
The Lost Lamb	*Richard Henry Stoddard*	293
The Auction	*Christine C. Brush*	315
The Poker Party	*Mary N. Murfree*	316
Too Late	*Fitz-Hugh Ludlow*	325
The Brothers	*Émile Gaboriau*	341
The Veteran	*Stephen Crane*	343
A Northern Vigil	*Bliss Carman*	362
Woodcutting	*André Theuriet*	367
Roses	*Louise Chandler Moulton*	370
At Tintern Abbey	*Louise Chandler Moulton*	377
The Washerwoman	*Blanche Willis Howard*	377
Spinning	*Helen Hunt Jackson*	378
The Romance of Certain Old Clothes	*Henry James*	388
Evening Primroses	*Helen Gray Cone*	389
The Puppy: A Portrait	*Louise Imogen Guiney*	408
George Borrow and the Publisher	*George Borrow*	409
A Ballad of London	*Richard Le Gallienne*	412
A Man of Great Projects	*Ivan Sergyevich Turgenief*	422
To-morrow	*Philip Bourke Marston*	424
Death of Barnier	*E. and J. de Goncourt*	436
Forgotten Airs	*Paul Verlaine*	436
The Bowden Reunion	*Sarah O. Jewett*	444
Prescience	*Thomas Bailey Aldrich*	445
The Adventures of a Fourth	*Thomas Bailey Aldrich*	456
Baby Bell	*Thomas Bailey Aldrich*	457
Monsieur Viple's Brother	*Paul Bourget*	464
On Hell-fer-Sartain Creek	*John Fox, Jr.*	467
Stories of Uncle Remus	*Joel Chandler Harris*	468
To Pépa	*Alfred de Musset*	477
What the Swallows Say	*Théophile Gautier*	485
		487

LIST OF ILLUSTRATIONS.

	PAGE
An Ancient Theatre	*Frontispiece*
Ferdinand Brunetière	*face p.* xi
F. Brunetière in his Study	*p.* xx *in Introduction*
Rev. H. R. Haweis	32
Westminster Abbey	68
"Aulestad," the Home of Björnstjerne Björnson in Norway	82
Bingen on the Rhine	90
Walt Whitman	104
The Home of George Meredith, Flint Cottage and "The Chalet," Box Hill, Surrey	110
Owen Meredith	124
Samuel Rutherford Crockett	126
Brest	148
Pierre Loti in his Study	154
François Coppée in his Study	166
Trinity College, Dublin	176
Ernest Renan in his Study	184
Thomas Henry Huxley	202
Great Temple of Karnak	222
Francis Parkman	230
Alexandre Dumas, Fils	248
Dumas Fils in his Study	252
Camille	256
William Dean Howells	262
Napoleon III.	294
Helen Hunt Jackson	388
Henry James' House at Rye	394
Henry James in his Study	404
Edmund de Goncourt in his Study	436
Thomas Bailey Aldrich	458
Paul Bourget in his Study	468

INTRODUCTION

"FRENCH POETRY IN THE NINETEENTH CENTURY"

BY

FERDINAND BRUNETIÈRE
Editor of the "Revue des Deux Mondes," Paris
Author of "History of French Literature," &c., &c.

Discount [illegible]. One of the [illegible] of the country, [illegible] the money market, [illegible] of last resort [illegible] either by re-discounting [illegible] a bank [illegible] than base rate with [illegible] 1998 [illegible] in the case [illegible]

[illegible]

Discount [illegible]. [illegible] should [illegible] money [illegible] house.)

Discounting [illegible]. Historically [illegible] discount houses, [illegible] known as [illegible] Overnight Advances [illegible] required for [illegible]

Discount [illegible]. A [illegible] bill [illegible] a bank [illegible]

$$\frac{[illegible] \times \text{Face Value}}{\text{Yield} \times \text{Days to [illegible]}}$$

[illegible] formula face value [illegible] governed by two [illegible] to maturity.

Discovery [illegible]. [illegible] insurance [illegible]

LA POÉSIE FRANÇAISE DU XIXe SIÈCLE

PAR FERDINAND BRUNETIÈRE

SI l'on en voulait croire la plupart des historiens du romantisme, et quelques-uns des romantiques eux-mêmes,—Sainte-Beuve, par exemple, ou Théodore de Banville,—c'est avec et par André Chénier que commencerait en France la poésie du dix-neuvième siècle. On ne saurait se tromper davantage. Grand poète et surtout grand artiste, à la manière de Racine ou de Ronsard, il est bien vrai que ces deux traits séparent et distinguent profondément André Chénier de tous les versificateurs de son temps, Lebrun, Delille, et ce Roucher, qu'on lui associe d'ordinaire, parce qu'ils montèrent tous deux le même jour sur l'échafaud, ou encore le chevalier de Parny. Mais d'ailleurs, il n'a rien d'un "romantique"; et de même que l'élégante et ardente sensualité de son siècle respire dans ses *Élégies*, c'est encore un "classique," c'est un contemporain de Ronsard, c'est un païen, c'est un Alexandrin, c'est un élève de Callimaque et de Théocrite, qu'on retrouve dans ses *Idylles*. Nous ajouterons que ses *Poésies*, dont on n'a connu pendant plus de vingt-cinq ans que des fragments épars, n'ont vu le jour pour la première fois qu'en 1819; et on pourrait bien signaler quelque trace de leur influence dans les premiers *Poèmes* d'Alfred de Vigny, qui parurent en 1822, mais on en chercherait en vain dans les premières *Odes* de Victor Hugo, qui sont de 1822, elles aussi, ou dans les *Premières Méditations* de Lamartine, qui sont datées de 1820.

En réalité, c'est l'inspiration de deux grands prosateurs et d'une femme de génie qu'on rencontre quand on remonte aux origines de la poésie française au dix-neuvième siècle : l'auteur des *Confessions*, Jean-Jacques Rousseau ; celui du *Génie du Christianisme*, Chateaubriand ; et l'auteur trop souvent et injustement oublié du livre *De l'Allemagne*, Mme de Staël. Le premier avait émancipé le Moi de la longue contrainte où l'avaient comme emprisonné, deux siècles durant, des habitudes littéraires fondées sur une conception essentiellement *sociale* de la littérature. Ni les Salons ni la Cour, qui faisaient et qui défaisaient alors les réputations, n'avaient admis, pendant deux cents ans, que l'on écrivît pour les entretenir de soi-même, de ses " affaires de cœur," ou de famille. La permission n'en était donnée qu'aux auteurs de *Mémoires* ou de *Correspondances*, et à la condition d'être préalablement morts. J.-J. Rousseau, dont l'œuvre entière n'est qu'une confidence à peine dissimulée, vint changer tout cela, et ainsi rouvrir, de toutes les sources de la grande poésie, non pas peut-être la plus abondante, ni toujours, on le verra, la plus pure, mais, en tout cas, l'une des principales et des plus profondément cachées. Chateaubriand fit davantage encore. Voyageur,—il rendit à une littérature devenue trop mondaine le sentiment de cette nature extérieure, mouvante, vivante et colorée, qu'elle avait, non pas précisément ignorée ni méconnue, dont elle avait même joui à Versailles ou à Fontainebleau, dans ses jardins à la française, mais qu'elle avait systématiquement subordonnée à l'observation de l'homme psychologique et moral. Historien,—il rendit à ses contemporains le sentiment de la diversité des époques : ils apprirent de lui combien un homme diffère d'un autre homme, un baron féodal d'un courtisan de Louis XV. Et chrétien, enfin,—il rendit à l'art ce sentiment religieux dont l'absence n'avait sans doute pas contribué médiocrement à la parfaite clarté, mais à la sécheresse et au prosaïsme aussi de nos poètes du dix-huitième siècle. Le dernier pas fut fait par Mme de Staël. Les modèles qui manquaient à nos poètes, elle les leur proposa dans les *Littératures du Nord*. Ou plutôt, et d'une manière plus générale, car on ne saurait dire que Lamartine, Hugo ni Vigny aient beaucoup imité Goethe ou Byron, elle élargit le champ de l'imagination française en nous ouvrant, par delà nos frontières, des horizons inexplorés.

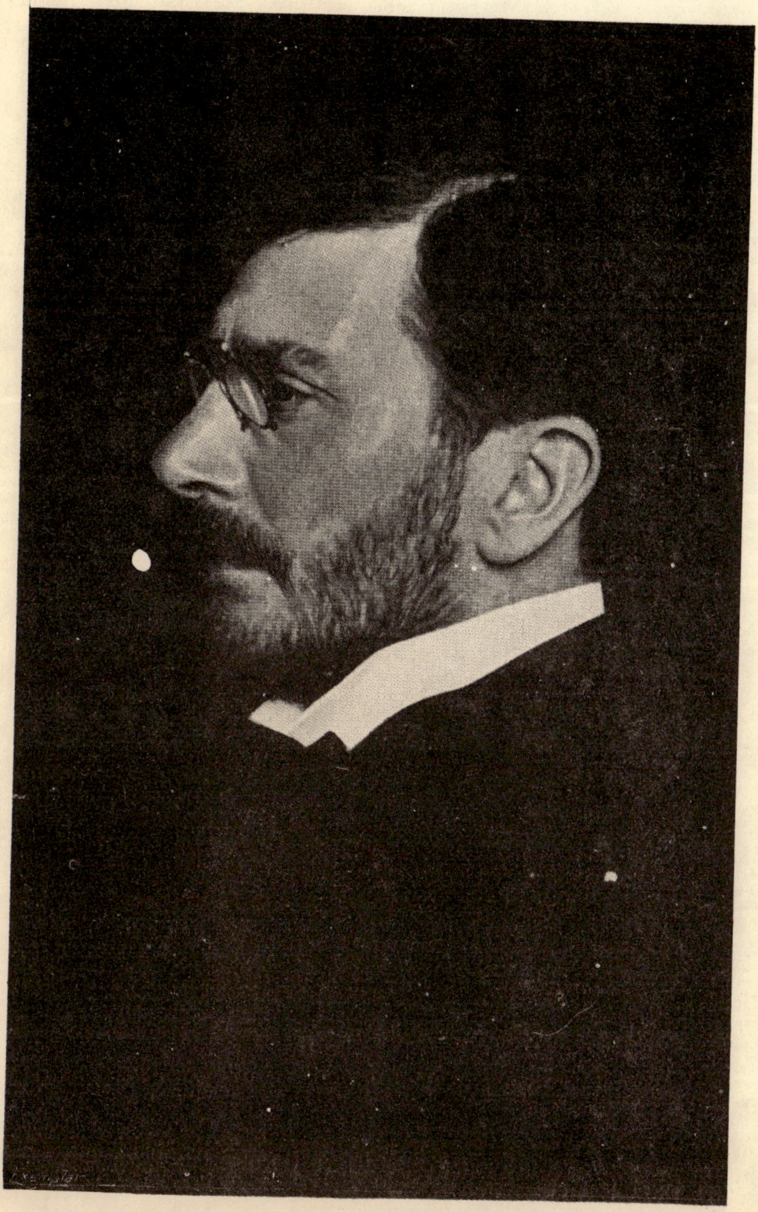

FERDINAND BRUNETIÈRE, OF THE FRENCH ACADEMY

Price discrimination is [illegible] with [illegible] aspect of monopolistic strategy. [illegible] [illegible] [illegible] transportation [illegible] [illegible] possibility and profitability of the [illegible] discrimination [illegible] adequately [illegible]

Discriminating Protection. The policy of protecting the [illegible] produced by newly established infant industries from the invasion of foreign goods through other nations of [illegible] [illegible]

Discrimination. [illegible] different [illegible] background, or union membership (or non-membership), concerning hiring, [illegible] promotion, training programs, or any other terms and conditions of employment. Discriminating against one group of workers [illegible] males over [illegible] benefits [illegible] or younger employees [illegible] if not actively support discriminatory practices. Consequently, although [illegible]

[illegible]

[illegible]

De nouvelles curiosités s'éveillèrent. Des doutes nous vinrent sur l'universalité de l'idéal dont nous nous étions contentés jusqu'alors. De nouveaux éléments s'insinuèrent dans la composition de l'esprit français. Et les poètes, s'il en surgissait, se trouvèrent ainsi assurés d'une liberté qui leur avait fait défaut jusqu'alors, et de cette espèce de complicité de l'opinion ou du *milieu*, sans laquelle rien n'est plus difficile,—même au génie,—que de déterminer une révolution littéraire.

Là est l'explication du succès des premières *Méditations* de Lamartine, qu'on pourrait comparer, dans l'histoire de notre poésie lyrique, au succès du *Cid* ou d'*Andromaque*, dans l'histoire du Théâtre Français. Mais on ne vit point alors, comme au temps d'*Andromaque* ou du *Cid*, de contradiction ni de lutte ; l'opinion fut unanime à reconnaître, à consacrer le poète ; et quand les *Nouvelles Méditations*, *La Mort de Socrate*, *Le Dernier Chant du Pèlerinage de Childe Harold*, les *Harmonies Poétiques* vinrent s'ajouter, de 1820 à 1830, aux *Méditations*, les derniers eux-mêmes et les plus obstinés des classiques durent avouer qu'une poésie nouvelle nous était née. Les *Poésies* d'Alfred de Vigny, parues en 1822, rééditées en 1826 ; et les *Odes* de Victor Hugo, 1822, suivies de ses *Ballades* en 1824, et de ses *Orientales* en 1829, achevaient promptement de caractériser cette poésie dans ses traits essentiels. Si ces trois grands poètes, en effet, avaient chacun son originalité, qui le distinguait profondément des deux autres, Lamartine plus clair, plus harmonieux, plus vague ; Hugo plus précis et plus coloré, plus sonore, plus rude aux oreilles françaises ; et Vigny plus discret, plus élégant, plus mystique, mais plus court d'haleine, ils ne laissaient pas d'avoir beaucoup de traits communs. S'ils avaient tous les trois des maîtres dans quelques-uns de leurs prédécesseurs du dix-huitième siècle, Lamartine dans Parny et dans Millevoye, Hugo dans Fontanes, dans Lebrun et dans Jean Baptiste Rousseau, Vigny dans Chénier, les différences apparaissaient quand on les comparait aux représentants encore vivants du pseudo-classicisme, tels que Casimir Delavigne, avec ses *Messéniennes* ou Béranger dans ses *Chansons*. Et peut-être une critique perspicace eut-elle pu prévoir qu'ils ne tarderaient pas à s'engager dans des voies divergentes : Lamartine plus idéaliste, Hugo plus réaliste, Vigny déjà plus "philosophe" ; mais pour le moment, c'est-à-dire entre 1820 et 1830, ils formaient groupe, s'ils n'étaient pas précisément une école, et c'est ce groupe qu'il nous faut essayer de caractériser.

Notons d'abord qu'aucun d'eux n'est ce qu'on appelait alors "Libéral," du parti de Benjamin Constant ou de Manuel, mais ils sont tous les trois "Royalistes," ultra-royalistes et Catholiques, du parti de Joseph de Maistre, de Bonald, et de Lamennais. C'est même Hugo qui est alors le plus absolu et le plus intransigeant des trois, et l'horreur ou la haine de la Révolution ne s'est nulle part déclarée plus énergiquement que dans ses premiers poèmes : *Les Vierges de Verdun, Quiberon, Buonaparte.* Leur religiosité n'est pas moins sincère ni moins ardente que leur royalisme, et, comme celle de leur maître, Chateaubriand, elle s'étend à toutes leurs idées. Ils se font de l'amour une conception *religieuse ;* c'est *religieusement* qu'ils admirent l'œuvre de Dieu dans la nature ; ils se font du rôle du poète une conception *religieuse.* Et, à la vérité, leur religion n'est pas toujours très sûre, ni très raisonnée. Elle n'est pas très orthodoxe : celle de Lamartine s'évaporera, pour ainsi dire, en une espèce de panthéisme hindou ; Hugo passera comme insensiblement du christianisme au Voltairianisme ; Vigny, d'année en année, s'acheminera vers un pessimisme très voisin de celui de Schopenhauer. Mais ce sera plus tard ; et, en attendant, la diffusion ou même l'exaltation du sentiment religieux fait un des caractères de la poésie française du dix-neuvième siècle à ses débuts.

Cette poésie est, en second lieu, *personnelle* ou *individuelle*, et nous voulons dire par là que le poète y est lui-même, comme homme, non seulement l'occasion, mais le principal objet et la matière habituelle de ses vers. Une *Ode* française, et même une *Élégie*, n'avaient guère été jusque là que des lieux communs, très généraux et très abstraits, qu'on dépouillait d'abord, pour les mieux développer, de tout ce qu'ils pouvaient avoir de trop particulier. Aussi se ressemblent-elles toutes. On ne voit pas de raisons pour qu'une *Élégie* de Chénier ne fût pas de Parny, et, si l'on eut imprimé les *Odes* de Lefranc de Pompignan, sous le nom de Lebrun,

these poems have the two characteristics of a work of art; each is "a philosophical thought presented in an epic or dramatic form"—the definition is his—and, above all, each is a *Poem.* By this last word one must understand something complete in itself, something of which the development is not left to the caprice or the fantasy of the poet, but depends upon the nature, the importance, and the compass of the subject. This is the limit imposed upon the liberty of purely romantic poetry.

Another poet of the same period restrained that liberty in another fashion: Victor de Laprade, whose *Psyché* in 1841, *Odes et Poèmes* in 1843, *Poèmes évangéliques* in 1852, unquestionably contain fine lines, but they are cold; they seem enveloped by some indefinable haze. There is no comparison between Victor de Laprade and Lamartine or Vigny, to whom he really owes less, though he may seem to owe more, than to two writers who are somewhat overlooked to-day: Ballanche, the Lyon's printer, who was Mme Récamier's friend, and Edgar Quinet, the friend of Michelet. Whatever may have been his inferiority, the purposes of Victor Laprade were profoundly interesting. Instinctively a pantheist, and an idealist as well, he laboured for ten or twelve years at the task of eliminating the poet's personality by reducing him to the office of an interpreter of the voice of nature. It was a sort of reversal of the romantic point of view, according to which nature herself only served as a pretext or an occasion for displaying the poet's personality. The subjective impression became, with Laprade, almost a matter of indifference; the truthful representation of the object was the important matter. Unfortunately for Laprade, he combined with this purpose, even in his verses, so many vague side-issues that one loses sight of his novel idea. And amid all this philosophy, which at times was little better than theosophy, the sense of form, of style, and even of prosody, was lost. Poets built their manner upon isolated examples of the work of Musset and of Lamartine, and thought that to be as careless, as often incorrect, as they, was the way to equal them.

Upon this theory a whole school of poets founded their

work, a school which the barbarous word "*Formistes*" was coined to describe. Happily the word has not survived the school. They did not at once formulate the doctrines of "art for art's own sake," but they were finding their way to that motto. The *Cariatides* of Théodore de Banville, 1842, and his *Stalactites*, 1846, were born of this suggestion. All that he appropriated from romanticism, and from the *Orientales* and the *Consolations* of Sainte-Beuve, was a scrupulous attention to form, to "pure beauty" as it was soon to be called. At the same time, however, he turned back to the Greek and Latin antiques, to the very source of classicism. He looked to André Chénier for inspiration, he sang the *Vénus de Milo*, the *Triomphe de Bacchus*, or the *Jugement de Pâris;* and all this was at once an abjuration of the romanticism of the Middle Ages and of that which might have been called Lamartine's neo-Christianism. The same must be said—or almost as much—of Théophile Gautier's collections *Emaux et Camées*, which appeared in 1852.

Banville and Gautier were true poets, true artists, over-anxious, indeed, to find new and singular expressions of art, but they had the misfortune to be also journalists and "men about town." From this combination there resulted a confusing association of incongruous ideals; strata of the quivering air of Paris and of the serene atmosphere of art. It is not always easy to distinguish their serious utterances from their æsthetic paradoxes. Were they sincere, or were they laughing at their readers? In the case of Banville the suspicion is stronger, for in the earlier work one perceives the "dandysm" of Musset, the Musset of *Mardoche* and of *Namouna*. The mere title of one of his collections, *Odes Funambulesques*, which appeared in 1857, sufficiently indicates the prankish side of his nature, and shows, too, why it is that his influence was so limited. Théophile Gautier, on the other hand, urged by the spur of need, did so much work of all sorts that the hack novelist pressed close upon the heels of the poet. The honour of becoming the true leader of the school was reserved for another; the author of the *Poèmes Antiques*, 1852, and the *Poèmes Barbares*, 1855, 1856: Leconte de Lisle, one of the foremost poets of contemporary France—if not the most perfect among them all.

He is certainly the most "objective," and in this regard he is the antithesis of the romantic poet and of the lyrical poet; in reality he is an epic poet. In all his works he only speaks of himself two or three times, and with splendid disinterestedness he soars above all the questions of his day, giving place in his verses only to the thoughts which he believed were for eternity, *sub specie aeternitatis.* It is this which gives him his sound and lasting value. He sang of the exchanging aspects of nature, the same before his time, in his time, and in our time. They fill his *Midi*, his *Juin*, the *Rêve du Jaguar*, the *Sommeil du Condor.* He celebrated, too, the traces which have been left to us by the great races and their successive civilisation: *Qaïn*, *Brahma*, *Khirôn*, the *Enfance d'Héraclès*, *Hypatie*, *Mouça al Kébyr*, the *Tête du Comte*, the *Epée d'Angantyr*, the *Cœur d'Hialmar.* He gave voice to the resistless melancholy which rises from the mass of ruins, from the dark void in which all human effort seems at last to be lost. He was a great artist, he always prepared himself for his work, adding the breadth of modern erudition to the scrupulous accuracy of the classic school. It was his ambition to give every line the precision of a bas-relief, the durability of bronze or marble. The larger public could hardly have been expected to turn with eagerness to so severe a form of art, but the poets promptly rendered their homage, and one is not surprised to learn that the influence of Leconte de Lisle was felt for a moment by Hugo himself.

This is plainly to be seen, if one compares the *Châtiments*, 1852, or the *Contemplations*, 1856, with the *Légende des Siècles*, 1859. In the two earlier collections we find Hugo still a lyric poet, and more than ever before a personal poet, but in the third he is manifestly inspired by the dominant note of the *Poèmes Antiques* and the *Poèmes Barbares.* With still greater truth he may be said to have been aroused by the sound of a rival's lyre, and, calling all his skill to his aid, he reasserts his sway over the empire which the newcomer had attacked. But the leopard skin which hangs from the poet's shoulder never altogether changes its spots, and although the *Légende des Siècles* contains some verses of truly epic ring—the *Sacre de la Femme,* for instance, or *Booz endormi*—the Hugo of the *Orientales* and the *Chants du Crépuscule* reappears in the other pieces, the Hugo to whom history and legend are no more than scene-painter's cloths, garnishing the stage from which he expresses his own, his most intimate sentiments. No matter how earnestly he tried to subordinate himself to his task, to mirror faithfully the scene he describes, his powerful imagination inevitably distorts the image, and it is always Hugo that we see. The other school aimed at a diametrically opposed result, and just as the romantic movement had spread from the field of poetry to that of the theatre, to history, and even to criticism, they tried now to impose the canons of the naturalist's æsthetics upon criticism and history, the theatre and the poetic art.

It was the first article of their code that the personality of the poet should be *subordinated to nature,* that he should become a sworn interpreter; not necessarily impassible, but yet quite impartial and incorruptible. It is no longer the question to know the poet's point of view, whether he is pleased or indignant, or with what sentiments he is agitated by the spectacle of nature or the events of history. It is his function to present things as they are, for what they are, independently of his personal opinions. A line of Horace expresses the new rule: *Non mihi res sed me rebus subjungere conor.* The nature of things is exterior, anterior, superior; it is not our task to correct or perfect, but to reproduce, and the first of all poetic qualities is the fidelity of presentiment. It is a painter's law, or a sculptor's, perhaps, as much as a poet's, and it may easily be carried to undue extremes; a law, indeed, that was afterwards to bring about strange results. But it worked a great change for good in the years that immediately preceded and followed 1860, it recalled the poet to the observation of nature, to the study of history, to respect for simple truth. We owed to it, between 1866 and 1875, the *Trophées* of M. J.-M. de Hérédia; the popular poems, the domestic and intimate verses of M. François Coppée; and, since we are not forbidden to study, in our own persons, the phenomena which Montaigne described as the "changing outlines of man's inner conditions," we owe to this same law some of the subtle and pathetic poems in which M. Sully-Prudhomme has so well expressed the complexity of the contemporary spirit.

These three authors, widely alike as they are, have a second characteristic in common; *each is almost perfect in his own field of work.* There are no more beautiful sonnets in the language than those of M. J.-M. de Hérédia. The Dutch painters, Gérard Dow, for instance, and Jean Steen, have painted no interiors more finished than the popular poems of M. Coppée. Finally, M. Sully-Prudhomme has touched our most secret fibres with verses of unparalleled delicacy and acuity. Perfection of form was indeed the second article, as the subjection of the poet's personality was the first article, of the new school's code. If critics forgave Victor Hugo the obscurities which were often darkened depths of meaning, and which never interfered with the correctness of his diction, they were pitiless to the carelessness of Lamartine and of Musset. The poet's art was no longer measured by the abundance or the strangeness of its inspiration, but by the richness and sonority of the rhythm, the fulness and soundness of the line, the precision and elegance of its French. There was a return to the opinions of the past, a renewed perception of "the power of the right word in the right place." People even began to discern in words many qualities which they do not possess. This was a logical change, no doubt, for there is only one way to imitate nature with fidelity, and that is to concentrate upon the perfection of form all the energy which has been repressed in the process of restricting the liberty of imagination.

To these two principles—*the perfection of form* and *the impersonality of the artist*—a third added itself: the principle that *art exists for art's sake only.* Art has no moral or didactic mission, and one has no right to question the poet's choice of a subject; his method of treatment is the only ground for the exercise of the critic's function. Gautier believed this to his last day; his work remains to prove it. Leconte de Lisle violated the principle in some of his poems, but he was not conscious that he did so, even when, finding his inspiration in the *Légende des Siècles*, he tried to rival Hugo's anti-religious ardour. M. de Hérédia has never swerved. It was this central idea that the Parnassians made their rallying-point in 1866. Some illustrious prose writers—Flaubert in the first rank—encouraged them. And if M. Sully-Prudhomme and M. François Coppée escaped from the strict yoke, it was because they were affected by another influence at the same time as Leconte de Lisle's—an influence more subtle and not less powerful, that of Charles Baudelaire and his *Fleurs du Mal.*

These poems appeared for the first time in 1857; but there are books which make themselves felt as soon as they appear, just as there are others which need, as it were, to be felt from a distance. Of such are, in the history of French prose, Stendhal's *Chartreuse de Parme*, and, in the history of French poetry, the *Fleurs du Mal*. At a first glance the critics imagined—fantastic as the idea seems to us—that they detected Catholicism in the *Fleurs du Mal;* and this was at the moment of a general reaction toward Paganism. The fact is that at a time when the elaboration of form was everything, Baudelaire's verses displayed the mosaicist's care, they suggested the prose writer who has with painful labour morticed a rime upon the end of every line. It was also a moment at which poetry tended to the impersonal; and the inspiration of Baudelaire betrays its debt to that of Vigny, and yet more to that of Sainte-Beuve,—the Sainte-Beuve of the *Confessions de Joseph Delorme.* He not only imitated, but exaggerated this strange morbidity. While the critics for these reasons despised even what there was of novelty in Baudelaire's product, the youth of his day recognised it, and felt its fascination. Beneath the declamatory tone, and the charlatanism, even, of his lament, they perceived the sincerity of a suffering which was not less genuine because it was purely intellectual. It has been said that of all the sensory suggestions the most material and the most diffusive are those which appeal to the olfactory perceptions, and that no others so immediately stir the memory. And if this be true, it must be remembered that the *Fleurs du Mal* are permeated by the whole gamut of exotic fragrance. They are full, too, of those subtle values of sensory co-ordination which Baudelaire himself indicates when he says that "forms and outlines and sounds all correspond the one to the other." There was novelty in all this, a fruitful and a lasting novelty, and as it did not seem to disagree with the lessons of the Parnassians, people listened obediently to the lofty teachings of Leconte de Lisle, but read Baudelaire with infinite delight, like children devouring a book in secret.

I remember trying, twenty-five years ago, in the pages of the *Revue des Deux Mondes,* to describe this influence which Baudelaire exerted upon M. François Coppée, M. Sully-Prudhomme upon M. Paul Bourget, too, whose first verses had then—in 1875—recently appeared, and upon other writers. François Buloz, who was still living at the time, was hugely displeased, although he had printed in the *Revue* Baudelaire's first verses. "So you take Baudelaire for a master, do you?" he cried. I thought that I had answered him when I said, "No, but he is a master in the eyes of the poets I named." But Buloz was not convinced. I little knew how amply time would justify me; I had not long to wait before a whole generation were invoking the name of the author of the *Fleurs du Mal,* the generation of Paul Verlaine and of Stephen Mallarmé.

Although they still continued to bow to the Parnassian discipline, they began to chafe under it. Despite the poet's dictum, *ut pictura poësis,* they began to perceive that poetry wilted in this dry perfection of execution. The precision of outline, the richness of metre, the unswerving fidelity of representation combined, embarrassed, cumbered, cramped the freedom of the imagination, the amplitude of visions. It was impossible to escape the accurate grasp of the artist, and when he had clutched you, there was no release. There was no background, no distant perspective, there was none of the indistinctness, the obscurity, the *chiaroscuro,* which is, nevertheless, one of the elements of true poetry. Save for some among M. Sully-Prudhomme's verses, everything was brought into the whitest light, and if, by chance, the meaning of any work, as a whole, was not quite clear, each line was in itself uncompromisingly distinct. People began to find, too, that this reproduction of nature was extended, in the past as in the present, to many objects which possessed no real interest. It does not follow that because an event has taken place it is necessarily a poetic event; nor is it true that everything that lives should be immortalised by art. It was said, too, that if ideas were plentiful enough in the masterpieces of the Parnassian School, no one idea ever passed beyond its original limits, or became the mantle and the veil of something more secret, more mysterious: the visible and palpable exterior of that which can neither be seen nor touched. There are, unquestionably, certain correspondences and associations between ourselves and the world in which we live: every sensation should lead us to an idea, and in that idea we ought to find something analogous to the sensation. The reality of things does not manifest itself in their mere exterior, they must be exposed to the light of the truth in accordance with which their forms are defined. Every representation which fails to base itself upon that fact is necessarily incomplete, superficial, mutilated. The Parnassians forgot this, and their forgetfulness created the school of symbolism.

It is difficult to see very clearly the inner meaning of Paul Verlaine's work. He was an "irregular" in the eyes of all the schools, and his emancipation had been no more than a return to the liberty of the Romantic School, and a step beyond even that liberty. He owes his reputation less to the profoundness and the ingenuity of his symbolism than to the cynicism of his *Confessions.* He was at once violent and feeble, ingeniously perverse, capable, by turn, of the worst sentiments and the most sincere repentances, inheriting from Baudelaire and from Sainte-Beuve the love of sin and of remorse. Poor "Lélian" wrote some wretched verses, and some that were detestable; but he wrote also some that were original and exquisite. His great merit is, perhaps, that he wrote exquisitely diaphanous lines, verse as lightly burdened as French verse ought to be. Stephen Mallarmé wrote the most incomprehensible verses, more obscure than any Lycophron ever had made before his time; but he had a poet's soul; he talked limpidly, if he wrote turgidly; he possessed the secret of clothing the strangest ideas in an enchanter's web of apparent truth; he has been, and will no doubt remain, the hierophant of symbolism, as Baudelaire was its precursor. I doubt whether he will be largely represented in the anthologies of the future, but no historian of nineteenth-century French poetry can refrain from mentioning his name. A certain Maurice Scève, of Lyons, played just such a rôle in the sixteenth century, only to disappear, when he had played it, in the effulgence of the great Ronsard.

There is one more observation that should perhaps be made before terminating this too hurried essay. It is a Ronsard that symbolism has lacked, and still lacks; it is a Ronsard that we have been awaiting for nearly ten years. It would be easy to name a dozen excellent craftsmen in verse, and three or four poets, among the younger men: M. Henri de Régnier, for instance, and M. Albert Samain. But however much talent, natural or acquired, they may have shown, it must be admitted that no work of theirs has aroused the immediate and universal emotion which Lamartine's *Méditations* and Ronsard's *Amours* kindled as soon as they appeared. Why is it so? Is it, perhaps, because the time is not favourable to poets, and that our poets lack the encouragement, the complicity of opinion, so to speak, which is more necessary to their development than to the development of any other sort of artists? Surely this is not the case. On the contrary, our poets find to-day a keener audience, not in France only, but abroad, than could have been hoped for ten, or twenty, or thirty years ago. Are fewer poets born, or is it more difficult for them to find the opportunity of appealing to the verdict of the public? is life less kind to them to-day than formerly? One can hardly say so, in view of the number of volumes of verse which appear each year. Is it that they ripen less rapidly, and that the standard they set themselves is higher, more complex, and demands longer effort? Are they awaiting a rounder maturity? As they are all young, let us hope that this is the case; and if the close of the nineteenth century, so abundant in poetic talent, is somewhat barren of poetic product, we can only wait, in the hope that the expected masterpiece is taking form, somewhere in silent seclusion, and that the sudden radiance of its appearance will greet the beginning of the new century. *Sic aliud ex alio nunquam desistit oriri.*

Ferdinand Brunetière

SONNETS.

By RICHARD GARNETT.

(*For biographical note, see Vol. XIV., page* 6755.)

TO AMERICA, AFTER READING SOME UNGENEROUS CRITICISMS.

WHAT though thy Muse the singer's art essay,
  With lip now over-loud, now over-low?
  'Tis but the augury that makes her so
Of the high things she hath in charge to say.
How shall the giantess of gold and clay,
  Girt with two oceans, crowned with Arctic snow,
  Sandalled with shining seas of Mexico,
Be pared to trim proportion in a day?
Thou art too great! Thy million-billowed surge
  Of life bewilders speech, as shoreless sea
  Confounds the ranging eye from verge to verge
With mazy strife or smooth immensity.
  Not soon or easily shall thence emerge
  A Homer or a Shakespeare worthy thee.

BISMARCK AND MOLTKE.

FIRE falters yet in the fatiguèd eyes;
  And now the slow blood stirs with sudden leap,
  And angry thunder daunts the spies that peep,
Exploring if the Lion lives or dies.
But cold upon the sand his fellow lies,
  The far-flung shadow of whose dawnless sleep
  The many-nationed world doth overcreep;
Not solely where Rhine's torrent seaward hies.

1

Day darkens, and uneasy Night must wake
  'Neath her blue vault, new sown with baleful stars.
  And chains of Slav and Gaul spontaneous shake;
As anciently at birth of Latin wars,
  Eager their appetite for blood to slake,
  Rome's weapons rattled in the fane of Mars.

April, 1891.

THE SANDS OF TIME.

Camest thou from the desert or the sea,
  Slow-raining sand, whose lapse of gleaming brown
  Stealeth the glassy horologe adown,
Arraying Time with visibility?
Helpmate in either hath he had in thee,
  Tombing the pride of temple or of town,
  Or withering with salt waste the herbless down,
As willed the varying wind's inconstancy.
Thou, joyless load on earth for ever laid,
  Yet plaything of all breezes as they pass,
  Recordest here what thou depictest well:
The thing like thee of streaming atoms made,
  Singly a nothing, measureless in mass,
  Mutation all, and yet unalterable!

JOY.

Joy is there made for all, transparent tide
  Of earth-embathing air, sun's general light,
  Sea, legioned stars, fields variously bright,
And in a common country common pride:
And joy to human multitudes denied,
  But solitary meed of soul of might,
  Pacing in lone content the silent height,
Save by his own thought unaccompanied:
Joy too, not made for many or for one,
  Flashing, as when the flying iron rings
  Sharp on smit stone beside the paven way,
As Love to Love in exultation springs:
  As fades the star of morn in morning's sun,
  All rosiest rapture to such joy is grey.

SONGS OF SION.

My harp upon the willows is not hung;
  Else had I anguish, dreading to forget
  The melody that soundeth sweetly yet,
Albeit in idle hearing idly sung.

Soul, if thou skillest aught of Sion's tongue,
  The more thou chide at Babylon's vain fret,
  The more thou Salem's strain must re-beget,
For Sion lives where Sion's lyre is strung.
To willowed brook or transitory breeze
  Trust nothing; not on such impends the weight
  Of duty on thyself divinely bound;
Thy Mother's songs, of old thy lullabies,
  Not only to revere but renovate,
  Not only to remember but resound.

THE DYER'S STORY.

By W. B. HOCKLEY.

(From "Tales of the Zenana; or, A Nuwab's Leisure Hours.")

[WILLIAM B. HOCKLEY, author of the following striking story, was born in 1792, and at an early age became an Indian civil servant on the Bombay establishment. After a few years' service he was detected in receiving bribes, and was dismissed, receiving however a compassionate allowance. Returning to England, he betook himself to literature, and between 1825 and 1830 produced "Pandurang Hari" and "Tales of the Zenana," which rank along with Meadows Taylor's as the best stories of Hindustan in English literature, until the appearance of Mr. Kipling. Other tales have been erroneously ascribed to him. He died about 1860.]

WHEN I parted from my friends Yasmin and Mohabet Ali I felt as if all attempts at obtaining riches without their aid must prove abortive, and my present condition shows how well-founded were my apprehensions. The first place I visited was Schiraz, where I hoped to obtain employment under the Governor's collectors. I tried in vain, by sundry well-written petitions, to bring myself to the notice of the Deewan or Vizier, then again to the secretary, to the treasurer, and to all junior scribes about court. This I soon found was only a waste of paper and time, without the least prospect of benefit, so I at last determined to apply to the secretary in person, although fully aware of the great difficulty in gaining access to him, knowing how little claim I had to his patronage.

I verily believe I might have waited until this moment at his door without seeing him. Rudely hustled by the guards and fortunate persons who enjoyed free ingress to his mansion, losing all patience, and convinced of my presumption in daring to expect that any of the proud men in power would provide for me, I departed from the court, and enlisted as a common soldier. In this capacity I had no idle time; for, what with guarding the treasury all day and cleaning my horse in the evening, preparatory to the next day's duty, I was nearly sick of my military occupation, and was meditating desertion, although I had bound myself to serve two years, when the Buckshee, the paymaster of the troops, came to deliver our monthly stipend. Requiring someone to make memorandums and take accounts, his own clerk being accidentally absent, he enquired if there were anyone amongst us who could write. I stepped forward, offering my services, which were accepted.

So active was I in my new capacity, that the Buckshee offered to appoint me to the situation of clerk under him, which I joyfully acceded to. Following him into the districts, I assumed the airs and consequence of a gentleman, treating the poor soldiers with neglect and contempt; so that I became no great favourite amongst them, especially as I made it my practice to clip their pay and pocket the money myself. The Buckshee himself hesitated not to adopt this mode of enriching himself; and by having a good understanding with the officers and muster-master, whose list contained the proper number of men, but whose ranks told a very different tale, we all, from first to last, made a tolerable harvest.

The clerk whose place I had taken *pro tempore* returned; but the Buckshee, finding I was by far the shrewder fellow of the two, dispensed with his attendance, desiring him to remain at his office at headquarters until his return. I imagine I must have given a triumphant grin as the crestfallen clerk passed me, for he intuitively put his hand on the hilt of his dagger, stopping immediately opposite to me. He said nothing, however, but walked away. There was, nevertheless, a diabolical expression of countenance on the man, which created in my bosom the most uncomfortable sensations, which his subsequent mysterious whisperings with the half-paid soldiers by no means tended to alleviate.

I foresaw a storm was gathering; nevertheless the Buckshee proceeded with his wonted audacity and impudence to cut, clip, and pocket as many toomauns as he possibly could. "We shall all be ruined," said I to myself; "this infuriated clerk will doubtless inform the Governor of our shameful system of fraud and peculation, in which I have entered too deeply to escape implication." Besides, I was well aware it was the invariable practice of the head of the department to lay all blame on his unhappy deputies; so that in all probability my eyes would be put out, or I should be subject to some dreadful punishment. The next time, therefore, I had an opportunity of fingering the cash I concealed as many toomauns around my body as I well could, and then decamped, leaving my master to answer both for his sins and my own.

I proceeded to a small town, where I procured a dye which stained my beard a light-brown colour, parted with my turban, and wore an Arab cap, so that it would have been a difficult matter to have recognized me. From Schiraz I somehow or other contrived to get to Bussorah; but not fancying myself quite far enough out of reach of the Schiraz governor, travelled on to Bagdad, where, soon after my arrival, I fell sick, and was conveyed by an Arab to his stables, where I was placed amongst the horses. When I recovered, what was my consternation at finding that my generous host, or his followers, having ridden me of my ill-gotten toomauns, had departed, leaving me again a beggar!

This was a pretty specimen of Arab hospitality, and I determined to take warning by it in future. To obtain a livelihood I served a merchant by filling all day bags of dates, which he daily dispatched into the interior. In Bagdad I could find no situation where my pen could advantageously be employed; and my labour was so heavy and constant, that I was entirely confined to the merchant's storehouses, without having a moment to spare to wander through the city. I thought myself, however, so very lucky in escaping the Schiraz governor, that I complained neither of my labour nor confinement.

My master one day fell sick, and in my anxiety to summon medical aid, no one being at that moment at hand, I ran about the city enquiring for a doctor. A shabby-looking fellow undertaking to conduct me to the abode of a clever physician, I followed him through narrow lanes and bye-streets, until we came to a lonely dwelling encompassed by a courtyard, the walls of which were built of coarse black granite, having a low door of solid iron. "Call aloud," said my conductor, "and someone will surely answer you."

Saying this he departed. I called aloud, and soon heard the rattling of chains and bolts, and the iron door grated on its massy hinges. But how can I describe the being that opened it? So hideous a little dwarf, I verily believe, no man ever set eyes upon. He was about three feet in height, with a head suited to the largest giant; his hair hung about his shoulders in the wildest and most disorderly manner, whilst his beard appeared neatly trimmed and dressed. Two eyes he had, but one would have imagined they had belonged to some other person, and been only borrowed by their present possessor—they were extremely bright and small, though every other feature of his face was large, in proportion to the gigantic head in which they were situated.

One of the arms of this monster was shrivelled and withered, but the other, his right one, strong and muscular; his nose was flat, and his mouth reached from ear to ear, which, on opening, displayed a set of large but regular teeth, whose whiteness formed a striking contrast to the sable exterior of this disgusting monster.

"Well," thought I, "with all my misfortunes, I am not reduced to the necessity of residing with this hideous object." I informed him of the sickness of the merchant, desiring him, if the doctor resided within those walls, to summon him immediately. The dwarf bowed, and went into the house, from whence he soon returned, followed by a venerable old man, with a white silvery beard reaching nearly to his middle; his fair countenance indicated mildness and benevolence, and I was quite struck with his noble and dignified mien.

The doctor kindly embraced me, bidding me lead the way towards the sick man's abode. I did so, and rushed into his apartment with joy, to announce the doctor's approach. Around the sick man's couch stood his mother, his wife, and lovely daughter, with whom I had frequently conversed, and on whom I gazed with more than ordinary interest. Umbah (so was the girl named) looked sternly at me as I entered the room, and motioned me to retire, her father being asleep. I informed the doctor of the sick man's slumbers, when he assured me that that was the very time he wished to behold the patient; upon which, without consulting Umbah or the other attendants in the chamber of sickness, I opened the door, and seizing the hand of the doctor, led him into the room.

No sooner had the mourning relatives beheld my venerable physician then one and all uttered violent screams, covering their faces with their hands, loading me with abuse, and desiring us both to be gone. The sick man, disturbed by the shrieks of his family, awoke, and sitting upright in his bed, beheld the doctor, when he also screamed, groaned, and fell backwards, to all appearance dead. Umbah flew out of the room, and the doctor whispered me, saying, "We had better be gone." I took the hint, and gaining the street, my companion in a low tone said, "Take my advice: go not near the merchant's house again; you will repent if you do!"

Now all this seemed to me most unaccountably strange. What had I done? What offence could I have given? My master was sick, and I called a doctor—and a more mild, civil, prepossessing man I never before beheld; but though I seemed so vastly pleased with the learned Hakeem, it appeared no one else was of the same opinion. His very appearance, which had so charmed me, disgusted everyone else. I thus walked on, as I imagined by the side of the doctor; but lifting up my eyes to make some few enquiries into the recent affair, to my astonishment he was gone, and I was alone in the middle of Bagdad, not knowing where to go or what to do. "Perhaps," thought I, still ruminating on the recent unaccountable behaviour of the merchant's family, "perhaps they have had some quarrel with this physician, and the very sight of him drives them distracted; yet this cannot surely be the case, or the doctor would not have accompanied me where he must have known his appearance alone would be attended with such direful consequences."

The whole was inexplicable, and I determined, on visiting the doctor, to enquire from him the probable cause of the agitation to which I had been witness, and in some measure the cause. I passed a long and sleepless night under a shed, and in the morning proceeded to the doctor's sombre abode. The whole place was surrounded by tall, graceful cypress trees, which shed a solemn gloom around the habitation truly awful to behold; and it was not until I had seriously debated with myself that I ventured to approach the iron door. At length, picking up a stone, I knocked with it, and called aloud. The dwarf once more appeared, bowing and grinning. I informed him I wished to speak with his master on particular business; he signed me to enter, and I obeyed.

The dwarf slammed the gate with a violence the noise of which frightened from her nest a raven of a prodigious size from one of the lofty cypress trees; and as she flew slowly over my head uttered three distinct and, as I thought, ominous screams. The dwarf, heedless of either bird or myself, hurried and shuffled on with his little bandy legs into the house, motioning me to stand still. I began heartily to repent my rashness, and essayed to open the iron gate, but it resisted my utmost efforts and remained firm as a rock.

The dwarf returned, beckoning me to follow him; tremblingly I obeyed, and just as my foot was on the threshold the ill-omened raven flapped its sable wings immediately over my head, repeating her screams. I therefore hesitated, saying to the dwarf, "If you please, I will call again to-morrow; I had rather not enter just now." A vile parrot, which hung in a cage over my head, in a large hall, paved with black marble, cried, "Come in, come in!" and seemed by its brain-rending laugh, which followed these words, to rejoice in my dilemma. The whole house now suddenly became perfumed so exquisitely that my senses became bewildered, and I entered.

My arrival at this singular mansion seemed to give universal delight to the inhabitants of this strange abode. The dwarf rubbed his hands and grinned; the parrot screamed more shrilly than before; and a great black cat came close to me, rubbing her sleek and glossy sides against my leg, mewing and whisking about a tremendous long tail. A monkey also capered and seemed ambitious of outdoing the dwarf in his grimaces; but what struck me as most unaccountable was, that parrot, cat, and monkey had each lost an eye. Having crossed the marble hall, I came to a flight of stone stairs. The dwarf placed his foot upon the first step, when up scampered cat and monkey, trying which should get first. Not so quickly did I ascend the stairs, and once turned back, half-determined to refuse proceeding any farther; but the dwarf scowling and looking displeased, I once more slowly ascended. Arrived at the top, the dwarf, monkey, and cat stopped at a black door studded with iron knobs; the cat was in ecstasies, and the monkey jumped on the dwarf's head, where he squeaked and showed evident signs of impatience. The dwarf gave three distinct knocks on the black door with his heavy fist, which slowly opened apparently of its own accord. The dwarf seizing my hand, led me over the threshold, whilst the cat and monkey contented themselves by peering with their single eyes into the half-darkened chamber. The physician was seated on a huge block of wood; and seeing me, arose and embraced me, which salute I coldly returned.

"What may be your commands with me?" cried the white-bearded doctor. I briefly told him the curiosity which the conduct of the merchant's family had excited in me, and that I had come to him for an explanation. "Young man," said he, "the merchant's family are ignorant people; but their reasons for the reception they gave me you had better, if you dare, demand from them. But I perceive you are a young man of education, and might, if you pleased, turn your acquirements to advantage."

"How?" cried I.

"Enter my service. Every convenience shall be afforded you, and your salary shall be handsome."

"What service is expected from me?" I enquired.

"A service," he answered, "which will profit you greatly. My professions are various. I am a physician and alchemist, and your labours will be the attention to the compounding of medicines, grinding colours, arranging shells, stuffing animals, and scraping skeletons' bones."

I shuddered at the composure with which the mysterious man mentioned the services I was expected to perform. I was silent, and the old fellow proceeded.

"You will gradually become acquainted with the mysteries of my profession, and, I foresee, will rise to great eminence."

"But," said I, "if in my professional character I, like you, terrify my patients to death, I am at a loss to understand what profit I am to reap."

"The fact is," said he, "you are impatiently curious; but you must know I am only called in by particular persons when at the last stage. No one will apply to me except the finger of death be on them. Now, the merchant was by no means in such imminent danger, and your mistake in bringing me to him will now reduce him to a lingering and miserable death."

I was still more and more astounded, but remained silent.

"Will you enter my service?" said the doctor.

I hesitated, for it was very clear the people of the city avoided this learned doctor, who doubtless was a magician and a man of bad character. He repeated his question, saying my salary should be five toomauns per diem; and if ever he failed to pay them every morning, I might be at liberty to quit his service.

"At liberty!" said I, "yes, whether you pay me or not, I conceive I should not be compelled to remain in a service which I disliked."

"There you mistake; you must let yourself for five years, or not at all."

"Then," said I, "my mind is soon made up. I beg permission to depart, and shall not approach your gate again."

"Oh, foolish man!" said he. "But, as you are determined to go, I must treat you as a visitor." Saying which he took up a vessel containing rose-water, which he sprinkled over my face in the most courteous manner, and then embracing me, opened the chamber door, saying: "Farewell! but I fancy you will soon find mine is the only gate that will henceforth be open to you, and when you come I shall be glad to see you."

This was strange, unaccountably strange, after my positive assurances of never intending to approach his house again. I looked the alchemist in the face, but he maintained the same dignified look, and called out aloud "Budnuzer!" Up came the frightful dwarf, accompanied by the cat and monkey. The doctor ordered him to open the iron door of the courtyard and allow his visitor to depart, saying, "Be at hand, however; he will soon return."

I turned round to demand an explanation, when the door of the apartment was shut-to, and the doctor disappeared. I followed the dwarf down the stairs, the cat mewing piteously, the monkey crying like a child, and the parrot in the hall shrieking in a most lamentable manner. Budnuzer, the dwarf, was, I imagine, dumb, or he would most probably have joined in the general mourning my departure occasioned. Arrived at the courtyard, I felt much relieved, and when the dwarf, with a melancholy face, opened the iron door I was in an ecstasy, and ran for a considerable distance, so delighted was I at escaping the horrors of the gloomy mansion. "The doctor," said I, "may be very learned, but, by Allah! I will disappoint him this time, and show him he can sometimes err in his prognostications, for I am determined never to go near the lane leading to his gate again. No, no; I am safe, and I mean to continue so."

The first person I met was an Arab labourer, who no sooner set eyes upon me than down he fell insensible, groaning most piteously. "Heavens!" I cried, "what can be the meaning of this extraordinary conduct?" I attempted to raise the poor fellow, but he only groaned and yelled the more, so I left him to his fate. When some distance from him I turned round, and beheld the man running so fast as never, I believe, an Arab had run before.

"Well," said I, "it seems strange that my appearance should have this extraordinary effect; however, I will go to a barber's and have my beard dressed; perhaps I have need of his scissors." I looked into a house to enquire where I could find a barber. No sooner did the people therein set eyes upon me than, like the labourer in the road, down they fell flat on their faces, roaring and screaming for mercy. I quickly retreated, feeling extremely uneasy at finding myself an object of horror to all the inhabitants of Bagdad. By chance I passed a barber's shop; it was full of customers waiting to be attended to. I entered; every head was turned towards me, and every mouth uttered a frightful yell; whilst some dropped down in a state of insensibility, and others hurried out of the shop, uttering dismal groans and muttering over prayers and portions of the Koran.

Determined to ascertain the cause of this terror which my appearance inspired, I seized the barber's mirror, and on viewing my face therein I was soon able to account for the mystery—my face being spotted all over with patches of blood, of so horrid a nature that I must have appeared like a creature from the other world. I had no doubt but this was to be attributed to the doctor's sweet-smelling rose-water, which, as I imagined, he had so courteously sprinkled over me. I flew to the water which stood in one corner of the shop and attempted to rub off the stain; but, alas! it was indelible. I most cordially cursed the doctor, being now under the necessity, notwithstanding my determination on the contrary, of once more knocking at his iron gate, to desire he would remove the bloody spots on my face; and, as he foretold, I soon returned.

Dire necessity compelled me once more to approach his horrid abode; I was shunned, abhorred, loathed; how could I, then, obtain a livelihood? "Oh, misery!" cried I, "the alchemist has indeed secured me; I must become his slave." With a heavy heart I knocked at the iron gate, which was instantly opened by the dwarf, who appeared as if expecting my return.

"Lead me to your master," cried I.

He bowed, and I followed him into the hall, the parrot once more crying, "Come in, come in!" and laughing most immoderately; the cat and monkey also testified their delight by a thousand antics and grimaces. Once more I was at the study door of the accursed doctor. He received me politely, saying, "I told you we should soon see you again—that mine was the only gate open to you in the world."

"Removed these accursed stains," cried I, pointing to my face, "and I shall then be enabled to obtain a livelihood."

"Impossible," said the doctor; "I must first have your services for five years. Be prudent; agree to remain with me, and after that period, if you obey me in every particular, you may bid adieu to service for ever and become independent. Reject my offers, and go abroad once more as you now are; but remember, my gate will not again be opened unto you."

"Oh! cruel fate that has led me hither!" cried I. "Curse the villain who pointed out this hellish place to me! What must I do?"

"Obey, serve, and honour me," said the doctor; "and as you diligently get through each year of servitude two of the ten spots on your face will vanish. I cannot, if I would, wipe them away by any other means."

"Will you promise," cried I, "that after five years I shall become rich, and be suffered to depart without stain?"

"It depends on yourself," said the doctor. "If you obey me, are not headstrong or imprudent, you shall retire wealthy, and perfect in appearance."

I consented to remain, and promised to obey. At this moment the monkey and the cat set up a scream of delight and hurried downstairs, I suppose to inform the parrot of the good news, for I soon after heard his thrilling shriek throughout the house. Budnuzer, the dwarf, entered the study, and the doctor drew forth a parchment, on which he wrote our agreement, he binding himself to pay me five toomauns per diem, and provide food and lodging for five years, after which he would have no farther claim upon me, provided I did not disobey his instructions and orders; in which case, though he might allow me to depart, I was to refund all the toomauns I might have received, or keep them, binding myself to stay for ten years more in his service, in which case I should be allowed to keep my money. I, on my part, bound myself to serve and obey, and signed my name, the dwarf being witness. From the deed I learned my master's name was Tabnag; and, oh! curse the day which first brought me near Tabnag and Budnuzer.

Being now regularly in the service of Tabnag, I was anxious to examine his gloomy abode, and so expressed myself to my master. He willingly undertook to conduct me about the premises. The first room into which we entered was a laboratory, containing surgical instruments, stuffed birds, and skeletons; in the second room, on the first floor, was a valuable collection of shells, with several curious swords, daggers, and matchlocks; but what struck me more forcibly, amongst the collection, was an enormous bow, made of buffalo's horn.

"Could you string it, think you?" said the doctor.

"I fear not," said I.

"Try," replied he. "I fancy you are strong, and that is one reason why I was anxious to secure your services."

The bow being taken down, I set to work with all my might, desirous of exhibiting my muscular powers, but nevertheless failed in my attempt. Tabnag assured me of all the assistants he ever had none had displayed so much strength as myself, adding, "And I am glad to see it, as you will need it, I assure you." I was somewhat alarmed at this speech, and enquired if it were impossible to string the bow. "There is only one person," said he, "who is able to string it, and that is Budnuzer. You shall see him." Saying which he took from his girdle a whistle, which applying to his mouth, he produced a noise, answered from below, not by the dwarf, but by the parrot, and soon after Budnuzer stood before us.

Tabnag pointed to the bow; and the dwarf, placing his foot upon it, with his strong and powerful arm strung it at one pull.

We passed on through many other rooms on this floor, some empty, and others containing medicines, bottles, and tools of all descriptions. The windows were all securely barred, but the shutters appeared to have felt the iron hand of time. We now descended the stairs and entered the hall, where the parrot welcomed us with his usual exclamation of "Come in, Come in!" and when the doctor informed me that the hall was paved with marble from a quarry near Mount Chasaqiri * the parrot cried, "Dur een che shuck?" †

* Caucasus. † "What doubt is there of this?"

"Your bird," said I, "seems able to converse."

"No, indeed," said Tabnag; "all he can say is 'Come in,' and 'What doubt is there of this?' I purchased him of a fakir from Hindustan, who was very unwilling to part with him."

Tabnag now opened a door to the right of the hall, which I had not before observed, which was strange, for close by it was another door—both painted black. The room into which we entered was spacious, and in the centre was placed a tremendous wheel, with leathern straps, which passed through into the adjoining apartment. Close to the great wheel was a smaller, placed horizontally, with cogs and springs, such as is used in many places to draw up water with from the wells. This I concluded was worked by an ox, although a very singularly constructed yoke lay on the floor.

"You will know more of this room shortly," said the doctor; "and I have now shown you as much as I intend—and seek to know no more."

"Are we not to look into the adjoining room?" enquired I.

"Young man," replied Tabnag, in the most solemn manner, "mark me—never presume to venture near the door of that room; the consequences of disobedience may be fatal to you. Be ready to-morrow at sunrise, when we will commence our labours. Budnuzer, conduct the young man to his apartment."

Saying which, he left me in charge of the dwarf, who conducted me to a low, damp cellar, where was a miserable bed, beside which stood an iron treasure-chest, which was open. The dwarf fastened the same, and put the key into my hands, by which I understood the box was intended for a place of deposit for my wages. I was allowed to walk around the spacious courtyard in the evening, and was joined by the doctor, who was pleasant and facetious enough, indulging in severe remarks on the ignorance of mankind in general, and contemning all forms of religion. To fathom this man was impossible, nor could I discover whether he was Suni, Sheeah, Turk, or infidel; he was undoubtedly a clever and experienced man, but certainly leagued with the evil one.

I joined my master at meals, and we were waited on by Budnuzer, who afterwards fed himself, the cat, monkey, and parrot

"Pray," said I, "what could make these animals so delighted at seeing me enter the house?"

"Why," said Tabnag, "they have had little or no food since my last assistant left me; and seeing another approach, they very sagaciously imagined their food would be continued to be given them as before."

"But why," said I, "did not you feed them until you had procured another assistant?"

"I ate but little myself," said the doctor; "I could not. But ask no questions."

"I must," said I, "ask one more question. How happens it that all your animals have but one eye?"

"Because," said he, "they all were imprudent, and dared to disobey me."

This was a very unsatisfactory answer, but I was constrained to be silent. I passed a quiet night, and was awakened by Budnuzer in the morning, and signed by him to enter the hall, where Tabnag was awaiting my coming. The dwarf conducted me into the room with the wheels, whilst the doctor entered the sacred and forbidden apartment. What was my dismay at finding the horizontal wheel, which I had imagined was constructed for an ox, intended for myself! And the curious yoke actually fastened on my neck by the ready dwarf ere I had well recovered from my surprise; my eyes were then blindfolded, I suppose to prevent dizziness, whilst each hand was placed on a bar, where they were tightly strapped; and here I stood like the patient ox, waiting the signal to move on. The signal soon came in the shape of a smart crack on my shoulders from the dwarf's whip, which I had not before observed him to carry. The labour was dreadful, and my knees tottered under me.

I continued at this truly bullock-work for half an hour, when a shrill whistle from the forbidden chamber, which I vainly imagined was the signal for cessation, brought the whip of the dwarf once more about my shoulders, and the shrill voice of old Tabnag, crying out, "Quick, quick!" I was obliged to strain every nerve to please both master and driver. At last a loud and continued whistle I found was the signal to discontinue my labour, for the dwarf, pulling me back, released me. I fell to the ground exhausted, and covered with perspiration. Presently in rushed the doctor, half-naked, and fell by my side, perspiring in every pore, panting and puffing, and calling for water, which the dwarf brought him forthwith.

I was of opinion that I had suffered greatly, but the

internal agony of old Tabnag baffles all description, whilst the dwarf appeared the only composed person in the house, for the mewing of the cat and the shrieks of the parrot and monkey were now become disagreeably audible. After some time the doctor arose, and was led out of the room by Budnuzer, leaving me to recover my fatigues as well as I could. I had experienced quite enough of the nature of my duties to make me anxious to quit so abominable a service, where the work of a beast was expected from me, in order to aid my master in some diabolical proceeding. What could I do? The demon doctor had fixed his accursed stamp on my face, and rendered me a loathed object, a monster on whom none for a moment dared rest their eyes.

With this most effectual preventive to escape, the doctor kindly allowed me egress from his infernal den whenever I was inclined. I determined to remonstrate with him before another day's labour commenced. The dwarf returned to me, and leading me from the room, fastened the door. I had great curiosity to know all that had been going on in the contiguous apartment; but as the dwarf was dumb, and I had been warned not to attempt gratifying my curiosity on the subject, I silently followed Budnuzer to my cellar, where, tired and hot, I laid down to sleep.

In the evening the dwarf called me, and I accompanied him to the study of my master, where I found him wearing the same serene and placid countenance as when I first beheld him. Before him were dishes of rice and sweetmeats, with sherbet and cool water, of which he politely invited me to partake.

"No," said I, "one who has been treated like a brute cannot now sit down as a human being to eat rice and pilau."

The doctor made no reply, but ate his fill, and then went to sleep. Being very hungry, however, I followed the dwarf out of the room with the dishes, intending to snatch a handful or two of rice; but lo! the cat and the monkey, ever watchful, jumped on the dwarf's shoulders, and soon between them cleared the dishes, with the exception of some sweetmeats, which Budnuzer reserved for the parrot.

"Well," thought I, "to-morrow I will be more prudent, and eat while I have it in my power."

The following day was productive of nearly the same misery to me. I was put to the handwheel, and as I turned it something in the adjoining chamber went round with a whizzing noise, accompanied by the sound of hammers and clinking of metal. Being greatly fatigued, I began to relax in my exertions; but the dwarf, who stood by me, immediately applied his hellish whip to my unfortunate shoulders. Irritated beyond measure, I left the wheel, and was approaching the dwarf to chastise him; but lifting up his arm, he levelled such a blow on my stomach as made me reel to the other end of the room, where I fell. All this time the operations, whatever they were, were at a stand, and in consequence in rushed Tabnag to enquire the cause. I explained to him how the dwarf had presumed to serve me.

"Presumed!" said Tabnag. "Why, 'tis his duty to keep the wheel going till he hears my whistle. If you are lazy of course you must be whipped; and I advise you not to attempt striking him—you are no match for him in strength. Come, to the wheel once more! I have not yet finished."

I assured him I was half-dead with hunger, and had not strength to turn the wheel any more that day.

"That is your own fault," said he; "I offered you food. If you did not choose to accept it, I don't see why my business should stand still in consequence." So saying, he nodded to the dwarf, who with his whip soon brought me from my corner again to the accursed wheel, where, after another hour's hard work, I was gratified by hearing the whistle from the next room. This being the signal for cessation, the doctor came smiling into the room and shook me by the hand, hoping, he said, to see me at dinner. I this day partook of his meal, and an excellent one it was.

Thus passed day after day. I was sometimes put to one wheel, then to another; but every time I was yoked to the heavy one the doctor, at the conclusion of my labour, evinced symptoms of terror similar to those I witnessed on the first day. My salary, according to agreement, was regularly paid me, and my food was excellent. I had remained with the doctor one year, during which time I had worked hard for my toomauns, and apparently gave great satisfaction. Two of the spots on my face disappeared as the doctor had assured me, so that I hoped, when my term should expire, to become quite free from the horrid stains. I shall not dwell upon the toil I endured for four years and a half, but proceed to relate events which then took place.

The doctor was summoned to the sick-bed of an Arab captain of a merchant vessel, who had come from Bussorah to visit his family, residing in Bagdad. The dwarf was occupied on the terrace of the house drying certain herbs for the doctor's use, and I was left alone and unemployed. I felt a strong inclination to peep into the forbidden apartment, and more than once found myself at the door; prudence, however, whispering in my ear, I turned away, considering, as my term of servitude was so near at an end, I would not run the risk of incurring the displeasure of the alchemist, although it would, I imagined, be next to impossible he should find me out. The doctor returned one day, informing me the Arab captain was quite recovered. "Yes," said he, "Maghroobia" (so was his patient named) "will ever bless the day he sent for me."

About one month after this event, as I was assisting the dwarf in his labours on the terrace, I heard the town crier proclaiming the sudden disappearance of a girl named Zenna, the daughter of Maghroobia, a captain of a merchant-vessel. Immense rewards were offered to anyone who could give information which would lead to her discovery. I was surprised, but mentioned not the circumstance to my master, who doubtless had heard the crier as well as myself.

Several days after I was again by chance left at liberty in the house, and fancied I heard a voice, sobbing and weeping bitterly, proceed from the forbidden apartment; it was unquestionably the voice of a female. "Heavens!" thought I, "it must be the daughter of the Arab captain. Oh!" said I, "were I certain this were the case, I would, when my term expires, give the distressed father information on the subject, and thus gain an immense reward, which, added to my savings, would possess me of a handsome sum of money to take with me to Yezd, where I anticipate the pleasure of sharing it with my two friends, Yazmin and Mohabet Ali, should they both be still in want.

No one was near, and I determined to hazard a peep into the mysterious chamber. Not a sound was to be heard in the house; the parrot, whose cage hung opposite the fatal door, was even sleeping, and the cat and monkey were reposing below. Cautiously did I, on my toes, creep towards the door. The female wept, and fain would I have called to her but for the parrot, who invariably, on hearing anyone talk, would scream violently, and thus bring down the dwarf. I tried the door; it was fastened. I placed my eye at the keyhole, when a flash of fire seemed to go through my brain, and my right eye was for ever destroyed, whilst my left felt painful and weak, and it was with difficulty I could bear the light. No sooner had this misery befallen me than the parrot gave a lengthened scream, and threw himself violently from one side of the cage to the other.

"What a fool I am!" cried I.

"What doubt is there of that?" said the parrot, whilst the dwarf came hobbling down the stairs.

I endeavoured to turn my back towards him, that he might not perceive my blindness, but to no purpose; he seemed to have divined what had taken place, for I found myself drawn by a strong cord and fastened to one of the pillars of the hall, so cruelly tight that the circulation of my blood was impeded; my eyes, particularly my left, ached violently, and I found I could see less and less every minute. I, however, saw the doctor enter, and beheld his chagrin at seeing me tied in the manner I describe.

"Fool!" said he, "did I not caution you against attempting to gratify your curiosity? You have got your reward. This day you go hence a beggar, and a blind one. Budnuzer," said he, "release the poor wretch, and turn him away for ever."

In vain I begged for a few toomauns; not one would the ill-natured Tabnag give me; my labour and toil for nearly five years was all clean forgotten by this one act of disobedience, although dearly had I been punished for it. Thus did I leave the mansion of Tabnag, not indeed quite blind, but nearly so; one eye, however, my right, had become dark and useless, and two of the red spots on my face to this day remain, but are, fortunately, on my chin, so that my beard, which I strive to make grow thick, completely covers them. I trust your Majesty will excuse my not showing them, having the greatest horror of having them exposed to view. I begged my way to Bussorah, and from thence by ship to Mocha, where, I should have said, the infernal doctor advised me to go, for what purpose I knew not, but soon comprehended his motive.

Arrived at Mocha, my left eye gradually recovered, and I could see to walk about. As I was one day begging in the street a stout fellow laid hold of me, and demanded his daughter.

"Heavens!" cried I, "what mean you? Who are you? I have no female in my possession!"

"I am," said he, "Maghroobia, and come to demand my daughter Zenna, whom the good Tabnag has assured me is under your protection, and that you have absconded from him on her account."

"Oh! sir," cried I, "call him not good; he is, I believe, the devil himself; and, not content with causing me to suffer toil and labour and blindness, has now deceived you, doubtless imagining you would sacrifice me to your fury. Thank heaven, you are a wise man, and have not proceeded so rashly. Your daughter, sir, is in the mansion of the doctor, at least so I have reason to fear; and it was my wish to be certain of the fact which has cost me my right eye, and ruined the vision of the other."

"Oh, Allah!" cried the captain, "can this be possible? Is the doctor indeed such a man? Now do I repent having called him in during my illness."

"Go," said I; "lose not a moment in returning to Bagdad to demand your child; you will find her in the second room on the right hand of the marble hall; but for heaven's sake be cautious, or your life may be forfeited."

"I will apply to the Governor," said the captain, "and have his house razed. Will you accompany me?"

"Excuse me," said I; "worlds should never tempt me to approach those detested walls again. Farewell! and may you succeed, noble captain."

Maghroobia was by no means surprised at my declining to accompany him, when he heard all my past sufferings. Some time after his departure I got into the service of a merchant, for whom I was employed in preparing coffee for exportation. My service requiring me on an estate about four miles distant from Mocha, I was one day proceeding thither on an Arab horse, when I missed my way, and got amongst wild and inaccessible places. At last, finding my horse could not proceed over the rocky and uneven ground, I fastened him to the stump of a tree, and ascended a hill, where I endeavoured to discover my lost path.

A venerable old man suddenly appeared, and I made him a salaam and enquired my road. He gave me the necessary information, and invited me to his cave close by, where, he said, he had resided for years retired from the world. I rather hesitated to trust myself a second time with the venerable-looking men of that country, but at last followed him to his retreat, where he produced milk, coarse bread, and dates. The heat of the day had caused my poor eye much pain, and I frequently put my hand before it.

"My friend," said my host, "you seem in much pain. How happens it that you have lost the use of your right eye, and appear to suffer much pain in your left?"

"Oh, sir," cried I, "I am the victim of a villain at Bagdad, who calls himself a doctor."

The hermit started, crying, "God forbid! have you served Tabnag?"

"Oh!" said I, "then thou knowest him?"

"I do," he replied; "he cured me when all other physicians had given me over; but I paid dearly for my recovery; my daughter was carried off, my wife died suddenly, and my ships (for I was a merchant) sunk, and I became a wanderer. When first I insisted on the attendance of Tabnag my friends were horror-struck, and fain would have turned me from my purpose, saying he could cure, but he would cause me sorrow for the remainder of my days. I heeded not their superstition, as I then deemed it. He came and cured my body, but wounded my peace of mind for ever. It is now about five years since I fell in with a man like yourself, blind in one eye, and suffering pain from the weakened state of the other; and he related to me his sufferings whilst under the roof of Tabnag; and you, like him, I imagine dared to peep into the forbidden apartment."

"I did," said I, and proceeded to relate everything that had happened to me.

"You are unfortunate," said he; "but in my inner cell is a poor wretch who, I fear, is dying, and one who has also served not only Tabnag, but Satan himself."

The hermit conducted me into a small cave, where on a pallet lay an emaciated being, apparently dying. I approached, and on examining his countenance what was my astonishment on recognizing the very man who had first pointed out to me the doctor's infernal abode!

Informing the hermit of the circumstance, he said this was very likely, "For as long as he could supply Tabnag with victims he lived; but all his attempts failing at the time of your emancipation, he is now about to suffer for his rash intimacy with the alchemist. His incoherence of speech and his dreadful agony of mind allow me to gather from him the following particulars:—He, it appears, was entrapped into the mansion of the doctor, and being poor and destitute, accepted his service; and unfortunately for him, did not peep into the forbidden apartment."

"Would I had been as unfortunate!" said I.

"Not so, my son," said the hermit; "you have reason to rejoice at rather than lament your disobedience. Listen to me. After the expiration of his term of servitude, the doctor, as he said, to reward him for his forbearance and strict obedience to his orders in not prying into his secrets, offered to conduct him into the mysterious chamber.

"Eagerly did he follow his master, when scarcely had he passed the threshold before a gigantic figure, with huge sable wings, touched him on the shoulder, crying, 'Mine, mine, mine for ever!' and instantly disappeared. The poor fellow sank to the earth overcome with terror, and on recovering begged an explanation from the alchemist, who coolly informed him that he was now the servant of Satan, but that provided he could procure for him a strong and able assistant every five years, or whenever he should require one, he should live wealthy and happy, and for this purpose he was allowed to be at large in the city; but if he failed, then would come his dreadful hour, and Satan would come and claim him.

"He succeeded in providing two assistants, whose curiosity lost them their eyes, but saved their souls. After you, the unhappy man, having been unable to provide an assistant, fled, vainly imagining he could elude the grasp of Satan; but in this wild and dreary place his enemy has overtaken him, and I dread the hour of his dissolution. He has also informed me that he verily believes the nature of his duty at the wheels in the alchemist's house was to draw up in one the devil, laden with gold and silver, and in the other to put in motion some machinery for the purpose of coining money.

"From your account I imagine that Tabnag, failing to obtain another assistant, has endeavoured to appease the devil by procuring a virgin, and this may account for his secreting the merchant's daughter."

"But," said I, "can you account for the horror I inspired by showing my spotted face in the city?"

"Yes," said the hermit. "This is one of the old fellow's tricks—a young man, a patient of his, having, it is said, come from the other world so marked, thus stalked through the streets, to the alarm and terror of the inhabitants. When you appeared, therefore, doubtless they imagined the same spectre had again visited them."

If this was all correct I had reason to rejoice at my getting off with the loss of an eye only. "What think you," said I, "has now become of old Tabnag, since he has failed to procure another assistant?"

"I cannot say," replied the hermit, "unless Satan has spared him, in consequence of his offering the merchant's daughter, though I question if he has been suffered to possess his immense wealth."

Whilst we were talking the sick man groaned and writhed in agony, crying, with a feeble voice, "He is coming! he is coming!" Alarmed, we rushed out of the cavern, not daring to venture near it again for an hour. The hermit at length summoned courage to peep into the inner cell, and returned to me, saying the place was filled with black smoke, so that nothing could be distinguished. After a short time he again repaired to the cell, followed by myself. The cave was free from smoke, but the victim was gone—not a trace of him was to be seen.

THE DESTRUCTION OF SENNACHERIB.

BY LORD BYRON.

The Assyrian came down like the wolf on the fold,
And his cohorts were gleaming in purple and gold;
And the sheen of their spears was like stars on the sea,
When the blue wave rolls nightly on deep Galilee.

Like the leaves of the forest when summer is green,
The host with their banners at sunset were seen:
Like the leaves of the forest when autumn hath blown,
That host on the morn lay withered and strewn.

For the Angel of Death spread his wings on the blast,
And breathed in the face of the foe as he passed,
And the eyes of the sleepers waxed deadly and chill,
And their heart but once heaved, and for ever grew still.

And there lay the steed with his nostril all wide,
But through it there rolled not the breath of his pride;
And the foam of his gasping lay white on the turf,
And cold as the spray of the rock-beating surf.

And there lay the rider distorted and pale,
With the dew on his brow and the rust on his mail;
And the tents were all silent, the banners alone,
The lances unlifted, the trumpet unblown.

And the widows of Ashur are loud in their wail,
And the idols are broke in the temple of Baal;
And the might of the Gentile, unsmote by the sword,
Hath melted like snow in the glance of the Lord.

HYMN OF APOLLO.

By PERCY BYSSHE SHELLEY.

I.

The sleepless Hours who watch me as I lie,
  Curtained with star-inwoven tapestries
From the broad moonlight of the sky,
  Fanning the busy dreams from my dim eyes,
Waken me when their Mother, the grey Dawn,
Tells them that dreams and that the moon is gone.

II.

Then I arise, and, climbing heaven's blue dome,
  I walk over the mountains and the waves,
Leaving my robe upon the ocean-foam;—
  My footsteps pave the clouds with fire; the caves
Are filled with my bright presence; and the air
Leaves the green Earth to my embraces bare.

III.

The sunbeams are my shafts, with which I kill
  Deceit, that loves the night and fears the day;
All men who do or even imagine ill
  Fly me, and from the glory of my ray
Good minds and open actions take new might,
Until diminished by the reign of night.

IV.

I feed the clouds, the rainbows, and the flowers,
  With their ethereal colours; the moon's globe,
And the pure stars in their eternal bowers,
  Are cinctured with my power as with a robe;
Whatever lamps on earth or heaven may shine
Are portions of one power, which is mine.

V.

I stand at noon upon the peak of heaven;
  Then with unwilling steps I wander down
Into the clouds of the Atlantic even;
  For grief that I depart they weep and frown.
What look is more delightful than the smile
With which I soothe them from the western isle?

VI.

I am the eye with which the universe
  Beholds itself, and knows itself divine;
All harmony of instrument or verse,
  All prophecy, all medicine, are mine,
All light of Art or Nature;—to my song
Victory and praise in its own right belong.

HOMER'S HYMN TO THE MOON.

TRANSLATED BY PERCY BYSSHE SHELLEY.

DAUGHTERS of Jove, whose voice is melody,
Muses, who know and rule all minstrelsy!
Sing the wide-wingèd Moon. Around the earth,
From her immortal head in heaven shot forth,
Far light is scattered—boundless glory springs;
Where'er she spreads her many-beaming wings,
The lampless air glows round her golden crown.
But, when the Moon divine from heaven is gone
Under the sea, her beams within abide;

Till, bathing her bright limbs in ocean's tide,
Clothing her form in garments glittering far,
And having yoked to her immortal car
The beam-invested steeds whose necks on high
Curve back, she drives to a remoter sky
A western crescent, borne impetuously.
Then is made full the circle of her light;
And, as she grows, her beams more bright and bright
Are poured from heaven where she is hovering then,
A wonder and a sign to mortal men.

NAPOLEON'S SANGAREE.

By RICHARD GARNETT.

NAPOLEON BONAPARTE sat in his garden at St. Helena, in the shadow of a fig-tree. Before him stood a little table, and upon the table stood a glass of sangaree. The day was hot and drowsy; the sea boomed monotonously on the rocks; the broad fig-leaves stirred not; great flies buzzed heavily in the sultry air. Napoleon wore a loose linen coat and a broad-brimmed planter's hat, and looked as red as the sangaree, but nowise as cool.

"To think," he said aloud, "that I should end my life here, with nothing to sweeten my destiny but this lump of sugar!"

And he dropped it into the sangaree, and little ripples and beads broke out on the surface of the liquid.

"Thou shouldst have followed me," said a voice.

"Me," said another.

And a steam from the sangaree rose high over Napoleon's head, and from it shaped themselves two beautiful female figures. One was fair and very youthful, with a Phrygian cap on her head, and eager eyes beneath it, and a slender spear in her hand. The other was somewhat older, and graver, and darker, with serious eyes; and she carried a sword, and wore a helmet, from underneath which her rich brown tresses escaped over her vesture of light steel armour.

"I am Liberty," said the first.

"I am Loyalty," said the second.

And Napoleon laid his hand in that of the first spirit, and instantly saw himself as he had been in the days of his youthful victories, only beset with a multitude of people who were offering him a crown, and cheering loudly. But he thrust it aside, and they cheered ten times more, and fell into each other's arms, and wept, and kissed each other. And troops of young maidens robed in white danced before him, strewing his way with flowers. And the debts of the debtor were paid, and the prisoners were released from their captivity. And the forty Academicians came bringing Napoleon the prize of virtue. And the Abbé Sieyès stood up, and offered Napoleon his choice of seventeen constitutions; and Napoleon chose the worst And he came to sit with five hundred other men, mostly advocates. And when he said "Yea," they said "Nay"; and when he said "white," they said "black." And they suffered him to do neither good nor evil, and when he went to war they commanded his army for him, until he was smitten with a great slaughter. And the enemy entered the country, and bread was scarce, and wine dear; and the people cursed Napoleon, and Liberty vanished from before him. But he roamed on, ever looking for her, and at length he found her lying dead in the public way, all gashed and bleeding, and trampled with the feet of men and horses; and the wheel of a tumbril was over her neck. And Napoleon, under compulsion of the mob, ascended the tumbril; and Abbé Sieyès and Bishop Talleyrand rode at his side, administering spiritual consolation. Thus they came within sight of the guillotine, whereon stood M. de Robespierre in his sky-blue coat, and his jaw bound up in a bloody cloth, bowing and smiling, nevertheless, and beckoning Napoleon to ascend to him. Napoleon had never feared the face of man; but when he saw M. de Robespierre great dread fell upon him, and he leapt out of the tumbril, and fled amain, passing mid the people as it were mid withered leaves, until he came where Loyalty stood awaiting him.

She took his hand in hers, and, lo! another great host of people proffering him a crown, save one little old man, who alone of them all wore his hair in a *queue* with powder.

"See," said the little old man, "that thou takest not what dost not belong to thee."

"To whom belongeth it then?" asked Napoleon, "for I am a plain soldier, and have no skill in politics."

"To Louis the Disesteemed," said the little old man, "for he is a great-great-nephew of the Princess of Schworfingen, whose ancestors reigned here at the Flood."

"Where dwells Louis the Disesteemed?" asked Napoleon.

"In England," said the little old man.

Napoleon therefore repaired to England, and sought for Louis the Disesteemed. But none could direct him, save that it behoved him to seek in the obscurest places. And one day, as he was passing through a mean street, he heard a voice of lamentation, and perceived a man whose coat and shirt were rent and dirty; but not so his pantaloons, for he had none.

"Who art thou, thou pantaloonless one?" asked he, "and wherefore makest thou this lamentation?"

"I am Louis the Esteemed, King of France," replied the distrousered personage, "and I lament for my pantaloons, which I have been enforced to pawn, inasmuch as the broker would advance nothing upon my coat or my shirt."

And Napoleon went upon his knees, and divested himself of his own nether garments, and arrayed the king therein, to the great diversion of those who stood about.

"Thou hast done wickedly," said the King, when he heard who Napoleon was, "in that thou hast presumed to fight battles and win victories without any commission from me. Go, nevertheless, and lose an arm, and a leg, and an eye in my service, then shall thy offence be forgiven thee."

And Napoleon raised a great army, and gained a great battle for the king, and lost an arm. And he gained another greater battle, and lost a leg. And he gained the greatest battle of all; and the king sat on the throne of his ancestors, and was called Louis the Victorious: but Napoleon had lost an eye. And he came into the King's presence, bearing his eye, his arm, and his leg.

"Thou art pardoned," said the King, "and I will even confer a singular honour upon thee. Thou shalt defray the expense of my coronation, which shall be the most splendid ever seen in France."

So Napoleon lost all his substance, and no man pitied him. But after certain days the keeper of the royal wardrobe rushed into the king's presence, crying, "Treason, treason! O Majesty, whence these republican and revolutionary pantaloons?"

"They are those I deigned to receive from the rebel Bonaparte," said the King. "It were meet to return them. Where abides he now?"

"Saving your Majesty's presence," they said, "he lieth upon a certain dunghill."

"If this be so," said the King, "life can be no gratification to him, and it were humane to relieve him of it. Moreover, he is a dangerous man. Go, therefore, and strangle him with his own pantaloons. Yet let a monument be raised to him, and engrave upon it, 'Here lies Napoleon Bonaparte, whom Louis the Victorious raised from the dunghill.'"

They went accordingly; but behold! Napoleon already lay dead upon the dunghill. And this was told unto the King.

"He hath ever been envious of my glory," said the King. "Let him therefore be buried underneath."

And it was so. And after no long space the King also died, and slept with his fathers. But when there was again a revolution in France, the people cast his bones out of the royal sepulchre, and laid Napoleon's there instead. And the dunghill complained grievously that it should be disturbed for so slight a cause.

And Napoleon withdrew his hand from the hand of Loyalty, saying, "Pish!" And his eyes opened, and he heard the booming of the sea, and the buzzing of the flies, and felt the heat of the sun, and saw that the sugar he had dropped into his sangaree had not yet reached the bottom of the tumbler.

TO A MOUSE.

By ROBERT BURNS.

(On turning her up in her nest with the plough, November, 1785.)

I.

Wee, sleekit, cowrin', tim'rous beastie,
O, what a panic's in thy breastie!
Thou need na start awa sae hasty
Wi' bickering brattle!
I wad be laith to rin an' chase thee
Wi' murdering pattle!

II.

I'm truly sorry man's dominion
Has broken Nature's social union,
An' justifies that ill opinion
Which makes thee startle
At me, thy poor, earth-born companion
An' fellow mortal!

III.

I doubt na, whyles, but thou may thieve;
What then? poor beastie, thou maun live!
A daimen icker in a thrave
'S a sma' request;
I'll get a blessin' wi' the lave,
An' never miss't!

IV.

Thy wee-bit housie, too, in ruin!
It's silly wa's the win's are strewin
An' naething, now, to big a new ane,
O' foggage green!
An' bleak December's win's ensuin'
Baith snell an' keen!

V.

Thou saw the fields laid bare an' waste,
An' weary winter comin' fast,
An' cozie here, beneath the blast,
Thou thought to dwell
Till crash! the cruel coulter past
Out thro' thy cell.

VI.

That wee bit heap o' leaves an' stibble
Hast cost thee monie a weary nibble!
Now thou's turned out, for a' thy trouble,
But house or hald
To thole the winter's sleety dribble,
An' cranreuch cauld!

VII.

But mousie, thou art no thy lane
In proving foresight may be vain:
The best-laid schemes o' mice an' men
Gang aft agley
An' lea'e us nought but grief an' pain
For promis'd joy!

VIII.

Still thou art blest, compared wi' me!
The present only toucheth thee:
But och! I backward cast my e'e,
On prospects drear!
An' forward tho' I canna see
I guess an' fear!

STREET MUSIC.[1]

By H. R. HAWEIS.

(From "Music and Morals.")

[Hugh Reginald Haweis: English clergyman and author; born at Egham, Surrey, April 3, 1838. After graduating at Cambridge he went to Italy at the time of the Italian Revolution, and was present at the siege of Capua, where he had several narrow escapes. He has been curate of St. James', Marylebone, since 1866; is interested in charitable work; and in 1895 made a lecturing and preaching tour of the world. Besides frequent contributions to periodicals, he has published: "Music and Morals," "Thoughts for the Time," "Speech in Season," "Christ and Christianity," a memoir of Garibaldi, and a life of Sir Morell Mackenzie.]

There are many problems in connection with national music which have never been solved. It would be difficult to find any country without some kind of popular music; but why have some nations called in the aid of science, and developed national schools of music, like France, Italy, Germany, while others, like Russia, Spain, and, above all, Ireland, Scotland, and Wales, have never got beyond rude national ballads? Again, how strange it is to find the old popular forms running side by side with the new scientific forms of modern music without losing their distinctive features!

Mr. Ap-Thomas tells us that the Welsh harper to this day preserves his ancient customs. "Now, as of old, he may be seen, as soon as the sun rises, in the large oak chair (which, as a fixture, stands at the entrance of every neat and tidy Welsh inn), welcoming, harp in hand, the weary traveler, or solacing the hours of friends never tired of listening to his national strains. Many of these harpists are blind and very old."

The primitive nature of the bagpipes would seem to need no comment; but, curiously enough, although the bagpipes play many of the old national tunes, they are not the old national instrument of Scotland, nor were the oldest tunes composed for the bagpipes, as is usually supposed. Up to the sixteenth century the harp was the national instrument of both Ireland and Scotland, and the national melodies of both countries were not dissimilar. The Irish and Scotch melodies, reduced to their simplest expressions, abound in thirds, fifths, and octaves. They were composed for the harp, which was

[1] By permission of Longmans, Green & Co. (Cr. 8vo. Price 7*s.* 6*d.*)

strung with wire, and very resonant. To avoid discord, it became necessary that every note should form a concord with the last, and hence the peculiar and forever pleasing character of Scotch and Irish melodies.

The abominable characteristics of the bagpipes are not really Scotch, but French. How the bagpipes superseded the harp in Scotland has always been considered a mystery. We believe it may be traced to French influence, and distinctly to the period of Mary Queen of Scots. At all events, about that time, toward the close of the sixteenth century, the harp went out of fashion, and the bagpipe came in. Is it unlikely that in the foreign train of Mary Stuart there may have been players of the national *cornemuse*, or French bagpipes, who managed to set a fashion which, for some reason or other, took root and has lasted ever since? The attempt to graft on Scotland foreign customs, instead of adopting Scotch ones, is entirely consistent with what we know of the Queen of Scots' policy.

But the cornemuse of southern France is perhaps the most striking instance of the way in which primitive national music may continue wholly uninfluenced by modern culture. The cornemuse has struck the keynote of all really national French music, and cornemuse forms of melody are not only to be found in the modern popular French ballads, but abound in the operas of Auber and Gounod; yet the cornemuse itself remains unchanged, nor are its melodies ever varied in the direction of modern music. Madame Sand, in one of her amusing digressions, gives an account of a conversation she had with a cornemuse player at a French fair. He did not make his tunes — they were all made by the woodcutters in the great forest: if a man wished to excel, he must go into the woods and catch the melodies from these wild men. The tunes were handed down from generation to generation, and might be endlessly varied; but there was no development, no change in their structure, nor had there been, as far as she could ascertain, for centuries.

Now, speaking generally, the state of music in Scotland, Ireland, Wales, France, Germany, Italy, Russia, and Spain is not wholly unintelligible. Scotland, Ireland, and Wales have no schools, but they have national ballads: music there is a wild germ, that, for some reason or other, has remained undeveloped by civilization. The same thing may be said of Spain

REV. H. R. HAWEIS

From a photo by Alexander Bassano

and Russia. In France a regular school of music has appropriated the rude popular elements (as a *point du départ*), which nevertheless remain alongside of the music school in all their primitive simplicity. In Italy the same phenomenon has occurred, only the connection between the Abruzzi mountaineer, with his pipe stuck into an inflated goatskin, and the Italian opera, is less obvious than that between the cornemuse player and modern French song.

In Germany, however, where music has attained its highest and most truly national development, the rude element will soon have reached the vanishing point; hardly an old melody of mountain or vale but what has received a new setting: our idea of a *Volkslied* is something in two or three parts by Mendelssohn, or, at all events, a charming air with a graceful accompaniment. Even the wild airs of Poland have been remodeled by Chopin. The "yodeling" of the peasants is generally heard in combination with delicious harmonies unknown to their forefathers, and the Swiss "hurdy-gurdy" is probably the last remnant of barbarism to be found in the direction of Germany.

But what shall be said of England? We can imagine the nations passing before us, each represented by its popular form of street music. Germany comes with a band of singers, followed by a band of men playing on all kinds of musical instruments. France comes fresh from the woods with her cornemuse. Italy issues from the mountains with that tuneful and fascinating goatskin and pipe, so finely rendered by M. Gounod in "Mirella." Spain comes with a bandoline; Scotland with the bagpipes; Ireland and Wales with harps of well-known national form and proportion. Even Russia sings a good bass tune, and blows a horn well, and England brings up the rear with — a policeman requesting an organ grinder to move on!

Indeed, that man plays all the favorite tunes. It is true he is not English, but he represents the popular tastes in music. Does he play national melodies? Not many — chiefly the melodies of other countries, or what will pass for them with the million; but he does *grind* certain English ballads too, claptrap sort of jingles — not especially national, or especially anything; he cannot be said to *play* them; no fancy, or originality, or taste is displayed, except by the monkey who sits on his shoulder; the performance from first to last is a *grind*. In the streets of other countries you seldom meet with foreign musicians — at least not in France, Germany, and Italy; but who will deny that the staple of street music in England is organ grinding? And the grinder is a foreigner, who only grinds a few English tunes under protest. In fact, "He's a Pal o' mine" and "Jolly Dogs" are used as gold leaf to gild pills like "Casta Diva" and the "Carnaval de Venise."

But as the organ grinder is a *great fact*, and perhaps, in a survey of street music in England, the most prominent fact, he deserves a few moments' calm consideration. There are big organs drawn by a donkey, and little organs carried by boys; nondescript boxes with a cradle at the top and two babies, drawn by a woman; uprights on a stick with a little handle, turned by a crazy old man; chests open in front and shut at the back, or shut in front and open at the back. There are flute organs, with a wonderful system of wooden pipes, visible through glass; great magnified accordions, played somehow with a handle — horrid things, which grind only the "Old Hundredth" and a chant on metal pipes. There are tinkling cupboards, which remind one of Dickens' pianoforte with the works taken out, so irregular and uncertain is the effect of the handle upon the tune. There are illustrated organs, with Chinese mandarins performing conjuring tricks in a row, or Nebuchadnezzar's band; and there are organs with a monkey, triangle, bones, tambourine, or whistle obligato. Every man has probably had moments in his life when he has not been sane upon the question of barrel organs. He has perhaps been placed in difficult circumstances. Let us say he occupies a corner house. On one side, at the bottom of the street, commences the "Chickaleary Bloke"; on the other side, at the bottom of another street, is faintly heard "Polly Perkins": both are working steadily up to a point — that point is his corner house — let us say your own corner house. You are in your study writing poetry; nearer and nearer draw the minstrels, regardless of each other, and probably out of each other's hearing, but both heard by you in your favorable position. As they near the point the discord becomes wild and terrible; you rush into the back study, but the *tom-tom* man is in the yard; you rush out of the front door to look for a policeman — there is none; you use any Italian words you can recollect; at the same time, pointing to your head, you explain that your father lies dangerously ill upstairs, and that several ladies are dying in the neighborhood; you implore the Italian to move on, and the scene ends in No. 1 slowly grinding down the street which No. 2 came up, and No. 2 grinding up the street which No. 1 has just come down. At such moments we are apt to speak recklessly on the great subject of barrel organs, and we sometimes—idle employment!—write letters to the newspapers, which are pardonably one-sided. The fact is, the organ question, like all other great questions, has two sides to it, although we seldom hear but one.

Let not those who write abusive letters to the newspapers, and bring in bills to abolish street music, think they will be able to loosen the firm hold which the barrel organist has over the British public. Your cook is his friend, your housemaid is his admirer; the policeman and the baker's young man look on him in the light of a formidable rival.

But, for once, let us speak a good word for him. We know all that can be said against him, let us now plead his cause a little. His sphere is large; he conquers more worlds than one; his popularity is not only wide, but varied: he enters many clean and spacious squares, and little chubby faces, well born and rosy, look out from high-railed nursery windows, and as they look out he looks up, and baby is danced at the bars and stops crying directly, and Tommy forgets his quarrel with Johnny, and runs to the window too, and tears are wiped and harmony is restored in many and many a nursery, and nurse herself finds the penny and smiles, and "organ man" pockets the penny and smiles, and plays five more tunes for the money, and lifts his hat, and waves "ta-ta!" in Italian, and walks off to "fresh fields and pastures new"—and isn't it worth the penny?

And where does he wander to now—that happy, easy-tempered son of the South? Ah! he has no proud looks; and, though he has just played to members of the aristocracy, he is willing to turn as merrily for the lowest of the people.

I meet him in the dingy alleys of the great city—I meet him in the regions of garbage and filth, where the atmosphere inhaled seems to be an impartial mixture of smoke and decomposition, and where the diet of the people seems to consist of fried herrings and potato parings: there is our organ man—and there, at least, we may bless him—grinding away to the miserable, sunken, and degraded denizens of Pigmire Lane or Fish Alley. Let him stay always there—let him grind ever thus. I confess it does my heart good to see those slatternly women come to their doors, and stand and listen, and the heavy, frowning, coal-besmeared men lean out of the windows with their pipes, and, forgetting hunger and grinding poverty, hushing also the loud oath and blasphemy for a little season, smile with the pleasure of the sweet sounds. Through that little black window with the cracked panes you can see the lame shoemaker look up for a moment, and, as he resumes the long-drawn-out stitches with both hands, it is with countenance relaxed, and almost pleasurable energy. The pale-faced tailor looks out from the top story (yes, like a beam of sunshine the music has struck through him); he forgets the rent, and the work, and the wages, and the wretchedness of life. It is the end of the day; it is lawful to rest for a moment and listen, and they do listen—the men and women clustering in groups on their door-steps, and leaning from the windows above, and the children—oh! the children! I look down the alley, and suddenly it is flooded with the light of the low sun; it smites the murky atmosphere into purple shades, and broad, warm, yellow light upon the pathway, and glitters like gold leaf upon the window panes; and the children—the children are dancing all down the alley, dancing in long vistas far down into the sunny mist, two and two, three and three, but all dancing, and dancing in time; and their faces—many poor pale faces, and some rosy ones too—their faces are so happy, and the whole alley is hushed, save only for the music and the dancing of the children.

I bless that organ man—a very Orpheus in hell! I bless his music. I stand in that foul street where the blessed sun shines, and where the music is playing; I give the man a penny to prolong the happiness of those poor people, of those hungry, pale, and ragged children, and, as I retire, I am saluted as a public benefactor; and was ever pleasure bought so cheap and so pure?

Toward evening we find the organ grinder fairly expelled from some quarters of the town—from the better streets and the more respectable squares. What we may have striven in vain to accomplish, what there was no policeman at hand to do, has been triumphantly effected by *the second great fact* of street music—THE GERMAN BAND. The full-blown brass band, with drums, plays fine music, and is patronized in high places. The men wear uniforms, and are from six to twelve in number.

The head man leads on the clarionet, arranges the music, and is generally a capital theoretical and practical musician. Every man carries his own stand of music, and, by an arrangement of strings and weights, can set it up and play through any moderate hurricane. The hardiness of these men is astonishing. They stand in cutting draughts at the corners of the streets; they will play through any ordinary shower. The cornet executes variations in the snow, the drum keeps himself warm in frosty weather by a close application to business, the flute chirps and twitters with the thermometer at zero, when other people cannot even whistle. The men with the great brass tubes and serpents pour forth volumes of breath on tropical nights, when other people can hardly breathe; the triangle man has the lightest time of it, but then he is expected to walk about and sue for coppers; indeed, that appears to be his real business — the triangle is only his pastime.

As we sit with our windows open in the summer evenings, we can hear them playing at the corner of the street. Now it is "Masaniello," dashed off with great fire, and generally taken too fast; then a selection from "Faust," or the last new opera chopped up, sometimes very cleverly, for street use. On these occasions the principal instruments play the "arias," and one often regrets that men who play so well have not had more opportunities of hearing the songs which they are the means of making so widely popular. The airs are constantly taken at a pace or in a style which proves that the player has never heard them on the stage, nor has the faintest notion of what they mean.

Although forced to play chiefly Italian and French overtures, opera selections, firework quadrilles, cataract waltzes, etc., to catch the public, the German feeling will creep out, and is not unkindly received. Homœopathic doses of Haydn, Mozart, or Beethoven are administered in the shape of a slow movement, allegretto, or minuet and trio out of some symphony, and these, inserted, sandwichlike, between a "Slap Bang" polka and "Fra Diavolo," go down very well. But as we contemplate the model German band, the scene changes, and we find ourselves, as in some bad dream, listening to a hideous parody. Four poor fellows have got together, the sport of a cruel destiny; none of their instruments are in tune; the public will not hear them or pay them; their own ears have become vitiated; they have learned to regard any brass instruments blown together anyhow as a German band. Of course, they do not long hang together; some of them get happily drafted into bigger bands, others pair off, and we thus have that form of street music which may be called the *Brass Band dissolved*. This may mean one of two things : it may mean either the *Brass without the Band*, or the *Band without the Brass*.

The *Brass without the Band* means generally a cornet and a serpent, who undertake to perform "Suono il Tromba Trepido"; sometimes the serpent does "Il Balen," or at least any part of it which happens to be within the compass of his instrument. On these occasions the cornet flourishes about wildly, and appears to be carrying on a kind of guerrilla warfare with his panting antagonist, which ends in the successful demolition of the latter, who finally wheezes and puffs himself to death, while the cornet screams a pæan of victory. At other times the cornet leads off with "Ah! che la morte," while the serpent, coming to life again, gasps in an explosive manner. Before long it usually happens that the serpent, jealous of the cornet's supremacy, absorbs himself into a band again, and the cornet, if he does not go and do likewise, wanders away to enter into a fruitless competition with the "organ man" in Fish Alley, or tries to get a precarious living off "The Blue Bells of Scotland" in front of a third-rate public house in a deserted quarter of the city.

If the *Brass without the Band* can fall to a lower depth still, it is when he seats himself on the top of a van full of tipsy Foresters, and after sharing their potations during the daytime, "joins in" frantically with the chorus of lunatics as they drive home through the streets of the city, making night hideous with bellow and blare. We may here take leave of the *Brass without the Band*.

The second part of the *Brass Band dissolved* is the *Band without the Brass*, which generally means a flute or a clarionet *solus*. Unlike the "brass," the "wood" never walk a road together. As they are both solo instruments, the rivalry would be too bitter; and, finding a lonely life intolerable, they soon join themselves to, or go to make up, what may be called *the third great fact* of street music — THE STRING BAND.

The highest form of the string band is too seldom seen. It consists of from six to twelve performers — two violins, tenor, violoncello or double bass, flute, clarionet, or the above doubled, or in such other various proportions as time and circumstances may allow of. We have met with them at seaside places in fine weather, and occasionally in the more retired parts of the city in the afternoon. But as stringed instruments in any perfection are delicate things, the expense of keeping them together in any number and efficiency is great; and the German bands, both louder and hardier in organization, drive them out of the field. For some reason, these large string bands are generally English; they play excellent music, but are not so popular or so well paid as their German rivals.

Another form of the string band, however, is the most popular and the best paid of any street music; but, from its very delicacy and excellence, its sphere of operation is restricted as to time and place, and few itinerant musicians seem to combine the necessary qualifications for success. Visitors to Brighton have all noticed the great rival to the excellent German band on the beach in the shape of four Italian musicians. The leader, Signor Beneventano, is a fine violin player out of doors, although the writer discovered that in a room he is somewhat coarse in tone and execution, which in great measure accounts for his success in the open air. He is accompanied by a harp, a second violin, and a flute. Each man is capital in his department, and each man knows his place. This little band of accomplished players forms the center for a group of attentive listeners, who are regaled with charming versions of the modern opera, the *primo violino* occasionally playing solos with excellent pathos and effect. We have seen shillings, half crowns, and even gold put into the cap, in return for which regular printed programmes are distributed. But at the first spot of rain or gust of wind — in the middle of a passage or "scena," however touching — Signor Beneventano signals to stop, packs up fiddle and bow, a cloth is hastily flung over the harp, the flute is unscrewed, the music folded up, all made "taut," and the artists retire. The brass band thinks them poor creatures.

But if we seldom hear either what we may call *the Orchestral String Band* or *the Italian Miniature Band*, *the String Band dissolved* is, alas! always with us. It is a harp and a fiddle. The harpist is generally a man with an ear for time, but not for tune; the fiddler has an ear for tune, but none for time. The fiddler can afford to be in tune, because he has only four strings, but the harpist, who has forty, very naturally cannot. We have heard people wonder how the harpists can keep their strings from breaking — they don't. Others ask how it is possible in the open air to have so many strings in any sort of tune — they never are. The picked Italian band *is* fairly in tune and that *is* a wonder. But though in the *String Band dissolved* there is much to regret, there is nothing to wonder at, except it be how such people ever get a living. The *sangfroid* of the harpist is great — one accompaniment does for all times and tunes; or, if he has different accompaniments, he never fits them on to their right tunes; and if for a couple of bars he blunders into the right measure, he does not notice it before he gets wrong again. A cat might walk over the wires with quite as much, probably a very similar, effect. But he is outdone by the determination of the violinist, who is superior to all accompaniment, and treats the harpist like a lackey. He does not tell him when he is going to begin, how long he is going on, or when he means to stop; indeed, he is generally much the better man of the two, and might play a respectable fourth-rate second violin at a third-class theater if he practiced hard, and did not show such overweening confidence in his variations on the "Carnaval de Venise." Where will that man end? Cross the street, and we can show you. Yonder comes an old blind man with a knowing dog who is constantly persuading him that it is necessary to move on whenever he is playing or begins to play a tune. He has thus got into the habit of walking. He is weak and old with drink before his time, and does not play much now except on the open strings. Sometimes it is his wife who leads him; now he is blind she keeps the drink from him, and prolongs his life a little. One day she will sell his old fiddle; they will go into the workhouse together, and the *String Band* will be completely *dissolved.*

We must here notice a large class of nondescript street musicians — chiefly self-made men. We may call these *the fourth great fact* in street music, and treat them under the head of MISCELLANEOUS ARTISTS. Many of them are men of strong original powers, subjected to the most eccentric development. We remember one strange man who bore the appearance of a

North American Indian armed to the teeth. He was hung round, saddled, propped up, sat upon, wedged in, and stuck all over generally with some two dozen or more instruments, and boasted that he could play most of them simultaneously. A drum, worked with a wire by one foot, rattled above his head; his mouth moved round a semicircle, blowing into such things as Pan pipes, flutes, clarionets, horns, and other tubes conveniently slung to his neck like an ox's cradle; one hand moved an accordion tied to his thigh, while a triangle jingled from his wrist; the other hand played the bones, while the elbow clapped a tambourine fixed to his side; on the inside of his knees were cymbals, which he kept knocking together. There was now only one foot and ankle left, and on that ankle he had bells, which rang with every motion. We describe from memory, and doubt whether we have detailed half the instruments. If Julius Cæsar had ever met that man, he would have felt quite ashamed of himself for not being able to do more than three things at a time.

Then we have, at the seaside, the Bohemian dwarfs on little three-legged stools, with tiny bandolines, strumming away almost inaudibly, but apparently quite content, and remunerated out of pity.

Then there is the piano on wheels, which goes about till one day it gets rained on unmercifully and bursts. And the harmonium on wheels, which in a very little time does nothing but "cipher," and has to retire into private life. There is the street Picco, who plays cleverly on the penny whistle, and the street Bonnay, who plays with hammers on a wooden instrument; another plays with hammers on bits of metal, another on bits of glass, another on regular musical glasses, another on bells, and another on strings; but the most original of this class is a man who produces singularly beautiful effects by using two balls of India rubber to set in vibration a perfectly tuned system of musical glasses. The India rubber is used to rub the edge of the glass as children rub dessert bowls with wet fingers, and the sound elicited is the same. This man plays pathetic tunes with great taste and extraordinary execution. He has lately substituted a series of glass tubes.

Having got thus far in my meditations, it occurred to me that it was time to pass from instrumental to vocal music; but the transition seemed abrupt: there must be a connecting link. I think I have discovered that missing link in the person of the *tom-tom* man. He is both vocal and instrumental. Many persons who have not studied the question may suppose that he only beats the tom-tom; but this is an error. On very hot days, if you go close up to him, you will perceive that he sings what are doubtless the national melodies of his native land. As far as we can make out, they are as simple as they are plaintive, and consist mainly in the constant repetition of

Yow, yow, aie! yagger, yow, yow.

Here, then, we may be said to have a link between instrumental and vocal street music.

Vocal street music divides itself naturally into ballad and chorus, or solo and part songs. The street ballads emanate from the music halls and penny gaffs. And, of all the encouraging facts in connection with popular music in England, this — our *fifth fact* — of BALLAD MUSIC is the least. This is the form in which whatever there is national in English music is uttered, and what utterances we have here! Every now and then, it is true, a really graceful ballad, such as, "When other lips," "Jeanette and Jeannot," gets into general vogue; but, as a rule, the really popular songs are those that minister to the lowest rollicking tastes, such as "Champagne Charley," or to the vulgar commonplaces of life, such as the "Postman's Knock," or to the feeblest sentimental fancies, such as "Sea Shells." About most of them there is a low affectation and a sense of unreality that pierces, and the people that troll them about the streets never sing them with earnestness or humor, like the Germans or the Italians, just because music is not to our lower orders a deep need, a means of expressing the pent-up and often oppressive emotions of the heart, but merely a noisy appendage to low pastimes. Even the less objectionable ballads which concern the most touching affections of our nature are full of vamped-up and artificial sentiment. What, for instance, can be more feeble in sentiment and false in taste than "Let me kiss him for his mother"? And yet, trash like this, which would be scouted in any other form by every national schoolboy, is considered finely pathetic by the lower orders when it comes to them in the disguise of a ballad, for music to them is an artificial thing, having artificial and unreal standards of propriety, and too often unconnected with their real interests and genuine emotions. And the consequence is that our street ballads last but from year to year, almost from month to month; they are constantly being replaced, not by songs that enrich the national stock, but by songs whose chief object seems to be to extinguish their predecessors, and when they have accomplished this, die themselves, like bees after discharging their sting. Who ever hears "Slap bang" now? Even "Old dog Tray," a really pathetic thing, seems dead at last, while the echoes of "Not for Joseph" seem finally to have died away.

There is a certain feeble prettiness about the Virginia Gabriel and Claribel school of ballads, but it is the "Baby asleep," "Papa, come to tea" style of thing, so eloquently condemned in the painting of the period, at the Royal Institution, by Mr. Ruskin; and when the ballad is not strictly social, spooney, or domestic, can we imagine any twaddle feebler than what is put forward to do duty for thought and feeling? In one ballad, for instance, the following ingenious conundrum is propounded: "What will to-morrow be?" The answer is, "Who can tell?" Of course nobody can, and this insult to our intelligence is repeated through several verses, to music nearly as exasperating. From the mud heaps of ballads lying around us we may no doubt pick out some gold nuggets; but the finest ballads are sure to be the least popular. All honor to Madame Sainton Dolby, Mr. Santley, and a few others, for keeping some really good ballads before the public. Let us only trust that Mr. Sullivan, the brightest hope of the young English school, will keep before him the high ballad ideal of his Shakespeare songs, and those lyrics which Mr. Tennyson has written for him, and not be tempted into the "Ever of thee" style by the tears of sopranos or the solemn warnings of publishers.

But if we have for a moment escaped from the streets, we are reminded by the shrill voice of a woman outside that it is with these, and not with the drawing-room, that we are now concerned. The poor creature, meanly clad, is singing "We may be happy yet," or "My pretty Jane." The crying baby has at last fallen asleep, but the song is almost more piteous. But we have only to go down one of the back streets, until we come to a third-class public house, and we reach at once the lowest depths to which the English ballad can descend. Two coarse and grimy ruffians, with greasy slips of thin paper, printed all over and adorned with villainous woodcuts, are tramping stoutly down the reeking alley, and chanting forth to admiring groups of the unwashed some account of the latest murder, in rhyme, or the interesting contest between Champion Tommy and the Charcoal Pet. Let us draw a veil over their proceedings as we pass with a sigh of relief to *the sixth fact* of street music, which consists of CHORUS and PART SONG in various forms.

The blind singers, who, with the assistance of a concertina, ply through the whole of London, are known to every one. They render their psalm tunes, soundly harmonized, in a hard *canto fermo* style, which has its legitimate attractions, and with that peculiar concentration and directness of purpose which characterizes blind people, and which has a pathos of its own. We fancy that regular bands of accomplished part singers are less common now than they were a few years ago. They may have been driven out of the field by the negro melodists, and have no doubt found a more congenial sphere in the various music halls which have been lately opened in great numbers all over the country. We must, however, notice the Præger family, who are unique in their excellent part singing and improvisations: we hear that it is not an uncommon thing for them, at the close of the Brighton or Folkestone season, to deposit several hundred pounds in the bank previous to their departure for the Continent. Out of the season the young ladies receive an excellent general education in one of the first French schools, and every year the return of the family is anxiously awaited by many thousands of discriminating admirers.

But there is a foreign band of singers—foreign only in appearance—that never leaves our shores—the *Negro Melodists.* The conquering nigger landed some years ago, and, after capturing this small island, caught many of the aborigines, blacked them over, and sent them off to proclaim the glories of Niggerdom throughout the length and breadth of this benighted land. The princes of the art sit in royal council at St. James' Hall, and it is an affecting thing to see the poor white men, who resort to their levees in crowds, welcomed by them as men and brethren. It is the fashion to smile at the "Christy Minstrels," and, indeed, uninterrupted gravity would be somewhat out of place in their assemblies; but we must not forget that they furnish one of the most remarkable and original elements of our street music. From St. James' Hall, and not from "Old Virginny," come constant supplies of new melodies. The original melodies such as "Lady Neale," "Uncle Ned," some of which were no doubt genuine American negro productions, are almost forgotten, but from that new source of negro pathos and humor numbers of songs and choruses continue to flow, some of them good imitations, and many of them retaining the characteristic form of the negro melody, viz., niggers *solus*, niggers *tutti*, interludes and brilliant finale by Bones, accompanied by the whole band. The real negro is passionately attached to music—his sorrows and joys are both accompanied by the banjo—and slave life, in which the present generation of negroes has been born and bred, is full of touching episodes and dramatic incidents. The English public were subdued by the power and beauty of these as depicted, or, as some say, overdrawn, in Mrs. Stowe's book, and it is not too much to presume that the lasting popularity and deep appreciation of negro fun and pathos in England is mainly due to the genius of "Uncle Tom's Cabin."

The gentlemen who nightly blacken their faces in order to portray to a sympathetic audience the life and manners of a hitherto oppressed race have certainly a fair claim upon our indulgent interest. There is something pathetic even about these worthy Englishmen themselves, and it is not without emotion that we gaze at the portraits of the most successful "Bones" of the age outside St. James' Hall, representing above the mighty W. P. Collins, black as to his face, and otherwise equipped for action, while underneath, the same face, only washed, looks appealingly at us, and seems to say, "You see the black all comes off. I am not so bad looking, either. You can hardly see me at night. But remember P. Collins is white, and, although his initial is P., he was not christened Pompey."

The street niggers are often excessively clever, but are forced to pander in a variety of ways to the popular taste. For the sake of an undiscerning public, English fun is mixed up with negro humor. Punch conducts with a bâton and a desk before him; light and flippant remarks are addressed to the crowd in good broad English; capers are cut in season and out of season, to the dismay of cab horses and omnibus drivers; and even practical jokes are played off on any who come too near "bones" or "tambourine." But a state of chronic fun is not without its penalties: the chorus over and the crowd dispersed, no faces look so downcast and woe-begone as the faces of the minstrels. They walk silently two and two, or follow each other, a string of lonely, dispirited men, down a back street into a public house. Not even there is rest. Two go in and immediately recommence, and banjo consumes a solitary pint outside, while fiddle and bones strike up within to earn another.

THE WIND IN A FROLIC.

By WILLIAM HOWITT.

[WILLIAM HOWITT: English miscellaneous writer; born at Heanor, Derbyshire, in 1792. In 1821 he married Mary Botham, and resided successively in Nottingham, London, Heidelberg, and Rome, where he died, March 3, 1879. In collaboration with his wife he wrote, "Literature and Romance of Northern Europe"; "Ruined Abbeys of Great Britain"; and independently, "History of Priestcraft," often reprinted; "Rural Life of England"; "Visits to Remarkable Places"; "Illustrated History of England." A visit to the Australian gold fields (1852–1854) resulted in "Land, Labor, and Gold" and "Discovery in Australia, Tasmania, and New Zealand."]

THE wind one morning sprang up from sleep
Saying, "Now for a frolic! now for a leap!
Now for a madcap galloping chase!
I'll make a commotion in every place."
So it swept with a bustle right through the great town,
Creaking the signs and scattering down
Shutters, and whisking, with merciless squalls
Old women's bonnets and gingerbread stalls.
There never was heard a much lustier shout
As the apples and oranges trundled about,
And the urchins, which stand with their thievish eyes
Forever on watch, ran off each with a prize.
Then away to the fields it went, blustering and humming,
And the cattle all wondered whatever was coming;
And tossed the colts' manes all over their brows
And pulled by their tails the matronly cows,
Till, offended at such a familiar salute,
They all turned their backs, and stood sullenly mute.
So on it went, capering and playing its pranks.
Whistling with reeds on the broad river's banks,
Puffing the birds as they sat on the spray,
Or the traveler grave on the king's highway;

It was not too nice to hustle the bags
Of the beggar and flutter his dirty rags;
'Twas so bold that it feared not to play its joke
With the doctor's wig or the gentleman's cloak.
Through the forest it roared and cried gayly, "Now,
You sturdy old oaks, I'll make you bow!"
And it made them bow without more ado,
And cracked their great branches through and through.
Then it rushed like a monster on cottage and farm,
Striking their dwellers with sudden alarm;
And they ran out like bees in a midsummer swarm.
There were dames with their kerchiefs tied over their caps
To see if their poultry were free from mishaps;
The turkeys they gobbled, the geese screamed aloud,
And the hens crept to rest in a terrified crowd;
There was raising of ladders, and logs laying on,
When the thatch from the roof threatened soon to be gone.
But the wind had passed on and had met in a lane
With a schoolboy who panted and struggled in vain,
For it tossed him and twirled him, then passed, and he stood
With his hat in a pool, and his shoe in the mud.
There was a poor man, hoary and old,
Cutting the heath in the open wold;
The strokes of his bill were faint and few
Ere this frolicsome wind upon him blew,
But behind him, before him, about him it came,
And the breath seemed gone from his feeble frame;
So he sat him down, with a muttering tone
Saying: "Plague on the wind! was the like ever known?
But nowadays every wind that blows
Tells me how weak an old man grows."
But away went the wind in its holiday glee,
And now it was far on the billowy sea,
And the lordly ship felt its staggering blow,
And the little boats darted to and fro;
But lo! it was night, and it sank to rest
On the sea birds' rock, in the gleaming west,
Laughing to think in its fearful fun
How little of mischief it had done.

CHARLES AUCHESTER.

By ELIZABETH SARA SHEPPARD.

[ELIZABETH SARA SHEPPARD, an English novelist, born at Blackheath, in 1830, who wrote "Charles Auchester," "Counterparts," "Rumor," etc. She died at Brixton in 1862.]

I HAVE never described Lenhart Davy, nor can I; but to use the keener words of my friend Dumas, he was one of the men the most "significant" I ever knew.

Arrived at his house,—that house, just what a house should be, to the purpose in every respect,—I flew in as if quite at home. I was rather amazed that I saw no woman creature about, nor any kind of servant. The door at the end of the passage was still open; I still saw out into the little lawny yard, but nobody was stirring. "The house was haunted!"

I believe it,—by a choir of glorious ghosts!

"Dear alto, you will not be alarmed to be locked in with me, I hope, will you?"

"Frightened, sir? Oh, no, it is delicious." I most truly felt it delicious. I preceded him up the staircase,—he remaining behind to lock the little door. I most truly felt it delicious. Allow me again to allude to the appetite. I was very hungry, and when I entered the parlor I beheld such preparation upon the table as reminded me it is at times satisfactory as well as necessary to eat and drink. The brown inkstand and company were removed, and in their stead I saw a little tray, of an oval form, upon which tray stood the most exquisite porcelain service for two I have ever seen. The china was small and very old,—I knew that, for we were rather curious in china at home; and I saw how very valuable these cups, that cream jug, those plates must be. They were of pearly clearness, and the crimson and purple butterfly on each rested over a sprig of honeysuckle entwined with violets.

"Oh, what beautiful china!" I exclaimed; I could not help it, and Lenhart Davy smiled.

"It was a present to me from my class in Germany."

"Did you have a class, sir, in Germany?"

"Only little boys, Charlie, like myself."

"Sir, did you teach when you were a little boy?"

"I began to teach before I was a great boy, but I taught only little boys then."

He placed me in a chair while he left the room for an instant. I suppose he entered the next, for I heard him close at hand. Coming back quickly, he placed a little spirit lamp upon the table, and a little bright kettle over it; it boiled very soon. He made such tea! — I shall never forget it; and when I told him I very seldom had tea at home, he answered, "I seldom drink more than one cup myself; but I think one cannot hurt even such a nervous person as you are, — and besides, tea improves the voice, — did you know that?"

I laughed, and drew my chair close to his. Nor shall I ever forget the tiny loaves, white and brown, nor the tiny pat of butter, nor the thin, transparent biscuits, crisp as hoar frost, and delicate as if made of Israelitish manna. Davy ate not much himself, but he seemed delighted to see me eat, nor would he allow me to talk.

"One never should," said he, "while eating."

Frugal as he was, he never for an instant lost his cheery smile and companionable manner, and I observed he watched me very closely. As soon as I had gathered up and put away my last crumb, I slipped out of my chair, and pretended to pull him from his seat.

"Ah! you are right, we have much to do."

He went out again, and returned laden with a wooden tray, on which he piled all the things and carried them downstairs. Returning, he laughed and said: —

"I must be a little put out to-night, as I have a visitor; so I shall not clear up until I have taken you home."

"My mother is going to send for me, sir; but I wish I might help you now."

"I shall not need help, — I want it at least in another way. Will you now come here?"

We removed to the piano. He took down from the shelves that overshadowed it three or four volumes in succession. At length, selecting one, he laid it upon the desk and opened it. I gazed in admiration. It was a splendid edition, in score, of Pergolesi's "Stabat Mater." He gathered from within its pages a separate sheet — the alto part, beautifully copied — and handed it to me, saying, "I know you will take care of it." So I did. We worked very hard, but I think I never enjoyed any exercise so much. He premised, with a cunning smile, that he should not let me run on at that rate if I had not to be brushed up all in a hurry; but then, though I was ignorant, I was apt and very ardent. I sang with an entire attention to his hints; and though I felt I was hurrying on too fast for my "understanding" to keep pace with my "spirit," yet I did get on very rapidly in the mere accession to acquaintance with the part. We literally rushed through the "Stabat Mater," which was for the first part of the first grand morning, and then, for the other, we began the "Dettingen Te Deum." I thought this very easy after the "Stabat Mater," but Davy silenced me by suggesting, "You do not know the difficulty until you are placed in the choir." Our evening's practice lasted about two hours and a half. He stroked my hair gently then, and said he feared he had fatigued me. I answered by thanking him with all my might, and begging to go on. He shook his head.

"I am afraid we have done too much now. This day week the 'Creation,'—that is for the second morning; and then, Charles, then the 'Messiah,'—last and best."

"Oh, the 'Messiah'! I know some of the songs,—at least, I have heard them. And are we to hear that? and am I to sing in 'Halleluiah'?" I had known of it from my cradle; and loving it *before* I heard it, how did I feel for it when it was to be brought so near me? I think that this oratorio is the most beloved of any by children and childlike souls. How strangely in it all spirits take a part!

Margareth, our ancient nurse, came for me at half-past eight. She was not sent away, but Davy would accompany us to our own door. Before I left his house, and while she was waiting in the parlor, he said to me, "Would you like to see where I sleep?" and called me into the most wonderful little room. A shower bath filled one corner; there was a great closet one whole side, filled with every necessary, exactly enough for one person. The bed was perfectly plain, with no curtains and but a headboard, a mattress, looking as hard as the ground, and a very singular portrait, over the head, of a gentleman, in line engraving, which does not intellectualize the contour. This worthy wore a flowing wig and a shirt bedecked with frills.

"That is John Sebastian Bach," said Lenhart Davy,—"at least, they told me so in Dresden. I keep it because it *means*

"Ah!" I replied; for I had heard the jaw-breaking name, which is dearer to many (though they, alas! too few, are scattered) than the sound of Lydian measures.

If I permit myself to pay any more visits to the nameless cottage, I shall never take myself to the festival; but I must just say that we entertained Davy the next Sunday at dinner. I had never seen my mother enjoy anybody's society so much; but I observed he talked not so much as he listened to her, and this may have been the secret. He went very early, but on the Tuesday he fetched me again. It was not in vain that I sang this time either,—my voice seemed to deliver itself from something earthly; it was joy and ease to pour it forth.

When we had blended the bass and alto of the "Creation" choruses, with a long spell at "The heavens are telling," Davy observed, "Now for the 'Messiah,' but you will only be able to look at it with me; to-morrow night is rehearsal at the hall, and your mother must let you go." Rehearsal at the hall! What words were those? They rang in my brain that night, and I began to grow very feverish. Millicent was very kind to me; but I was quite timid of adverting to my auspices, and I dared not introduce the subject, as none of them could feel as I did. My mother watched me somewhat anxiously,—and no wonder; for I was very much excited. But when the morrow came, my self-importance made a man of me, and I was calmer than I had been for days.

I remember the knock which came about seven in the evening, just as it was growing gray. I remember rushing from our parlor to Lenhart Davy on the doorstep. I remember our walk, when my hands were so cold and my heart was so hot, so happy. I remember the pale, pearly shade that was falling on street and factory, the shop-lit glare, the mail coach thundering down High Street. I remember how I felt entering, from the dim evening, the chiaro-oscuro of the corridors, just uncertainly illustrated by a swinging lamp or two; and I remember passing into the hall. Standing upon the orchestra, giddy, almost fearful to fall forwards into the great unlighted chaos, the windows looked like clouds themselves, and every pillar, tier, and cornice stood dilated in the unsubstantial space. Lenhart Davy had to drag me forwards to my nook among the altos, beneath the organ, just against the conductor's desk. The orchestra was a dream to me, filled with dark shapes, flitting and hurrying, crossed by wandering sounds, whispers, and laughter. There must have been four or five hundred of us up there, but it seems to me like a lampless church, as full as it could be of people struggling for room.

Davy did not lose his hold upon me, but one and another addressed him, and flying remarks reached him from every quarter. He answered in his hilarious voice; but his manner was decidedly more distant than to me when alone with him. At last some one appeared at the foot of the orchestra steps with a taper; some one or other snatched it from him, and in a moment a couple of candles beamed brightly from the conductor's desk. It was a strange, candle-light effect then. Such great, awful shadows threw themselves down the hall, and so many faces seemed darker than they had, clustered in the glooming twilight. Again some hidden hand had touched the gas, which burst in tongues of splendor that shook themselves immediately over us; *then* was the orchestra a blaze defined as day. But still dark, and darkening, like a vast abyss, lay the hall before us; and the great chandelier was itself a blot, like a mystery hung in circumambient nothingness.

I was lost in the light around me, and striving to pierce into that mystery beyond, when a whisper thrilled me: "Now, Charles, I must leave you. You are Mr. Auchester at present. Stand firm and sing on. Look alone at the conductor, and think alone of your part. Courage!" What did he say "courage" for? As if my heart could fail me then and there!

I looked steadfastly on. I saw the man of many years' service in the cause of music looking fresh as any youth in the heyday of his primal fancy. A white-haired man, with a patriarchal staff besides, which he struck upon the desk for silence, and then raised in calm, to dispel the silence.

I can only say that my head swam for a few minutes, and I was obliged to shut my eyes before I could tell whether I was singing or not. I was very thankful when somebody somewhere got out as a fugue came in, and we were stopped, because it gave me a breathing instant. But then again, breathless,—nerveless, I might say, for I could not distinguish my sensations,—we rushed on, or I did, it was all the same; I was not myself yet. At length, indeed, it came, that restoring sense of self which is so precious at some times of our life. I recalled exactly where I was. I heard myself singing, felt myself standing; I was as if treading upon air, yet fixed as rock. I arose and fell upon those surges of sustaining sound ; but it was as with an undulating motion itself rest. My spirit straightway soared. I could imagine my own voice, high above all the others, to ring as a lark's above a forest, tuneful with a thousand tones more low, more hidden ; the attendant harmonies sank as it were beneath me ; I swelled above them. It was my first idea of paradise.

And it is perhaps my last.

Let me not prose where I should, most of all, be poetical. The rehearsal was considered very successful. St. Michel praised us. He was a good old man, and, as Davy had remarked, very steady. There was a want of unction about his conducting, but I did not know it, certainly not feel it, that night. The "Messiah" was more hurried through than it should have been, because of the late hour, and also because, as we were reminded, "it was the most generally known." Besides, there was to be a full rehearsal with the band before the festival, but I was not to be present, Davy considerately deeming the full effect would be lost for me were it in any sense to be anticipated.

I feel I should only fail if I should attempt to delineate my sensations on the first two days of performance, for the single reason that the third morning of that festival annihilated the others so effectually as to render me only master at this moment of its unparalleled incidents. *Those* I bear on my heart and in my life even to this very hour, and shall take them with me, yea, as a part of my essential immortality.

The second night I had not slept so well as the first, but on the third morning I was, nathless, extraordinarily fresh. I seemed to have lived ages, but yet all struck me in perfect unison as new. I was only too intensely happy as I left our house with Davy, he having breakfasted with us.

He was very much pleased with my achievements. I was very much pleased with everything; I was saturated with pleasure. That day has lasted me — a light — to this. Had I been stricken blind and deaf afterwards, I ought not to have complained, — so far would my happiness, in degree and nature, have outweighed any other I can imagine to have fallen to any other lot. Let those who endure, who rejoice, alike pure in passion, bless God for the power they possess — innate, unalienable, intransferable — of suffering all they feel.

I shall never forget that scene. The hall was already

crowded when we pressed into our places half an hour before the appointed commencement. Every central speck was a head; the walls were pillared with human beings; the swarm increased, floating into the reserved places, and a stream still poured on beneath the gallery.

As if to fling glory on music not of its own, it was a most splendid day, — the finest, warmest, and serenest we had had for weeks. Through the multitudinous panes the sky was a positive blaze of blue; the sunshine fell upon the orchestra from the great arched window at the end of the vaulted building, and through that window's purple and orange border radiated gold and amethyst upon the countenances of the entering crowd. The hands of the clock were at the quarter now; we in the chorus wondered that St. Michel had not come. Again they moved, those noiseless hands, and the "tongue" of iron told eleven. We all grew anxious. Still, as all the clocks in the town were not alike, we might be the mistaken ones by ours. It now struck eleven, though, from the last church within our hearing, and there was not yet St. Michel. We were all in the chorus fitted in so nicely that it would have been difficult for some to get out, or if out, impossible to get in. They were all in the orchestra placed as closely as possible, amidst a perfect grove of music stands. The reserved seats were full, the organist was seated, the score lay wide open upon the lofty desk; but St. Michel did not come!

I shall never forget how we wearied and wondered, and how I, at least, racked myself, writhed, and agonized. The door beneath the orchestra was shut, but every instant or two a hand turned the lock outside; one agitated face peeped in, then another, but were immediately withdrawn. I scarcely suppose the perfect silence lasted three minutes; it was like an electrical suspension, and as quickly snapped. The surcharging spleen of the audience began to break in a murmuring, humming, and buzzing, from center to gallery. The confusion of forms and faces became a perfect dream, it dazzled me dizzy, and I felt quite sick. A hundred fans began to ply in the reserved seats, the gentlemen bent over the ladies; the sound gathered strength and portentous significance from the non-explanatory calm of the orchestra force; but all eyes were turned, all chins lengthened, towards the orchestra door. At precisely a quarter past eleven the door opened wide, and up came a gentleman in a white waistcoat. He stood somewhere in front, but he could not get his voice out at first. Oh, the hisses then! the shouts! the execrations! But it was a musical assembly, and a few cries of "Shame!" hushed the storm sufficiently to give our curiosity vent.

The speaker was a member of the committee, and very woebegone he looked. He had to say (and it was of course his painful duty) that the unprecedented delay in the commencement of the performance was occasioned by an inevitable and most unexpected accident. Mr. St. Michel, in riding from his house a few miles out, had been thrown from his horse at the corner of the market place, and falling on his right arm, had broken it below the elbow.

The suddenness of the event would account for the delay sufficiently; all means at present were being employed to secure the services of an efficient resident professor, and it was trusted he would arrive shortly. Otherwise, should there among the enlightened audience be present any professor able and willing to undertake the responsible office of conductor *pro tempore*, the committee would feel — A hurricane of noes tore up the rest of the sentence in contempt, and flung it in the face of the gentleman in the white waistcoat. He still stood. It was well known that not a hand could be spared from the orchestra; but of course a fancy instantly struck me of Lenhart Davy. I looked up wistfully at him, among the basses, and endeavored to persuade him with my eyes to come down. He smiled upon me, and his eye was kindled; otherwise he seemed determined to remain as he was. Davy was very proud, though one of the most modest men I ever knew.

A fresh volley of hisses broke from the very heart of the hall. Still, it did not circulate, though the confusion seemed increasing in the center; and it was at that very instant — before poor Merlington had left his apologetic stand — that a form, gliding light, as if of air, appeared hovering on the steps at the side of the orchestra.

It was a man at least, if not a spirit; but I had not seen where that gliding form came from, with its light and stealthy speed.

Swift as a beam of morning he sprang up the steps, and with one hand upon the balustrade bowed to the audience. In a moment silence seemed to mantle upon the hall.

He stood before the score, and as he closed upon the time stick those pointed fingers, he raised his eyes to the chorus, and then let them fall upon the band. Those piercing eyes recalled us. Every hand was on the bow, every mouthpiece lifted. There was still silence, but we "heard" no "voice." He raised his thin arm: the overture began. The curiosity of the audience had dilated with such intensity that all who had been standing still stood, and not a creature stirred. The calm was perfect upon which the "Grave" broke. It was not interpretation alone, it was inspiration. All knew that "Grave," but few had heard it as it had been spoken that day. It was *then* a heard voice, — "a voice from heaven." There seemed not a string that was not touched by fire.

The tranquil echo of the repeat enabled me to bear it sufficiently to look up and form some notion of him on whom so much depended. He was slight, so slight that he seemed to have grown out of the air. He was young, so young that he could not have numbered twenty summers; but the heights of eternity were far-shadowed in the forehead's marble dream.

A strange transparency took the place of bloom upon that face of youth, as if from temperament too tender, or blood too rarefied; but the hair betrayed a wondrous strength, clustering in dark curls of excessive richness. The pointed fingers were pale, but they grasped the time stick with an energy like naked nerve.

But not until the violins woke up, announcing the subject of the allegro, did I feel fully conscious of that countenance absolved from its repose of perfection by an excitement itself divine.

It would exhaust thought no less than words to describe the aspect of music, thus revealed, thus presented. I was a little child then, my brain was unused to strong sensation, and I can only say I remembered not how he looked after all was over. The intense impression annihilated itself, as a white, dazzling fire struck from a smith's anvil dies without ashy sign. I have since learned to discover, to adore, every express lineament of that matchless face; but then I was lost in gazing, in a spiritual, ebbless excitement, — then I was conscious of the composition that he had made one with himself, that became one with him.

The fire with which he led, the energy, the speed, could only have been communicated to an English orchestra by such accurate force. The perfection with which the conductor was endued must surely have passed electrically into every player.

—there fell not a note to the ground. Such precision was well-nigh oppressive; one felt some hand must drop.

From beginning to end of the allegro not a disturbing sound arose throughout the hall; but on the closing chord of the overture there burst one deep toll of wonderful applause. I can only call it a "toll"; it was simultaneous. The conductor looked over his shoulder, and slightly shook his head. It was enough, and silence reigned as the heavenly sympathy of the recitative trembled from the strings surcharged with fire. Here it was as if he whispered "Hush!" for the sobbing staccato of the accompaniment I never heard so low,—it was silvery, almost awful. The baton stirred languidly, as the stem of a wind-swept lily, in those pointed fingers.

Nor would he suffer any violence to be done to the solemn brightness of the aria. It was not until we all arose that he raised his arm, and impetuously, almost imperiously, fixed upon us his eyes. He glanced not *a moment* at the score, he never turned a leaf, but he urged the time majestically, and his rapturous beauty brightened as the voices firmly, safely, swelled over the sustaining chords, launched in glory upon those waves of sound.

I almost forgot the festival. I am not certain that I remembered who I was, or where I was, but I seemed to be singing at every pore. I seemed pouring out my life instead of my voice; but the feeling I had of being irresistibly borne along was so transporting that I can conceive of nothing else like it, until after death.

I walked home also, and was tolerably tired. Entering the house as one at home there, I found nobody at home, no Starwood,—no Chevalier. I lay upon the sofa in a day dream or two, and when rested, went out into the garden. I searched every corner, too, in vain; but wandering past the dividing hedge, a voice floated articulately over the still afternoon.

All was calm and warm. The slightest sound made way, and I hesitated not to scale the green barrier, nowhere too high for me to leap it, and to approach the parlor of the cottage in that unwonted fashion. I was in for pictures this while, I suppose; for when I reached the glass doors, that swept the lawn wide open, and could peep through them without disturbing foot on that soft soil, I saw, indeed, another, a less impressive, not less expressive, view. Clara sat at her piano, her side face was in the light. His own, which I was sure to find there, in profile also, was immediately behind her; but as he stood, the shade had veiled him, the shade from the trembling leaves without, through which one sunbeam shot, and upon the carpet kissed his feet. She was singing, as I could hear, scarcely see, for her lips opened not more than for a kiss, to sing. The strains molded themselves imperceptibly, or as a warble shaken in the throat of a careless nightingale that knew no listener.

Seraphael, as he stood apart drinking in the notes with such eagerness that his lips were also parted, had never appeared to me so borne out of himself, so cradled in a second nature. I could scarcely have believed that the face I knew so well had yet an expression hidden I knew not of; but it was so: kindled at another fire than that which his genius had stolen from above, his eye was charged, his cheek flushed.

So exquisitely beautiful they looked together, — he in that soft shadow, she in that tremulous light, — that at first I noticed not a third figure, now brought before me. Behind them both, but sitting so that she could see his face, was Laura, — or rather she half lay; some antique figures carved in statuary have an attitude as listless, that bend on monuments, or crouch in relievo. She had both her arms outspread upon the little work table, hanging over the edge, the hands just clasped together, as reckless in repose; her face all colorless, her eyes all clear, but with scarcely more tinting, were fixed, rapt, upon Seraphael.

I could not tell whether she was feeding upon his eye, his cheek, or his beauteous hair; all her life came forth from her glance, but it spent itself without expression. Still, that deep, that feeding gaze was enough for me; there was in it neither look of hope nor of despair, as I could have interpreted it. I did not like to advance, and waited till my feet were stiff; but neither could I retire.

I waited while Clara, without comment on her part or request of his, glided from song to *scena*, from the romance of a wilderness to the simplest troll. Her fingers just touched the keys as we touch them for the violin solo, — supporting, but unnoticeable. At last, when afraid to be caught, — for the face of the Chevalier in its new expression I rather dreaded, — I went back, like a thief, the way I came, and still more like a thief in that I carried away a treasure of remembrance from those who knew not they had lost it.

I found Starwood yet out, and roved very impatiently all over the house until, at perhaps five o'clock, Seraphael came in for something. The dog in the yard barked out; but I was in no humor to let him loose, and ran straight into the hall.

"Carlomein," said the Chevalier, "I thought you were in London. Is it possible, my child, that you have not dined?" and he gave orders for an instant preparation. "I am truly vexed that I did not know it, but Stern is gone to his father, and will stay till the last coach to-night. I thought you would be absent also."

"And so, sir, I suppose you had determined to go without your dinner?"

He smiled.

"Not at all, Carlomein. The fact is, I *have* dined. I could not resist La Benetta benedetta. I never knew what young potatoes were until I tasted them over there."

"I dare say not," I thought; but I was wise enough to hold my tongue.

"Then, sir, I shall dine alone; and very much I shall enjoy it. There is nothing I like so well as dining alone, except to dine alone with you."

"Carl! Carl! hadst thou been in that devil when he tempted Eve! Pardon, but I have come home for a few things, and have promised to return."

"Sir, if you will not think it rude, I must say that for once in your life you are enjoying what you confer upon others. I am so glad!"

"I thought it says, 'It is better to give than to receive.' I do like receiving; but perhaps that is because I cannot give this which I now receive. Carlomein, there is a spell upon thee; there is a charm about thee, that makes thee lead all thou lovest to all they love! It is a thing I cannot comprehend, but am too content to feel."

He ran into his study, and returning, just glanced into the room with an air of *allegresse* to bid me adieu; but what had he in his arms, if it were not the score of his oratorio? I knew its name by this time; I saw it in that nervous writing which I could read at any earthly distance, — what was to be done with it, and what then? Was he going to the rehearsal, or a rehearsal of his own?

I had not been half an hour quiet, playing to myself, having unpacked my fiddle for the first time since I came to London, when the lady of the scanty silk arrived at my door and aroused me. Some gentlemen had called to see the Chevalier, and as he was supposed to be absent, must see me. I went down into a great, dampish dining room we had not lived in at all, and found three or four worthies, a deputation from the band and chorus, who had helplessly assembled two hours ago in London, and were at present waiting for the conductor.

It was no pleasant task to infringe the fragrant privacy of the cottage, but I had to do it. I went to the front gate this time, and sent up a message, that I might not render myself more intrusive than necessary. He came down as upon the wings of the wind, with his hat half falling from his curls, and flew to the deputation without a syllable to me; they carried him off in triumph so immediately that I could only fancy he looked annoyed, and may have been about that matter mistaken.

Certainly Clara was not annoyed, whom I went indoors to see; Laura had vanished, and she herself was alone in the room, answering my first notes of admiration merely, "Yes, I have sung to him a good while." I was, however, so struck with the change, not in manner, but in her mien, that I would stay on to watch, at the risk of being in the way more than ever in my days. Since I had entered, she had not once looked up; but an unusual flush was upon her face, she appeared serious, but intent, — something seemed to occupy her. At last, after turning about the music sheets that strewed the chamber everywhere, and placing them by in silence, — and a very long time she took, — she raised her eyes. Their luster was indeed quickened; never saw I so much excitement in them; they were still not so grave as significant, — full of unwonted suggestions. I ventured to say then: —

"And now, Miss Benette, I may ask you what you feel about the personality of this hero?"

I could not put it better; she replied not directly, but came and sat beside me on the sofa, by the window. She laid her little hands in her lap, and her glance followed after them. I could see she was inexpressibly burdened with some inward revelation. I could not for a moment believe she trembled, but certainly there was a quiver of her lips; her silken curls, so calm, did not hide the pulsation, infantinely rapid, of those temples where the harebell-azure veins penciled the rose-flower skin. After a few moments' pause, during which she evidently collected herself, she addressed me, her own sweet voice as clear as ever, but the same trouble in it that touched her gaze.

"Sir, I am going to tell you something, and to ask your advice besides."

"I am all attention!" indeed, I was in an agony to attend and learn.

"I have had a strange visitor this morning, — very sudden, and I was not prepared. You will think me very foolish when you hear what is the matter with me, that I have not written to Mr. Davy; but I prefer to ask you. You are more enlightened, though you are so young."

"Miss Benette, I know your visitor; for on returning home next door, I missed my master, and I knew he could be only here. What has he done that could possibly raise a difficulty, or said that could create a question? He is my unerring faith, and should be yours."

"I do not wonder; but I have not known him so long, you see, and contemplate him differently. I had been telling him, as he requested to know my plans, of the treatment I had received at the opera, and how I had not quite settled whether to come out now or next year as an actress. He answered: —

"'Do neither.'

"I inquired why?

"'You must not accept any engagement for the stage in England, and pray do not hold out to them any idea that you will.'

"Now, what does he mean? Am I to give up my only chance of being able to live in England? For I wish to live here. And am I to act unconscientiously? For my conscience tells me that the pure-hearted should always follow their impulses. Now, I know very few persons; but I am born to be known of many, — at least I suppose so, or why was I gifted with this voice, my only gift?"

"Miss Benette, you cannot suppose the Chevalier desires your voice to be lost. Has he not been informing and interpenetrating himself with it the whole morning? He has a higher range in view for you, be assured, or he had not persuaded you, *I* am certain, to annul your present privileges. He has the right to will what he pleases."

"And are we all to obey him?"

"Certainly; and only him, — in matters musical. If you knew him as I do, you would feel this."

"But is it like a musician to draw me away from my duty?"

"Not obviously; but there may be no duty here. You do not know how completely, in the case of dramatic, and indeed of all other art, the foundations are out of course."

"You mean they do not fulfill their first intentions. But then nothing does, except, certainly, as it was first created. We have lost that long."

"Music, Miss Benette, it appears to me, so long as it preserves its purity, may consecrate all the forms of art by raising them into its own atmosphere, — govern them as the soul the body. But where music is itself degraded, its very type defaced, its worship rendered ridiculous, its nature mere name, by its own master the rest falls. I know not much about it, but I know how little the drama depends on music in this country, and how completely, in the first place, one must lend one's self to its meanest effect in order to fulfill the purpose of the writer. All writers for the stage have become profane, and dramatic writers whom we still confess to are banished from the stage in proportion to the elevation of their works. I even go so far as to think an artist does worse who lends an incomparable organ to such service than an unheeded player (myself, for example), who should form one in the ranks of such an orchestra as that of our opera houses, where the bare notion or outline of harmony is all that is provided for us. While the idea of the highest prevails with us, our artist life must harmonize, or Art will suffer, — and it suffers enough now. I have said too long a say, and perhaps I am very ignorant; but this is what I think."

"You cannot speak too much, sir, and you know a great deal more than I do. My feeling was that I could perhaps have shown the world that simplicity of life is not interfered with by a public career, and that those who love what is beautiful must also love what is good, and endeavor to live up to it besides. I have spoken to several musicians abroad, who came to me on purpose; they all extolled my voice, and entreated me to sing upon the stage. I did so then because I was poor and had several things I wished to do; but I cannot say I felt at home with music on the stage in Italy. The gentleman who was here to-day was the first who disturbed my ideas and dissuaded me. I was astonished, not because I am piqued, — for you do not know how much I should prefer to live a quiet life,

— but because everybody else had told me a different story. I do not like to think I shall only be able to sing in concerts, for there are very few concerts that content me, and I do so love an orchestra. Am I to give it all up? If this gentleman had said, 'Only sing in this opera or that,' I could have made up my mind. But am I never to sing in any? Am I to waste my voice that God gave me as he gives to others a free hand or a great imagination? You cannot think so, with all your industry and all your true enthusiasm."

"Miss Benette, you must not be shocked at what I shall now say, because I mean it with all reverence. I could no more call in question the decision of such genius than I could that of Providence if it sent me death sickness or took away my friends. I am certain that the motive, which you cannot make clear just yet, is that you would approve of."

"And you also, sir?"

"And I also, though it is as dark to me as to you. Let it stand over, then; but for all our sakes do not thwart him, — he has suffered too much to be thwarted."

"Has he suffered? I did not know that."

"Can such a one live and not suffer? A nature which is all love, — an imagination all music?"

"I thought that he looked delicate, but very happy, — happy as a child or an angel. I have seen your smile turn bitter, sir, — pardon, — but never his. I am sure, if it matters to him that I should accede, I will do so, and I cannot thank you enough for telling me."

"Miss Benette, if you are destined to do anything great for music, it may be in one way as well as in another; that is, if you befriend the greatest musician, it is as much as if you befriended music. Now you cannot but befriend him if you do exactly as he requests you."

"In all instances, you recommend?"

"*I*, at least, could refuse him nothing. The nourishment such a spirit requires is not just the same as our own, perhaps, but it must not the less be supplied. If I could, now, clean his boots better than any one else, or if he liked my cookery, I would give up what I am about and take a place in his service."

"What! you would give up your violin, your career, your place among the choir of ages?"

"I would; for in rendering a single hour of his existence on earth unfretted, — in preserving to him one day of ease and comfort,—I should be doing more for all people, all time, at least for the ideal, who will be few in every age, but many in all the ages, and who I believe leaven society better than a priesthood. I would not say so except to a person who perfectly understands me; for as I hold laws to be necessary, I would infringe no social or religious *régime* by one heterodox utterance to the ear of the uninitiated: still, having said it, I keep to my text, that you must do exactly as he pleases. He has not set a seal upon your throat at present, if you have been singing all the morning."

"I have been singing from his new great work. There is a contralto solo, 'Art Thou not from Everlasting?' which spoiled my voice; I could not keep the tears down, it was so beautiful and entreating. He was a little angry at me; at least he said, 'You must not do that.' There is also a very long piece which I scarcely tried, we had been so long over the other, which he made me sing again and again until I composed myself. What a mercy Mr. Davy taught us to read so fast! I have found it help me ever since. Do you mean to go to this oratorio?"

"I am to go with Miss Lawrence. How noble, how glorious she is!"

"Your eyes sparkle when you speak of her. I knew you would there find a friend."

"I hope you, too, will hear it, Miss Benette. I shall speak to the Chevalier about it."

"I pray you not to do so; there will not be any reason, for I find out all about those affairs. Take care of yourself, Mr. Auchester, or rather make Miss Lawrence take care of you; she will like to have to do so."

"I must go home, if it is not to be just yet, and return on purpose for the day."

"But that will fatigue you very much,—cannot you prevent it? One ought to be quiet before a great excitement."

"Oh! you have found that. I cannot be quiet until afterwards."

"I have never had a great excitement," said Clara, innocently; "and I hope I never may. It suits me to be still."

"May that calm remain in you and for you with which you never fail to heal the soul within your power, Miss Benette!"

"I should indeed be proud, Mr. Auchester, to keep you quiet; but that you will never be until it is forever."

"In that sense no one could, for who could ever desire to awaken from that rest? And from all rest here it is but to awaken."

I felt I ought to go, or that I might even remain too long. It was harder at that moment to leave her than it had ever been before; but I had a prescience that for that very reason it was better to depart. Starwood had returned, I found, and was waiting about in the evening, before the candles came.

We both watched the golden shade that bound the sunset to its crimson glow, and then the violet dark, as it melted downwards to embrace the earth. We were both silent, Starwood from habit (I have never seen such power of abstraction), I by choice. An agitated knock came suddenly, about nine, and into the room bounced the big dog, tearing the carpet up with his capers. Seraphael followed, silent at first as we; he stole after us to the window, and looked softly forth. I could tell even in the uncertain silver darkness of that thinnest shell of a moon that his face was alight with happiness, an ineffable gentleness, — not the dread alien air of heaven, soothing the passion of his countenance. He laid for long his tiny hand upon my shoulder, his arm crept round my neck, and drawing closer still, he sighed rather than said, after a thrilling pause: —

"Carlomein, wilt thou come into my room? I have a secret for thee; it will not take long to tell."

"The longer the better, sir."

We went out through the dark drawing-room, we came to his writing chamber; here the white sheets shone like ghosts in the bluish blackness, for we were behind the sunset.

"We will have no candles, because we shall return so soon. And I love secrets told in the dark, or between the dark and light. I have prevented that child from taking her own way. It was very naughty, and I want to be shriven. Shrive me, Charles."

"In all good part, sir, instantly."

"I have been quarreling with the manager. He was very angry, and his whiskers stood out like the bristles of a cat; for I had snatched the mouse from under his paw, you see."

"The mouse must have been glad enough to get away, sir. And you have drawn a line through her engagement? She has told me something of it, and we are grateful."

"I have canceled her engagement! Well, this one, — but I am going to give her another. She does not know it, but she

5

will sing for me at another time. Art thou angry, Carl? Thou art rather a dread confessor."

"I could not do anything but rejoice, sir. How little she expects to bear such a part! She is alone fitted for it; an angel, if he came into her heart, could not find one stain upon his habitation."

"The reason you take home to you, then, Carlomein?"

"Sir, I imagine that you consider her wanting in dramatic power; or that as a dramatic songstress under the present dispensation she would but disappoint herself, and perhaps ourselves; or that she is too delicately organized, — which is no new notion to me."

"All of these reasons, and yet not one, — not even because, Carlomein, in all my efforts I have not written directly for the stage, nor because a lingering recollection ever forbids profane endeavor. There is yet a reason, obvious to myself, but which I can scarcely make clear to you. Though I would have you know, and learn as truth, that there is nothing I take from this child I will not restore to her again, nor shall she have the lesson to be taught to feel that in heaven alone is happiness."

He made a long, long pause. I was in no mood to reply, and it was not until I was ashamed of my own silence that I spoke; then my own accents startled me. I told Seraphael I must return on the morrow to my own place if I were to enjoy at length what Miss Lawrence had set before me. He replied that I must come back to him when I came, and that he would write to me meantime.

"If I can, Carlomein; but I cannot always write, even, my child, to thee. There is one thing more between us, — a little end of business."

He lit with a waxen match a waxen taper, which was coiled into a brazen cup; he brought it from the mantelshelf to the table; he took a slip of paper and a pen. The tiny flame threw out his hand, of a brilliant ivory, while his head remained in flickering shadow, — I could trace a shadow smile.

"Now, Carlomein, this brother of yours. His name is David, I think?"

"Lenhart Davy, sir."

"Has he many musical friends?"

"Only his wife particularly so, — the class are all neophytes."

"Well, he can do as he pleases. Here is an order."

He held out the paper in a regal attitude, and in the other

hand brought near the tremulous taper, that I so might read. It was : —

ABBEY CHOIR WESTMINSTER.

Admit Mr. Lenhart Davy and party 21st June.

SERAPHAEL.

I could say nothing, nor even essay to thank him, — indeed he would not permit it, as I could perceive. We returned directly to the drawing-room, and roused Starwood from a blue study, as the Chevalier expressed it.

"I am ready, and Miss Lemark is tired of waiting for both of us," said Miss Lawrence, as she entered that crown of days, the studio; "I have left her in the drawing-room. And, by the way, though it is nothing to the purpose, she has dressed herself very prettily."

"I do not think it is nothing to the purpose, — people dress to go to church, and why not, then, to honor music? You have certainly succeeded also, Miss Lawrence, if it is not impertinent that I say so."

"It is not impertinent. You will draw out the colors of that bit of canvas, if you gaze so ardently."

It was not so easy to refrain. That morning the pictured presence had been restored to its easel, framed and ready for inspection. I had indeed lost myself in that contemplation; it was hard to tear myself from it even for the embrace of the reality. The border, dead gold, of great breadth and thickness, was studded thickly with raised bright stars, polished and glittering as points of steel. The effect thus seemed conserved and carried out where in general it abates. I cannot express the picture; it was finished to that high degree which conceals its own design, and mantles mechanism with pure suggestion. I turned at length and followed the paintress; my prospects more immediate rushed upon me.

Our party, small and select as the most seclusive spirit could ask for, consisted of Miss Lawrence and her father, — a quiet but genuine amateur he, — of Miss Lemark, whom my friend had included without a question, with Starwood and myself. We had met at Miss Lawrence's, and went together in her carriage. She wore a deep blue muslin dress, — blue as that summer heaven; her scarf was gossamer, the hue of the yellow butterfly, and her bonnet was crested with feathers drooping like golden hair. Laura was just in white; her Leghorn hat lined with grass-green gauze; a green silk scarf waved around her. Both ladies carried flowers. Geraniums and July's proud roses were in Miss Lawrence's careless hand, and Laura's bouquet was of myrtle and yellow jasmine.

We drove in that quiet mood which best prepares the heart. We passed so street by street, until at length, and long before we reached it, the gray Abbey towers beckoned us from beyond the houses, seeming to grow distant as we approached, as shapes of unstable shadow, rather than time-fast masonry.

Into the precinct we passed, we stayed at the mist-hung door. It was the strangest feeling — mere physical sensation — to enter from that searching heat, those hot blue heavens, into the cool, the dream of dimness, where the shady marbles clustered, and the foot fell dead and awfully, where hints more awful pondered, and for our coming waited. Yea, as if from far and very far, as if beyond the grave descending, fell wondrous unwonted echoes from the tuning choir unseen. Involuntarily we paused to listen, and many others paused, — those of the quick hand or melodious forehead, those of the alien aspect who ever draw after music. Now the strings yearned fitfully, — a sea of softest dissonances; the wind awoke and moaned; the drum detonated and was still; past all the organ swept, a thundering calm.

Entering, still hushed and awful, the center of the nave, we caught sight of the transept already crowded with hungering, thirsting faces; still they too, and all there hushed and awful. The vision of the choir itself, as it is still preserved to me, is as a picture of heaven to infancy. What more like one's idea of heaven than that height, that aspiring form — the arches whose sun-kissed summits glowed in distance, whose vista stretched its boundaries from the light of rainbows at one end, on the other to the organ, music's archetype? Not less powerful, predominating, this idea of our other home, because no earthly flowers nor withering garlands made the thoughts recoil on death and destiny, — the only flowers there, the rays transfused through sun-pierced windows; the blue mist strewing aisle and wreathing arch, the only garlands. Nor less because for once an assembly gathered of all the fraternities of music, had the unmixed element of pure enthusiasm thrilled through the "electric chain" from heart to heart. Below the organ stood Seraphael's desk, as yet unhaunted; the orchestra; the chorus, as a cloud-hung company, with starlike faces in the lofty front.

WESTMINSTER ABBEY

From a photo by Valentine & Sons, Ltd., Dundee

to penetrate the mystery of our roundabout way of enlivening him. He pored over the journals in perplexity, and talked of his indignation, mainly to his pretty partners at balls, who told him they were lesser Andromedas of his dear Andromeda country, but pouted and chatted and were gay, and said they were sure he would defend them. The men he addressed were cool. They listened to him sometimes with smiles and sometimes with laughter, but approvingly, liking the lad's quick spirit. They were accustomed to the machinery employed to give our land a shudder and to soothe it, and generally remarked that it meant nothing. His uncle Everard, and his uncle's friend, Stukely Culbrett, expounded the nature of such panics to him, saying that they were uneasy when not periodically thrashed; it would be cruel to deny them their joy beforehand; and so the pair of gentlemen pooh-poohed the alarm; agreeing with him, however, that we had no great reason to be proud of our appearance, and the grounds they assigned for this were the activity and the prevalence of the ignoble doctrines of Manchester — a power whose very existence was unknown to Mr. Beauchamp. He would by no means allow the burden of our national disgrace to be cast on one part of the nation. We were insulted, and all in a poultry flutter, but no one seemed to feel it but himself! Outside the Press and Parliament, which must necessarily be the face we show to the foreigner, absolute indifference reigned. Navy men and redcoats were willing to join him or anybody in sneers at a pinching and paring miserly Government, but they were insensible to the insult, the panic, the startled-poultry show, the shame of our exhibition of ourselves in Europe. It looked as if the blustering French Guard were to have it all their own way. And what would they, what could they but, think of us! He sat down to write them a challenge.

He is not the only Englishman who has been impelled by a political chivalry to do that. He is perhaps the youngest who ever did it, and consequently there were various difficulties to be overcome. As regards his qualifications for addressing Frenchmen, a year of his pre-neptunal time had been spent in their capital city for the purpose of acquiring French of Paris, its latest refinements of pronunciation and polish, and the art of conversing. He had read the French tragic poets and Molière; he could even relish the Gallic-classic — "Qu'il mourût," and he spoke French passably, being quite beyond the Bullish treat-

I knew not much about London orchestras, and was taking a particular stare, when Miss Lawrence whispered in a manner that only aroused, not disturbed me: "There is our old friend Santonio. Do look and see how little he is altered!"

I caught his countenance instantly,—as fine, as handsome, a little worn at its edges, but rather refined by that process than otherwise. "I did not ask about him, because I did not know he was in London. He is, then, settled here; and is he very popular?"

"You need not ask the question; he is too true to himself. No, Santonio will never be rich, though he is certainly not poor."

Then she pointed to me one head and another crowned with fame; but I could only spare for them a glance,—Santonio interested me still. He was reminding me especially of himself as I remembered him, by laying his head, as he used to do, upon the only thing he ever really loved,—his violin,—when, so quietly as to take us by surprise, Seraphael entered, I may almost say rose upon us, as some new-sprung star or sun.

Down the nave the welcome rolled, across the transept it overflowed the echoes; for a few moments nothing else could be felt, but there was, as it were, a tender shadow upon the very reverberating jubilance,—it was subdued as only the musical subdue their proud emotions; it was subdued for the sake of one whose beauty, lifted over us, appeared descending, hovering from some late-left heaven, ready to depart again, but not without a sign, for which we waited. Immediately, and while he yet stood with his eyes of power upon the whole front of faces, the solo singers entered also and took their seats all calmly.

There were others besides Clara, but besides her I saw nothing, except that they were in colors, while she wore black, as ever; but never had I really known her loveliness until it shone in contrast with that which was not so lovely. More I could not perceive, for now the entering bar of silence riveted; we held our breath for the coming of the overture.

It opened like the first dawn of lightening, yet scarce yet lightened, morning, its vast subject introduced with strings alone in that joyous key which so often served him, yet as in the extreme of vaulting distance; but soon the first trombone blazed out, the second and third responding with their stupendous tones, as the amplifications of fugue involved and spread themselves more and more, until, like glory filling up and flooding the height of heaven from the heaven of heavens itself, broke in the organ, and brimmed the brain with the calm of an utter and forceful expression, realized by tone. In sympathy with each instrument, it was alike with none, even as the white and boundless ray of which all beams, all color tones, are born. The perfect form, the distinct conception of this unbrothered work, left our spirits as the sublime fulfillment confronted them. For once had genius, upon the wings of aspiration, that alone are pure, found all it rose to seek, and mastered without a struggle all that it desired to embrace; for the pervading purpose of that creation was the passioned quietude with which it wrought its way. The vibrating harmonies, pulselike, clung to our pulses, then drew up, drew out each heart, deep-beating and distracted, to adore at the throne above from whence all beauty springs. And opening and spreading thus, too intricately, too transcendentally for criticism, we do not essay, even feebly, to portray that immortal work of a music-veiled immortal.

Inextricable holiness, precious as the old Hebrew psalm of all that hath life and breath, exhaled from every modulation, each dropped celestial fragrances, the freshness of everlasting spring. Suggestive, — our oratorio suggested nothing here, nothing that we find or feel; all that we seek and yearn to clasp, but rest in our restlessness to discover is beyond us! In nothing that form of music reminded of our forms of worship, — in the day of Paradise it might have been dreamed of, an antepast of earth's last night, and of eternity at hand, — or it might be the dream of heaven that haunts the loving one's last slumber.

I can no more describe the hush that hung above and seemed to spiritualize the listeners until, like a very cloud of mingling souls, they seemed congregated to wait for the coming of a Messiah who had left them long, promising to return; nor how, as chorus after chorus, built up, sustained, and self-supported, gathered to the stricken brain, the cloud of spirits sank, as in slumber sweeter than any dreamful stir, upon the alternating strains and songs, all softness, — all dread soothing, as the fire that burned upon the strings seemed suddenly quenched in tears. Faint supplications wafted now, now deep acclaims of joy; but all, all surcharged the spirit alike with the mysterious thrall and tenderness of that uncreate and unpronounceable Name, whose eternal love is all we need to assure us of eternal life.

It was with one of those alternate strains that Clara rose to sing, amidst silence yet unbroken, and the more impressive because of the milder symphony that stole from the violoncello, its meandering pathos asking to support and serve her voice. Herself penetrated so deeply with the wisdom of genius, she failed to remind us of herself; even her soft brow and violet eyes — violet in the dense glory of the Abbey afternoon light — were but as outward signs and vivid shadows of the spirit that touched her voice. Deeper, stiller than the violoncello notes, hers seemed as those articulated, surcharged with a revelation beyond all sound.

Calm as deep, clear as still, they were not yet passionless; though they clung and molded themselves strictly to the passion of the music, lent not a pulse of their own; nor disturbed it the rapt serenity of her singing to gaze upon her angel face. No child could have seemed less sensitive to the surrounding throng, nor have confided more implicitly in the father of its heart, than she leaned upon Seraphael's power.

I made this observation afterwards, when I had time to think; at present I could only feel, and feeling know, that the intellect is but the servant of the soul. When at length those two hours, concentrating such an eternity in their perfection of all sensation, had reached their climax, or rather when, brightening into the final chorus, unimprisoned harmonies burst down from stormy-hearted organ, from strings all shivering alike, from blasting, rending tubes, and thus bound fast the Alleluia, — it was as if the multitude had sunk upon their knees, so profound was the passion-cradling calm. The blue-golden luster, dim and tremulous, still crowned the unwavering arches, — tender and overwrought was laid that vast and fluctuating mind. So many tears are not often shed as fell in that silent while, — dew-stilly they dropped and quickened; but still not all had wept.

Many wept then who had never wept before; many who had wept before could not weep now, — among them I. Our party were as if lost to me; as I hid my face my companion did not disturb me, — she was too far herself in my own case. I do not know whether I heard, but I was aware of a stretching and breathing; the old bones stirring underneath the pavement would have shaken me less, but could not have been less to my liking; the rush, however soft, the rustle, however subdued, were agony, were torment: I could only feel, "Oh that I were in heaven! that I might never return to earth!" But then it came upon me, to that end we must all be changed. This was sad, but of a sadness peculiarly soothing; for could we be content to remain forever as we are here, even in our holiest, our strongest moments?

During the last reverberations of that unimaginable Alleluia I had not looked up at all; now I forced myself to do so, lest I should lose my sight of *him*, — his seal upon all that glory. As Seraphael had risen to depart, the applause, stifled and trembling, but not the less by heartfuls, rose for him.

He turned his face a moment, — the heavenly half-smile was there; then at that very moment the summer sun, that, falling downwards in its piercing glare, glowed gorgeous against the flower-leaf windows, flung its burning bloom, its flushing gold, upon that countenance. We all saw it, we all felt it, — the seraph strength, the mortal beauty, — and that it was pale as the cheek of the quick and living changed in death, — that his mien was of no earthly triumph!

THE CANE-BOTTOMED CHAIR.

By W. M. THACKERAY.

In tattered old slippers that toast at the bars,
And a ragged old jacket perfumed with cigars,
Away from the world and its toils and its cares,
I've a snug little kingdom up four pairs of stairs.

To mount to this realm is a toil, to be sure,
But the fire there is bright and the air rather pure;
And the view I behold on a sunshiny day
Is grand through the chimney pots over the way.

This snug little chamber is crammed in all nooks
With worthless old knickknacks and silly old books,
And foolish old odds and foolish old ends,
Cracked bargains from brokers, cheap keepsakes from friends.

Old armor, prints, pictures, pipes, china (all cracked),
Old rickety tables, and chairs broken-backed;
A twopenny treasury, wondrous to see;
What matter? 'tis pleasant to you, friend, and me.

No better divan need the Sultan require,
Than the creaking old sofa that basks by the fire;
And 'tis wonderful, surely, what music you get
From the rickety, ramshackle, wheezy spinet.

That praying rug came from a Turcoman's camp;
By Tiber once twinkled that brazen old lamp;
A Mameluke fierce yonder dagger has drawn:
'Tis a murderous knife to toast muffins upon.

Long, long through the hours, and the night, and the chimes,
Here we talk of old books, and old friends, and old times;
As we sit in a fog made of rich Latakie
This chamber is pleasant to you, friend, and me.

But of all the cheap treasures that garnish my nest,
There's one that I love and I cherish the best;
For the finest of couches that's padded with hair
I never would change thee, my cane-bottomed chair.

'Tis a bandy-legged, high-shouldered, worm-eaten seat,
With a creaking old back, and twisted old feet;
But since the fair morning when Fanny sat there,
I bless thee and love thee, old cane-bottomed chair.

If chairs have but feeling, in holding such charms,
A thrill must have passed through your withered old arms!
I looked, and I longed, and I wished in despair;
I wished myself turned to a cane-bottomed chair.

It was but a moment she sat in this place,
She'd a scarf on her neck, and a smile on her face!
A smile on her face, and a rose in her hair,
And she sat there, and bloomed in my cane-bottomed chair.

And so I have valued my chair ever since,
Like the shrine of a saint, or the throne of a prince;
Saint Fanny, my patroness sweet I declare,
The queen of my heart and my cane-bottomed chair.

When the candles burn low, and the company's gone,
In the silence of night as I sit here alone—
I sit here alone, but we yet are a pair—
My Fanny I see in my cane-bottomed chair.

She comes from the past and revisits my room;
She looks as she then did, all beauty and bloom;
So smiling and tender, so fresh and so fair,
And yonder she sits in my cane-bottomed chair.

THE FISHER LASSIE.[1]

By BJÖRNSTJERNE BJÖRNSON.

[BJÖRNSTJERNE BJÖRNSON, a leading Norwegian novelist and dramatist, was born December 8, 1832, at Kvikne, Norway, where his father was pastor, and attended the university of Christiania. He has figured prominently as theatrical manager, journalist, and lecturer, and is the foremost Norwegian advocate of republicanism in politics. In 1880 he visited the United States and lectured in the principal cities. Recently he has lived upon his estate, Olestad, in the Gausdal. His best-known novels are: "Arne," "Synnöve Solbakken," and "The Fisher Lassie," all of which have been popular in English translations. His numerous dramatic works include: "Halte Hulda," the trilogy of "Sigurd Slembe," "The Newly Married Pair," "Between the Battles," etc.]

GUNLAUG OF THE HILL.

WHEN the herring has fixed upon any place along the coast for its constant and regular haunt, a town grows up there bit by bit, if it is otherwise a likely place. Towns such as these may not only be said to have been actually cast up by the sea, but even still, at some distance off, look like bits of wreckage or timber that the waves have washed ashore, or like upturned boats, under which the fishermen have crept for shelter against the stormy night. Draw nearer, and you will see in what a casual fashion the town has been built: crags lie in the midst of thoroughfares; the sea divides the hamlet into three or four parts; and the streets curve and wind about at will.

But one property is possessed by all these towns alike: they have shelter in the harbors for the largest ships; within them, the water is smooth as in a basin; and therefore these inlets are very welcome to vessels that come with sails torn, and bulwarks shattered, scudding away from the high seas to seek for breathing time.

In such townlets, all is stillness: everything that is a source of noise is relegated to the quays, where the villagers' boats lie fast, and ships load and unload.

In our little town, the only street runs along the quays,

[1] From "Arne and the Fisher Lassie." By permission of Geo. Bell & Sons. (Price 3*s.* 6*d.*)

facing which are white and red painted houses, one or two stories high, with walls not touching one another, but with bright strips of garden in between, the whole forming a long and broad road, on which you get the scent of whatever happens to be on the quays, if the wind is blowing from the sea.

All is quiet here,—not from fear of the policeman, for as a rule there is none,—but from fear of what people say, for everybody in the place is known to everybody else. Should you walk down the street, you must give a greeting at every window you pass, and the old dame sitting at it will pleasantly greet you in return. Exchange a greeting, too, with every one you meet; for all these quiet folk go about their business considering what is the most fitting conduct for the world in general and for themselves in particular, and any one who oversteps the limits proper to his rank and station in life loses his good name; for not alone is *he* known, but his father and his grandfather before him; and immediately folks set themselves to find out if, at any previous time, any tendency towards impropriety has been manifested in the family.

To our quiet town there came many years ago a man much respected by all, Per Olsen by name. He had come from the country, where he had earned his livelihood as a peddler and fiddler, and he opened a shop in the town for his old customers, selling bread and brandy in addition to his peddler's wares. You might hear him walking up and down in the back room behind the shop, playing jigs and wedding marches. Every time, as he passed the door, he peeped through the glass panels, and if he caught sight of a customer coming, he finished up his tune with a flourish and went into the shop.

His business prospered, he married, and had a son, whom he called after himself, naming him, however, not "Per," but "Peter."

Little Peter was to be what Per felt he himself was not—a cultivated man; and with this end in view the boy was sent to the Latin school.

The lads who ought to have been his comrades beat him home from their games, because he was the son of Per Olsen; and Per Olsen beat him back again to them, because it was impossible for him to be educated otherwise. In consequence, little Peter, finding himself isolated at school, grew so idle, and by degrees so completely inured to the whole affair, that his father could strike neither tear nor smile out of him; so Per gave up the beating process, and put him into the shop.

Judge of his surprise when he saw the lad serve every customer with exactly what he asked for, never giving a grain too much, nor ever himself eating so much as a currant; weighing, counting, or invoicing, with immovable countenance; never talking, if he could avoid so doing; very slow in all his movements, but unimpeachable in his exactitude.

Then the father's hope sprang up anew, and he sent him (in a fishing boat) to Hamburg, that he might go into the Commercial Institute and learn good manners.

After eight months' absence — long enough, in all conscience — he returned, provided with six new suits, which, when he landed, he wore one over the other: "for what one wears and walks in," as the saying is, "pays no customhouse duty."

Next day, when he was seen in the street, he had lost some of his bulk, but otherwise he looked much the same. He walked stiff and straight, holding his hands close by his sides; he saluted with a sudden jerk, bowing as if deprived of the use of his joints, and immediately becoming quite stiff again. He was politeness personified, but silent in his manners, and, after a fashion, shy.

His name he no longer wrote "Olsen," but "Ohlsen," which gave the town wag a chance for the following display of wit: *Question.* "How far did Peter Olsen get in Hamburg?" *Answer.* "As far as the letter H." He had had thoughts of calling himself "Pedro," but he suffered so much annoyance for the sake of an H, that he gave up that idea, and wrote himself "P. Ohlsen."

He did much to extend his father's business, and when only in his two and twentieth year he married a red-handed shopkeeper's lass, that he might have some one to look after the household; for the father had just become a widower, and a wife is more trustworthy than a housekeeper. Just a year after their marriage, she bore him a son, who, within a week of his birth, was named Pedro.

Now that worthy Per Olsen was a grandfather, he felt an inner call to become old; so he handed the business over to his son, took his seat on a bench in the open air, and smoked twist out of a short pipe. And when one day he began to grow somewhat weary of his life, he uttered a wish that he might soon die, and this wish of his was as quietly granted as all the rest of his desires had been.

Now, just as the son Peter had inherited one side exclusively of his father's powers, viz., his business aptitude, so the grandson Pedro seems to have been sole heir to the other—his musical faculties. It was long before he learned to read, but he very quickly knew how to sing. He played the flute so well that it could not escape notice. He was weak of sight and yielding in disposition. All this, however, only vexed the father, who wanted the boy to possess his own punctilious accuracy; so if ever he neglected anything, he was not scolded and beaten, as his father had been, but pinched. This was done in a quiet, an affable, well-nigh a polite manner; but it was done on the very smallest provocation. Every night as the mother undressed him, she counted and kissed the blue and yellow marks, but she made no resistance, for she herself knew what it was to be pinched. For every rent in his clothes—which were those his father had brought from Hamburg, cut down and altered for the son's use—for every smudge on his schoolbooks, she had to bear the blame. Hence all day long it was "Don't do that, Pedro!" "Take care, Pedro!" "Mind what you're doing, Pedro!" till the boy grew afraid of his father and weary of his mother. Among his schoolmates he came to no particular harm, because he always fell a crying, begging them not to hurt his clothes: they nicknamed him "Touchwood," and troubled themselves no more about him. He was like a sickly, featherless duckling, ever limping along behind the rest of the brood, and sneaking quickly off with any little bit he could steal for himself: nobody shared with him, and so he shared with nobody.

But he soon found out that it was very different for him among the poor children of the town; they had far more patience with him, because he was better off than themselves. A tall, strongly built lass, who was queen of the whole crew, took a liking to him. He was never tired of looking at her. She had raven-black hair that curled about her head and was never combed save by her fingers; eyes of perfect blue beneath her narrow forehead, and an expression that betokened single-hearted determination. She was always actively engaged, whether in sport or in work, going about in summer time with arms and legs bare, and face tanned by the sun, while in winter her clothing was such as others wear in summer. Her father was a pilot and fisherman: she dashed about selling his fish, holding his boat still against wind and tide, and — when he was away acting as pilot — did the fishing alone. No one who saw her could help turning round and taking another look at her, she seemed such a picture of self-reliance. Her name was Gunlaug, but she was called "The Fisher Lassie," a name she accepted as a title proper to her rank. In all games she was always to be found on the weaker side; she seemed to need somebody to care for, so now she took charge of this sickly boy. In her boat he might blow his flute, which was forbidden him at home, because it was believed to divert his thoughts from his lessons. She used to row him out on the fjord; she began to take him out with her on longer fishing expeditions, and, before long, let him accompany her on her night tours as well. On such occasions they rowed off in the silent summer twilight as the sun sank to rest, and he would play his flute, or listen to her as she told him all the tales that she knew of mermen and of monsters, of strange adventures, foreign lands, and black men, just as the sailors had told them to her. She shared her food with him just as she did her knowledge, and he partook of both alike without making any return; for he had neither eatables to bring with him from home, nor fancy from school. They rowed till the sun went down behind the snow-capped hills, and then anchored off some craggy islet, where they landed and made a fire; that is to say, she collected sticks and branches, he sat and looked on. She brought one of her father's seaman's jackets and a blanket in the boat with her, and in these she wrapped him round. She looked after the fire and he went to sleep, while she kept herself awake by singing bits of psalms and songs; she sang in a clear firm voice until he fell asleep, and then she sang in a lower tone. When the sun rose again across the water, darting pale yellow rays over the mountain tops to herald his approach, she would wake him. The woods still stood in blackness, and the country still lay darkened, but began to be reddish and glowing until the ridge of hills shone clear, and every color gleamed forth bright and distinct. Then they dragged the boat into the water again, and quickly it shot through the waves before the fresh morning breeze, and soon it lay moored among the other fishing boats.

When the winter came, and the expeditions came to an end, he used to visit her at her home. He would often sit looking at her as she worked, but neither he nor she spoke much; it was as if they were sitting together waiting for summer. But alas! when it came, their hopes were destined to come to naught, for Gunlaug's father died, and she left the town, while the boy, at his schoolmaster's advice, was put into the shop. There he stood beside his mother, for little by little the father had become the color of the groats he was always weighing out, and was at last obliged to keep to his bed in the back room; yet he still wished to take part in all that went on and to know what sales each of them made. He would act as if he did not hear, until he got them near enough, and then pinch them. At length the oil ran quite dry in this little lamp one night, and the light flickered out. The wife wept, hardly knowing why she did so, but the son had not a tear to squeeze forth. Having money enough to live on, they gave up the business, removed everything that might have reminded them of it, and made the shop into a sitting room; there the mother sat by the window and knitted stockings, while Pedro sat in the room on the other side of the passage and blew his flute. But as soon as the summer came, he bought a little light sailing boat, bent his course to the rocky islet, and lay where Gunlaug had lain.

One day, as he lay there among the heather, he saw a boat steering straight for him; it brought up close by his resting place, and out stepped Gunlaug. She had not altered at all, save that she was full-grown, and taller than other women; but as her eyes fell upon him, she turned aside a little and slackened her pace, for it had never occurred to her that he was now a man.

The thin, mealy face was unknown to her, for it was no longer ailing and delicate-looking; it was dull and heavy; but as he looked at her, his eyes were lit up as if by the light of his former dreams, and as she advanced, for every step she came it seemed as if a year fell from him, and when she stood by him he had sprung up and stood laughing and talking like a boy. Beneath the old face lay the visage of a child; he had got older, it is true, but he had not grown up.

Such as he was, it was just such a child she was seeking, though now that she had found him again, she hardly knew what more she would have. She laughed and blushed. Involuntarily he seemed to feel a sort of power within him; it was the first time in his life, and at that instant he was actually handsome; it lasted perhaps more than a moment, but in that moment she was captivated.

Gunlaug was one of those natures that can only love whatever is weak, whatever they have borne in their arms. She had meant to stay in the town two days, — she remained two months.

In those two months he developed more than in all the rest of his life. He was so far aroused from his dreamy apathy as to form plans for the future: he decided that he would go away and learn music! But when he talked of this to her one day, she turned pale, and said, "Yes; but first we must be married!"

He looked at her, and she looked steadfastly back at him; both blushed red as fire; and then, "What will people say to that?" said he.

It had never occurred to Gunlaug that his wishes could be other than hers, just because her wishes had till then never been other than his. But now it flashed upon her that, deep down in his heart, he had never for an instant had any intention of sharing anything with her, except what *she* gave him. In that instant it stood revealed to her that it had been so in all their intercourse. She had begun by pitying, and ended by loving, the being she herself had fostered. Ah! if now she had only exercised a moment's self-control! — for he saw her anger blazing up, and in fear he cried out, "I will!" She heard him; but her anger at her own blindness and his littleness, at her own shame and his cowardice, seethed up with burning speed to boiling point, and never did a love that began in childhood in the evening sunshine, that had been rocked on the billows beneath the rays of the moon and accompanied by the melody of the flute and of soft singing, come to a more pitiable ending. She grasped him with both her hands, she raised him from the ground, and struck him with all the passion of her heart; then she rowed straight back to the town, and, never swerving, took her course over the hills.

He had sailed out a youth deep in love, and on his way to achieve manhood; he returned an old man, for whom manhood had never been. His life had but one memory, and that he had in his folly thrown away: one spot only on earth did he care for, and thither no longer durst he go. Brooding over his own misery and how it had come upon him, his newborn vigor sank as in a quagmire, never to emerge again. The little town boys soon noticed his strange bearing, and began to plague him ; and as he was an obscure person to his fellow-townsmen, who knew neither what he lived on nor how, it fell out that he found no one to defend him. Before long he no longer dared to venture out—at any rate, not in the public thoroughfares. His whole existence became a warfare with the boys, who were, perhaps, of the same use as flies are in the heat of summer; without them he would have sunk into complete torpor.

Nine years later Gunlaug came back to the town just as unexpectedly as she had left it. She was accompanied by a little girl about eight years of age, who looked just as Gunlaug used to in former days, save that she was more delicate in her features and bearing, and had a look about her as if she had stepped out of a dream. Gunlaug had been married, it was said ; she had inherited some money, and had come back to the town to open an inn for seamen.

She managed her house in such a way that merchants and skippers came to her to hire sailors, and sailors came to her to get hired. Besides this, all the town ordered fish of her. And though she never took a shilling for her services as agent, she wielded despotically the power her position gave her. Certainly she was the most influential person in the town, though she was a woman, and a woman, too, who never left her own house. She was known as "Fish-Gunlaug," or "Gunlaug of the Hill" ; while the title of "The Fisher Lassie" descended to her little daughter, who was always to be found skipping about at the head of the small boys of the town.

Her history it is which we are about to tell. She had something of her mother's strong nature, and she had occasion to use it.

PETRA'S CHILDHOOD.

The many pretty gardens of the town, now clad in their second and third blossoms, were fragrant after the rain. The sun was sinking to rest behind the everlasting mountains of snow, and the whole heavens far around seemed all on fire, making even the snow peaks give back a subdued reflection. The nearer mountains stood in the shadow, but were bright, notwithstanding, with many-hued autumnal foliage. The rocky islets with their dense woods, coming one after another in the middle of the fjord, like a stream of boats rowing in, afforded a still stronger display of color, for they were not far off. The sea was still as glass: a big ship was slowly being towed in. People were sitting about on the wooden steps before their doors, where the rosebushes grew thick about them: they were talking to one another from door to door, running over to each other's dwellings, or exchanging greetings with the passers-by, who were on their way to the long, leafy lanes beyond the town. Here and there a piano might be heard through an open window: save that, no sound broke upon their talk. The last gleams of the setting sun over the sea seemed to add to the feeling of utter calm.

All of a sudden, there arose a sound in the middle of the town as if it were being stormed. Boys were screaming, girls crying, other boys hurrahing, old women scolding and shrieking out orders; the policeman's big dog was barking his loudest, and every dog in the town barked in answer. Nobody that heard it could stop indoors. So great was the uproar, that the Amtmand himself turned on his threshold, and was heard to say, "Why, there must be something the matter!"

"What is it?" was the constant question of those who came from the lanes to those on the steps.

"Dear me! what can it be?" every one was asking now, whenever anybody came from the middle of the town.

But the town lies in a half moon along a gently curving bay, and so it was a good while before those at each end had heard the answer:—

"Oh! it's only the Fisher Lassie!"

That venturesome spirit, bold in the protection of a redoubtable mother, and sure of help from every seaman in the town (for such service always got them a free dram from Gunlaug), had put herself at the head of her horde of small boys, and fallen upon a great apple tree in Pedro Ohlsen's garden.

The plan of assault was as follows: certain of the boys were to lure Pedro to the front of the house by making his rosebush beat against his window; at the same time, one of the others was to shake the apple tree, which stood in the midst of the garden, and the rest were to throw the apples over the fence in all directions — not to steal them — far from it! — but just for fun. This ingenious plan had that very evening been hatched behind Pedro's garden; but as luck would have it, Pedro himself happened to be sitting on the other side of the fence, and heard every word!

"AULESTAD," THE HOME OF BJÖRNSTJERNE BJÖRNSON, IN NORWAY

Somewhat before the appointed time, he got the town policeman (a tippling fellow) and his big dog into his back parlor, where he gave both of them refreshment. When the Fisher Lassie's curly black hair was seen above the palings, and a number of little faces peeped over on every side, Pedro let the young scamps in front of the house dash his rosebushes against the window panes to their heart's content, while he quietly waited in the room at the back of the house. But when they had all gathered in perfect silence round the tree, and the Fisher Lassie, with bare arms and scratched legs, had climbed up to shake it, the garden door suddenly sprang open, and Pedro and the policeman dashed out with sticks in their hands and the huge dog close behind them!

A scream of terror rose from among the boys. A lot of little girls, who were innocently playing "touch" on the other side of the fence, thought that somebody was being murdered in the garden, and began crying in the most heartrending way. The boys who had escaped shouted "Hurrah"; those who were still struggling over the fence screamed under the blows of the cudgels; and, to complete the confusion, there arose from the depths certain old women—they always do, when boys begin to shriek—and joined in the chorus. Pedro and the policeman were dismayed themselves at the uproar, and tried to still the old women: meanwhile, the boys took to their heels, and the dog (whom most they feared) dashed over the fence after them—that was *his* part of the game! And now the screams, the boys, the girls, and the dog flew like wildfire all over the town.

All this time, the Fisher Lassie had been sitting quite still up in the tree, thinking that nobody had noticed her; crouching up at the very top, she could follow through the leaves the course of the fray. But as soon as the policeman had in desperation gone out to the old women, and Pedro Ohlsen was alone in the garden, he came right under the tree, looked up, and shouted:—

"Come down with you at once, you rascal!"

Not a sound from the tree.

"Will you come down, I say? I know you're up there!"

Still unbroken silence.

"I shall go and get my gun and shoot you! I will!" and he made a movement as if to go.

"Boo-hoo-hoo!" came a sound from the tree.

"Yes, you may well begin to squall! You shall get a whole barrel full of shot in you, you shall!"

"Oo-hoo, oo-hoo!" cried a voice like an owl's; "I am so frightened!"

"Ah! it's you, you little devil, is it? You're the worst limb of mischief of the whole lot; but I've got you now!"

"Oh! de good kind sir! I'll never do it again!" and at the same moment she flung a rotten apple clean in his face, and a peal of laughter accompanied it.

The apple burst all over him, and while he was wiping it off, she slipped down from the tree, and was struggling over the palings before he could get near her. She would have got right off in safety, if she had not been so afraid of his being close behind her that she slipped back in her haste.

As soon as he touched her, she gave a scream — a scream so piercing, loud, thrilling, and shrill, that he was quite taken aback, and let go his hold. At her signal of distress, people began to gather round the fence. She heard this, and plucked up courage straightway.

"Let me go!" she threatened, "or I'll tell mother!" and her face was now all ablaze with passion.

Then he knew that look, and shouted wildly: "Your mother! who *is* your mother?"

"Gunlaug, Gunlaug of the Hill, Fish-Gunlaug," reiterated the girl in triumph, for she saw he was frightened.

Nearsighted as he was, he had never seen the child till now, and was the only person in the town who did not know who she was; he did not even know that Gunlaug was in the town.

"What is your name?" he cried, like one possessed.

"Petra!" came the answer, in still higher tones.

"Petra!" cried Pedro — and turned and dashed into the house as if he had spoken with the fiend.

Now, the paleness of fear is very like that of anger; Petra thought he had gone for his gun; terror seized her — already she felt the shots pursuing her. The garden gate had at that moment been burst open from the outside, and she rushed off through it, with her black hair streaming wild behind her, her eyes flashing fire, and the dog, whom she met, following and baying after her. Thus she burst upon her mother, who was coming from the kitchen with a bowl of soup, and down went the girl, with the soup all over her and the floor.

"Drat the girl!" from Gunlaug.

But, lying there in the spilt soup, she cried out: "He's coming to shoot me, mother! he's coming to shoot me!"

"Shoot you! *who's* going to shoot you, you little imp?"

"He — he — Pedro Ohlsen — we were taking his apples." She never dared tell aught but the truth.

"Whom are you talking of, child?"

"Of Pedro Ohlsen; he's after me with a big gun! he's coming to shoot me!"

"Pedro Ohlsen!" shrieked the mother; and then she laughed, and seemed somehow to have grown taller.

The child began to whimper and tried to make off; but the mother sprang upon her, with her white teeth shining as if for prey, and, gripping her by the shoulders, stopped her from going.

"Did you say who you were?"

"Yes, yes, yes, yes!" cried the child, holding up her hands entreatingly.

Then the mother drew herself up to her full height: —

"So he has got to know at last! Well, what did he say?"

"He ran in for his gun; he was going to shoot me!"

"*He* shoot *you!*" laughed Gunlaug, in huge scorn; but the child, in great terror, and all bespattered with the soup, had crept away into the corner, and was standing drying her clothes and shedding tears.

"If ever you go near him again," said the mother, coming up to her once more, seizing her and shaking her, "or talk to him, or listen to what he says, may God help both him and you! — Tell him that from me!" she added threateningly as the child did not at once answer.

"Yes, yes, yes, yes!"

"Tell — him — that — from — me!" she repeated once more, in a lower tone, as she walked away, stopping to nod her head at every word.

The child washed herself, changed her clothes, and went and sat out on the steps in her Sunday frock. But when she thought of the peril she had been in, her tears again began to fall.

"What are you weeping for, childie?" asked a voice, more kindly than any she had ever heard before.

She looked up; there stood before her a gracefully built, intellectual-looking man with spectacles. She stood up at once, for it was Hans Oedegaard, a young man in whose presence every one in the town stood.

"What are you weeping for, childie?" repeated the voice.

She looked up at him, and said that she and "some other boys" had been trying to get the apples in Pedro Ohlsen's garden; but Pedro and the policeman had come after them, and ——;" but she called to mind that her mother had shaken her faith in the shooting, so she dared not tell that part of the story —she gave a long deep sigh to make up for it.

"Is it possible," cried he, "that a child of your age could think of committing so great a sin?"

Petra stared at him; she knew well enough that it was a sin, but she had always been used to being told so by hearing herself called "You imp of the devil! you black-haired little fiend!" Now, somehow, she felt ashamed.

"How is it you don't go to school and learn God's Commandments to us about what is good and what is evil?"

She stood tugging at her frock, as she made shift to answer that her mother did not want her to go to school.

"You cannot even read, I suppose?" he said.

"Yes," replied she, she could read.

He took out a little book and gave it her. She opened it, turned it over, and then looked at the cover.

"I can't read such fine print," she said.

But he would not let her off so, and straightway she became most marvelously stupid: her eyes and lips drooped, and all her limbs seemed to hang loose.

"T-h-e the, L-o-r-d Lord, G-o-d God, the Lord God, s-a-i-d said, the Lord God said to M—M—M—"

"Good gracious!" he broke in, "you can't even read! And you ten or eleven years old! Wouldn't you be glad to be able to read?"

She managed to jerk out that she would be glad enough.

"Come with me, then; we must set to work at once."

She moved away a little, to look into the house.

"Yes, go and tell your mother about it," he said; and just then Gunlaug passed the door. Seeing the child talking with a stranger, she came out on to the flagstones.

"He wants to teach me to read, mother," said the child, looking at her with doubtful eyes.

The mother made no answer, but set both her arms akimbo, and looked at Oedegaard.

"Your child is very ignorant," said he. "You cannot answer it before God or man for letting her go on so."

"Who are you?" returned Gunlaug, sharply.

"Hans Oedegaard, son of your priest."

Her face cleared a little, for she had heard nothing but good of him.

"When I was at home before," he went on, "I noticed this child. To-day my attention has been called to her afresh. She must no longer accustom herself to doing only what is bad."

"What is that to you?" said the mother's face plainly enough, but he continued quietly: —

"Surely you would like her to learn something?"

"No!"

A slight flush passed over his face as he asked: —

"Why not?"

"Are folks any the better for learning?" — she had only had one experience of it, but she stuck fast to that.

"I am astonished that any one can ask such a question."

"Yes, of course; I know you are. I know people are none the better for it;" and she moved to the steps, to put an end to such ridiculous talk.

But he planted himself right in her way.

"Here is a duty," said he, "which you *shall* not pass by. You are a most injudicious mother."

Gunlaug measured him from head to foot.

"Who has told you," said she, "what I am?"

"You — you yourself; just now; or else you must have seen that your child was going on the way to ruin."

Gunlaug turned, and her eye met his; she saw he was in earnest in what he had said, and she began to feel afraid of him. She had always had to do with seamen and tradesfolk; talk such as his she had never heard.

"What do you want to do with my child?" she asked.

"Teach her what is right for her soul's welfare, and see what is to be made of her."

"My child shall be just what I want."

"No indeed she shan't! she shall be what God wants."

Gunlaug was at a loss what to answer. She drew nearer to him and said: —

"What do you mean by that?"

"I mean," he replied, "she ought to learn whatever her powers allow; for God has given them her for that."

Gunlaug now drew close up to him.

"Am I not to decide what is best for her — I, the child's mother?" she asked, as if really wishing to be informed.

"That you shall; but you must act on the advice of those who know better than you. You must do the Lord's will."

Gunlaug stood still for a moment.

"What if she learns too much?" she said at last — "a poor woman's child," she added, looking tenderly at her daughter.

"If she learns too much for her own rank, she will thereby have attained another," he said.

She grasped his meaning at once, and looking more and more fondly at her child, she said (as if to herself): —

"That is dangerous."

"That is not the question," he returned gently; "the question is, what is right?"

A strange expression came into her keen eyes; she looked at him piercingly, but there was so much earnestness in his voice, his words, and his face, that Gunlaug felt herself conquered. She went up to the child, and laid her hands on her head, but she spoke not a word.

"I shall read with her from now till the time when she is confirmed," he said, hoping to make things easier for Gunlaug. "I wish to take charge of the child."

"And do you want to take her away from me?"

He hesitated, and looked at her inquiringly.

"Of course, you know far better than I," she said, speaking with difficulty; "but if it hadn't been for what you said about the Lord ——" here she stopped. She had been smoothing down her daughter's hair, and now she took off her own kerchief and bound it round Petra's neck. Thus, in no other way, did she say the child was to go with him; but she hastened back into the house, as if she could not bear to see it.

Oedegaard began suddenly to feel afraid of what, in his youthful zeal, he had done. The child, for her part, felt afraid of him, for he was the first person who had ever got the best of her mother. And so, with mutual fears, they went to their first lesson.

Day by day, as it seemed to him, her cleverness and knowledge increased; and it often happened that their conversation seemed, of its own accord, to take one peculiar bent. He would bring before her eyes characters from the Bible or from history, in such a way as to point out to her the call that God had given them. He would tell her of Saul leading his wild life, or of the young David tending his father's flocks, till Samuel came and laid on him the hands of the Lord. But greatest of all was the Call when the Lord walked upon earth, tarried among the fisherfolk, and called them to His work. And the humble fishermen arose and followed after Him — to suffering — yea, even to Death; for the feeling of the holy Call bears men up through all tribulation.

The thought of this took such hold of her that she could not refrain from asking him about her own "Call." He looked steadfastly at her; she grew red beneath his gaze; and then he answered that through work every man finds out his vocation: that that might be insignificant and unimportant, but that it existed for every one. Then a great zeal came upon her; it drove her to work with all her might; it entered into her games, and it made her wan and thin.

Strange longings for adventure came over her. Oh! to cut short her hair, dress like a boy, and go out to take part in the struggle! But when one day her teacher told her that her hair would be so pretty if only she would take a little care of it, she got fond of her long tresses, and for their sake sacrificed her chance of a heroine's fame. After this, to be a girl became a more precious thing to her than ever, and henceforth her work went peacefully on, with the ever-changing dreams of girlhood floating around her.

BINGEN ON THE RHINE.

BY CAROLINE NORTON.

[MRS. NORTON (Caroline Elizabeth Sarah Sheridan), English poet and novelist, was the granddaughter of Richard Brinsley Sheridan, and was born in London, in 1808. In 1827 she married the Hon. George Chapple Norton, but the union proved an unfortunate one and a separation followed a few years later. She died June 14, 1877, shortly after her second marriage, to Sir W. Stirling-Maxwell. Among Mrs. Norton's works are the poems "Sorrows of Rosalie" and "The Undying One," and the novels "Lost and Saved," "Stuart of Dunleath," and "Old Sir Douglas."]

A SOLDIER of the Legion lay dying in Algiers,
There was lack of woman's nursing, there was dearth of woman's
tears;

But a comrade stood beside him, while the life blood ebbed away,
And bent with pitying glances to hear what he might say.
The dying soldier faltered, as he took that comrade's hand,
And he said: "I never more shall see my own — my native land!
Take a message and a token to some distant friends of mine,
For I was born at Bingen — at Bingen on the Rhine!

"Tell my brothers and companions, when they meet and crowd around,
To hear the mournful story in the pleasant vineyard ground,
That we fought the battle bravely, and when the day was done,
Full many a corse lay ghastly pale, beneath the setting sun;
And midst the dead and dying were some grown old in wars,
The death wound on their gallant breasts, the last of many scars!
But some were young, and suddenly beheld life's morn decline, —
And *one* had come from Bingen — fair Bingen on the Rhine!

"Tell my mother that her other sons shall comfort her old age,
For I was still a truant bird that thought his home a cage;
For my father was a soldier, and even when a child,
My heart leaped forth to hear him tell of struggles fierce and wild;
And when he died, and left us to divide his scanty hoard,
I let them take whate'er they would, but kept my father's sword!
And with boyish love I hung it where the bright light used to shine,
On the cottage wall at Bingen — calm Bingen on the Rhine!

"Tell my sister not to weep for me, and sob with drooping head,
When the troops come marching home again, with glad and gallant tread;
But to look upon them proudly, with a calm and steadfast eye,
For her brother was a soldier, too, and not afraid to die!
And if a comrade seek her love, I ask her in my name
To listen to him kindly, without regret and shame;
And to hang the old sword in its place (my father's sword and mine),
For the honor of old Bingen — dear Bingen on the Rhine!

"There's another — not a sister! In the happy days gone by
You'd have known her by the merriment that sparkled in her eye;
Too innocent for coquetry, too fond for idle scorning, —
O friend! I fear the lightest heart makes sometimes heaviest mourning!
Tell her the last night of my life (for, ere the moon be risen,
My body will be out of pain, my soul be out of prison),
I dreamed I stood with her, and saw the yellow sunlight shine
On the vine-clad hills of Bingen — fair Bingen on the Rhine!

BINGEN ON THE RHINE

"I saw the blue Rhine sweep along, — I heard, or seemed to hear,
The German songs we used to sing, in chorus sweet and clear;
And down the pleasant river, and up the slanting hill,
The echoing chorus sounded, through the evening calm and still;
And her glad blue eyes were on me, as we passed, with friendly talk,
Down many a path beloved of yore, and well-remembered walk;
And her little hand lay lightly, confidingly, in mine, —
But we'll meet no more at Bingen — loved Bingen on the Rhine!"

His trembling voice grew faint and hoarse, his gasp was childish weak;
His eyes put on a dying look — he sighed and ceased to speak;
His comrade bent to lift him, but the spark of life had fled —
The soldier of the Legion in a foreign land was dead!
And the soft moon rose up slowly, and calmly she looked down
On the red sand of the battle field, with bloody corses strown.
Yes; calmly on that dreadful scene her pale light seemed to shine,
As it shone on distant Bingen — fair Bingen on the Rhine!

THE DEATH OF THE PRINCE IMPERIAL.[1]

By ARCHIBALD FORBES.

(From "Memories and Studies of War and Peace.")

[Archibald Forbes: A Scotch war correspondent and author; born in Morayshire, in 1838. After studying at Aberdeen University, he served for several years in the Royal Dragoons, and then engaged in journalism. He was special correspondent of the London *Daily News* during the Franco-Prussian War (1870–1871), saw fighting with the Carlists in Spain, and reported the Servian, Russo-Turkish, Afghanistan, and Zululand campaigns. He afterwards lectured on his experiences, in Great Britain, America, and Australia. His publications include: "Glimpses through the Cannon Smoke" (1880), lives of "Chinese" Gordon, Havelock, Emperor William I., and Emperor Napoleon III., "Barracks, Bivouacs, and Battles," "Studies of War and Peace," "Tzar and Sultan."]

It was in Zululand, on the evening of June 1, 1879. A little group of us were at dinner in the tent of General Marshall, who commanded the cavalry brigade in the British army which was marching on Ulundi, King Cetewayo's royal kraal. The sun was just going down when Colonel Harrison, the quartermaster general, put his head inside the tent door, and called aloud in a strange voice, "Good God! the Prince Imperial is killed!" Harrison, though stolid, sometimes jested, and for the moment this announcement was not taken seriously. Lord Downe, Marshall's aid-de-camp, threw a crust of bread

[1] From "Memoirs and Studies of Peace and War" by Archibald Forbes. (Price 6s.) By permission of Cassell & Co., Ltd.

at his head, and Herbert Stewart, then Marshall's brigade major, afterwards killed during the desert march in the Soudan, laughed aloud.

But, sitting near the door, I discerned in the faint light of the dying day the horror in Harrison's face, and sprang to my feet instinctively. The news was only too fatally true; and when the dismal, broken story of the survivors of the party had been told, throughout the force there was a thrill of sorrow for the poor gallant lad, a burning sense of shame that he should have been so miserably left to his fate, and a deep sympathy for the forlorn widow in England on whom fortune seemed to rejoice in heaping disaster on disaster, bereavement on bereavement.

I knew the Prince well. On the first two occasions I saw him it was through a binocular from a considerable distance. On August 2, 1870, the day on which the boy of fourteen in the words of his father "received his baptism of fire," I was watching from the drill ground above Saarbrücken in company with the last remaining Prussian soldiers, the oncoming swarm attack of Battaille's tirailleurs firing as they hurried across the plain. The tirailleurs had passed a little knoll which rose in the plain about midway between the Spicheren hill and where I stood, and presently it was crowned by two horsemen followed by a great staff. The glass told me that without a doubt the senior of the foremost horsemen was the Emperor Napoleon, and that the younger, shorter and slighter — a mere boy he looked — was the Prince Imperial, whom we knew to be with his father in the field.

A fortnight later, in the early morning of the 15th, the day before Mars-la-Tour, when the German army was as yet only east and south of Metz, I accompanied a German horse battery which, galloping up to within five hundred paces of the chateau of Longueville, around which was a French camp of some size, opened fire on chateau and camp. After a few shells had been fired great confusion was observed about the chateau and in the camp, and I distinctly discerned the Emperor and his son emerge from the building, mount, and gallop away, followed by suite and escort.

Years later in Zululand, when the day's work was done for both of us and the twilight was falling on the rolling veldt, the Prince was wont occasionally to gossip with me about those early days of the great war which we had witnessed from opposite sides, and he told me his experiences of the morning just mentioned. A crash awoke him with a start and he was sitting up in bed, bewildered, when his father entered with the exclamation, "Up, Louis! up and dress! The German shells are crashing through the roofs." As the Prince looked out of the window while he was hurriedly dressing, he saw a shell fall and burst in a group of officers seated in the garden at breakfast, and when the smoke lifted three of them lay dead. That the story of his nerves having been shattered by the bullet fire at Saarbrücken was untrue was proved by an episode he related to me of that same morning an hour later. On the steep ascent of the *chaussée* up to Châtel, the imperial party was wedged in the heart of a complete block of troops, wagons, and guns. A long delay seemed inevitable. But the lad had noticed a wayside gate whence a track led up through the vineyard. He followed it to the crest and marked its trend; then, riding back, he called aloud, "This way, papa!" The Prince's side track turned the block, and presently the party were in the new quarters in the house which is now the post office of Gravelotte.

That excellent American publication, "Johnson's Universal Cyclopedia," errs for once in stating that after the downfall of the empire the Prince "escaped with his mother to England." He never saw his mother after leaving Paris for the seat of war until she came to him in Hastings after the revolution in Paris. When the shadows were darkening on MacMahon's ill-fated march, the Emperor sent his son away from the front; and the story of the vicissitudes and dangers the lad encountered before reaching England after Sedan would make of itself a long chapter.

When his parents settled at Chislehurst, the Prince, then in his fifteenth year, entered the Royal Academy at Woolwich to receive a scientific military education. He had not undergone the usual preparation, and he might have joined without the preliminary examination; but never, then nor through the course, would he accept any indulgence, and his "preliminary" was satisfactory in spite of his want of familiarity with the language. In the United States West Point affords the same instruction to all cadets alike, those who are most successful passing into the scientific branches; but in England the cadets for the Line are educated at Sandhurst, and the severer tuition of Woolwich is restricted to candidates for the engineer and artillery branches. The Prince took his chance with his comrades both at work and play. His mathematical instructor has stated that he had considerable powers, evincing an undoubtedly clear insight into the principles of the higher mathematics ; but he added that he often failed to bring out specifically his knowledge at examinations, owing to his imperfect grasp of the necessary formulæ and working details. Indeed, details wearied him, then and later. In Zululand he more than once told me that he "hated desk work"; and M. Deleage, his countryman and friend, who accompanied the Zululand expedition, wrote that on the day before his death, after he had left the staff office tent, "Lieutenant Carey found the Prince's work done with so much haste and inattention that he had to sit up all night correcting it." In spite of this defect in steady concentration, at the end of his Woolwich course he passed seventh in a class of thirty-five, and had he gone into the English service he would have been entitled to choose between the engineers and artillery. He would have stood higher but that, curiously enough, he comparatively failed in French. He was an easy first in equitation. During his Woolwich career he won the love and respect of his comrades; his instructors spoke warmly of his modesty, conscientiousness, and uprightness, and pronounced him truthful and honorable in a high degree.

After leaving Woolwich he lived mostly with his widowed mother at Chislehurst, but he traveled on the Continent occasionally, and mixed a good deal in London society, where from time to time I met him. After he attained manhood it was understood that a marriage was projected between him and the Princess Beatrice, the youngest of the Queen's daughters, who is now the wife of Prince Henry of Battenberg. The attainment of his majority was made a great occasion by the Imperialist adherents, as a test of their adherence to a cause which they refused to consider lost. More than 10,000 Frenchmen of all ranks and classes congregated on Chislehurst Common that day. The tricolor waved along the route to the little Roman Catholic chapel on the outskirts of the quiet Kentish village; as the members of the Imperial family passed from Camden Place to the religious service, every head was uncovered; and shouts of "Vive l'Empereur !" rose from the ardent partisans, numbers of whom had already paid homage to the remains of their dead Emperor lying in the marble sarcophagus in front of the high altar of the chapel. Later in the day the large company of French people assembled in the park of Camden Place, in rear of the deputations from the different provinces of France, each deputation headed by a leader bearing the provincial banner. The Prince, with his mother by his side, stood forward; behind them the princes, nobles, and statesmen of the late empire, and many Imperialist ladies of rank. When the Duc de Padoue had finished reading a long address expressive of attachment and devotion, the young Prince spoke to his supporters with great dignity, earnestness, and modesty. I heard the final sentences of his speech, the manly tone of which I can never forget. "If the time should ever arrive when my countrymen shall honor me with a majority of the suffrages of the nation, I shall be ready to accept with proud respect the decision of France. If for the eighth time the people pronounce in favor of the name of Napoleon, I am prepared to accept the responsibility imposed upon me by the vote of the nation." Once again, and only once, I heard the Prince speak in public. It was at the annual dinner of an institution known as the "Newspaper Press Fund." Lord Salisbury, one of the most brilliant speakers of our time, was in the chair. Cardinal Manning, the silver-tongued, Lord Wolseley, good speaker and brilliant commander, and Henry M. Stanley, fresh from "darkest Africa," were among the orators. But, quite apart from his position, the short address made by the Prince Imperial was unanimously regarded as the speech of the evening.

In features, with his long, oval face, black hair and eyes — attributes of neither of his parents, and his lean, shapely head, the Prince was a Spaniard of the Spaniards. One recognized in him no single characteristic of the Frenchman; he was a veritable hidalgo, with all the pride, the melancholy, the self-restraint yet ardor to shine, the courage trenching on an ostentatious recklessness, and indeed the childishness in trifles which marked that now but all extinct type. Whether there was in his veins a drop of the Bonapartist blood (remembering the suspicions of King Louis of Holland with regard to Hortense) is a problem now probably insoluble. Certainly neither he nor his father had any physical feature in common with the undoubted members of the race. The Montijos, although the house in its latest developments had somewhat lost caste and had a bourgeois strain on the distaff side, were ancestrally of the bluest blood of Spain; and it has always been my idea that the Prince Imperial illustrated the theory of atavism by throwing back to the Guzmans, the Corderas, or the Baros, all grand old Spanish families whose blood was in his veins. How strong was his self-restraint even in youth, an anecdote told in Miss Barlee's interesting book of his Woolwich days may evidence. Hearing one day that a Frenchman was visiting the academy, he sent to say that he should be glad to see his countryman. The person, who as it happened was a bitter anti-Imperialist, was presented, and the Prince asked him from what part of France he came. The fellow, looking the youth straight in the face with a sarcastic smile, uttered the one word "Sedan," and grinningly waited for the effect of his brutality. The Prince flushed, and his eye kindled; then he conquered himself, and, quietly remarking, "That is a very pretty part of France," closed the interview with a bow.

I never saw dignity and self-control more finely manifested in union than when the lad, not yet seventeen, wearing a black cloak over which was the broad red ribbon of the Legion of Honor, followed his father's coffin as chief mourner along the path lined by many thousand French sympathizers; and his demeanor was truly royal when later on that trying day the masses of French artisans hailed him with shouts of "Vive Napoleon IV.!" He stopped the personal acclaim by saying: "My friends, I thank you; but your Emperor is dead. Let us join in the cry of 'Vive la France!'"—baring at the same time his head and leading off the cheering. His craving for effect curiously displayed itself during a parade in Scotland of a number of Clydesdale stallions, at which were present the Prince of Wales and a number of noblemen and gentlemen. One horse, which was plunging violently, was described as never having allowed a rider to remain on its back. At the word the Prince Imperial vaulted on to the bare back of the animal, mastered its efforts to dislodge him, and rode the conquered stallion round the arena amid loud applause.

The forced inaction of his life irked him intensely. His good sense and true patriotism induced him steadily to decline the urgency of young and ardent Imperialists, that he should disturb the peace of France either by intrigue or by more active efforts to restore the dynasty. It stung him to the quick that the scurrilous part of the French press taunted him with the quietness of his life, which it chose to attribute to cowardice and lack of enterprise. In Zululand he told me of a circumstance which I have nowhere seen mentioned, that a year before he had applied to the French Government for permission to join the French troops fighting in Tonquin; that MacMahon, who was then President, was in his favor; but that the Ministry refused the request. The English war of 1879 in Zululand was his opportunity. His constant belief was that ten years would be the term of his exile. "Dix ans de patience, et après!" he used to mutter in his daydreams. The ten years were nearly up. And what prestige would not accrue to him if he should have the good fortune to distinguish himself in the field, which he was resolved to do at any cost! The disaster of Isandlwana, to retrieve which troops were being hurried out, and the heroic defense of Rorke's Drift, were lost opportunities at which he chafed. He felt that he was forfeiting chances which, taken advantage of, might have aided his progress to the Imperial throne. Determined to lose no more chances, he went to the British Commander in Chief and begged to be permitted to go on service to South Africa.

His attitude and yearnings were quite intelligible, and were in no sense blameworthy. He desired to further the means towards a specific and obvious end, if England only would give him the helping hand. But this ultimate aim of his being so evident, it was singularly improper and ill-judged on the part of the English authorities to give well-grounded umbrage to the friendly power across the Channel, by forwarding an enterprise the purpose of which was to help toward changing Republican France into Imperial France, and to contribute toward the elevation of this young man to the throne which his father had lost. The Commander in Chief had his scruples, for he is a man of some discretion; but they were overruled. And it was from Windsor, bidden Godspeed by the Sovereign, that the Prince departed to embark. France sullenly watched his career in South Africa. Had it ended differently the mood would have become intensified. If it be asked why for the last sixteen years France has never for an hour worn a semblance of cordial accord with the insular power its neighbor, the answer is that this attitude of chronic umbrage has one of its sources in the intrigue which sent the Prince Imperial to Zululand.

At the news of Isandlwana I had hurried from the Khyber Pass to South Africa, and the Prince had already joined the army when first I met him in May, 1879, at Sir Evelyn Wood's camp of Kambula, which he was visiting with Lord Chelmsford and the headquarters' staff. The Duke of Cambridge had specially confided him to his lordship's care. But poor Lord Chelmsford's nerve had been sore shaken by the tragedy of Isandlwana, after which he had begged to be relieved. Like Martha, he was careful and troubled about many things; his will power was limp and fickle, and the Prince was to him in the nature of a white elephant. The latter, for his part, was ardent for opportunities of adventurous enterprise, while the harassed Chelmsford had been bidden to dry nurse him assiduously. The military arrangements were lax and the Prince had been able to share in several somewhat hazardous reconnaissances, in the course of which he had displayed a rash bravery which disquieted the responsible leaders. After one of these scouting expeditions, in which he actually had come to close quarters with a party of Zulus, and it was asserted had whetted his sword, he was said to have remarked naïvely: "Such skirmishes suit my taste exactly, yet I should be au désespoir did I think I should be killed in one. In a great battle, if Providence so willed it, all well and good; but in a petty reconnaissance of this kind—ah! that would never do."

His penultimate reconnaissance was with a detachment of Frontier Light Horse under the command of Colonel Buller, V.C., now Sir Redvers Buller, Adjutant General of the British Army. The Zulus gathered and a fight seemed impending, to the Prince's great joy; but they dispersed. A few, however, were seen skulking at a distance, and against them he rode at full gallop in a state of great excitement. He had to be supported, which occasioned inconvenience; during the night, which was bitterly cold and during which the Prince's excitement continued, he tramped up and down constantly, singing at intervals "Malbrook s'en va-t-en-guerre," not wholly to the contentment of the phlegmatic Britons around him. Colonel Buller reported his inconvenient recklessness, protested against accepting responsibility for him when his military duties called for all his attention, and suggested that he should be employed in camp on staff duty instead of being permitted to risk himself on reconnaissance service. Thereupon Lord Chelmsford detailed him to desk work in the quartermaster general's department, and gave Colonel Harrison a written order that the Prince should not quit the camp without the express permission of his lordship. The Prince, made aware of this order, obeyed, for he had a high sense of discipline; but he did not conceal his dislike to the drudgery of plan making in a tent. He was fond of and expert in sketching in the field.

The orders issued to the little army in the Koppie Allein camp on the 31st of May for the morrow were that the infantry should march direct to a camping ground on the Itelezi hill about eight miles forward, the cavalry to scout several miles farther and then to fall back to the Itelezi camp. Early on the morning of June 1st the Prince, dead tired of routine desk work, begged Colonel Harrison to allow him to make a sketching expedition with an escort, beyond the ground to be covered by the cavalry. The matter was under discussion—Harrison reluctant to consent, when Lieutenant Carey, a staff officer of the department, suggested that he should accompany the Prince, and proposed that the expedition should extend into the Ityotyozi valley, where the next camp beyond the Itelezi was to be and a sketch of which he (Carey) had two days previously left unfinished. Harrison then made no further objection, consenting the more readily because the whole terrain in advance had been thoroughly scouted over recently. He instructed Carey to requisition a mounted escort of six white men and six Basutos, and he subsequently maintained that he had intrusted the command of the escort to Carey. This Carey denied, repudiating all responsibility in regard to the direction of the escort since the Prince in his rank of honorary captain was his superior officer, and holding that his function as regarded the latter was simply that of friendly adviser. I was afterwards told that before leaving camp the Prince wrote a letter—the last he ever wrote—to his mother, and that hearing I was about to ride back to the post office at Landmann's Drift, he left the message for me with his best regards, that he should be greatly obliged by my carrying down his letter. As it happened, I did not quit the camp until I did so as the bearer to the telegraph wire of the tidings of the Prince's death.

I was with Herbert Stewart, the cavalry brigade major, when Carey came to him with Harrison's warrant for an escort. Carey did not mention, nor did the document state, that the escort was for the Prince Imperial. Stewart ordered out six men of Beddington's Horse—a curiously mixed handful of diverse nationalities—and he told Carey that he would send Captain Shepstone an order for the Basuto detail of the escort, but that time would be saved if Carey himself on his way back to headquarters would hand Shepstone the order and give his own instructions. Carey chose the latter alternative and departed. An hour later, while I was still with Stewart, the six Basutos paraded in front of his tent. Either Carey or Shepstone had blundered in the instructions given them, that was clear; but nothing could now be done but to order the Basutos to hurry forward and try to overtake the other installment of the escort. Meanwhile the Prince had been impatient; and he, Carey, and the white section of the escort had gone on. Carey made no demur to the scant escort, since nothing was to be apprehended and since he himself had been recently chaffed for being addicted to requisitioning inordinately large escorts. Harrison later met the party some miles out, and sanctioned its going forward notwithstanding that the Basutos had not joined, which indeed they never succeeded in doing. The party then consisted of the Prince, Carey, a sergeant, a corporal, four troopers, and a black native guide — nine persons in all.

When Harrison had announced the tidings of the tragedy, I went to my tent and sent for each of the four surviving troopers in succession. They were all bad witnesses, and I could not help suspecting that they were in collusion to keep something back. All agreed, however, that Lieutenant Carey headed the panic flight; and next day it transpired that, when a mile away from the scene and still galloping wildly, he was casually met by Sir Evelyn Wood and Colonel Buller, to whom he exclaimed: "Fly! Fly! The Zulus are after me and the Prince Imperial is killed!" The evidence I took on the night of the disaster, and that afterwards given before the court of inquiry and the court martial on Carey, may now be briefly summarized.

The site of the intended camp having been planned out by the Prince and Carey, the party ascended an adjacent hill and spent an hour there in sketching the contours of the surrounding country. No Zulus were visible in the wide expanse surveyed from the hilltop. At its base, on a small plain at the junction of the rivers Tambakala and Ityotyozi, was the small Zulu kraal of Etuki, the few huts of which, according to the Zulu custom, stood in a rough circle which was surrounded on three sides at a little distance by a tall growth of "mealies" (Indian corn) and the high grass known as "Kaffir corn."

The party descended to this kraal, off-saddled, fed the horses, made coffee, ate food, and then reclined, resting against the wall of a hut in full sense of assured safety. Some dogs skulking about the empty kraal and the fresh ashes on the hearths might have warned them, but they did not heed the suggestion thus afforded. About three o'clock Corporal Grubbe, who understood the Basuto language, reported the statement of the guide that he had seen a Zulu entering the mealie field in their front. Carey proposed immediately saddling up. The Prince desired ten minutes' longer rest, and Carey did not expostulate. Then the horses were brought up and saddled. Carey stated that at this moment he saw black forms moving behind the screen of tall grain, and informed the Prince. Throughout the day the latter had acted in command of the escort, and he now in soldierly fashion gave the successive orders, "Prepare to mount!" "Mount!" Next moment, according to the evidence, a volley of twenty or thirty bullets — one witness said forty bullets — were fired into the party.

Let me be done with Carey for good and all. He had mounted on the inner, the safe, side of the hut, and immediately galloped off. On the night of the event he expressed the opinion that the Prince had been shot dead at the kraal, but owned that the first actual evidence of misfortune of which he became cognizant was the Prince's riderless horse galloping past him. The men were either less active or less precipitate than was the officer. One of their number fell at the kraal, another on the grassy level some 150 yards wide, between the kraal and a shallow "donga," or gully, across which ran the path towards the distant camp. As to the Prince the testimony was fairly unanimous. Sergeant Cochrane stated that he never actually mounted, but had foot in stirrup when at the Zulu volley his horse, a spirited gray, sixteen hands high and always difficult to mount, started off, presently broke away, and later was caught by the survivors. Then the Prince tried to escape on foot, and was last seen by Cochrane running into the donga, from which he never emerged. Another trooper testified that he saw the Prince try to mount, but that, not succeeding, he ran by his horse's side for some little distance making effort after effort to mount, till he either stumbled or fell in a scrambling way and seemed to be trodden on by his horse. But the most detailed evidence was given by trooper Lecocq, a Channel Islander. He stated that after their volley the Zulus bounded out of cover, shouting "Usuta!" ("Cowards!"). The Prince was unable to mount his impatient horse, scared as it was by the fire. One by one the troopers galloped by the Prince, who, as he ran alongside his now maddened horse, was endeavoring in vain to mount. As Lecocq passed lying on his stomach across the saddle, not yet having got his seat, he called to the Prince, "Dépêchez-vous, s'il vous plait, Monseigneur!" The Prince made no reply and was left alone to his fate. His horse strained after that of Lecocq, who then saw the doomed Prince holding his stirrup leather with one hand, grasping reins and pommel with the other, and trying to remount on the run. No doubt he made one desperate effort, trusting to the strength of his grasp on the band of leather crossing the pommel from holster to holster. That band tore under the strain. I inspected it next day and found it no leather at all, but paper faced—so that the Prince's fate really was attributable to shoddy saddlery. Lecocq saw the Prince fall backwards, and his horse tread on him and then gallop away. According to him the Prince regained his feet and ran at full speed towards the donga on the track of the retreating party. When for the last time the Jerseyman turned round in the saddle, he saw the Prince still running, pursued only a few yards behind by some twelve or fourteen Zulus, with assegais in hand, which they were throwing at him. None save the slayers saw the tragedy enacted in the donga.

Early next morning the cavalry brigade marched out to recover the body, for there was no hope that anything save the body was to be recovered. As the scene was neared, some of us rode forward in advance. In the middle of the little plain was found a body, savagely mutilated; it was not that of the Prince, but of one of the slain troopers. We found the dead Prince in the donga, a few paces on one side of the path. He was lying on his back, naked save for one sock; a spur bent out of shape was close to him. His head was so bent to the right that the cheek touched the sward. His hacked arms were lightly crossed over his lacerated chest, and his face, the features of which were in no wise distorted but wore a faint smile that slightly parted the lips, was marred by the destruction of the right eye from an assegai stab. The surgeons agreed that this wound, which penetrated the brain, was the first and the fatal hurt, and that the subsequent wounds were inflicted on a dead body. Of those there were many, in throat, in chest, in side, and on arms, apart from the nick in the abdomen which is the Zulu fetish custom, invariably practiced on slain enemies as a protection against being haunted by their ghosts. His wounds bled afresh as we moved him. Neither on him nor on any of the three other slain of the party was found any bullet wound; all had been killed by assegai stabs. Round the poor Prince's neck his slayers had left a little gold chain on which were strung a locket set with a miniature of his mother, and a reliquary containing a fragment of the true Cross which was given by Pope Leo III. to Charlemagne when he crowned that great Prince Emperor of the West, and which dynasty after dynasty of French monarchs had since worn as a talisman. Very sad and solemn was the scene as we stood around, silent all and with bared heads, looking down on the untimely dead. The Prince's two servants were weeping bitterly and there was a lump in many a throat. An officer, his bosom friend at Woolwich, detached the necklet and placed it in an envelope with several locks of the Prince's short dark hair for transmission to his mother, who a year later made so sad a pilgrimage to the spot where we now stood over her dead son. Then the body, wrapped in a cloak, was placed on the lance shafts of the cavalrymen, and on this extemporized bier the officers of the brigade bore it up the ascent to the ambulance wagon which was in waiting. The same afternoon a solemn funeral service was performed in the Itelezi camp, and later in the evening the body, escorted by a detachment of cavalry, began its pilgrimage to England, in which exile, in the chapel at Farnborough, where the widowed wife and childless mother now resides, the remains of husband and son now rest side by side in their marble sarcophagi. The sword worn in South Africa by the Prince, the veritable sword worn by the first Napoleon from Arcola to Waterloo — in reference to which the Prince had been heard to say, "I must earn a better right to it than that which my name alone can give me" — had been carried off by his Zulu slayers, but was restored by Cetewayo when Lord Chelmsford's army was closing in upon Ulundi.

To be slain by savages in an obscure corner of a remote continent was a miserable end, truly, for him who once was the Son of France.

DEATH'S VALLEY

By WALT WHITMAN.

NAY, do not dream, designer dark,
Thou hast portrayed or hit thy theme entire:
I, hoverer of late by this dark valley, by its confines, having glimpses of it,
Here enter lists with thee, claiming my right to make a symbol too.
For I have seen many wounded soldiers die,
After dread suffering — have seen their lives pass off with smiles;
And I have watched the death hours of the old; and seen the infant die;
The rich, with all his nurses and his doctors;
And then the poor, in meagerness and poverty;
And I myself for long, O Death, have breathed my every breath
Amid the nearness and the silent thought of thee.

And out of these and thee,
I make a scene, a song, brief (not fear of thee,
Nor gloom's ravines, nor bleak, nor dark — for I do not fear thee,
Nor celebrate the struggle, or contortion, or hard-tied knot),
Of the broad blessed light and perfect air, with meadows, rippling tides, and trees and flowers and grass,
And the low hum of living breeze — and in the midst God's beautiful eternal right hand,
Thee, holiest minister of Heaven — thee, envoy, usherer, guide at last of all;
Rich, florid, loosener of the stricture knot called life,
Sweet, peaceful, welcome Death.

FROM "BEAUCHAMP'S CAREER."[1]

By GEORGE MEREDITH.

[GEORGE MEREDITH, English novelist and poet, is a native of Hampshire and was born February 12, 1828. After studying for some time in Germany, he commenced his literary career with the publication of a volume of poems (1851), which was followed by the burlesque poem, "The Shaving of Shagpat," and his first novel, "The Ordeal of Richard Feverel" (1859). Subsequent novels are: "Emilia in England" (now known as "Sandra Belloni"), "Rhoda Fleming," "Vittoria" (sequel to "Sandra Belloni"), "The Adventures of Harry Richmond," "Beauchamp's Career," "The Egoist," "Diana of the Crossways,"

[1] By permission of Author and A. Constable & Co. (Cr. 8vo. Price 6s.)

Walt Whitman

"One of the Conquerors," "Lord Ormont and his Aminta," and "The Amazing Marriage." Besides the poems mentioned above he published: "Farina," "Modern Love," "Poems and Lyrics of the Joy of Earth." Mr. Meredith resides at Boxhill, Surrey. In 1892 he was elected president of the British Society of Authors in succession to Lord Tennyson.]

THE CHAMPION OF HIS COUNTRY.

WHEN young Nevil Beauchamp was throwing off his midshipman's jacket for a holiday in the garb of peace, we had across Channel a host of dreadful military officers flashing swords at us for some critical observations of ours upon their sovereign, threatening Afric's fires and savagery. The case occurred in old days now and again, sometimes, upon imagined provocation, more furiously than at others. We were unarmed, and the spectacle was distressing. We had done nothing except to speak our minds according to the habit of the free, and such an explosion appeared as irrational and excessive as that of a powder magazine in reply to nothing more than the light of a spark. It was known that a valorous General of the Algerian wars proposed to make a clean march to the capital of the British empire at the head of ten thousand men; which seems a small quantity to think about, but they wore wide red breeches blown out by Fame, big as her cheeks, and a ten thousand of that sort would never think of retreating. Their spectral advance on quaking London through Kentish hop gardens, Sussex cornfields, or by the pleasant hills of Surrey, after a gymnastic leap over the ribbon of salt water, haunted many pillows. And now those horrid shouts of the legions of Cæsar, crying to the inheritor of an invading name to lead them against us, as the origin of his title had led the army of Gaul of old gloriously, scared sweet sleep. We saw them in imagination lining the opposite shore; eagle and standard bearers, and *gallifers*, brandishing their fowls and their banners in a manner to frighten the decorum of the universe. Where were our men?

The returns of the census of our population were oppressively satisfactory, and so was the condition of our youth. We could row and ride and fish and shoot, and breed largely: we were athletes with a fine history and a full purse: we had first-rate sporting guns, unrivaled park hacks and hunters, promising babies to carry on the renown of England to the next generation, and a wonderful Press, and a Constitution the highest reach of practical human sagacity. But where were our armed men? where our great artillery? where our proved captains, to resist a sudden sharp trial of the national mettle? Where was the first line of England's defense, her navy? These were questions, and Ministers were called upon to answer them. The Press answered them boldly, with the appalling statement that we had no navy and no army. At the most we could muster a few old ships, a couple of experimental vessels of war, and twenty-five thousand soldiers indifferently weaponed.

We were in fact as naked to the Imperial foe as the merely painted Britons.

This being apprehended, by the aid of our own shortness of figures and the agitated images of the red breeched only waiting the signal to jump and be at us, there ensued a curious exhibition that would be termed, in simple language, writing to the newspapers, for it took the outward form of letters: in reality, it was the deliberate saddling of our ancient nightmare of Invasion, putting the postilion on her, and trotting her along the highroad with a winding horn to rouse old Panic. Panic we will, for the sake of convenience, assume to be of the feminine gender and a spinster, though properly she should be classed with the large mixed race of mental and moral neuters which are the bulk of comfortable nations. She turned in her bed at first like the sluggard of the venerable hymnist; but once fairly awakened, she directed a stare toward the terrific foreign contortionists, and became in an instant all stormy nightcap and fingers starving for the bell rope. Forthwith she burst into a series of shrieks, howls, and high piercing notes that caused even the parliamentary Opposition, in the heat of an assault on a parsimonious Government, to abandon its temporary advantage and be still awhile. Yet she likewise performed her part with a certain deliberation and method, as if aware that it was a part she had to play in the composition of a singular people. She did a little mischief by dropping on the stock markets; in other respects she was harmless, and, inasmuch as she established a subject for conversation, useful.

Then, lest she should have been taken too seriously, the Press, which had kindled, proceeded to extinguish her with the formidable engines called leading articles, which fling fire or water, as the occasion may require. It turned out that we had ships ready for launching, and certain regiments coming home from India; hedges we had, and a spirited body of yeomanry; and we had pluck and patriotism, the father and mother of volunteers innumerable. Things were not so bad.

Panic, however, sent up a plaintive whine. What country had anything like our treasures to defend? — countless riches, beautiful women, an inviolate soil! True, and it must be done. Ministers were authoritatively summoned to set to work immediately. They replied that they had been at work all the time, and were at work now. They could assure the country that, though they flourished no trumpets, they positively guaranteed the safety of our virgins and coffers.

Then the people, rather ashamed, abused the Press for unreasonably disturbing them. The Press attacked old Panic and stripped her naked. Panic, with a desolate scream, arraigned the parliamentary Opposition for having inflated her to serve base party purposes. The Opposition challenged the allegations of Government, pointed to the trimness of army and navy during its term of office, and proclaimed itself watchdog of the country, which is, at all events, an office of a kind. Hereupon the ambassador of yonder ireful soldiery let fall a word, saying, by the faith of his Master, there was no necessity for watchdogs to bark; an ardent and a reverent army had but fancied its beloved chosen Chief insulted; the Chief and chosen held them in; he, despite obloquy, discerned our merits and esteemed us.

So, then, Panic, or what remained of her, was put to bed again. The Opposition retired into its kennel, growling. The People coughed like a man of two minds, doubting whether he has been divinely inspired or has cut a ridiculous figure. The Press interpreted the cough as a warning to Government; and Government launched a big ship with hurrahs, and ordered the recruiting sergeant to be seen conspicuously.

And thus we obtained a moderate reënforcement of our arms.

It was not arrived at by connivance all round, though there was a look of it. Certainly it did not come of accident, though there was a look of that as well. Nor do we explain much of the secret by attributing it to the working of a complex machinery. The housewife's remedy of a good shaking for the invalid who will not arise and dance away his gout, partly illustrates the action of the Press upon the country: and perhaps the country shaken may suffer a comparison with the family chariot of the last century, built in a previous one, commodious, furnished agreeably, being all that the inside occupants could require of a conveyance, until the report of horsemen crossing the heath at a gallop sets it dishonorably creaking and complaining in rapid motion, and the squire curses his miserly purse that would not hire a guard, and his dame says, I told you so! — Foolhardy man, to suppose, because we have constables in the streets of big cities, we have dismissed the highwayman to limbo. And here he is, and he will cost you fifty times the sum you would have laid out to keep him at a mile's respectful distance! But see, the wretch is bowing: he smiles at our carriage, and tells the coachman that he remembers he has been our guest, and really thinks we need not go so fast. He leaves word for you, sir, on your peril to denounce him on another occasion from the magisterial Bench, for that albeit he is a gentleman of the road, he has a mission to right society, and succeeds legitimately to that bold Good Robin Hood who fed the poor. — Fresh from this polite encounter, the squire vows money for his personal protection: and he determines to speak his opinion of Sherwood's latest captain as loudly as ever. That he will, I do not say. It might involve a large sum per annum.

Similes are very well in their way. None can be sufficient in this case without leveling a finger at the taxpayer — nay, directly mentioning him. He is the key of our ingenuity. He pays his dues; he will not pay the additional penny or two wanted of him, that we may be a step or two ahead of the day we live in, unless he is frightened. But scarcely anything less than the wild alarum of a tocsin will frighten him. Consequently the tocsin has to be sounded; and the effect is woeful past measure; his hugging of his army, his kneeling on the shore to his navy, his implorations to his yeomanry and his hedges, are sad to note. His bursts of pot-valiancy (the male side of the maiden Panic within his bosom) are awful to his friends. Particular care must be taken after he has begun to cool and calculate his chances of security, that he do not gather to him a curtain of volunteers and go to sleep again behind them; for they cost little in proportion to the much they pretend to be to him. Patriotic taxpayers doubtless exist: prophetic ones, provident ones, do not. At least we show that we are wanting in them. The taxpayer of a free land taxes himself, and his disinclination for the bitter task, save under circumstances of screaming urgency — as when the night gear and bed linen of old convulsed Panic are like the churned Channel sea in the track of two hundred hostile steamboats, let me say — is of the kind the gentle schoolboy feels when death or an expedition has relieved him of his tyrant, and he is entreated notwithstanding to go to his books.

Will you not own that the working of the system for scaring him and bleeding is very ingenious? But whether the ingenuity comes of native sagacity, as it is averred by some, or whether it shows an instinct laboring to supply the deficiencies of stupidity, according to others, I cannot express an opinion. I give you the position of the country undisturbed by any moralizings of mine. The youth I introduce to you will rarely let us escape from it; for the reason that he was born with so extreme and passionate a love for his country, that he thought all things else of mean importance in comparison: and our union is one in which, following the counsel of a sage and seer, I must try to paint for you what it is, not that which I imagine. This day, this hour, this life, and even politics, the center and throbbing heart of it (enough, when unburlesqued, to blow the down off the gossamer stump of fiction at a single breath, I have heard tell), must be treated of: men, and the ideas of men, which are — it is policy to be emphatic upon truisms — are actually the motives of men in a greater degree than their appetites: these are my theme; and may it be my fortune to keep them at blood heat, and myself calm as a statue of Memnon in prostrate Egypt! He sits there waiting for the sunlight; I here, and readier to be musical than you think. I can at any rate be impartial; and do but fix your eyes on the sunlight striking him and swallowing the day in rounding him, and you have an image of the passive receptivity of shine and shade I hold it good to aim at, if at the same time I may keep my characters at blood heat. I shoot my arrows at a mark that is pretty certain to return them to me. And as to perfect success, I should be like the panic-stricken shopkeepers in my alarm at it; for I should believe that genii of the air fly above our tree tops between us and the incognizable spheres, catching those ambitious shafts they deem it a promise of fun to play pranks with.

Young Mr. Beauchamp at that period of the panic had not the slightest feeling for the taxpayer. He was therefore unable to penetrate the mystery of our roundabout way of enlivening him. He pored over the journals in perplexity, and talked of his indignation nightly to his pretty partners at balls, who knew not they were lesser Andromedas of his dear Andromeda country, but danced and chatted and were gay, and said they were sure he would defend them. The men he addressed were civil. They listened to him, sometimes with smiles and sometimes with laughter, but approvingly, liking the lad's quick spirit. They were accustomed to the machinery employed to give our land a shudder and to soothe it, and generally remarked that it meant nothing. His uncle Everard, and his uncle's friend Stukely Culbrett, expounded the nature of Frenchmen to him, saying that they were uneasy when not periodically thrashed; it would be cruel to deny them their crow beforehand; and so the pair of gentlemen pooh-poohed the affair; agreeing with him, however, that we had no great reason to be proud of our appearance, and the grounds they assigned for this were the activity and the prevalence of the ignoble doctrines of Manchester — a power whose very existence was unknown to Mr. Beauchamp. He would by no means allow the burden of our national disgrace to be cast on one part of the nation. We were insulted, and all in a poultry-flutter, yet no one seemed to feel it but himself! Outside the Press and Parliament, which must necessarily be the face we show to the foreigner, absolute indifference reigned. Navy men and redcoats were willing to join him or anybody in sneers at a clipping and paring miserly Government, but they were insensible to the insult, the panic, the startled-poultry show, the shame of our exhibition of ourselves in Europe. It looked as if the blustering French Guard were to have it all their own way. And what would they, what could they but, think of us! He sat down to write them a challenge.

He is not the only Englishman who has been impelled by a youthful chivalry to do that. He is perhaps the youngest who ever did it, and consequently there were various difficulties to be overcome. As regards his qualifications for addressing Frenchmen, a year of his pre-neptunal time had been spent in their capital city for the purpose of acquiring French of Paris, its latest refinements of pronunciation and polish, and the art of conversing. He had read the French tragic poets and Molière; he could even relish the Gallic-classic — "Qu'il mourut!" and he spoke French passably, being quite beyond the Bullish treat-

THE HOME OF GEORGE MEREDITH, FLINT COTTAGE AND THE "CHALET," BOX HILL, SURREY

By Permission of Messrs. A. Constable & Co.

ment of the tongue. Writing a letter in French was a different undertaking. The one he projected bore no resemblance to an ordinary letter. The briefer the better, of course; but a tone of dignity was imperative, and the tone must be individual, distinctive, Nevil Beauchamp's, though not in his native language. First he tried his letter in French, and lost sight of himself completely. "Messieurs de la Garde Française," was a good beginning; the remainder gave him a false air of a masquerader, most uncomfortable to see; it was Nevil Beauchamp in mustache and imperial, and bag breeches badly fitting. He tried English, which was really himself, and all that heart could desire supposing he addressed a body of midshipmen just a little loftily. But the English, when translated, was bald and blunt to the verge of offensiveness.

GENTLEMEN OF THE FRENCH GUARD, — I take up the glove you have tossed us. I am an Englishman. That will do for a reason.

This might possibly pass with the gentlemen of the English Guard. But read: —

MESSIEURS DE LA GARDE FRANÇAISE, — J'accepte votre gant. Je suis Anglais. La raison est suffisante.

And imagine French Guardsmen reading it!

Mr. Beauchamp knew the virtue of punctiliousness in epithets and phrases of courtesy toward a formal people, and as the officers of the French Guard were gentlemen of birth, he would have them to perceive in him their equal at a glance. On the other hand, a bare excess of phrasing distorted him to a likeness of Mascarille playing Marquis. How to be English and think French! The business was as laborious as if he had started on the rough sea of the Channel to get at them in an open boat.

The lady governing his uncle Everard's house, Mrs. Rosamund Culling, entered his room and found him writing with knitted brows. She was young, that is, she was not in her middle age; and they were the dearest of friends; each had given the other proof of it. Nevil looked up and beheld her lifted finger.

"You are composing a love letter, Nevil!" The accusation sounded like irony.

"No," said he, puffing; "I wish I were."

"What can it be, then?"

He thrust pen and paper a hand's length on the table, and gazed at her.

"My dear Nevil, is it really anything serious?" said she.

"I am writing French, ma'am."

"Then I may help you. It must be very absorbing, for you did not hear my knock at your door."

Now, could he trust her? The widow of a British officer killed nobly fighting for his country in India was a person to be relied on for active and burning sympathy in a matter that touched the country's honor. She was a woman, and a woman of spirit. Men had not pleased him of late. Something might be hoped from a woman.

He stated his occupation, saying that if she would assist him in his French she would oblige him; the letter must be written and must go. This was uttered so positively that she bowed her head, amused by the funny semitone of defiance to the person to whom he confided the secret. She had humor, and was ravished by his English boyishness, with the novel blush of the heroical-nonsensical in it.

Mrs. Culling promised him demurely that she would listen, objecting nothing to his plan, only to his French.

"Messieurs de la Garde Française!" he commenced.

Her criticism followed swiftly.

"I think you are writing to the Garde Impériale."

He admitted his error, and thanked her warmly.

"Messieurs de la Garde Impériale!"

"Does not that," she said, "include the non-commissioned officers, the privates, and the cooks of all the regiments?"

He could scarcely think that, but thought it provoking the French had no distinctive working title corresponding to gentlemen, and suggested "Messieurs les Officiers": which might, Mrs. Culling assured him, comprise the barbers. He frowned, and she prescribed his writing, "Messieurs les Colonels de la Garde Impériale." This he set down. The point was that a stand must be made against the flood of sarcasms and bullyings to which the country was exposed in increasing degrees, under a belief that we would fight neither in the mass nor individually. Possibly, if it became known that the colonels refused to meet a midshipman, the gentlemen of our Household troops would advance a step.

Mrs. Culling's adroit efforts to weary him out of his project were unsuccessful. He was too much on fire to know the taste of absurdity.

Nevil repeated what he had written in French, and next the English of what he intended to say.

The lady conscientiously did her utmost to reconcile the two languages. She softened his downrightness, passed with approval his compliments to France and the ancient high reputation of her army, and, seeing that a loophole was left for them to apologize, asked how many French colonels he wanted to fight.

"I do not *want*, ma'am," said Nevil.

He had simply taken up the glove they had again flung at our feet: and he had done it to stop the incessant revilings, little short of positive contempt, which we in our indolence exposed ourselves to from the foreigner, particularly from Frenchmen, whom he liked; and precisely because he liked them he insisted on forcing them to respect us. Let his challenge be accepted, and he would find backers. He knew the stuff of Englishmen: they only required an example.

"French officers are skillful swordsmen," said Mrs. Culling. "My husband has told me they will spend hours of the day thrusting and parrying. They are used to dueling."

"We," Nevil answered, "don't get apprenticed to the shambles to learn our duty on the field. Dueling is, I know, sickening folly. We go too far in pretending to despise every insult pitched at us. A man may do for his country what he wouldn't do for himself."

Mrs. Culling gravely said she hoped bloodshed would be avoided, and Mr. Beauchamp nodded.

She left him hard at work.

He was a popular boy, a favorite of women, and therefore full of engagements to Balls and dinners. And he was a modest boy, though his uncle encouraged him to deliver his opinions freely and argue with men. The little drummer attached to wheeling columns thinks not more of himself because his short legs perform the same strides as the grenadiers'; he is happy to be able to keep the step; and so was Nevil; and if ever he contradicted a senior, it was in the interests of the country. Veneration of heroes, living and dead, kept down his conceit. He worshiped devotedly. From an early age he exacted of his flattering ladies that they must love his hero. Not to love his hero was to be strangely in error, to be in need of conversion, and he proselytized with the ardor of the Moslem. His uncle Everard was proud of his good looks, fire, and nonsense, during the boy's extreme youth. He traced him by cousinships back to the great Earl Beauchamp of Froissart, and would have it so; and he would have spoilt him had not the young fellow's mind been possessed by his reverence for men of deeds. How could he think of himself, who had done nothing, accomplished nothing, so long as he brooded on the images of signal Englishmen whose names were historic for daring, and the strong arm, and artfulness, all given to the service of the country? — men of a magnanimity overcast with simplicity, which Nevil held to be pure insular English; our type of splendid manhood, not discoverable elsewhere. A method of enraging him was to distinguish one or other of them as Irish, Scotch, or Cambrian. He considered it a dismemberment of the country. And notwithstanding the pleasure he had in uniting in his person the strong red blood of the chivalrous Lord Beauchamp with the hard and tenacious Romfrey blood, he hated the title of Norman. We are English — British, he said. A family resting its pride on mere ancestry provoked his contempt, if it did not show him one of his men. He had also a disposition to esteem lightly the family which, having produced a man, settled down after that effort for generations to enjoy the country's pay. Boys are unjust; but Nevil thought of the country mainly, arguing that he should not accept the country's money for what we do not ourselves perform. These traits of his were regarded as characteristics hopeful rather than the reverse; none of his friends and relatives foresaw danger in them. He was a capital boy for his elders to trot out and banter.

Mrs. Rosamund Culling usually went to his room to see him and dote on him before he started on his rounds of an evening. She suspected that his necessary attention to his toilet would barely have allowed him time to finish his copy of the letter. Certain phrases had bothered him. The thrice recurrence of "ma patrie" jarred on his ear. "Sentiments" afflicted his acute sense of the declamatory twice. "C'est avec les sentiments du plus profond regret:" and again, "Je suis bien sûr que vous comprendrez mes sentiments, et m'accorderez l'honneur que je réclame au nom de ma patrie outragée." The word "patrie" was broadcast over the letter, and "honneur" appeared four times, and a more delicate word to harp on than the others!

"Not to Frenchmen," said his friend Rosamund. "I would put 'Je suis convaincu:' it is not so familiar."

"But I have written out the fair copy, ma'am, and that alteration seems a trifle."

"I would copy it again and again, Nevil, to get it right."

"No: I'd rather see it off than have it right," said Nevil, and he folded the letter.

How the deuce to address it, and what direction to write on it, were further difficulties. He had half a mind to remain at home to conquer them by excogitation.

Rosamund urged him not to break his engagement to dine at the Halketts', where perhaps from his friend Colonel Halkett, who would never imagine the reason for the inquiry, he might learn how a letter to a crack French regiment should be addressed and directed.

This proved persuasive, and as the hour was late Nevil had to act on her advice in a hurry.

His uncle Everard enjoyed a perusal of the manuscript in his absence.

Baronial Views of the Present Time.

Upon the word of honor of Rosamund, the letter to the officers of the French Guard was posted.

"Post it, post it," Everard said, on her consulting him, with the letter in her hand. "Let the fellow stand his luck." It was addressed to the Colonel of the First Regiment of the Imperial Guard, Paris. That superscription had been suggested by Colonel Halkett. Rosamund had been in favor of addressing it to Versailles, Nevil to the Tuileries; but Paris could hardly fail to hit the mark, and Nevil waited for the reply, half expecting an appointment on the French sands; for the act of posting a letter, though it be to little short of the Pleiades even, will stamp an incredible proceeding as a matter of business, so ready is the ardent mind to take footing on the last thing done. The flight of Mr. Beauchamp's letter placed it in the common order of occurrences for the youthful author of it. Jack Wilmore, a messmate, offered to second him, though he should be dismissed the service for it. Another second would easily be found somewhere; for, as Nevil observed, you have only to set these affairs going, and British blood rises:

we are not the people you see on the surface. Wilmore's father was a parson, for instance. What did he do? He could not help himself: he supplied the army and navy with recruits! One son was in a marching regiment, the other was Jack, and three girls had vowed never to quit the rectory save as brides of officers. Nevil thought that seemed encouraging; we were evidently not a nation of shopkeepers at heart; and he quoted sayings of Mr. Stukely Culbrett's, in which neither his ear nor Wilmore's detected the under-ring Stukely was famous for: as that England had saddled herself with India for the express purpose of better obeying the Commandments in Europe; and that it would be a lamentable thing for the Continent and our doctrines if ever beef should fail the Briton, and such like. "Depend upon it we're a fighting nation naturally, Jack," said Nevil. "How can we submit! . . . however, I shall not be impatient. I dislike dueling, and hate war, but I will have the country respected." They planned a defense of the country, drawing their strategy from magazine articles by military pens, reverberations of the extinct voices of the daily and weekly journals, customary after a panic, and making bloody stands on spots of extreme pastoral beauty, which they visited by coach and rail, looking back on unfortified London with particular melancholy.

Rosamund's word may be trusted that she dropped the letter into a London post office in pursuance of her promise to Nevil. The singular fact was that no answer to it ever arrived. Nevil, without a doubt of her honesty, proposed an expedition to Paris; he was ordered to join his ship, and he lay moored across the water in the port of Bevisham, panting for notice to be taken of him. The slight of the total disregard of his letter now affected him personally; it took him some time to get over this indignity put upon him, especially because of his being under the impression that the country suffered, not he at all. The letter had served its object: ever since the transmission of it the menaces and insults had ceased. But they might be renewed, and he desired to stop them altogether. His last feeling was one of genuine regret that Frenchmen should have behaved unworthily of the high estimation he held them in. With which he dismissed the affair.

He was rallied about it when he next sat at his uncle's table, and had to pardon Rosamund for telling.

Nevil replied modestly: "I dare say you think me half a

fool, sir. All I know is, I waited for my betters to speak first. I have no dislike of Frenchmen."

Everard shook his head to signify, "not *half.*" But he was gentle enough in his observations. "There's a motto, Ex pede Herculem. You stepped out for the dogs to judge better of us. It's an infernally tripping motto for a composite structure like the kingdom of Great Britain and Manchester, boy Nevil. We can fight foreigners when the time comes." He directed Nevil to look home and cast an eye on the cotton spinners, with the remark that they were binding us hand and foot to sell us to the biggest buyer, and were not Englishmen but "Germans and Jews, and Quakers and hybrids, diligent clerks and speculators, and commercial travelers, who have raised a fortune from foisting drugged goods on an idiot population."

He loathed them for the curse they were to the country. And *he* was one of the few who spoke out. The fashion was to pet them. We stood against them; were half-hearted, and were beaten; and then we petted them, and bit by bit our privileges were torn away. We made lords of them to catch them, and they grocers of us by way of a return. "Already," said Everard, "they have knocked the nation's head off, and dry-rotted the bone of the people."

"Don't they," Nevil asked, "belong to the Liberal party?"

"I'll tell you," Everard replied, "they belong to any party that upsets the party above them. They belong to the GEORGE FOX party, and my poultry roosts are the mark they aim at. You shall have a glance at the manufacturing district some day. You shall see the machines they work with. You shall see the miserable lank-jawed, half-stewed pantaloons they've managed to make of Englishmen there. My blood's past boiling. They work young children in their factories from morning to night. Their manufactories are spreading like the webs of the devil to suck the blood of the country. In that district of theirs an epidemic levels men like a disease in sheep. Skeletons can't make a stand. On the top of it all they sing Sunday tunes!"

This behavior of corn-law agitators and protectors of poachers was an hypocrisy too horrible for comment. Everard sipped claret. Nevil lashed his head for the clear idea which objurgation insists upon implanting, but batters to pieces in the act.

"Manchester's the belly of this country!" Everard continued. "So long as Manchester flourishes, we're a country governed and led by the belly. The head and the legs of the country are sound still; I don't guarantee it for long, but the middle's rapacious and corrupt. Take it on a question of foreign affairs, it's an alderman after a feast. Bring upon home politics, you meet a wolf."

The faithful Whig veteran spoke with jolly admiration of the speech of a famous Tory chief.

"That was the way to talk to them! Denounce them traitors! Up whip, and set the ruffians capering! Hit them facers! Our men are always for the too-clever trick. They pluck the sprouts and eat them, as if the loss of a sprout or two thinned Manchester! Your policy of absorption is good enough when you're dealing with fragments. It's a devilish unlucky thing to attempt with a concrete mass. You might as well ask your head to absorb a wall by running at it like a pugnacious nigger. I don't want you to go into Parliament ever. You're a fitter man out of it; but if ever you're bitten, —and it's the curse of our country to have politics as well as the other diseases,—don't follow a flag, be independent, keep a free vote: remember how I've been tied, and hold foot against Manchester. Do it blindfold; you don't want counseling, you're sure to be right. I'll lay you a blooded brood mare to a cab-stand skeleton, you'll have an easy conscience and deserve the thanks of the country."

Nevil listened gravely. The soundness of the head and legs of the country he took for granted. The inflated state of the unchivalrous middle, denominated Manchester, terrified him. Could it be true that England was betraying signs of decay? and signs how ignoble! Half a dozen crescent lines cunningly turned, sketched her figure before the world, and the reflection for one ready to die upholding her was that the portrait was no caricature. Such an emblematic presentation of the land of his filial affection haunted him with hideous mockeries. Surely the foreigner hearing our boasts of her must compare us to showmen bawling the attractions of a Fat Lady at a fair!

Swoln Manchester bore the blame of it. Everard exulted to hear his young echo attack the cotton spinners. But Nevil was for a plan, a system, immediate action; the descending among the people, and taking an initiative, LEADING them, insisting on their following, not standing aloof and shrugging.

"We lead them in war," said he; "why not in peace? There's a front for peace as well as war, and that's our place rightly. We're pushed aside; why, it seems to me we're treated like old-fashioned ornaments! The fault must be ours. Shrugging and sneering is about as honorable as blazing fireworks over your own defeat. Back we have to go! that's the point, sir. And as for jeering the cotton spinners, I can't while they've the lead of us. We let them have it! And we have thrice the stake in the country. I don't mean properties and titles."

"Deuce you don't," said his uncle.

"I mean our names, our histories; I mean our duties. As for titles, the way to defend them is to be worthy of them."

"Damned fine speech," remarked Everard. "Now you get out of that trick of prize orationing. I call it snuffery, sir; it's all to your own nose. You're talking to me, not to a gallery. 'Worthy of them!' Cæsar wraps his head in his robe; he gets his dig in the ribs for all his attitudinizing. It's very well for a man to talk like that who owns no more than his bare-bodkin life, poor devil. Tall talk's his jewelry: he must have his dandification in bunkum. You ought to know better. Property and titles are worth having, whether you are 'worthy of them,' or a disgrace to your class. The best way of defending them is to keep a strong fist, and take care you don't draw your fore foot back more than enough."

"Please propose something to be done," said Nevil, depressed by the recommendation of that attitude.

Everard proposed a fight for every privilege his class possessed. "They say," he said, "a nobleman fighting the odds is a sight for the gods: and I wouldn't yield an inch of ground. It's no use calling things by fine names — the country's ruined by cowardice. Poursuivez! I cry. Haro! at them! The biggest heart wins in the end. I haven't a doubt about that. And I haven't a doubt we carry the tonnage."

"There's the people," sighed Nevil, entangled in his uncle's haziness.

"What people?"

"I suppose the people of Great Britain count, sir."

"Of course they do; when the battle's done, the fight lost and won."

"Do you expect the people to look on, sir?"

"The people always wait for the winner, boy Nevil."

The young fellow exclaimed despondingly, "If it were a race!"

"It's like a race, and we're confoundedly out of training," said Everard.

There he rested. A mediæval gentleman with the docile notions of the twelfth century, complacently driving them to grass and wattling them in the nineteenth, could be of no use to a boy trying to think, though he could set the youngster galloping. Nevil wandered about the woods of Steynham, disinclined to shoot and lend a hand to country sports. The popping of the guns of his uncle and guests hung about his ears much like their speech, which was unobjectionable in itself, but not sufficient; a little hard, he thought, a little idle. He wanted something, and wanted them to give their time and energy to something, that was not to be had in a market. The nobles, he felt sure, might resume their natural alliance with the people, and lead them, as they did of old, to the battle field. How might they? A comely Sussex lass could not well tell him how. Sarcastic reports of the troublesome questioner represented him applying to a nymph of the country for enlightenment. He thrilled surprisingly under the charm of feminine beauty. "The fellow's sound at bottom," his uncle said, hearing of his having really been seen walking in the complete form proper to his budding age, that is, in two halves. Nevil showed that he had gained an acquaintance with the struggles of the neighboring agricultural poor to live and rear their children. His uncle's table roared at his enumeration of the sickly little beings, consumptive or bandy-legged, within a radius of five miles of Steynham. Action was what he wanted, Everard said. Nevil perhaps thought the same, for he dashed out of his mooning with a wave of the Tory standard, delighting the ladies, though in that conflict of the Lion and the Unicorn (which was a Tory song) he seemed rather to wish to goad the dear lion than crush the one-horned intrusive upstart. His calling on the crack corps of Peers to enroll themselves forthwith in the front ranks, and to anticipate opposition by initiating measures, and so cut out that funny old crazy old galleon, the People, from under the batteries of the enemy, highly amused the gentlemen.

Before rejoining his ship, Nevil paid his customary short visit of ceremony to his great-aunt Beauchamp — a venerable lady past eighty, hitherto divided from him in sympathy by her dislike of his uncle Everard, who had once been his living hero. That was when he was in frocks, and still the tenacious fellow could not bear to hear his uncle spoken ill of.

"All the men of that family are heartless, and he is a man of wood, my dear, and a bad man," the old lady said. "He should have kept you at school, and sent you to college. You want reading and teaching and talking to. Such a house as that is should never be a home for you." She hinted at Rosamund. Nevil defended the persecuted woman, but with no better success than from the attacks of the Romfrey ladies; with this difference, however, that these descried the woman's vicious arts, and Mistress Elizabeth Mary Beauchamp put all the sin upon the man. Such a man! she said. "Let me hear that he has married her, I will not utter another word." Nevil echoed, "Married!" in a different key.

"I am as much of an aristocrat as any of you, only I rank morality higher," said Mrs. Beauchamp. "When you were a child I offered to take you and make you my heir, and *I* would have educated you. You shall see a great-nephew of mine that I did educate; he is eating his dinners for the bar in London, and comes to me every Sunday. I shall marry him to a good girl, and I shall show your uncle what my kind of man making is."

Nevil had no desire to meet the other great-nephew, especially when he was aware of the extraordinary circumstance that a Beauchamp great-niece, having no money, had bestowed her hand on a Manchester man defunct, whereof this young Blackburn Tuckham, the lawyer, was issue. He took his leave of Mrs. Elizabeth Beauchamp, respecting her for her constitutional health and brightness, and regretting for the sake of the country that she had not married to give England men and women resembling her. On the whole he considered her wiser in her prescription for the malady besetting him than his uncle. He knew that action was but a temporary remedy. College would have been his chronic medicine, and the old lady's acuteness in seeing it impressed him forcibly. She had given him a peaceable two days on the Upper Thames, in an atmosphere of plain good sense and just-mindedness. He wrote to thank her, saying: "My England at sea will be your parlor window looking down the grass to the river and rushes; and when you do me the honor to write, please tell me the names of those wild flowers growing along the banks in Summer." The old lady replied immediately, inclosing a check for fifty pounds: "Colonel Halkett informs me you are under cloud at Steynham, and I have thought you may be in want of pocket money. The wild flowers are willow-herb, meadowsweet, and loosestrife. I shall be glad when you are here in Summer to see them."

Nevil dispatched the following: "I thank you, but I shall not cash the check. The Steynham tale is this: I happened to be out at night, and stopped the keepers in chase of a young fellow trespassing. I caught him myself, but recognized him as one of a family I take an interest in, and let him run before they came up. My uncle heard a gun; I sent the head gamekeeper word in the morning to out with it all. Uncle E. was annoyed, and we had a rough parting. If you are rewarding me for this, I have no right to it."

Mrs. Beauchamp rejoined: "Your profession should teach you subordination, if it does nothing else that is valuable to a Christian gentleman. You will receive from the publisher the 'Life and Letters of Lord Collingwood,' whom I have it in my mind that a young midshipman should task himself to imitate. Spend the money as you think fit."

Nevil's ship, commanded by Captain Robert Hall (a most gallant officer, one of his heroes, and of Lancashire origin, strangely!), flew to the South American station, in and about Lord Cochrane's waters; then as swiftly back. For, like the frail Norwegian bark on the edge of the Maelstrom, liker to a country of conflicting interests and passions, that is not mentally on a level with its good fortune, England was drifting into foreign complications. A paralyzed Minister proclaimed it. The governing people, which is looked to for direction in grave dilemmas by its representatives and reflectors, shouted that it had been accused of pusillanimity. No one had any desire for war, only we really had (and it was perfectly true) been talking gigantic nonsense of peace, and of the everlastingness of the exchange of fruits for money, with angels waving raw groceries of Eden in joy of the commercial picture. Therefore, to correct the excesses of that fit, we held the standing by the Moslem, on behalf of the Mediterranean (and the Moslem is one of our customers, bearing an excellent reputation for the payment of debts), to be good, granting the necessity. We deplored the necessity. The Press wept over it. That, however, was not the politic tone for us while the Imperial berg of Polar ice watched us keenly; and the Press proceeded to remind us that we had once been bulldogs. Was there not an animal within us having a right to turn now and then? And was it not (Falstaff, on a calm world, was quoted) for the benefit of our constitutions now and then to loosen the animal? Granting the necessity, of course. By dint of incessantly speaking of the necessity, we granted it unknowingly. The lighter hearts regarded our period of monotonously lyrical prosperity as a man sensible of fresh morning air looks back on the snoring bolster. Many of the graver were glad of a change. After all that maundering over the blessed peace which brings the raisin and the currant for the pudding, and shuts up the cannon with a sheep's head, it became a principle of popular taste to descant on the vivifying virtues of war; even as, after ten months of money mongering in smoky London, the citizen hails the sea breeze and an immersion in unruly brine, despite the cost, that breeze and brine may make a man of him, according to the doctor's prescription: sweet is home, but health is sweeter! Then was there another curious exhibition of us. Gentlemen, to the exact number of the Graces, dressed in drab of an ancient cut, made a pilgrimage to the icy despot, and besought him to give way for Piety's sake. He, courteous, colossal, and immovable, waved them homeward. They returned and were hooted for belying the bellicose by their mission, and interpreting too well the peaceful. They were the unparalyzed Ministers of the occasion, but helpless.

And now came war, the purifier and the pestilence.

The cry of the English people for war was pretty general, as far as the criers went. They put on their Sabbath face concerning the declaration of war, and told with approval how the Royal hand had trembled in committing itself to the form of signature to which its action is limited. If there was money to be paid, there was a bugbear to be slain for it; and a bugbear is as obnoxious to the repose of commercial communities as rivals are to kings.

The cry for war was absolutely unanimous, and a supremely national cry, Everard Romfrey said, for it excluded the cotton spinners.

He smacked his hands, crowing at the vociferations of disgust of those negrophiles and sweaters of Christians, whose isolated clamor amid the popular uproar sounded of gagged mouths.

One of the half-stifled cotton spinners, a notorious one, a spouter of rank sedition and hater of aristocracy, a political poacher, managed to make himself heard. He was tossed to the Press for a morsel, and tossed back to the people in strips. Everard had a sharp return of appetite in reading the daily and weekly journals. They printed logic, they printed sense; they abused the treasonable barking cur unmercifully. They printed almost as much as he would have uttered, excepting the strong salt of his similes, likening that rascal and his crew to the American weed in our waters, to the rotting wild bee's nest in our trees, to the worm in our ships' timbers, and to lamentable afflictions of the human frame, and of sheep, oxen, honest hounds. Manchester was in eclipse. The world of England discovered that the peace party which opposed was the actual cause of the war: never was indication clearer.

THE WARFARE OF LIFE.[1]

By OWEN MEREDITH.

(From "Lucile.")

[Edward Robert Bulwer-Lytton, first Earl of Lytton, better known to literature as "Owen Meredith," was the only son of the famous novelist, and was born in London, November 8, 1831. He began his diplomatic career as private secretary to his uncle, Sir H. L. Bulwer, at Washington, D.C., and afterwards held various important posts in Europe. He was viceroy of India (1876–1880), and ambassador at Paris from 1887 until his death, November 24, 1891. The chief events of his viceroyalty were the Afghan War and the proclamation of Queen Victoria as Empress of India. Under the pen name of "Owen Meredith" he published: "Lucile," a novel in verse, his principal production; "Clytemnestra"; "The Wanderer"; "Orval"; "Julian Fane"; "Glenaveril"; "After Paradise"; and "The Ring of Amasis," a prose romance.]

I.

Man is born on a battle field. Round him, to rend
Or resist, the dread Powers he displaces attend,
By the cradle which Nature, amidst the stern shocks
That have shattered creation, and shapen it, rocks.
He leaps with a wail into being; and lo!
His own mother, fierce Nature herself, is his foe.
Her whirlwinds are roused into wrath o'er his head:
'Neath his feet roll her earthquakes: her solitudes spread

[1] By permission of Lady Lytton and the Publishers, Longmans, Green & Co.

EDWARD ROBERT BULWER-LYTTON
(OWEN MEREDITH)
From a photo by Elliott & Fry

To daunt him: her forces dispute his command:
Her snows fall to freeze him: her suns burn to brand:
Her seas yawn to engulf him: her rocks rise to crush:
And the lion and leopard, allied, lurk to rush
On their startled invader.
In lone Malabar,
Where the infinite forest spreads breathless and far,
'Mid the cruel of eye and the stealthy of claw
(Striped and spotted destroyers!) he sees, pale with awe,
On the menacing edge of a fiery sky
Grim Doorga, blue-limbed and red-handed, go by,
And the first thing he worships is Terror.
Anon,
Still impelled by necessity hungrily on,
He conquers the realms of his own self-reliance,
And the last cry of fear wakes the first of defiance.
From the serpent he crushes its poisonous soul:
Smitten down in his path see the dead lion roll!
On toward Heaven the son of Alcmena strides high on
The heads of the Hydra, the spoils of the lion:
And man, conquering Terror, is worshiped by man.

A camp has this world been since first it began!
From his tents sweeps the roving Arabian; at peace,
A mere wandering shepherd that follows the fleece;
But, warring his way through a world's destinies,
Lo from Delhi, from Bagdad, from Cordova, rise
Domes of empiry, dowered with science and art,
Schools, libraries, forums, the palace, the mart!

New realms to man's soul have been conquered. But those,
Forthwith they are peopled for man by new foes!
The stars keep their secrets, the earth hides her own,
And bold must the man be that braves the Unknown!
Not a truth has to art or to science been given,
But brows have ached for it, and souls toiled and striven;
And many have striven, and many have failed,
And many died, slain by the truth they assailed.

But when Man hath tamed Nature, asserted his place
And dominion, behold! he is brought face to face
With a new foe — himself!
Nor may man on his shield
Ever rest, for his foe is forever afield,
Danger ever at hand, till the armèd Archangel
Sound o'er him the trump of earth's final evangel.

II.

Silence straightway, stern Muse, the soft cymbals of pleasure,
Be all bronzen these numbers, and martial the measure!
Breathe, sonorously breathe, o'er the spirit in me
One strain, sad and stern, of that deep Epopee
Which thou, from the fashionless cloud of far time,
Chantest lonely, when Victory, pale, and sublime
In the light of the aureole over her head,
Hears, and heeds not the wound in her heart fresh and red
Blown wide by the blare of the clarion, unfold
The shrill clanging curtains of war!
                                        And behold
A vision!
            The antique Heraclean seats;
And the long Black Sea billow that once bore those fleets,
Which said to the winds, "Be ye, too, Genoese!"
And the red angry sands of the chafed Chersonese;
And the two foes of man, War and Winter, allied
Round the Armies of England and France, side by side
Enduring and dying (Gaul and Briton abreast!)
Where the towers of the North fret the skies of the East.

FROM "THE STICKIT MINISTER."[1]

BY S. R. CROCKETT

[SAMUEL RUTHERFORD CROCKETT, Scotch author, was born at Little Duchrae, New Galloway, September 24, 1860, and studied at Edinburgh University, where he supported himself by tutoring and journalistic work. After a residence abroad as tutor he returned to Edinburgh, entered a theological school, and in 1886 became a Free Church minister at Penicuik. He has written: "The Stickit Minister," "The Raiders," "Mad Sir Uchtred of the Hills," "The Play Actress," "The Men of the Moss Hags," "Cleg Kelly," "The Gray Man," "The Red Ax." Mr. Crockett's books have been exceedingly popular in America, and have been translated into several European languages.]

ENSAMPLES TO THE FLOCK.

THE family of the late Tyke M'Lurg consisted of three loons and a lassie. Tyke had never done anything for his children except share with a short-lived and shadowy mother the responsibility of bringing them into the world. The time that he could spare from his profession of poacher, he had systematically devoted to neglecting them. Tyke had solved suc-

[1] By permission of the Author and Mr. T. Fisher Unwin.

SAMUEL RUTHERFORD CROCKETT

cessfully for many years the problem of how to live by the least possible expenditure of labor. Kind ladies had taken him in hand time and again. They had provided clothes for his children, which Tyke had primarily converted into coin of the realm, and indirectly into liquid refreshment, at Lucky Morgan's rag store in Cairn Edward. Work had been found for Tyke, and he had done many half days of labor in various gardens. Unfortunately, however, before the hour of noon, it was Tyke's hard case to be taken with a "grooin' in his inside" of such a nature that he became rapidly incapacitated for further work.

"No, mem, I canna tak' it. It's mony a year since I saw the evil o't. Ye'll hae to excuse me, but I really couldna. Oh, thae pains! Oh, sirce, my inside! Weel, gin ye insist, I'll juist hae to try a toothfu' to oblige ye, like."

But Tyke's toothfu's were over for this world, and his shortcomings were lying under four feet of red mold. Half a dozen kindly folk who pitied his "three loons and a lassie" gathered a few pounds and gave him a decent burial, not for his own sake, but in order that the four little scarecrows might have a decent start in life. It is the most fatal and indestructible of reproaches in the south of Scotland to have a father buried by the parish.

The lassie was the eldest of the children. She was thirteen, and she hardly remembered what it was to have a mother or a new frock. But ever since she was eleven she had never had a dirty one. The smith's wife had shown her how to wash, and she had learned from the teacher how to mend. "Leeb" had appeared on the books of the school as Elizabeth M'Lurg, and she had attended as often as she could—that is, as often as her father could not prevent her; for Tyke, being an independent man, was down on the compulsory clause of the Education Act, and had more than once got thirty days for assaulting the school-board officer.

When he found out that Leeb was attending school at the village, he lay in wait for her on her return, with a stick, and after administering chastisement on general principles, he went on to specify his daughter's iniquities:—

"Ye upsettin' blastie, wad ye be for gangin' to their schule, learnin' to look doon on yer ain faither that has been at sic pains to rare ye"—(a pause for further correction, to which poor Leeb vocalized an accompaniment). "Let me see gin ye can read! Hae, read that!" he said, flinging a tattered lesson book, which the teacher had given her, to his daughter. Leeb opened the book, and, punctuating the lesson with her sobs, she read in the high and level shriek of a locomotive engine, "And so brave Bobby, hav'ing sa-ved the tr-r-r-em-bling child, re-turn-ed with the res-cu-ed one in his mouth to the shore."

"Davert! but ye *can* read!" said her father, snatching the book and tearing it up before her eyes. "Noo, listen; I'll hae nane o' my bairns teached to despise their faither by no school boards. Look you here, Leeb M'Lurg, gin ever I catch you within a mile o' the schule, I'll skin ye!"

But for all this tremendous threat, or maybe all the more because of it, and also because she so much desired to be able to do a white seam, Leeb so arranged it that there were few days when she did not manage to come along the mile and a half of loch-side road which separated her from the little one-roomed, whitewashed schoolhouse on the face of the brae. She even brought one of the "loons" with her pretty often; but as Jock, Rob, and Benny (otherwise known as Rag, Tag, and Bobtail) got a little older, they more easily accommodated themselves to the wishes of their parent; and, in spite of Leeb's blandishments, they went into "hidie holes" till the school-board officer had passed by.

M'Lurg's Mill, where the children lived, was a tumble-down erection, beautiful for situation, set on the side of the long loch of Kenick. The house had once been a little farm-house, its windows brilliant with geraniums and verbenas; but in the latter days of the forlorn M'Lurg's it had become be-trampled as to its doorsteps by lean swine, and bespattered as to its broken floor by intrusive hens. It was to M'Lurg's Mill that the children returned after the funeral. Leeb had been arrayed in the hat and dress of a neighbor's daughter for the occasion, but the three loons had played "tig" in the intervals of watching their father's funeral from the broomy knoll be-hind the mill. Jock, the eldest, was nearly eleven, and had been taken in hand by the kind neighbor wife at the same time as Leeb. At one time he looked as though he would even better repay attention, for he feigned a sleek-faced submission and a ready compliance which put Mistress Auld of the Ark-land off her guard. Then as soon as his sister, of whom Jock stood much in awe, was gone out, he snatched up his ragged clothes and fled to the hill. Here he was immediately joined by the other two loons. They caught the Arkland donkey grazing in the field beside the milldam, and having made a parcel of the good black trousers and jacket, they tied them to the donkey and drove him homeward with blows and shoutings. A funeral was only a dull procession to them, and the fact that it was their father's made no difference.

Next morning Leeb sat down on the "stoop" or wooden bench by the door, and proceeded to cast up her position. Her assets were not difficult to reckon. A house of two rooms, one devoted to hens and lumber; a mill which had once sawed good timber, but whose great circular saw had stood still for many months; a mill lade broken down in several places, three or four chairs and a stool, a table, and a washtub. When she got so far she paused. It was evident that there could be no more school for her, and the thought struck her that now she must take the responsibility for the boys, and bring them up to be useful and diligent. She did not and could not so express her resolve to herself, but a still and strong determination was in her sore little heart not to let the boys grow up like their father.

Leeb had gone to Sabbath school every week, when she could escape from the tyranny of home, and was, therefore, well known to the minister, who had often exercised himself in vain on the thick defensive armor of ignorance and stupidity which encompassed the elder M'Lurg. His office bearers and he had often bemoaned the sad example of this ne'er-do-weel family which had intrenched itself in the midst of so many well-doing people. M'Lurg's Mill was a reproach and an eye-sore to the whole parish, and the M'Lurg "weans" a gratuitous insult to every self-respecting mother within miles. For three miles round the children were forbidden to play with, or even to speak to, the four outcasts at the mill. Consequently their society was much sought after.

When Leeb came to set forth her resources, she could not think of any except the four-pound loaf, the dozen hens and a cock, the routing wild Indian of a pig, and the two lean and knobby cows on the hill at the back. It would have been possible to have sold all these things, perhaps, but Leeb looked upon herself as trustee for the rest of the family. She resolved, therefore, to make what use of them she could, and having most of the property under her eye at the time, there was the less need to indite an inventory of it.

But, first, she must bring her brothers to a sense of their position. She was a very Napoleon of thirteen, and she knew that now that there was no counter authority to her own, she could bring Jock, Rob, and Benny to their senses very quickly. She therefore selected with some care and attention a hazel stick, using a broken table knife to cut it with a great deal of deftness. Having trimmed it, she went out to the hill to look for her brothers. It was not long before she came upon them engaged in the fascinating amusement of rooting for pignuts in a green bankside. The natural Leeb would instantly have thrown down her wand of office and joined them in the search, but the Leeb of to-day was a very different person. Her second thought was to rush among them and deal lusty blows with the stick, but she fortunately remembered that in that case they would scatter, and that by force she could only take home one or at most two. She therefore called to her assistance the natural guile of her sex.

"Boys, are ye hungry?" she said. "There's sic a graun' big loaf come frae the Arkland!" By this time all her audience were on their feet. "An' I'll milk the kye, an' we'll hae a feast."

"Come on, Jock," said Rob, the second loon, and the leader in mischief, "I'll race ye for the loaf."

"Ye needna do that," said Leeb, calmly; "the door's lockit."

So as Leeb went along she talked to her brothers as soberly as though they were models of good behavior and all the virtues, telling them what she was going to do, and how she would expect them to help her. By the time she got them into the mill yard, she had succeeded in stirring their enthusiasm, especially that of Jock, to whom with a natural tact she gave the wand of the office of "sairgint," a rank which, on the authority of Sergeant M'Millan, the village pensioner, was understood to be very much higher than that of general, "Sairgint" Jock foresaw much future interest in the disciplining of his brothers, and entered with eagerness into the new ploy. The out-of-doors livestock was also committed to his care. He was to drive the cows along the roadside and allow them to pasture on the sweetest and most succulent grasses, while Rob scouted in the direction of the village for supposititious "poalismen" who were understood to take up and sell for the queen's benefit all cows found eating grass on the public highway. Immediately after Jock and Rob had received a hunch of the Arkland loaf and their covenanted drink of milk, they went off to drive the cows to the loch road, so that they might at once begin to fill up their lean sides. Benny, the youngest, who was eight past, she reserved for her own assistant. He was a somewhat tearful but willing little fellow, whose voice haunted the precincts of M'Lurg's Mill like a wistful ghost. His brothers were constantly running away from him, and he pattering after them as fast as his fat little legs could carry him, roaring with open mouth at their cruelty, the tears making clean water courses down his grimy cheeks. But Benny soon became a new boy under his sister's exclusive care.

"Noo, Benny," she said, "you an' me's gaun to clean the hoose. Jock an' Rob will no' be kennin' it when they come back!" So, having filled the tub with water from the mill lade, and carried every movable article of furniture outside, Leeb began to wash out the house and rid it of the accumulated dirt of years. Benny carried small bucketfuls of water to swill over the floor. Gradually the true color of the stones began to shine up, and the black incrustation to retreat toward the outlying corners.

"I'm gaun doon to the village," she said abruptly. "Benny, you keep scrubbin' alang the wa's."

Leeb took her way down rapidly to where Joe Turner, the village mason, was standing by a newly begun pig stye or swine ree, stirring a heap of lime and sand.

"G'ye way oot o' that!" he said instantly, with the threatening gesture which every villager except the minister and the mistress of Arkland instinctively made on seeing a M'Lurg. This it is to have a bad name.

But Leeb stood her ground, strong in the consciousness of her good intentions.

"Maister Turner," she said, "could ye let me hae a bucketfu' or twa o' whitewash for the mill kitchen, an' I'll pey ye in hen's eggs. Oor hens are layin' fine, an' your mistress is fond o' an egg in the mornin'."

Joe stopped and scratched his head. This was something new, even in a village where a good deal of business is done according to the rules of truck or barter.

"What are ye gaun to do wi' the whitewash?" he inquired, to get time to think. "There was little whitewash in use about M'Lurg's Mill in yer faither's time!"

"But I'm gaun to bring up the boys as they should," said Leeb, with some natural importance, sketching triangles on the ground with her bare toe.

"An' what's whitewash got to do wi' that?" asked Joe, with some asperity.

Leeb could not just put the matter into words, but she instinctively felt that it had a good deal to do with it. Whitewash was her badge of respectability both inside the house and out, in which Leeb was at one with modern science.

"I'll gie three dizzen o' eggs for three bucketfu's," she said.

"An' hoo div I ken that I'll ever see ane o' the eggs?" asked Joe.

"I've brocht a dizzen wi' me noo!" said Leeb, promptly, producing them from under her apron.

Leeb got the whitewash that very night and the loan of a brush to put it on with. Next morning the farmer of the Crae received a shock. There was something large and white down on the loch side, where ever since he came to the Crae he had seen nothing but the trees which hid M'Lurg's Mill.

"I misdoot it's gaun to be terrible weather. I never saw that hoose o' Tyke M'Lurg's aff our hill afore!" he said.

The minister came by that day and stood perfectly aghast at the new splendors of the M'Lurg mansion. Hitherto when he had strangers staying with him, he took them another way, in order that his parish might not be disgraced. Not only were the walls of the house shining with whitewash, but the windows were cleaned, a piece of white muslin curtain was pinned across each, and a jug with a bunch of heather and wild flowers looked out smiling on the passers-by. The minister bent his steps to the open door. He could see the two M'Lurg cows pasturing placidly with much contented head tossing on the roadside, while a small boy sat above laboring at the first rounds of a stocking. From the house came the shrill voice of singing. Out of the fir wood over the knoll came a still smaller boy bent double with a load of sticks.

In the window, written with large, sprawling capitals on a leaf of a copy book under the heading "Encourage Earnest Endeavor," appeared the striking legend:—

SOWING & MENDING DUN
GOOD COWS MILK
STICKS FOR FIREWOOD CHEEP
NEW LAID EGGS
BY ELIZABETH MC LURG

The minister stood regarding, amazement on every line of his face. Leeb came out singing, a neatly tied bundle of chips made out of the dry débris of the sawmill in her hand.

"Elizabeth," said he, "what is the meaning of this?"

"Will ye be pleased to step ben?" said Leeb. The minister did so, and was astonished to find himself sitting down in a spotless kitchen, the walls positively painfully white, the wooden chairs scoured with sand till the very fiber of the wood was blanched, and on a floor, so clean that one might have dined off it, the mystic whorls and crosses of whiting which connect all good Galloway housekeepers with Runic times.

Before the minister went out of M'Lurg's Mill he had learned the intentions of Leeb to make men of her brothers. He said:—

"You are a woman already, before your time, Elizabeth!" which was the speech of all others best fitted to please Leeb M'Lurg. He had also ordered milk and eggs for the manse to be delivered by Benny, and promised that his wife would call upon the little head of the house.

As he went down the road by the loch side he meditated, and this was the substance of his thought, "If that girl brings up her brothers like herself, Tyke M'Lurg's children may yet be ensamples to the flock."

But as to this we shall see.

The Siege of M'Lurg's Mill.

Elizabeth M'Lurg had been over at the village for her groceries. Dressed in her best—clean pinafored, lilac sunbonneted—she was a comely picture. Half a dozen years had made a difference in the coltish lassie who had dragooned her three loons of brothers into decency and school attendance after her father's funeral. There was now not a better doing family in the parish than that over which the rule of Leeb M'Lurg had the unquestioned force of an autocracy. Leeb had saved enough from her cows and poultry to employ Sanny MacQuhatt, the traveling millwright, to put the old sawmill in order against that approaching day when John M'Lurg, her eldest brother, would be out of his time at the shop of Rob Johnstone, joiner and cartwright in Whunnyliggate. Affairs had marched well with the M'Lurgs. Rob, the second, was still at school, but there was word of his getting into a Cairn Edward bank; and it was the desire of Leeb's life to see her favorite Benny turned into a dominie. She had already spoken to the minister about having him made a pupil teacher at the next vacancy.

Elizabeth had a word for every one as she walked sedately up the narrow, unpaved street — modest for the minister, shy for young Will Morton, the teacher of the village school where her brothers were alternately at the head of the highest class in sharp fraternal emulation — no other pupil coming within a mile of them; straightforward with the women folk, who came to their doors to look down the street every ten minutes or so on the chance of seeing a cadger, or even a red farm cart, whose clanking passage might break the soundless monotony.

The village lads would also cry, "Hoo's a' wi' ye the day, Leeb?" in an offhand way which did not conceal from that sharp-eyed young woman their desire to stand well with her.

"She's the only lass i' the parish that kens hoo to lift her feet aff the grund," said Saunders Paterson to Rab Affleck, as they watched Leeb's progress up the street.

"Ay, man, ye're richt; there's nae glaur'll [mud] stick to Leeb's coat tail."

But this morning many came to look after Leeb M'Lurg, of M'Lurg's Mill, who had hitherto paid small attention to her comings and goings. For it was the village talk that Timothy M'Lurg, Tyke M'Lurg's younger brother, otherwise known as "Tim the Tairger," had come back, and had been seen and heard on the skirts of the public house declaring that he had come as trustee of his brother to take possession of M'Lurg's Mill, its cattle and sheep, house gear and bestial, and to administer the same for the behoof of the children of the departed. It was a noble ambition, and when declared among the choice company assembled at the "public," it elicited warm commendations there, for Timothy M'Lurg had always spent other people's money like a man.

But when the better spirits of the village heard of it, there were many who grieved for the children who had made so gallant a fight. So when Elizabeth M'Lurg went up the street that day there was many a one who watched her with a wae heart. Yet it was not until David Clark, the village shopkeeper, had finished serving her with tea and sugar that he said to Leeb, in a friendly way: —

"I hear ye've gotten your uncle Timothy back." Leeb whitened to the lips at that name of dread. She remembered the wild nights when Timothy brought his companions with him, and turned the little world of M'Lurg's Mill upside down.

"No," she answered, determined not to show any emotion to the watchful eyes of David Clark, "I didna ken."

She spoke as though the news were some ordinary and unimportant gossip.

"Where has he come frae?" she asked.

David Clark knew that he had come from a long sojourn in her majesty's prisons, owing to the death of a keeper in one of Tim's poaching affrays. But David was not a man to commit himself unnecessarily when a well-paying customer was concerned.

"They were sayin' that he was up aboot the public, an' that he cam' frae Cairn Edward in the bottom o' a coal cairt."

Calmly Leeb settled her reckoning with the eggs and butter which she had brought, and received the balance in good queen's silver. Calmly she took her sedate way down the street, no step discomposed or hurried. But in her heart there was a deadly tumult.

Her scheme of life, so carefully constructed and so sturdily worked for, came tumbling about her ears. She had no idea what her uncle's powers might be — whether he could take the mill or claim the cows. She only knew that he would certainly do all the ill he was capable of, and she thought of her fortress lying open and unguarded at her enemy's mercy, with only old Sanny MacQuhatt hammering and grumbling to himself over the reconstruction of the rickety sawmill. As soon as she was clear of the village Leeb took to her heels, and glinted light foot through the poplar avenues along the skirts of the bright June meadows, where the hemlock was not yet overtopped by the meadowsweet, as in a week or two it would be.

She struck across the hill above the loch, which lay below her rippleless and azure as the blue of a jay's wing. The air from off the heather was warm and honey-scented. At the second stile, when she turned into her own hill pasture, some vague fear struck her heart. She dared not take the first look at the homestead which she had given her young life to make worthy of her vow to bring up her brothers as they should. As she set her foot on the lowest stone of the high, uncouth stile in the drystone dike, something grunted heavily on the other side.

There was something so bestially human and superfluously degraded in the noise that Leeb knew that it could not be produced by any of the "lower" animals. Gathering her skirts about her for a spring, and turning up a supercilious nose, she peeped over the top of the dike. Beneath her lay Tim M'Lurg, sleeping stertorously, with his head recumbent on the lowest step, by which she must descend. A swarm of flies buzzed and crawled over his face, unhealthily flushed through its prison sallowness by drink and the June sun.

Leeb, whose tastes were dainty as those of any other lady, glanced at him with such extreme disfavor that her fear was for the time being swallowed up in disgust. She paused for half a dozen long moments, finally reached down an experimental toe, and with a sharp side push on the close-cropped head she undid the precarious balance of her relative, who collapsed flaccidly sideways on the heather like an overset bolster.

His niece sprung over his prostrate hulk, took two or three rapid steps, faced about, and gazed fixedly at him, to show that she was not in the least afraid, then walked slowly up the path to the crest of the hill, where she was out of sight of the stile; then, with heart beating wildly, her terror came upon her, and she ran as hard as she could toward M'Lurg's Mill, which lay peacefully among the trees at the foot of the hill.

As she came down the woodside she caught up the tough branch of a fir tree, and drove the two cows, now no longer lean and ill-favored, and the young bull, to which Leeb had been looking to pay her rent that year, toward the byre. She sent Jock and his mother on with vicious blows till they were safely stabled in their stalls, with fresh bundles of clover grass before them. Then Leeb locked the byre door with a ponderous, seldom-used key, and went down to the mill to warn Sanny MacQuhatt.

"Ay, an' yer uncle's come hame," muttered Sanny. "That's no, sae guid; an' ill yin him a' the days o' him. Tim the Tairger they ca' him — no' withoot raison. Ay, ay, an ill yin Tim."

"You'll no' let him within the mill, wull ye, Sanny?"

"Certes, he'll no' come here as long as I'm responsible for pittin' the auld ramshackle in order — mair fule me for takin' on the job. It's never worth it: guid for nocht but firewood."

And Sanny grumbled away till his words were lost in the snuffling produced by repeated pinches of brown Taddy from his waistcoat pocket. Leeb stood patiently by, knowing that at this juncture the word of Sanny MacQuhatt, ill-tempered old curmudgeon of a millwright though he might be, was to her a tower of strength.

The cattle put under lock and key, the mill garrisoned, Leeb proceeded to the house, where she carefully locked every door and put the hasp on every window. Those which had no defense of this kind she secured with nails. While she was still employed about this last operation, there came a loud knock at the front door, which Leeb had secured first of all.

"Wha's there?" challenged the besieged, sharp and clear.

"Open the door, Leeb," returned a thick voice, which Leeb knew instinctively to be that of her uncle. "It's me come hame."

"I ken naebody that's to come hame," returned Leeb. "Wha micht 'me' be?"

"D'ye no' mind yer uncle Timothy?" said the thick voice outside, subsiding into a whine. "Let me come ben, Leeb; I'm comed to look efter ye, an' to work for ye a'."

"Na," said Leeb, "I've worked for mysel' a' thae years that ye've been lyin' in the jail, a disgrace to us a', and I'm no' gaun to let ye scatter what I hae gathered, sae just e'en tak' yersel' aff to where ye cam' frae. This is nae hame o' yours!"

The wrath of the still half-tipsy man rose in a flash. His voice became an unsteady scream.

"Then tak' heed to yersel', Leeb M'Lurg!" he shouted through the keyhole. "Gin ye dinna let me in I'll burn the riggin' ower yer heid — mill first and then the hoose — ye ill-set, ungratefu' besom!"

"Ay, Uncle Timothy, ye can try either o' the twa," said Leeb, from the safe vantage of a little staircase window, which, made of a single pane, opened inward. "Gae awa' frae my door this minute!" she said.

The jail bird beneath threw himself furiously against the old wooden door, which opened in the middle; but the oak bolt was firm, and held. Still, the whole house shook with the shock of his onslaught.

Leeb hesitated no longer, but snatched a black "goblet" from the side of the kitchen fire, and sent the contents out of the window with a deft hand. There was an answering howl of pain.

"Ye've scadded me! I'll hae the law on ye, ye randy! I'll hae yer life!"

"There's a' potfu' mair on the fire for ye, gin ye dinna gang awa' quaitly wi' what ye hae gotten!" said Tim M'Lurg's hard-hearted niece.

He now took himself off in the direction of the barn. Hardly had he disappeared on the other side when Leeb's favorite brother, Benny, came whistling round the corner opposite to that at which Tim had disappeared. He stood astonished to see the front door shut. Leeb hurried down, unlocked the door, and called to him to run. He came slowly toward her with a bewildered countenance. She pulled him inside, told him hurriedly what had happened, and sent him off through the back window, which abutted on the moor, with a message to Will Morton, the schoolmaster. Benny flew like the wind. He knew that it was his part to bring up reënforcements while his sister kept the castle. Leeb watched till Benny was safe over the hill, then she herself slipped out of the house, locking the door behind her, and went toward the mill, from which rose the sound of angry voices. Before she got there, however, the commotion was evidently reaching its climax, and Leeb deemed it best to slip into the byre, through one of the wickets of which she could see the mill door. Through that wide-open square tumbled Tim the Tairger, bareheaded and in disarray, and behind him appeared the burly figure of old Sanny MacQuhatt, with his millwright mallet in his hand.

"I wad be wae to strike the like o' you, Tim," said the old man. "Ye michtna need anither, but dinna ye come back here to interfere wi' my wark. Gang awa' an' collogue wi' yer cronies, poachers, an' siclike, an' lea' decent folk abee!"

Timothy gathered himself up. He had had enough of the millwright, who, having done his part, went staidly back to his interrupted work. The ill-treated one came toward the byre, and seeing the door open, he went in. Leeb sprung into the bauks above the stall of the bull just in time. Her uncle looked the cattle over with a dissatisfied eye. He seemed to Leeb to be reckoning how much Crummie and Specklie would bring in the auction mart. She resolved that he should also have a look at Jock, and so be able to decide on his market value as well.

Stooping over, she undid his binding, and lashed him at the same time sharply across the nose with the rope. Jock lowered his head, and backed indignantly out of his stall. As he turned he found himself face to face with an intruder, a man whose red neckcloth proved him evidently his enemy and assailant. Jock's charge was instant and effective. With a snort he cleared the byre, and pursued across the open square of the yard, tail in air and horns to the ground. Timothy M'Lurg could not complain of the warmth of his reception in the home of his ancestors.

He sought refuge from the bull in the big water hole under the mill wheel. Here, waiting the bull's retirement, Leeb interviewed him from the mill window, under the protection of Sanny MacQuhatt, and offered him a pound note to go away. This compromise had the weakness of a woman's compunction, and was strongly disapproved of by her ally.

"Gie that craitur a poun' to drink — he'll sune come back on ye for anither," said Sanny, who knew the breed. "I'd 'pound' him," he muttered.

But Tim the Tairger, also thinking that this offer gave signs of yielding, rejected it with oaths and contumely. On the contrary, he would sell them up, bag and baggage. The whole place belonged to him. He had deeds that could prove it. Stock, plenishing, water power — all were his.

"Gin the water poo'er be yours, ma man," said Sanny, "ye can hae that, an' welcome."

Sanny's humor was of the entirely practical kind.

He went to the mill lade, and turned on the stream. The whole force of M'Lurg's milldam took its way smoothly down the repaired lade, and flashed with a solid leap over the old green wheel upon Timothy, as he stood between the bull to landward and the plunging mill wheel. Sanny grimly kept up his end of the jest.

"Hae, ma man, ye'll no' say that we keepit ye oot o' yer richts. 'Water poo'er,'" quo' he; "nae pound notes ye'se get i' this pairish, but it'll no' be Sanny MacQuhatt that'll keep ye oot o' the use o' yer ain water poo'er!"

Tim the Tairger was in a woeful case. The old man looked from the mill window, and confronted him with crusty humor, the points of which were all too obvious. The cold water plunged upon him from the mill wheel, it deepened about his knees, and Jock, the young bull, pawed the ground and snorted murderously for his blood. He was completely sobered now, and vowed repeatedly that if they would only give him the pound note he would go and never disturb them more.

But Sanny had taken things into his own hands, and would not allow Leeb to interfere.

"Bide ye where ye are, ma man; ye're braw and caller doon there. Ye were aye a drouthy lad, Tim, since ever I kenned ye. Ye're in the way o' being slockened noo! An' in a wee there'll be a bonny lad wi' silver buttons comin' up that road to look for ye. Benny, yer ain bluid relative, he's gane for him, an' he'll hae him here the noo. It was a blessin' he was in the district onyway; it's no' that often a polisman's where he's wantit."

"Here he's come!" cried Leeb, from her post of observation in the mill gable.

Tim the Tairger took one look down the road, one link of which he could see as it wound round the loch. He saw the sun glitter on the white buttons of a policeman's coat, who came stalking majestically along. Whatever evil Tim had on his conscience of prison breaking or ticket of leave unreported, we do not know, but the fear of the officer of the law overpowered even his fear of Jock's horns. With a wild skelloch of desperation he dashed out of the pool, and took down the road, doubling from the bull like a hunted hare.

The schoolmaster — masquerading according to Leeb's orders, in Sergeant M'Millan's old policeman's coat — saw Timothy M'Lurg leap the low loaning dike and tear down the road. After him thundered the bull, routing in blood-curdling wrath. From a high knoll he watched the chase, till hunter and hunted were lost in the shades of Knock-angry Wood. The bull was found next day wandering near Dalry, with a clouted deer-stalking cap transfixed on one horn; but as for Tim the Tairger, he was never more heard tell of in stewartry or in shire.

The mystery is not likely to be solved now, for the secrets of that chase are only known to Jock, and he ran his earthly race to the beef tub half a dozen years ago without unburdening his conscience to any. From his uncertain temper it is however suspected that he had something on his mind.

As for Sanny MacQuhatt, he says that he is "muckle feared that Tim the Tairger is gane whaur he wad be michty gled o' the water poo'er o' M'Lurg's mill lade; whilk," concludes Sanny, "I defy him to say that I ever denied him!"

ON BEING HARD UP.[1]

By JEROME K. JEROME.

(From the "Idle Thoughts of an Idle Fellow.")

[JEROME KLAPKA JEROME, English humorous writer, was born at Walsall, May 2, 1859, and has been successively a clerk, schoolmaster, shorthand writer, reporter, actor, and journalist. In 1892 he became associated with Mr. Robert Barr as joint editor and proprietor of the *Idler*, and in 1893 started *To-Day*, a weekly magazine journal. His works comprise: "Three Men in a Boat," which established his reputation; "On the Stage and Off"; "Idle Thoughts of an Idle Fellow"; "Stageland"; "Diary of a Pilgrimage"; "John Ingerfield"; "Sketches in Lavender"; besides several successful comedies.]

It is a most remarkable thing. I sat down with the full intention of writing something clever and original; but for the life of me I can't think of anything clever and original — at least — not at this moment. The only thing I can think about now is being hard up. I suppose having my hands in my pockets has made me think about this. I always do sit with my hands in my pockets, except when I am in the company of my sisters, my cousins, or my aunts; and they kick up such a shindy — I should say expostulate so eloquently upon the subject — that I have to give in and take them out — my hands I mean. The chorus to their objections is that it is not gentlemanly. I am hanged if I can see why. I could understand its not being considered gentlemanly to put your hands in other people's pockets (especially by the other people), but how, O ye sticklers for what looks this and what looks that, can putting his hands in his own pockets make a man less gentle! Perhaps you are right, though. Now I come to think of it, I have heard some people grumble most savagely when doing it. But they were mostly old gentlemen. We young fellows, as a rule, are never quite at ease unless we have our hands in our pockets. We are awkward and shifty. We are like what a music-hall Lion Comique would be without his opera hat, if such a thing can be imagined. But let us put our hands in our trousers pockets, and let there be some small change in the right-hand one and a bunch of keys in the left, and we will face a female post-office clerk.

It is a little difficult to know what to do with your hands, even in your pockets, when there is nothing else there. Years

[1] By permission of Author and The Leadenhall Press. (Price 2*s.* 6*d.*)

ago, when my whole capital would occasionally come down to "what in town the people call a bob," I would recklessly spend a penny of it, merely for the sake of having the change, all in coppers, to jingle. You don't feel nearly so hard up with elevenpence in your pocket as you do with a shilling. Had I been "La-di-da," that impecunious youth about whom we superior folk are so sarcastic, I would have changed my penny for two ha'pennies.

I can speak with authority on the subject of being hard up. I have been a provincial actor. If further evidence be required, which I do not think likely, I can add that I have been a "gentleman connected with the press." I have lived on fifteen shillings a week. I have lived a week on ten, owing the other five; and I have lived for a fortnight on a greatcoat.

It is wonderful what an insight into domestic economy being really hard up gives one. If you want to find out the value of money, live on fifteen shillings a week, and see how much you can put by for clothes and recreation. You will find out that it is worth while to wait for the farthing change, that it is worth while to walk a mile to save a penny, that a glass of beer is a luxury to be indulged in only at rare intervals, and that a collar can be worn for four days.

Try it just before you get married. It will be excellent practice. Let your son and heir try it before sending him to college. He won't grumble at a hundred a year pocket money then. There are some people to whom it would do a world of good. There is that delicate blossom, who can't drink any claret under ninety-four, and who would as soon think of dining off cats' meat as off plain roast mutton. You do come across these poor wretches now and then, though, to the credit of humanity, they are principally confined to that fearful and wonderful society known only to lady novelists. I never hear of one of these creatures discussing a *menu* card, but I feel a mad desire to drag him off to the bar of some common East End public house, and cram a sixpenny dinner down his throat — beefsteak pudding, fourpence; potatoes, a penny; half a pint of porter, a penny. The recollection of it (and the mingled fragrance of beer, tobacco, and roast pork generally leaves a vivid impression) might induce him to turn up his nose a little less frequently in the future at everything that is put before him. Then, there is that generous party, the cadger's delight, who is so free with his small change, but who never thinks of paying his debts. It might teach even him a little common sense. "I always give the waiter a shilling. One can't give the fellow less, you know," explained a young government clerk with whom I was lunching the other day in Regent Street. I agreed with him as to the utter impossibility of making it elevenpence ha'penny; but, at the same time, I resolved to one day decoy him to an eating house I remembered near Covent Garden, where the waiter, for the better discharge of his duties, goes about in his shirt sleeves — and very dirty sleeves they are too, when it gets near the end of the month. I know that waiter. If my friend gives him anything beyond a penny, the man will insist on shaking hands with him then and there, as a mark of his esteem; of that I feel sure.

There have been a good many funny things said and written about hardupishness, but the reality is not funny, for all that. It is not funny to have to haggle over pennies. It isn't funny to be thought mean and stingy. It isn't funny to be shabby, and to be ashamed of your address. No, there is nothing at all funny in poverty — to the poor. It is hell upon earth to a sensitive man; and many a brave gentleman, who would have faced the labors of Hercules, has had his heart broken by its petty miseries.

It is not actual discomforts themselves that are hard to bear. Who would mind roughing it a bit, if that were all it meant? What cared Robinson Crusoe for a patch on his trousers? — Did he wear trousers? I forget; or did he go about as he does in the pantomimes? What did it matter to him if his toes did stick out of his boots? and what if his umbrella was a cotton one, so long as it kept the rain off. His shabbiness did not trouble him: there were none of his friends round about to sneer at him.

Being poor is a mere trifle. It is being known to be poor that is the sting. It is not cold that makes a man without a greatcoat hurry along so quickly. It is not all shame at telling lies — which he knows will not be believed — that makes him turn so red when he informs you that he considers greatcoats unhealthy, and never carries an umbrella on principle. It is easy enough to say that poverty is no crime. No; if it were, men wouldn't be ashamed of it. It's a blunder, though, and is punished as such. A poor man is despised the whole world over; despised as much by a Christian as by a lord, as much by a demagogue as by a footman, and not all the copybook maxims ever set for ink-stained youth will make him respected. Appearances *are* everything, so far as human opinion goes, and the man who will walk down Piccadilly arm in arm with the most notorious scamp in London, provided he is a well-dressed one, will slink up a back street to say a couple of words to a seedy-looking gentleman. And the seedy-looking gentleman knows this — no one better — and will go a mile round to avoid meeting an acquaintance. Those that knew him in his prosperity need never trouble themselves to look the other way. He is a thousand times more anxious that they should not see him than they can be; and as to their assistance, there is nothing he dreads more than the offer of it. All he wants is to be forgotten; and in this respect he is generally fortunate enough to get what he wants.

One becomes used to being hard up, as one becomes used to everything else, by the help of that wonderful old homeopathic doctor, Time. You can tell at a glance the difference between the old hand and the novice; between the case-hardened man who has been used to shift and struggle for years, and the poor devil of a beginner, striving to hide his misery, and in a constant agony of fear lest he should be found out. Nothing shows this difference more clearly than the way in which each will pawn his watch. As the poet says somewhere: "True ease in pawning comes from art, not chance." The one goes into his "Uncle's" with as much composure as he would into his tailor's — very likely with more. The assistant is even civil and attends to him at once, to the great indignation of the lady in the next box, who, however, sarcastically observes that she don't mind being kept waiting "if it is a regular customer." Why from the pleasant and businesslike manner in which the transaction is carried out, it might be a large purchase in the Three per Cents. Yet what a piece of work a man makes of his first "pop." A boy popping his first question is confidence itself compared with him. He hangs about outside the shop, until he has succeeded in attracting the attention of all the loafers in the neighborhood, and has aroused strong suspicions in the mind of the policeman on the beat. At last, after a careful examination of the contents of the windows, made for the purpose of impressing the bystanders with the notion that he is going in to purchase a diamond bracelet or some such trifle, he enters, trying to do so with a careless swagger, and giving himself really the air of a member of the swell mob. When inside, he speaks in so low a voice as to be perfectly inaudible, and has to say it all over again. When, in the course of his rambling conversation about a "friend" of his, the word "lend" is reached, he is promptly told to go up the court on the right, and take the first door round the corner. He comes out of the shop with a face that you could easily light a cigarette at, and firmly under the impression that the whole population of the district is watching him. When he does get to the right place he has forgotten his name and address and is in a general condition of hopeless imbecility. Asked in a severe tone how he came by "this," he stammers and contradicts himself, and it is only a miracle if he does not confess to having stolen it that very day. He is thereupon informed that they don't want anything to do with his sort, and that he had better get out of this as quickly as possible, which he does, recollecting nothing more until he finds himself three miles off, without the slightest knowledge how he got there.

By the way, how awkward it is, though, having to depend on public houses and churches for the time. The former are generally too fast, and the latter too slow. Besides which, your efforts to get a glimpse of the public-house clock from the outside are attended with great difficulties. If you gently push the swing door ajar and peer in, you draw upon yourself the contemptuous looks of the barmaid, who at once puts you down in the same category with area sneaks and cadgers. You also create a certain amount of agitation among the married portion of the customers. You don't see the clock, because it is behind the door: and in trying to withdraw quietly you jam your head. The only other method is to jump up and down outside the window. After this latter proceeding, however, if you do not bring out a banjo and commence to sing, the youthful inhabitants of the neighborhood, who have gathered round in expectation, become disappointed.

I should like to know, too, by what mysterious law of nature it is that, before you have left your watch "to be repaired" half an hour, some one is sure to stop you in the street and conspicuously ask you the time. Nobody even feels the slightest curiosity on the subject when you've got it on.

Dear old ladies and gentlemen, who know nothing about being hard up — and may they never, bless their gray old heads — look upon the pawnshop as the last stage of degradation; but those who know it better (and my readers have, no doubt,

10

noticed this themselves) are often surprised, like the little boy who dreamed he went to Heaven, at meeting so many people there that they never expected to see. For my part, I think it a much more independent course than borrowing from friends, and I always try to impress this upon those of my acquaintance who incline toward "wanting a couple of pounds till the day after to-morrow." But they won't all see it. One of them once remarked that he objected to the principle of the thing. I fancy if he had said it was the interest that he objected to he would have been nearer the truth; twenty-five per cent certainly does come heavy.

There are degrees in being hard up. We are all hard up, more or less — most of us more. Some are hard up for a thousand pounds; some for a shilling. Just at this moment I am hard up myself for a fiver. I only want it for a day or two. I should be certain of paying it back within a week at the outside, and if any lady or gentleman among my readers would kindly lend it me, I should be very much obliged indeed. They could send it to me under cover to Messrs. Field & Tuer, only, in such case, please let the envelope be carefully sealed. I would give you my I O U as security.

AN ANCIENT MARINER.

(Translated from the French of Pierre Loti by Helen B. Dole.)

[Pierre Loti is the pseudonym of Louis Marie Julien Viaud, a French naval officer, novelist, and Academician; born at Rochefort, in 1850. He entered the French navy at seventeen, and has served with distinction in campaigns in Oceanica, Japan, Senegal, and Tonkin. During the naval operations off the coast of Annam (1883) he sent to the *Figaro* a series of letters descriptive of the cruelties practiced by the French soldiers at the storming of Hué. In consequence of this imprudence he was court-martialed, and put on half pay for twelve months. In 1891 he was appointed an Academician, succeeding Octave Feuillet. He has published: "Le Mariage de Loti"; "Le Roman d'un Spahi"; "Mon Frère Yves"; "Pêcheur d'Islande," awarded the Prix Vitet by the Academy; "Madame Chrysanthème"; "Fantôme d'Orient"; "Ramuntcho." a Basque story.]

He dwelt in a very old-fashioned little house halfway up the cliff on the road from Brest to the lighthouse at Portzic. All along the road, in other dwellings like his, many retired sailors were living out their days.

His own backed up against the granite bulwarks, looked out from a considerable height on the dark, gray roadstead, Point Cormorandière — and the narrow entrance from the open sea, through which came the ships.

A little garden with a very low wall separated it from the passer-by; through bushes now grown old and almost exhausted it could be seen crouching gloomily against the open rocks. It was constantly buffeted by the west winds, the equinoctial gales, or the long winter storms.

When the sky was clear the man who dwelt there all alone would sit before the door. His grayish white beard contrasted vividly with his brown face, which looked as if it had been roughly hewn from a block of dead wood.

He wore earrings and bore himself very erect. One could see that he was worn out, worn out completely, but in a peculiar way. His was an old age different from that of other people; it was impossible to look at him and tell the number of his years.

For an occasional pedestrian, or for the workmen returning home from Brest at night after their work was done, he never raised his head. Only when some sailor passed by did he seem interested; he would get up then to gaze, and his eyes would follow the swaying figure that stood out against the gray background of the sea as it moved along.

On both sides, toward Brest and toward Le Portzic, the road disappeared as it ascended and seemed to end suddenly in the mist hanging over sea and sky; travelers would rise abruptly into sight at one end and then disappear at the other, as though they had been swallowed up. On all sides were granite rocks, heather, and thorns; at the very gates of the great town that indescribable longing and melancholy peculiar to the Breton country began to be felt.

In summer, when the days were very fine, he would bring out into his little garden a gray parrot, from Gaboon, with a red tail, whose perch was of some foreign wood, and his food bits of cocoa. He showed great anxiety about this old bird, which sat silent and crestfallen on its roost.

If, indeed, it happened to be warm, both seemed to revive. The parrot began to talk; without ever stirring he would repeat in a ventriloquial voice the slang of the sea. The man, as though he were in some tropical country, would put fresh water into an Arabian water cooler, dress himself in a nankeen cloak of Chinese pattern, and fan himself with a palm-leaf fan.

When the windows were open one could see through the branches of a flowering veronica a corner of this hermit's home. It was tidy, and as clean as though cared for by the hands of the most careful housewife; on his mantelpiece he had two vases, some shells, and other curiosities from foreign lands.

In June and July a pale sunbeam would steal in toward evening and seem to linger, surprised to find such things there.

Then, after the melancholy of these short summers, the gloomy fogs came again for long months, enveloping and obscuring everything.

Neighbors who had lived a long time in the place remembered how they saw this old man come there some ten years before. He was even then broken down, although his eyes were a little less dim, his beard a little less gray. He settled down by himself, arranging everything with egotistic care, as though he had still a long life before him.

But he had failed, failed from year to year, from season to season. His sad face was almost frightful from having lost all expression of life. He still retained the erectness of bearing which gave him the gait of a phantom, and he moved slowly with the stiffness, *the all-of-a-pieceness* of a great mummy.

He remembered that he had been young. That time had had a very real existence. It came back to him sometimes in confused visions, brightening his dull eyes.

But under the tension of his mind, eager to grasp them, they would suddenly slip away and become extinct, and these efforts of his aged memory left afterwards in his empty brain something like the impression of physical pain.

Just as when, on waking, we are surprised to find suddenly that the dream of the night before has fled. We try to fasten it, to bring it into relation with others, so as to form a connected whole, with its possibility of wondrous charm. But, on the contrary, it all the more quickly vanishes, intangible, leaving in the mind a blank, a sort of black nothingness.

He remembered that he had been handsome, alert, and strong.

Oh, his strength; what could bring it back to him now? Oh, his sailor veins, his brawny arms, which, when contracted, swelled to the hardness of marble, which were able to break anything with their power, which on the swinging, shaking yardarms held fast like iron clamps!

BREST

Now they ached and trembled at the mere lifting of a chair.

When the brigs of the training school put out into the offing with every sail spread to the west wind, he would stand at his window to see them pass. Those young children of the sea were scattered up among the rigging like white specks, climbing to the sound of silver whistles, climbing in the air along slender threads, climbing with hands and feet like young monkeys.

He who watched them no longer understood the utter fullness of their young lives, that exhilaration of motion which enabled them to climb so easily. No; but his own childhood had been passed on this roadstead learning to follow this healthful, hardy livelihood; he watched them long, and experienced, as he saw them, feelings of melancholy — which were almost undefined, so faint and far away were they.

He remembered that he had had sweethearts. It was at the time when his eyes flashed under their black lashes, throwing right and left their youthful, virile flame, their overpowering brilliancy.

He had been longed for, sought after, adored. Women had sighed beneath the kisses from his lips — now the scurvy and the dampness of the sea had left their ravening traces upon them, his beautiful white teeth, once the delight of the young girls, had become those yellow, unequal ones, in the middle of which his clay pipe had worn a round gap.

Women, bronzed women, black women, white women with fair tresses. . . . From time to time his memory brought back, now the face of one, now the tender words and soft hands of another; they passed slowly like spectral forms, confused, without focus, too far away to be grasped.

He did not even regret them any longer, and was only astonished that he had once been able to give them so much of that life, of which he was to-day so fond.

Love, longing looks which are all-absorbing, lips put up to be kissed, the everlasting charm which makes all creatures seek and find their mates — all that was at an end, was dead. But he did not try to explain it; there was now something lacking in him so that he could not understand it; the key of the delicious mystery was for him forever lost. . . . His thoughts were occupied with what he should eat, with preparing his little supper alone by the light of his feeble lamp, before stretching himself out early upon his chilly couch.

He remembered that he had had a wife. That had lasted one single springtide, that love making through the April evenings, in the sober propriety of a simple home.

He was getting to be rather old for a sailor — thirty-one years — when he took that young girl in marriage at Port Louis.

There had been a wedding procession, with violins and a honeymoon at Lorient. At first he had enjoyed the novelty of having her all to himself; he had found a charm in saying "my wife," in giving her his arm in broad daylight when they went to walk; in coming back in the evening with her to their little home that he had furnished with the savings from his voyages. Two or three of his comrades had followed his example that same spring, and likewise amused themselves by playing the Benedict in the long interval between two voyages. And they exchanged dignified greetings when they met out walking along the roadside already green. One fine day there came an order to sail on the "Pomona" for a three years' cruise in the Pacific Ocean!

On his return she was living with a rich old man in the town who gave her costly dresses.

He remembered that he had had a child, a daughter. . . .

A sailor had stolen her from him one fine morning in May, in a year when the spring in Brittany was beautiful and the nights warm. The memory of this touched him still, but it was the only one.

It came over him when his eyes fell on a little shell frame where he kept her picture taken in her first communion dress, with a candle in her hand. Then his features would instantly contract to a sort of grimace, heartrending from its very absurdity; and he would weep: two tears only, which trickled down his old shriveled cheeks into the wrinkles, and that was all.

His wife, when she had deserted him, left the frail little creature two years old. Oh, she was very like him. She had his forehead, his eyes, his complexion; and he constantly beheld himself in this child's face, which was no other than her own, but refined, intensified with candor and youth, and as it were remodeled in virgin wax. Yes; for sixteen years of his life he had deprived himself of much on his cruises; he had patched his garments himself, washed his linen, in order to have more money on his return, saving everything for this little one. She was delicate and pale, with an air of the aristocratic young lady about her, and he loved her all the more for it; he, so rough and uncouth.

An old woman, in whom he placed confidence, brought her up at Pontanezen. On his return he always found her grown larger; each time she was almost a new person. He brought her things from foreign lands that he had bought for her: Chinese ornaments, Brazilian birds, a paroquet. During his short visits to Brest he wanted her to be well dressed and happy.

At last she became a young girl, tall and supple, with something distinguished about her rather slow walk.

A sailor had stolen her from him on a certain evening in May, in a year when the spring nights were still and warm. He was a deck hand. He was twenty-three years old. She met him at her first ball, where she had gone to attend a wedding.

He began to pay her attention, and one evening the innocent old woman, who was her guardian, allowed them to go out together. She was full of joy in his company, she who had been always alone with uncongenial strangers, always shut up with ugly-faced old women occupied with sewing, and never loved, never caressed, except by that far-away father, who seldom came back. He said childish things to her and very sweet words. With an air so honest, so respectful towards her. He laughed with a good, frank laugh, throwing back his bronze-colored neck — a way that open-hearted people have — and showing his white teeth, all even, all just alike. A balmy warmth and the fragrance of hawthorn blossoms filled the air. One could see the roadstead still and gray, with streaks of very faint light, die away in the night. Poor lonely little one.

About ten months later, one winter day, Jean Kervella returned to Brest, from his fourth voyage to China. The first of all to leap on shore, he hastened to the suburb of Pontanezen, carrying on his back the gifts for his daughter, in a bag ornamented with a painting representing a ship under full sail.

But before the door of the house, which he was about to enter so joyfully, the old guardian of his child froze him to the spot with her foreboding face. Trembling, terrified at seeing him, she clung to him and wouldn't let him pass.

What! What was the matter? Was his daughter dead? He had felt all at once a sudden and cruel blow. No, it was not that. Very ill then? Perhaps — yes; but no, not exactly that. What, then? He begged her to speak quickly, seizing her by the arm, while she still barred the way to the door. Where was she, anyway? Upstairs, in her little chamber? Where had they put her?

Other women came downstairs, showing assiduity, the good matrons, with their sighs at seeing him, their mysterious whisperings. Ah! he understood. It flashed upon him. It came to him intuitively what her misfortune was, and he spoke the word brutally. Yes, it was even so.

And then he went upstairs quickly, but with trembling limbs, and feeling a stifling sense of shame, feeling a frightfully painful anger, increasing at every step.

But when he saw her so wan, in her poor little bed, her nostrils already pinched with coming death, he found not a word to say. Beneath the frightened, supplicating look that she fixed upon him he simply broke down and wept.

In a low voice he made inquiries of the women who were there. And little by little his anger disappeared. It was a man from the "Flora," who had promised to marry her. He was called Peter Daniel, and he was a deck hand.

At first he had feared that it was some city coxcomb — for money. A topman; he liked that better. They should be married at the return of the "Flora."

Indeed, he must be a good fellow, this Peter Daniel. Surely, if he had known, if he had suspected, he would have come back to marry her, the poor little thing, that he might not cause pain to her nor to her father, a second mate, a seafarer like himself. But the "Flora" was far away. Nobody had come to tell him that, the poor boy. And one pay day at Peru, he had deserted.

In the evening she died in giving birth to the sailor's child, who soon followed its mother.

For a long time, for a very long time, this scene remained alive and harrowing in his memory, in his dreams, in his cruel waking moments.

That was forgotten now, as well as all the rest.

The picture of the little communicant grew yellow in its frame of shells, which was coming unglued from the dampness of the winters. It dated from the infancy of photography.

She, who was really very pretty, looked like a poor little foolish monkey, holding her candle as though she were afraid of being beaten. He had had it reproduced several times, carried it with him on many ships; and, in spite of all, it resembled her still. In this very small, droll figure, now more vague than a sketch, in which two yellow spots represented her eyes, there remained an indescribable, indestructible emanation of herself — all that remained on earth of the poor little dead girl.

Now, for nearly twenty years she had been in the churchyard, and the memory of her, kept alive only in the mind of this old man, was beginning already to die out there.

Almost immediately after he had laid her in the ground he went to sea again, and became one of those stern men who roam about without any aim in life. His word of command and his whistle acquired a new sound, — short and imperative. Night and day he busied himself only with sails or cordage, and managed his men roughly, without a word of commendation when they had done well. He never sang now in the evening, and he was constantly up late.

Once from Hong Kong he sent a large sum of money to the woman who had taken care of his daughter, to purchase the little piece of Breton soil where she had been buried, and to set up a tombstone.

When he came back to Brest this woman had become an imbecile pauper, and could no longer remember receiving anything. She had spent it all on drink. And he, for five years of cruises and adventures, under the devouring heat of the equatorial sun, had had no other thought during his night watches, during his sleepless nights, than to preserve that young girl's grave under the foggy skies of Brittany.

He ran in haste to her little grave. The earth had been freshly turned, and a new cross had been placed there, bearing the name of an old man whom he didn't know. On the walks of the graveyard, in the midst of other melancholy débris of vases and flowers, he saw the last gift that he had made to his dead child, — a crown of pearls with its motto.

Ah, well; all was ended. Her dust had been thrown in the common grave.

And at nightfall he came back alone from the cemetery.

Years and years had passed since then. His cruises, his times of weariness, his nights of watching, of pleasure or of pain, had continued to accumulate, one upon another, in every climate under the sun. An admiral, who sometimes figured even now in his feeble recollections, took a fancy to him, and then he became ambitious.

During an expedition to Africa he had been decorated for having saved the life of an officer.

Finally he had reached the honorable and lucrative rank of first mate.

Jean Kervella was already a battered hulk when he first came to the sailor's retreat at Brest, yet he was still neat and trim in his mate's uniform, with a red ribbon in his buttonhole.

And it was then that he bought the little house on the road from Portzic, to end his days in view of the sea and the ships.

The day of his retirement was a day like every other. Neither people nor things seemed to pay much attention to this old servant who was about to leave them forever.

At the usual hour for cleaning the decks, long before dawn, in those large rooms of the division which have assumed something of the roughness and smell of ships, the sailors leaped down from their hammocks, hung up in a row on iron bars. He alone felt troubled on awaking, with an indefinable consciousness that it was his last day.

Then followed the usual routine of the morning, the sound of drums and bugles, and then the sun — the slightly hazy sun of autumn — rose, too, at its accustomed hour.

Before the dinner at noon, Kervella had passed the inspection with his company, in his newest uniform, worn in honor of this last time. Some of the mates, coming across him, congratulated him; he had reached that period which few sailors have the good fortune to attain; he was at last going to rest, to have a little garden, and, as they expressed it, live on his income. Others, on the contrary, knowing that he was getting old, called him "My poor Kervella," with that air of pity which we use in speaking of some one on his deathbed. Then there were "good-bys" and hand shaking. He believed himself very happy, and forced himself to find cheerful things to say to them.

Around him continued the familiar routine of those great barracks, which is, as it were, the true headquarters, the mother home of sailors.

The hour for rest had come. Between the great smooth walls, which it was impossible to scale, the sailors were walking

PIERRE LOTI IN HIS STUDY

back and forth in groups. They showed to advantage in their loose garments, with the shambling or impatient gait of imprisoned children. Those who had been to sea, the real, settled mariners, whose faces had grown dark beneath the sun of the tropics, were smoking and relating their adventures, exchanging amorous confidences about the young girls of the neighborhood, or else spending their superfluous energy on the iron bars of the gymnasium. And the newcomers, round-faced youngsters, fresh from their fishing boats or villages on the Breton coast, were looking a little frightened, with innocent eyes, impatiently waiting for the blue collar and tufted cap that would be given to them ; these were stared at by the old sailors, who exchanged remarks about them, and in the midst of their harsh criticisms might be heard from time to time these words of hearty praise : —

"He is green yet, but he will come out all right."

All day long, in his new uniform, he had walked carelessly back and forth among these groups; and then over the stairs where the young men were rushing down four at a time, making a noise like a runaway horse, and through the great halls, through which blew the wind, bringing in the smell of freshly washed boards and tar water.

On all sides were recollections of every period in his life. When a man has served forty years in the fleet, he has often stopped in this part of Brest; very often, when returning from a cruise, he has entered here with joy, his pocket full of money; very often he has gone away, again descending the granite steps which lead to the port, his two linen sacks on his back — perhaps still happy, or possibly broken-hearted — leaving for distant and unknown shores. And Kervella wished to see all these nooks once more. He had business to transact at the bureau where the quartermasters reign, papers to fill out, signatures to obtain, in fact, all that is customary on the eve of a final departure. Above all, he felt a desire to bestir himself, to be on the move, and, in spite of his undeniable contentment, a necessity to forget himself.

That evening, in his little room in the barracks, he experienced the first feeling of heartache when he exchanged his uniform for a black suit, which made him look already several years older, and then, having finished with the state, which had amply paid him for his life work, he went forth from the home.

At the door, some young fellows who were coming in drunk,

pitiless in the exuberance of their spirits, jostled against this civilian, whom they no longer recognized. But his friends, seeing him about to take his solitary departure, rejoined him out of courtesy, to see him off for the last time; together they went to drink the health of this fortunate man of property.

Darkness was falling when he found himself alone outside the walls of Brest, on the road to Portzic. The west wind, bringing the scent of seaweed, fanned his cheeks.

Night had come when he opened the gate to his little garden and entered his hermit cottage, where he was going to sleep for the first time.

In a place of honor, above the fireplace, he hung up his silver whistle, never more to be taken down. It was strange what an unexpected melancholy now seized him, as if this evening had marked for him the end of everything. His room was well arranged, and he had taken care that it should look attractive. Many of the ornaments in this old viking's home, trophies or plunder from the four corners of the earth, had an extraordinary appearance, recalling distant lands. Near his bed, the picture of the little dead daughter, not so dim at that time, looked vaguely out as she held her candle. He took the shell frame in both his hands, his heart melted, and in spite of himself, on this happy evening, a single tear trickled down to his grizzly beard. He was a true Breton sailor, and these men of rough appearance, who live on the sea, keep always at the bottom of their hearts the unique and ineffaceable memory of some village nook or of some little sweet face that once they loved.

The west wind whistled under the door; behind his lonely house, in the damp court overhung by rocks and furze bushes, it was blowing hard; far below in the offing a tempest seemed to be approaching, and the night threatened to be rough. But he had done forever with these anxieties, done with these dark and disastrous nights, with the great noise of raging waters, with all those terrors of the sea that make one turn pale with chilly fear; all the winds might whistle now, and rage outside; never, never would that concern him again. How happy he was going to be! No more dangers, no more labor, no more trouble; every evening he would sleep peacefully in a veritable bed, all the night long; he would cultivate a little garden—a thing quite new to him, that he had always wished for—and then he would take care of himself. With all the rest and all the precautions that he was going to take, surely he couldn't fail to spend yet many happy years, even to grow young again. Nevertheless, he continued to weep; his tears, at first slowly gathering, like the sweat of cold stones, now fell faster and thicker, like a heavy rainstorm.

And then, what was it that seized him? It was not alone longing for his departed daughter; it was a deep, inward distress; his great happiness of the day was now melting away into mighty sobs, and to a desire to die at once.

The following day he awoke very early in the morning, struck with the perfect silence, astonished to find himself alone in his own house, realizing for the first time that he was nothing but an old man.

And thereupon began for him that life of decay which from week to week savored more and more of death. He grew feeble in spite of all the care he took of himself, in spite of all the rest. Left to his own resources, in the sudden calmness of this retired life, he now felt the burden of the fatigue of forty years at sea, and he was conscious, only too late, of being irrevocably broken down.

After five years of this quiet life, destruction had worked so swiftly, that he was almost obliged to introduce himself when he met any of his old friends, in order to be recognized by them.

More than all else the nights wore upon him. He had night sweats and troubled dreams. It seemed as though his brain was completely exhausted with the nightmares and the mysterious labor that he underwent in his sleep. When he awoke, his arms and legs pained him; he felt exhausted, just as he did in his youth, after some great expenditure of strength which had made his muscles so powerful. But it had the opposite effect upon his body now; his limbs grew smaller and smaller during these nightly experiences, and the bony framework began to protrude beneath his wrinkled skin.

Such scenes as these were constantly coming up in his dreams. He would think he was on board ship in his bunk, without air, in a great storm, between decks with the hatches closed; then somebody would come to look for him, reminding him that it was his watch, and that they were taking in sail. He would be in a hurry to dress himself, try to run, exasperated that he had failed of his duty, seized with a frightful anxiety to think what might happen in the rigging. But he would be unable to find his clothes, or there would be no way to get on deck, and he couldn't tell where he was. Or, perhaps, if he succeeded in getting on deck, and knew what to do, his whistle would make no sound, his arms would no longer have any strength in them, and he would struggle long and mightily against this strange inertia. At last he would awake, bathed in perspiration, hearing only the familiar sound of the west wind, soughing beneath the door, or of the winter rain, falling on the roof; little by little, he would remember that all these scenes of the deep were forever at an end, and that he was now an old man almost ready to die. And this was more terrible to him than the horrors of his dreams.

He had enough to live upon with his pension, his cross, and the money he had invested.

All the most minute details of his life were regulated for each day with precision, from the habit of order acquired by those who have long served on board ship.

He prepared his meals himself, made his bed, put his room in order, washed his linen on certain days in the week in his little back yard.

An old woman from Portzic, called Mother Le Gall, who passed by every morning, did his marketing for him. There were many, however, of these retired seafaring men whom the calling had left without families, — the scarred faces of old adventurers, or respectable brave men, with red or yellow ribbons in their buttonholes, — there were many of these who went openly, with a basket on their arm, to buy the provisions for table, their solitary table, themselves. To be sure there was nothing dishonorable in the little market basket, in the discussions and bargaining with the tradespeople, but it was all distasteful to him.

However, like all sailors, he was in the habit of doing things that people on shore generally leave to women. An old man of still noble appearance, he might be seen in his little home, mending his garments, changing the buttons on his uniform to give it the appearance of citizen's clothes, and sewing quite briskly with his rough, tattooed hands, which had once been so prodigiously strong.

The flowers grew luxuriously in his little garden, and that was the last and only pleasure which had not disappointed his expectations.

The coming in of the ships, the uproar made by the sailors

only one in all the river's course, but he had not expected it so soon, and he was alarmed.

The buoys which had suddenly appeared in the midst of the gray sea in his dream were very many; they were accumulated as if for some supernatural and unspeakable danger. They assumed all sorts of strange and unknown forms; perched on very long poles, they stretched out like arms, making signs, tossing about, with the despairing powerlessness of mute things trying to cry out, and trace magic writing across the pale heavens.

And he awoke seized with the profoundest terror, as if some fatal event which could not be averted were approaching. A danger announced in this manner must be something frightful. He thought that it signified death.

And yet the year passed away without bringing anything unusual.

There was only one change in his habits. He became very gluttonous, and continually complained that Mother Le Gall, who acted the part of houses keeper, didn't market well, that she didn't buy good enough things; so much so that one day he took his little basket himself with determination — and from that time he was seen every morning in Recouvrance, waiting about to argue with the market people like any housewife.

Clean and well brushed in his old sailor cloak — that garment of a material that never wears out, and which retired mariners wear to the day of their death — he would start out at quite a quick pace, having a determined air and bearing; but he puffed a good deal on his way home.

One morning, having taken a drink with another old man like himself, he came home staggering a little; then for the first time in his life, he was shamefully scolded by a woman, by this same Mother Le Gall, who never lost her temper except of a Sunday evening, and that not every week.

It occurred to him now — and this was a sign that the end was near — to mingle with the other pensioners, who assembled in pleasant weather near the fortifications, at the gate of Recouvrance. All the sea coats were there, brushed and brushed again, turned and threadbare, wrapped about bony backs, bodies ready to drop into the grave.

They amused themselves with quoits, and games such as are played on board ship, having kept all through their lives as sailors, a naïveté, a childlike simplicity, which, in old men, was sad to see. Sometimes, seated in little pitiful groups, they would tell the history of their lives: When I was on the "Melpomena." . . . And when I was on board the "Semiramis," one evening when they were taking in the third reef, the admiral said to me: "Jizeguet, your turn!"

They would all talk at once, each speaking for himself. And these ships they were talking about might no longer be in existence; and the commanders, who appeared in their tales like legendary characters, if not already dead many years, had become sad phantoms, who, having finished an admirable career of bravery, devotion, and honor, walked slowly through the streets in black clothes, with a red rosette in their buttonholes, or else were wheeled about in rolling chairs on days whenever there was a bit of sunshine.

Near this gate of Recouvrance were footpaths following the great granite ramparts, full of grass and lichens, until they diverged and were lost in the settled portions of the suburbs; these green footpaths were very favorable to lovers, and the sailors were fond of walking there with the young girls of the town. Naturally enough all the old men chose the entrance to these ways as a meeting place, giving it the appearance of the entrance to a cemetery. Drawn hither by habit, it was always encumbered with a melancholy crowd of them, some sober and dignified in their everlasting close-buttoned cloaks; others dirty, stupid with drink, unpleasant to see.

All, worn out in the service of their country, which gave them enough to keep them from starvation, had once been smart and strong. There were those among them who had been so good and brave that what was left of them was even yet, in spite of everything, looked upon as venerable, almost sacred.

The young people, in their low-cut shirts of blue, with their sweethearts on their arm, passed by these old ruins of what were once brave men, and hastened to penetrate by the grassy walks, beneath the young elms on the ramparts.

Before these, life and the sea were great openings, calling to them by all sorts of spells. They were in the full bloom of youth, which with sailors is more vigorous than that of other men, and without dreaming that it would pass away all the more quickly without noticing these specters, who had once been like them, they passed gayly along, like children reveling in health and strength; they passed along at the evening hour when these old men, wagging their heads, were on their way home, leaning on their canes for support.

One winter the shaking palsy seized him suddenly. He let everything fall that he touched, and broke many things in his little household.

A malady that he had once had under the equator came upon him again. Doctors on board ship called it hemeralopia, and it comes to sailors in hot countries who sleep in the wind with their eyes exposed to the air. He was unable to see after the sun had gone down, and did not dare to move without feeling his way like a blind person.

His life was going out like a candle. A veil seemed to be woven over everything about him.

His head always felt heavy, although it had hardly an idea in it. Sometimes at night a Chinese figure seemed to make faces at him near his bed; then he would be enraged and use abusive language, becoming much excited, — imagining that he could really fight with them.

He never looked now at the picture of the little communicant, who was still holding her candle, but continued to fade year by year.

He spent much money for good wine and strengthening things. But sores appeared on his legs, and as he wanted to keep sweet and clean, every morning in his little yard alone he washed the linen with which he used to dress them.

His body became deformed; he seemed much smaller than heretofore, and his shoulder blades grew out.

All day long his face looked perfectly blank, and he thought of nothing but taking care of himself and eating; it was only in the morning that intelligence came back to him very clearly, when he awoke, always alone by himself, after the sort of rest that the last hours of the night had brought him. Then he remained motionless and forbidding with the fixed gaze of one who understands and remembers.

Poor wreck, of whose destruction the sea is innocent; lonely old man with no one to watch his falling tears! Why had he not died before, in the beauty of his youth?

Still another spring found him more palsied, more feeble, seated in his garden.

However, his slumbers were no longer disturbed by troubled dreams. They were only recollections of wide spaces and burning suns; there were great wastes of blue before him, or expanses continually changing, like never-ending depths of water; and, in the foreground, there always stood out some striking detail, like rigging, masts, a yard, a sail, or shrouds. At the bottom of his brain, whose powers were passing away, there remained these last impressions of his youth spent among the rigging, or perhaps, by some mysterious transmission, there would come back still more distant recollections of his ancestors, sailors like himself.

Each nightfall brought with it the fear that he might end his days by dying alone; but Mother Le Gall, who for pay was now willing to stay with him every day, refused to sleep there, pretending that it would cause scandal.

In May he again tried to do some gardening, vexing himself greatly about two little borders which had grown wild, and where the grass was growing very high as about a neglected grave.

May came in very beautiful; the swallows which had nests under his roof sang their notes of joyful love from morning till night; everywhere in the country the new verdure was growing thick and the flowers were opening.

He went and came, bending over laboriously to root out the recalcitrant weeds. An old fuchsia, which had grown into a tree in the mild climate of Brittany, blocked up the walk with its drooping branches; at the top it was almost dead, but the lower part had put forth flowers anew in profusion, like a young plant; and when the old man passed along all the coral-colored flowers, as they brushed against his sailor's cloak, covered the worn cloth with the fresh powder of their yellow pollen. But men cannot grow young in their old age like the trees.

Another summer passed. The heat revived him a little. He put on for the last time his nankeen paletot, and fanned himself with the palm-leaf fan. But winter brought new trouble. And he nursed himself with all the greater care, growing foolish in this one idea of preserving his life. Who knew; with great precaution perhaps he might reach another springtime?

But no. One night in March Death, passing along on his way to Brest to finish some consumptives, stopped to put an end to him. He twisted his mouth, rolled up his eyes, shriveled up his fingers, and went on his way, leaving him stiff upon his bed.

The next morning Mother Le Gall coming in found him lying there: —

"A'mighty God! The old man is dead!"

He was buried by the sailors; that had been his desire, like most old mariners. On account of his decoration he had a military escort.

This was right and honorable.

For a long time afterwards there was to be seen in the front of an old-clothes shop, in the lower quarter of Brest, the nankeen paletot, the palm-leaf fan, and the picture of the little communicant in its shell frame.

DIED AT SEA.

By FRANÇOIS COPPÉE.

(Translated by Marion Lamson.)

[FRANÇOIS ÉDOUARD JOACHIM COPPÉE, generally known as François Coppée, was born at Paris January 12, 1842, and first made his reputation as a poet, afterward writing for the stage. He was for a period on the staff of the Senate Library, in 1878 became archivist of the Comédie Française, and in 1884 was elected to the French Academy. He is the author of "The Reliquary," "The Humble," "Olivier," and other poems, besides several volumes of prose sketches. Among his plays are: "Le Passant," in which Bernhardt appeared; "The Abandoned"; "Severo Torelli"; "The Jacobites," produced on the American stage under the title of "For Bonnie Prince Charlie"; "For the Crown," his latest and greatest success.]

SOME years ago I passed several weeks in a fishing village on the Breton coast. What a hole it was, but how picturesque! A beach for ten boats at the most; a single street, very steep, and resembling the bed of a torrent; and up above, on the first plateau of the cliff, the church, a Gothic gem, in the midst of a cemetery full of wild oats, and commanding a view of the ocean. Finding myself situated favorably for work, I had lingered in this corner till the end of the month of September, which, by a chance rare enough in rainy Finisterre, was exceptionally clear and mild.

I was staying at the only inn of the village, and occupied a large whitewashed room, meagerly but neatly furnished, with the window facing the open ocean. Seated on a straw-bottomed chair, at a wooden table, I composed at that time a whole poem to the solemn and soothing noise of the great waves, which seemed to say to me incessantly that rhythm is a law of nature.

But a man cannot always make verses or write, and long walks were my tonic and distraction. I used to go most often along the shore, having at my right the dry and monumental cliff, and at my left the tracts uncovered by the low tide, an immense desert of sand, spotted only by black groups of rocks. The solitude was complete. Hardly two or three times did I exchange a greeting with some patrol of the customs who was making his rounds with his gun slung over his shoulder. I was so quiet and peaceful a stroller that the sea swallows were not afraid of my red jersey, and hopped about a few steps from me, impressing their starry tracks on the damp sand. I used to walk in this manner four or five miles a day, and always returned with my pockets full of those delicate shells that one finds by excavating with the hand the little beach pebbles always wet by the tide.

This was my favorite walk. However, on the days when there was a high gale and violent surf, I used to leave the beach, and ascending the village street I would loiter about the moor. Or else I established myself with a book on an old bench in the cemetery, where I was sheltered from the west wind by the body of the church.

An ideal spot for melancholy and dreaming. Towards the autumn sky, where clouds were floating, rose the spire, devout and slender. The crows that nested there flew out and in, cawing, and the shadows of their great wings continually glided over the graves scattered in the tall grass. Between two half-ruined buttresses of the church, where the gray stone, eaten by the sea wind, supported here and there a waving cluster of little yellow flowers, there was picketed a black goat, which was almost terrifying, with his fiery eyes and satanic beard, as he bleated and pulled at his rope. In the evening above all, when, athwart the skeleton of an old dead apple tree, with rugged branches, one could see far away on the horizon the setting sun bleeding over the sea, this wild cemetery filled the soul with piercing melancholy.

It was on such an evening that, in wandering among the gravestones — many, below a sailor's name, bore the sinister

FRANÇOIS COPPÉE IN HIS STUDY

inscription, "Died at Sea" — I read, on a cross still new, these words that astonished and touched me: —

HERE RESTS

NONA LE MAGUET,

Died at sea, October 26, 1878, aged nineteen years.

Died at sea! A young girl! Women, however, never embark on the fishing boats. How had this misfortune happened?

"Indeed, sir!" said suddenly behind me a rough voice, "are you looking at the grave of our poor Nona?"

I turned, and recognized an old sailor with a wooden leg, whose good graces I had gained by a few glasses of brandy, offered in the public room of the inn.

"Yes," I answered. "But I supposed that all you fishermen refused to admit a woman on board. I have even been told that it brings ill luck."

"And it is the truth," replied the good man. "Likewise Nona never went on board a boat. — You would like to know how she died, our dear one? Well, I will tell you about it.

"First of all I must tell you that her father, Pierre Le Maguet, was an old topman like me, an old comrade of mine. At Bourget, when the admiral, La Roncière, put his gilt-trimmed cap at the end of his saber, and hurled us, our axes in our hands, against the fortified houses, Pierre and I marched shoulder to shoulder, and it was he who caught me in his arms when those cursed Prussians sent a bullet into my leg. That evening also, at the ambulance of the fort, Pierre held my hand to encourage me while the major chopped me up. And he was still there, the good Pierre, the day that the admiral brought my medal to me in bed. But, at last, those beggarly Prussians came out ahead. The treaty of peace was signed, and we were sent home. I, with my wooden leg, had nothing to do but to idle away my time like a worn-out dog. But Pierre, who had all his limbs entire, engaged in the fisherman's trade. Soon after, his wife died of an ague, and left him alone with this little Nona, who was nearly ten years old.

"Naturally, while the widower was at sea, it was I, the sailor, I, the old bachelor, who took care of the little girl. A good and quiet child, sir, very brave and very gentle. We used very often to go together over the shelving rocks at low tide, to gather large crabs, shrimps, and now and then a lobster. Oh! we were a pair of good friends.

"Things went on like this for two years. Nona had had her first communion and was growing like a sand thistle. But one tempestuous day the 'Amélie,' the boat which carried Le Maguet, had great difficulty in getting back to the beach. The skipper did not haul down his jib and spanker in time, and was lost, life and goods, on that reef which you see from here — no, a little more to starboard. There were four men on board, the skipper, two sailors, of whom my poor Pierre was one, and the cabin boy. However, the sea did not wish to return but three of the bodies to the shore, and kept my comrade for its own. Now that Nona was an orphan, I of course did my best to take her father's place. But the child, even after the first shock of grief, would not be consoled. And can you guess why, above all? On account of an idea cherished by all the women of the place. They imagine, you see, that it is necessary to be buried in consecrated ground, lest the soul suffer in torment until the Great Judgment. We do not believe in all those stupid tales, we men, who know what takes place after there has been a death on board ship. I know the ceremony well: the body in a bag of tarred sacking, a cannon ball at the foot, on a plank near the rail, and the commander bareheaded, the book in his hand, reading aloud the service for the dead. But the women about here are very religious, as you know well, and Nona began to burn candles in all the Pardons of the neighborhood, that her father's soul might have repose.

"Still, in spite of all, time is a famous dealer in forgetfulness, and Nona, after several years had passed, seemed to me to be somewhat consoled. Moreover, her grief had not kept her from growing tall and beautiful; and it is not because I loved her like a father that I say so, but on my word of honor, she was the freshest and prettiest young girl in the parish. We lived so happily together! We were not rich, most assuredly, but we got along just the same. I have my pension and my medal, and besides, Nona and I used to go lobster hunting among the rocks. The business is not a bad one, and there is only one danger, that of being caught by the rising tide. Alas! it is thus that she perished, poor little girl!

"One day that my rheumatism kept me chained in the

house, she went alone for the lobsters, a day like to-day, with a clear sky and a high wind. But the other gatherers of shell-fish, coming back with full baskets, noticed that Nona was missing. There was no doubt possible, good God! She had delayed, she had been cut off by the tide, she had died at sea! Oh! what a night I passed! At my age, yes, old tough-as-leather as I am, I sobbed like a woman. And the thought kept coming back to me, of the poor girl's belief, that to go to heaven one must be buried in the cemetery. Therefore, as soon as the sea began to ebb, I dragged myself down to the beach, and set out with the others to search for the body.

"And we found her, my Nona," went on the old sailor, whose voice was breaking. "We found her on a rock covered with seaweed, where, seeing herself lost, the brave darling, she had made herself ready to die. Yes, she had fastened her skirts below her knees with her neckerchief, for the sake of decency, and, still adhering to her old belief, she had tied her hair to the seaweed, her beautiful black hair, certain in this way that she would be found and buried in consecrated ground. And I can tell you, I, who know well what bravery is, there is hardly a man bold enough to do the like."

The old man ceased speaking. In the last gleam of twilight I saw two great tears roll down his tanned cheeks. We went down towards the village, side by side, without speaking a word. I was deeply moved by the courage of this simple girl, who, even in the agony of death, had preserved the modesty of her sex and the piety of her race. And before me, in the distant spaces, in the somber solitude of sky and sea, gleamed the lighthouses and the stars.

Oh! brave people of the sea! Oh! noble Brittany!

LOTUS FARM.[1]

By FRÉDÉRIC MISTRAL.

(From "Mirèio": translated by Harriet W. Preston.)

[Frédéric Mistral is one of a group of writers called "Les Félibriges," whose aim is the restoration of the Provençal literature. He was born near Maillane, in the department of Bouches-du-Rhône, September 8, 1830, and

[1] Copyright, 1872, by Roberts Brothers. Published by permission of Little, Brown & Co.

studied law at Avignon. His masterpiece is the epic "Mirèio" (1859), which gained the poet's prize of the French Academy and secured for the author the Cross of the Legion of Honor. Other works are: the poems "Calendau" and "The Golden Isles," "Nerto," a novel, and a Provençal-French lexicon.]

I SING the love of a Provençal maid;
How through the wheat fields of La Crau she strayed,
Following the fate that drew her to the sea.
Unknown beyond remote La Crau was she;
And I, who tell the rustic tale of her,
Would fain be Homer's humble follower.

What though youth's aureole was her only crown?
And never gold she wore nor damask gown?
I'll build her up a throne out of my song,
And hail her queen in our despisèd tongue.
Mine be the simple speech that ye all know,
Shepherds and farmer folk of lone La Crau.

God of my country, who didst have Thy birth
Among poor shepherds when Thou wast on earth,
Breathe fire into my song! Thou knowest, my God,
How, when the lusty summer is abroad,
And figs turn ripe in sun and dew, comes he,—
Brute, greedy man,—and quite despoils the tree.

Yet on that ravaged tree thou savest oft
Some little branch inviolate aloft,
Tender and airy up against the blue,
Which the rude spoiler cannot win unto:
Only the birds shall come and banquet there,
When, at St. Magdalene's, the fruit is fair.

Methinks I see yon airy little bough:
It mocks me with its freshness even now;
The light breeze lifts it, and it waves on high
Fruitage and foliage that cannot die.
Help me, dear God, on our Provençal speech,
To soar until the birds' own home I reach!

Once, then, beside the poplar-bordered Rhone,
There lived a basket weaver and his son,
In a poor hut set round with willow trees
(For all their humble wares were made from these);
And sometimes they from farm to farm would wend,
And horses' cribs and broken baskets mend.

And so one evening, as they trudged their round
With osier bundles on their shoulders bound,
"Father," young Vincen said, "the clouds look wild
About old Magalouno's tower uppiled.
If that gray rampart fell, 'twould do us harm:
We should be drenched ere we had gained the farm."

"Nay, nay!" the old man said, "no rain to-night!
'Tis the sea breeze that shakes the trees. All right!
A western gale were different." Vincen mused:
"Are many plows at Lotus farmstead used?"
"Six plows!" the basket weaver answered slow:
"It is the finest freehold in La Crau.

"Look! There's their olive orchard, intermixt
With rows of vines and almond trees betwixt.
The beauty of it is, that vineyard hath
For every day in all the year a path!
There's ne'er another such the beauty is;
And in each path are just so many trees."

"O heavens! How many hands at harvest tide
So many trees must need!" young Vincen cried.
"Nay: for 'tis almost Hallowmas, you know,
When all the girls come flocking in from Baux,
And, singing, heap with olives green and dun
The sheets and sacks, and call it only fun."

The sun was sinking, as old Ambroi said;
On high were little clouds aflush with red;
Sideways upon their yokèd cattle rode
The laborers slowly home, each with his goad
Erect. Night darkened on the distant moor;
'Twas supper time, the day of toil was o'er.

"And here we are!" the boy cried. "I can see
The straw-heaped threshing floor, so hasten we!"
"But stay!" the other. "Now, as I'm alive,
The Lotus Farm's the place for sheep to thrive—
The pine woods all the summer, and the sweep
Of the great plain in winter. Lucky sheep!

"And look at the great trees that shade the dwelling,
And look at that delicious stream forth welling
Inside the vivary! And mark the bees!
Autumn makes havoc in their colonies;

But every year, when comes the bright May weather,
Yon lotus grove a hundred swarms will gather."

"And one thing more!" cried Vincen, eagerly,
"The very best of all, it seems to me, —
I mean the maiden, father, who dwells here.
Thou canst not have forgotten how, last year,
She bade us bring her olive baskets two,
And fit her little one with handles new."

So saying, they drew the farmhouse door anigh,
And, in the dewy twilight, saw thereby
The maid herself. Distaff in hand she stood,
Watching her silkworms at their leafy food.
Then Master Ambroi let his osiers fall,
And sang out cheerily, "Good even, all!"

"Father, the same to you!" the damsel said.
"I had come out my distaff point to thread,
It grows so dark. Whence come you now, I pray?
From Valabrègo?" Ambroi answered, "Yea.
I said, when the fast-coming dark I saw,
'We'll sleep at Lotus Farm, upon the straw.'"

Whereat, with no more words, father and son
Hard by upon a roller sat them down,
And fell to their own work right busily.
A half-made cradle chanced the same to be.
Fast through the nimble fingers of the two
The supple osier bent and crossed and flew.

Certes, our Vincen was a comely lad.
A bright face and a manly form he had,
Albeit that summer he was bare sixteen.
Swart were his cheeks; but the dark soil, I ween,
Bears the fine wheat, and black grapes make the wine
That sets our feet adance, our eyes ashine.

Full well he knew the osier to prepare,
And deftly wrought: but ofttimes to his share
Fell coarser work; for he the panniers made
Wherewith the farmers use their beasts to lade,
And divers kinds of baskets, huge and rough,
Handy and light. Ay, he had skill enough!

And likewise brooms of millet grass, and such, —
And baskets of split cane. And still his touch
Was sure and swift; and all his wares were strong,
And found a ready sale the farms among.
But now, from fallow field and moorland waste,
The laborers were trooping home at last.

Then hasted sweet Mirèio to prepare,
With her own hands and in the open air,
Their evening meal. There was a broad flat stone
Served for a table, and she set thereon
One mighty dish, where each man plunged his ladle.
Our weavers wrought meanwhile upon their cradle.

Until Ramoun, the master of the farm,
Cried, "How is this?" — brusque was his tone and warm.
"Come to your supper, Ambroi: no declining!
Put up the crib, my man: the stars are shining.
And thou, Mirèio, run and fetch a bowl:
The travelers must be weary, on my soul!"

Wherefore the basket weaver, well-content,
Rose with his son and to the table went,
And sat him down and cut the bread for both;
While bright Mirèio hasted, nothing loath,
Seasoned a dish of beans with olive oil,
And came and sat before them with a smile.

Not quite fifteen was this same fair Mirèio.
Ah, me! the purple coast of Font Vièio,
The hills of Baux, the desolate Crau plain,
A shape like her will hardly see again.
Child of the merry sun, her dimpled face
Bloomed into laughter with ingenuous grace.

Eyes had she limpid as the drops of dew;
And, when she fixed their tender gaze on you,
Sorrow was not. Stars in a summer night
Are not more softly, innocently bright:
And beauteous hair, all waves and rings of jet;
And breasts, a double peach, scarce ripened yet.

MORALITY INDEPENDENT OF UTILITY.[1]

BY W. E. H. LECKY.

(From "History of European Morals.")

[WILLIAM EDWARD HARTPOLE LECKY: An English historian; born at Newtown Park, near Dublin, Ireland, March 26, 1838. He was educated at Trinity College, Dublin; honorary member of the Royal Academy, 1895; made member of Parliament for Dublin University in 1895, and became a privy councilor in 1897. His works include: "The Religious Tendencies of the Age" (1860), "The Leaders of Public Opinion in Ireland" (1861), "History of the Rise and Influence of the Spirit of Rationalism in Europe" (2 vols., 1865), "History of European Morals" (2 vols., 1869), "A History of England in the Eighteenth Century" (8 vols., 1878–1890), "A History of Ireland in the Eighteenth Century" (5 vols., 1892), "Poems" (1891), "The Political Value of History" (1892), "The Empire, its Value and its Growth" (1893), and "Democracy and Liberty" (2 vols., 1896).]

WHEN moralists assert that what we call virtue derives its reputation solely from its utility, and that the interest or pleasure of the agent is the one motive to practice it, our first question is naturally how far this theory agrees with the feelings and with the language of mankind. But if tested by this criterion, there never was a doctrine more emphatically condemned than utilitarianism. In all its stages, and in all its assertions, it is in direct opposition to common language and to common sentiments. In all nations and in all ages, the ideas of interest and utility on the one hand and of virtue on the other have been regarded by the multitude as perfectly distinct, and all languages recognize the distinction. The terms honor, justice, rectitude, or virtue, and their equivalents in every language, present to the mind ideas essentially and broadly differing from the terms prudence, sagacity, or interest. The two lines of conduct may coincide, but they are never confused, and we have not the slightest difficulty in imagining them antagonistic. When we say a man is governed by a high sense of honor, or by strong moral feeling, we do not mean that he is prudently pursuing either his own interests or the interests of society. The universal sentiment of mankind represents self-sacrifice as an essential element of a meritorious act, and means by self-sacrifice the deliberate adoption of the least pleasurable course without the prospect of any pleasure in return. A self-

[1] By permission of the Author and Longmans, Green & Co. (Cr. 8vo. 16s.)

ish act may be innocent, but cannot be virtuous, and to ascribe all good deeds to selfish motives is not the distortion but the negation of virtue. No Epicurean could avow before a popular audience that the one end of his life was the pursuit of his own happiness without an outburst of indignation and contempt. No man could consciously make this — which according to the selfish theory is the only rational and indeed possible motive of action — the deliberate object of all his undertakings, without his character becoming despicable and degraded.

Whether we look within ourselves or examine the conduct either of our enemies or of our friends, or adjudicate upon the characters in history or in fiction, our feelings on these matters are the same. In exact proportion as we believe a desire for personal enjoyment to be the motive of a good act is the merit of the agent diminished. If we believe the motive to be wholly selfish, the merit is altogether destroyed. If we believe it to be wholly disinterested, the merit is altogether unalloyed. Hence, the admiration bestowed upon Prometheus, or suffering virtue constant beneath the blows of Almighty malice, or on the atheist who with no prospect of future reward suffered a fearful death rather than abjure an opinion which could be of no benefit to society, because he believed it to be the truth. Selfish moralists deny the possibility of that which all ages, all nations, all popular judgments, pronounce to have been the characteristic of every noble act that has ever been performed. Now, when a philosophy which seeks by the light of consciousness to decipher the laws of our moral being proves so diametrically opposed to the conclusions arrived at by the great mass of mankind, who merely follow their consciousness without endeavoring to frame systems of philosophy, that it makes most of the distinctions of common ethical language absolutely unmeaning, this is, to say the least, a strong presumption against its truth. If Molière's hero had been speaking prose all his life without knowing it, this was simply because he did not understand what prose was. In the present case we are asked to believe that men have been under a total delusion about the leading principles of their lives which they had distinguished by a whole vocabulary of terms.

It is said that the case becomes different when the pleasure sought is not a gross or material enjoyment, but the satisfaction of performed virtue. I suspect that if men could persuade themselves that the one motive of a virtuous man was the certainty that the act he accomplished would be followed by a glow of satisfaction so intense as more than to compensate for any sacrifice he might have made, the difference would not be as great as is supposed. In fact, however — and the consciousness of this lies, I conceive, at the root of the opinions of men upon the subject — the pleasure of virtue is one which can only be obtained on the express condition of its not being the object sought. Phenomena of this kind are familiar to us all. Thus, for example, it has often been observed that prayer, by a law of our nature and apart from all supernatural intervention, exercises a reflex influence of a very beneficial character upon the minds of the worshipers. The man who offers up his petitions with passionate earnestness, with unfaltering faith, and with a vivid realization of the presence of an Unseen Being has risen to a condition of mind which is itself eminently favorable both to his own happiness and to the expansion of his moral qualities. But he who expects nothing more will never attain this. To him who neither believes nor hopes that his petitions will receive a response such a mental state is impossible. No Protestant before an image of the Virgin, no Christian before a pagan idol, could possibly attain it. If prayers were offered up solely with a view to this benefit, they would be absolutely sterile and would speedily cease.

Thus again, certain political economists have contended that to give money in charity is worse than useless, that it is positively noxious to society, but they have added that the gratification of our benevolent affections is pleasing to ourselves, and that the pleasure we derive from this source may be so much greater than the evil resulting from our gift, that we may justly, according to the "greatest happiness principle," purchase this large amount of gratification to ourselves by a slight injury to our neighbors. The political economy involved in this very characteristic specimen of utilitarian ethics I shall hereafter examine. At present it is sufficient to observe that no one who consciously practiced benevolence solely from this motive could obtain the pleasure in question. We receive enjoyment from the thought that we have done good. We never could receive that enjoyment if we believed and realized that we were doing harm. The same thing is preëminently true of the satisfaction of conscience. A feeling of satisfaction follows the accomplishment of duty for itself, but if the duty be performed solely through the expectation of a mental pleasure conscience refuses to ratify the bargain.

TRINITY COLLEGE, DUBLIN

From a photo by W. Lawrence, Dublin

There is no fact more conspicuous in human nature than the broad distinction, both in kind and degree, drawn between the moral and the other parts of our nature. But this on utilitarian principles is altogether unaccountable. If the excellence of virtue consists solely in its utility or tendency to promote the happiness of men, we should be compelled to canonize a crowd of acts which are utterly remote from all our ordinary notions of morality. The whole tendency of political economy and philosophical history which reveal the physiology of societies is to show that the happiness and welfare of mankind are evolved much more from our selfish than from what are termed our virtuous acts. The prosperity of nations and the progress of civilization are mainly due to the exertions of men who, while pursuing strictly their own interests, were unconsciously promoting the interests of the community. The selfish instinct that leads men to accumulate confers ultimately more advantage upon the world than the generous instinct that leads men to give. A great historian has contended with some force that intellectual development is more important to societies than moral development. Yet who ever seriously questioned the reality of the distinction that separates these things? The reader will probably exclaim that the key to that distinction is to be found in the motive; but it is one of the paradoxes of the utilitarian school that the motive of the agent has absolutely no influence on the morality of the act. According to Bentham, there is but one motive possible, the pursuit of our own enjoyment. The most virtuous, the most vicious, and the most indifferent of actions, if measured by this test, would be exactly the same, and an investigation of motives should therefore be altogether excluded from our moral judgments. Whatever test we adopt, the difficulty of accounting for the unique and pre-eminent position mankind have assigned to virtue will remain. If we judge by tendencies, a crowd of objects and of acts to which no mortal ever dreamed of ascribing virtue contribute largely to the happiness of man. If we judge by motives, the moralists we are reviewing have denied all generic difference between prudential and virtuous motives. If we judge by intentions, it is certain that however much truth or chastity may contribute to the happiness of mankind, it is not with philanthropic intentions that those virtues are cultivated.

It is often said that intuitive moralists in their reasonings are guilty of continually abandoning their principles by themselves appealing to the tendency of certain acts to promote human happiness as a justification, and the charge is usually accompanied by a challenge to show any confessed virtue that has not that tendency. To the first objection it may be shortly answered that no intuitive moralist ever dreamed of doubting that benevolence or charity, or in other words, the promotion of the happiness of man, is a duty. He maintains that it not only is so, but that we arrive at this fact by direct intuition, and not by the discovery that such a course is conducive to our own interest. But while he cordially recognizes this branch of virtue, and while he has therefore a perfect right to allege the beneficial effects of a virtue in its defense, he refuses to admit that all virtue can be reduced to this single principle. With the general sentiment of mankind he regards charity as a good thing only because it is of use to the world. With the same general sentiment of mankind he believes that chastity and truth have an independent value, distinct from their influence upon happiness. To the question whether every confessed virtue is conducive to human happiness, it is less easy to reply, for it is usually extremely difficult to calculate the remote tendencies of acts, and in cases where, in the common apprehension of mankind, the morality is very clear, the consequences are often very obscure. Notwithstanding the claim of great precision which utilitarian writers so boastfully make, the standard by which they profess to measure morals is itself absolutely incapable of definition or accurate explanation. Happiness is one of the most indeterminate and undefinable words in the language, and what are the conditions of "the greatest possible happiness" no one can precisely say. No two nations, perhaps no two individuals, would find them the same. And even if every virtuous act were incontestably useful, it by no means follows that its virtue is derived from its utility.

It may be readily granted that as a general rule those acts which we call virtuous are unquestionably productive of happiness, if not to the agent, at least to mankind in general, but we have already seen that they have by no means that monopoly or preëminence of utility which, on utilitarian principles, the unique position assigned to them would appear to imply. It may be added that if we were to proceed in detail to estimate acts by their consequences, we should soon be led to very startling conclusions. In the first place, it is obvious that if virtues are only good because they promote, and vices only evil because they impair the happiness of mankind, the degrees of excellence or criminality must be strictly proportioned to the degrees of utility or the reverse. Every action, every disposition, every class, every condition of society, must take its place on the moral scale precisely in accordance with the degree in which it promotes or diminishes human happiness. Now it is extremely questionable whether some of the most monstrous forms of sensuality, which it is scarcely possible to name, cause as much unhappiness as some infirmities of temper, or procrastination or hastiness of judgment. It is scarcely doubtful that a modest, diffident, and retiring nature, distrustful of its own abilities, and shrinking with humility from conflict, produces on the whole less benefit to the world than the self-assertion of an audacious and arrogant nature, which is impelled to every struggle, and develops every capacity. Gratitude has no doubt done much to soften and sweeten the intercourse of life, but the corresponding feeling of revenge was for centuries the one bulwark against social anarchy, and is even now one of the chief restraints to crime. On the great theater of public life, especially in periods of great convulsions when passions are fiercely roused, it is neither the man of delicate scrupulosity and sincere impartiality, nor yet the single-minded religious enthusiast, incapable of dissimulation or procrastination, who confers most benefit upon the world. It is much rather the astute statesman earnest about his ends but unscrupulous about his means, equally free from the trammels of conscience and from the blindness of zeal, who governs because he partly yields to the passions and the prejudices of his time. But however much some modern writers may idolize the heroes of success, however much they may despise and ridicule those far nobler men whose wide tolerance and scrupulous honor rendered them unfit leaders in the fray, it has scarcely yet been contended that the delicate conscientiousness which in these cases impairs utility constitutes vice. If utility is the sole measure of virtue, it is difficult to understand how we could look with moral disapprobation on any class who prevent greater evils than they cause. But with such a principle we might find strange priestesses at the utilitarian shrine. "Aufer meretrices de rebus humanis," said St. Augustine, "turbaveris omnia libidinibus."

Let us suppose an inquirer who intended to regulate his life consistently by the utilitarian principle; let us suppose him to have overcome the first great difficulty of his school, arising from the apparent divergence of his own interests from his duty, to have convinced himself that that divergence does not exist, and to have accordingly made the pursuit of duty his single object, it remains to consider what kind of course he would pursue. He is informed that it is a pure illusion to suppose that human actions have any other end or rule than happiness, that nothing is intrinsically good or intrinsically bad apart from its consequences, that no act which is useful can possibly be vicious, and that the utility of an act constitutes and measures its value. One of his first observations will be that in very many special cases acts such as murder, theft, or falsehood, which the world calls criminal, and which in the majority of instances would undoubtedly be hurtful, appear eminently productive of good. Why, then, he may ask, should they not in these cases be performed?

The answer he receives is that they would not really be useful, because we must consider the remote as well as the immediate consequences of actions, and although in particular instances a falsehood or even a murder might appear beneficial, it is one of the most important interests of mankind that the sanctity of life and property should be preserved, and that a high standard of veracity should be maintained. But this answer is obviously insufficient. It is necessary to show that the extent to which a single act of what the world calls crime would weaken these great bulwarks of society is such as to counterbalance the immediate good which it produces. If it does not, the balance will be on the side of happiness, the murder or theft or falsehood will be useful, and therefore, on utilitarian principles, will be virtuous. Now even in the case of public acts, the effect of the example of an obscure individual is usually small, but if the act be accomplished in perfect secrecy, the evil effects resulting from the example will be entirely absent.

It has been said that it would be dangerous to give men permission to perpetrate what men call crimes in secret. This may be a very good reason why the utilitarian should not proclaim such a principle, but it is no reason why he should not act upon it. If a man be convinced that no act which is useful can possibly be criminal, if it be in his power by perpetrating what is called a crime to obtain an end of great immediate utility, and if he is able to secure such absolute secrecy as to render it perfectly certain that his act cannot become an example, and cannot in consequence exercise any influence on the general standard of morals, it appears demonstrably certain that on utilitarian principles he would be justified in performing it. If what we call virtue be only virtuous *because* it is useful, it can only be virtuous *when* it is useful. The question of the morality of a large number of acts must therefore depend upon the probability of their detection, and a little adroit hypocrisy must often, not merely in appearance but in reality, convert a vice into a virtue.

The only way by which it has been attempted with any plausibility to evade this conclusion has been by asserting that the act would impair the disposition of the agent, or in other words predispose him on other occasions to perform acts which are generally hurtful to society. But in the first place a single act has no such effect upon disposition as to counteract a great immediate good, especially when, as we have supposed, that act is not a revolt against what is believed to be right, but is performed under the full belief that it is in accordance with the one rational rule of morals, and in the next place, as far as the act would form a habit it would appear to be the habit of in all cases regulating actions by a precise and minute calculation of their utility, which is the very ideal of utilitarian virtue.

If our inquirer happens to be a man of strong imagination and of solitary habits, it is very probable that he will be accustomed to live much in a world of imagination, a world peopled with beings that are to him as real as those of flesh, with its joys and sorrows, its temptations and its sins. In obedience to the common feelings of our nature, he may have struggled long and painfully against sins of the imagination, which he was never seriously tempted to convert into sins of action. But his new philosophy will be admirably fitted to console his mind. If remorse be absent, the indulgence of the most vicious imagination is a pleasure, and if this indulgence does not lead to action it is a clear gain, and therefore to be applauded. That a course may be continually pursued in imagination without leading to corresponding actions he will speedily discover, and indeed it has always been one of the chief objections brought against fiction that the constant exercise of the sympathies in favor of imaginary beings is found positively to indispose men to practical benevolence.

Proceeding farther in his course, our moralist will soon find reason to qualify the doctrine of remote consequences, which plays so large a part in the calculations of utilitarianism. It is said that it is criminal to destroy human beings, even when the crime would appear productive of great utility, for every instance of murder weakens the sanctity of life. But experience shows that it is possible for men to be perfectly indifferent to one particular section of human life, without this indifference extending to others. Thus among the ancient Greeks, the murder or exposition of the children of poor parents was continually practiced with the most absolute callousness, without exercising any appreciable influence upon the respect for adult life. In the same manner what may be termed religious unveracity, or the habit of propagating what are deemed useful superstitions, with the consciousness of their being false, or at least suppressing or misrepresenting the facts that might invalidate them, does not in any degree imply industrial unveracity. Nothing is more common than to find extreme dishonesty in speculation coexisting with scrupulous veracity in business. If any vice might be expected to conform strictly to the utilitarian theory, it would be cruelty; but cruelty to animals may exist without leading to cruelty to men, and even where spectacles in which animal suffering forms a leading element exercise an injurious influence on character, it is more than doubtful whether the measure of human unhappiness they may ultimately produce is at all equivalent to the passionate enjoyment they immediately afford.

This last consideration, however, makes it necessary to notice a new and, as it appears to me, almost grotesque development of the utilitarian theory. The duty of humanity to animals, though for a long period too much neglected, may, on the principles of the intuitive moralist, be easily explained and justified. Our circumstances and characters produce in us many and various affections towards all with whom we come in contact, and our consciences pronounce these affections to be good or bad. We feel that humanity or benevolence is a good affection, and also that it is due in different degrees to different classes. Thus it is not only natural but right that a man should care for his own family more than for the world at large, and this obligation applies not only to parents who are responsible for having brought their children into existence, and to children who owe a debt of gratitude to their parents, but also to brothers who have no such special tie. So too we feel it to be both unnatural and wrong to feel no stronger interest in our fellow-countrymen than in other men. In the same way we feel that there is a wide interval between the humanity it is both natural and right to exhibit towards animals, and that which is due to our own species. Strong philanthropy could hardly coexist with cannibalism, and a man who had no hesitation in destroying human life for the sake of obtaining the skins of the victims, or of freeing himself from some trifling inconvenience, would scarcely be eulogized for his benevolence. Yet a man may be regarded as very humane to animals who has no scruple in sacrificing their lives for his food, his pleasures, or his convenience.

Towards the close of the last century an energetic agitation in favor of humanity to animals arose in England, and the utilitarian moralists, who were then rising into influence, caught the spirit of their time and made very creditable efforts to extend it. It is manifest, however, that a theory which recognized no other end in virtue than the promotion of human happiness, could supply no adequate basis for the movement. Some of the recent members of the school have accordingly enlarged their theory, maintaining that acts are virtuous when they produce a net result of happiness, and vicious when they produce a net result of suffering, altogether irrespective of the question whether this enjoyment or suffering is of men or animals. In other words, they place the duty of man to animals on exactly the same basis as the duty of man to his fellow-men, maintaining that no suffering can be rightly inflicted on brutes, which does not produce a larger amount of happiness to man.

The first reflection suggested by this theory is that it appears difficult to understand how, on the principles of the inductive school, it could be arrived at. Benevolence, as we have seen, according to these writers, begins in interest. We first of all do good to men, because it is for our advantage, though the force of the habit may at last act irrespective of interest. But in the case of animals which cannot resent barbarity, this foundation of self-interest does not for the most part exist. Probably, however, an association of ideas might help to solve the difficulty, and the habit of benevolence generated originally from the social relations of men might at last be extended to the animal world; but that it should be so to the extent of placing the duty to animals on the same basis as the duty to men, I do not anticipate, or (at the risk of being accused of great inhumanity), I must add, desire. I cannot look forward to a time when no one will wear any article of dress formed out of the skin of an animal, or feed upon animal flesh, till he has ascertained that the pleasure he derives from doing so exceeds the pain inflicted upon the animal, as well as the pleasure of which by abridging its life he has deprived it. And supposing that with such a calculation before him, the utilitarian should continue to feed on the flesh of animals, his principle might carry him to further conclusions, from which I confess I should recoil. If, when Swift was writing his famous essay in favor of employing for food the redundant babies of a half-starving population, he had been informed that, according to the more advanced moralists, to eat a child, and to eat a sheep, rest upon exactly the same ground; that in the one case as in the other, the single question for the moralist is, whether the repast on the whole produces more pleasure than pain, it must be owned that the discovery would have greatly facilitated his task.

The considerations I have adduced will, I think, be sufficient to show that the utilitarian principle if pushed to its full logical consequences would be by no means as accordant with ordinary moral notions as is sometimes alleged; that it would, on the contrary, lead to conclusions utterly and outrageously repugnant to the moral feelings it is intended to explain.

THE LAST JOURNEY TO JERUSALEM.[1]

By ERNEST RENAN.

(From "The Life of Jesus." Translated by Wm. G. Hutchison.)

[Joseph Ernest Renan: Noted French historian and essayist; born at Tréguier, Brittany, February 27, 1823; died at Paris, October 2, 1892. He was educated for the priesthood, but being beset by doubts concerning the accepted tenets of faith, he left the seminary of St. Sulpice and devoted himself to science and literature. He made a careful study of the Semitic languages and of religious history. Among his principal works are: "General History of the Semitic Languages" (1856), "Studies of Religious History" (1857), "Translation of the Book of Job" (1858), "The Origin of Language" (1858), "Essays, Moral and Critical" (1859), "The Life of Jesus" (1863), "The Apostles" (1866), "St. Paul" (1869), "Antichrist" (1873), "The Gospels" (1877), "The Christian Church" (1879), "Marcus Aurelius" (1881), "New

[1] By permission of the translator, and of Walter Scott, Ltd. (Cloth, 1s. 6d.)

ERNEST RENAN IN HIS STUDY

Studies in Religious History" (1884), "Discourses and Conferences" (1884), and the dramas "Caliban" (1878), "Fountain of Youth" (1880), "The Priest of Némi" (1885), and "The Abbess of Jouarre" (1886).]

For a long time Jesus had been aware of the dangers surrounding him. During a period of time which may be estimated at eighteen months, he avoided going on pilgrimage to Jerusalem. At the feast of Tabernacles of the year 32 (according to the hypothesis we have adopted) his relatives, always malevolent and skeptical, pressed him to go there. The evangelist John seems to insinuate that in this invitation there was some hidden project to ruin Jesus. "Depart hence, and go into Judæa, that thy disciples also may behold thy works which thou doest. For no man doeth anything in secret, and himself seeketh to be known openly. If thou doest these things, manifest thyself to the world." Jesus, suspecting some treachery, at first refused; but when the caravan of pilgrims had started, he set out on the journey, unknown to every one, and almost alone. It was the last farewell that he bade to Galilee. The feast of Tabernacles fell at the autumnal equinox. Six months had still to elapse before the fatal consummation. But during this interval Jesus never again saw his beloved northern land. The days of pleasantness have passed away; step by step he must now traverse the path of sorrows that will only end in the anguish of death.

His disciples, and the pious women who followed him, met him again in Judæa. But how greatly was all changed for him here! In Jerusalem Jesus was a stranger. Here he felt a wall of resistance he could not penetrate. Hemmed in by snares and difficulties, he was unceasingly dogged by the enmity of the Pharisees. Instead of that illimitable faculty of belief, the happy gift of youthful natures, which he found in Galilee — instead of those good and gentle folk, amongst whom objections (which are always in part the fruit of evil thinking and indocility) had no existence, here at every step he met with an obstinate skepticism, upon which the means of action that had succeeded in the north so well had little effect. His disciples were despised as being Galileans. Nicodemus, who, on one of the former visits of Jesus, had had a nocturnal interview, almost compromised himself with the Sanhedrim by his desire to defend him. "Art thou also of Galilee?" they said to him. "Search and see that out of Galilee ariseth no prophet."

The city, as we have already remarked, displeased Jesus. Until now he had always avoided great centers, preferring rural districts and towns of small importance for his field of action. Many of the precepts which he gave to his apostles were absolutely inapplicable, except in a simple community of humble folk. Since he had no conception of the world, and was accustomed only to the kindly communism of Galilee, remarks constantly escaped him, the simplicity of which might well appear odd at Jerusalem. His imagination and his love of nature felt constraint within its walls. It is not the destiny of true religion to emerge from the tumult of towns, but from the tranquil quietude of the fields.

The arrogance of the priests made the courts of the Temple disagreeable to him. One day some of his disciples, who knew Jerusalem better than he, wished him to notice the beauty of the Temple buildings, the admirable choice of materials, and the richness of the votive offerings which covered the walls. "See ye not all these things," said he; "verily I say unto you there shall not be left here one stone upon another." He refused to admire anything, unless it was a poor widow who passed at that moment and threw a small coin into the box. "This poor widow cast in more than they all," said he; "for all these did of their superfluity cast in unto their gifts: but she of her want did cast in all the living that she had." This habit of criticising all that was going on at Jerusalem, of exalting the poor who gave little, of slighting the rich who gave much, and of rebuking the wealthy priests who did nothing for the good of the people, naturally exasperated the sacerdotal caste. As the seat of a conservative aristocracy, the Temple, like the Mussulman *Haram* which has succeeded it, was the last place in the world in which revolutions could triumph. Imagine a reformer going in our own time to preach the overthrow of Islamism round the Mosque of Omar! The Temple, however, was the center of Jewish life, the point at which victory or death was essential. On this Calvary, where Jesus assuredly suffered more than at Golgotha, his days were passed in disputation and bitterness, in the midst of tedious controversies about canonical law and exegesis, for which his great moral grandeur, far from giving him any advantage, positively unfitted him.

In his troubled life at this period, the sensitive and kindly heart of Jesus was able to find a refuge, where he enjoyed much tranquillity. After having passed the day disputing in the Temple, Jesus used to descend at evening into the valley of Kedron, and rest awhile in the orchard of a kind of farm (probably a place where oil was made) called Gethsemane, which served as a pleasure garden to the inhabitants. Thence he would proceed to pass the night upon the Mount of Olives, which shuts in the horizon of the city on the east. This district is the only one, in the neighborhood of Jerusalem, presenting an aspect that is in any way pleasing and verdant. Groves of olives, figs, and palms were numerous there, and gave their names to the villages, farms, or inclosures of Bethphage, Gethsemane, and Bethany. Upon the Mount of Olives were two great cedars, the memory of which was long cherished amongst the dispersed Jews; their branches served as a refuge for bevies of doves, and under their shade were established small bazaars. The whole precinct was in a manner the abode of Jesus and his disciples; they evidently knew it field by field and house by house.

In particular the village of Bethany, situated at the summit of the hill, upon the slope which commands the Dead Sea and the Jordan, at a journey of an hour and a half from Jerusalem, was the place especially loved by Jesus. There he made the acquaintance of a family of three persons, two sisters and a third member, whose friendship had a great charm for him. Of the two sisters, the one called Martha was an obliging, kind woman, assiduous in her attentions; while the other, Mary, on the contrary, pleased Jesus by a kind of languor, and by her highly developed speculative tendencies. Seated at the feet of Jesus, she often forgot, in listening to his words, the duties of everyday life. Her sister, upon whom all these duties devolved at such times, gently complained. "Martha, Martha," said Jesus to her, "thou art anxious and troubled about many things; but one thing is needful. For Mary hath chosen the good part, which shall not be taken away from her." A certain Simon the Leper, who was the owner of the house, was apparently the brother of Mary and Martha, or at least formed part of the family. It was there that, in the midst of pious friendship, Jesus forgot the vexations of public life. In this quiet home he consoled himself for the wrangling which the Scribes and the Pharisees never ceased to raise around him. He often sat on the Mount of Olives, facing Mount Moriah, having under his eyes the splendid perspective of the terraces of the Temple, and its roofs covered with glittering plates of metal. This view used to strike strangers with admiration; at sunrise especially the holy mountain dazzled the eyes, and seemed as it were a mass of snow and gold. But a profound feeling of sadness poisoned for Jesus the spectacle that filled all other Israelites with joy and pride. "O Jerusalem, Jerusalem which killeth the prophets, and stoneth them that are sent unto her! how often would I have gathered thy children together, even as a hen gathereth her chickens under her wings, and ye would not."

It was not that many honest souls here, as in Galilee, were not touched; but such was the weight of the dominant orthodoxy, that very few dared to avow it. Men feared to discredit themselves in the eyes of the Hierosolymites by placing themselves in the school of a Galilean. They would have risked expulsion from the synagogue, which, in a mean and bigoted society, was the greatest degradation possible. Excommunication besides carried with it confiscation of all property. By ceasing to be a Jew, a man did not become a Roman; he remained defenseless under the power of a theocratic legislation of the most atrocious severity. One day the lower officers of the Temple, who had been present at one of the discourses of Jesus, and had been enchanted with it, came to confide their doubts to the priests: "Hath any of the rulers believed on him, or of the Pharisees?" was the reply to them; "but this multitude who knoweth not the Law are accursed." Jesus thus remained at Jerusalem, a provincial admired by provincials like himself, but rejected by all the aristocracy of the nation. Chiefs of schools and of sects were too numerous for any one to be stirred by seeing one more appear. His voice made little impression in Jerusalem. Racial and sectarian prejudices, the open enemies of the spirit of the Gospel, were too deeply rooted.

His teaching in this new world necessarily became greatly modified. His beautiful discourses, the effect of which was always marked upon hearers with youthful imaginations and consciences morally pure, here fell upon stone. He who was so much at ease on the shores of his charming little lake felt constrained and in a strange land when he confronted pedants. His perpetual self-assertion took a somewhat fastidious tone. He had to become controversialist, jurist, exegetist, and theologian. His conversations, generally so full of grace, were transformed into a rolling fire of disputes, an interminable series of scholastic battles. His harmonious genius was wasted away in insipid argumentations upon the Law and the Prophets, in which we should have preferred not to see him sometimes play the part of aggressor. With a regrettable condescension he lent himself to the captious criticisms to which tactless cavilers subjected him. As a rule he extricated himself from difficulties with much skill. His reasonings, it is true, were often subtle (for simplicity of mind and subtlety are akin; when simplicity reasons, it is always a little sophistical); we find that he sometimes courted misconceptions, and intentionally prolonged them; his reasoning, judged by the rules of Aristotelian logic, was very weak. But when the unparalleled charm of his mind could be shown, he was triumphant. One day it was intended to embarrass him by presenting an adultress to him, and asking him what should be done with her. We know the admirable response of Jesus. The fine raillery of a man of the world, tempered by a divine charity, could not be more exquisitely expressed. But the wit allied to moral grandeur is that which fools can least forgive. With his words so just and pure in their taste: "He that is without sin among you, let him first cast a stone at her," Jesus pierced hypocrisy to the heart, and with the same stroke sealed his own death warrant.

It is probable indeed that, but for the exasperation caused by so many bitter shafts, Jesus might have long been able to remain unnoticed, and might have lost himself in the terrible storm which was soon to overwhelm the whole Jewish nation. The higher priesthood and the Sadducees rather disdained than hated him. The great sacerdotal families, the *Boëthusim*, the family of Hanan, were only fanatical when their peace was threatened. The Sadducees, like Jesus, rejected the "traditions" of the Pharisees. By a very strange singularity, it was these skeptics, denying the resurrection, the oral Law, and the existence of angels, who were the true Jews. Or rather, since the old Law in its simplicity no longer satisfied the religious wants of the time, those who held strictly to it and rejected modern inventions were regarded by devotees as impious, just as an evangelical Protestant of the present day is considered an unbeliever in Catholic countries. At all events, from a party such as this no very strong reaction against Jesus could proceed. The official priesthood, with its attention concentrated on political power and closely connected with the former party, did not understand enthusiastic movements of this kind. It was the middle-class Pharisees, the innumerable *Soferim* or Scribes making a living by the science of "traditions," who took the alarm; and it was their prejudices and interests that in reality were threatened by the doctrine of the new Master.

One of the most constant efforts of the Pharisees was to draw Jesus into the political arena, and to compromise him as being attached to the party of Judas the Gaulonite. Their tactics were clever; for all the deep wisdom of Jesus was required to avoid embroilment with the Roman authority, in his preaching of the kingdom of God. They desired to cut through his ambiguity, and force him to explain himself. One day a group of Pharisees, and of those politicians who were called "Herodians" (probably some of the *Boëthusim*), approached him and, under the pretense of pious zeal, said, "Master, we know that thou art true, and teachest the way of God in truth, and carest not for any one. . . . Tell us therefore, What thinkest thou? Is it lawful to give tribute unto Cæsar, or not?" They hoped for a response which would give them a pretext for delivering him up to Pilate. The answer of Jesus was admirable. He made them show him the image on a coin: "Render therefore," said he, "unto Cæsar the things that are Cæsar's; and unto God the things that are God's." Such were the profound words which decided the future of Christianity! Words of the most perfect spirituality, and of marvelous justice, which established the separation of the spiritual from the temporal, and laid the foundation of true liberalism and true civilization!

His gentle and irresistible genius inspired him, when alone with his disciples, with accents full of tenderness. "Verily, verily, I say unto you, He that entereth not by the door unto the fold of the sheep, but climbeth up some other way, the same is a thief and a robber. But he that entereth in by the door is the shepherd of the sheep. . . . The sheep hear his voice: and he calleth his own sheep by name, and leadeth them out. . . . He goeth before them, and the sheep follow him; for they know his voice. . . . The thief cometh not, but that he may steal, and kill, and destroy. . . . He that is an hireling and not a shepherd, whose own the sheep are not, beholdeth the wolf coming, and leaveth the sheep, and fleeth. . . . I am the good shepherd and I know mine own, and mine own know me . . . and I lay down my life for the sheep." The idea that the crisis of humanity was close at hand frequently recurred to him: "Now," said he, "from the fig tree learn her parable: When her branch is now become tender, and putteth forth its leaves, ye know that the summer is nigh." "Lift up your eyes, and look on the fields; for they are white already to harvest."

His powerful eloquence always burst forth when he had to contend with hypocrisy. "The Scribes and the Pharisees sit on Moses' seat; all things therefore whatsoever they bid you, these do and observe: but do not ye after their works; for they say, and do not. Yea, they bind heavy burdens and grievous to be borne, and lay them on men's shoulders; but they themselves will not move them with their finger.

"But all their works do they for to be seen of men: for they make broad their phylacteries and enlarge the borders of their garments, and love the chief place at feasts, and the chief seats in the synagogues, and the salutation in the market places, and to be called of men, Rabbi. . . .

"But woe unto you, Scribes and Pharisees, hypocrites! because ye shut the kingdom of heaven against men: for ye enter not in yourselves, neither suffer ye them that are entering in to enter. Woe unto you, Scribes and Pharisees, hypocrites! for ye devour widows' houses, even while for a pretense ye make long prayers: therefore ye shall receive greater condemnation. Woe unto you, for ye compass sea and land to make one proselyte; and when he is become so, ye make him twofold more a son of hell than yourselves!" "Woe unto you! for ye are as the tombs which appear not, and the men that walk over them know it not."

"Woe unto you, Scribes and Pharisees, hypocrites! for ye tithe mint and anise and cumin, and have left undone the weightier matters of the law, judgment, and mercy, and faith: but these ye ought to have done, and not to have left the other undone. Ye blind guides, which strain out the gnat and swallow the camel.

"Woe unto you, Scribes and Pharisees, hypocrites! for ye cleanse the outside of the cup and of the platter, but within they are full from extortion and excess. Thou blind Pharisee, cleanse first the inside of the cup and of the platter, that the outside thereof may become clean also.

"Woe unto you, Scribes and Pharisees, hypocrites! for ye are like unto whited sepulchers, which outwardly appear beautiful, but inwardly are full of dead men's bones, and of all uncleanness. Even so ye also outwardly appear righteous unto men, but inwardly ye are full of hypocrisy and iniquity.

"Woe unto you, Scribes and Pharisees, hypocrites! for ye build the sepulchers of the prophets, and garnish the tombs of the righteous, and say, If we had been in the days of our fathers, we should not have been partakers with them in the blood of the prophets. Wherefore, ye witness to yourselves, that ye are sons of them that slew the prophets. Fill ye up then the measure of your fathers. . . .

"Therefore, behold, I will send unto you prophets, and wise men, and scribes: some of them shall ye kill and crucify; and some of them shall ye scourge in your synagogues, and persecute from city to city. That upon you may come all the righteous blood shed on the earth, from the blood of Abel the righteous unto the blood of Zachariah, son of Barachiah, whom ye slew between the sanctuary and the altar. Verily, I say unto you, all these things shall come upon this generation."

His terrible doctrine of the substitution of the Gentiles—the idea that the kingdom of God was about to be passed over to others, because those for whom it was destined would not receive it, used to recur as a fearful menace against the aristocracy. The title "Son of God," which he openly assumed in vivid parables, wherein his enemies were depicted as murderers of the heavenly messengers, was an open defiance to the Judaism of the Law. The bold appeal he addressed to the poor was yet more seditious. He declared that he had come, "that they which see not may see, and that they which see may become blind." One day, his dislike of the Temple evoked an imprudent speech from him: "I will destroy this Temple that is made with hands, and in three days I will build another made without hands." We do not know what meaning Jesus attached to this saying, in which his disciples sought for strained allegories; but, as only a pretext was wanted, it was quickly fastened upon. It reappeared in the preamble of his death warrant, and rang in his ears amid the last agonies of Golgotha. These irritating discussions always ended in tumult. The Pharisees cast stones at him; in doing which they only fulfilled an article in the Law, which commanded that every prophet, even a thaumaturgist, who should turn the people from the ancient worship, was to be stoned without a hearing. At other times they called him mad, possessed, a Samaritan, and even sought to slay him. His words were noted in order to draw down upon him the laws of an intolerant theocracy, which had not yet been abrogated by the Roman power.

MOTHER COUNTRY.[1]

By CHRISTINA G. ROSSETTI.

[1830–1894.]

Oh what is that country
  And where can it be,
Not mine own country,
  But dearer far to me?
Yet mine own country,
  If I one day may see
Its spices and cedars,
  Its gold and ivory.

As I lie dreaming
  It rises, that land;
There rises before me
  Its green golden strand,
With the bowing cedars
  And the shining sand;
It sparkles and flashes
  Like a shaken brand.

Do angels lean nearer
  While I lie and long?
I see their soft plumage
  And catch their windy song,
Like the rise of a high tide
  Sweeping full and strong;
I mark the outskirts
  Of their reverend throng.

Oh what is a king here,
  Or what is a boor?
Here all starve together,
  All dwarfed and poor;

[1] By permission of the Publishers, Macmillan & Co., Ltd.

Here Death's hand knocketh
  At door after door,
He thins the dancers
  From the festal floor.

Oh what is a handmaid,
  Or what is a queen?
All must lie down together
  Where the turf is green,
The foulest face hidden,
  The fairest not seen;
Gone as if never
  They had breathed or been.

Gone from sweet sunshine
  Underneath the sod,
Turned from warm flesh and blood
  To senseless clod;
Gone as if never
  They had toiled or trod,
Gone out of sight of all
  Except our God.

Shut into silence
  From the accustomed song,
Shut into solitude
  From all earth's throng,
Run down though swift of foot,
  Thrust down though strong;
Life made an end of,
  Seemed it short or long.

Life made an end of,
  Life but just begun;
Life finished yesterday,
  Its last sand run;
Life new born with the morrow,
  Fresh as the sun:
While done is done forever;
  Undone, undone.

And if that life is life,
  This is but a breath,
The passage of a dream
  And the shadow of death;

But a vain shadow
  If one considereth;
Vanity of vanities,
  As the Preacher saith.

THE HEART.[1]

By JEAN MACÉ.

(From "The History of a Mouthful of Bread.")

[JEAN MACÉ: A French writer; born in Paris in 1815. His parents were poor, but gave the boy an unusually good education for one of his class. He took a course in the Collège Stanislaus; became instructor in history there in 1836; served three years in the French army; sympathized with the revolutionists in 1848, and was banished at the restoration of the Empire. During his exile he taught at a private school for girls at Beblenheim, in Alsace, and used his leisure time in writing stories for the young. On his return to Paris, after ten years' absence, he established the popular *Magazine d'Éducation et de Récréation*, and later organized a League of Instruction. His best-known work is "Home Fairy Tales" (1862). Among the others are: "History of a Mouthful of Bread" (1861), "Servants of the Stomach" (1866), and "France before the Franks" (1881).]

THERE was once upon a time a banker, a millionaire, who could reckon his wealth not by millions only, but by hundreds of millions and more; who was, in fact, so tremendously rich that he did not know what to do with his money — a difficulty in which nobody had ever been before.

This man took it into his head to build a palace infinitely superior to anything that had hitherto been seen. Marbles, carpets, gildings, silk hangings, pictures, and statues — in fact, the whole mass of commonplace luxuries as one sees them even in the grandest royal abodes, fell short of his magnificent pretensions. He was an intelligent man, and thoroughly understood the respect due to his riches; and the common fate of kings seemed to him far too shabby for the entertainment of his dynasty, which he looked upon as very superior to all the families of crowned heads in the world. In consequence he sent to the four quarters of the globe for the most illustrious professors, the most skillful engineers, the cleverest and most ingenious workmen in every department, and giving them

[1] By permission of Geo. Bell & Sons.

unlimited permission as to expenditure, ordered them to adorn his palace with all the wonders of science and human industry.

Science, and human industry, and unlimited means — what will they not accomplish? No wonder that nothing was talked of for a hundred miles around but the magic building — of which, by the way, I do not venture to give you a description, because it would carry me too far away. Let it suffice to say that never Emperor of China, Caliph of Bagdad, or Great Mogul had such a habitation as our banker, and for a very good reason — he was twenty times as rich as any such gentry as I have named ever were in their lives.

When all was finished, one trifling flaw was discovered: the place was not supplied with water. A spring seeker, who was summoned to the premises, could only discover a small subterranean watercourse, a sort of zigzag pipe, formed by nature, between two beds of clay, in which the rain of the neighborhood collected as in a sort of reservoir. The water was neither very clear nor very plentiful, as you may imagine; and the professor appointed to examine it, having begun by tasting it, made a horrible face, and declared there was no use in proceeding any further, for it had a stagnant flavor which would not be agreeable to my lord.

To the amazement of everybody, my lord jumped for joy when he heard this unpleasant news. It was proposed to him to fetch water from a river which flowed a few miles' distance off; but he would hear of nothing of the sort. What he wanted was something new, unexpected, impossible — that was his object throughout. He took a pen and drew up at a sitting the following programme, which caused our poor professors to open their eyes in dismay: —

First. We will use the water on the premises.

Second. It shall flow night, day, and in all parts of the palace at once.

Third. There shall be plenty of it, and it shall be good.

The professors looked at each other for some time without speaking, and the gravest of them, whose fortunes and characters had been long ago established, suggested that they should simply give my lord and his money the slip, and so teach him to make fools of people another time!

But the youngsters, less easily discouraged, cried out against this with one accord. They declared that the honor of science was at stake, and that they ought to return impudence for impudence, by executing to the letter the impertinent programme! At length, after much discussion and many propositions made against all hope, and thrown aside one after the other as impracticable, a sudden inspiration crossed the brain of an engineer who had not yet spoken; and the following is what he proposed: —

What prevented the water from being sweet and fit to drink was the want of movement and air. What had to be done, therefore, was to erect a pump, but a pump provided with numberless small pipes, extending to the watercourse in all directions, and so arranged that by means of them it should be able to draw up the water from all the corners and windings where it lay stagnating, and then forcing it forward into a pipe terminating in a rose, like that of a watering pot, whence it should gush out to fall down in fine rain, into a reservoir in the open air. From thence another action of the pump was to bring it back well aërated, to send it once more into a large pipe with numerous lesser ramifications, which should convey it into every corner of the palace.

Up to this point all seemed practicable, but the hardest part had not yet come. The great difficulty was how to supply this enormous consumption with so slender a runnel of water as the one at their disposal. But our engineer had provided for this by a stroke of genius.

Under each of the taps (always kept open), which were dispersed all over the palace, he would place a small cistern, from the bottom of which should go a pipe communicating with the body of the force pump which drew up the water from the original watercourse. By which means the water which ran from the taps would be taken up again and go back to feed the reservoir in the open air; whence it would again return to supply the taps; and so on and on, the same water continually keeping the game alive, as people call it. Have you not sometimes seen at a circus or theater a large army represented by a hundred supernumeraries, who file in close columns before the audience, going out at one side of the stage and coming in at the other, following close at each other's heels indefinitely? By a similar artifice the engineer would change his meager little runnel into an inexhaustible fountain. The water drawn up from the watercourse by each stroke of the pump would fully compensate for what was used in its passage through the palace by the inhabitants. Lastly, as it might sometimes happen that the said inhabitants washed their hands under the taps, the water on its return to the cisterns was to pass through a series of small filters, in order to cleanse it from any impurity it might have contracted by the way. Always flowing, always limpid, it would soon lose every trace of its original source, and might defy comparison with the water of any river in the world!

A unanimous buzz of congratulations welcomed this plan, at once so simple and so bold, and our professors thought their troubles were over; but they were not at the end of their difficulties yet. When it came to the actual erection of the machine (naturally a most complicated one, as it had to set going a quintuple system of pipes — pipes from the watercourse to the pump, pipes from the pump to the reservoir, pipes from the reservoir to the pump, from the pump to the taps, and from the taps to the pump again), — our banker, who had got amused and excited as they went on, conducted them to a small dark closet, only a few square feet in size, concealed in a corner of the large apartments, and informed them with a laugh that he had no other place to offer them. Besides which, he made them understand that on account of its situation, there could be no question of furnaces or boilers being set up there (he detested equally coal smoke, fires, and explosions) — nor of workmen employed about the machine (it would not be decent to have them going up and down the front staircase) — nor above all, of the frightful brake wheels always screeching and grinding, the unwieldy pistons rising and falling with a noise sufficient to give one the headache. He himself slept near the little dark closet, and the slightest noise was fatal to his repose. Having explained all this, the rich man curtly made his bow and retired.

For once our professors owned themselves beaten. They had come forward quite proud of their invention, and now they were received, not with ecstasies of delight, but with fresh demands, more ridiculous even than the first. They were decidedly being mystified, and were preparing in consequence to pack up and be gone, furious, and swearing by all their gods that they would never again expose science to see itself disgraced by a purse-proud vulgarian's scorn; when, lo! happily, a good fairy, the special friend of learned men, came passing by that way. She raised her enchanted wand with the tip of her finger, and all at once a little girl dressed in rags appeared in the midst of our astonished professors. Without giving them time to recover themselves, the child put her hand into the little patched waist of her dress, and drew forth a rounded object, about the size of her closed fist, from which hung a quantity of tubes spreading in all directions.

"See!" cried she; "here is the machine your banker demands of you."

Picture to yourself a small closed bag, narrowing to a point at the end, and separated within into two very distinct compartments by a fleshy partition which went across the inside from the top to the bottom. Such was the object held up by the little girl. From each of these compartments issued a thick tube, ramifying into endless smaller ones; and they were moreover each surmounted by a sort of pouch, into which ran another tube, of the same description as the first. Each of these four portions (the two compartments and their pouches) was in constant but independent motion, distending and contracting alternately; and by carefully examining the noiseless play of this singular machine (the walls of which were, by the magic power of the fairy, rendered transparent to the bystanders), the learned assembly were very soon enabled to convince themselves that it fulfilled all the monstrous conditions exacted of them by the fantastic millionaire.

All was in movement together, I told you; but let us begin at one end. The right-hand compartment and its pouch represented the first pump—the pump employed to draw, by the same stroke, the water from the stagnant channel, and that from the taps. It was perfectly easy to distinguish the two systems of pipes, and how they united together at the small pouch on their arrival. When this was distended, a vacuum was created inside, which was instantly filled by the liquid from the tube which ran into it (do not ask me why or how; I will explain that presently). When it contracted again, the liquid which had just entered was not able to get back, being prevented from so doing by a very ingenious and simple contrivance, which requires a brief explanation.

Take off the lock from your chamber door, which opens inside; then, standing outside, push against it with your shoulder, and you will get in without any difficulty. But when you are in, try to push the door open again with your shoulder in order to get outside into the passage, and you will find that you will not be able to pass through, and this simply because it does not open on that side.

Which was exactly what happened to the liquid in the pouch!

The door between the tube and the pouch only opened inwardly, and the liquid, finding itself pressed on all sides in proportion as the pouch contracted more and more, and unable to return, was obliged at last to make its way through another similar door which led to the large compartment below. Here the same game recommenced. The compartment which had distended itself to receive it contracted in its turn, and the liquid, finding the road again barred behind it, had no choice but to force its way through the tube which led to the air reservoir.

Here commenced the work of the second pump, — the pump of the left compartment. The little pouch, when distended, was filled by the liquid from the reservoir, and then forced it forward into the large compartment below, always by means of the same process. This compartment again drove it, by a powerful contraction, into the large conducting tube charged with the office of its general distribution throughout the body. At the end of all which, it returned once more into the right-hand pump as before, to pursue the same course again, etc.

Thus, as you see, the whole mechanism turned upon two little points of detail, of the simplest description possible; namely, first, on the entrance doors only opening on one side; and secondly, on the elastic covers of the pouches and compartments distending and contracting spontaneously. It was the prettiest thing in the world to see this unpretending-looking little bag working thus, quite naturally, without a suspicion that it was solving a problem which so many men, proud of their science, had given up as hopeless. Certainly here was a machine which made no noise! Once installed in its dark closet, it would have been necessary to place your hand upon it to find out that it moved at all. My lord could certainly sleep beside it without disturbance.

"How much do you want for it?" said they to the poor little beggar girl. "Name your price; have no fear; we will pay you anything you wish."

"I cannot give it to you," replied the child; "I need it too much myself: IT IS MY HEART. Now that you have seen it, make another like it, if you can." And she disappeared.

It is said that the engineer, who longed to see his idea carried out, tried hard to construct a similar machine with gutta-percha and iron wires, and to set it in motion by electricity. But history does not tell us that he succeeded, and we have yet to ask ourselves whether the richest man in the world, aided by the wisest men in the world, could ever provide himself with a miracle of wonder, such as the ragged child had received as a free gift from the hands of a gracious Creator.

THE INVESTIGATION OF LIFE.[1]

BY T. H. HUXLEY.

(From "The Physical Basis of Life.").

[THOMAS HENRY HUXLEY, famous English biologist, was born at Ealing May 24, 1825, and was educated at Ealing School (of which his father was one of the masters) and at Charing Cross Hospital. He served as assistant surgeon on H.M.S. "Victory" and "Rattlesnake," and during the cruise of the latter vessel in Australian waters made important observations on oceanic hydrozoa. Returning to England, he was made professor of natural history in the Royal School of Mines, and of physiology at the Royal Institution. He has also held other professorships; was lord rector of Aberdeen University (1872), Rede lecturer at Cambridge, president of the Royal Society, etc. He greatly interested himself in educational questions, and with Darwin, Tyndall, and Herbert Spencer brought about the general acceptance of the doctrine of evolution. His publications include: "Man's Place in Nature," "Lay Sermons," "Science and Culture," "Essays on Controverted Questions," and "Evolution and Ethics." He died at Eastbourne, June 29, 1895.]

WHAT is the ultimate fate, and what the origin, of the matter of life?

Is it, as some of the older naturalists supposed, diffused throughout the universe in molecules, which are indestructible and unchangeable in themselves, but, in endless transmigration, unite in innumerable permutations, into the diversified forms of life we know? Or, is the matter of life composed of ordinary matter, differing from it only in the manner in which its atoms are aggregated? Is it built up of ordinary matter, and again resolved into ordinary matter when its work is done?

Modern science does not hesitate a moment between these alternatives. Physiology writes over the portals of life —

Debemur morti nos nostraque [We and ours must die],

[1] By permission of the Publishers, Macmillan & Co., Ltd.

with a profounder meaning than the Roman poet attached to that melancholy line. Under whatever disguise it takes refuge, whether fungus or oak, worm or man, the living protoplasm not only ultimately dies and is resolved into its mineral and lifeless constituents, but is always dying, and, strange as the paradox may sound, could not live unless it died.

In the wonderful story of the "Peau de Chagrin," the hero becomes possessed of a magical wild ass' skin, which yields him the means of gratifying all his wishes. But its surface represents the duration of the proprietor's life; and for every satisfied desire the skin shrinks in proportion to the intensity of fruition, until at length life and the last handbreadth of the *peau de chagrin* disappear with the gratification of a last wish.

Balzac's studies had led him over a wide range of thought and speculation, and his shadowing forth of physiological truth in this strange story may have been intentional. At any rate, the matter of life is a veritable *peau de chagrin*, and for every vital act it is somewhat the smaller. All work implies waste, and the work of life results, directly or indirectly, in the waste of protoplasm.

Every word uttered by a speaker costs him some physical loss; and, in the strictest sense, he burns that others may have light — so much eloquence, so much of his body resolved into carbonic acid, water, and urea. It is clear that this process of expenditure cannot go on forever. But, happily, the protoplasmic *peau de chagrin* differs from Balzac's in its capacity of being repaired, and brought back to its full size, after every exertion.

For example, this present lecture, whatever its intellectual worth to you, has a certain physical value to me, which is, conceivably, expressible by the number of grains of protoplasm and other bodily substance wasted in maintaining my vital processes during its delivery. My *peau de chagrin* will be distinctly smaller at the end of the discourse than it was at the beginning. By and by, I shall probably have recourse to the substance commonly called mutton, for the purpose of stretching it back to its original size. Now this mutton was once the living protoplasm, more or less modified, of another animal — a sheep. As I shall eat it, it is the same matter altered, not only by death, but by exposure to sundry artificial operations in the process of cooking.

But these changes, whatever be their extent, have not ren-

THOMAS HENRY HUXLEY

dered it incompetent to resume its old functions as matter of life. A singular inward laboratory, which I possess, will dissolve a certain portion of the modified protoplasm; the solution so formed will pass into my veins; and the subtle influences to which it will then be subjected will convert the dead protoplasm into living protoplasm, and transubstantiate sheep into man.

Nor is this all. If digestion were a thing to be trifled with, I might sup upon lobster, and the matter of life of the crustacean would undergo the same wonderful metamorphosis into humanity. And were I to return to my own place by sea, and undergo shipwreck, the crustacea might, and probably would, return the compliment, and demonstrate our common nature by turning my protoplasm into living lobster. Or, if nothing better were to be had, I might supply my wants with mere bread, and I should find the protoplasm of the wheat plant to be convertible into man, with no more trouble than that of the sheep, and with far less, I fancy, than that of the lobster.

Hence it appears to be a matter of no great moment what animal, or what plant, I lay under contribution for protoplasm, and the fact speaks volumes for the general identity of that substance in all living beings. I share this catholicity of assimilation with other animals, all of which, so far as we know, could thrive equally well on the protoplasm of any of their fellows, or of any plant; but here the assimilative powers of the animal world cease. A solution of smelling salts in water, with an infinitesimal proportion of some other saline matters, contains all the elementary bodies which enter into the composition of protoplasm; but, as I need hardly say, a hogshead of that fluid would not keep a hungry man from starving, nor would it save any animal whatever from a like fate. An animal cannot make protoplasm, but must take it ready made from some other animal, or some plant — the animal's highest feat of constructive chemistry being to convert dead protoplasm into that living matter of life which is appropriate to itself.

Therefore, in seeking for the origin of protoplasm, we must eventually turn to the vegetable world. The fluid containing carbonic acid, water, and ammonia, which offers such a Barmecide feast to the animal, is a table richly spread to multitudes of plants; and, with a due supply of only such materials, many a plant will not only maintain itself in vigor, but grow and multiply until it has increased a million-fold, or a million

million-fold, the quantity of protoplasm which it originally possessed — in this way building up the matter of life, to an indefinite extent, from the common matter of the universe.

Thus the animal can only raise the complex substance of dead protoplasm to the higher power, as one may say, of living protoplasm; while the plant can raise the less complex substances — carbonic acid, water, and ammonia — to the same stage of living protoplasm, if not to the same level. But the plant also has its limitations. Some of the fungi, for example, appear to need higher compounds to start with; and no known plant can live upon the uncompounded elements of protoplasm. A plant supplied with pure carbon, hydrogen, oxygen, and nitrogen, phosphorus, sulphur, and the like, would as infallibly die as the animal in his bath of smelling salts, though it would be surrounded by all the constituents of protoplasm. Nor, indeed, need the process of simplification of vegetable food be carried so far as this, in order to arrive at the limit of the plant's thaumaturgy. Let water, carbonic acid, and all the other needful constituents be supplied with ammonia, and an ordinary plant will still be unable to manufacture protoplasm.

Thus the matter of life, so far as we know it (and we have no right to speculate on any other), breaks up, in consequence of that continual death which is the condition of its manifesting vitality, into carbonic acid, water, and ammonia, which certainly possess no properties but those of ordinary matter. And out of these same forms of ordinary matter, and from none which are simpler, the vegetable world builds up all the protoplasm which keeps the animal world a going. Plants are the accumulators of the power which animals distribute and disperse.

But it will be observed that the existence of the matter of life depends on the preëxistence of certain compounds; namely, carbonic acid, water, and ammonia. Withdraw any one of these three from the world, and all vital phenomena come to an end. They are related to the protoplasm of the plant, as the protoplasm of the plant is to that of the animal. Carbon, hydrogen, oxygen, and nitrogen are all lifeless bodies. Of these, carbon and oxygen unite, in certain proportions and under certain conditions, to give rise to carbonic acid; hydrogen and oxygen produce water; nitrogen and hydrogen give rise to ammonia. These new compounds, like the elementary bodies of which they are composed, are lifeless. But when they are brought together, under certain conditions they give rise to the still more complex body, protoplasm, and this protoplasm exhibits the phenomena of life.

I see no break in this series of steps in molecular complication, and I am unable to understand why the language which is applicable to any one term of the series may not be used to any of the others. We think fit to call different kinds of matter carbon, oxygen, hydrogen, and nitrogen, and to speak of the various powers and activities of these substances as the properties of the matter of which they are composed.

When hydrogen and oxygen are mixed in a certain proportion, and an electric spark is passed through them, they disappear, and a quantity of water, equal in weight to the sum of their weights, appears in their place. There is not the slightest parity between the passive and active powers of the waters and those of the oxygen and hydrogen which have given rise to it. At 32° Fahrenheit, and far below that temperature, oxygen and hydrogen are elastic gaseous bodies, whose particles tend to rush away from one another with great force. Water, at the same temperature, is a strong though brittle solid, whose particles tend to cohere into definite geometrical shapes, and sometimes build up frosty imitations of the most complex forms of vegetable foliage.

Nevertheless we call these, and many other strange phenomena, the properties of the water, and we do not hesitate to believe that, in some way or another, they result from the properties of the component elements of the water. We do not assume that a something called "aquosity" entered into and took possession of the oxide of hydrogen as soon as it was formed, and then guided the aqueous particles to their places in the facets of the crystal, or amongst the leaflets of the hoarfrost. On the contrary, we live in the hope and in the faith that, by the advance of molecular physics, we shall by and by be able to see our way as clearly from the constituents of water to the properties of water, as we are now able to deduce the operations of a watch from the form of its parts and the manner in which they are put together.

Is the case in any way changed when carbonic acid, water, and ammonia disappear, and in their place, under the influence of preëxisting living protoplasm, an equivalent weight of the matter of life makes its appearance?

It is true that there is no sort of parity between the properties of the components and the properties of th. resultant, but neither was there in the case of the water. It is also true that what I have spoken of as the influence of preëxisting living matter is something quite unintelligible; but does anybody quite comprehend the *modus operandi* of an electric spark, which traverses a mixture of oxygen and hydrogen?

What justification is there, then, for the assumption of the existence in the living matter of a something which has no representative, or correlative, in the not living matter which gave rise to it? What better philosophical status has "vitality" than "aquosity"? And why should "vitality" hope for a better fate than the other "itys" which have disappeared since Martinus Scriblerus accounted for the operation of the meat jack by its inherent "meat-roasting quality," and scorned the "materialism" of those who explained the turning of the spit by a certain mechanism worked by the draught of the chimney?

If scientific language is to possess a definite and constant signification whenever it is employed, it seems to me that we are logically bound to apply to the protoplasm, or physical basis of life, the same conceptions as those which are held to be legitimate elsewhere. If the phenomena exhibited by water are its properties, so are those presented by protoplasm, living or dead, its properties.

If the properties of water may be properly said to result from the nature and disposition of its component molecules, I can find no intelligible ground for refusing to say that the properties of protoplasm result from the nature and disposition of its molecules.

But I bid you beware that, in accepting these conclusions, you are placing your feet on the first rung of a ladder which, in most people's estimation, is the reverse of Jacob's, and leads to the antipodes of heaven. It may seem a small thing to admit that the dull vital actions of a fungus, or a foraminifer, are the properties of their protoplasm, and are the direct results of the nature of the matter of which they are composed. But if, as I have endeavored to prove to you, their protoplasm is essentially identical with, and most readily converted into, that of any animal, I can discover no logical halting place between the admission that such is the case, and the further concession that all vital action may, with equal propriety, be said to be the result of the molecular forces of the protoplasm which displays it. And if so, it must be true, in the same sense and to the same extent, that the thoughts to which I am now giving utterance, and your thoughts regarding them, are the expression of molecular changes in that matter of life which is the source of our other vital phenomena.

Past experience leads me to be tolerably certain that, when the propositions I have just placed before you are accessible to public comment and criticism, they will be condemned by many zealous persons, and perhaps by some few of the wise and thoughtful. I should not wonder if "gross and brutal materialism" were the mildest phrase applied to them in certain quarters. And, most undoubtedly, the terms of the propositions are distinctly materialistic. Nevertheless two things are certain: the one, that I hold the statements to be substantially true; the other, that I, individually, am no materialist, but, on the contrary, believe materialism to involve grave philosophical error.

This union of materialistic terminology with the repudiation of materialistic philosophy I share with some of the most thoughtful men with whom I am acquainted. And, when I first undertook to deliver the present discourse, it appeared to me to be a fitting opportunity to explain how such a union is not only consistent with, but necessitated by, sound logic. I purposed to lead you through the territory of vital phenomena to the materialistic slough in which you find yourselves now plunged, and then to point out to you the sole path by which, in my judgment, extrication is possible.

An occurrence of which I was unaware until my arrival here last night renders this line of argument singularly opportune. I found in your papers the eloquent address "On the Limits of Philosophical Inquiry," which a distinguished prelate of the English Church delivered before the members of the Philosophical Institution on the previous day. My argument, also, turns upon this very point of the limits of philosophical inquiry; and I cannot bring out my own views better than by contrasting them with those so plainly and, in the main, fairly stated by the Archbishop of York.

But I may be permitted to make a preliminary comment upon an occurrence that greatly astonished me. Applying the name of the "New Philosophy" to that estimate of the limits of philosophical inquiry which I, in common with many other men of science, hold to be just, the Archbishop opens his address by identifying this "New Philosophy" with the Positive Philosophy of M. Comte (of whom he speaks as its "founder"), and then proceeds to attack that philosopher and his doctrines vigorously.

Now, so far as I am concerned, the most reverend prelate might dialectically hew M. Comte in pieces, as a modern Agag, and I should not attempt to stay his hand. In so far as my study of what specially characterizes the Positive Philosophy has led me, I find therein little or nothing of any scientific value, and a great deal which is as thoroughly antagonistic to the very essence of science as anything in ultramontane Catholicism. In fact, M. Comte's philosophy in practice might be compendiously described as Catholicism *minus* Christianity.

But what has Comtism to do with the "New Philosophy," as the Archbishop defines it in the following passage?

> Let me briefly remind you of the leading principles of this new philosophy.
>
> All knowledge is experience of facts acquired by the senses. The traditions of older philosophies have obscured our experience by mixing with it much that the senses cannot observe, and until these additions are discarded our knowledge is impure. Thus metaphysics tell us that one fact which we observe is a cause, and another is the effect of that cause; but, upon a rigid analysis, we find that our senses observe nothing of cause or effect: they observe, first, that one fact succeeds another, and, after some opportunity, that this fact has never failed to follow—that for cause and effect we should substitute invariable succession. An older philosophy teaches us to define an object by distinguishing its essential from its accidental qualities: but experience knows nothing of essential and accidental; she sees only that certain marks attach to an object, and, after many observations, that some of them attach invariably, whilst others may at times be absent. . . . As all knowledge is relative, the notion of anything being necessary must be banished with other traditions.

There is much here that expresses the spirit of the "New Philosophy," if by that term be meant the spirit of modern science; but I cannot but marvel that the assembled wisdom and learning of Edinburgh should have uttered no sign of dissent, when Comte was declared to be the founder of these doctrines. No one will accuse Scotchmen of habitually forgetting their great countrymen; but it was enough to make David Hume turn in his grave, that here, almost within earshot of his house, an instructed audience should have listened, without a murmur, while his most characteristic doctrines were attributed to a French writer of fifty years' later date, in whose dreary and verbose pages we miss alike the vigor of thought and the exquisite clearness of style of the man whom I make bold to term the most acute thinker of the eighteenth century — even though that century produced Kant.

But I did not come to Scotland to vindicate the honor of one of the greatest men she has ever produced. My business is to point out to you that the only way of escape out of the crass materialism in which we just now landed is the adoption and strict working-out of the very principles which the Archbishop holds up to reprobation.

Let us suppose that knowledge is absolute, and not relative, and therefore that our conception of matter represents that which it really is. Let us suppose, further, that we do know more of cause and effect than a certain definite order of succession among facts, and that we have a knowledge of the necessity of that succession — and hence, of necessary laws — and I, for my part, do not see what escape there is from utter materialism and necessarianism. For it is obvious that our knowledge of what we call the material world is, to begin with, at least as certain and definite as that of the spiritual world, and that our acquaintance with law is of as old a date as our knowledge of spontaneity. Further, I take it to be demonstrable that it is utterly impossible to prove that anything whatever may not be the effect of material and necessary cause, and that human logic is equally incompetent to prove that any act is really spontaneous. A really spontaneous act is one which, by the assumption, has no cause; and the attempt to prove such a negative as this is, on the face of the matter, absurd. And while it is thus a philosophical impossibility to demonstrate that any given phenomenon is not the effect of a material cause, any one who is acquainted with the history of science will admit that its progress has, in all ages, meant, and now, more than ever, means, the extension of the province of what we call matter and causation, and the concomitant gradual banishment from all regions of human thought of what we call spirit and spontaneity.

I have endeavored, in the first part of this discourse, to give you a conception of the direction towards which modern physiology is tending; and I ask you, what is the difference between the conception of life as the product of a certain disposition of material molecules, and the old notion of an Archæus governing and directing blind matter within each living body, except this — that here, as elsewhere, matter and law have devoured spirit and spontaneity? And as surely as every future grows out of past and present, so will the physiology of the future gradually extend the realm of matter and law until it is coextensive with knowledge, with feeling, and with action.

The consciousness of this great truth weighs like a nightmare, I believe, upon many of the best minds of these days. They watch what they conceive to be the progress of materialism, in such fear and powerless anger as a savage feels, when, during an eclipse, the great shadow creeps over the face of the sun. The advancing tide of matter threatens to drown their souls; the tightening grasp of law impedes their freedom; they are alarmed lest man's moral nature be debased by the increase of his wisdom.

If the "New Philosophy" be worthy of the reprobation with which it is visited, I confess their fears seem to me to be well founded. While, on the contrary, could David Hume be consulted, I think he would smile at their perplexities, and chide them for doing even as the heathen, and falling down in terror before the hideous idols their own hands have raised.

For, after all, what do we know of this terrible "matter," except as a name for the unknown and hypothetical cause of states of our own consciousness? And what do we know of that "spirit" over whose threatened extinction by matter a great lamentation is arising, like that which was heard at the death of Pan, except that it is also a name for an unknown and hypothetical cause, or condition, of states of consciousness? In other words, matter and spirit are but names for the imaginary substrata of groups of natural phenomena.

And what is the dire necessity and "iron" law under which men groan? Truly, most gratuitously invented bugbears. I suppose if there be an "iron" law, it is that of gravitation; and if there be a physical necessity, it is that a stone, unsupported, must fall to the ground. But what is all we really know, and can know, about the latter phenomenon? Simply that, in all human experience, stones have fallen to the ground under these conditions; that we have not the smallest reason for believing that any stone so circumstanced will not fall to the ground; and that we have, on the contrary, every reason to believe that it will so fall. It is very convenient to indicate that all the conditions of belief have been fulfilled in this case, by calling the statement that unsupported stones will fall to the ground "a law of nature." But when, as commonly happens, we change *will* into *must*, we introduce an idea of necessity which most assuredly does not lie in the observed facts, and has no warranty that I can discover elsewhere. For my part, I utterly repudiate and anathematize the intruder. Fact I know; and Law I know; but what is this Necessity, save an empty shadow of my own mind's throwing?

But, if it is certain that we can have no knowledge of the nature of either matter or spirit, and that the notion of necessity is something illegitimately thrust into the perfectly legitimate conception of law, the materialistic position that there is nothing in the world but matter, force, and necessity is as utterly devoid of justification as the most baseless of theological dogmas. The fundamental doctrines of materialism, like those of spiritualism, and most other "isms," lie outside "the limits of philosophical inquiry," and David Hume's great service to humanity is his irrefragable demonstration of what these limits are. Hume called himself a skeptic, and therefore others cannot be blamed if they apply the same title to him; but that does not alter the fact that the name, with its existing implications, does him gross injustice.

If a man asks me what the politics of the inhabitants of the moon are, and I reply that I do not know; that neither I, nor any one else, have any means of knowing; and that, under these circumstances, I decline to trouble myself about the subject at all, I do not think he has any right to call me a skeptic. On the contrary, in replying thus, I conceive that I am simply honest and truthful, and show a proper regard for the economy of time. So Hume's strong and subtle intellect takes up a great many problems about which we are naturally curious, and shows us that they are essentially questions of lunar politics, in their essence incapable of being answered, and therefore not worth the attention of men who have work to do in the world. And he thus ends one of his essays:—

> If we take in hand any volume of Divinity, or school metaphysics, for instance, let us ask, *Does it contain any abstract reasoning concerning quantity or number?* No. *Does it contain any experimental reasoning concerning matter of fact and existence?* No. Commit it then to the flames; for it can contain nothing but sophistry and illusion.

Permit me to enforce this most wise advice. Why trouble ourselves about matters of which, however important they may be, we do know nothing, and can know nothing? We live in a world which is full of misery and ignorance, and the plain duty of each and all of us is to try to make the little corner he can influence somewhat less miserable and somewhat less ignorant than it was before he entered it. To do this effectually it is necessary to be fully possessed of only two beliefs: the first, that the order of nature is ascertainable by our faculties to an extent which is practically unlimited; the second, that our volition counts for something as a condition of the course of events.

Each of these beliefs can be verified experimentally, as often as we like to try. Each, therefore, stands upon the strongest foundation upon which any belief can rest, and forms one of our highest truths. If we find that the ascertainment of the order of nature is facilitated by using one terminology, or one set of symbols, rather than another, it is our clear duty to use the former; and no harm can accrue, so long as we bear in mind that we are dealing merely with terms and symbols.

In itself it is of little moment whether we express the phenomena of matter in terms of spirit; or the phenomena of spirit, in terms of matter: matter may be regarded as a form of thought, thought may be regarded as a property of matter—each statement has a certain relative truth. But with a view to the progress of science, the materialistic terminology is in every way to be preferred. For it connects thought with the other phenomena of the universe, and suggests inquiry into the nature of those physical conditions, or concomitants of thought, which are more or less accessible to us, and a knowledge of which may, in future, help us to exercise the same kind of control over the world of thought as we already possess in respect of the material world; whereas the alternative, or spiritualistic, terminology is utterly barren, and leads to nothing but obscurity and confusion of ideas.

Thus there can be little doubt that the further science advances, the more extensively and consistently will all the phenomena of nature be represented by materialistic formulæ and symbols.

But the man of science who, forgetting the limits of philosophical inquiry, slides from these formulæ and symbols into what is commonly understood by materialism seems to me to place himself on a level with the mathematician, who should mistake the *x*'s and *y*'s with which he works his problems for real entities — and with this further disadvantage, as compared with the mathematician, that the blunders of the latter are of no practical consequence, while the errors of systematic materialism may paralyze the energies and destroy the beauty of a life.

THE PETRIFIED FERN.

By MARY L. B. BRANCH.

[1840–.]

In a valley, centuries ago,
  Grew a little fern leaf green and slender,
  Veining delicate and fibers tender,
Waving when the wind crept down so low.
  Rushes tall, and moss, and grass grew round it;
  Playful sunbeams darted in and found it;
  Drops of dew stole down by night and crowned it;
But no foot of man e'er came that way; —
Earth was young and keeping holiday.

Monster fishes swam the silent main;
  Stately forests waved their giant branches;
  Mountains hurled their snowy avalanches;
Mammoth creatures stalked across the plain.
  Nature reveled in grand mysteries;
  But the little fern was not like these,
  Did not number with the hills and trees,
Only grew and waved its sweet, wild way;
No one came to note it day by day.

Earth, one time, put on a frolic mood,
  Heaved the rocks, and changed the mighty motion
  Of the strong, dread currents of the ocean;
Moved the hills, and shook the haughty wood;
  Crushed the little fern in soft, moist clay,
  Covered it, and hid it safe away.
  O, the long, long centuries since that day!
O, the changes! O, life's bitter cost,
Since the little useless fern was lost!

Useless? Lost? There came a thoughtful man,
  Searching Nature's secrets far and deep;
  From a fissure in a rocky steep
He withdrew a stone, o'er which there ran
  Fairy pencilings, a quaint design, —
  Leafage, veining, fibers, clear and fine —
  And the fern's life lay in every line.
So, I think, God hides some souls away,
Sweetly to surprise us the Last Day.

CHECKS TO THE INCREASE OF GENIUS.[1]

By FRANCIS GALTON.

(From "Hereditary Genius.")

[FRANCIS GALTON, anthropologist, was born at Duddeston, England, February 16, 1822. He attended King Edward's School, Birmingham, studied medicine at Birmingham Hospital and King's College, London, and was graduated an M.A. from Trinity College, Cambridge, 1844. He traveled in Africa and elsewhere, and in 1850 received the gold medal from the Geographical Society. He was general secretary of the British Association 1863–1868, president of the anthropological sections 1885–1886, and held many other honorary positions in learned societies. He invented composite photography. He was given the degree of D.C.L., 1894, and that of D.Sc., 1895. His principal works are: "Travels in South Africa" (1853), "Art of Travel" (1855), "Meteorographica" (1863), "Hereditary Genius" (1869), "English Men of Science" (1874), "Composite Portraits" (1878), "Inquiries into Human Faculty" (1889), and "Finger Points" (3 books, 1892–1893 and 1895).]

I TRUST the reader will realize the heavy doom which figures pronounce against all subsections of prolific races in which it is the custom to put off the period of marriage until middle age. It is a maxim of Malthus that the period of marriage ought to be delayed in order that the earth may not be overcrowded by a population for whom there is no place at the great table of nature. If this doctrine influenced all classes alike, I should have nothing to say about it here, one way or another, for it would hardly affect the discussions in this book; but, as it is put forward as a rule of conduct for the prudent part of mankind to follow, whilst the imprudent are necessarily left free to disregard it, I have no hesitation in saying that it is a most pernicious rule of conduct in its bearing upon race. Its

[1] By permission of the Publishers, Macmillan & Co., Ltd.

effect would be such as to cause the race of the prudent to fall, after a few centuries, into an almost incredible inferiority of numbers to that of the imprudent, and it is therefore calculated to bring utter ruin upon the breed of any country where the doctrine prevailed. I protest against the abler races being encouraged to withdraw in this way from the struggle for existence. It may seem monstrous that the weak should be crowded out by the strong, but it is still more monstrous that the races best fitted to play their part on the stage of life should be crowded out by the incompetent, the ailing, and the desponding.

The time may hereafter arrive, in far-distant years, when the population of the earth shall be kept as strictly within the bounds of number and suitability of race as the sheep on a well-ordered moor or the plants in an orchard house; in the mean time, let us do what we can to encourage the multiplication of the races best fitted to invent and conform to a high and generous civilization, and not, out of a mistaken instinct of giving support to the weak, prevent the incoming of strong and hearty individuals.

The long period of the dark ages under which Europe has lain is due, I believe, in a very considerable degree, to the celibacy enjoined by religious orders on their votaries. Whenever a man or woman was possessed of a gentle nature that fitted him or her to deeds of charity, to meditation, to literature, or to art, the social condition of the time was such that they had no refuge elsewhere than in the bosom of the Church. But the Church chose to preach and exact celibacy. The consequence was that these gentle natures had no continuance, and thus, by a policy so singularly unwise and suicidal that I am hardly able to speak of it without impatience, the Church brutalized the breed of our forefathers. She acted precisely as if she had aimed at selecting the rudest portion of the community to be, alone, the parents of future generations. She practiced the arts which breeders would use, who aimed at creating ferocious, currish, and stupid natures. No wonder that club law prevailed for centuries over Europe; the wonder rather is that enough good remained in the veins of Europeans to enable their race to rise to its present very moderate level of natural morality.

A relic of this monastic spirit clings to our Universities, who say to every man who shows intellectual powers of the kind they delight to honor, "Here is an income of from one to two hundred pounds a year, with free lodging and various advantages in the way of board and society; we give it to you on account of your ability; take it and enjoy it all your life if you like: we exact no condition to your continuing to hold it but one, namely, that you shall not marry."

The policy of the religious world in Europe was exerted in another direction, with hardly less cruel effect on the nature of future generations, by means of persecutions which brought thousands of the foremost thinkers and men of political aptitudes to the scaffold, or imprisoned them during a large part of their manhood, or drove them as emigrants into other lands. In every one of these cases the check upon their leaving issue was very considerable. Hence the Church, having first captured all the gentle natures and condemned them to celibacy, made another sweep of her huge nets, this time fishing in stirring waters, to catch those who were the most fearless, truth-seeking, and intelligent, in their modes of thought, and therefore the most suitable parents of a high civilization, and put a strong check, if not a direct stop, to their progeny. Those she reserved on these occasions, to breed the generations of the future, were the servile, the indifferent, and, again, the stupid. Thus, as she — to repeat my expression — brutalized human nature by her system of celibacy applied to the gentle, she demoralized it by her system of persecution of the intelligent, the sincere, and the free. It is enough to make the blood boil to think of the blind folly that has caused the foremost nations of struggling humanity to be the heirs of such hateful ancestry, and that has so bred our instincts as to keep them in an unnecessarily long-continued antagonism with the essential requirements of a steadily advancing civilization. In consequence of this inbred imperfection of our natures, in respect to the conditions under which we have to live, we are, even now, almost as much harassed by the sense of moral incapacity and sin, as were the early converts from barbarism; and we steep ourselves in half-unconscious self-deception and hypocrisy, as a partial refuge from its insistence. Our avowed creeds remain at variance with our real rules of conduct, and we lead a dual life of barren religious sentimentalism and gross materialistic habitudes.

The extent to which persecution must have affected European races is easily measured by a few well-known statistical facts. Thus, as regards martyrdom and imprisonment, the

Spanish nation was drained of free thinkers at the rate of 1000 persons annually, for the three centuries between 1471 and 1781,—an average of 100 persons having been executed and 900 imprisoned every year during that period. The actual data during those three hundred years are 32,000 burnt, 17,000 persons burnt in effigy (I presume they mostly died in prison or escaped from Spain), and 291,000 condemned to various terms of imprisonment and other penalties. It is impossible that any nation could stand a policy like this, without paying a heavy penalty in the deterioration of its breed, as has notably been the result in the formation of the superstitious, unintelligent Spanish race of the present day.

Italy was also frightfully persecuted at an earlier date. In the diocese of Como, alone, more than 1000 were tried annually by the inquisitors for many years, and 300 were burnt in the single year 1416.

The French persecutions, by which the English have been large gainers, through receiving their industrial refugees, were on a nearly similar scale. In the seventeenth century three or four hundred thousand Protestants perished in prison, at the galleys, in their attempts to escape, or on the scaffold, and an equal number emigrated. Mr. Smiles, in his admirable book on the Huguenots, has traced the influence of these and of the Flemish emigrants on England, and shows clearly that she owes to them almost all her industrial arts and very much of the most valuable lifeblood of her modern race. There has been another emigration from France of not unequal magnitude, but followed by very different results, namely that of the Revolution in 1789. It is most instructive to contrast the effects of the two. The Protestant emigrants were able men, and have profoundly influenced for good both our breed and our history; on the other hand, the political refugees had but poor average stamina, and have left scarcely any traces behind them.

It is very remarkable how large a proportion of the eminent men of all countries bear foreign names, and are the children of political refugees,—men well qualified to introduce a valuable strain of blood. We cannot fail to reflect on the glorious destiny of a country that should maintain, during many generations, the policy of attracting eminently desirable refugees, but no others, and of encouraging their settlement and the naturalization of their children.

No nation has parted with more emigrants than England, but whether she has hitherto been on the whole a gainer or a loser by the practice, I am not sure. No doubt she has lost a very large number of families of sterling worth, especially of laborers and artisans; but, as a rule, the very ablest men are strongly disinclined to emigrate; they feel that their fortune is assured at home, and unless their spirit of adventure is overwhelmingly strong, they prefer to live in the high intellectual and moral atmosphere of the more intelligent circles of English society, to a self-banishment among people of altogether lower grades of mind and interests. England has certainly got rid of a great deal of refuse through means of emigration. She has found an outlet for men of adventurous and Bohemian natures, who are excellently adapted for colonizing a new country, but are not wanted in old civilizations; and she has also been disembarrassed of a vast number of turbulent radicals and the like, men who are decidedly able but by no means eminent, and whose zeal, self-confidence, and irreverence far outbalance their other qualities.

The rapid rise of new colonies and the decay of old civilizations is, I believe, mainly due to their respective social agencies, which in the one case promote, and in the other case retard, the marriages of the most suitable breeds. In a young colony, a strong arm and an enterprising brain are the most appropriate fortune for a marrying man, and again, as the women are few, the inferior males are seldom likely to marry. In an old civilization, the agencies are more complex. Among the active, ambitious classes, none but the inheritors of fortune are likely to marry young; there is especially a run against men of classes C, D, and E, — those, I mean, whose future fortune is not assured except through a good deal of self-denial and effort. It is almost impossible that they should succeed well and rise high in society, if they hamper themselves with a wife in their early manhood. Men of classes F and G are more independent, but they are not nearly so numerous, and therefore their breed, though intrinsically of more worth than E or D, has much less effect on the standard of the nation at large. But even if men of classes F and G marry young, and ultimately make fortunes and achieve peerages or high social position, they become infected with the ambition current in all old civilizations, of founding families. Thence result the evils I have already described, in speaking of the marriages of eldest sons with heiresses and of the suppression of the marriages of the younger sons. Again, there is a constant tendency of the best men in the country to settle in the great cities, where marriages are less prolific and children are less likely to live. Owing to these several causes, there is a steady check in an old civilization upon the fertility of the abler classes; the improvident and unambitious are those who chiefly keep up the breed. So the race gradually deteriorates, becoming in each successive generation less fitted for a high civilization, although it retains the external appearances of one, until the time comes when the whole political and social fabric caves in and a greater or less relapse to barbarism takes place, during the reign of which the race is perhaps able to recover its tone.

The best form of civilization in respect to the improvement of the race would be one in which society was not costly; where incomes were chiefly derived from professional sources, and not much through inheritance; where every lad had a chance of showing his abilities and, if highly gifted, was enabled to achieve a first-class education and entrance into professional life, by the liberal help of the exhibitions and scholarships which he had gained in his early youth; where marriage was held in as high honor as in ancient Jewish times; where the pride of race was encouraged (of course I do not refer to the nonsensical sentiment of the present day, that goes under that name); where the weak could find a welcome and a refuge in celibate monasteries or sisterhoods, and lastly, where the better sort of emigrants and refugees from other lands were invited and welcomed, and their descendants naturalized.

THE TOMBS OF THE KINGS.[1]

BY MATHILDE BLIND.

[1847-1896.]

WHERE the mummied Kings of Egypt, wrapped in linen fold on fold,
Couched for ages in their coffins, crowned with crowns of dusky gold,

Lie in subterranean chambers, biding to the day of doom,
Counterfeit life's hollow semblance in each mazy mountain tomb,

[1] From "Birds of Passage: Songs of the Orient and Occident." By permission of Chatto & Windus. (Cr. 8vo. Price 6*s.* net.)

Grisly in their gilded coffins, mocking masks of skin and bone,
Yet remain in change unchanging, balking Nature of her own;

Mured in mighty Mausoleums, walled in from the night and day,
Lo, the mortal Kings of Egypt hold immortal Death at bay.

For — so spake the Kings of Egypt — those colossal ones whose hand
Held the peoples from Pitasa to the Kheta's conquered land;

Who, with flash and clash of lances and war chariots, stormed and won
Many a town of stiff-necked Syria to high-towering Askalon:

"We have been the faithful stewards of the deathless gods on high;
We have built them starry temples underneath the starry sky.

"We have smitten rebel nations, as a child is whipped with rods:
We the living incarnation of imperishable gods.

"Shall we suffer Death to trample us to nothingness? and must
We be scattered, as the whirlwind blows about the desert dust?

"No! Death shall not dare come near us, nor Corruption shall not lay
Hands upon our sacred bodies, incorruptible as day.

"Let us put a bit and bridle, and rein in Time's headlong course;
Let us ride him through the ages as a master rides his horse.

"On the changing earth unchanging let us bide till Time shall end,
Till, reborn in blest Osiris, mortal with Immortal blend."

Yea, so spake the Kings of Egypt, they whose lightest word was law,
At whose nod the far-off nations cowered, stricken dumb with awe.

And Fate left the haughty rulers to work out their monstrous doom;
And, embalmed with myrrh and ointments, they were carried to the
tomb;

Through the gate of Bab-el-Molouk, where the sulphur hills lie bare,
Where no green thing casts a shadow in the noon's tremendous glare;

Where the unveiled Blue of heaven in its bare intensity
Weighs upon the awe-struck spirit with the world's immensity;

Through the Vale of Desolation, where no beast or bird draws breath,
To the Coffin Hills of Tuat — the Metropolis of Death.

Down—down—down into the darkness, where, on either hand, dread fate
In the semblance of a serpent, watches by the dolorous gate;

Down—down—down into the darkness, where no gleam of sun or star
Sheds its purifying radiance from the living world afar;

Where in labyrinthine windings, darkly hidden, down and down,—
Proudly on his marble pillow, with old Egypt's double crown,

And his mien of cold commandment, grasping still his staff of state,
Rests the mightiest of the Pharaohs, whom the world surnamed the great.

Swathed in fine Sidonian linen, crossed hands folded on the breast,
There the mummied Kings of Egypt lie within each painted chest.

And upon their dusky foreheads Pleiades of flaming gems,
Glowing through the nether darkness, flash from luminous diadems.

Where is Memphis? Like a Mirage, melted into empty air:
But these royal gems yet sparkle richly on their raven hair.

Where is Thebes in all her glory, with her gates of beaten gold?
Where Syenê, or that marvel, Heliopolis of old?

Where is Edfu? Where Abydos? Where those pillared towns of yore
Whose auroral temples glittered by the Nile's thick-peopled shore?

Gone as evanescent cloudlands, Alplike in the afterglow;
But these Kings hold fast their bodies of four thousand years ago.

Sealed up in their Mausoleums, in the bowels of the hills,
There they hide from dissolution and Death's swiftly grinding mills.

Scattering fire, Uræus serpents guard the Tombs' tremendous gate;
While Troth holds the trembling balance, weighs the heart and seals its fate.

And a multitude of mummies in the swaddling clothes of death,
Ferried o'er the sullen river, on and on still hasteneth.

And around them and above them, blazoned on the rocky walls,
Crowned with stars, enlaced by serpents, in divine processionals,

Ibis-headed, jackal-featured, vulture-hooded, pass on high,
Gods on gods through Time's perspectives — pilgrims of Eternity.

There, revealed by fitful flashes, in a gloom that may be felt,
Wild Chimeras flash from darkness, glittering like Orion's belt.

And on high, o'er shining waters, in their barks the gods sail by,
In the Sunboat and the Moonboat, rowed across the rose-hued sky.

Night, that was before Creation, watches sphinxlike, starred with eyes,
And the hours and days are passing, and the years and centuries.

But these mummied Kings of Egypt, pictures of a perished race,
Lie, of busy Death forgotten, face by immemorial face.

Though the glorious sun above them, burning on the naked plain,
Clothes the empty wilderness with the golden, glowing grain;

Though the balmy Moon above them, floating in the milky Blue,
Fills the empty wilderness with a silver fall of dew;

Though life comes and flies unresting, like the shadow which a dove
Casts upon the Sphinx, in passing, for a moment from above; —

Still these mummied Kings of Egypt, wrapped in linen, fold on fold,
Bide through ages in their coffins, crowned with crowns of dusky gold.

Had the sun once brushed them lightly, or a breath of air, they must
Instantaneously have crumbled into evanescent dust.

Pale and passive in their prisons, they have conquered, chained to death;
And their lineaments look living now as when they last drew breath!

Have they conquered? Oh, the pity of those Kings within their tombs,
Locked in stony isolation in those petrifying glooms!

Motionless where all is motion in a rolling Universe,
Heaven, by answering their prayer, turned it to a deadly curse.

Left them fixed where all is fluid in a world of star-winged skies;
Where, in myriad transformations, all things pass and nothing dies;

Nothing dies but what is tethered, kept when Time would set it free,
To fulfill Thought's yearning tension upward through Eternity.

GREAT TEMPLE OF KARNAK

(OLD THEBES)

JIUJUTSU.

BY LAFCADIO HEARN.

(From "Out of the East."[1])

[LAFCADIO HEARN: An American writer; born of English and Greek parentage, at Santa Maura, Ionian Islands, June 27, 1850. He received his education in England and removed to America, engaging in journalism in Cincinnati and New Orleans. He afterward lived in New York city, and in 1890 removed to Japan. Among his works are: "Stray Leaves from Strange Literature" (1884), "Some Chinese Ghosts" (1887), "Chita: A Memory of Last Island" (1889), "Two Years in the French West Indies" (1890), "Youma" (1890), "Out of the East" (1894), "Glimpses of Unfamiliar Japan" (2 vols., 1894), "Korkovo: Hints and Echoes of Japanese Inner Life" (1896), and "Gleanings in Buddha Fields" (1897).]

"Man at his birth is supple and weak; at his death, firm and strong. So is it with all things. . . . Firmness and strength are the concomitants of death; softness and weakness, the concomitants of life. Hence he who relies on his own strength shall not conquer." — TAO-TE-KING.

THERE is one building in the grounds of the Government College quite different in structure from the other edifices. Except that it is furnished with horizontally sliding glass windows instead of paper ones, it might be called a purely Japanese building. It is long, broad, and of one story; and it contains but a single huge room, of which the elevated floor is thickly cushioned with one hundred mats. It has a Japanese name, too, — Zuihōkwan, — signifying "The Hall of Our Holy Country"; and the Chinese characters which form that name were painted upon the small tablet above its entrance by the hand of a Prince of the Imperial blood. Within there is no furniture; nothing but another tablet and two pictures hanging upon the wall. One of the pictures represents the famous "White Tiger Band" of seventeen brave boys who voluntarily sought death for loyalty's sake in the civil war. The other is a portrait in oil of the aged and much-beloved Professor of Chinese, Akizuki of Aidzu, a noted warrior in his youth, when it required much more to make a soldier and a gentleman than it does to-day. And the tablet bears Chinese characters written by the hand of Count Katsu, which signify: "Profound knowledge is the best of possessions."

[1] Copyright by Houghton, Mifflin & Co.

But what is the knowledge taught in this huge unfurnished apartment? It is something called jiujutsu. And what is jiujutsu?

Here I must premise that I know practically nothing of jiujutsu. One must begin to study it in early youth, and must continue the study a very long time in order to learn it even tolerably well. To become an expert requires seven years of constant practice, even presupposing natural aptitudes of an uncommon order. I can give no detailed account of jiujutsu, but merely venture some general remarks about its principle.

Jiujutsu is the old samurai art of fighting without weapons. To the uninitiated it looks like wrestling. Should you happen to enter the Zuihōkwan while jiujutsu is being practiced, you would see a crowd of students watching ten or twelve lithe young comrades, barefooted and barelimbed, throwing each other about on the matting. The dead silence might seem to you very strange. No word is spoken, no sign of approbation or of amusement is given, no face even smiles. Absolute impassiveness is rigidly exacted by the rules of the school of jiujutsu. But probably only this impassibility of all, this hush of numbers, would impress you as remarkable.

A professional wrestler would observe more. He would see that those young men are very cautious about putting forth their strength, and that the grips, holds, and flings are both peculiar and risky. In spite of the care exercised, he would judge the whole performance to be dangerous play, and would be tempted, perhaps, to advise the adoption of Western "scientific" rules.

The real thing, however, — not the play, — is much more dangerous than a Western wrestler could guess at sight. The teacher there, slender and light as he seems, could probably disable an ordinary wrestler in two minutes. Jiujutsu is not an art of display at all: it is not a training for that sort of skill exhibited to public audiences; it is an art of self-defense in the most exact sense of the term; it is an art of war. The master of that art is able, in one moment, to put an untrained antagonist completely *hors de combat*. By some terrible legerdemain he suddenly dislocates a shoulder, unhinges a joint, bursts a tendon, or snaps a bone, — without any apparent effort. He is much more than an athlete: he is an anatomist. And he knows also touches that kill — as by lightning. But this fatal knowledge he is under oath never to communicate except under such conditions as would render its abuse almost impossible. Tradition exacts that it be given only to men of perfect self-command and of unimpeachable moral character.

The fact, however, to which I want to call attention is that the master of jiujutsu never relies upon his own strength. He scarcely uses his own strength in the greatest emergency. Then what does he use? Simply the strength of his antagonist. The force of the enemy is the only means by which that enemy is overcome. The art of jiujutsu teaches you to rely for victory solely upon the strength of your opponent; and the greater his strength, the worse for him and the better for you. I remember that I was not a little astonished when one of the greatest teachers of jiujutsu told me that he found it extremely difficult to teach a certain very strong pupil, whom I had innocently imagined to be the best in the class. On asking why, I was answered: "Because he relies upon his enormous muscular strength, and uses it." The very name "jiujutsu" means *to conquer by yielding.*

I fear I cannot explain at all; I can only suggest. Every one knows what a "counter" in boxing means. I cannot use it for an exact simile, because the boxer who counters opposes his whole force to the impetus of the other; while a jiujutsu expert does precisely the contrary. Still there remains this resemblance between a counter in boxing and a yielding in jiujutsu, — that the suffering is in both cases due to the uncontrollable forward impetus of the man who receives it. I may venture then to say, loosely, that in jiujutsu there is a sort of counter for every twist, wrench, pull, push, or bend: only, the jiujutsu expert does not oppose such movements at all. No: he yields to them. But he does much more than yield to them. He aids them with a wicked sleight that causes the assailant to put out his own shoulder, to fracture his own arm, or, in a desperate case, even to break his own neck or back.

With even this vaguest of explanations, you will already have been able to perceive that the real wonder of jiujutsu is not in the highest possible skill of its best professor, but in the uniquely Oriental idea which the whole art expresses. What Western brain could have elaborated this strange teaching, — never to oppose force to force, but only to direct and utilize the power of attack; to overthrow the enemy solely by his own strength, — to vanquish him solely by his own effort?

Surely none! The Occidental mind appears to work in straight lines; the Oriental, in wonderful curves and circles. Yet how fine a symbolism of Intelligence as a means to foil brute force! Much more than a science of defense is this jiujutsu: it is a philosophical system; it is an economical system; it is an ethical system (indeed, I had forgotten to say that a very large part of jiujutsu training is purely moral); and it is, above all, the expression of a racial genius as yet but faintly perceived by those Powers who dream of further aggrandizement in the East.

* * * * * * *

Before me lies an album more than thirty years old. It is filled with photographs taken at the time when Japan was entering upon her experiments with foreign dress and with foreign institutions. All are photographs of samurai or daimyō; and many possess historical value as reflections of the earliest effects of foreign influence upon native fashions.

Naturally the military class were the earliest subjects of the new influence; and they seem to have attempted several curious compromises between the Western and the Eastern costume. More than a dozen photographs represent feudal leaders surrounded by their retainers, — all in a peculiar garb of their own composition. They have frock coats, waistcoats, and trousers of foreign style and material; but under the coat the long silk girdle or obi is still worn, simply for the purpose of holding the swords. (For the samurai were never in a literal sense *traîneurs de sabre;* and their formidable but exquisitely finished weapons were never made to be slung at the side, — besides being in most cases much too long to be carried in the Western way.) The cloth of the suits is broadcloth; but the samurai will not surrender his mon, or crest, and tries to adapt it to his novel attire by all manner of devices. One has faced the lappets of his coat with white silk; and his family device is either dyed or embroidered upon the silk six times — three mon to each lappet. All the men, or nearly all, wear European watches with showy guards; one is examining his timepiece curiously, probably a very recent acquisition. All wear Western shoes, too, — shoes with elastic sides. But none seem to have yet adopted the utterly abominable European hat — destined, unfortunately, to become popular at a later day. They still retain the jingasa, — a strong wooden headpiece, heavily lacquered in scarlet and gold. And the jingasa and the silken girdle remain the only satisfactory parts of their astounding uniform. The trousers and coats are ill-fitting; the shoes are inflicting slow tortures; there is an indescribably constrained, slouchy, shabby look common to all thus attired. They have not only ceased to feel free: they are conscious of not looking their best. The incongruities are not grotesque enough to be amusing; they are merely ugly and painful. What foreigner in that time could have persuaded himself that the Japanese were not about to lose forever their beautiful taste in dress?

Other photographs show still more curious results of foreign influences. Here are samurai who refuse to adopt the Western fashions, but who have compromised with the new mania by having their haori and hakama made of the heaviest and costliest English broadcloth, — a material utterly unsuited for such use both because of its weight and its inelasticity. Already you can see that creases have been formed which no hot iron can ever smooth away.

It is certainly an æsthetic relief to turn from these portraits to those of a few conservatives who paid no attention to the mania at all, and clung to their native warrior garb to the very last. Here are nagabakama worn by horsemen, — and jin-baori, or war coats, superbly embroidered, — and kamishimo, — and shirts of mail, — and full suits of armor. Here also are various forms of kaburi, — the strange but imposing headdresses anciently worn on state occasions by princes and by samurai of high rank, — curious cobwebby structures of some light black material. In all this there is dignity, beauty, or the terrible grace of war.

But everything is totally eclipsed by the last photograph of the collection, — a handsome youth with the sinister, splendid gaze of a falcon, — Matsudaira Buzen-no-Kami, in full magnificence of feudal war costume. One hand bears the tasseled signal wand of a leader of armies; the other rests on the marvelous hilt of his sword. His helmet is a blazing miracle; the steel upon his breast and shoulders was wrought by armorers whose names are famed in all the museums of the West. The cords of his war coat are golden; and a wondrous garment of heavy silk — all embroidered with billowings and dragonings of gold — flows from his mailed waist to his feet, like a robe of fire. And this is no dream; — this was! — I am gazing at a solar record of one real figure of mediæval life! How the man flames in his steel and silk and gold, like some splendid iridescent beetle, — but a War beetle, all horns and mandibles and menace despite its dazzlings of jewel color!

From the princely magnificence of feudal costume as worn by Matsudaira-Buzen-no-Kami to the nondescript garments of the transition period, how vast a fall! Certainly the native dress and the native taste in dress might well have seemed doomed to pass away forever. And when even the Imperial Court had temporarily adopted Parisian modes, few foreigners could have doubted that the whole nation was about to change garb. As a fact, there then began in the chief cities that passing mania for Western fashions which was reflected in the illustrated journals of Europe, and which created for a while the impression that picturesque Japan had become transformed into a land of "loud" tweeds, chimney-pot hats, and swallowtail coats. But in the capital itself to-day, among a thousand passers-by, you may see scarcely one in Western dress, excepting, of course, the uniformed soldiers, students, and police. The former mania really represented a national experiment; and the results of that experiment were not according to Western expectation. Japan has adopted various styles of Western uniform, with some excellent modifications, for her army, her navy, and her police, simply because such attire is the best possible for such callings. Foreign civil costume has been adopted by the Japanese official world, but only to be worn during office hours in buildings of Western construction furnished with modern desks and chairs. At home even the general, the admiral, the judge, the police inspector, resume the national garb. And, finally, both teachers and students in all but the primary schools are expected to wear uniform, as the educational training is partly military. This obligation, once stringent, has, however, been considerably relaxed, in many schools the uniform being now obligatory only during drill time and upon certain ceremonial occasions. In all Kyūshū schools, except the Normal, the students are free to wear their robes, straw sandals, and enormous straw hats, when not on parade. But everywhere after class hours both teachers and students return at home to their kimono and their girdles of white crape silk.

In brief, then, Japan has fairly resumed her national dress; and it is to be hoped that she will never again abandon it. Not only is it the sole attire perfectly adapted to her domestic habits; it is also, perhaps, the most dignified, the most comfortable, and the most healthy in the world. In some respects, indeed, the native fashions have changed during the era of Meiji much more than in previous eras; but this was largely due to the abolition of the military caste. As to forms, the change has been slight; as to color, it has been great. The fine taste of the race still appears in the beautiful tints and colors and designs of those silken or cotton textures woven for apparel. But the tints are paler, the colors are darker, than those worn by the last generation; — the whole national costume, in all its varieties, not excepting even the bright attire of children and of young girls, is much more sober of tone than in feudal days. All the wondrous old robes of dazzling colors have vanished from public life: you can study them now only in the theaters, or in those marvelous picture books reflecting the fantastic and beautiful visions of the Japanese classic drama, which preserves the Past.

LINES ON LEAVING ITALY.

By Adam Gottlob Oehlenschläger.

[1779-1850.]

Once more among the old gigantic hills
 With vapors clouded o'er;
The vales of Lombardy grow dim behind,
 The rocks ascend before.

They beckon me, the giants, from afar,
 They wing my footsteps on;
Their helms of ice, their plumage of the pine,
 Their cuirasses of stone.

My heart beats high, my breath comes freer forth, —
 Why should my heart be sore?
I hear the eagle and the vulture's cry,
 The nightingale's no more.

Where is the laurel, where the myrtle's blossom?
 Bleak is the path around;
Where from the thicket comes the ringdove's cooing?
 Hoarse is the torrent's sound.

Yet should I grieve, when from my loaded bosom
A weight appears to flow?
Methinks the Muses come to call me home
From yonder rocks of snow.

I know not how, — but in yon land of roses
My heart was heavy still,
I startled at the warbling nightingale,
The zephyr on the hill.

They said, the stars shone with a softer gleam, —
It seemed not so to me;
In vain a scene of beauty beamed around,
My thoughts were o'er the sea.

CANADIAN ABSOLUTISM.[1]

By FRANCIS PARKMAN.

(From "The Old Régime in Canada.")

[Francis Parkman: An American historian; born at Boston, September 16, 1823; died at Jamaica Plain, Mass., November 8, 1893. He was graduated from Harvard in arts in 1844, and in law in 1846, and then made a journey to the far West to study the Indians, living for five months in the lodge of a Dakota chief. This journey undermined his health and was the beginning of lifelong illness. He was honored with the degree of LL.D. from several American colleges. He published: "The Oregon Trail: Prairie and Rocky Mountain Life" (1849), "History of the Conspiracy of Pontiac" (2 vols., 1851), "The Pioneers of France in the New World" (1865), "The Jesuits in North America" (1866), "La Salle and the Discovery of the Great West" (1869), "The Old Régime in Canada" (1874), "Count Frontenac and New France under Louis XIV." (1877), "Montcalm and Wolfe" (2 vols., 1884), and "A Half-Century of Conflict" (2 vols., 1892).]

It is easy to see the nature of the education, past and present, which wrought on the Canadians and made them what they were. An ignorant population, sprung from a brave and active race, but trained to subjection and dependence through centuries of feudal and monarchical despotism, was planted in the wilderness by the hand of authority, and told to grow and flourish. Artificial stimulants were applied, but freedom was

[1] Copyright, 1874, by Francis Parkman. Used by permission of Little, Brown & Co.

FRANCIS PARKMAN

withheld. Perpetual intervention of government, regulations, restrictions, encouragements sometimes more mischievous than restrictions, a constant uncertainty what the authorities would do next, the fate of each man resting less with himself than with another, volition enfeebled, self-reliance paralyzed.

But this was not all. Against absolute authority there was a counter influence, rudely and wildly antagonistic. Canada was at the very portal of the great interior wilderness. The St. Lawrence and the Lakes were the highway to that domain of savage freedom; and thither the disfranchised, half-starved seignior, and the discouraged *habitant* who could find no market for his produce, naturally enough betook themselves. Their lesson of savagery was well learned, and for many a year a boundless license and a stiff-handed authority battled for the control of Canada. Nor, to the last, were church and state fairly masters of the field. The French rule was drawing towards its close when the intendant complained that though twenty-eight companies of regular troops were quartered in the colony, there were not soldiers enough to keep the people in order. One cannot but remember that in a neighboring colony, far more populous, perfect order prevailed, with no other guardians than a few constables chosen by the people themselves.

Whence arose this difference, and other differences equally striking, between the rival colonies? It is easy to ascribe them to a difference of political and religious institutions; but the explanation does not cover the ground. The institutions of New England were utterly inapplicable to the population of New France, and the attempt to apply them would have wrought nothing but mischief. There are no political panaceas, except in the imagination of political quacks. To each degree and each variety of public development there are corresponding institutions, best answering the public needs; and what is meat to one is poison to another. Freedom is for those who are fit for it. The rest will lose it, or turn it to corruption. Church and state were right in exercising authority over a people which had not learned the first rudiments of self-government. Their fault was not that they exercised authority, but that they exercised too much of it, and, instead of weaning the child to go alone, kept him in perpetual leading strings, making him, if possible, more and more dependent, and less and less fit for freedom.

In the building up of colonies, England succeeded and France failed. The cause lies chiefly in the vast advantage drawn by England from the historical training of her people in habits of reflection, forecast, industry, and self-reliance, — a training which enabled them to adopt and maintain an invigorating system of self-rule, totally inapplicable to their rivals.

The New England colonists were far less fugitives from oppression than voluntary exiles seeking the realization of an idea. They were neither peasants nor soldiers, but a substantial Puritan yeomanry, led by Puritan gentlemen and divines in thorough sympathy with them. They were neither sent out by the king, governed by him, nor helped by him. They grew up in utter neglect, and continued neglect was the only boon they asked. Till their increasing strength roused the jealousy of the Crown, they were virtually independent; a republic, but by no means a democracy. They chose their governor and all their rulers from among themselves, made their own government and paid for it, supported their own clergy, defended themselves, and educated themselves. Under the hard and repellent surface of New England society lay the true foundations of a stable freedom, — conscience, reflection, faith, patience, and public spirit. The cement of common interests, hopes, and duties compacted the whole people like a rock of conglomerate, while the people of New France romained in a state of political segregation, like a basket of pebbles held together by the inclosure that surrounds them.

It may be that the difference of historical antecedents would alone explain the difference of character between the rival colonies; but there are deeper causes, the influence of which went far to determine the antecedents themselves. The Germanic race, and especially the Anglo-Saxon branch of it, is peculiarly masculine, and, therefore, peculiarly fitted for self-government. It submits its action habitually to the guidance of reason, and has the judicial faculty of seeing both sides of a question. The French Celt is cast in a different mold. He sees the end distinctly, and reasons about it with an admirable clearness; but his own impulses and passions continually turn him away from it. Opposition excites him; he is impatient of delay, is impelled always to extremes, and does not readily sacrifice a present inclination to an ultimate good. He delights in abstractions and generalizations, cuts loose from unpleasing facts, and roams through an ocean of desires and theories.

While New England prospered and Canada did not prosper, the French system had at least one great advantage. It favored military efficiency. The Canadian population sprang in great part from soldiers, and was to the last systematically reënforced by disbanded soldiers. Its chief occupation was a continual training for forest war; it had little or nothing to lose, and little to do but fight and range the woods. This was not all. The Canadian government was essentially military. At its head was a soldier nobleman, often an old and able commander, and those beneath him caught his spirit and emulated his example. In spite of its political nothingness, in spite of poverty and hardship, and in spite even of trade, the upper stratum of Canadian society was animated by the pride and fire of that gallant *noblesse* which held war as its only worthy calling, and prized honor more than life. As for the *habitant*, the forest, lake, and river were his true school; and here, at least, he was an apt scholar. A skillful woodsman, a bold and adroit canoeman, a willing fighter in time of need, often serving without pay, and receiving from government only his provisions and his canoe, he was more than ready at any time for any hardy enterprise; and in the forest warfare of skirmish and surprise there were few to match him. An absolute government used him at will, and experienced leaders guided his rugged valor to the best account.

The New England man was precisely the same material with that of which Cromwell formed his invincible "Ironsides"; but he had very little forest experience. His geographical position cut him off completely from the great wilderness of the interior. The sea was his field of action. Without the aid of government, and in spite of its restrictions, he built up a prosperous commerce, and enriched himself by distant fisheries, neglected by the rivals before whose doors they lay. He knew every ocean from Greenland to Cape Horn, and the whales of the north and of the south had no more dangerous foe. But he was too busy to fight without good cause, and when he turned his hand to soldiering it was only to meet some pressing need of the hour. The New England troops in the early wars were bands of raw fishermen and farmers, led by civilians decorated with military titles, and subject to the slow and uncertain action of legislative bodies. The officers had not learned to command, nor the men to obey. The remarkable exploit of the capture of Louisburg, the strongest fortress in America, was the result of mere audacity and hardihood, backed by the rarest good luck.

One great fact stands out conspicuous in Canadian history, — the Church of Rome. More even than the royal power she shaped the character and the destinies of the colony. She was its nurse and almost its mother; and, wayward and headstrong as it was, it never broke the ties of faith that held it to her. It was these ties which, in the absence of political franchises, formed under the old régime the only vital coherence in the population. The royal government was transient; the church was permanent. The English conquest shattered the whole apparatus of civil administration at a blow, but it left her untouched. Governors, intendants, councils, and commandants, all were gone; the principal seigniors fled the colony; and a people who had never learned to control themselves or help themselves were suddenly left to their own devices. Confusion, if not anarchy, would have followed but for the parish priests, who in a character of double paternity, half spiritual and half temporal, became more than ever the guardians of order throughout Canada.

This English conquest was the grand crisis of Canadian history. It was the beginning of a new life. With England came Protestantism, and the Canadian church grew purer and better in the presence of an adverse faith. Material growth, an increased mental activity, an education real though fenced and guarded, a warm and genuine patriotism, all date from the peace of 1763. England imposed by the sword on reluctant Canada the boon of rational and ordered liberty. Through centuries of striving she had advanced from stage to stage of progress deliberate and calm, never breaking with her past, but making each fresh gain the base of a new success, enlarging popular liberties while bating nothing of that height and force of individual development which is the brain and heart of civilization; and now, through a hard-earned victory, she taught the conquered colony to share the blessings she had won. A happier calamity never befell a people than the conquest of Canada by the British arms.

NORTH AND SOUTH.[1]

BY NORA PERRY.

[NORA PERRY, American poet and author, was born in Webster, Mass., in 1841, and spent her girlhood in Providence, R.I. She began to write verse for the magazines at the age of eighteen, and was in later life Boston correspondent of the *Chicago Tribune* and the *Providence Journal*. She wrote: "After the Ball, and other Poems" and "New Songs and Ballads"; and the popular juvenile books "A Flock of Girls," "A Rosebud Garden of Girls," and "Hope Benham." Miss Perry died at Dudley, Mass., May 13, 1896.]

FORT ADAMS.

I. 1860.

SHE leaped up, laughing, all alone
Upon the rampart's sodden stone,

And, laughing, hid behind the mouth
Of the great cannon, facing south.

"Ah! will he find me here?" she said,
Then hushed her laugh and shook her head.

"Nay, will he miss me from the rest,
And, missing, care to come in quest?"

But dancing eyes deride the doubt,
The deprecating lips breathe out,

And waiting, waiting all alone,
Upon the rampart's sodden stone,

She looks across the cannon's mouth,
The silent cannon facing south;

Across the great ships riding down
In stately silence to the town;

Across the sea just where the mist
Melts all the blue to amethyst,

From whence the wind o'er all the sails
Blew soft that day its southern gales.

[1] By permission of Houghton, Mifflin & Co.

But white-sailed ships that rode the sea,
Nor dusky cannon's mouth saw she,

With those young eyes whose wistful gaze
Went dreaming thwart the purple haze;

Instead, beyond the white-sailed ships,
Beyond the cannon's dusky lips,

Beyond the sea just where the mist
Melts all the blue to amethyst,

The tall palmettoes darkly rise
Before her dream-enchanted eyes,

And waiting, waiting all alone
Upon the rampart's sodden stone,

In dreams she stands beneath the shade
Of southern palms, — this little maid,

Whose morning face and tender eyes
Took all their hue from Northern skies.

And standing thus enchanted there,
Within her castle of the air,

The rippling tide, that sinks and swells,
Comes to her ear like wedding bells;

And through her castle's airy halls,
From room to room a low voice calls,

And calling, calling, near, so near,
That half in dream and half in fear

She turns, and swift her vision flies
Before the vision of her eyes;

For some one scales the rampart mound,
And some one laughs: "Ah, truant, found!"

And face to face she meets him there,
Her fairy castle's lordly heir!

So, North and South, the pine and palm,
United, in that summer calm

Of idle summer days they stand,
By prosperous gales and breezes fanned.

II. 1862.

No summer guests with curious gaze
Stroll now beneath the "covered ways,"

And gayly laugh and speculate
Upon the old Fort's useless state.

Where last year's lonely arches rang
With idle voices, girls who sang

Their airy songs, or sent their call
From sodden stone or rampart wall,

There echoes now the martial tread
Of soldier sentinels instead.

And they who, sailing through the mist,
Came hither for a lover's tryst,

And vowed next year again to stand
Thus face to face, thus hand to hand,

Upon the old Fort's moldering mound,—
Where find they now a trysting ground?

Upon Manassas' bloody plain
One keeps a tryst with death and pain;

And one, grown old before her years
Of youth have fled, with anguished tears

Wrung from despair, far out of reach
Of love's last touch, of love's last speech,

By Narragansett's rushing tide
Walks desolate,—a widowed bride.

NIHILIST CIRCLES IN RUSSIA.[1]

BY GEORG BRANDES.

(From "Impressions of Russia": translated by Samuel C. Eastman.)

[GEORG BRANDES is one of the most eminent of Scandinavian critics. He was born of Jewish parentage in Copenhagen, Denmark, February 4, 1842, and after graduating at the university in that city, traveled and lectured in all parts of Europe. In 1883 he returned to Denmark, his fellow-countrymen having guaranteed him an income of four thousand crowns for ten years, with the single stipulation that he should deliver public lectures on literature. The most important of his publications, over thirty in number, are: "Æsthetic Studies," "Criticisms and Portraits," "Principal Tendencies in the Literature of the Nineteenth Century," "Danish Poets," "Impressions of Russia," "Benjamin D'Israeli," and "William Shakespeare."]

Two thousand women annually, of their own accord, accompany the exiles to Siberia, frequently to hard labor. In this way a lady of high rank, Baroness Rehbinder, some years ago went with the celebrated physician, Dr. Weimar, who was implicated in the trials for the attempts at assassination.

It can generally be said of those who "go out among the people," that when the home life is oppression or obstruction, they seek emancipation from it at any cost. It was in this view that what at the time was called *sham marriage* was invented, though it has nearly gone out of use. The young girl found a comrade of the same views of life as herself, who consented to marry her *pro forma*, but who neither had nor claimed any control over her, and by whose aid she escaped from the surveillance of her family. Sometimes it happens that the two (as in Mrs. Gyllembourg's "Light Nights"), after having become better acquainted, actually marry; in other cases the man is said to have abused the rights formally conferred upon him and a separation is the result. Generally the newly married couple have separated from each other immediately after the wedding, each being free and independent. As is well known, in "Virgin Soil" Turgenief has described a kindred case, the relation of brother and sister in the case of Nezhdanof and Marianne, after he carried away the young girl.

[1] By permission of T. Y. Crowell & Co., New York, and Walter Scott, Ltd. (Cr. 8vo. Price 2*s*. 6*d*.)

However much these young women feel themselves drawn towards the common people, it very seldom happens that they fall in love or marry out of their own rank; and, if it does happen, it usually brings its own punishment. The following is an instance from my own circle of acquaintance: A young girl loved a man of her own, the higher, classes. They were both exiled by the administrative process, but were sent to the opposite ends of Siberia and could never learn the least thing about each other. In the country town where the young girl was, after the lapse of a few years, she became acquainted with a young workman exiled for the same political reasons she was. She met him daily. He fell passionately in love with her; they had a child. Other exiles, on the way home, came to the town. Among them was a young man of the same class in society as the young girl, who knew something about her lover. She was never wearied of asking him questions, and sat and talked with him through the whole night. At daybreak, as she was sitting with the child at her breast, the workman killed her in a fit of jealous frenzy. He thought that in her face he read regret for having stooped down to him. Two years after, the child was brought to St. Petersburg, to her parents.

Very significant and instructive is an unprinted and prohibited novel of Korolenko, the title of which is "Strange," and the plot as follows:—

A woman has been sent in exile to a distant province. One of the gendarmes who has accompanied the young lady is the narrator. She has not been able in advance to find out where she is to be sent to, and is thus, by two gendarmes, taken almost through the whole of Siberia. One of the gendarmes, an uncultivated but fine fellow, feels so deeply affected by her youth and charms that he actually falls in love with her, and cannot obey his orders. He tells her the name of the town which is selected for her abode. "Good!" she says; "there are several of *ours* there." Immediately on her arrival, she goes to a young man, whose name she knows, but whom she has never seen, and takes lodgings in his house. She falls ill of a lung disease.

A month later the gendarme comes again through the town, seeks her out, and finds the young man by her bedside, and with astonishment hears them still using the formal "you" to each other. It is impossible for him to understand what kind of bond it is which unites them; it is clear that it is not love; but the companionship of ideas is foreign to his scope of comprehension. He makes known to the young girl his attachment for her, but she drives him away with the greatest abhorrence. She does not dislike him personally; but solely because he is a gendarme, from principle, from love for the cause to which she has devoted her life; he is for her not a human being, only an instrument in the hand of an evil power. The poor gendarme cannot possibly understand this any more than what has been stated above.

An author, who has a European reputation, gave me the following account of his connection with this circle: "About ten years ago, while I was living in Berlin, I frequently received letters from discontented Russians, of both sexes, some of them asking me to write for them some pamphlets, which they could translate and distribute among the peasants; and others, in relation to a monograph I had written about a celebrated revolutionary individual, — a book to which I am chiefly indebted for my popularity in certain social circles in Russia. A juvenile naïveté shone through the style of some of the letters; but the tone of warm juvenile enthusiasm, united to an energy of style, — which is uncommon even in men of ability, — in one letter, where the Christian name of the writer was only indicated by an initial, awakened great surprise in me. As I remarked, in my answer, that it was not new to me to find enthusiasm and energy among the young men in Russia, I received, to my amazement, the following reply: 'It is very possible that you have been accustomed to find these qualities among our young men; but it does not apply to my case, for I have for some years already been a grandmother.' An extended correspondence was the result of this letter. But, after the lapse of some time, this, and other correspondence of a similar nature, had to be suspended, on account of the innumerable precautions my correspondents were obliged to take. As several of my books had at that time just been forbidden in Russia, they did not dare to write my name on the envelopes. They changed the name, so that I was obliged to inform the letter carriers of it. At the time of the attempts at assassination, all correspondence of this kind was suspended."

Not infrequently they are very young children who embark upon the peculiarly Russian plans for the improvement of the world. For, even if the old sometimes possess a youthful enthusiasm, yet in Russia, as elsewhere, it is the rule that years and experience bring both men and women to regard the existing state of things as stronger than it is, and the prospect of being able to overthrow it, as much less promising than it appeared to them in their youth. The observation has also long since been made that, in the numerous political trials of the last twenty years, hardly any one has been convicted who was over thirty years old; even those who were twenty-five years old were uncommon, the ages of the majority varying from seventeen to twenty-three.

In the spring of 1887, a young girl of sixteen was arrested in St. Petersburg, whose parents were well known everywhere in good society. Out of regard to the high standing of her father, she was set at liberty; but yet with such conditions that she now remains under the surveillance of the police. A group of young students had a weekly meeting in her mother's house,—to read Shakespeare aloud in Russian, as it was said. The fact of these six or seven students meeting together so regularly aroused suspicion; and the police sent a warning, received an explanation, and answered: "It would be better to abandon these readings."

They apparently complied. Then the young students were arrested. A manuscript translation of a little socialistic tract, written by a man by the name of Thun, was found in the rooms of one of them; and a card of invitation was found, in the same handwriting, signed with the young girl's name. It was of no avail that she denied all knowledge of the tract contained in the manuscript.

She was very peculiar: homely, with beautiful eyes; difficult to become acquainted with, for a little thing would silence her. In the presence of a dashing woman of the world or a beautiful coquette, she opened not her mouth. She contended that it was impossible to say a word in the presence of that kind of woman. She had the whole severity of youth; forbearance was a virtue she knew only by name. And she had youth's naïve faith in the efficacy of every kind of propaganda. Her mother, a lady of thirty-five years of age, was high-spirited and passionate, with all the luxurious vital powers of the Russian blood. The whole emotional life of the daughter had been absorbed by the intellectual; she managed her mother as if the latter had been her own grown-up child.

Still more rare than this type, there is among these women

16

the patient, light-hearted, on whom no opposition makes any impression. A letter from a young married woman, who had been exiled to a town in Siberia, but without being confined in prison, was somewhat to this effect: "Dear Friends, — I can imagine that you are somewhat uneasy about me. But never in my life have I been happier. It is quite pleasant to be separated for a while from my beloved husband, who was beginning to tire me. But that is truly one of the most unimportant things. I have been received here not as a criminal, but as a queen. The whole town is made up of exiles, descendants of exiles, friends of exiles. They actually vie with each other in showing me kindness — nay, homage. Every other evening, I am at a ball, and never off the floor. This place is a true ball paradise," etc.

More frequent than this arrogance is a humility, a profound, boundless modesty, which is genuinely Slavic. In a small house with a garden, in a remote quarter of Moscow, lived an extremely finely endowed young girl, who for many years had been severely ill; and, as a result, from time to time, especially when excited, lost the power of speech. She lived a purely intellectual life, wholly absorbed in intellectual pursuits; and, on account of her poor health and weakness, was hardly a woman. But a purer and stronger intellectual enthusiasm, and more arduous exertions in that direction, are not often seen. She translated a great deal from foreign languages, and also wrote, herself. There was a combination of energy and the most profound humility, which struck the stranger who conversed with her. Her father had been a well-known professor of mathematics. She and her two sisters, bright and healthy girls, supported themselves respectably, orphans as they were, without aid. The worship of the gifted invalid by the two sisters, especially by the younger, was very touching.

One evening, in a company, a distinguished foreigner, who had spent some time in St. Petersburg, described another young girl of the same turn of mind and of the same plane of culture, only seventeen years old, and of far bolder temperament. "I have," he continued, "met her for a short time in society, but we were almost immediately separated. I merely noticed that she had beautiful, clear eyes, and cordial but very decided manners. The day before my departure, I received a long letter from her, which seemed to me to be very interesting, because it gave me the impression of being characteristic of a whole family. She wrote: —

"'Permit me to express to you in writing what I had not any opportunity to say otherwise. I do not speak in my own name alone, but in behalf of a large part of the young people of Russia, with whom you have not had time to become adequately acquainted. I should have said it to you day before yesterday, at the D——s', but could not in the few moments we talked together. You regretted having known, comparatively, so few of the young people. That is partly because the time of your visit was very unfortunately chosen, so far as the Russian youth are concerned. It is just the time of examination in all of the public institutions of education. But, entirely apart from that, the Russian youth could not make themselves known to you. Life deprives us of its highest good, — freedom, and all the happiness which is inseparable from it; but do not believe us insensible to that which alone gives meaning and value to human life. Quite the contrary. If fate has sent us so few blessings, we love those we do receive all the more dearly, and prize them the more highly. We prize above everything the science which emancipates. It is not allowed to the Russian youth to express in writing what they feel; but it would pain me, as a patriot, if you should get an unjust impression of them. You once called Rudin the typical representative of the Russian weakness of character. "Weakness!" I exclaimed to myself when I heard it. Oh, no! Do not forget that the Russian literature is only an incomplete reflex of the life and character of the Russian people. Do not forget that they would make us deaf and dumb, and that we are still too few in number not to be compelled to be so. But we are really not like Rudin. Rudin is intelligent, and has a certain quality of intellectual perception, but has no depth of soul; he loves no one and no thing. He is allured by the beauty of ideas; he is not drawn on by true and earnest love for the human race. It is on this account that he is a failure in his relation to Nathalie, and especially in life, even if he does not succeed as a hero. But, great God! — do not believe about us that we are a failure in the wearisome battle of life, which we are in, day in and day out. How unjust! my strong and living faith is that Russia will some day come forth cured of its political disease, and disclose itself liberally and manfully. I believe not only in the Russian people, but

I believe in our intelligent youth, in their receptiveness of everything which is true and therefore beautiful. It betrays itself in the profound respect for the men who understand how to find out and unveil the meaning of things, and to open for us wider horizons.'"

There is, perhaps, nothing in this letter indicative of uncommon abilities, and the seventeen-year-old child is visible behind it; nevertheless, there is a personality in it which may be typically Russian, and which it would be impossible to find in a Scandinavian girl of that age, — and a will gleams out through the words, flashing like a steel blade, a will which is full of promise.

One can form a vivid conception of this progressive youth of both sexes, as they enter upon life, face to face with the common people, whose elevation is the object of their aspirations.

These young people represent the highest culture of the age; among the peasants there is an ignorance which renders it almost impossible to begin the communication of information. An exiled mathematician, who had returned from Siberia, a very practical young man, told me that in the country town he was regarded as a man with a supernatural insight, simply on account of his large library; and after he had taught some peasants there, in the spring, how to graft fruit trees, they came to him the next day from the whole neighborhood with sick children and sick cattle, and besought him to undertake a general cure: "Make them well, little father! make them well!" When he assured them that he had not the power to do it, there was not one of them who would believe him. They begged, cried, asked him what they had done to him that he would not help them: "You know very well you can, if you will!"

In Benjamin Constant's old work on "Religion," it is related that at the beginning of this century, when a Russian general in full uniform rode out into a country town in a part of Siberia but little frequented, he was regarded by the natives as God himself, and that the memory of his appearance got such a firm hold among the people that when ten years later a Russian colonel came to the same place he was greeted as the "Son of God."

That would hardly be possible now. Still, the following happened last year. A cultured Russian passed through a town inhabited by Cossacks of Little Russia. He was asked the question: "Will you be so good as to tell us if you have been in the other world?" He was offended, since he supposed that the inhabitants meant to indicate to him that they did not believe what he had said. But the fact was that one of the inhabitants of the town had returned from a pilgrimage and had told them that he came from the other world, and those recently deceased in the town had requested him to bring greetings to their relatives. He had gone away again, loaded with rustic presents, to the departed relatives of the credulous Cossacks. Now they wanted to find out from the Russian gentleman whether these gifts had reached their proper destination.

In the presence of such ignorance and naïveté, mutual understanding is difficult, — most difficult, perhaps, because the peasant does not like to be treated as children are by their teachers. As a matter of course, he does not like to have morals preached to him. When an attempt was lately made on an estate to give a new drama of Tolstoï, aimed against intoxicating liquors, and in which the devil personally appears as the maker and distributer of spirits, the peasants expressed their disgust at it. It was, they said, a tale for children.

But the same peasants would readily believe that, if the harvest was poor this year, it was because the priests were now on a fixed salary. Heretofore the latter said the mass earnestly, to get a good harvest and rich tithe: this year it was all the same to them; therefore they prayed negligently and without real heartiness. Drought followed. And the same peasants explained the last Russian-Turkish war by saying that in the country of the Turks there lies in the ground a huge beast, of great age, and under the claw of his left hind leg an immense treasure of gold is buried, which the Tsar wanted to wrest from the Turk.

It must not be forgotten that by the last returns seventy-six out of one hundred of the soldiers could neither read nor write.

On the other hand, let us examine the moral idea which underlies the whole struggle of the intelligent people of Russia: The wish to be useful, to see those about them happy in freedom. This idea crops out in many different guises, now in the costume of the utilitarianism of Bentham and Mill, now in the garb of Tchernuishevski's phalanstery, now in Dostoyevski's strait-jacket, but it is the basis of the philosophy of the enlightened reformers of the fatherland and their friends of reform.

In speaking of the relations of the two sexes, attention has been called to the equality between the man and woman, and to the greatest possible sum of human freedom as the right of both. On this point we can compare the manner of thought and action prevailing among the peasants. External considerations are almost wholly excluded from the marriage question in this class. Nowhere else in Europe does the heart play so small a rôle in affairs of this kind. That early marriages do not indeed of themselves bestow the happiness of love is shown here; for as a rule the age at which they marry is eighteen for the men and sixteen for the women. A result of the extreme youth of these marriages is that the "old man," the head of the family, is often a man less than forty years old and who uses to the full extent his power and the respect which must be shown to him. For a long time past he has sent his sons into the fields and been at home alone with the son's wives. For centuries he has gone about among all the young women in the house, like a Turkish sultan, and none of them has dared to defy him. A whole range of Russian national songs treat of the cane of the father-in-law. The result is that the Russian peasant never has treated woman as man's equal helpmate. The proverbs run: "Love your wife as your own soul and beat her like your fur!"—"If you cannot thrash your wife, whom can you thrash?"—"It is my wife—my thing."—Even in the seventeenth century the father, on giving his daughter in marriage, bought a new whip to give her the last domestic discipline coming from him, and then gave it solemnly to the son-in-law, with the direction to use it early and unsparingly. On entering the bridal chamber, the ceremonial custom was for the bridegroom to give his bride one or two lashes over the shoulders, with the words: "Now forget your father's will and suit yourself to mine." The national song, nevertheless, directs him to take a "silken whip."

What a stride it is from this to the conceptions of the youngest generation about the right of women freely to give themselves away and freely recede, and their ideas of the common work of the sexes for the freedom and happiness of the masses!

And yet, if the distance is enormous between these alert and sprightly young people and those for whom and among whom they would labor, the contrast between an *intelligentia* with its system of morals and the official world of Russia, which holds in its hands the whole administration and all the material means of the country, is not less immense.

Here is an intelligent *élite*, for whom the rule of ethics is not the official patent morality, — nay, even not the legal — for the motto, "Nothing unlawful," is, for many who belong to it, the stamp of the Philistine, — but for whom above all ethics stands that which they call *the divine spark*, — this spark which Dostoyevski traces out and finds even in criminals and the partially insane, and for whom morality is what they call "the unconscious condition," — that is, that in which the individual does what is right without exertion, without self-conquest, because it agrees with his nature.

Imagine an *intelligentia* with these rules of ethics, as a spiritual guiding power in a state which is ruled and governed as Russia, — where the most ignorant bigotry, in the darkest of the Christian creeds, is the law and fashion, which from the court is diffused downwards, and where a single man's will, even if he has none, is the supreme controlling law.

These two underlying powers are drawing away from each other on every side. What does it lead to? Can any mortal draught the parallelogram of these forces, the resulting tendency and its course?

We are reminded, in considering it, of the passage in Gogol's "Dead Souls," where Tchitchikof's *kibitka* is lost in the distance, driven with mad haste : —

"And dost not thou, Russia, drive away, like a *troïka*, not to be overtaken! The road smokes behind thee, the bridges creak. Thou leavest all behind thee. The beholders, amazed, stop and say, — 'Was it a flash of lightning? what means this blood-curdling course? what is the secret power in these horses? What kind of horses are you? have you whirlwinds in your withers? have you recognized tones from above, and do you now force your iron limbs, without touching the earth with your hoofs, to fly hence through the air, as if inspired by a God? Russia, answer whither thou art driving!' There comes no answer. We can hear the little bells on the horses tinkling strangely; there is a groaning in the air, increasing like a storm; and the Russian land continues its wild flight, and the other nations and kingdoms of the earth step timorously aside, without checking its career."

LIBERTY.

By WILLIAM LLOYD GARRISON.

[1805-1879.]

High walls and huge the body may confine,
And iron gates obstruct the prisoner's gaze,
And massive bolts may baffle his design,
And vigilant keepers watch his devious ways;
But scorns the immortal mind such base control;
No chains can bind it, and no cell inclose.
Swifter than light it flies from pole to pole,
And in a flash from earth to heaven it goes.
It leaps from mount to mount; from vale to vale
It wanders, plucking honeyed fruits and flowers;
It visits home to hear the fireside tale
And in sweet converse pass the joyous hours;
'Tis up before the sun, roaming afar,
And in its watches wearies every star.

CAMILLE AND ARMAND.

By ALEXANDRE DUMAS, Fils.

(From "Camille": translated by Matilda Heron.)

[Alexandre Dumas, Fils: A French dramatist and author; born in Paris, July 27, 1824; died at Marly, November 28, 1895. He was educated at the Collège Bourbon, and published his first book, "The Sins of Youth," at the age of seventeen. His principal novels are "Camille" (1848) and "The Clémenceau Case" (1864). His plays include: "Camille" (1852), "Diana of the Lily" (1853), "The Other Half-World" (1855), "The Natural Son" (1857), "A Prodigal Father" (1859), "The Friend of Women" (1864), "A Woman's Torture" (1865), "Madame Aubray's Ideas" (1867), "A Wedding Call" and "The Princess Georges" (1868), "Claude's Wife" (1873), "Monsieur Alphonse" (1873), "The Danicheffs" (1876), "Joseph Belsamo" (1878), "The Princess of Bagdad" and "Françillon" (1887).]

Present: Camille. *Enter* Duval.

Duval — Mademoiselle Camille Gauthier?

Camille — It is I, sir. To whom have I the honor of speaking?

ALEXANDRE DUMAS, FILS

Duval — To Monsieur Duval.

Camille — Monsieur Duval?

Duval — Yes, Mademoiselle, Armand's father.

Camille — Monsieur Armand is not here, sir.

Duval — I know it. But I would speak with you, and I wish you to listen. You are not only compromising, but ruining, my son.

Camille — You are deceived, sir. I am here beyond the reach of scandal; and I accept nothing from your son.

Duval — Which means that he has fallen so low as to be a sharer of the gain which you accept from others.

Camille — Pardon me, sir. I am a woman, and in my own house, — two reasons that should plead in my behalf to your more generous courtesy. The tone in which you addressed me is not what I have been accustomed to, and more than I can listen to from a gentleman whom I have the honor to see for the first time. I pray you will allow me to retire.

Duval — Stay, Mademoiselle, when one finds himself face to face with you, it is hard to think those things are so. Oh, I was told that you are a dangerous woman.

Camille — Yes, sir! dangerous to myself.

Duval — It is not less true, however, that you are ruining my son.

Camille — Sir, I repeat, with all the respect I have for Armand's father, that you are wrong.

Duval — Then what is the meaning of this letter to my lawyer, which apprises me of Armand's intention to dispose of his property, the gift of a dying mother? [*Gives her a letter.*

Camille — I assure you, sir, that if this is Armand's act, he has done so without my knowledge; for he knew well that had he offered such a gift, I should refuse it.

Duval — Indeed! you have not always spoken thus!

Camille — True, sir; but I have not always loved.

Duval — And now ——

Camille — I am no longer what I was.

Duval — These are very fine words.

Camille — What can I say to convince you? I swear by the love I bear your son, the holiest thing that ever filled my heart, that I was ignorant of the transaction.

Duval — Still, you must live by some means?

Camille — You force me, sir, to be explicit. So far from resembling other associations of my life, this has made me penniless. I pray you, read that paper. [*Handing a paper.*] It contains a list of all that I possess on earth. When you were announced just now, I thought you were the person to whom I had sold them.

Duval — A bill of sale of all your furniture, pictures, plate, and other things, with which to pay your creditors — the surplus to be returned to you. Have I been deceived?

Camille — You have, sir. I know that my life has been clouded. — Oh, you do not know me, sir! You can never know how purely I love your son, and how he loves me! It is his love that has saved me from myself, and made me what I am. I have been so happy for three months! And you, sir, are his father. You are good, I am sure. I know you would not harm me. Then let me entreat you will not tell him ill of me, or he will believe you, for he loves you so; and I also love and honor you, because you are *his father!*

Duval — Pardon me for the manner in which I presented myself to you. I was angry at my son, for his ingratitude to his dead mother, in disposing of her gift to him. I pray you, pardon.

Camille — Oh, sir, it is you have everything to pardon. I can only bless you for those kind words. I pray you take a chair.

Duval — In the name of these sentiments, which, you say, are so sacred to you, I am about to ask of you a sacrifice greater than any you have yet performed.

Camille — Oh, heaven!

Duval — Listen, my child, and patiently, to what I have to say.

Camille — Oh, sir, I pray you let us speak no more. I know you are going to ask something terrible of me. I have been expecting this. I was too happy. Yet over my brightest hour there has always hung a cloud. It was the shadow of your frown.

Duval — Camille, I am not going to chide, but to *supplicate.* You love my son — so do I. We are both desirous of his happiness — jealous of those who could contribute to it more than we. I speak to you as a father and ask of you the happiness of both my children.

Camille — Of both your children?

Duval — Yes, Camille, of both. I have a daughter, young, beautiful, and pure as an angel. She loves as you do. That love has been the dream of her life. But the family of the man about to marry her has learned the relation between you and Armand, and declared the withdrawal of their consent unless he gives you up. You see, then, how much depends on you. Let me entreat you in the name of your love for her brother, to save my daughter's peace.

Camille — You are very good, sir, to deign to speak such words as these. I understand you, and you are right. I will at once leave Paris, and remain away from Armand for some time. It will be a sacrifice, I confess; but I will make it for *your* sake. Besides, his joy at my return will make amends for my absence. You will allow him to write me after your daughter is married?

Duval — Thanks, my child; but I fear you do not wholly understand me. I would ask more.

Camille — What could I do more?

Duval — A temporary absence will not suffice.

Camille — Ah, you would not have me quit Armand forever?

Duval — You must.

Camille — Never! To separate us now would be more than cruel — it would be a crime. Oh, sir! you have never loved! You know not what it is to be left without a home, a friend, a father, or a family. When Armand forgave my faults he swore to be all these. I have grafted life and hope on him till they and he are one. Oh, do not tear him from me the little while I have to live! I am not well, sir. I have been ill for months. A sudden shock would kill me. Ask anything but this. Oh, do not drive me to despair! See, I am at your feet!

Duval — Rise, Camille! I know that I demand a great sacrifice from your heart! but one that, for your own good, you are fatally forced to yield. Listen. You have known Armand three months, and you love him. Are you sure you have not deceived yourself, and that even now you do not begin to tire of your new choice, and long for other conquests?

Camille — Oh, spare me, sir! Unworthy as the offering of my love may seem, Armand's heart was the first shrine in which it ever sought a sanctuary, and there it shall remain forever!

Duval — You think so now, perhaps; but sooner or later the truth must come. Youth is prodigal — old age exacting. Do you listen?

Camille — Do I listen? Oh, heaven!

Duval — You are willing to sacrifice everything for my son; but should he accept this, what sacrifice could he make you in return? Say that Armand Duval is an honest man, and would marry you, — what kind of union would that be which has neither purity nor religion to recommend it to the grace of heaven, the smile of friends, or the esteem of the world? And what will be your fate to see the man who sacrificed position, honor, all for you, bowed down with shame of her who ought to be his pride?

Camille — Oh, my punishment is come!

Duval — Avoid what may yet follow. Say that both of you love, as none has ever loved. The warmest sun will set at eve. And when the evening of your life steals on, Armand will seek elsewhere the charms he can no longer find in you; and with every trace of age on *your* brow, a blush will rise on *his*, accusing him of youth, and hopes, and honor, lost for you!

Camille — My dream is past!

Duval — Dream no more, Camille; but wake to duty to yourself, and to the man you love.

Camille — Why — why do I live?

Duval — And should you die, would you have your husband stand upon your grave, ashamed to breathe the name of her who lies there? No, Camille, you are too proud for that. I leave to your heart, to your reason, to your affection for my son, the sacrifice I might demand. You will be proud some day of having saved Armand from a fate he would have regretted all his life — which would have brought on him the idle jest and scorn of every honorable man. Pardon me, Camille; but you know the world too well to doubt the truth of what I say. It is a father who implores you to save his child. Come, *prove* to me you love my son. Give me your hand. Courage, Camille, courage! [*She slowly gives her hand.*] Bless you, bless you! You have done your duty.

Camille — You desire, sir, that I separate from your son for his good, his honor, and his fortune. What am I to do? Speak — I am ready.

Duval — You must tell him that you do not love him.

Camille — He will not believe me.

Duval — You must leave Paris.

Camille — He will follow me.

DUMAS FILS IN HIS STUDY

Duval — What *will* you do?

Camille — I must teach him to despise me.

Duval — But, Camille, I fear ——

Camille — Ah, fear nothing! He will hate me! I will teach him. I know how; for I have taught myself.

Duval — Armand must not know of this.

Camille — Sir, you do not know me yet; for I swear by the love I bear your son, that he shall never know from my lips what has transpired between us.

Duval — You are a noble girl! Is there aught that I can do for you?

Camille — When the heart that now is breaking lies pulseless in the grave — when the world records my very virtues to my blame — when Armand's voice shall rise with curses on my memory — tell him — oh! tell him how I loved him! And now, I pray you will withdraw into that room. He may return each moment, and discover our purpose.

Duval — Camille, you have saved my life — nay, more, you have preserved my honor. Heaven bless you for the sacrifice.

[*Exit* DUVAL. CAMILLE *staggers to table to write.*

Camille — Oh, I cannot! Every word I trace seems to tear from my heart a hope that never can take root again. [*After a struggle writes.*] What shall I say? [*Reads what she has written.*] "*Armand, in a few hours from this, the little flowers you gave me this morning will be withered on my breast, and in their place, Camellias, the badge of that life in which alone I can find happiness.*" Oh! heaven, forgive the injuries these words may bring to him, and the injustice they do my heart!

[*Folds the letter.*

Enter ARMAND.

Armand — Ah, Camille, here I am! What are you doing there?

Camille — Armand! Nothing!

Armand — You were writing as I entered.

Camille — No! That is — yes!

Armand — What does this mean? You are pale! To whom were you writing? Camille, let me see that letter.

Camille — I cannot.

Armand — I thought we had done with mystery.

Camille — And with suspicion.

Armand — Pardon me, Camille, — I was wrong. I entered excited, and saw in you my own embarrassment. My father is arrived.

Camille — Have you seen him?

Armand — No; but he left at my house a letter, in which he reproaches me very bitterly. He has learned that I am here, and doubtless will pay me a visit this evening. Some idle tongues have been busy in informing him of our retreat. But let him come. I wish him to see you — to talk with you. He will be sure to love you. Or should he remain stern for a while, and refuse his smiles, what of it? He can withhold his patronage from me; but he cannot separate me from your love. I will work, toil, labor for you, and think it a privilege and a joy, if I have but your smile to repay me at its close.

Camille — How he loves me! But you must be wise, and not anger your father unnecessarily; for you know he has much cause to blame. He is coming, you say. Then I will retire awhile until he speaks with you — then I will return, and be with you again. I will fall at his feet, and implore him not to part us.

Armand — Camille, there is something passing in your mind that you would hide from me. It is not my words that agitate you so. You can scarcely stand. There is something wrong here. It is this letter. [*Snatches the letter from her.*

Camille — Armand — that letter must not be read.

Armand — What does it contain?

Camille — A proof of my love for you. In the name of that love, return it to me unread, and ask to know no more.

Armand — Take it, Camille. [*Returns letter.*] I know it all. Madam Prudence told me this morning, and it was that which took me to Paris. I know the sacrifice you would make, and while you were considering my happiness, I was not unmindful of yours. I have arranged it all unknown to you. Ah, Camille, how can I ever return such devotion, truth, and love?

Camille — Well, now that you are satisfied and know all, let us part ——

Armand — Part?

Camille — I mean, let me retire. Your father will be here, you remember, and I would rather he would see you alone. I will be in the garden with Nichette and Gustave. You can call me when you want me. Oh, how — how can I ever part from you? You will calm your father, if he be irritated, and win him to forgive you. Will you not? Then we will be so happy — happy as we have always been since first we met! And you are happy — are you not? And have nothing to reproach me for — have you? Since first I met you I welcomed in my heart of hearts your love, believing it a sign from heaven that the past had been forgiven. If I have ever caused your heart a pang, you will forgive me — will you not? And when you recall, one day, the little proofs of love I have bestowed on you, you will not despise or curse my memory! Oh, do not — do not curse me when you learn how I have loved you!

Armand — Camille, what does this mean?

Camille — Love for you!

Armand — But why these tears?

Camille — Oh, let them fall! I had forgotten. Do not heed them. I am such a silly girl! You know I often love to weep. See, I am calm now. They are all gone. Come, chase them away. [*He kisses her brow.*] See, now, they are all gone. No more tears, but smiles. You, too, are smiling. Ah! I will live on that smile until we meet again! See, I too can smile! You can read until your father comes, and think of me; for I shall never cease to think of you. Adieu [*Aside*] forever!

[*Exit.*

Armand — It is too late. The world would be a blank without her. [*Calls*] Ninnette! [*Enter* NANINE.] A gentleman, my father, will arrive here presently. If he ask to see Madam, say that I am here awaiting him.

Nanine — I will, sir.

ARMAND'S REVENGE.

Camille — What's to be done? I must continue to deceive him. I made a sacred promise to his father. It must not be broken. Oh, heaven! give me strength to keep it. But this duel! How to prevent it! Peril honor, life, for me! Oh! No, no, no! Rather let him hate, despise me! Oh! he is here!

Enter ARMAND.

Armand — Madam, did you send for me?

Camille — I did, Armand! I would speak with you.

Armand — Speak! I listen.

Camille — I have a few words to say to you — not of the past ——

Armand — Oh, no! Let that be buried in the shame that shrouds it.

Camille — Oh! do not crush me with reproach. See how I am bowed before you, pale, trembling, supplicating. Listen to me without hate, and hear me without anger. Say that you will forget the past, and — give me your hand.

Armand [*rejecting her hand*] — Pardon me, Mademoiselle. If your business with me is at an end, I will retire.

Camille — Stay — I will not detain you long. Armand, you must leave Paris.

Armand — Leave Paris? And why, Mademoiselle?

Camille — Because the Count de Varville seeks to quarrel with you, and I wish you to avoid him. I alone am to blame, and I alone should suffer.

Armand — And it is thus you would counsel me to play the *coward's* part, and *flec — flee* from Count de Varville! What other counsel could come from such a source?

Camille — Armand, by the memory of the woman whom you once loved — in the name of the pangs it cost her to destroy your faith — and in the name of her who smiled from heaven upon the act that saved her son from shame — even in her name — your mother's name — Armand Duval, I charge you leave me! Flee — flee — anywhere from here — from me — or you will make me human!

Armand — I understand, Mademoiselle. You tremble for your lover — your wealthy Count — who holds your fortune in his hands. You shudder at the thought of the event which would rob you of his gold, or, perhaps, his title, which, no doubt, erelong you hope to wear.

Camille — I tremble for *your life!*

Armand — You tremble for my life! Oh, you jest! What is my life or death to you? Had you such a fear when you wrote that letter? [*Takes out a letter and reads.*] "*Armand forget me. The Count has offered me his protection. I accept it, for I know he loves me.*" Love you! Oh, had he loved you, you would not have been *here* to-night. These were your words. That they did not kill me was no fault of yours — and that I am not dead is because I *cannot* die until I am avenged; because I *will not* die until I see the words you have graven on my brain imprinted on the blood of him who wronged me! And should your lifestrings crack to part with him, he shall not live; for I have sworn it!

Camille — Armand, you wrong him! De Varville is innocent of all that has occurred!

Armand — He loves you, Madam! *That* is his crime — the sin that he must answer for!

SARAH BERNHARDT AS CAMILLE

Camille — Oh, could you but know his thoughts, they would tell you that I *hate* him!

Armand — Why are you *his?* Why *here* — the plaything of his vanity, the trophy of his gold?

Camille — Oh, heaven! Armand! No — no! this must not be. You may retire! I have no more to say. Do not ask me, for I cannot tell!

Armand — Then I will tell you! Because you are heartless, truthless, and make a sale of what you call love to him who bids the highest! Because when you found a man who truly loved you, who devoted every thought and act to bless and guard you, you fled from him at the very moment you were mocking him with a sacrifice you had not the courage to make. Horses, house, and jewels had to be parted with, and all for love! Oh, no! that could not be! They had to remain unsold, and so they did! They were returned, and with them, what? The bitter pangs of anguish and remorse that fill your breast, even while it heaves beneath a weight of gems! — the fixed despair on that brow on which those diamonds look down in mockery! And this is what the man you love has done for you! These are *his* triumphs — the wages of *your* shame!

Camille — Armand, you have pierced my heart — you have bowed me in the dust! Is it fit that you should die for such a wretch as you have drawn? Is it fit that you should taint your name in such a cause as hers? Remember those who love you, Armand! — your sister, father, friends, Camille! For her sake do not peril life and honor! Do not meet the Count again! Leave Paris! Forget your wrongs for *my* sake! See, at your feet I ask it in my name?

Armand — On condition that you fly from Paris with me!

Camille — Oh, you are mad!

Armand — I am indeed! I stand upon the brink of an abyss, whence I must soar or fall! You can save me. A moment since I thought I hated you. I tried to smother in my breast the truth, that it was love — *love for you!* All shall be forgotten — forgiven! We will fly from Paris and the past! We will go to the ends of the earth — away from man — where not an eye shall feast a glance upon your form, nor sound disturb your ear less gentle than the echoes that repeat our tales of love!

Camille — This cannot be!

Armand — Again!

Camille — I would give a whole eternity of life to purchase one short hour of bliss like that you have pictured now! But it must not be! There is a gulf between us which I dare not cross! I have sworn to forget you — to avoid you — to tear you from my thoughts, though it should uproot my reason!

Armand — You have sworn to whom?

Camille — To one who had the right to ask me!

Armand — To the Count de Varville, who loves you! Now say that you love *him*, and I will part with you forever!

Camille [*faltering*] — Yes, I love the Count de Varville!

Armand [*rushes to supper-room door, and violently dashes it open*] — Enter all!

[*All the characters in the act rush in.*

Camille — What would you do?

Armand — You will see! [*To guests*] You see that woman!

Olimpe — Camille?

Armand — Yes! Camille Gauthier! Do you know what she has done?

All — No!

Armand — But you shall! She once sold her horses, carriage, diamonds — all to live with me, so much she loved me! This was generous — was it not? But what did I do? You shall hear! I accepted this sacrifice at her hands without repaying her! But it is not too late! I have repented — and now that I am rich, I am come to pay it back! You all bear witness that I have paid that woman, and that I owe her nothing!

[*He throws a shower of notes and gold upon* CAMILLE, *who has thrown herself at his feet.* DE VARVILLE *advances suddenly and strikes him.*

Varville — 'Tis false! You owe me revenge!

[*Music* — ARMAND *springs at him, but is held by* GUSTAVE *and* GASTON — CAMILLE *leaning on* Madame PRUDENCE — *Tableaux.*

FLOWERS OF EVIL.

By CHARLES BAUDELAIRE.

[1821-1867.]

I.

I ADORE thee as much as the vaults of night,
O vase full of grief, taciturnity great,
And I love thee the more because of thy flight.
It seemeth, my night's beautifier, that you
Still heap up those leagues — yes! ironically heap! —
That divide from my arms the immensity blue.

I advance to attack, I climb to assault,
Like a choir of young worms at a corpse in the vault;
Thy coldness, oh cruel, implacable beast!
Yet heightens thy beauty, on which my eyes feast!

II.

Two warriors come running, to fight they begin,
With gleaming and blood they bespatter the air;
These games, and this clatter of arms, is the din
Of youth that's a prey to the surgings of love.

The rapiers are broken! and so is our youth,
But the dagger's avenged, dear! and so is the sword,
By the nail that is steeled and the hardened tooth.
Oh, the fury of hearts aged and ulcered by love!

In the ditch, where the ounce and the pard have their lair,
Our heroes have rolled in an angry embrace;
Their skin blooms on brambles that erewhile were bare.
That ravine is a fiend-inhabited hell!
Then let us roll in, oh woman inhuman,
To immortalize hatred that nothing can quell!

APRIL HOPES.[1]

By W. D. HOWELLS.

[William Dean Howells: An American novelist and critic; born a Martin's Ferry, Ohio, March 1, 1837. He learned the printer's trade of hi father; was later on the editorial staffs of the *Cincinnati Gazette* and the *Ohi State Journal;* was United States consul at Venice, 1861–1865; and editor in chie of the *Atlantic Monthly*, 1871–1881; afterwards devoting himself entirely to liter ary work. Among his published volumes are: "Poems of Two Friends" (wit John J. Piatt, 1860), "Venetian Life" (1866), "Italian Journeys" (1867) "Suburban Sketches" (1871), "Their Wedding Journey" (1872), "A Chanc Acquaintance" (1873), "A Foregone Conclusion" (1875), "Out of the Ques tion" (1877), "A Counterfeit Presentment" (1877), "The Lady of the Aroos took" (1879), "The Undiscovered Country" (1880), "A Fearful Responsibility" (1881), "Doctor Breen's Practice" (1881), "A Modern Instance" (1882), "A Woman's Reason" (1883), "The Rise of Silas Lapham" (1884), "India Summer" (1885), "The Minister's Charge" (1887), "April Hopes" (1888) "Annie Kilburn" (1889), "A Hazard of New Fortunes" (1890), "The Shadow of a Dream" (1890), "A Boy's Town" (1890), "The Quality o Mercy" (1892), "The Coast of Bohemia" (1893), "The World of Chance" (1893), "A Traveler from Altruria" (1894), and "The Landlord at Lion's Head" (1897).]

From his place on the floor of the Hemenway Gymnasium, Mr. Elbridge G. Mavering looked on at the Class Day gayety with the advantage which his stature gave him over most people there. Hundreds of these were pretty girls, in a great variety of charming costumes, such as the eclecticism of modern fashion permits, and all sorts of ingenious compromises between walking dress and ball dress. It struck him that the young men on whose arms they hung, in promenading around the long oval within the crowd of stationary spectators, were very much younger than students used to be, whether they wore the dress coats of the Seniors or the cutaways of the Juniors and Sophomores; and the young girls themselves did not look so old as he remembered them in his day. There was a band playing somewhere, and the galleries were well filled with spectators seated at their ease, and intent on the party-colored turmoil of the floor, where from time to time the younger promenaders broke away from the ranks into a waltz, and after some turns drifted back, smiling and controlling their quick breath, and resumed their promenade. The place was intensely light, in the candor of a summer day which had no reserves; and the

[1] Copyright, 1887, by William Dean Howells. Used by permission of Harper and Brothers.

brilliancy was not broken by the simple decorations. Ropes of wild laurel twisted up the pine posts of the aisles, and swung in festoons overhead; masses of tropical plants in pots were set along between the posts on one side of the room; and on the other were the lunch tables, where a great many people were standing about, eating chicken and salmon salads, or strawberries and ice cream, and drinking claret cup. From the whole rose that blended odor of viands, of flowers, of stuffs, of toilet perfumes, which is the characteristic expression of all social festivities, and which exhilarates or depresses according as one is new or old to it.

Elbridge Mavering kept looking at the faces of the young men as if he expected to see a certain one; then he turned his eyes patiently upon the faces around him. He had been introduced to a good many persons, but he had come to that time of life when an introduction, unless charged with some special interest, only adds the pain of doubt to the wearisome encounter of unfamiliar people; and he had unconsciously put on the severity of a man who finds himself without acquaintance where others are meeting friends, when a small man, with a neatly trimmed reddish-gray beard and prominent eyes, stopped in front of him, and saluted him with the "Hello, Mavering!" of a contemporary.

His face, after a moment of question, relaxed into joyful recognition. "Why, John Munt! is that you?" he said, and he took into his large moist palm the dry little hand of his friend, while they both broke out into the incoherencies of people meeting after a long time. Mr. Mavering spoke in a voice soft yet firm, and with a certain thickness of tongue, which gave a boyish charm to his slow utterance, and Mr. Munt used the sort of bronchial snuffle sometimes cultivated among us as a chest tone. But they were cut short in their intersecting questions and exclamations by the presence of the lady who detached herself from Mr. Munt's arm as if to leave him the freer for his hand shaking.

"Oh!" he said, suddenly recurring to her, "let me introduce you to Mrs. Pasmer, Mr. Mavering," and the latter made a bow that creased his waistcoat at about the height of Mrs. Pasmer's pretty little nose.

His waistcoat had the curve which waistcoats often describe at his age; and his heavy shoulders were thrown well back to balance this curve. His coat hung carelessly open; the Panama hat in his hand suggested a certain habitual informality of dres but his smoothly shaven large handsome face, with its jaw slowly ruminant upon nothing, intimated the consequence of man accustomed to supremacy in a subordinate place.

Mrs. Pasmer looked up to acknowledge the introductio with a sort of pseudo-respectfulness which it would be har otherwise to describe. Whether she divined or not that sh was in the presence of a magnate of some sort, she was rathe superfluously demure in the first two or three things she said and was all sympathy and interest in the meeting of these ol friends. They declared that they had not seen each other fo twenty years, or, at any rate, not since '59. She listened whil they disputed about the exact date, and looked from time t time at Mr. Munt, as if for some explanation of Mr. Mavering but Munt himself, when she saw him last, had only just begu to commend himself to society, which had since so full accepted him, and she had so suddenly, the moment before found herself hand in glove with him that she might well hav appealed to a third person for some explanation of Munt. Bu she was not a woman to be troubled much by this momentar mystification, and she was not embarrassed at all when Mun said, as if it had all been prearranged, "Well, now, Mrs. Pasmer, if you'll let me leave you with Mr. Mavering a moment, I'll go off and bring that unnatural child *to* you; no use dragging you round through *this* crowd any longer."

He made a gesture intended, in the American manner, to be at once polite and jocose, and was gone, leaving Mrs. Pasmer a little surprised, and Mr. Mavering in some misgiving, which he tried to overcome by pressing his jaws together two or three times without speaking. She had no trouble in getting in the first remark. "Isn't all this charming, Mr. Mavering?" She spoke in a deep low voice, with a caressing manner, and stood looking up at Mr. Mavering with one shoulder shrugged and the other drooped, and a tasteful composition of her fan and hands and handkerchief at her waist.

"Yes, ma'am, it is," said Mr. Mavering. He seemed to say *ma'am* to her with a public or official accent, which sent Mrs. Pasmer's mind fluttering forth to poise briefly at such conjectures as "Congressman from a country district? judge of the Common Pleas? bank president? railroad superintendent? leading physician in a large town?—no, Mr. Munt said *Mister*," and then to return to her pretty blue eyes, and to center

WILLIAM DEAN HOWELLS

there in that pseudo-respectful attention under the arch of her neat brows and her soberly crinkled gray-threaded brown hair and her very appropriate bonnet. A bonnet, she said, was much more than half the battle after forty, and it was now quite after forty with Mrs. Pasmer; but she was very well dressed otherwise. Mr. Mavering went on to say, with a deliberation that seemed an element of his unknown dignity, whatever it might be, "A number of the young fellows together can give a much finer spread, and make more of the day, in a place like this, than we used to do in our rooms."

"Ah, then you're a Harvard man too!" said Mrs. Pasmer to herself, with surprise, which she kept to herself, and she said to Mavering: "Oh, yes, indeed! It's altogether better. *Aren't* they nice-looking fellows?" she said, putting up her glasses to look at the promenaders.

"Yes," Mr. Mavering assented. "I suppose," he added, out of the consciousness of his own relation to the affair—"I suppose you've a son somewhere here?"

"Oh dear, no!" cried Mrs. Pasmer, with a mingling, superhuman, but for her, of ironical deprecation and derision. "Only a daughter, Mr. Mavering."

At this feat of Mrs. Pasmer's, Mr. Mavering looked at her with question as to her precise intention, and ended by repeating hopelessly, "Only a daughter?"

"Yes," said Mrs. Pasmer, with a sigh of the same irony, "only a poor, despised young girl, Mr. Mavering."

"You speak," said Mr. Mavering, beginning to catch on a little, "as if it were a misfortune," and his dignity broke up into a smile that had its queer fascination.

"Why, isn't it?" asked Mrs. Pasmer.

"Well, I shouldn't have thought so."

"Then you *don't* believe that all that old-fashioned chivalry and devotion have gone out? You *don't* think the young men are all spoiled nowadays, and expect the young ladies to offer *them* attentions?"

"No," said Mr. Mavering, slowly, as if recovering from the shock of the novel ideas. "Do you?"

"Oh, I'm such a stranger in Boston—I've lived abroad so long—that I don't know. One hears all kinds of things. But I'm *so* glad you're not one of those—pessimists!"

"Well," said Mr. Mavering, still thoughtfully, "I don't know that I can speak by the card exactly. I can't say how it is now. I haven't been at a Class Day spread since my own Class Day; I haven't even been at Commencement more than once or twice. But in my time here we didn't expect the young ladies to show us attentions; at any rate, we didn't wait for them to do it. We were very glad to be asked to meet them, and we thought it an honor if the young ladies would let us talk or dance with them, or take them to picnics. I don't think that any of them could complain of want of attention."

"Yes," said Mrs. Pasmer, "that's what I preached, that's what I prophesied, when I brought my daughter home from Europe. I told her that a girl's life in America was one long triumph; but they say now that girls have more attention in London even than in Cambridge. One hears such dreadful things!"

"Like what?" asked Mr. Mavering, with the unserious interest which Mrs. Pasmer made most people feel in her talk.

"Oh, it's too vast a subject. But they tell you about charming girls moping the whole evening through at Boston parties, with no young men to talk with, and sitting from the beginning to the end of an assembly and not going on the floor once. They say that unless a girl fairly throws herself at the young men's heads she isn't noticed. It's this terrible disproportion of the sexes that's at the root of it, I suppose; it reverses everything. There aren't enough young men to go half round, and they know it, and take advantage of it. I suppose it began in the war."

He laughed, and "I should think," he said, laying hold of a single idea out of several which she had presented, "that there would always be enough young men in Cambridge to go round."

Mrs. Pasmer gave a little cry. "In Cambridge!"

"Yes; when I was in college our superiority was entirely numerical."

"But that's all passed *long* ago, from what I hear," retorted Mrs. Pasmer. "I know very well that it used to be thought a great advantage for a girl to be brought up in Cambridge, because it gave her independence and ease of manner to have so many young men attentive to her. But they say the students all go into Boston now, and if the Cambridge girls want to meet them, they have to go there to. Oh, I assure you that, from what I hear, they've changed all that since *our* time, Mr. Mavering."

Mrs. Pasmer was certainly letting herself go a little more than she would have approved of in another. The result was apparent in the jocosity of this heavy Mr. Mavering's reply.

"Well, then, I'm glad that I was of our time, and not of this wicked generation. But I presume that unnatural supremacy of the young men is brought low, so to speak, after marriage?"

Mrs. Pasmer let herself go a little further. "Oh, give us an equal chance," she laughed, "and we can always take care of ourselves, and something more. They say," she added, "that the young married women now have all the attention that girls could wish."

"H'm!" said Mr. Mavering, frowning. "I think I should be tempted to box my boy's ears if I saw him paying another man's wife attention."

"What a Roman father!" cried Mrs. Pasmer, greatly amused, and letting herself go a little further yet. She said to herself that she really must find out who this remarkable Mr. Mavering was, and she cast her eye over the hall for some glimpse of the absent Munt, whose arm she meant to take, and whose ear she meant to fill with questions. But she did not see him, and something else suggested itself. "He probably wouldn't let you see him, or if he did, you wouldn't know it."

"How not know it?"

Mrs. Pasmer did not answer. "One hears such dreadful things. What do you say — or you'll think I'm a terrible gossip —— "

"Oh no," said Mr. Mavering, impatient for the dreadful thing, whatever it was.

Mrs. Pasmer resumed: " — to the young married women meeting last winter just after a lot of pretty girls had come out, and magnanimously resolving to give the Buds a chance in society?"

"The Buds?"

"Yes, the Rosebuds — the *débutantes;* it's an odious little word, but everybody uses it. Don't you think that's a strange state of things for America? But I can't believe all those things," said Mrs. Pasmer, flinging off the shadow of this lurid social condition. "*Isn't* this a pretty scene?"

"Yes, it *is,*" Mr. Mavering admitted, withdrawing his mind gradually from a consideration of Mrs. Pasmer's awful instances. "Yes!" he added, in final self-possession. "The young fellows certainly do things in a great deal better style nowadays than we used to."

"Oh yes, indeed! And all those pretty girls *do* seem to be having such a good time!"

"Yes; they don't have the despised and rejected appearance that you'd like to have one believe."

"Not in the least!" Mrs. Pasmer readily consented. "They look radiantly happy. It shows that you can't trust anything that people say to you." She abandoned the ground she had just been taking without apparent shame for her inconsistency. "I fancy it's pretty much as it's always been: if a girl is attractive, the young men find it out."

"Perhaps," said Mr. Mavering, unbending with dignity, "the young married women have held another meeting, and resolved to give the Buds one more chance."

"Oh, there are some pretty mature Roses here," said Mrs. Pasmer, laughing evasively. "But I suppose Class Day can never be taken from the young girls."

"I hope not," said Mr. Mavering. His wandering eye fell upon some young men bringing refreshments across the nave toward them, and he was reminded to ask Mrs. Pasmer, "Will you have something to eat?" He had himself had a good deal to eat, before he took up his position at the advantageous point where John Munt had found him.

"Why, yes, thank you," said Mrs. Pasmer. "I ought to say, 'An ice, please,' but I'm really hungry, and——"

"I'll get you some of the salad," said Mr. Mavering, with the increased liking a man feels for a woman when she owns to an appetite. "Sit down here," he added, and he caught a vacant chair toward her. When he turned about from doing so, he confronted a young gentleman coming up to Mrs. Pasmer with a young lady on his arm, and making a very low bow of relinquishment.

The men looked smilingly at each other without saying anything, and the younger took in due form the introduction which the young lady gave him.

"My mother, Mr. Mavering."

"Mr. Mavering!" cried Mrs. Pasmer, in a pure astonishment, before she had time to color it with a polite variety of more conventional emotions. She glanced at the two men, and gave a little "Oh?" of inquiry and resignation, and then said demurely, "Let me introduce *you* to Mr. Mavering, Alice," while the young fellow laughed nervously, and pulled out his handkerchief, partly to hide the play of his laughter, and partly to wipe away the perspiration which a great deal more laughing had already gathered on his forehead. He had a vein that showed prominently down its center, and large, mobile, girlish blue eyes under good brows, an arched nose, and rather a long face and narrow chin. He had beautiful white teeth; as he laughed these were seen set in a jaw that contracted very much toward the front. He was tall and slim, and he wore with elegance the evening dress which Class Day custom prescribes for the Seniors; in his buttonhole he had a club button.

"I shall not have to ask an introduction to Mr. Mavering; and you've robbed me of the pleasure of giving him one to you, Mrs. Pasmer," he said.

She heard the young man in the course of a swift review of what she had said to his father, and with a formless resentment of the father's not having told her he had a son there; but she answered with the flattering sympathy she had the use of, "Oh, but you won't miss one pleasure out of so many to-day, Mr. Mavering; and think of the little dramatic surprise!"

"Oh, perfect," he said, with another laugh. "I told Miss Pasmer as we came up."

"Oh, then you were *in* the surprise, Alice!" said Mrs. Pasmer, searching her daughter's eyes for confession or denial of this little community of interest. The girl smiled slightly upon the young man, but not disapprovingly, and made no other answer to her mother, who went on: "Where in the world have you been? Did Mr. Munt find you? Who told you where I was? Did you see me? How did you know I was here? Was there ever anything so droll?" She did not mean her questions to be answered, or at least not then; for, while her daughter continued to smile rather more absently, and young Mavering broke out continuously in his nervous laugh, and his father stood regarding him with visible satisfaction, she hummed on, turning to the young man: "But I'm quite appalled at Alice's having monopolized even for a few minutes a whole Senior—and probably an official Senior at that," she said, with a glance at the pink and white club button in his coat lapel, "and I can't let you stay another instant, Mr. Mavering. I know very well how many demands you have upon you, and you must go back directly to your sisters and your cousins and your aunts, and all the rest of them; you must indeed."

"Oh no! Don't drive me away, Mrs. Pasmer," pleaded the young man, laughing violently, and then wiping his face. "I assure you that I've no encumbrances of any kind here except my father, and he seems to have been taking very good care of himself." They all laughed at this, and the young fellow hurried on: "Don't be alarmed at my button; it only means a love of personal decoration, if that's where you got the notion of my being an official Senior. This isn't my spread; I shall hope to welcome you at Beck Hall after the Tree; and I *wish* you'd let me be of use to you. Wouldn't you like to go round to some of the smaller spreads? I think it would amuse you. And have you got tickets to the Tree, to see us make fools of ourselves? It's worth seeing, Mrs. Pasmer, I assure you."

He rattled on very rapidly, but with such a frankness in his urgency, such amiable kindliness, that Mrs. Pasmer could not feel that it was pushing. She looked at her daughter, but she stood as passive in the transaction as the elder Mavering. She was taller than her mother, and as she waited, her supple figure described that fine lateral curve which one sees in some Louis Quinze portraits; this effect was enhanced by the fashion of her dress of pale sage green, with a wide stripe or sash of white dropping down the front, from her delicate waist. The same simple combination of colors was carried up into her hat, which surmounted darker hair than Mrs. Pasmer's, and a complexion of wholesome pallor; her eyes were gray and grave, with black brows, and her face, which was rather narrow, had a pleasing irregularity in the sharp jut of the nose; in profile the parting of the red lips showed well back into the cheek.

"I don't know," said Mrs. Pasmer, in her own behalf; and she added in his, "about letting you take so much trouble," so smoothly that it would have been quite impossible to detect the point of union in the two utterances.

"Well, don't call it names, anyway, Mrs. Pasmer," pleaded the young man. "I thought it was nothing but a pleasure and a privilege ——"

"The fact is," she explained, neither consenting nor refusing, "that we were expecting to meet some friends who had tickets for us"—young Mavering's face fell—"and I can't imagine what's happened."

"Oh, let's hope something dreadful," he cried.

"Perhaps you know them," she delayed further. "Professor Saintsbury?"

"Well, rather! Why, they were here about an hour ago — both of them. They must have been looking for you."

"Yes; we were to meet them here. We waited to come out with other friends, and I was afraid we were late." Mrs. Pasmer's face expressed a tempered disappointment, and she looked at her daughter for indications of her wishes in the circumstances; seeing in her eye a willingness to accept young Mavering's invitation, she hesitated more decidedly than she had yet done, for she was, other things being equal, quite willing to accept it herself. But other things were not equal, and the whole situation was very odd. All that she knew of Mr. Mavering the elder was that he was the old friend of John Munt, and she knew far too little of John Munt, except that he seemed to go everywhere, and to be welcome, not to feel that his introduction was hardly a warrant for what looked like an impending intimacy. She did not dislike Mr. Mavering; he was evidently a country person of great self-respect, and no doubt of entire respectability. He seemed very intelligent, too. He was a Harvard man; he had rather a cultivated manner, or else naturally a clever way of saying things. But all that was really nothing, if she knew no more about him, and she certainly did not. If she could only have asked her daughter who it was that presented young Mavering to her, that might have formed some clew, but there was no earthly chance of asking this, and, besides, it was probably one of those haphazard introductions that people give on such occasions. Young Mavering's behavior gave her still greater question: his self-possession, his entire absence of anxiety, or any expectation of rebuff or snub, might be the ease of unimpeachable social acceptance, or it might be merely adventurous effrontery; only something ingenuous and good in the young fellow's handsome face forbade this conclusion. That his face was so handsome was another of the complications. She recalled, in the dreamlike swiftness with which all these things passed through her mind, what her friends had said to Alice about her being sure to meet her fate on Class Day, and she looked at her again to see if she had met it.

"Well, mamma?" said the girl, smiling at her mother's look.

Mrs. Pasmer thought she must have been keeping young

Mavering waiting a long time for his answer. "Why, of course, Alice. But I really don't know what to do about the Saintsburys." This was not in the least true, but it instantly seemed so to Mrs. Pasmer, as a plausible excuse will when we make it.

"Why, I'll tell you what, Mrs. Pasmer," said young Mavering, with a cordial unsuspicion that both won and reassured her, "we'll be sure to find them at some of the spreads. Let me be of that much use, anyway; you must."

"We really oughtn't to let you," said Mrs. Pasmer, making a last effort to cling to her reluctance, but feeling it fail, with a sensation that was not disagreeable. She could not help being pleased with the pleasure that she saw in her daughter's face.

Young Mavering's was radiant. "I'll be back in just half a minute," he said, and he took a gay leave of them in running to speak to another student at the opposite end of the hall.

The party went to half a dozen spreads, some of which were on a scale of public grandeur approaching that of the Gymnasium, and others of a subdued elegance befitting the more private hospitalities in the students' rooms. Mrs. Pasmer was very much interested in these rooms, whose luxurious appointments testified to the advance of riches and of the taste to apply them since she used to visit students' rooms in far-off Class Days. The deep window nooks and easy-chairs upholstered in the leather that seems sacred alike to the seats and the shelves of libraries; the æsthetic bookcases, low and topped with bric-a-brac; the etchings and prints on the walls, which the elder Mavering went up to look at with a mystifying air of understanding such things; the foils crossed over the chimney, and the mantel with its pipes, and its photographs of theatrical celebrities tilted about over it—spoke of conditions mostly foreign to Mrs. Pasmer's memories of Harvard. The photographed celebrities seemed to be chosen chiefly for their beauty, and for as much of their beauty as possible, Mrs. Pasmer perceived, with an obscure misgiving of the sort which an older generation always likes to feel concerning the younger, but with a tolerance, too, which was personal to herself; it was to be considered that the massive thought and honest amiability of Salvini's face, and the deep and spiritualized power of Booth's, varied the effect of these companies of posturing nymphs.

At many places she either met old friends with whom she clamored over the wonder of their encounter there, or was made acquainted with new people by the Saintsburys. She kept a mother's eye on her daughter, to whom young Mavering presented everybody within hail or reach, and whom she could see, whenever she looked at her, a radiant center of admiration. She could hear her talk sometimes, and she said to herself that really Alice was coming out; she had never heard her say so many good things before; she did not know it was in her. She was very glad then that she had let her wear that dress; it was certainly distinguished, and the girl carried it off, to her mother's amusement, with the air of a superb lady of the period from which it dated. She thought what a simple child Alice really was, all the time those other children, the Seniors, were stealing their glances of bold or timid worship at her, and doubtless thinking her a brilliant woman of the world. But there could be no mistake that she was a success.

THE SIGHTLESS.[1]

By MAURICE MAETERLINCK.

(Translated by Laurence Alma-Tadema.)

[Maurice Maeterlinck, known as the "Belgian Shakespeare," was born at Ghent, in 1864. Since 1890 he has published a number of remarkable plays which have been widely read and admired outside of his own country. They include: "The Princess Maleine," "The Intruder," "The Blind," "Aglavaine and Selysette," and "Pelleas and Melisande," recently produced with success in London. In addition to his dramatic works Maeterlinck has written "The Treasure of the Humble," a volume of essays.]

Persons:

The Priest. Three that were born Blind. The Oldest Blind Man. The Fifth Blind Man. The Sixth Blind Man. Three Old Blind Women praying. The Oldest Blind Woman. A Young Blind Woman. A Mad Blind Woman.

A very ancient northern forest, eternal of aspect, beneath a sky profoundly starred. — In the midst, and towards the depths of night, a very old priest is seated wrapped in a wide black

[1] By permission of Walter Scott, Ltd. (Price 1s. 6d.)

cloak. His head and the upper part of his body, slightly thrown back and mortally still, are leaning against the bole of an oak tree, huge and cavernous. His face is fearfully pale and of an inalterable waxen lividity; his violet lips are parted. His eyes, dumb and fixed, no longer gaze at the visible side of eternity, and seem bleeding beneath a multitude of immemorial sorrows and of tears. His hair, of a most solemn white, falls in stiff and scanty locks upon a face more illumined and more weary than all else that surrounds it in the intent silence of the gloomy forest. His hands, extremely lean, are rigidly clasped on his lap.—To the right, six old blind men are seated upon stones, the stumps of trees, and dead leaves.—To the left, separated from them by an uprooted tree and fragments of rock, six women, blind also, are seated facing the old men. Three of them are praying and wailing in hollow voice and without pause. Another is extremely old. The fifth, in an attitude of mute insanity, holds on her knees a little child asleep. The sixth is strangely young, and her hair inundates her whole being. The women, as well as the old men, are clothed in ample garments, somber and uniform. Most of them sit waiting with their elbows on their knees and their faces between their hands; and all seem to have lost the habit of useless gesture, and no longer turn their heads at the stifled and restless noises of the island. Great funereal trees, yews, weeping willows, cypresses, enwrap them in their faithful shadows. Not far from the priest, a cluster of long and sickly daffodils blossoms in the night. It is extraordinarily dark in spite of the moonlight that here and there strives to dispel for a while the gloom of the foliage.

First Blind Man—Is he not coming yet?

Second Blind Man—You have waked me!

First Blind Man—I was asleep too.

Third Blind Man—I was asleep too.

First Blind Man—Is he not coming yet?

Second Blind Man—I hear nothing coming.

Third Blind Man—It must be about time to go back to the asylum.

First Blind Man—We want to know where we are!

Second Blind Man—It has grown cold since he left.

First Blind Man—We want to know where we are!

The Oldest Blind Man—Does any one know where we are?

The Oldest Blind Woman — We were walking a very long time; we must be very far from the asylum.

First Blind Man — Ah! the women are opposite us?

The Oldest Blind Woman — We are sitting opposite you.

First Blind Man — Wait, I will come next to you. [*He rises and gropes about.*] Where are you? Speak! that I may hear where you are!

The Oldest Blind Woman — Here; we are sitting on stones.

First Blind Man [*steps forward stumbling against the fallen tree and the rocks*] — There is something between us . . .

Second Blind Man — It is better to stay where one is!

Third Blind Man — Where are you sitting? Do you want to come over to us?

The Oldest Blind Woman — We dare not stand up!

Third Blind Man — Why did he separate us?

First Blind Man — I hear praying on the women's side.

Second Blind Man — Yes; the three old women are praying.

First Blind Man — This is not the time to pray!

Second Blind Man — You can pray by and by in the dormitory! [*The three old women continue their prayers.*

Third Blind Man — I should like to know next to whom I am sitting?

Second Blind Man — I think I am next you.

[*They grope about them with their hands.*

Third Blind Man — We cannot touch each other.

First Blind Man — And yet we are not far apart. [*He gropes about him, and with his stick hits the fifth blind man, who gives a dull moan.*] The one who cannot hear is sitting next us.

Second Blind Man — I don't hear everybody; we were six just now.

First Blind Man — I am beginning to make things out. Let us question the women too; it is necessary that we should know how matters stand. I still hear the three old women praying; are they sitting together?

The Oldest Blind Woman — They are sitting beside me, on a rock.

First Blind Man — I am sitting on dead leaves!

Third Blind Man — And the beauty, where is she?

The Oldest Blind Woman — She is near those that are praying.

Second Blind Man — Where are the mad woman and her child?

The Young Blind Woman — He is asleep; don't wake him!

First Blind Man — Oh! how far from us you are! I thought you were just opposite me!

Third Blind Man — We know, more or less, all that we need know; let us talk a little, till the priest comes back.

The Oldest Blind Woman — He told us to await him in silence.

Third Blind Man — We are not in a church.

The Oldest Blind Woman — You don't know where we are.

Third Blind Man — I feel frightened when I am not talking.

Second Blind Man — Do you know where the priest has gone?

Third Blind Man — It seems to me that he is leaving us alone too long.

First Blind Man — He is growing too old. It appears that he has hardly been able to see for some time himself. He will not own it, for fear that another should come and take his place among us; but I suspect that he can hardly see any more. We ought to have another guide; he never listens to us now, and we are becoming too many for him. The three nuns and he are the only ones in the house that can see; and they are all older than we are! — I am sure that he has led us astray, and is trying to find the way again. Where can he have gone? — He has no right to leave us here . . .

The Oldest Blind Man — He has gone very far; I think he said so to the women.

First Blind Man — Then he only speaks to the women now? — Do we not exist any more? — We shall have to complain in the end!

The Oldest Blind Man — To whom will you carry your complaint?

First Blind Man — I don't yet know; we shall see, we shall see. — But where can he have gone? — I am asking it of the women.

The Oldest Blind Woman — He was tired, having walked so long. I think he sat down a moment in our midst. He has been very sad and very weak for some days. He has been uneasy since the doctor died. He is lonely. He hardly ever speaks. I don't know what can have happened. He insisted on going out to-day. He said he wanted to see the Island one last time, in the sun, before winter came. It appears that the winter will be very cold and very long, and that ice is already coming down from the north. He was anxious too; they say that the great storms of these last days have swelled the stream, and that all the dikes are giving way. He said too that the sea frightened him; it appears to be agitated for no reason, and the cliffs of the Island are not high enough. He wanted to see for himself; but he did not tell us what he saw. — I think he has gone now to fetch some bread and water for the mad woman. He said that he would perhaps have to go very far. We shall have to wait.

The Young Blind Woman — He took my hands on leaving; and his hands trembled as if he were afraid. Then he kissed me . . .

First Blind Man — Oh! oh!

The Young Blind Woman — I asked him what had happened. He told me that he did not know what was going to happen. He told me that the old men's reign was coming to an end, perhaps . . .

First Blind Man — What did he mean by that?

The Young Blind Woman — I did not understand him. He told me that he was going towards the great lighthouse.

First Blind Man — Is there a lighthouse here?

The Young Blind Woman — Yes, north of the Island. I think we are not far from it. He told me that he could see the light of the beacon falling here, upon the leaves. He never seemed to me sadder than to-day, and I think that for some days he had been crying. I don't know why, but I cried too, without seeing him. I did not hear him go. I did not question him further. I could hear that he was smiling too solemnly; I could hear that he was closing his eyes and wished for silence . . .

First Blind Man — He said nothing to us of all this!

The Young Blind Woman — You never listen to him when he speaks!

The Oldest Blind Woman — You all murmur when he speaks!

Second Blind Man — He merely said "Good night" on leaving.

Third Blind Man — It must be very late.

First Blind Man — He said "Good night" two or three times on leaving, as if he were going to sleep. I could hear that he was looking at me when he said, "Good night; good night." — The voice changes when one looks at some one fixedly.

Fifth Blind Man — Have pity on those that cannot see!

First Blind Man — Who is talking in that senseless way?

Second Blind Man — I think it is the one who cannot hear.

First Blind Man — Be quiet! — this is not the time to beg!

Third Blind Man — Where was he going for the bread and water?

The Oldest Blind Woman — He went towards the sea.

Third Blind Man — One does not walk towards the sea in that way at his age!

Second Blind Man — Are we near the sea?

The Oldest Blind Woman — Yes; be quiet an instant; you will hear it.

[*A murmur of the sea near at hand and very calm against the cliffs.*

Second Blind Man — I only hear the three old women praying.

The Oldest Blind Woman — Listen well, you will hear it through their prayers.

Second Blind Man — Yes; I hear something that is not far from us.

The Oldest Blind Woman — It was asleep; it seems as if it were waking.

First Blind Man — It was wrong of him to lead us here; I don't like hearing that noise.

The Oldest Blind Man — You know very well that the Island is not large, and that one can hear it as soon as ever one leaves the walls of the asylum.

Second Blind Man — I never listened to it.

Third Blind Man — It seems to me that it is next us to-day; I don't like hearing it so close.

Second Blind Man — Nor I; besides, we never asked to leave the asylum.

Third Blind Man — We have never been as far as this; it was useless to bring us so far.

The Oldest Blind Woman — It was very fine this morning; he wanted us to enjoy the last days of sunshine, before shutting us up for the whole winter in the asylum . . .

First Blind Man — But I prefer staying in the asylum!

The Oldest Blind Woman — He said too that we ought to

know something of the little Island we live in. He himself has never been all over it; there is a mountain that no one has climbed, valleys which no one likes to go down to, and caves that have not been entered to this day. He said, in short, that one must not always sit waiting for the sun under the dormitory roof; he wanted to bring us to the seashore. He has gone there alone.

The Oldest Blind Man — He is right; one must think of living.

First Blind Man — But there is nothing to see out of doors!

Second Blind Man — Are we in the sun, now?

Third Blind Man — Is the sun still shining?

Sixth Blind Man — I think not; it seems to me to be very late.

Second Blind Man — What o'clock is it?

The Others — I don't know. — Nobody knows.

Second Blind Man — Is it still light? [*To the sixth blind man*] Where are you? — Come, you who can see a little, come!

Sixth Blind Man — I think it is very dark; when the sun shines, I see a blue line under my eyelids; I saw one a long while ago; but now I can see nothing at all.

First Blind Man — As for me, I know that it is late when I am hungry, and I am hungry.

Third Blind Man — But look up at the sky; you will see something perhaps!

[*They all lift their heads towards the sky, save the three that were born blind, who continue to look on the ground.*

Sixth Blind Man — I don't know that we are under the sky.

First Blind Man — Our voices resound as if they were in a cave.

The Oldest Blind Man — I rather think they resound so because it is evening.

The Young Blind Woman — It seems to me that I feel the moonlight on my hands.

The Oldest Blind Woman — I think there are stars; I hear them.

The Young Blind Woman — I too.

First Blind Man — I can hear no sound.

Second Blind Man — I can only hear the sound of our breathing!

The Oldest Blind Man — I think the women are right.

First Blind Man — I never heard the stars.

Second and Third Blind Men — Neither did I.

[*A flight of night birds alights suddenly amidst the foliage.*

Second Blind Man — Listen! listen! — What is that above us? — Do you hear?

The Oldest Blind Man — Something passed between the sky and us.

Sixth Blind Man — There is something moving above our heads; but we cannot reach it!

First Blind Man — I don't know the nature of that sound. — I want to go back to the asylum.

Second Blind Man — We want to know where we are!

Sixth Blind Man — I have tried to stand up; there are thorns, nothing but thorns about me; I dare not spread my hands out any more.

Third Blind Man — We want to know where we are!

The Oldest Blind Man — We cannot know it!

Sixth Blind Man — We must be very far from the house; I can no longer make out a single noise.

Third Blind Man — For a long while, I have smelt the smell of dead leaves.

Sixth Blind Man — Did any one of us see the Island in past days, and could he tell us where we are?

The Oldest Blind Woman — We were all blind when we came here.

First Blind Man — We have never been able to see.

Second Blind Man — Let us not be unnecessarily anxious; he will soon return; let us wait a little longer; but in future. we will not go out with him again.

The Oldest Blind Man — We cannot go out alone!

First Blind Man — We will not go out at all, I prefer not going out.

Second Blind Man — We had no wish to go out, nobody had asked to do so.

The Oldest Blind Woman — It was a holiday on the Island; we always go out on great holidays.

Third Blind Woman — He came and hit me on the shoulder when I was still asleep, saying: Get up, get up, it is time; the sun is shining! — Was there any sun? I was not aware of it. I have never seen the sun.

The Oldest Blind Man — I saw the sun when I was very young.

The Oldest Blind Woman — I too; it was long ago, when I was a child; but I hardly remember it now.

Third Blind Man — Why does he want us to go out every time the sun shines? Which of us is any the wiser? I never know whether I am walking out at midday or at midnight.

Sixth Blind Man — I prefer going out at midday; I suspect great brightness then, and my eyes make great efforts to open.

Third Blind Man — I prefer staying in the refectory by the coal fire; there was a big fire there this morning . . .

Second Blind Man — He could bring us out into the sun in the yard; there one has the shelter of the walls; one cannot get out, there is nothing to fear when the door is shut. — I always shut it. — Why did you touch my left elbow?

First Blind Man — I did not touch you; I cannot reach you.

Second Blind Man — I tell you that somebody touched my elbow.

First Blind Man — It was none of us.

Second Blind Man — I want to go away!

The Oldest Blind Woman — O God! O God! tell us where we are!

First Blind Man — We cannot wait here forever!

[*A very distant clock strikes twelve very slowly.*

The Oldest Blind Woman — Oh! how far we are from the asylum!

The Oldest Blind Man — It is midnight!

Second Blind Man — It is midday! — Does any one know? — Speak!

Sixth Blind Man — I don't know. But I think we are in the shade.

First Blind Man — I can make nothing out; we slept too long.

Second Blind Man — I am hungry.

The Others — We are hungry and thirsty!

Second Blind Man — Have we been here long?

The Oldest Blind Woman — It seems to me that I have been here centuries!

Sixth Blind Man — I am beginning to make out where we are . . .

Third Blind Man — We ought to go towards where midnight struck. [*All the night birds exult suddenly in the gloom.*

First Blind Man — Do you hear? — Do you hear?

Second Blind Man — We are not alone!

Third Blind Man — I have had my suspicions for a long time; we are being overheard. — Has he come back?

First Blind Man — I don't know what it is; it is above us.

Second Blind Man — Did the others hear nothing? — You are always silent!

The Oldest Blind Man — We are still listening.

The Young Blind Woman — I hear wings about me!

The Oldest Blind Woman — O God! O God! tell us where we are!

The Sixth Blind Man — I am beginning to make out where we are . . . The asylum is on the other side of the big river; we have crossed the old bridge. He has brought us to the north side of the Island. We are not far from the river, and perhaps we should hear it if we were to listen a moment . . . We shall have to go down to the edge of the water, if he does not come back . . . Night and day great ships pass there, and the sailors will see us standing on the banks. It may be that we are in the forest that surrounds the lighthouse; but I don't know the way out of it . . . Is somebody willing to follow me?

First Blind Man — Let us keep seated! — Let us wait, let us wait; — we don't know the direction of the big river, and there are bogs all round the asylum; let us wait, let us wait . . . He will come back; he is bound to come back!

Sixth Blind Man — Does any one know which way we came here? He explained it to us as we walked.

First Blind Man — I paid no attention.

Sixth Blind Man — Did any one listen to him?

Third Blind Man — We must listen to him in future.

Sixth Blind Man — Was any one of us born on the Island?

The Oldest Blind Man — You know quite well that we come from elsewhere.

The Oldest Blind Woman — We come from the other side of the sea.

First Blind Man — I thought I should have died crossing.

Second Blind Man — I too; — we came together.

Third Blind Man — We are all three of the same parish.

First Blind Man — They say that one can see it from here in clear weather; — towards the north. — It has no steeple.

Third Blind Man — We landed by chance.

The Oldest Blind Woman — I come from another direction . . .

Second Blind Man — From where do you come?

The Oldest Blind Woman — I no longer dare think of it . . . I can hardly call it to mind when I speak of it . . . It was too long ago . . . It was colder there than here . . .

The Young Blind Woman — And I, I come from very far . . .

First Blind Man — Where do you come from then?

The Young Blind Woman — I could not tell you. How should I be able to describe it? — It is too far from here; it is beyond the seas. I come from a big country . . . I could only explain it to you by signs, and we cannot see . . . I have wandered too long . . . But I have seen the sun and water and fire, and mountains, and faces and strange flowers . . . There are none like them on this Island; it is too dismal here and too cold . . . I have never known the scent again, since I lost my sight . . . But I saw my parents and my sisters . . . I was too young then to know where I was . . . I still played about on the seashore . . . Yet how well I remember having seen! . . . One day, I looked at the snow from the top of a mountain . . . I was just beginning to distinguish those that are to be unhappy . . .

First Blind Man — What do you mean?

The Young Blind Woman — I can still distinguish them by the sound of their voice at times . . . I have memories that are clearer when I am not thinking of them . . .

First Blind Man — I have no memories, I . . .

[*A flight of big birds of passage passes clamoring above the foliage.*

The Oldest Blind Man — There is something passing again beneath the sky!

Second Blind Man — Why did you come here?

The Oldest Blind Man — To whom are you speaking?

Second Blind Man — To our young sister.

The Young Blind Woman — They had told me that he could cure me. He says that I shall see again some day; then I shall be able to leave the Island . . .

First Blind Man — We should all like to leave the Island!

Second Blind Man — We shall stay here forever!

Third Blind Man — He is too old; he will never have time to cure us!

The Young Blind Woman — My eyelids are closed, but I feel that my eyes are alive . . .

First Blind Man — Mine are open . . .

Second Blind Man — I sleep with my eyes open.

Third Blind Man — Let us not speak of our eyes!

Second Blind Man — You have not been here long?

The Oldest Blind Man — One evening, during prayers, I heard on the women's side a voice I did not know; and I could tell by your voice that you were young . . . I wanted to see you, having heard your voice . . .

First Blind Man — I never noticed it.

Second Blind Man — He never lets us know anything!

Sixth Blind Man — They say that you are beautiful, like some woman come from afar.

The Young Blind Woman — I have never seen myself.

The Oldest Blind Man — We have never seen each other. We question each other, and we answer each other; we live together, we are always together, but we know not what we are! . . . It is all very well to touch each other with both hands; eyes know more than hands . . .

Sixth Blind Man — I see your shadows sometimes when you are in the sun . . .

The Oldest Blind Man — We have never seen the house in which we live; it is all very well to touch the walls and the windows; we know nothing of where we live . . .

The Oldest Blind Woman — They say it is an old castle, very gloomy and very wretched; one never sees a light there, save in the tower where the priest's room is.

First Blind Man — Those who cannot see need no light.

Sixth Blind Man — When I am keeping the flocks, round about the asylum, the sheep go home of themselves when, at evening, they see that light in the tower . . . They have never led me astray.

The Oldest Blind Man — For years and years we have lived together and we have never beheld each other! One would say we were always alone! . . . One must see to love . . .

The Oldest Blind Woman — I sometimes dream that I can see . . .

The Oldest Blind Man — I only see when I am dreaming . . .

First Blind Man — I only dream, as a rule, at midnight.

Second Blind Man — Of what can one dream when one's hands are motionless?

[*A squall shakes the forest, and the leaves fall in dismal showers.*

Fifth Blind Man — Who was it touched my hands?

First Blind Man — There is something falling round us.

The Oldest Blind Man — It comes from above; I don't know what it is . . .

Fifth Blind Man — Who was it touched my hands? — I was asleep; let me sleep!

The Oldest Blind Man — Nobody touched your hands.

Fifth Blind Man — Who was it took my hands? Answer loud, I am rather hard of hearing . . .

The Oldest Blind Man — We don't ourselves know.

Fifth Blind Man — Have they come to warn us?

First Blind Man — It is of no use answering; he can hear nothing.

Third Blind Man — It must be admitted that the deaf are very unfortunate!

The Oldest Blind Man — I am tired of sitting down!

Sixth Blind Man — I am tired of being here!

Second Blind Man — We seem to me so far from one another . . . Let us try to draw a little closer together; — it is beginning to be cold . . .

Third Blind Man — I dare not stand up! It is better to stay where one is.

The Oldest Blind Man — There is no knowing what there may be between us.

Sixth Blind Man — I think both my hands are bleeding; I wanted to stand up.

Third Blind Man — I can hear that you are leaning towards me.

[*The blind mad woman rubs her eyes violently, moaning, and persistently turning towards the motionless priest.*

First Blind Man — I hear another noise . . .

The Oldest Blind Woman — I think it is our poor sister rubbing her eyes.

Second Blind Man — She never does anything else; I hear her every night.

Third Blind Man — She is mad; she never says anything.

The Oldest Blind Woman — She has never spoken since she had her child. She seems always to be afraid . . .

The Oldest Blind Man — Are you not afraid here then?

First Blind Man — Who?

The Oldest Blind Man — All the rest of us!

The Oldest Blind Woman — Yes, yes, we are afraid!

The Young Blind Woman — We have been afraid a long time!

First Blind Man — Why do you ask that?

The Oldest Blind Man — I don't know why I ask it? . . . There is something I cannot make out . . . It seems as if I heard a sudden sound of crying in our midst! . . .

First Blind Man — It does not do to be afraid; I think it is the mad woman . . .

The Oldest Blind Man — There is something else besides . . . I am sure there is something else besides . . . It is not only that which frightens me . . .

The Oldest Blind Woman — She always cries when she is about to suckle her child.

First Blind Man — She is the only one that cries so!

The Oldest Blind Woman — They say that she can still see at times . . .

First Blind Man — One never hears the others cry . . .

The Oldest Blind Man — One must see to weep . . .

The Young Blind Woman — I smell a scent of flowers round about us . . .

First Blind Man — I only smell the smell of the earth!

The Young Blind Woman — There are flowers, there are flowers near us!

Second Blind Man — I only smell the smell of the earth!

The Oldest Blind Woman — I have just smelt flowers on the wind . . .

Third Blind Man — I only smell the smell of the earth!

The Oldest Blind Man — I think the women are right.

Sixth Blind Man — Where are they? — I will go and pick them.

The Young Blind Woman — To your right, stand up.

[*The sixth blind man rises slowly, and, knocking himself against trees and bushes, gropes his way towards the daffodils, which he treads down and crushes as he goes.*

The Young Blind Woman — I can hear that you are snapping green stems! Stop! stop!

First Blind Man — Never mind about the flowers, but think about getting back!

Sixth Blind Man — I dare not retrace my steps!

The Young Blind Woman — You must not come back! — Wait. [*She rises.*] — Oh! how cold the earth is! It is going to freeze. [*She moves without hesitation towards the strange pale daffodils, but she is stopped by the fallen tree and the rocks, in the neighborhood of the flowers.*] — They are here! — I cannot reach them; they are on your side.

Sixth Blind Man — I think I am picking them.

[*Groping about him, he picks what flowers are left, and offers them to her; the night birds fly away.*

The Young Blind Woman — It seems to me that I once saw these flowers . . . I have forgotten their name . . . But how ill they are, and how limp their stalks are! I hardly know them again . . . I think they are the flowers of the dead . . .

[*She plaits the daffodils in her hair.*

The Oldest Blind Man — I hear the sound of your hair.

The Young Blind Woman — Those are the flowers . . .

The Oldest Blind Man — We shall not see you . . .

The Young Blind Woman — I shall not see myself . . . I am cold.

[*At this moment the wind rises in the forest and the sea roars suddenly and with violence against the neighboring cliffs.*

First Blind Man — It is thundering!

Second Blind Man — I think it is a storm rising.

The Oldest Blind Woman — I think it is the sea.

Third Blind Man — The sea? — Is it the sea? — But it is at two steps from us! — It is beside us! I hear it all round me! — It must be something else!

The Young Blind Woman — I hear the sound of waves at my feet.

First Blind Man — I think it is the wind in the dead leaves.

The Oldest Blind Man — I think the women are right.

Third Blind Man — It will be coming here!

First Blind Man — Where does the wind come from?

Second Blind Man — It comes from the sea.

The Oldest Blind Man — It always comes from the sea; the sea hems us in on all sides. It cannot come from elsewhere . . .

First Blind Man — Let us not think of the sea any more!

Second Blind Man — But we must think of it, as it is going to reach us!

First Blind Man — You don't know that it is the sea.

Second Blind Man — I hear its waves as if I were going to dip both hands in! We cannot stay here! They may be all around us!

The Oldest Blind Man — Where do you want to go?

Second Blind Man — No matter where! No matter where! I will not hear the sound of that water any more! Let us go! Let us go!

Third Blind Man — It seems to me that I hear something else besides. — Listen!

[*A sound of footsteps, swift and distant, is heard among the dead leaves.*

First Blind Man — There is something coming towards us!

Second Blind Man — He is coming! He is coming! He is coming back!

Third Blind Man — He is taking little steps, like a little child . . .

Second Blind Man — Let us reproach him nothing to-day!

The Oldest Blind Woman — I think it is not the step of a man!

[*A big dog enters the forest and passes before them. — Silence.*

First Blind Man — Who is there? — Who are you? — Have pity on us, we have been waiting so long! . . . [*The dog stops, and returning, lays his front paws on the blind man's knees.*] Ah! ah! what have you put on my knees? What is it? . . . Is it an animal? I think it is a dog? . . . Oh! oh! it is the dog! it is the dog from the asylum! Come here! come here! He has come to deliver us! Come here! come here!

The Others — Come here! come here!

First Blind Man — He has come to deliver us! He has followed our traces! He is licking my hands as if he had found me after hundreds of years! He is howling for joy! He will die of joy! Listen! listen!

The Others — Come here! come here!

The Oldest Blind Man — He has perhaps run on in front of somebody? . . .

First Blind Man — No, no, he is alone. — I hear nothing coming. — We need no other guide; there is none better. He will lead us wherever we want to go; he will obey us . . .

The Oldest Blind Woman — I dare not follow him.

The Young Blind Woman — Nor I.

First Blind Man — Why not? He sees better than we do.

Second Blind Man — Let us not listen to the women!

Third Blind Man — I think that something has changed in the sky; I breathe freely; the air is pure now . . .

The Oldest Blind Woman — It is the sea breeze that is blowing round us.

Sixth Blind Man — It seems to me that it is going to get light; I think the sun is rising . . .

The Oldest Blind Man — I think it is going to be cold . . .

First Blind Man — We shall find the way. He is dragging me along. He is drunk with joy! — I can no longer hold him back! . . . Follow me! follow me! We are going home! . . .

[*He rises, dragged along by the dog, who leads him towards the motionless priest, and there stops.*

The Others — Where are you? Where are you? — Where are you going? Take care!

First Blind Man — Wait! wait! Don't follow me yet; I will come back . . . He is standing still. — What is it? — Ah! ah! I have touched something very cold!

Second Blind Man — What are you saying? I can hardly hear your voice any more.

First Blind Man — I have touched . . . I think I am touching a face!

Third Blind Man — What are you saying? — One can hardly understand you any more. What is the matter with you? — Where are you? — Are you already so far away from us?

First Blind Man — Oh! oh! oh! I don't yet know what it is . . . — There is a dead man in our midst!

The Others — A dead man in our midst? — Where are you? where are you?

First Blind Man — There is a dead man among us, I tell you! Oh! oh! I have touched a dead face! — You are sitting next to a dead body! One of us must have died suddenly! But speak then, that I may know which are alive! Where are you? — Answer! answer all together!

[*They answer in succession save the mad woman and the deaf man; the three old women have ceased praying.*

First Blind Man — I can no longer distinguish your voices! . . . You are all speaking alike! . . . They are all trembling!

Third Blind Man — There are two who did not answer . . . Where are they? [*He touches with his stick the fifth blind man.*

Fifth Blind Man — Oh! oh! I was asleep; let me sleep!

Sixth Blind Man — It is not he. — Is it the mad woman?

The Oldest Blind Woman — She is sitting next me; I can hear her live . . .

First Blind Man — I think . . . I think it is the priest! — He is standing! Come! come! come!

Second Blind Man — He is standing?

Third Blind Man — Then he is not dead!

The Oldest Blind Man — Where is he?

Sixth Blind Man — Come and see! . . .

[*They all rise, save the mad woman and the fifth blind man, and grope their way towards the dead.*

Second Blind Man — Is he here? — Is it he?

Third Blind Man — Yes! yes! I recognize him!

First Blind Man — O God! O God! what is to become of us!

The Oldest Blind Woman — Father! father! — Is it you? Father, what has happened? — What is the matter with you? — Answer us! — We are all gathered round you . . . Oh! oh! oh!

The Oldest Blind Man — Bring some water; he is perhaps still alive . . .

Second Blind Man — Let us try . . . He will perhaps be able to lead us back to the asylum . . .

Third Blind Man — It is useless; I cannot hear his heart. — He is cold . . .

First Blind Man — He died without a word.

Third Blind Man — He ought to have warned us.

Second Blind Man — Oh! how old he was! . . . It is the first time I ever touched his face . . .

Third Blind Man [*feeling the corpse*] — He is taller than we are! . . .

Second Blind Man — His eyes are wide open; he died with clasped hands . . .

First Blind Man — He died, so, for no reason . . .

Second Blind Man — He is not standing, he is sitting on a stone . . .

The Oldest Blind Woman — O God! O God! I did not know all . . . all! . . . He had been ill so long . . . He must have suffered to-day! Oh! oh! oh! — He never complained! . . . He only complained in pressing our hands . . . One does not always understand . . . One never understands! . . . Let us pray around him. Kneel down . . . [*The women kneel, moaning.*

First Blind Man — I dare not kneel down . . .

Second Blind Man — One does not know what one is kneeling on here . . .

Third Blind Man — Was he ill? . . . He never told us . . .

Second Blind Man — I heard him whisper something as he went . . . I think he was speaking to our young sister; what did he say?

First Blind Man — She will not answer.

Second Blind Man — You will not answer us any more? — But where are you then? — Speak!

The Oldest Blind Woman — You made him suffer too much; you have killed him . . . You would go no further; you wanted to sit down on the stones by the roadside to eat; you grumbled all day . . . I heard him sigh . . . He lost courage . . .

First Blind Man — Was he ill? did you know it?

The Oldest Blind Man — We knew nothing . . . We had never seen him . . . When have we ever known of anything that passed before our poor dead eyes? . . . He never complained . . . Now it is too late . . . I have seen three die . . . but never so . . . Now it is our turn . . .

First Blind Man — It is not I that made him suffer. — I never said anything . . .

Second Blind Man — Nor I; we followed him without a word . . .

Third Blind Man — He died going to fetch water for the mad woman . . .

First Blind Man — What are we to do now? Where shall we go?

Third Blind Man — Where is the dog?

First Blind Man — Here; he will not leave the dead.

Third Blind Man — Drag him away! Drive him off! drive him off!

First Blind Man — He will not leave the dead!

Second Blind Man — We cannot wait beside a dead man! . . . We cannot die thus in the dark!

Third Blind Man — Let us keep together; let us not move away from one another; let us hold hands; let us all sit down on this stone . . . Where are the others? Come here! come! come!

The Oldest Blind Man — Where are you?

Third Blind Man — Here; I am here. Are we all together? — Come nearer to me. Where are your hands? — It is very cold.

The Young Blind Woman — Oh! how cold your hands are!

Third Blind Man — What are you doing?

The Young Blind Woman — I was putting my hands to my eyes. I thought I was going to see all at once . . .

First Blind Man — Who is that crying?

The Oldest Blind Woman — It is the mad woman sobbing.

First Blind Man — Yet she does not know the truth?

The Oldest Blind Man — I think we shall die here . . .

The Oldest Blind Woman — Some one will come perhaps . . .

The Oldest Blind Man — Who else would be likely to come? . . .

The Oldest Blind Woman — I don't know.

First Blind Man — I think the nuns will come out of the asylum . . .

The Oldest Blind Woman — They never go out of an evening.

The Young Blind Woman — They never go out at all.

Second Blind Man — I think that the men from the big lighthouse will see us . . .

The Oldest Blind Man — They never come down from their tower.

Third Blind Man — They might see us . . .

The Oldest Blind Woman — They are always looking towards the sea.

Third Blind Man — It is cold!

The Oldest Blind Man — Listen to the dead leaves; I think it is freezing.

The Young Blind Woman — Oh! how hard the earth is!

Third Blind Man — I hear to my left a noise that I cannot make out . . .

The Oldest Blind Man — It is the sea moaning against the rocks.

Third Blind Man — I thought it was the women.

The Oldest Blind Woman — I hear the ice breaking under the waves . . .

First Blind Man — Who is it that is shivering so? He is making us all shake on the stone!

Second Blind Man — I can no longer open my hands.

The Oldest Blind Man — I hear another noise that I cannot make out . . .

First Blind Man — Which of us is it that is shivering so? He is shaking the stone!

The Oldest Blind Man — I think it is a woman.

The Oldest Blind Woman — I think the mad woman is shivering most.

Third Blind Man — I cannot hear her child.

The Oldest Blind Woman — I think he is still sucking.

The Oldest Blind Man — He is the only one that can see where we are!

First Blind Man — I hear the north wind.

Sixth Blind Man — I think there are no more stars; it is going to snow.

Second Blind Man — Then we are lost!

Third Blind Man — If one of us falls asleep he must be waked.

The Oldest Blind Man — I am sleepy though.

[*A squall makes the dead leaves whirl.*

The Young Blind Woman — Do you hear the dead leaves? I think some one is coming towards us!

Second Blind Man — It is the wind; listen!

Third Blind Man — No one will come now!

The Oldest Blind Man — The great cold is coming . . .

The Young Blind Woman — I hear some one walking in the distance!

First Blind Man — I only hear the dead leaves!

The Young Blind Woman — I hear some one walking very far from us!

Second Blind Man — I only hear the north wind.

The Young Blind Woman — I tell you that some one is coming towards us!

The Oldest Blind Woman — I hear a sound of very slow footsteps . . .

The Oldest Blind Man — I think the women are right.

[*It begins to snow in great flakes.*

First Blind Man — Oh! oh! what is that falling so cold on my hands?

Sixth Blind Man — It is snowing!

First Blind Man — Let us draw up close to one another!

The Young Blind Woman — But listen to the sound of the footsteps!

The Oldest Blind Woman— For God's sake! be still an instant!

The Young Blind Woman — They are drawing nearer! they are drawing nearer! listen then!

[*Here the mad woman's child begins to wail suddenly in the dark.*

The Oldest Blind Man — The child is crying!

The Young Blind Woman — It sees! it sees! It must see something as it is crying! [*She seizes the child in her arms and moves forward in the direction whence the sound of footsteps seems to come; the other women follow her anxiously and surround her.*] I am going to meet it!

The Oldest Blind Man — Take care!

The Young Blind Woman — Oh! how he is crying! — What is it? — Don't cry. — Don't be afraid; there is nothing to be afraid of; we are here all about you. — What do you see? — Fear nothing! — Don't cry so! — What is it that you see? — Tell us, what is it that you see?

The Oldest Blind Woman — The sound of footsteps is drawing nearer; listen! listen!

The Oldest Blind Man — I hear the rustling of a dress among the dead leaves.

Sixth Blind Man — Is it a woman?

The Oldest Blind Man — Is it the sound of footsteps?

First Blind Man — It is perhaps the sea on the dead leaves.

The Young Blind Woman — No, no! they are footsteps! they are footsteps! they are footsteps!

The Oldest Blind Woman — We shall soon know; listen to the dead leaves.

The Young Blind Woman — I hear them, I hear them, almost beside us! listen! listen! — What is it that you see? What is it that you see?

The Oldest Blind Woman — Which way is he looking?

The Young Blind Woman — He always follows the sound of the footsteps! — Look! Look! When I turn him away he turns back to look . . . He sees! he sees! he sees! — He must see something strange! . . .

The Oldest Blind Woman [*coming forward*] — Lift him above us, that he may see.

The Young Blind Woman — Step aside! step aside! [*She lifts the child above the group of the sightless.*] The footsteps have stopped right among us! . . .

The Oldest Blind Man — They are here! They are here in our midst!

The Young Blind Woman — Who are you? [*Silence.*

The Oldest Blind Woman — Have pity on us!

[*Silence. The child cries more desperately.*

LIGHT.

BY FRANCIS W. BOURDILLON.

[1852–.]

THE night has a thousand eyes,
  And the day but one;
Yet the light of the bright world dies
  With the dying sun.

The mind has a thousand eyes,
  And the heart but one:
Yet the light of a whole life dies
  When its day is done.

HOW BRICHANTEAU ALMOST SAVED THE EMPEROR.[1]

BY JULES CLARETIE.

(From "Brichanteau, Actor.")

[ARSÈNE ARNAUD CLARETIE, called Jules Claretie, a French author, was born at Limoges, December 3, 1840. He was educated in Paris and became a journalist, corresponding for the leading French and Belgian papers during the Austrian and Franco-Prussian wars. In 1885 he became director of the Théâtre Français, and in 1888 was chosen a member of the French Academy. He became an officer of the Legion of Honor in 1889. He has published many novels and plays, including "Madeleine Berten" (1868), "The Million" (1882), "Monsieur the Minister" (1882), "Noris, Manners of the Time" (1883), "The American Woman" (1892), "Brichanteau, Comédien" (1896), "L'Accusateur" (1897), and many historical works.]

WELL, yes, I nearly saved France! It is a matter of history. The late Monsieur le Baron Taylor, who knew all about

[1] Copyright, 1897, by Little, Brown & Co. Published by permission.

the affair, could have vouched for the truth of what I am about to tell you. But I have no need of witnesses to induce belief in my word. Everybody knows Brichanteau; he has never lied. My life may seem an extraordinary one, but the fact is that life is a dream, as has been said by — by — that Spaniard. Well, then, this is how it happened.

It was in the last days of the siege. Life was terribly wearisome in Paris. September, October, November, December, January, those months seemed like years. At first, people said: "Patience, we are going to be relieved, we shall crush the enemy under our walls, the North is bestirring itself, the South is rising, it is only a matter of a few weeks; we can surely give credit to the country, — the country is doing well, it is being born again!" But the days passed, nothing came; we could not leave the city, we became mere snails on the ramparts, we were horribly bored — there is no other word for it, we were bored to death. But with great dignity, eating little and that unfit to eat, atrocious bread, horseflesh, refuse. And with it all the smallpox and the cold. There is no use talking, it was not cheerful. I did my duty like the others, you understand. I mounted guard in my turn, I passed nights on guard, and when the battalion marched out of the fortifications, ah, messeigneurs, I thought that my *chassepot* was going to open the road to Berlin and the King of Prussia had best look to himself! . . .

I was still saying to myself that there was certainly "something else to be done," when a cutting from a provincial newspaper, which reached Paris by balloon, stirred within me all the conjoined fibers of patriotism and of art. A man of heart, a Frenchman living at Buenos Ayres, had raised a gallant legion, the Argentine legion, to come to France and defend his natal soil; and the brave fellows had just landed at Bordeaux, where their leader, an ex-subaltern in the army of Africa, ex-colonel in the army of General Lee during the War of Secession, was drilling and organizing them. He proposed, with them, to join Bourbaki's army, which was still intact. But the thing that impressed me in the news contained in the *Victoire* newspaper of Bordeaux, the thing that stirred my imagination, always in love with the picturesque, was this: the ex-colonel, being unable to procure the uniforms that he desired for his command ready made when they disembarked, had purchased the costumes of a theatrical manager who was called upon for com-

LOUIS NAPOLEON

pulsory military service, — among others those of "Les Trois Mousquetaires"; and he himself, insanely, I grant you, but heroically, you must admit, was about to defy the bullets of the Dreysse muskets in the hat and riding coat of D'Artagnan.

Ah! that newspaper cutting! The possibility of realizing a chimerical vision, of being one of Dumas' *mousquetaires*, not only between the wings and in front of a canvas background, but in the open air, in a real battle! To protect our country, arrayed in the felt hat and plume of the defenders of the Saint-Gervais bastion! To live in peril, wearing the costume of a dream! The thought intoxicated me, it went to my brain, it drove me mad. I conceived a loathing for my black trousers with the red stripe, my broadcloth jacket, my laced hat, my woolen girdle; I fancied myself, sword in hand, cleaving helmets, and I determined, oh! I determined, by hook or crook, despite closed gates, despite the blockade, despite Monsieur de Bismarck, despite the devil, despite everything, to go to Bordeaux and join the red-coated legion from Buenos Ayres!

When a man with a will like mine has an idea, he puts it into execution. To go from Paris to Bordeaux was no easy matter. But I would find my way out of Paris; I would play the part of a peasant as far as Rouen, a market gardener returning to his village, and so I would reach Havre, — the Germans were not in possession of Havre, — and go thence to Bordeaux by sea; I would make my escape by the valley of the Seine. In the main it was the plan, the famous plan, of Trochu, over which people made so merry, and which the governor did not undertake to carry out because, instead of operating upon Rouen, the Tours authorities decided to operate upon Orléans. That is an historical fact which will come to light later. I give it to you by the way.

To cut the matter short, my plan was a good one. Ought I to intrust it to any one? That was a question that I put to myself, and, after all, as long as I intended to go, it was quite as well to turn my departure to some good use. The government, which sent out information and instructions by balloon, might have some mission to intrust to a sure man. Through an influential colleague, a *sociétaire* of the Comédie Française, I sent word to a member of the government that I was ready to pass through the lines and to carry to any desired point a written or verbal order, whichever they chose.

My influential colleague went so far as to present me to the chief of staff of the Governor of Paris, who looked me over — I standing as erect under his soldierly glance as I would have done before the enemy's bullets — and said to me: —

"Your mind is made up, my boy?"

"Fully made up, general. I am stifling in Paris. I propose to fight in the provinces."

"Yes, you dream of a breath of fresh air. You don't want very much. We are all quartered in the same inn. And you would undertake to carry a message to the governor at Tours?"

"Yes, general, if I am not killed on the road!"

"But suppose you are the bearer of a message in writing, and you are arrested?"

"I will swallow the message in writing. That is the *a b c* of the trade."

"And suppose you are questioned?"

"I will not say a word. I have played that part in 'Masséna, or L'Enfant Chéri de la Victoire.'"

"Oh! but there are ways of making people speak!"

"Not a word should pass my lips, general, though they should put me to the torture. There are certain secrets that die with some men. I will remember Coconnas in 'La Reine Margot.' It is a sympathetic rôle. I came near creating it at Montparnasse."

Faith, it seems that I inspired confidence in the chief of staff. He bade me return to the Place the next day. I returned with military promptness. They gave me my credentials to the government at Tours on a little paper no bigger than that, written very fine; and they handed me, with a dispatch in cipher, a passport for the French outposts. The general informed me that, all the information obtainable about me being satisfactory, they had decided to intrust to me the mission that I solicited. If I succeeded in reaching Tours, I was to deliver my credentials and my dispatch, and the government there was, it seems, instructed to reward me.

"Oh! general," I said hastily, when the subject of reward was mentioned, "let us not mention that, I beg of you. I am sufficiently rewarded by your confidence and your esteem."

"Very well. But have you money in your pocket for the journey?"

"I have, general. Base metal is not the patriot's viaticum."

The general smiled at that phrase, which came quite naturally to my lips and which I have never forgotten. Then he wished me *bon voyage*. I had not dared to say to him that if I rendered the country the service that was expected of me, there was a reward, craved by many gallant men, which would have made me mad with pride. But not only did I not dare to mention it, I dared not even think of it. Decorated! I, Brichanteau, a chevalier of the Legion of Honor! It would have been too much. No, seriously, I can honestly say that I did not even think of it. I thought only of escaping, of passing through the lines, of obtaining a breath of fresh air, as the general had said, and of joining the legion of *mousquetaires* from Buenos Ayres. . . .

I had arranged for myself a very simple costume of a worthy rustic who had taken refuge in Paris. Nothing grotesque, not the *café-concert* peasant who sings at Jean-Pierre's wedding; not a *Brasseur* rôle either. A realistic peasant, close-shaven chin, cloth jacket, blouse with a blue-black cape and melon-shaped hat. With the rest, a stout stick for marauders, because there was no sense in being armed against the Prussian. My conscience was my weapon.

Off at last. I carried my passport, and, rolled up like two balls of dough in my pocket, my dispatch and my credentials to the authorities at Tours. I left neither love nor relations in Paris, so that my heart, as it happened, was free; and even if I had been in love, I would have sacrificed that attachment, caprice, or passion to the prospect of making myself useful to my country and of fighting with the Argentine *mousquetaires*.

I left the city by the Neuilly gate. Beautiful weather favored my journey, which I began with a self-assured demeanor. Mont-Valérien, which was firing from time to time, seemed to salute my departure as if I were a ship. The winter sun, the smoke from the cannon floating in the clear air, all seemed to me of good augury, and I walked on, deliberately, not allowing my emotions to be stirred even by the lamentable spectacle of war,—trees felled, houses gutted, walls razed to the ground,—which I met at every step. It was for the purpose of avenging and repairing this destruction that I walked straight ahead, bound on an important mission!

Everything went well as I passed through the dismantled suburb, until I had passed our outposts on the Sèvres road. I remember the last warning word of the officer of the flying column, when I showed him my passport, which he kept, as I had no further use for it.

"You know *they* are not far away! How are you going to cross the Seine? Beware: it rains bullets!"

How was I going to cross the Seine? Upon my word I had no idea. By swimming? Impossible. Once on the other side, I must apply to the Germans for a chance to dry my clothes. It was not probable that I could find a boat in some creek or other. I walked along the river, crouching as best I could behind the leafless trees and shrubbery, and I said to myself that I should probably have to return as I came, the very first day. I was hungry. I sat down at the foot of a birch and ate some bread — siege bread — washed down with wine from my flask. It was delicious, that repast in the open air! I said to myself: "If the Parisians were here, how happy they would be! They would be free!"

No, not so free as they might be! The Seine was there, quite as effective as a wall, and I watched it flowing in the sunlight. It reflected the houses on the other bank, where there were, perhaps, where there certainly were Prussians. But I could not see them. They were inside, smoking or reading or playing cards. At one time I heard, far away, very far away, a refrain from an operetta, an Offenbach air that was wafted to my ears through the branches. It was one of them playing "La Belle Hélène" on a piano which they had not yet burned for firewood.

And if you knew how melancholy that refrain from Offenbach sounded to me at that moment! I had heard it sung not long before at the Théâtre de Mourmelon, before our poor soldiers, formerly so gay and reckless! Ah! to avenge them, also, in the red coat of a *mousquetaire!* That thought restored all my confidence, and I waited for nightfall, saying to myself, as in "Victorine," that the night brings counsel.

Night came in due time, very cold,—luckily quite dark, even after the beautiful day,—and I shivered infernally on the bank. I even deliberated whether I had not better fall back on our outposts and get under cover until daylight. But that would have reminded me of the *retreat in good order* which we are constantly hearing about in bulletins, and, as I was near my goal, I must remain there. It was well for me that I came to that decision, for it is probable that, if I had retraced my steps toward Paris, the rain of bullets would have been a French shower, and who knows, monsieur, if I should be here?

I said to myself: "I will remain, I will wait!" And I longed to stamp on the ground to warm myself, but I was afraid of making a noise. The better plan was to look along the river for some hovel where I could lie until daybreak; and as it turned out, while I was looking for the hovel, I found the boat and the ferryman who carried me to the other bank.

It was like this. I had discovered, from a distance, something very high, like a wall, with something ragged and full of holes on top, like a roof riddled with shells; a sort of shed it was, and I said to myself, "That's just what I want for a nap;" but, as I was going in, I heard somebody, whom I could not see, moving near me, then a voice growled in French: —

"Who goes there?"

I replied instinctively: —

"France!"

I should have made the same reply, on my word of honor, if the question had been, "*Wer da?*"

The person on the ground approached. He was some vagabond or other who came at night to try and catch fish, in order to sell them the next day at an exorbitant price at the Halle or at Brébant's, — one of the redskins of civilization, who live on everything and nothing, and would find a silk thread in an egg. There in that shed, under a pile of bricks and straw, he had an old skiff that he used on occasion, at the risk of receiving ten bullets in his head for one. I learned all this by talking with him, at a safe distance, my staff in hand; for, to tell the truth, he seemed to be a famous rascal, did my new friend!

Rascal or not, he was brave! He agreed to set me across the river for ten francs. That was not a high price to pay. The least sound of oars might arouse the Germans, and the whole shore would have taken fire. But nothing venture, nothing have. I poured out a glass of wine for my ferryman, which he clinked against my flask, and we drank to France, — for perhaps the rascal was a good sort of fellow, after all, — and off we went.

Behold us in the skiff.

Not a star. I thought of Mordaunt aboard his boat in the fifth act of "Vingt Ans Après." I said to myself that we must cast Chinese shadows against the clearer background of the water, and I expected, every moment, to receive a volley. I had my two rolls of paper beween my fingers ready to be swallowed, if I had time, before the death agony.

But there is a God. Not a shot. *They*, the Germans, were sound asleep.

My boatman deposited me on the bank.

I gave him twelve francs — two francs *pourboire* — and said to him : —

" At least let me know the name of the stranger who has assisted me in my flight."

" What's my name to you ? " he replied. " My name is Auguste ! "

Whatever he may have been, I have kept that baptismal name, Auguste, engraven on my heart, and I associate it with my most heroic memory. Wherever thou art, Auguste, if thou still livest, my blessing on thee !

I was on the other side of the river, but I was not at the end of my troubles. I repeated the words of Rysoor, — there's a part that I would like to act, a fine Dumaine ! — *No, the trouble is not finished, it is but beginning !* And I felt that I was in the enemy's country. The darkness, the night, the silence, everything seemed hostile to me. The simplest plan was not to stir. When day broke, I would find my road. And I kept myself out of sight, cowering in a ditch on the hard ice, frozen stiff, — absolutely frozen.

With the first ray of dawn I began to walk, to drive away the numbness, to bring the blood back to my feet. I had a sort of rush of blood to my brain. I was walking straight ahead, not at random, for I knew the roads, I was walking toward Saint-Germain, when suddenly — oh ! my odyssey was not of long duration ! — I walked straight into a German patrol as if I had banged my head against a closed door.

Ah ! it was no longer the *Qui vive ?* of my friend Auguste. I heard the dreaded *Wer da ?* The crossed muskets stopped me short. A corporal asked me something in German. As I made no reply, a soldier pushed me behind, and I was taken, surrounded by tall, red-bearded devils, before a very light, very thin officer, who, as he stared at me through a monocle, seemed to me to be very tired, either because he had risen so early, or because he had passed the night in the little cottage where he was warming his boots, by the light of a kerosene lamp still lighted.

The officer spoke French very well, with a very slight accent that vaguely resembled the Gascon accent. He asked me what I was doing in the German lines, and where I came from.

I replied concisely : —

"From Paris."

"What, from Paris? You have undertaken to escape from a besieged city?"

Thereupon I summoned all my skill in the matter of make-up, and, if I do say it, I acted the Norman peasant as he has rarely been acted on the stage. I felt that it was an excellent performance. I was in the good fellow's skin, — a Bouffé or a Paulin Ménier.

Have I told you, by the way, that while the red-beards were escorting me to the cottage I had deftly swallowed the two balls of paper intended for the authorities at Tours? That is the alphabet of the juggler's art. Pass, *muscades!* And the Germans had seen nothing! I said to myself : —

"Farewell to your dispatch, Brichanteau! Even if you reach Tours, my boy, you will not receive the reward you have dreamed of!"

But I added that, after all, I might, even without the papers, which by the way had nearly strangled me, like overlarge pills, furnish sufficient information for them to recognize my zeal.

And then, too, I had not set out in search of compliments, but of blows. I wanted to fight! To fight in the costume of D'Artagnan. The rest was incidental.

"Why did you leave Paris?" the officer asked me in a satirical tone.

"Because I was tired of staying there."

"Ah! then you're not a Parisian?"

"No, officer; I *was* a poor farmer in the outskirts of Rouen — at Saint-Pierre; I don't know if you know Saint-Pierre?"

"No, I don't know it."

"Well, that's where my people are. I took refuge in Paris, or I should say I had business there, grain to sell, and I was shut up there when the siege began. At first I says to myself: 'Pshaw! this won't last long! They'll raise the siege,'" — the officer smiled as if I had said an absurd thing; — "but, you see, they didn't do it, and it seemed as if I couldn't stand it, to stay there without seeing my people; so I came out, yes, I came out, that's the truth, preferring to risk everything rather than stay shut up there like my hens in the hencoop. And that's the good God's true truth, officer!"

As I told you, I played my part admirably, although peasants, the second comedian's parts, like Alain in "L'École des

Femmes," are not in my line. But I have played many other parts that were not in my line! The gesture, the accent, the curl of the lip, everything was there, and the tall, thin officer stared into the whites of my eyes while I was talking my patois to him. That stare would have confused me if I had been on the stage, although I am not easily put out of countenance. The fellow magnetized me!

But, pshaw! I was master of myself, and I determined to bewilder him with *dames* and *bédames!*

"Look you, peasant, aren't you an emissary (*émissaire*) of the government of Paris?" inquired the officer, finally.

I made this reflection: "Brichanteau, if you understand the word *émissaire*, you are lost."

I stammered and stuttered: —

"*Émi — émis — père —* What was that word, officer?"

"*Émissaire?* Spy, if you prefer."

"Spy? me! Ah! *bon Dieu de bon Dieu!* me, a spy! Spy on who? spy on what?"

"In the first place, what's your name?"

"Bonnin, Jean-Marie."

The officer wrote the name on his notebook.

That name suddenly came to my lips in memory of "François le Champi" and Madame Sand, who saw me play "Claudie" at La Châtre. Jean Bonnin! I shall never forget it.

"You were born?"

"At Saint-Pierre-du-Vauvray, the 3d December, 1830."

"Good. We will keep you and see what the inquiry will bring forth."

He made a sign to his soldiers; they took me by the shoulders once more and carried me to a vile barrack, where they locked me up and kept me in sight, without food or drink. I must have remained there from five or six o'clock in the morning until noon, something like that, when the door of my barrack opened and a great longshanks of a German growled at me, "Come!" and with a gesture bade me follow him.

A detachment was waiting at the door.

I glanced instinctively at the Dreysse muskets. I said to myself: "Oho! suppose they are loaded for you, my old Brichanteau!"

The squad escorted me through divers streets to a large dwelling house, in front of which a whole general's staff was parading up and down, dragging their swords behind them.

There were hussar officers all in blue, others all in red, and old officers, whom by their helmets and their plumes I knew to be generals. One of them, a beggarly little fellow, with spectacles and not a hair of beard, looked me over when they led me before him, and the villain said to me abruptly, without a trace of accentuation :—

"You come from Paris?"

"Yes, I come from Paris."

"You were a bearer of dispatches?"

"I, good God! I was bearer of nothing at all."

"Where are your dispatches?"

"Ah! *dame bédame*, if you look for them you'll waste your time like the devil. I'm a poor man who escaped from Paris because he wants to see his wife and his little ones and the old folks. *Voilà!*"

"You are married?"

"Yes."

"You have children?"

"Three."

Perhaps it was not a lie. One never can tell!

"And your name is Bonnin, born ——"

"At Saint-Pierre-du-Vauvray, the 3d December, 1830. Bonnin, Jean-Marie, son of Bonnin, Pierre-Lavinien."

"Enough!" said the little old man.

He turned to his officers; they whispered together for a moment, and a little red hussar, all bedecked with gold lace, left the group and made a sign to the squad that had brought me thither, whereupon it drew up in front of me.

The whole staff looked on.

They motioned to me to take up my position in front of a wall which, in the bright sunlight, looked perfectly white — like a winding sheet. The devil! that had a bad look. The curious part of it is that I noticed everything.

I knew where I was.

At Rueil. I had noticed the house particularly one day when I had come to Rueil to recite poetry at a concert for the benefit of a municipal Fanfare. I recognized the street. I saw the distant landscape and, through the clear air, Mont-Valérien, thundering away, with its little columns of smoke floating upward.

And behind it I fancied that I could see Paris, — Rue de Bondy where my lodgings were, the Porte-Saint-Martin, the

Gaiété, the Châtelet, the Conservatory from which I had graduated, the Comédie Française, where I ought to have been engaged! — my whole life! And it was all ended! These men in high boots, wrapped in their cloaks, with heavy pie-shaped helmets on their heads, were going to finish it all up, and adieu, Brichanteau! Curtain! The lights are going out.

The staff did not stir. A subaltern planted me in front of the wall, facing the squad, and the tall, thin devil of an officer who had questioned me in the morning — I did not know he was there — made his appearance and drew his sword.

"Prepare arms!"

I am not quite sure if that was what he said, but I think so. However I distinctly heard the word *arms*, which he pronounced with an *h* before it: *harms!* — how that would have made my teacher, Monsieur Beauvallet, squirm!

I folded my arms like Laferrière in "La Barrière de Clichy," or Monsieur Alexandre in "Les Cosaques."

The little gold-bespangled red hussar came toward me and very courteously asked me this question: —

"His Excellency the general asks you if you have no disclosure to make."

"Nothing," I replied.

"You have nothing to say? Nothing?"

An idea came into my mind, a wild temptation. I longed to show those swashbucklers what a dramatic artist's soul really is, and I felt that I was on the point of replying: —

"I have to say that I die for my country," and shouting: "*Vive la France!*"

It was the only reply for a man who wants to die. But why die? And if I had yielded to that natural but heroic impulse, I should have ceased to be Jean-Marie Bonnin, Norman peasant, and have become Sébastien Brichanteau once more; but I should have had a dozen bullets in my brain or my breastbone.

I had the courage to reply: —

"*Dame*, I have to say that I wish you'd send word if you can to my wife and Père Bonnin at Saint-Pierre-du-Vauvray that I wanted to kiss my children and it brought me bad luck! That's all!"

The pretty red hussar went back to the little old general. My officer of the morning still held his sword in the air. The soldiers had their guns ready. A charming tableau. But I said to myself: "When he lowers his sword, the beast, it will be very nice!" And I already imagined the tall, white, sunlight-mottled wall spattered with my blood. One has curious ideas at such moments.

Then I thought: —

"You will not join the Buenos Ayres legion, Brichanteau, and you will never, never enter the Comédie-Française!"

That disgusted me. Suddenly the little hussar, after talking with his general, returned to the officer commanding the squad, and I saw — I half saw, for all this going and coming was beginning to make my head and my eyes rather dizzy — the soldiers *grounding harms!* The general, stepping toward me, stared at me again through his spectacles, then he and his staff all turned their backs on me.

Thereupon the red hussar, always polite, said to me: —

"You're not afraid. You are to be taken to Versailles. Your affair is worth the trouble of being looked into."

"My affair!"

"To be sure. For all we know, you're a dangerous fellow. We shall see how that is!"

For my part, I saw but one thing. I had escaped the squad of execution for the moment and destiny led me back after many hardships to Versailles, my native place, where, thank God! I had left too few reminders and acquaintances for any one to recognize in Jean Bonnin, Norman peasant — second comedian — little Sébastien who played hopscotch on Avenue de Paris, or the young Brichanteau who made his début in "Horace" on the boards of the theater of his native town. It was so long ago! — 1849! Think of it!

And there I was! The staff had gone, the squad was going, and they bestowed me once more in my hovel. I uttered an *ouf!* as in a fifth act, when the young girl or the mother or the kind magistrate brings the pardon of the condemned man. And I said to myself that such excitement makes a horrible void in a man, and that I would eat a morsel. On that point the Germans were very cautious. Bread and water. A little sausage. My first banquet did not ruin them, and the expense of keeping me did not necessitate an inroad on their war treasure. But a man fresh from Paris was not likely to be exacting, and that food seemed to me worthy of the Maison-d'Or. Never, no, never have I eaten with better appetite.

I passed the night in that dog kennel, and the next day,

with cords about my wrists, like Lesurques in the last tableau of the "Courrier de Lyon," I started for Versailles on foot. I had the pleasure of espying the palace from afar. I saw that the streets and avenues of my poor great city were swarming with pointed helmets, and I was taken to the prison, where I have been so many times when a child, to watch the condemned men come out, and gazed at the door, the great nails, the heavy knocker, never suspecting that the day would come — but let us be philosophers, everything comes to pass.

And it was there, in the prison at Versailles, that I conceived a plan which, if it had succeeded — and it might have succeeded — would perhaps have saved our country, and would in any event — I say it boldly — have changed the course of history.

I say this, and I will prove it. This is the story.

In the first place they threw me into a dungeon like a cell in a cloister. Good. I knew all about dungeons. I had played Buridan and Latude. I had heard bolts shoot and had seen the sinister faces of jailers appear in doorways. But in the prison at Versailles the bolts were not put on by stage carpenters, and the massive door bore little resemblance to the doors of painted canvas. The jailer was a subaltern officer in the German gendarmerie, and from time to time I was taken before some stipendiary of the provostry, who tried to make me confess that my name was not Jean Bonnin, that I was not a Norman from Normandie, and that I had left Paris with "evil designs." So did they qualify my patriotic purposes.

But King William's provosts exerted their cunning to no purpose; they did not succeed in making me forget the part I was playing. I was Jean Bonnin from top to toe, and, *bédame*, I thought of nothing but getting back to my province, and I laughed well — *jarnigué* — at the Parisians who persisted in firing cannon to prevent my sleeping at night.

After a few days my *cellular* imprisonment ceased. They allowed me to walk for two hours daily in a sort of courtyard with other prisoners, all French. There were soldiers there, and thieves, a little of everything, a curious collection of people picked up here and there around Paris by the German authorities: poachers suspected of having fired at an Uhlan by moonlight; freebooters who pretended to be deserters, and who had, perhaps, like myself, been intrusted with a commission by General Trochu. Poor devils, locked up they hardly knew why, because they were prowling about homeless, picking up cabbages and greens in the outskirts of Paris. Gardeners from Seine-et-Oise, some old soldiers of the Crimea, who had made insolent replies to the questions of the conquerors, — everybody raging against the Prussians, growling, and picketed there like a herd of angry beasts. In all, thirty or forty individuals, — thirty-seven, to be exact, — young and old, but *gars*, I promise you.

And the herd assembled twice a day, taking the air between four walls, under the surveillance of sentinels with loaded guns. We heard the cannon on Mont-Valérien, the crackling of musketry, and sometimes, when the noise seemed to come nearer, we would look at one another, saying in undertones: —

"*They* are leaving the city! *They* are coming!"

In Paris when we said *they*, we meant the Prussians. Outside of Paris *they* were the French.

The days passed, however, and the weeks, and *they* did not come. We had ended by becoming pretty thoroughly acquainted with one another, meeting as we did at stated hours. Sometimes one of us was missing at the promenade. Then we would ask the sentinel, in stumbling German, what had become of our comrade. No reply. Perhaps they had sent him to Germany, to Spandau, to the devil, or God knows where; perhaps they had shot him, against a wall or at the corner of a wood. That might happen to any one of us one of those fine mornings. But, strangely enough, as soon as one had gone another appeared. They would bring us some French prisoner who had rebelled, some newly caught marauder, and there were always just thirty-seven of us, by chance, I think. If we had risen to forty, we would have made a cross and imagined we were at the Academy.

Thirty-seven stanch men, all with fire in their eyes, tired of being behind bolts, annoyed at having eaters of sauerkraut for jailers, tired of hearing cannon shots and musket shots in the distance without fighting, — even thirty-seven men are something; and I said to myself that they might be put to some use, and that the *mousquetaires* were only four when they shook the world.

Fate seemed to have pointed out my duty to me by allotting to me, a child of Versailles, a dungeon in my native city. I knew that the prison in which I was eating the bread of captivity was situated near the Avenue de Paris; it is only two hundred and sixty-four paces — I have counted them since — and I knew the distance by heart — from Rue Saint-Pierre, or rather from Place des Tribunaux, to the Avenue de Paris. I knew also that on that Avenue de Paris stood the prefecture of the department, and that it was there, in the buildings of the prefecture, that King William lodged, slept, breathed, and took his repose!

"Well, well," I said to myself, "it would put a strangely different face on the war, if the King of Prussia should wake suddenly from a sound sleep to find himself a prisoner in the hands of a few determined Frenchmen! Yes, that would be a dream! And such a dream! The conqueror sleeps. The prisoners are on the alert. They throw themselves upon their jailers, they seize their weapons, they gag or kill the sentinels, they are free, and with one accord they rush toward the prefecture which is contaminated by the presence of the enemy. A grating embellished with the imperial bees forbids entrance to the building. They break it down. The post guarding the entrance is gagged. Doubtless some German sentinel will fire and give the alarm; but before any one has time to come from the neighboring barracks, the apartments where the sovereign sleeps are invaded, the chancellors, the staff officers are taken prisoners, and the old king sees at his pillow a determined man, the leader of the expedition, who, holding him in awed subjection under the barrel of a German revolver snatched from one of his soldiers, says to him: —

"'Not a word, not an outcry, not a movement, Sire! You are our prisoner!'"

Ah! as soon as that idea took root in my brain, it sowed fever there, — a generous fever! All my blood boiled at the prospect of the adventure, and I no longer regretted my failure to join the Buenos Ayres legion. No, no, I no longer regretted it. Was not my present project, this thing that I could attempt there in Versailles, superior to all that the mobilized provincial legions tried to accomplish? They attacked the instruments, the subordinates, the supernumeraries. I, Brichanteau, would smite the invasion at its head. It was heaven that ordained that I should be arrested at Rueil and thrown like a bandit into the prison of Versailles. Fate pointed out my duty to me.

To kidnap the King of Prussia — the idea was rank madness, wise men will say. Yes, to-day, when our head rests quietly on our pillows, it seems like madness. But it was not, it was audacity. It was theatrical, and honestly theatrical. Is not the stage life? Did not Athos, Porthos, Aramis, and D'Artagnan come near rescuing the King of England? They would have saved Charles I. if history had not been against them. Whereas I had before me history not yet made, a scheme which permitted the realization of all sorts of possibilities. Once the king was my prisoner I would dictate to his Majesty such conditions as I pleased. Ah! it would be a very different thing from the commonplace information given me to carry to the authorities at Tours, in the shape of a bullet!

"You will raise the siege of Paris at once, Sire." — "Very well." — "You will evacuate Champagne." — "It is done." — "You will recall to Germany all your garrisons in Alsace and Lorraine. — Ah! not a word, not an outcry, not a movement, Sire! I have you fast. Well played, King William, but my country has its revenge!"

And I calculated that, however heroic a handful of thirty-seven men might be, they would quickly have been surrounded and wiped out in the prefecture, surrounded as it was by the German garrison at Versailles. But we should have our hostage, the most precious of hostages, — the king! We should have him cowering at the muzzles of our guns, his guns. And we would not give him up until our retreat, assured by his presence in the midst of us, was safely effected. Yes, until we had regained our lines we would keep King William in custody. The slightest movement on the part of one of his soldiers and it would have been all up with him. I repeated to myself the words from "Les Funérailles de l'Honneur," which I uttered so proudly at the moment I was about to stab Don Pedro the Cruel: "One does not kill a sleeping man!" To which I replied, as in the drama: "I will awaken him!" Even so. And if, by reason of some unforeseen necessity which one must always provide against under such circumstances, we should be obliged to consent to set the king at liberty on conditions less rigorous for him, less satisfactory to us, than those I had fixed upon in my own mind, our *minimum* would be the raising of the siege and the withdrawal of the invader's troops to a distance of twenty-five leagues from Paris. Oh! upon those points, even though we should be constrained to take the monarch's life and to leave our own on the spot, we would agree to no compromise, I would agree to no compromise!

And I already imagined myself, on a dark night—it was essential *to select* a night when there was no moon, when the footlights were not lighted—I imagined myself at the head of the thirty-seven captive heroes, gliding along like shadows to the prefecture, after depriving our jailers of their weapons; in thought I was present at that epic scene: the scaling of the iron fence, the sudden irruption into the prefect's salon, and William's sudden awakening beneath that gilded canopy, reconquered by France. And the flag! We had no tricolored flag, but we would at all events strike the black and white flag of the King of Prussia, or the black, white, and red flag of Germany that was probably waving over the prefecture! That would serve the purpose. Ah! to hurl that black eagle down into the courtyard with a loud shout of triumph, while some one of us—surely there would be a pianist in our number—played the "Marseillaise" on Madame la Préfète's piano! What ecstasy!

I tell you, it was possible. It was practicable. It would change the whole face of affairs. The thing that does not happen seems mad, but not more mad, I swear, than the thing that actually happens. And I said to myself: "This shall be done!—Brichanteau, perhaps thou mayst never enter the Comédie Française, but thou shalt make an irruption into history!"

But I could not make the irruption all by myself. I must have collaborators, I will not say accomplices. At first I intrusted my plan to only one or two among those of my companions who inspired most confidence in me. There might be *sheep* among the prisoners. I opened my heart and mind freely to an old Crimean Zouave who dreamed of nothing but wounds and bruises, and was forever mumbling in his grizzled red beard his rage at not having *brought down* a Prussian.

He stared at me in amazement at first and asked me if it were practicable.

"To throw one's self on a jailer, gag him and disarm him," I replied, "is the *a b c* of art. Have you never read 'Latude, or Thirty-five Years of Captivity'?"

"No."

There was nothing literary about him. But he assented very quickly. "If there are blows to strike, I am in it, I'll strike! I took Malakoff; that should be more difficult than to take a prefecture!" It was not quite the same thing.

After the Crimean I sounded the poacher. He confessed to me under his breath that he did really *bring down* the Uhlan, because the cavalier had hugged his niece too tight. We talked about these matters in low tones, sometimes in a sort of half-Parisian, half-military slang, so that the sentinel, if he were listening, could not understand. And little by little, one by one, I enlisted recruits. I told them the plan I had formed; I held up the hope of victory before their eyes. I dazzled them with visions of their future glory. I said to them: —

"Will you?"

And all answered: —

"We will."

Thereupon I pledged them to secrecy, and told them to wait until the time came. They would be notified.

"Be always ready! *Ad augusta per augusta!*"

They were not familiar with Hugo, but they shuddered instinctively, which proves that the drama is true to nature.

I said to each neophyte: —

"Mouth closed, heart mute, tongue prudent, hate concealed," and I went on to the next. Not one refusal. My idea made an indelible impression. Eyes blazed, fingers moved nervously, as if they were already pressing the trigger of a musket.

They all said to me: —

"Whenever you choose!"

I replied: —

"Confidence. Patience. Silence and mystery."

And I waited. I had said to Martineau the poacher, and to the old Zouave: —

"You must leap upon the first sentinel, gag him, choke him, strangle him. That's your business."

They had answered: —

"It shall be done, and done in good shape. At your orders."

One morning in January, my jailer, who spoke French, said to me with a sneer: —

"Well, it's done. We have no King of Prussia now!"

That gave me a start. Had fate anticipated me? Was the conqueror dead?

"No," the man went on, "we have a German Emperor! His Majesty was proclaimed yesterday in the great Galerie des Glaces. Ha! ha! how your Louis XIV. must have laughed!"

I cannot say whether Louis XIV. laughed very heartily, but I myself was blind with anger. I remembered the fourth act of "Hernani," Charles the Fifth's monologue, and it seemed to me that the guns of Mont-Valérien protested against the proclamation of the Kaiser. However, it made no change in my plan. None. Instead of carrying off a king, I would carry off an emperor, that was all!

The Emperor was ours! He was the same old William. But that last insult suggested to me to hasten the catastrophe. Were we all notified? All. Were we all ready? All. Solemnly, in mysterious silence, — everything had been decided upon, and repeated from ear to ear, — putting out our hands without a word, we had sworn inwardly to make the attempt at the risk of losing — what? a thing of small consequence, our skins; and I said to myself: —

"Now, Brichanteau, to work!"

What was I waiting for? I have told you. A moonless night. Darkness. I must have darkness. I said to myself, "To-morrow! To-morrow!" And once more I imagined the admirable scene; the gagging of the sentries, the soldiers of the post bound hand and foot, strangled, the open door, the street, the prefecture. I should have done it, we should have done it. Determined men all. Heroes, jaguars. I had fixed the date, January 19th.

But the Governor of Paris was not notified. He attempted a last sortie: Buzenval. We heard the cannonading in the depths of our prison, and our hearts skipped about like little goats! The German Emperor was present, of course, away off, we had no idea where. Perhaps he would not return to the prefecture that night, but would sleep in some cottage near the field of battle, unless he should be — delicious hypothesis — driven from Versailles by our victorious troops. At all events we had to wait, and to wait again the next day. What had been the result of the battle? Had the day been glorious or disastrous to us? Our plan hung upon that interrogation point.

Oh! but we did not wait long before finding out that it was another defeat!

"An unsuccessful sortie," said my jailer, gayly. "Parisians shut up like rats. Rats! They can eat one another."

He was in high spirits, the imbecile!

Thereupon I said to myself: —

"Ah! destiny has spoken Now let us act!"

And I prepared to act. I was simply meditating whether, instead of making our way to the prefecture by the Avenue de Paris, we should not do better to enter by the door leading to the offices, on Rue Saint-Pierre, that being much nearer: a hundred and seventeen paces, instead of two hundred and sixty-four. Bah! we should see! That would depend on the soldier who happened to be on guard there. But the devil took a hand in the affair. My friend Martineau the poacher, the man whom I had selected, with the Zouave, to leap upon the sentinel during our evening promenade,—the poacher, a redoubtable, daring fellow, was taken to the infirmary. Oh! he would have left his bed, ready to go on, even though he was sick. But the jailer told me that the surgeon feared an attack of fever, and proposed to keep the man in that devilish infirmary to avoid contagion. Should we attempt the blow without that gallant fellow's sturdy arm? I had confidence in him, absolute confidence. He was game to the end. For the first bold stroke I needed Martineau! So I said to myself: "Let us have all the aces in the game. Let us wait till to-morrow."

And the others repeated beneath their breath:—

"When you say the word!"

I had my troupe well in hand. The play was ready, we could go on.

Ah! I shall never forgive myself for having waited! Ah! that rascal of a Martineau! Monsieur Scribe is quite right: small causes, the *glass of water!* Always small causes, scraps of paper, grains of sand! Small causes produce great effects!

If Martineau doesn't get better, so much the worse for him; if Martineau doesn't come back, we will act without him! I will give his rôle to somebody else and up goes the curtain!

We should be thirty-six fighting men, thirty-six heroes, instead of thirty-seven!

But, alas! what a crushing of our hopes! The parleying, the shameful parleying, between Paris and the German army had begun; Monsieur Jules Favre made his appearance on the bridge at Sèvres; the flags of truce came face to face. They parleyed and parleyed, and when Martineau, coming from the infirmary, resolute and bubbling over with enthusiasm, said to me:—

"Well, great chief, here I am! Is it to be to-night?"

I replied with a hopeless gesture and pointed to the insulting smile of the sentinels. . . .

It was all over. I had missed my great day. I have missed many others. I have gone over to the believers in immortality!

But, at all events, I shall die with that fair dream. And, when the pessimism that afflicts the latest generations threatens to invade my essentially sentimental and, I do not hesitate to say, spiritual and optimistic nature, I remember my thirty-six comrades in the prison at Versailles, the débris of defeat, marauders or adventurers, all of whom shared my generous dream, my chimera if you will, all of whom would have given their lives to accomplish it, all of whom were ready to undertake that magnificent game of stake-all, and not one of whom, not a single one, would have been tempted to barter for a little gold, to betray, in exchange for his liberty, the project of a madman whose madness at all events took the form of patriotism.

Ah! how far away it seems! How sad it was! How glorious it might have been! I ought to say that the German authorities did not even wait for the conclusion of peace before setting me at liberty.

"You can go back now to your Normandie," said the little red hussar, who was on hand to give me my freedom, and who knew — they all knew them — Frédéric Bérat's novels, which we have forgotten.

I began to laugh, a stupid laugh.

"Ah! *dame*, to see one's province again is always pleasant, *bédame*, yes!"

And I took my passport for Saint-Pierre-du-Vauvray. But I resorted to strategy to return to Paris, as I had done to leave the city, and I found myself once more, sad and lonely, in my lodgings on Rue de Bondy.

"Hallo!" said my concierge, staring hard at me, "we thought you were dead. Have you come back for the elections?"

The elections? Go to!

I returned for art's sake. I opened Corneille, my old Corneille. That comforted me.

Since then I have never been able to hear an actor imitate the Norman dialect on the stage without a vague desire to weep. And for what do I weep? You can guess. The irreparable. A vanished dream! If I were not telling a true story, your patriotism might be stung, wounded. One does not joke about defeat. But, whether it was the dream of a sick man or a fool, this that I have told you of was very near accomplishment. Ah! that 19th of January, that 19th of January! Had it not been for General Trochu's sortie, the Emperor was ours!

THE LOST LAMB.

By RICHARD HENRY STODDARD.

[1825-.]

The little Tartar maiden
  That tends my master's sheep—
She makes a lamb her pillow,
  When she lies down to sleep.

She parts her gray tent curtains
  Before the morn is seen,
And drives our flocks together,
  To pastures fresh and green.

My heart goes with the maiden,
  For when I wake I find
No heart within my bosom,
  No happy peace of mind.

I track the lost lamb's footsteps,
  And find it fast asleep,
Beside the little maiden
  Among my master's sheep.

THE AUCTION.[1]

BY CHRISTINE C. BRUSH.

(From "The Colonel's Opera Cloak.")

[CHRISTINE (CHAPLIN) BRUSH: The author of "The Colonel's Opera Cloak"; born in Providence, R.I., in May, 1842; died in Brooklyn, N.Y., February 3, 1892. She was the daughter of the Rev. Jeremiah and Jane (Dunbar) Chaplin and the wife of the Rev. Alfred H. Brush. She was an artist of considerable ability, studied painting in Paris in 1877, and in 1879 published in the "No Name" series "The Colonel's Opera Cloak," her most famous book. Her other works are: "Inside our Gate" (1889), "One Summer's Lessons in Perspective" (1890), and contributions to periodical literature.]

AT last, at dark, in a pouring rain, they reached the house.

Pomp had made a fire in the furnace. Mrs. St. John's spirits rose as she grew warm.

"We may as well go to the Colonel at once," she said. "We could start to-morrow, if it wasn't for our things here. What shall we do with them? We shall have to auction them off, I think. I'm sure we have paid this landlord enough, without giving him the things we have bought ourselves. But I am afraid it will be a heap of trouble to have an auction."

"Oh, no, it won't," said Pomp. "It isn't never no trouble to sell tings: it's trouble to buy 'em. Why, ef yer buy, yer has to go out, an' yer has to spend yer money; but, in sellin', yer jes stays in de house, an' gits money fur tings yer doesn't want an' can't kerry off wid yer, nohow."

"But everything is a trouble," returned Mrs. St. John. "If it wasn't for the heat it would make in the house, I'd burn all our things up, to save the trouble of selling them."

"Yer couldn't burn de piano up," said Pomp. "Yer couldn't git it into de furnace."

"What an old fool you are!" said Mrs. St. John. "Let us look over the things, Leslie, and make a list. Here's the piano, and that red velvet chair, and those vases, and——"

"And the towel rack, and the foot rest, and the slipper case I bought at the church fair," added Leslie.

"Yes; and the gilt shaving stand the Colonel bought, the last time he came on.

[1] Copyright, 1897, by Roberts Brothers. Used by permission of Little, Brown & Co.

"I suppose," she added, turning to Pomp, "that there are heaps of broken things."

"Yes, missus; but all on 'em ain't ourn. We've broke a good many of de lan'lord's. We ain't no right to sell dem, hev we?"

"We'll put all our broken things into barrels, and get rid of them in that way," said Mrs. St. John.

"De barrels is all done broke dereselfs," replied Pomp.

"Well, trunks, then," said Mrs. St. John. "Don't pick me up so, Pomp!"

"De trunks! Massy gracious!" cried Pomp. "Yer doesn't want to sell yer trunks, full o' broken traps, and kerry yer clo'es Souf in yer han's, does yer?"

"We shall have some on us," said Mrs. St. John, with dignity. "Very few people travel without clothes in this country, if they do in yours.

"But if you won't use trunks," she added, "tie the things up in sheets."

"De sheets ain't ourn: dey b'longs to de house. Dey wouldn't hold much, anyway. De boys hes used 'em so much fur tents, an' hes wrastled so in bed, an' fired de pillers roun' so free, dat de cases is — well, yer kin git in mos' anywhar, an' out mos' anywhar too; an' de fedders flies out o' dem pillers like as ef yer was shakin' a chicken. Ef I was yer, Miss Marie, I'd leave dem broke tings fur de lan'lord to cl'ar up."

"So I will. Horrid old thing! It would serve him just right," said Mrs. St. John.

"Now look at that ceiling, Leslie," she added; "did you ever see anything like it?"

"The boys did that," said Leslie.

"Well," said Mrs. St. John, "they learned to make them here. I'm sure I never heard of a 'spitball' until I came North. What a house this was to let to a gentleman's family! We have paid rent enough for it. Just look at that spot on the sofa. Ugh! it is sticky."

"I reckon that was some of our medicine, that we've had round. That isn't anything," said Clarence.

"And those lace curtains! What a color! The landlord will do those up before he lets the house again, if he has any kind of decency, — which I shouldn't judge he had," said Mrs. St. John.

"They were fresh when we came," said Leslie.

"Of course they were: he couldn't expect to let a house with soiled curtains, could he?"

"I reckon de piano'll fotch a heap," said Pomp, who had been attentively listening to the conversation. "We ought to 'tend to de auction tings now."

"You must rub up the piano, Pomp," said Leslie. "You know Clarence and Wilfrid used to spring on it dreadfully, when they ran round the parlor over all the furniture."

"I wonder you would allow them to act so, Leslie," said Mrs. St. John. "I should no more think of jumping on a piano than on a looking-glass."

"I danced a clog dance on it one night," said Clarence; "and we put paper inside of it, and Arthur thumped on the keys like a banjo. Oh, it was awful funny music!"

Pomp examined the piano critically.

"Some parts shows de boot heels, but it ain't so bad as it mought be," said he,—it took a great deal to surprise Pomp,—"I thinks a little grease would put it in putty good shape."

"All the keys don't go," said Clarence. "There's a pin in one. I can see it."

"You can shut it down, for the auction," said his mother. "Oh, no, you can't, either. I'll wager a good bit they'll want to hear the tone: it would be just like these Yankees. That chair is all right, isn't it?"

"Yes," said Leslie. "The springs are good—only, aunty, I think there are moths in it."

"Very likely. It was bought North," said Mrs. St. John. "I wouldn't trust a Northerner while I turned my head round. It was bought with moths in it, if they are there. We can't sell a chair better than we buy it, of course.

"You can pin a tidy over that stained place on the back, Leslie, and it can go with the chair.

"We must put a high price on everything," she continued, "because I've always heard that people insist on beating down, at auctions."

"Who's going to say, 'Going, going, gone'?" asked Clarence.

"I s'pose I is," said Pomp. "I does 'mos' ev'ryting."

"No," said Mrs. St. John, "I shall send for a man who makes a business of it. If I am going to have an auction, I'll have one."

Pomp went at once to the grocer, who directed him to an auctioneer.

The man came to look over the house, and was surprised to see how little was to be sold; but that was none of his business. He said he would set the day, and then advertise it a few times.

"Advertise it!" exclaimed Mrs. St. John. "What in the world would you advertise it for? You don't suppose people are coming here from the four corners of the earth, to buy a few old things, do you? Besides, I am going away day after to-morrow. I'll have the auction to-morrow. You've got a flag, haven't you? I never heard of an auctioneer who had not.

"But be sure," she called after him, "not to put up a small-pox flag, and make the people afraid to come in."

When the flag was flung to the breeze, Mrs. St. John seated herself at a front window, to inspect the people who came up the steps.

When any one appeared whose looks did not please her, she called to Pomp not to let him in, or to tell him it wasn't time, and that he would better come back day after to-morrow; adding, in a low tone, "when we shall be all cleared up and gone."

Before the auction began, Mrs. St. John and Leslie seated themselves in the back parlor, where they could see what was going on, through a crack between the sliding doors.

Pomp stayed in the front parlor, where the auction was to take place, to keep an eye on things, and see that the auctioneer did his duty.

Several of the neighbors, to whom the St. Johns had afforded a great deal of excitement, and who knew that the house had been let furnished, came in to look on.

About thirty people had assembled in the hall and parlor at the appointed hour.

"Pomp! Pomp!" called Mrs. St. John. Pomp went to the crack, and looked in with one eye.

"I don't like the looks of those men over there," said the lady, in a loud whisper, loud enough to be heard by those standing near. "You must keep a sharp eye on them. They look like Jews. We ought to have had a policeman here, to watch."

The people looked at each other, and felt like pickpockets.

The auctioneer's voice broke the silence.

"The first thing offered for sale in this elegant house is a superb piano, for which seven hundred and fifty dollars was paid, six short months ago."

"What a whopper!" said Clarence. "It only cost three hundred,—the legs were so scratched up."

"The lady assures me that seven hundred and fifty dollars was its price," said the man, looking threateningly at the impudent boy who was trying to ruin his sale.

Leslie glanced inquiringly at her aunt.

"The man said it was marked at that price, and was worth it,—only he let me have it cheap," said Mrs. St. John, in answer to her look.

"Clarence!" she called. "Come into this room, this moment."

Every one turned toward the back parlor.

"The tone is equal to that of a Steinway," continued the auctioneer. "I might play 'Greenville' myself, but I suppose some one here can display it to better advantage."

No one stirred; and so he ran his fingers over the keys, and soon knocked off the instrument for one hundred and fifty dollars,—"Which was enough for the old thing," Mrs. St. John said.

"Well, here is a clock. Who will bid on this? It is an elegant French clock,—runs a week."

"It runs two, if you run with it," said Wilfrid: and he and Arthur laughed.

"Did we buy that, or does it belong to the house?" whispered Mrs. St. John to Leslie.

"To the house, I think," she replied. "I wasn't here at the first, you know."

"I'll give you five dollars," said a man.

"Five-fifty," said another.

"Six dollars."

Mrs. St. John beckoned to Pomp.

"Nobody can't buy dat," Pomp called out, in a loud voice, "'cause it doesn't b'long to us. We forgot. Dat's de lan'-lord's clock."

Every one laughed.

"Well, here," said the man, "is a towel rack, not owned by the landlord, and worked by fair fingers, doubtless. Some young bachelor would find this priceless. Five dollars it is marked. It is a bunch of white lilies worked on a background of--of—blue."

"Gaslight green," said a young lady near him.

"On a background of gaslight green," he repeated. "It is useful as well as ornamental, and worth double its price."

"I only paid three for it," whispered Leslie.

"I knew they would beat him down, and so I marked it five," replied her aunt, with a businesslike air.

"One dollar," called a voice from the hall.

"What a mean man!" said Mrs. St. John, in a loud whisper, which was heard in the front parlor.

"One dollar twenty-five,—one-fifty,—two dollars."

"Gone,—at two dollars!"

"Stingy enough, I am sure," said Mrs. St. John, half aloud.

"This red velvet chair is in good condition. Springs in order. Tidy goes with it, and gives it a feminine and homelike air. As the poet asks,—

"What's a chair without a tidy?"

"It's a chair," giggled Wilfrid's voice from behind the door.

The people looked at each other, and laughed. They had never attended such a sale before. The auctioneer was amused, too: it seemed like playing at auction.

At length, after various bids, the chair was sold.

A vase was just being carried off, when Mrs. St. John remembered that that wasn't hers.

"The pink pair are mine,—on the mantelpiece," she called, through the crack.

The woman who had bought the large vase was very angry.

"Why do you have an auction," she asked, "if you haven't anything to sell?"

"We have," replied Mrs. St. John, through the crack.

"Why don't you sell it, then, and know your own mind?"

"Why don't you buy the things we own, and not the things which belong to the landlord?" replied again the invisible proprietress.

"These pink vases," said the auctioneer, pointing to the mantelpiece, "are very rare, I am told. The pictures on them are gems of art,—shepherd and shepherdess, surrounded by flock,—landscape in the distance. I have never seen a pair like them before. I should judge they were *Sèvres* or Dresden china, only that the mark of seven dollars shows that they must be of less value. But perhaps their value was not known. At any rate, they are very beautiful, and evidently a great bargain, such as one meets with only once in a lifetime."

"I didn't know they were so valuable," said Mrs. St. John, in a low tone, to Leslie. "I bought them at a ninety-nine-cent store; but, if they are such a bargain, I'll just keep them myself."

The people were beginning to bid, when Mrs. St. John called out:—

"You need not sell those vases. I think I'll keep them myself."

A laugh went around the room.

"The slipper case and foot rest,—will you keep those too, Madame?" asked the auctioneer, turning toward the crack.

"You can sell them, if you get their value: otherwise, I will keep them myself," called out the voice. "I want ten dollars for the foot rest, and seven for the slipper case."

Nobody bid, and the auctioneer laid them aside.

Pomp came forth from the back parlor.

"Missus says she don't know as she keers for de slipper case, after all, an' she'll let it go for free dollars, ef somebody'll buy de foot rest for four."

Several spoke at once. A laugh was raised, and the articles were knocked down.

"Is this satin furniture for sale?" asked some one in the hall.

"No."

"These draperies and mirrors?"

"No, sir."

"Anything in the other parts of the house?"

"No, Madame."

"What *is* for sale?"

"Here is a trunk, for one thing,—locked,—key can't be found,—sold on speculation."

"Two dollars," said a second-hand-clothes man, who looked like a second-hand man.

"Two seventy-five," said his neighbor.

"Massy gracious!" cried Pomp, "don't bid no more! I done forgot till dis blessed minute dat dat ar trunk was Massa Cavello's. I 'spect dar ain't much in it, or he'd ha' sent fur it. Anyhow, dat ain't ourn, an' we ain't got no right to sell it. I'll fin' out whar his club is, an' sen' it to him. though he don't desarve to git it."

"This gilt shaving stand," resumed the auctioneer, after Pomp's episode, as he moved aside the trunk, "will go at a good bargain. In the morning, when the light is perhaps rather dim, or at eve, when the bureau glass does not catch a good light, this small stand can be easily moved about, and afford comfort to the man who would otherwise appear to his friends with black court-plaster covering ghastly wounds, made not by 'the envious Casca,' but by his own hand."

A slight young man, who had the air of a piano tuner, and who had bid off the piano, attracted the eye of the auctioneer. He had light hair, smooth cheeks, and a thin mustache.

"Here, young man, it would serve your purpose well! Shall I look to you for a bid?"

"You'd better help him get more hair: he can't raise what he wants now," cried Wilfrid, from behind the hall door.

The young man wanted to kill him.

At last, the shaving stand was disposed of.

"Here's a boy's jacket, with a jackknife in the pocket, and a few marbles."

The auctioneer could not help laughing: it seemed so absurd to sell one old jacket, in this elegant house.

At the words "jackknife" and "marbles," Clarence rushed into the parlor, and when he beheld the jacket he burst into a flood of tears.

"Give me that jacket, you old fool!" said he. "Those are the things I gave Jasper when he was sick, and he's dead now. I tell you, give it to me. It's his jacket!"

"Oh, yes," said Pomp, the tears running down his cheeks: "dat don't go. I dunno whar dat ar' jacket come from now. Dat war what my poor little gran'son hed on to him when he died, a lyin' on dat very red satin soffy. No, no: we can't sell little dead boys' clo'es! Miss Marie ain't so pore as dat yit."

Two ladies got up hastily from the sofa: one of them had to stop to pull away her sash fringes, which adhered to the cover.

The auctioneer handed the jacket to Pomp, hardly knowing whether to swear or laugh.

"Well," said he, "we will try once more, hoping that the party to whom this belongs is in fine health and spirits, and willing to part with his clothes."

"Here is a fine cloak,—a military cloak, I should say. It is of fine ——"

"Oh! Nobody mustn't make no bid on dat," called Pomp, in a loud voice. "Dat can't be sold, nohow: dat b'longs to de Colonel, an' wa'n't never meant to be sold. Massy gracious! Why, don't you know! Dat's de Colonel's op'ra cloak,— Colonel St. John's."

"No, don't sell that!" cried Mrs. St. John, through the crack. "Of course that can't be sold: anybody might have known that. We are not second-hand-clothes men."

"What did you put it here for, if it wasn't to be sold?" asked the auctioneer, in a little temper.

"I didn't put it dar," said Pomp. "It hed to be somewhar or 'noder, didn't it? I don't 'spect yer to sell yer own clo'es, jes' 'cause dey happens to be in dis house."

"I vouldn't puy dat gloak, if dare vant notin' more to puy in de vorld," said the little Jew to his friend. "Dat gloak gum near to geddin' me inder drouble. I dought de devil vas in him dat night."

"But he vas a goot gloak," said his friend, regretfully, looking after it. "And de leedle goat,—das vas a goot leedle goat. I likes to puy gloes mit bockets in 'em. I finds dings in de bockets, somedimes."

The little Jew looked admiringly at his friend: he had learned a new point in business.

"Well, is there anything else to be sold?" asked the auctioneer.

"No," said Pomp. "Yer hev sold all dere is and more'n dere is."

"And now I hope you are satisfied," said Mrs. St. John, in a low voice. "That man is a monomaniac, Leslie. He wants to sell everything he can lay his hands on."

The people were soon gone, and Mrs. St. John proceeded to settle with the auctioneer.

"How much do you ask for selling these things? Not much, of course, for they were my own things."

"Well, five dollars will satisfy me," said the man.

"I should think it might! You hadn't rent to pay, or anything that other people have to spend money for. Yours must be a very paying business," she said.

Sinking into an easy-chair, after the auctioneer was gone, she cried: "I declare, I am almost tired to death. I was never so sick of anybody in my life as I was of that auctioneer. I thought he never would get off till he had sold every one of us;

and you'd think, to hear him go on about things, that he owned them all. I pity his wife, if his tongue runs that way all the time."

"It makes yer feel kind o' solemn too, doesn't it," said Pomp, "to see tings go out o' de house yer's used to seein' in it,—kind o' like a funereal. I wanted to grab dem men by de ha'r, when dey kerried off our pianner."

"It would have been a pretty sight," said Mrs. St. John, "to have had the police in. Dear, dear, dear! How can the Colonel leave all this care on me?"

THE POKER PARTY.[1]

By MARY N. MURFREE.

(From "Where the Battle was Fought.")

[MARY NOAILLES MURFREE: An American author; born near Murfreesboro, Tenn., about 1850. When she was a child she became lame from a stroke of paralysis and spent her youth chiefly in study. She wrote for the magazines under the pen name of Charles Egbert Craddock, for several years before her sex or identity became known. Among her works are: "In the Tennessee Mountains" (1884), "Where the Battle was Fought" (1884), "Down the Ravine" (1885), "The Prophet of the Great Smoky Mountains" (1885), "In the Clouds" (1886), "The Story of Keedon Bluffs" (1887), "The Despot of Broomsedge Cove" (1888), "In the Stranger People's Country" (1891), "His Vanished Star" (1894), "The Mystery of Witch-Face Mountain" (1896), and "The Young Mountaineer" (1897).]

ESTWICKE slept little that night. For long hours he lay gazing at the pallid wintry moonlight as it crept, barred with the shadow of the tiny window panes, across the floor of his room at the village hotel. The winds had died away. The world without was mute. Within, the intense quietude was broken only by the light sound of his watch under his pillow checking off the seconds. It seemed loud and strident, and its monotonous iteration jarred upon his nerves. He drew it forth presently and stopped the works. And then he could hear only his passionate pulses beat. These he might not silence so lightly.

He rose after a time, stirred the failing fire, dressed, and lighted a cigar. He drew a chair to the window and sat aimlessly looking out upon the street. More than once he sighed

[1] Copyright, 1898, by Houghton, Mifflin & Co. Used by permission.

heavily, — heavily. The shadows and the moonlight shifted about the "Square." The sonorous clangor of the clock, in the courthouse tower, ever and anon warned the world how the time wore on. He watched a mist rise, and hover, and drift away. He looked to the east for the flush of dawn. But clouds were gathering silently, and in the morning they hung low and dense.

This assisted the somewhat dreary aspect of the place, for the pretty homes of Chattalla and the graces of its social life were well out of sight behind the two-story business blocks that surrounded the muddy, ill-paved Square, in the center of which was the courthouse yard and the Temple of Justice itself. A gaunt sycamore tree overhung this red brick structure; the grass was covered with dank withered leaves; to the iron fence saddle horses were hitched in time-honored defiance of the august legislation of the county court. As Estwicke strolled out in front of the hotel after breakfast, he was impressed by a certain military aspect about the citizens. The teamsters standing near their wagons, loaded with wood or country produce, shouldered their long-handled whips in a soldierly fashion, implying a similar habitude with a far deadlier weapon. An equestrian group, that might well have served a painter for a study of cavalry, had gathered about the town scales, where the weighing of cattle was in progress. A dry-goods clerk, middle-aged and iron-gray, came out of a store and crossed the Square to the bank. Estwicke's eyes followed the erect figure with its practiced, measured gait.

"That man has marched a thousand miles to the throb of the drum," he said.

When the rain began to fall heavily in myriads of dun-colored lines, it drove the population within doors, except the teamsters, still lounging near their horses' heads, and Saturday's crowd of black humanity that surged about a row of Jew stores denominated by common consent "Jerusalem."

The contemplation of this picture from the hotel window was his only resource during the morning, and he regarded the approach of the belated train as in the nature of a rescue.

He established himself with a newspaper and a cigar in the smoking car, and did not look up until his name was called.

"Glad to see you back," said a young man who was entering from the "ladies' car." He smiled agreeably and offered his hand, then leaned unsteadily against the arm of the seat while he struck a match and applied it to his cigarette. He was a tall, supple, dandyish young fellow, with a sparkling clever face, a girl's complexion, a long, silky, brown mustache, and hair and eyes of the same shade. The officer moved to give room, and he slipped into the place assigned him with a pantherlike ease and grace that habitually characterized his motions, and made heavier and more muscular men seem a trifle awkward and clumsy in comparison.

"I'm not going to tell you we've missed you. And why? Because you have come among us too lately to believe me," he declared lightly.

"Don't think you overtax my credulity, Mr. Meredith," said Estwicke, somewhat satirically. "I can fancy how the society of Yankee officers must be prized among you."

Meredith laughed coolly. He had been too young to bear his share on this historic plain that stretched so far around them on every side; he had grown happily into manhood under the new *régime*. He held something of the old theories, but in the revolving years his mind had been caught on the cogs of new ideas, and revolved with them. He looked with unruffled serenity at his companion.

"You are so eager in helping us to keep the peace that you never forget your mission. It had escaped me for the instant. Do you find it hard work? Very arduous, eh?"

Estwicke laughed, too. "Well, on the whole you are not so bad as the Indians," he said temperately. "But you are duller, — far! There is some healthy snap and go on the frontier."

"That pleasing uncertainty about being scalped is the one redeeming feature of your profession — otherwise it is too painfully definite," said Meredith, philosophically. "If you keep your scalp — when it is gray you'll still be *Captain* Estwicke, unless we can get up a foreign war or a civil commotion for your advancement. Whereas *I*," with a hopeful rising inflection, "may in the course of time, and by the force of talent alone, be a Chief Justice — and then again, by the force of talent alone, I mayn't. Room for speculation, eh?"

"Strikes me, on the contrary, that your prospects are painfully definite, too," said Estwicke. "Your father and his partner will take you in as a third after a while. So you'll be perpetually bringing up the rear, overcrowed by the two big lawyers. Your father will think he ought to do something for you — that's the way he'll do it."

"Not he—not he," protested Meredith. "I wish he would. My father has a theory that if a young lawyer is not helped he will help himself—to any stray litigation that may be afloat, as it were, in the air. He has left me to illustrate this theory."

"How does it work?" asked Estwicke, with interest.

"I pray God I mayn't starve," said Meredith, tersely.

"Room for speculation, eh?" suggested Estwicke.

Chattalla had faded in the distance, and now the earthworks loomed up through the low-lying vapors and the blurring rain, vague and distorted but always grim and grewsome. As the train thundered with a hollow roar on the railroad bridge, there could be caught a fleeting glimpse of the isolated piers, and of the ferryboat, pausing in mid stream that Tom Toole might gaze after the cloud of smoke, which lay on the top of the cars, and drifted back to the redoubts and hung about the empty embrasures suggestively.

Estwicke, oblivious of the landscape, was absorbed in the conversation. He was essentially a man of this world. He craved the companionship of other men. He could not live apart from it. He had none of those intimate inner resources that make solitude sweet. Except for some principles of gunnery, bearing upon a still unperfected improvement of his own, he cared nothing for the study of science. Apart from the history of splendid achievement, some stirring martial lyrics, the biographies of great commanders, he had no fondness for reading. His books were the men about him; their experience, their lives, formed his interest, and as in the ever-shifting combinations of human events they lapsed upon his own life he too bore a part in this sentient literature. He had a quick understanding of men, and a passionate sympathy with them. He did not even affect an appreciation of art; he looked blankly at its results. But an unrecognized something in the burnished sunlight, the silver-shotted moonlit mists, the haze on the purple hills, the sound of the melancholy autumn wind, subtly thrilled to his heart and prevailed within him mightily. He found a wondrous sensuous exaltation in the mystery and the joy of being. He felt that his blood was swift in his veins; he stretched his limbs; he admired his muscles; he took cognizance of an involuntary alertness of his mental faculties; he knew that he was strong, and well, and graciously endowed. But he had no questions to ask of

Heaven or Earth. He was too definite for mere abstractions, and adhered mechanically to the faith of the fathers.

Despite his imperfectly tempered aggressiveness, he possessed certain qualities of good comradeship, — his zest in life, his soldierly frankness, and his ardor commended themselves to Meredith, who was presently surprised in the midst of the desultory talk, which was neither wise nor witty, to see that the twenty miles had slipped past, that billowy sweeps of hills were on every side, that the city was elusively appearing and disappearing, miragelike, in the purple distance.

They parted at the depot, and until evening Estwicke was greatly harassed with loneliness, for his regiment had but recently been stationed in the vicinity, and he knew few of the citizens. Nothing was going on at either of the theaters, and he could only mitigate the tedium after tea by lounging about the hotel with a promiscuous crowd of smokers, who habitually congregated here, for Marston boasted no clubhouses. A fountain in the center of the tessellated floor was tossing up pretty corolla-shaped jets of spray, that sparkled in the gaslight. The clerks bullied the incoming travelers. A mocking bird in a cage sang shrilly; the cheerful click of billiard balls was heard from behind a colonnade, and through its vistas might be descried delicately poised cues and nimbly attitudinizing figures.

The scene soon palled upon Estwicke. He began to think of driving out to the barracks to-night instead of in the morning, but Meredith came in from the street, and the resolve faded.

"I'm glad to see that you are still in town," said the lawyer, as they met.

Following, as was often the case, in Meredith's footsteps, was his cousin, Tom West, a jaunty young sprig, some twenty or twenty-two years old, who effusively claimed Estwicke's acquaintance. As they shook hands, the officer became aware of a close scrutiny directed upon him from over the tall, young fledgeling's shoulder. It emanated from a pair of cold, fishy eyes, set in an impassive, florid face, which belonged to a stout, middle-aged, soberly dressed, responsible-looking party. Estwicke could not have said explicitly why he was so unfavorably impressed, nor why when West, with callow self-sufficiency, introduced the stranger as his friend, Mr. Casey, it seemed so very odd that he should have a friend like this. Estwicke, mechanically extending his hand, looked at Casey with wonted fierce intentness, and noted the indefinable but strong intimations lurking about him of solid commercial pursuits. Somehow his breadth of waistcoat, his sparingness of speech, his quiet, grave manner, assisted this effect. The man who knew men could not reconcile it with the look in his eye and stony countenance.

He showed a disposition to devote himself to West, and said little to Estwicke, who presently turned back in relief to Meredith.

"How do you get away with these long evenings?" he demanded.

"Professional study, generally; regular midnight-oil business."

"Nice boy!" ejaculated Estwicke.

"Sometimes," said Meredith, signifying by a gesture that he desired the favor of a light from Estwicke's cigar, "sometimes clients get as scarce as hen's teeth, and the justice's court — most of my practice is in that humble modern *pie poudre* — the justice's court knows me no more. Then I make up my mind to renounce the profession before it is in everybody's mouth that the profession has renounced me. So I play billiards in the evening, or go to the theater, or call on the young ladies."

"Oh, the young ladies!" cried Estwicke, stroking his whiskers. "That's mighty bad!"

He looked at Meredith, and laughed as he received his cigar back.

A band of itinerant musicians suddenly struck up a popular waltz, and the rotunda was filled with surging waves of sound. "This is insufferable," said Meredith. "Suppose we go up to my room, where we can have a quiet smoke and talk."

As they passed the fountain, West approached them. "Going upstairs?" he asked of his cousin.

Meredith nodded. "Will you come with us?"

"And I'll bring Casey," West declared agreeably, very slightly lowering his voice; "that is if you have no objection. I'm under great obligations to him, and as he knows nobody in town but us I feel bound to see him through and make his stay as pleasant as possible."

Meredith frowned, and hesitated. But Casey was standing at no great distance, and had evidently overheard the conversation. Estwicke experienced a twinge of uneasiness. Despite his ill-defined antipathy toward Casey, and although the suggestion that he should join them had destroyed every prospect of pleasure, it seemed to Estwicke almost a cruelty to refuse publicly so slight and apparently so reasonable a request. He watched Meredith with expectant eyes.

"Certainly, if you like," the young lawyer assented, not too graciously, and turned away.

"That's a boon," he muttered to Estwicke, who made no reply, for at that moment they stepped into the elevator, and stood silent and with their cigars held low and reversed, like the muskets of privates at a military funeral, in deference to a group of ladies within.

"I roost high," said Meredith, when they had gotten out on an upper story. "It comes cheaper up here, and there's better ventilation. 'Beggars all, but, marry, good air.'"

After they were seated before the blazing fire in Meredith's room, West seemed altogether unaware of the reluctant toleration with which his entertainer regarded the amendment to the quiet smoke and talk. With his gay, youthful self-sufficiency, he absorbed the conversation as far as he might. He was facetious, and flippantly fraternized with Casey.

"Captain," he said to Estwicke, with an explanatory wave of his hand toward his solemn red-faced friend, "there is the great original David! And I am Jonathan! Wasn't it David who saved Jonathan's life?" He pulled at his mustache and laughed and smoked his big cigar with manly gusto.

"Oh, it was nothing, nothing whatever," declared Casey. His manner suggested that from good nature he was content to lightly waive recognition of a feat.

The sharp young lawyer apprehended the intimation.

"Nothing?" he repeated satirically. "Nothing to save Tom West's life? Why, it was a public benefaction!"

Estwicke, with his quick interest in exploits, his love of danger, his enthusiastic admiration of bravery, turned to Casey with a sudden sense of respect.

"May I ask how that came about?"

Casey hesitated, and Estwicke presently recognized in this a tact which was hardly consonant with such a slow-seeming man, for West, after waiting expectantly for a moment, plunged into an account of a recent railroad accident, that might have been very disastrous, but had resulted in nothing worse than cooping him up in the débris, whence by some exercise of thews and sinews — of which Mr. Casey was amply capable — he was extricated. His rescue had evidently involved no risk, but it had served as an introduction of Casey, who was adroitly abetting West in magnifying its importance. Estwicke listened with contemptuous amusement, and Meredith's efforts to conceal his impatience had grown so lame that his relief was very evident when a knock at the door interrupted the conversation, and a card was brought in. He glanced at it in surprise.

"Show the gentleman up," he said, and the brisk and grinning bell boy disappeared.

The interval that ensued was expectant. Perhaps this was the reason the newcomer appeared upon the scene with the impressiveness of the principal character of a drama. Perhaps it might be that life had always cast Maurice Brennett for the leading business, and he bore himself in a manner befitting the title *rôle*. His eyes had a peculiar brilliancy, and were capable of an intent expression so concentrated that when suddenly elicited it had a sinister effect, and put its subject instinctively on guard. He was tall, thin, angular, and dressed with an elaborate fastidiousness that was somehow oddly incongruous with his pale, powerful, intellectual face — he seemed rather the type of man who scorns the minutiæ of externals. Between his mobile eyebrows many a scheme had registered itself in subtle hieroglyphics. There was a look of severely maintained repression about the hard lines of his lips as if the controlling influences of his nature had had a struggle for ascendency over other wild and turbulent forces. Even now the slight annoyance of finding a group here instead of the man he wanted had brought a quiver to the thin, sensitive nostrils of his sharp, hooked, and delicately chiseled nose. His pallor was the pallor of late hours — not such as these young fellows kept, but the anxious vigils of thought, the canvassing of opportunity, and the inception of plans. He had his hat in his hand, and the gaslight revealed such glimmers here and there in his dark hair, clipped close about a shapely head, and in his full, dark mustache, as might intimate that he was fast growing gray, which is premature at forty.

His presence exerted a singular influence upon the other men; their personal peculiarities were suddenly abnormally pronounced.

Casey seemed trebly slow, stolid, rubicund. West looked

very callow, and felt very callow too; Meredith's dainty complexion, his silky mustache, his sparkle, were almost effeminate. Estwicke silently measured the stranger with challenging eyes.

"I have hardly time for this," Brennett said, as he took the cigar which Meredith tendered him. "My business with you is rather imperative."

Meredith was a trifle confused, having naturally enough supposed that the visit at this place and hour had only a social significance. Upon the word business, the others made a motion as if to take leave.

"I fear I am interrupting you," Brennett continued, looking round at the group. "I feel rather like the ghost of fiction who routs a pleasure party. It is a hackneyed theme, but no one has adequately considered the embarrassing position of the ghost."

There was a laugh at this and a momentary hesitation.

"You will greatly alleviate it if you won't allow me to put you to flight. I only want a few minutes' consultation with Mr. Meredith. I ventured to look you up out of office hours and on Saturday night," he continued, turning to the young lawyer, "because I have information that a debtor of mine is about to run off his cotton on a Sunday freight, and this may be my last opportunity to get out an attachment."

"I insist that you don't go," said Meredith, addressing himself specially to Estwicke. "This won't keep me long — meantime suppose you have a game of cards. I am not going to my office — we can talk the matter over here."

He flung a pack of cards on the table; then he and Brennett turned away to a desk which was on the opposite side of the room. The trio at the table chatted for a few moments in a desultory strain, but presently West, glancing at lawyer and client now fairly immersed in business, shrugged his shoulders, gathered up the cards, and with a juvenile leer at the others, proposed to deal for "draw."

"I haven't played for so long, I scarcely remember the game," protested Casey.

West laughed jeeringly; he joyed so in his amiable wickedness.

"Oh, Casey's afraid of getting turned out of church. We'll take you in out of the wet — won't we, Captain? We belong to the 'big church' — we do."

Estwicke made no reply; he hardly relished even a "big church" membership with Casey.

"I suppose we play with a limit?" he asked impatiently, showing some eagerness to begin.

West's *was* an amiable wickedness. In fact it was only a weak-kneed semblance — that would, yet might not, be. He quaked at the bare suggestion of the alternative.

"Captain, you shock me," he declared. "Of course we play with a limit — fifty cents — say."

They talked very little when once fairly at it. For a time Meredith, who sat with his back toward them, only knew vaguely that somebody was "passing" or "straddling the blind," or "seeing and going better." Once or twice West laughed out loud and long in triumph. And again his voice rose in excited remonstrance, to which his companions seemed to pay no attention. Then the room was quiet for a time, and the lawyer lost cognizance of everything except the complications of Brennett's liens and his debtor's duplicity.

"How many bales do you suppose he has there?" Meredith asked, after a meditative pause.

There was no answer.

He glanced up impatiently. Brennett's face was instinct with an alert interest. His eyes, lighted by some inward sardonic laughter, were fixed upon the group by the fire.

Meredith turned quickly, and at this moment Estwicke — his coat thrown off upon the floor, his hat thrust on the back of his head, the hot blood crimsoning his sunburned cheek, the perspiration standing thick in his close-clipped red hair, his eyes blazing with that most unholy fire, the gambler's passion — cocked his cigar between his set teeth and raised the blind one hundred dollars.

West had passed out of the game, had drawn away from the table, and was gazing with dismayed surprise at the swollen proportions of the pool and at the impassive, stony countenance of Casey. Not a feather was ruffled as he looked coolly into Estwicke's burning eyes; he was as decorously florid, his waistcoat as commercially rotund as ever, but his demeanor was the demeanor of the professional expert.

He stolidly made good — and then he drew one card, Estwicke standing pat. After this, for a few moments, each seemed cautious, making very small bets. But presently, when Estwicke raised him fifty dollars, Casey "saw it" and went a hundred better.

Then the slow, cumbrous fellow, according to his habit, laid his cards, face downward, on the table in front of him, with a single chip upon them to hold them in place, and clasping his hands lightly upon his substantial stomach, calmly awaited Estwicke's "say."

And all at once Estwicke looked hard at the man, with a change on his expressive face. There was an eager surprise in his eyes; the flush of sheer excitement deepened to an angry glow; he seemed lost for an instant in a sort of doubting confusion. Suddenly he made good, and "called."

Meredith was thunderstruck as he realized the full significance of the scene. He rose hastily. "Gentlemen," he said sternly, "this is going entirely too far."

They took no heed. With one hand Casey laid his cards, a straight flush — ace, king, queen, jack, and ten of diamonds — upon the table beside Estwicke's jack full, while with the other hand he gathered the pool toward him, giving no sign of elation.

"I protest," began Meredith. He stopped suddenly short.

Brennett sprang to his feet with a sharp exclamation.

It happened in an instant. There was a swift movement of Estwicke's intent figure; he thrust his hand behind him, and seemed to draw from his pistol pocket a glancing, steely flash of light; there was a sharp, metallic click — of a peculiarly nerve-thrilling quality; he lunged across the table, and held the weapon at full cock at the man's head.

Warned by Estwicke's motion, Casey had made an effort to draw his pistol. His hand grasped it in his pocket.

"Move your right arm and you're a dead man," said Estwicke between his set teeth. They were strong and white, and unconsciously he showed them. The veins that crossed his forehead were black and swollen. His breath came hot and fast and with a sibilant sound. He seemed to think as Brennett sprang up that there would be an effort to disarm him.

"If you interfere," he said in a low voice, — "if you touch me — I will kill you — I will kill you!"

It was a moment of terrible suspense, but as Brennett moved hastily back, he laughed aloud — a short, ungenial laugh, nervous perhaps — or was the fancy so absurd that he should interfere!

Meredith's motion toward Estwicke was arrested by his next words. "Drop that card out of your sleeve — the card I dealt you."

Casey gazed abjectly at him, turning even paler than before, and made a weak, spasmodic effort to speak, to deny.

"No use talking," said Estwicke, cutting him short. "Drop the card." His finger by accident or design quivered slightly on the trigger.

The sharper shook his sleeve, and the three of diamonds fell upon the table.

"The exchange was quick as lightning — but I *saw* it!" Estwicke declared.

Without lowering his eyes or moving the weapon, he placed with his left hand the three of diamonds on the table beside the straight flush to illustrate the self-evident fact that, no matter which of the cards Casey had substituted for it, the hand after the draw was merely a flush.

"And a full outranks a flush!" he proclaimed, with a fierce, dictatorial air.

Casey sat before him, silent, cowed, helpless, the revolver that he still grasped in his pocket as useless as if his right hand was palsied.

"My full raked the pool!" thundered Estwicke. "I won it all! I'll have it all! Fork! With your left hand — mind."

As Casey hastily pushed the money across the table, a modest nickel that had served in the half-dollar-limit game with which they began fell to the floor and rolled away among the shadows.

He had surrendered utterly — it was all over. A breath of relief was beginning to inflate his lungs, which in the surprise and fright had seemed to forget and bungle their familiar functions. The other men moved slightly as they stood, — an involuntary expression of the relaxation of the tension, — the creak of Tom West's boots was to him like the voice of a friend. Then they realized, with the shock of an infinite surprise, that Estwicke sat as motionless as if he were carved in stone, his pistol still held at the cheat's head. The room was so silent that they might hear the rumble of the elevator on its missions up and down, the throb of the engine in the cellar, the faint rattle of the dishes in the dining room far, far below the high story where the young man's room was perched. They understood at last, and it came upon them with the amazing effect of a flash of lightning from a clear sky.

Estwicke was waiting for the nickel!

The card sharper was panting, failing, almost losing consciousness. He did not dare to stoop and search for the coin — he could not summon his voice for speech. The tears sprang into his eyes when he saw that the situation was at length comprehended by the others.

West hastily knelt on the floor, passed his tremulous fingers over the dark carpet, clutched the coin and placed it on the table.

To the two men who knew Estwicke best the episode was a frightful illustration of a certain imperious exactingness which they had discovered even in their short acquaintance was a notable characteristic of his nature. For one instant longer he looked hard at the sharper. Then he brought his heavy hand down upon the table in the midst of the pile of greenbacks, with a vehemence that sent a shiver through every glass in the room.

"Damn you!" he cried out fiercely. "Keep it!"

He thrust his pistol into his pocket. Without another word he strode heavily out of the room, leaving Casey staring blankly at the money so strangely relinquished, and the others standing petrified under the yellow gas jets gazing after the receding figure that marched through the shadowy vagueness of the dimly lighted hall without.

When he was fairly gone, Meredith turned to Casey. The sharper had before hardly seemed able to breathe. He was on his feet now and ready to walk. His god was good to him. The touch of it had made him whole.

"I have never before had occasion," said Meredith, sternly, "to show a man the door." He waved his hand toward it.

The hardened creature insolently lifted his cold, fishy eye and grinned. His plethoric pocketbook was overflowing in his hands; he tucked the other bills into the pockets of his respectable, commercial-looking waistcoat.

"Sorry to have any disagreement, I'm sure. Your friend is a little too choleric — apt to be the fault of military men. I have to thank you for a most delightful evening. I'll come again soon. Bye-bye, West!"

He bowed and grinned and grimaced at the door. Meredith was scarlet with indignation. Tom West thrust his hands into his pockets and turned sheepishly away. Brennett flung himself against the mantelpiece and laughed with an intense enjoyment so chilling, so derisive, so repellent in its quality that Casey paused in the hall and glanced back through the open door in surprise and a vague distrust. Meredith saw among the shadows his white, heavy-jawed face, from which the smile had faded in an expression of inexplicable wonder, of fear. Then he turned once more and disappeared.

Meredith hastily handed Brennett his memoranda and, with a promise to return in a few moments, started toward the door.

"Where are you going?" West demanded inquisitively.

"To look up Captain Estwicke," Meredith replied curtly.

The "elevator boy" knew the number of Estwicke's room on the transient floor by reason of having had the key left with him during the evening. Estwicke had hardly entered and closed the door when Meredith knocked. He looked around with a flushed face as the young lawyer came in.

"I hope you will remember how that blackguard was forced upon me," Meredith began hotly. "I don't usually consort with cheats. I am not responsible for your meeting such company in my room."

Estwicke gave a bitter laugh.

"What does it matter to me where I met him?"

"It matters to me," said Meredith, tersely.

Estwicke was tramping back and forth the length of the room.

"I thought I had given that thing up!" he cried in a tumult of despair. "I haven't touched a card for years. I can't play in moderation. I can't, you see. I go wild — wild! It's an hereditary passion."

Meredith was a lawyer, and an acute one. He changed his base with a celerity that did infinite credit to his acumen. Estwicke was taking himself to task — not his entertainer. He briskly joined the onslaught.

"Oh, hereditary!" he sneered. "I have often noticed that a man credits his father with his own pet vices. What was the reason you let the rascal have the money?"

"I had no reason — no positive idea; it was only an impulse," said Estwicke. "Somehow when I got it — I — couldn't touch it. That *I* should brawl with a fellow like that for money! But why not?" he added after a sullen pause. "He is as good as I am — that is, I am as bad as he is."

"Bless me!" exclaimed Meredith, satirically, "I wouldn't say *that*."

"I know better. He doesn't."

"But some of it was yours on the strictest moral construction."

Estwicke stood in the middle of the floor staring at his visitor.

"I mean the money you originally bet," Meredith explained.

This was a distinction that Estwicke could not grasp. "It was *all* mine!" he bawled. "My — full — raked — the — pool!" He came hastily and sat down in the green-rep armchair, expounding how the game stood, checking off his cards and Casey's on the fingers of his right and left hands respectively. His excited words in their confused haste stumbled and tripped up over each other in his throat; his eyes were eager and earnest; he trembled with the intensity of his interest. Even the wordy lawyer could not interrupt.

"Well," he said, when Estwicke had concluded, "I knew all that before — and it's a nice business. You told me once that you have nothing but your pay. I should think," he continued exasperatingly, "this night's work would make a considerable hole in it. I hope you feel that you have invested your time and money to the best advantage."

"Oh, I got disgusted with the money. I couldn't endure to keep step, morally, you know, with that contemptible, poor devil. I tell you he looked at the money with tears in his eyes."

Meredith stared.

"This is rather a belated sympathy with the 'poor devil,'" he said sarcastically. "Captain Estwicke," he continued, "I don't pretend to understand you, but I feel it almost a duty to tell you how heartily I disapprove of your conduct to-night. Pistoling a man at a card table for cheating is a practically unprovoked, cruel, and abhorrent crime."

"Didn't do it," said Estwicke, grimly, on the defensive.

"You would have done it — if he had not instantly yielded."

"Ha-a-rdly," drawled Estwicke. The tone was significant. Meredith looked at him expectantly. Estwicke glanced uneasily up at the ceiling, then down at his boots. As he turned doubtfully toward Meredith their eyes met, and he broke into an uproarious peal of laughter.

"Why, man!" he cried hilariously, "the pistol wasn't loaded!"

He drew the weapon from his pocket and held it at arm's length, revolving its empty chambers, and setting the walls to echoing its sharp click.

Meredith laughed, too, partly in sympathy with the other's boisterous enjoyment of what he considered so exquisitely flavored a joke and partly in relief. "I'm glad you let me know this," he declared. "Forget what I said when I didn't know it." Presently he added with a view of contingencies of which Estwicke seemed utterly incapable—"but suppose that that fellow had persisted in heaving up the thing *he* had in his pocket?"

"Oh, but I was sure he wouldn't. Moral suasion, you know. There's a wonderful deal of moral suasion in giving a man a peep down an iron tube. It puts the best of us out of countenance." After a pause he said gravely,—"Nothing would have induced me to hurt the man—besides, I *couldn't.* All I wanted was my own money."

"And you didn't want that little long."

"I feel like the devil," said Estwicke, impatiently. "I'm so much like the devil to-night that I don't know us apart."

"Well," persisted Meredith, "you've given us a fine sensation. I never saw a man so entertained as that fellow Brennett."

"I don't care to set up as a show," said Estwicke, sulkily.

"A cat may look at a king."

"I doubt if it is altogether safe for the cat."

"In the light of late events, I certainly should not take the liberty if I were a cat," said Meredith, with a laugh.

"He is not a cat," rejoined Estwicke, with that sudden insight into character which was so marked a quality of his mind. "He has a hawk's face and a hawk's eyes—the most startlingly brilliant eyes I ever saw. I never met a human hawk before—though I've known human wolves, and monkeys, and dogs, and cats. We don't want to claim kin with our poor relations. But some of us can't help ourselves. We will look like 'em, and sometimes we will behave like 'em." He stretched out his legs to the fire, and thrust his hands in his pockets. "I'm misanthropic, ain't I?" He glanced up with a laugh. After a pause he asked—"What's his business?"

"Getting rich."

"I could have guessed as much," declared Estwicke. "That man has his soul in his pocket. And his pocket doesn't bulge. Such a soul as that won't crowd things."

"Don't know about his soul, but he certainly has an instinct for money. He speculates heavily in cotton futures. And he owns a half-interest in a mine out west that they used to say was as good as a mint."

The young lawyer had risen to take leave. With an almost affectionate impulse he paused at the door. "Estwicke," he said, "I want to tell you — you're a good fellow."

"That I am," said Estwicke, mockingly, "I'm mighty good."

He looked about him wearily, with a haggard, hunted face after the door had closed. Then suddenly he rang the bell, called for his bill, packed his traps dexterously, methodically, and in surprisingly small compass — one of his military accomplishments — and the full moon was hardly swinging past the meridian before he was bowling swiftly along the turnpike among the hills that encompassed the city. Through the carriage windows he saw it lying behind him in many an undulation, its domes and its mansard roofs idealized in the glamour and the distance to a castellated splendor. It had faded away in the dusky shadows long before he caught sight of the white-framed barrack buildings. His heart warmed at the thought of his friends so close at hand, of the familiar surroundings, and the old routine. He saw the sentry's bayonet glisten in the moonlight, and catch on its point a star of fire. And the evening and the scene he had left slipped into the dark corners of his recollection.

TOO LATE.

By FITZ-HUGH LUDLOW.

[1837–1870.]

"Ah! si la jeunesse savait, — si la vieillesse pouvait!"

THERE sat an old man on a rock,
  And unceasing bewailed him of Fate, —
That concern where we all must take stock,
  Though our vote has no hearing or weight;

And the old man sang him an old, old song,—
Never sang voice so clear and strong
That it could drown the old man's for long,
For he sang the song "Too late! too late!"

"When we want, we have for our pains
The promise that if we but wait
Till the want has burned out of our brains,
Every means shall be present to state;
While we send for the napkin the soup gets cold,
While the bonnet is trimming the face grows old,
When we've matched our buttons the pattern is sold,
And everything comes too late,—too late!

"When strawberries seemed like red heavens,—
Terrapin stew a wild dream,—
When my brain was at sixes and sevens,
If my mother had 'folks' and ice cream,
Then I gazed with a lickerish hunger
At the restaurant man and fruit monger,—
But oh! how I wished I were younger
When the goodies all came in a stream! in a stream!

"I've a splendid blood horse, and—a liver
That it jars into torture to trot;
My rowboat's the gem of the river,—
Gout makes every knuckle a knot!
I can buy boundless credits on Paris and Rome,
But no palate for *ménus*,—no eyes for a dome,—
Those belonged to the youth who must tarry at home,
When no home but an attic he'd got,—he'd got!

"How I longed, in that lonest of garrets,
Where the tiles baked my brains all July,
For ground to grow two pecks of carrots,
Two pigs of my own in a sty,
A rosebush, a little thatched cottage,—
Two spoons—love—a basin of pottage!—
Now in freestone I sit,—and my dotage,—
With a woman's chair empty close by, close by!

"Ah! now, though I sit on a rock,
I have shared one seat with the great;
I have sat—knowing naught of the clock—
On love's high throne of state;

But the lips that kissed, and the arms that caressed,
To a mouth grown stern with delay were pressed,
And circled a breast that their clasp had blessed,
Had they only not come too late, — too late!"

THE BROTHERS.[1]

BY ÉMILE GABORIAU.

(From "File No. 113.")

[ÉMILE GABORIAU, a French author, was born in Saujon, November 9, 1835; died in Paris, September 28, 1873. His books consist chiefly of detective stories, which are of a high order and have been translated into almost every modern tongue. They include: "The Lerouge Affair" (1866), "The Crime of Orcival" (1867), "File No. 113" (1867), "Slaves of Paris" (1869), "M. Lecoq" (1869), "The Infernal Life" (1870), "The Fall" (1871), and "The Rope about the Neck" (1873).]

ABOUT two leagues from Tarascon, on the left bank of the Rhone, not far from the wonderful gardens of M. Audibert, stood the Château of Clameran, a weather-stained, neglected, but massive structure.

Here lived, in 1841, the old Marquis de Clameran and his two sons, Gaston and Louis.

The marquis was an eccentric old man. He belonged to the race of nobles, now almost extinct, whose watches stopped in 1789 and who kept time with the past century.

More attached to his illusions than to his life, the old marquis insisted upon considering all the stirring events which had happened since the first revolution as a series of deplorable practical jokes.

Emigrating with the Count D'Artois, he did not return to France until 1815 with the allies.

He soon became accustomed to the free and indolent life of a country gentleman.

Possessing fifteen thousand francs a year, he spent twenty-five or thirty thousand, borrowing from every source, saying that a genuine restoration would soon take place, and that then he would regain possession of all his properties.

Following his example, his younger son lived extravagantly. Louis was always in pursuit of adventure, and idled away his

[1] By permission of G. Routledge & Sons.

time in drinking and gambling. The elder son, Gaston, anxious to participate in the stirring events of the time, prepared himself for action by quietly working, studying, and reading certain papers and pamphlets surreptitiously received, the very mention of which was considered a hanging matter by his father.

Altogether the old marquis was the happiest of mortals, living well, drinking high, hunting much, tolerated by the peasants, and execrated by the gentlemen of the neighborhood, who regarded him with contempt and raillery.

Time never hung heavy on his hands, except in midsummer, when the valley of the Rhone was intensely hot; and even then he had infallible means of amusement, always new, though ever the same.

He detested, above all, his neighbor, the Countess de la Verberie.

The Countess de la Verberie, the *bête noire* of the marquis, as he ungallantly termed her, was a tall, dry woman, angular in appearance and character, cold and arrogant toward her equals, and domineering over her inferiors.

Like her noble neighbor, she too had emigrated; and her husband was afterward killed at Lützen, but unfortunately not in the French ranks.

In 1815 the countess came back to France. But while the Marquis de Clameran returned to comparative ease, she could obtain nothing from royal munificence but the small estate and Château of La Verberie.

It is true that the Château of La Verberie would have contented most people; but the countess never ceased to complain of her unmerited poverty, as she called it.

The pretty château was more modest in appearance than the manor of the Clamerans; but it was equally comfortable, and much better regulated by its proud mistress.

The countess had but one child — a lovely girl of eighteen, named Valentine: fair, slender, and graceful, with large, soft eyes, beautiful enough to make the stone saints of the village church thrill in their niches when she knelt piously at their feet.

The renown of her great beauty, carried on the rapid waters of the Rhone, was spread far and wide.

Often the bargemen and the robust wagoners, driving their powerful horses along the road, would stop to gaze with admiration upon Valentine seated under some grand old tree on the banks of the river, absorbed in her book.

At a distance her white dress and flowing tresses made her seem a mysterious spirit from another world, these honest people said; they thought it a good omen when they caught a glimpse of her as they passed up the river. All along between Arles and Valence she was spoken of as the "lovely fairy" of La Verberie.

If M. de Clameran detested the countess, Mme. de la Verberie execrated the marquis. If he nicknamed her "the witch," she never called him anything but "the old gander."

And yet they should have agreed, for at heart they cherished the same opinions, with different ways of viewing them.

He considered himself a philosopher, scoffed at everything, and had an excellent digestion. She nursed her rancor, and grew yellow and thin from rage and envy.

Nevertheless, they might have spent many pleasant evenings together, for, after all, they were neighbors. From Clameran could be seen Valentine's greyhound running about the park of La Verberie; from La Verberie glimpses were had of the lights in the dining-room windows of Clameran.

And, as regularly as these lights appeared every evening, the countess would say in a spiteful tone: —

"Ah, now their orgies are about to commence."

The two châteaux were only separated by the fast-flowing Rhone, which at this spot was rather narrow.

But between the two families existed a hatred deeper and more difficult to avert than the course of the Rhone.

What was the cause of this hatred?

The countess, no less than the marquis, would have found it difficult to tell.

It was said that under the reign of Henry IV. or Louis XIII., a La Verberie betrayed the affection of a fair daughter of the Clamerans.

This misdeed led to a duel and bloodshed.

This groundwork of facts had been highly embellished by fiction; handed down from generation to generation, it had now become a long tragic history of robbery, murder, and rapine, which precluded any intercourse between the two families.

The usual result followed, as it always does in real life, and often in romances, which, however exaggerated they may be, generally preserve a reflection of the truth which inspires them.

Gaston met Valentine at an entertainment; he fell in love with her at first sight.

Valentine saw Gaston, and from that moment his image filled her heart.

But so many obstacles separated them!

For over a year they both religiously guarded their secret, buried like a treasure in the inmost recesses of their hearts.

And this year of charming, dangerous reveries decided their fate. To the sweetness of the first impression succeeded a more tender sentiment; then came love, each having endowed the other with superhuman qualities and ideal perfections.

Deep, sincere passion can only expand in solitude; in the impure air of a city it fades and dies, like the hardy plants which lose their color and perfume when transplanted to the hothouse.

Gaston and Valentine had only seen each other once, but seeing was to love; and as the time passed, their love grew stronger, until at last the fatality which had presided over their first meeting brought them once more together.

They both happened to be spending the day with the old Duchess d'Arlange, who had returned to the neighborhood to see her property.

They spoke to each other, and like old friends, surprised to find that they both entertained the same thoughts and echoed the same memories.

Again they were separated for months. But soon, as if by accident, they happened to be at a certain hour on the banks of the Rhone, and would sit and gaze across at each other.

Finally, one mild May evening, when Mme. de la Verberie had gone to Beaucarie, Gaston ventured into the park, and appeared before Valentine.

She was not surprised or indignant. Genuine innocence displays none of the startled modesty assumed by conventional innocence. It never occurred to Valentine that she ought to bid Gaston to leave her.

She leaned upon his arm, and strolled up and down the grand old avenue of oaks. They did not say they loved each other, they felt it; but they did say that their love was hopeless. They well knew that the inveterate family feud could never be overcome, and that it would be folly to attempt it.

They swore never, never to forget each other, and tearfully resolved never to meet again; never, not even once more!

Alas! Valentine was not without excuse. With a timid, loving heart, her expansive affection was repressed and chilled by a harsh mother. Never had there been one of those long private talks between the Countess de la Verberie and Valentine which enable a good mother to read her daughter's heart like an open book.

Mme. de la Verberie saw nothing but her daughter's beauty. She was wont to rub her hands and say: —

"Next winter I will borrow enough money to take the child to Paris, and I am much mistaken if her beauty does not win her a rich husband who will release me from poverty."

She called this loving her daughter.

The second meeting was not the last. Gaston dared not trust to a boatman, so he was obliged to walk a league in order to cross the bridge. Then he thought it would be shorter to swim the river; but he could not swim well, and to cross the Rhone where it ran so rapidly was rash for the most skillful swimmers.

One evening, however, Valentine was startled by seeing him rise out of the water at her feet.

She made him promise never to attempt this exploit again. He repeated the feat and the promise next evening and every successive evening.

As Valentine always imagined he was being drowned in the furious current, they agreed upon a signal. At the moment of starting, Gaston would put a light in his window at Clameran, and in fifteen minutes he would be at his idol's feet.

What were the projects and hopes of the lovers? Alas! they projected nothing, they hoped for nothing.

Blindly, thoughtlessly, almost fearlessly, they abandoned themselves to the dangerous happiness of a daily rendezvous; regardless of the storm that must erelong burst over their devoted heads, they reveled in their present bliss.

Is not every sincere passion thus? Passion subsists upon itself and in itself; and the very things which ought to extinguish it, absence and obstacles, only make it burn more fiercely. It is exclusive and undisturbed, reflects neither of the past nor of the future; excepting the present, it sees and cares for nothing.

Moreover, Valentine and Gaston believed every one ignorant of their secret.

They had always been so cautious! they had kept such strict watch! They had flattered themselves that their conduct had been a masterpiece of dissimulation and prudence.

Valentine had fixed upon the hour when she was certain her mother would not miss her. Gaston had never confided to any one, not even to his brother Louis. They never breathed each other's name. They denied themselves a last sweet word, a last kiss, when they felt it would be more safe.

Poor blind lovers! As if anything could be concealed from the idle curiosity of country gossips; from the slanderous and ever-watchful enemies who are incessantly on the lookout for some new bit of tittle-tattle, good or bad, which they improve upon, and eagerly spread far and near.

They believed their secret well kept, whereas it had long since been made public: the story of their love, the particulars of their rendezvous, were topics of conversation throughout the neighborhood.

Sometimes, at dusk, they would see a bark gliding along the water, near the shore, and would say to each other: —

"It is a belated fisherman, returning home."

They were mistaken. The boat contained malicious spies, who delighted in having discovered them, and hastened to report, with a thousand false additions, the result of their expedition.

One dreary November evening, Gaston was awakened to the true state of affairs. The Rhone was so swelled by heavy rains that an inundation was daily expected. To attempt to swim across this impetuous torrent would be tempting God. Therefore Gaston went to Tarascon, intending to cross the bridge there, and walk along the bank to the usual place of meeting at La Verberie. Valentine expected him at eleven o'clock.

Whenever Gaston went to Tarascon, he dined with a relative living there; but on this occasion a strange fatality led him to accompany a friend to the hotel of the Three Emperors.

After dinner, they went not to the Café Simon, their usual resort, but to the little *café* in the market place, where the fairs were held.

The small dining hall was filled with young men. Gaston

and his friend called for a bottle of beer, and began to play billiards.

After they had been playing a short time, Gaston's attention was attracted by peals of laughter from a party at the other end of the room.

From this moment, preoccupied by this continual laughter, of which he was evidently the subject, he knocked the balls carelessly in every direction. His conduct surprised his friend, who said to him : —

"What is the matter? You are missing the simplest shots."

"It is nothing."

The game went on awhile longer, when Gaston suddenly turned as white as a sheet, and, throwing down his cue, strode toward the table which was occupied by five young men, playing dominoes and drinking wine.

He addressed the eldest of the group, a handsome man of twenty-six, with fierce-looking eyes, and a heavy mustache, named Jules Lazet.

"Repeat, if you dare," he said, in a voice trembling with passion, "the remark you just now made!"

"I certainly will repeat it," said Lazet, calmly. "I said, and I say it again, that a nobleman's daughter is no better than a mechanic's daughter; that virtue does not always accompany a titled name."

"You mentioned a particular name!"

Lazet rose from his chair, as if he knew his answer would exasperate Gaston, and that from words they would come to blows.

"I did," he said, with an insolent smile; "I mentioned the name of the pretty little fairy of La Verberie."

All the coffee drinkers, and even two traveling agents who were dining in the *café*, rose and surrounded the two young men.

The provoking looks, the murmurs, or rather shouts, which welcomed him as he walked up to Lazet, proved to Gaston that he was surrounded by enemies.

The wickedness and evil tongue of the old marquis were bearing their fruit. Rancor ferments quickly and fiercely among the people of Provence.

Gaston de Clameran was not a man to yield, even if his foes were a hundred, instead of fifteen or twenty.

"No one but a coward," he said, in a clear, ringing voice, which the pervading silence rendered almost startling, "no one but a contemptible coward would be infamous enough to calumniate a young girl who has neither father nor brother to defend her honor."

"If she has no father or brother," sneered Lazet, "she has her lovers, and that suffices."

The insulting words, "her lovers," enraged Gaston beyond control; he slapped Lazet violently in the face.

Every one in the *café* simultaneously uttered a cry of terror. Lazet's violence of character, his herculean strength and undaunted courage were well known. He sprang across the table between, and seized Gaston by the throat. Then arose a scene of excitement and confusion. Clameran's friend, attempting to assist him, was knocked down with billiard cues, and kicked under a table.

Equally strong and agile, Gaston and Lazet struggled for some minutes without either gaining an advantage.

Lazet, as loyal as he was courageous, would not accept assistance from his friends. He continually called out: —

"Keep away; let me fight it out alone!"

But the others were too excited to remain inactive spectators of the scene.

"A quilt!" cried one of them, "a quilt to make the marquis jump!"

Five or six young men now rushed upon Gaston, and separated him from Lazet. Some tried to throw him down, others to trip him up.

He defended himself with the energy of despair, exhibiting in his furious struggles a strength of which he himself had not been conscious. He struck right and left as he showered fierce epithets upon his adversaries for being twelve against one.

He was endeavoring to get around the billiard table so as to be near the door, and had almost succeeded, when an exultant cry arose: —

"Here is the quilt! the quilt!" they cried.

"Put him in the quilt — the pretty fairy's lover!"

Gaston heard these cries. He saw himself overcome and suffering an ignoble outrage at the hands of these enraged men.

By a dexterous movement he extricated himself from the grasp of the three who were holding him, and felled a fourth to the ground.

His arms were free; but all his enemies returned to the charge.

Then he seemed to lose his head, and, seizing a knife which lay on the table where the traveling agents had been dining, he plunged it into the breast of the first man who rushed upon him.

This unfortunate man was Jules Lazet. He dropped to the ground.

There was a second of silent stupor.

Then four or five of the young men rushed forward to raise Lazet. The landlady ran about wringing her hands, and screaming with fright. Some of the assailants rushed into the street shouting, "Murder! Murder!"

The others once more turned upon Gaston with cries of "Vengeance! kill him!"

He saw that he was lost. His enemies had seized the first objects they could lay their hands upon, and he received several wounds. He jumped upon the billiard table, and, making a rapid spring, dashed through the large window of the *café*. He was fearfully cut by the broken glass and splinters, but he was free.

Gaston had escaped, but he was not yet saved. Astonished and disconcerted at his desperate feat, the crowd for a moment were stupefied; but recovering their presence of mind, they started in pursuit of him.

The weather was bad, the ground wet and muddy, and heavy dark clouds were rolling westward; but the night was not dark.

Gaston ran on from tree to tree, making frequent turnings, every moment on the point of being seized and surrounded, and asking himself what course he should take.

Finally he determined, if possible, to regain Clameran.

With incredible rapidity he darted diagonally across the fair ground, in the direction of the levee which protected the valley of Tarascon from inundations.

Unfortunately, upon reaching this levee, planted with magnificent trees which made it one of the most charming walks of Provence, Gaston forgot that the entrance was closed by a gate with three steps, such as are always placed before walks intended for foot passengers, and rushed against it with such violence that he was thrown back and badly bruised.

He quickly sprang up; but his pursuers were upon him.

This time he could expect no mercy. The infuriated men at his heels yelled that fearful cry which in the evil days of lawless bloodshed had often echoed in that valley: "In the Rhone with him! In the Rhone with the marquis!"

His reason had abandoned him; he no longer knew what he did. His forehead was cut, and the blood trickled from the wound into his eyes, and blinded him.

He must escape, or die in the attempt.

He had tightly clasped the bloody knife with which he had stabbed Lazet. He struck his nearest foe; the man fell to the ground with a heavy groan.

A second blow gained him a moment's respite, which gave him time to open the gate and rush along the levee.

Two men were kneeling over their wounded companion, and five others resumed the pursuit.

But Gaston flew fast, for the horror of his situation tripled his energy; excitement deadened the pain of his wounds; with elbows held tight to his sides, and holding his breath, he went along at such a speed that he soon distanced his pursuers; the noise of their feet became gradually more indistinct, and finally ceased.

Gaston ran on for a mile, across fields and over hedges; fences and ditches were leaped without effort, and when he knew he was safe from capture he sank down at the foot of a tree to rest.

This terrible scene had taken place with inconceivable rapidity. Only forty minutes had elapsed since Gaston and his friend entered the *café*.

But during this short time how much had happened! These forty minutes had given him more cause for sorrow and remorse than the whole of his previous life put together.

Entering the tavern with head erect, and a happy heart, enjoying present existence and looking forward to a yet better future, he left it ruined; for he was a murderer! Henceforth he would be under a ban — an outcast!

He had killed a man, and still convulsively held the murderous instrument; he cast it from him with horror.

He tried to account for the dreadful circumstances which had just taken place, — as if it were of any importance to a man lying at the bottom of an abyss to know which stone had slipped and precipitated him from the summit.

Still, if he alone had been ruined! But Valentine was

dragged down with him: she was disgraced yet more than himself; her reputation was gone. And it was his want of self-command which had cast to the wind her honor, confided to his keeping, and which he held far dearer than his own.

But he could not remain here bewailing his misfortune. The police must soon be on his track. They would certainly go to the Château of Clameran to seek him; and before leaving home, perhaps forever, he wished to say good-by to his father, and once more press Valentine to his heart.

He started to walk, but with great pain, for the reaction had come, and his nerves and muscles, so violently strained, had now begun to relax; the intense heat caused by his struggling and fast running was replaced by a cold perspiration, aching limbs, and chattering teeth. His hip and shoulder pained him almost beyond endurance. The cut on his forehead had stopped bleeding, but the coagulated blood around his eyes blinded him.

After a painful walk he reached his door at ten o'clock.

The old valet who admitted him started back terrified.

"Good heavens, monsieur! what is the matter?"

"Silence!" said Gaston, in the brief compressed tone always inspired by imminent danger, "silence! where is my father?"

"Monsieur the Marquis is in his room with M. Louis. He has had a sudden attack of the gout, and cannot put his foot to the ground; but you, monsieur ——"

Gaston did not stop to listen further. He hurried to his father's room.

The old marquis, who was playing backgammon with Louis, dropped his dicebox with a cry of horror, when he looked up and saw his eldest son standing before him covered with blood.

"What is the matter? what have you been doing, Gaston?"

"I have come to embrace you for the last time, father, and to ask for assistance to escape abroad."

"Do you wish to fly the country?"

"I must fly, father, and instantly; I am pursued, the police may be here at any moment; I have killed two men."

The marquis was so shocked that he forgot the gout, and attempted to rise; a violent twinge made him drop back in his chair.

"Where? when?" he gasped.

"At Tarascon, in a *café*, an hour ago; fifteen men attacked me, and I seized a knife to defend myself."

23

"The old tricks of '93," said the marquis. "Did they insult you, Gaston? What was the cause of the attack?"

"They insulted in my presence the name of a noble young girl."

"And you punished the rascals? *Jarnibleu!* You did well. Who ever heard of a gentleman allowing insolent puppies to speak disrespectfully of a lady of quality in his presence? But who was the lad you defended?"

"Mademoiselle Valentine de la Verberie."

"What!" cried the marquis, "what! the daughter of that old witch? Those accursed De la Verberies have always brought misfortune upon us."

He certainly abominated the countess; but his respect for her noble blood was greater than his resentment toward her individually, and he added: —

"Nevertheless, Gaston, you did your duty."

Meanwhile, the curiosity of St. Jean, the marquis' old valet, made him venture to open the door, and ask: —

"Did Monsieur the Marquis ring?"

"No, you rascal," answered M. de Clameran; "you know very well I did not. But now you are here, be useful. Quickly bring some clothes for M. Gaston, some fresh linen, and some warm water: hasten and dress his wounds."

These orders were promptly executed, and Gaston found he was not so badly hurt as he had thought. With the exception of a deep stab in his left shoulder, his wounds were not serious.

After receiving all the attentions which his condition required, Gaston felt like a new man, ready to brave any peril. His eyes sparkled with renewed energy and excitement.

The marquis made a sign to the servants to leave the room.

"Do you still think you ought to leave France?" he asked Gaston.

"Yes, father."

"My brother ought not to hesitate," interposed Louis; "he will be arrested here, thrown into prison, vilified in court, and — who knows?"

"We all know well enough that he will be convicted," grumbled the old marquis. "These are the benefits of the immortal revolution, as it is called. Ah, in my day we three would have taken our swords, jumped on our horses, and, dashing into Tarascon, would soon have — But those good old days are past. To-day we have to run away."

"There is no time to lose," observed Louis.

"True," said the marquis, "but to fly, to go abroad, one must have money; and I have none by me to give him."

"Father!"

"No, I have none. Ah, what a prodigal old fool I have been! If I only had a hundred louis!"

Then he told Louis to open the secretary, and hand him the money box.

The box contained only nine hundred and twenty francs in gold.

"Nine hundred and twenty francs," cried the marquis; "it will never do for the eldest son of our house to fly the country with this paltry sum."

He sat lost in reflection. Suddenly his brow cleared, and he told Louis to open a secret drawer in the secretary, and bring him a small casket.

Then the marquis took from his neck a black ribbon to which was suspended the key of the casket.

His sons observed with what deep emotion he unlocked it and slowly took out a necklace, a large cross, several rings, and other pieces of jewelry.

His countenance assumed a solemn expression.

"Gaston, my dear son," he said, "at a time like this your life may depend upon bought assistance; money is power."

"I am young, father, and have courage."

"Listen to me. The jewels belonged to the marquise, your sainted mother, a noble, holy woman, who is now in heaven watching over us. These jewels have never left me. During my days of misery and want, when I was compelled to earn a livelihood by teaching music in London, I piously treasured them. I never thought of selling them; and to mortgage them, in the hour of direst need, would have seemed to me a sacrilege. But now you must take them, my son, and sell them for twenty thousand livres."

"No, father, no; I cannot take them!"

"You must, Gaston. If your mother were on earth, she would tell you to take them, as I do now. I command you to take and use them. The salvation, the honor, of the heir of the house of Clameran must not be imperiled for want of a little gold."

With tearful eyes Gaston sank on his knees, and, carrying his father's hand to his lips, said: —

"Thanks, father, thanks! In my heedless, ungrateful presumption, I have hitherto misjudged you. I did not know your noble character. Forgive me. I accept, yes, I accept these jewels worn by my dear mother; but I take them as a sacred deposit, confided to my honor, and for which I will some day account to you."

In their emotion, the marquis and Gaston forgot the threatened danger. But Louis was not touched by the affecting scene.

"Time presses," he said: "you had better hasten."

"He is right," cried the marquis; "go, Gaston, go, my son; and God protect the heir of the Clamerans!"

Gaston slowly got up, and said with an embarrassed air: —

"Before leaving you, my father, I must fulfill a sacred duty. I have not told you everything. I love Valentine, the young girl whose honor I defended this evening."

"Oh!" cried the marquis, thunderstruck, "oh, oh!"

"And I entreat you, father, to ask Mme. de la Verberie for the hand of her daughter. Valentine will gladly join me abroad and share my exile."

Gaston stopped, frightened at the effect of his words. The old marquis had become crimson, or rather purple as if struck by apoplexy.

"Preposterous!" he gasped. "Impossible! Perfect folly!"

"I love her, father, and have promised never to marry another."

"Then always remain a bachelor."

"I shall marry her!" cried Gaston, excitedly. "I shall marry her because I have sworn I would, and I will not be so base as to desert her."

"Nonsense!"

"I tell you Mademoiselle de la Verberie must and shall be my wife. It is too late for me to draw back. Even if I no longer loved her, I would still marry her."

Gaston's confession, forced from him by circumstances, produced a very different impression from that which he had expected. The enraged marquis instantly became cool, and his mind seemed relieved of an immense weight. A wicked joy sparkled in his eyes, as he replied: —

"Aha! she yielded to his entreaties, did she? *Jarnibleu!* I am delighted. I congratulate you, Gaston: they say she is a pretty little fool."

"Monsieur," interrupted Gaston, indignantly, "I have told you that I love her, and have promised to marry her. You seem to forget."

"Ta, ta, ta!" cried the marquis, "your scruples are absurd. You know full well that her great-grandfather led our great-grandmother astray. Now we are quits! I am delighted at the retaliation, for the old witch's sake."

"I swear by the memory of my mother, that Valentine shall be my wife!"

"Do you dare assume that tone toward me?" cried the exasperated marquis. "Never, understand me clearly, never will I give my consent. You know how dear to me is the honor of our house. Well, I would rather see you tried for murder, and even chained to the galleys, than married to this worthless jade!"

This last word was too much for Gaston.

"Then your wish shall be gratified, monsieur. I will remain here, and be arrested. I care not what becomes of me! What is life to me without the hope of Valentine? Take back these jewels; they are useless now."

A terrible scene would have taken place between the father and son, had they not been interrupted by a domestic who rushed into the room and excitedly cried: —

"The gendarmes! here are the gendarmes!" At this news the old marquis started up, and seemed to forget his gout, which had yielded to more violent emotions.

"Gendarmes!" he cried, "in my house at Clameran! They shall pay dear for their insolence! You will help me, will you not, my men?"

"Yes, yes," answered the servants. "Down with the gendarmes! down with them!"

Fortunately Louis, during all this excitement, preserved his presence of mind.

"To resist would be folly," he said. "Even if we repulsed the gendarmes to-night, they would return to-morrow with reënforcements."

"Louis is right," said the marquis, bitterly. "Might is right, as they said in '93. The gendarmes are all-powerful. Do they not even have the impertinence to come up to me while I am hunting, and ask to see my shooting license? I, a Clameran, show a license!"

"Where are they?" asked Louis of the servants.

"At the outer gate," answered La Verdure, one of the grooms. "Does not monsieur hear the noise they are making with their sabers?"

"Then Gaston must escape over the garden wall."

"It is guarded, monsieur," said La Verdure, "and the little gate in the park besides. There seems to be a regiment of them. They are even stationed along the park walls."

This was only too true. The rumor of Lazet's death had spread like wildfire throughout the town of Tarascon, and everybody was in a state of excitement. Not only mounted gendarmes, but a platoon of hussars from the garrison, had been sent in pursuit of the murderer.

At least twenty young men of Tarascon were volunteer guides to the armed force.

"Then," said the marquis, "we are surrounded?"

"Not a single chance for escape," groaned St. Jean.

"We shall see about that. *Jarnibleu!*" cried the marquis. "Ah, we are not the strongest, but we can be the most adroit. Attention! Louis, my son, you and La Verdure go down to the stable, and mount the fastest horses; then, as quietly as possible station yourselves, you, Louis, at the park gate, and you, La Verdure, at the outer gate. Let each of you others post yourselves at a door. Upon the signal I shall give by firing a pistol, let every door be instantly opened, whilst Louis and La Verdure dash through the gates, and make the gendarmes pursue them."

"I will make them fly," said La Verdure.

"Listen. During this time, Gaston, aided by St. Jean, will scale the park wall, and hasten along the river to the cabin of Pilorel, the fisherman. He is an old sailor of the republic, and devoted to our house. He will take Gaston in his boat; and when they are once on the Rhone, there is nothing to be feared save the wrath of God. Now go, all of you, fly!"

Left alone with his son, the old man slipped the jewels into a silk purse, and, handing them once more to Gaston, said, as he stretched out his arms toward him:—

"Come here, my son, and let me embrace you, and bestow my blessing."

Gaston hesitated.

"Come," insisted the old man, in broken tones, "I must embrace you for the last time: I may never see you again. Save yourself, save your name, Gaston, and then—you know how I love you, my son: take back the jewels. Come."

For an instant the father and son clung to each other, overpowered by emotion.

But the continued noise of the gates now reached their ears.

"We must part!" said M. de Clameran, "go!" And, taking from his desk a little pair of pistols, he handed them to his son, and added with averted eyes, "You must not be captured alive, Gaston!"

Gaston did not immediately descend to the park.

He yearned to see Valentine and give her one last kiss before leaving France, and determined to persuade Pilorel to stop the boat as they went by the park of La Verberie.

He hastened to his room, placed the signal in the window so that Valentine might know he was coming, and waited for an answering light.

"Come, M. Gaston," entreated old St. Jean, who could not understand this strange conduct. "For God's sake make haste! your life is at stake!"

At last he came running down the stairs, and had just reached the vestibule when a pistol shot, the signal given by the marquis, was heard.

The loud swinging open of the large gate, the rattling of the sabers of the gendarmes, the furious galloping of many horses, and a chorus of loud shouts and angry oaths, were next heard.

Leaning against the window, his brow beaded with cold perspiration, the Marquis of Clameran breathlessly awaited the issue of this expedient, upon which depended the life of his eldest son.

His measures were excellent, and deserved success. As he had ordered, Louis and La Verdure dashed out through the gate, one to the right, the other to the left, each one pursued by a dozen mounted men. Their horses flew like arrows, and kept far ahead of the pursuers.

Gaston would have been saved but for the interference of fate; but was it fate, or was it malice?

Suddenly Louis' horse stumbled, and fell to the ground with his rider. The gendarmes rode up, and at once recognized the second son of M. de Clameran.

"This is not the assassin!" they cried. "Let us hurry back, else he will escape!"

They turned just in time to see, by the uncertain light of the moon peeping from behind a cloud, Gaston climbing the garden wall.

"There is our man!" exclaimed the corporal. "Keep your eyes open, and follow after him!"

They spurred their horses, and hastened to the spot where Gaston had jumped from the wall.

In a wooded piece of ground, even if it be hilly, an agile man, if he preserves his presence of mind, can escape a number of horsemen. The ground on this side of the park was favorable to Gaston. He found himself in an immense madder field; and, as is well known, as this valuable root must remain in the ground three years, the furrows are necessarily plowed very deep. Horses cannot even walk over its uneven surface; indeed, they can scarcely stand steadily upon it.

This circumstance brought the gendarmes to a dead halt.

Four rash hussars ventured in the field, but they and their beasts were soon rolling between the hillocks.

Jumping from ridge to ridge, Gaston soon reached a large field, freshly plowed, and planted with young chestnuts.

As his chances of escape increased, the excitement grew more intense. The pursuers urged each other on and called out to head him off, every time they saw Gaston run from one clump of trees to another.

Being familiar with the country young De Clameran was confident of eluding his pursuers. He knew that the next field was a thistle field, and was separated from the chestnuts by a long, deep ditch.

He resolved to jump into this ditch, run along the bottom, and climb out at the further end, while they were looking for him among the trees.

But he had forgotten the swelling of the river. Upon reaching the ditch he found it full of water.

Discouraged but not disconcerted, he was about to jump across, when three horsemen appeared upon the opposite side.

They were gendarmes who had ridden around the madder field and chestnut trees, knowing they could easily catch him on the level ground of the thistle field.

At the sight of these three men, Gaston stood perplexed.

He should certainly be captured if he attempted to run through the field, at the end of which he could see the cabin of Pilorel the ferryman.

To retrace his steps would be surrendering to the hussars.

At a little distance on his right was a forest, but he was separated from it by a road, upon which he heard the sound of approaching horses. He would certainly be caught there.

Foes in front of him, foes behind him, foes on the right of him. What was on the left?

On his left was the foaming, surging river.

What hope was left? The circle of which he was the center was fast narrowing.

Must he, then, fall back upon suicide? Here in an open field, tracked by police like a wild beast, must he blow his brains out? What a death for a De Clameran!

No! he would seize the one chance of salvation left him; a forlorn, desperate, perilous chance, but still a chance—the river.

Holding a pistol in either hand, he ran and leaped upon the edge of a little promontory projecting three yards into the Rhone.

This cape of refuge was formed by the immense trunk of a fallen tree.

The tree swayed and cracked fearfully under Gaston's weight, as he stood on the extreme end, and looked around upon his pursuers; there were fifteen of them, some on the right, some on the left, all uttering cries of joy.

"Do you surrender?" called out the corporal.

Gaston did not answer, he was weighing his chances. He was above the park of La Verberie: would he be able to swim there, granting that he was not swept away and drowned the instant he plunged into the angry torrent before him?

He pictured Valentine, at this very moment, watching, waiting, and praying for him on the opposite shore.

"For the last time I command you to surrender!" cried the corporal.

The unfortunate man did not hear; he was deafened by the waters which were roaring and rushing around him.

In a supreme moment like this, with his foot upon the threshold of another world, a man sees his past life rise before him, and seldom does he find cause for self-approval.

Although death stared him in the face, Gaston calmly considered which would be the best spot to plunge into, and commended his soul to God.

"He will stand there until we go after him," said a gendarme, "so we might as well advance."

Gaston had finished his prayer.

He flung his pistols in the direction of the gendarmes; he was ready.

He made the sign of the cross, then, with outstretched arms, dashed head foremost into the Rhone.

The violence of his spring detached the few remaining roots of the old tree; it oscillated a moment, whirled over, and then drifted away.

The spectators uttered a cry of horror and pity; anger seemed to have deserted them in their turn.

"That is the end of him," muttered one of the gendarmes. "It is useless for one to fight against the Rhone: his body will be picked up at Arles to-morrow."

The hussars seemed really remorseful at the tragic fate of this brave, handsome young man, who, a moment before, they had pursued with so much bitter zeal. They admired his spirited resistance, his courage, and especially his resignation, his resolution to die.

True French soldiers, their sympathies were now all upon the side of the vanquished, and every man of them would have done all in his power to assist in saving the drowning man and aiding his escape.

"An ugly piece of work!" grumbled the old quartermaster who had command of the hussars.

"*Basta!*" exclaimed the philosophic corporal, "the Rhone is no worse than the court of assizes; the result would be the same. Right about, men; march! The thing that troubles me is the idea of that poor old man waiting to hear his son's fate. I would not be the one to tell him what has happened. March!"

THE VETERAN.[1]

By STEPHEN CRANE.

(From "The Little Regiment.")

[STEPHEN CRANE: An American novelist; born in Newark, N.J., in 1870. He was educated at Lafayette College and Syracuse University, and in 1886 began newspaper work. His first novel, published in 1891, was written under the pen name Johnson Smith, and is entitled "Maggie: a Girl of the Streets."

[1] By permission of Author and Mr. Wm. Heinemann. (Cloth. 3s. net.)

A volume of verses, — "The Black Riders," — written in less than three days, appeared in 1895, and was soon followed by "The Red Badge of Courage," a lurid and highly popular novel. He made journalistic tours through Mexico; was at the seat of war in Greece in 1886–1887 as correspondent of the New York *Journal*, and represented the same paper in Cuba in the Spanish-American war in 1898. His other books are: "The Little Regiment" (1896), "The Third Violet" (1897), and "The Open Boat" (1898).]

OUT of the low window could be seen three hickory trees placed irregularly in a meadow that was resplendent in springtime green. Farther away, the old, dismal belfry of the village church loomed over the pines. A horse meditating in the shade of one of the hickories lazily swished his tail. The warm sunshine made an oblong of vivid yellow on the floor of the grocery.

"Could you see the whites of their eyes?" said the man who was seated on a soap box.

"Nothing of the kind," replied old Henry, warmly. "Just a lot of flitting figures, and I let go at where they 'peared to be the thickest. Bang!"

"Mr. Fleming," said the grocer — his deferential voice expressed somehow the old man's exact social weight — "Mr. Fleming, you never was frightened much in them battles, was you?"

The veteran looked down and grinned. Observing his manner, the entire group tittered. "Well, I guess I was," he answered finally. "Pretty well scared, sometimes. Why, in my first battle I thought the sky was falling down. I thought the world was coming to an end. You bet I was scared."

Every one laughed. Perhaps it seemed strange and rather wonderful to them that a man should admit the thing, and in the tone of their laughter there was probably more admiration than if old Fleming had declared that he had always been a lion. Moreover, they knew that he had ranked as an orderly sergeant, and so their opinion of his heroism was fixed. None, to be sure, knew how an orderly sergeant ranked, but then it was understood to be somewhere just shy of a major general's stars. So, when old Henry admitted that he had been frightened, there was a laugh.

"The trouble was," said the old man, "I thought they were all shooting at me. Yes, sir, I thought every man in the other army was aiming at me in particular, and only me. And it seemed so darned unreasonable, you know. I wanted to explain to 'em what an almighty good fellow I was, because I thought then they might quit all trying to hit me. But I couldn't explain, and they kept on being unreasonable — blim! — blam! — bang! So I run!"

Two little triangles of wrinkles appeared at the corners of his eyes. Evidently he appreciated some comedy in this recital. Down near his feet, however, little Jim, his grandson, was visibly horror-stricken. His hands were clasped nervously, and his eyes were wide with astonishment at this terrible scandal, his most magnificent grandfather telling such a thing.

"That was at Chancellorsville. Of course, afterward I got kind of used to it. A man does. Lots of men, though, seem to feel all right from the start. I did, as soon as I 'got on to it,' as they say now; but at first I was pretty well flustered. Now, there was young Jim Conklin, old Si Conklin's son — that used to keep the tannery — you none of you recollect him — well, he went into it from the start just as if he was born to it. But with me it was different. I had to get used to it."

When little Jim walked with his grandfather, he was in the habit of skipping along on the stone pavement in front of the three stores and the hotel of the town and betting that he could avoid the cracks. But upon this day he walked soberly, with his hand gripping two of his grandfather's fingers. Sometimes he kicked abstractedly at dandelions that curved over the walk. Any one could see that he was much troubled.

"There's Sickles's colt over in the medder, Jimmie," said the old man. "Don't you wish you owned one like him?"

"Um," said the boy, with a strange lack of interest. He continued his reflections. Then finally he ventured, "Grandpa — now — was that true what you was telling those men?"

"What?" asked the grandfather. "What was I telling them?"

"Oh, about your running."

"Why, yes, that was true enough, Jimmie. It was my first fight, and there was an awful lot of noise, you know."

Jimmie seemed dazed that this idol, of its own will, should so totter. His stout boyish idealism was injured.

Presently the grandfather said: "Sickles's colt is going for a drink. Don't you wish you owned Sickles's colt, Jimmie?"

The boy merely answered, "He ain't as nice as ourn." He lapsed then into another moody silence.

* * * * * * *

One of the hired men, a Swede, desired to drive to the

county seat for purposes of his own. The old man loaned a horse and an unwashed buggy. It appeared later that one of the purposes of the Swede was to get drunk.

After quelling some boisterous frolic of the farm hands and boys in the garret, the old man had that night gone peacefully to sleep, when he was aroused by clamoring at the kitchen door. He grabbed his trousers, and they waved out behind as he dashed forward. He could hear the voice of the Swede, screaming and blubbering. He pushed the wooden button, and, as the door flew open, the Swede, a maniac, stumbled inward, chattering, weeping, still screaming: "De barn fire! Fire! Fire! De barn fire! Fire! Fire! Fire!"

There was a swift and indescribable change in the old man. His face ceased instantly to be a face; it became a mask, a gray thing, with horror written about the mouth and eyes. He hoarsely shouted at the foot of the little rickety stairs, and immediately, it seemed, there came down an avalanche of men. No one knew that during this time the old lady had been standing in her night clothes at the bedroom door, yelling: "What's th' matter? What's th' matter? What's th' matter?"

When they dashed toward the barn it presented to their eyes its usual appearance, solemn, rather mystic in the black night. The Swede's lantern was overturned at a point some yards in front of the barn doors. It contained a wild little conflagration of its own, and even in their excitement some of those who ran felt a gentle secondary vibration of the thrifty part of their minds at sight of this overturned lantern. Under ordinary circumstances it would have been a calamity.

But the cattle in the barn were trampling, trampling, trampling, and above this noise could be heard a humming like the song of innumerable bees. The old man hurled aside the great doors, and a yellow flame leaped out at one corner and sped and wavered frantically up the old gray wall. It was glad, terrible, this single flame, like the wild banner of deadly and triumphant foes.

The motley crowd from the garret had come with all the pails of the farm. They flung themselves upon the well. It was a leisurely old machine, long dwelling in indolence. It was in the habit of giving out water with a sort of reluctance. The men stormed at it, cursed it; but it continued to allow the buckets to be filled only after the wheezy windlass had howled many protests at the mad-handed men.

With his opened knife in his hand old Fleming himself had gone headlong into the barn, where the stifling smoke swirled with the air currents, and where could be heard in its fullness the terrible chorus of the flames, laden with tones of hate and death, a hymn of wonderful ferocity.

He flung a blanket over an old mare's head, cut the halter close to the manger, led the mare to the door, and fairly kicked her out to safety. He returned with the same blanket, and rescued one of the work horses. He took five horses out, and then came out himself, with his clothes bravely on fire. He had no whiskers, and very little hair on his head. They soused five pailfuls of water on him. His eldest son made a clean miss with the sixth pailful, because the old man had turned and was running down the decline and around to the basement of the barn, where were the stanchions of the cows. Some one noticed at the time that he ran very lamely, as if one of the frenzied horses had smashed his hip.

The cows, with their heads held in the heavy stanchions, had thrown themselves, strangled themselves, tangled themselves: done everything which the ingenuity of their exuberant fear could suggest to them.

Here, as at the well, the same thing happened to every man save one. Their hands went mad. They became incapable of everything save the power to rush into dangerous situations.

The old man released the cow nearest the door, and she, blind drunk with terror, crashed into the Swede. The Swede had been running to and fro babbling. He carried an empty milk pail, to which he clung with an unconscious, fierce enthusiasm. He shrieked like one lost as he went under the cow's hoofs, and the milk pail, rolling across the floor, made a flash of silver in the gloom.

Old Fleming took a fork, beat off the cow, and dragged the paralyzed Swede to the open air. When they had rescued all the cows save one, which had so fastened herself that she could not be moved an inch, they returned to the front of the barn and stood sadly, breathing like men who had reached the final point of human effort.

Many people had come running. Some one had even gone to the church, and now, from the distance, rang the tocsin note of the old bell. There was a long flare of crimson on the sky, which made remote people speculate as to the whereabouts of the fire.

The long flames sang their drumming chorus in voices of the heaviest bass. The wind whirled clouds of smoke and cinders into the faces of the spectators. The form of the old barn was outlined in black amid these masses of orange-hued flames.

And then came this Swede again, crying as one who is the weapon of the sinister fates. "De colts! De colts! You have forgot de colts!"

Old Fleming staggered. It was true; they had forgotten the two colts in the box stalls at the back of the barn. "Boys," he said, "I must try to get 'em out." They clamored about him then, afraid for him, afraid of what they should see. Then they talked wildly each to each. "Why, it's sure death!" "He would never get out!" "Why, it's suicide for a man to go in there!" Old Fleming stared absent-mindedly at the open doors. "The poor little things!" he said. He rushed into the barn.

When the roof fell in, a great funnel of smoke swarmed toward the sky, as if the old man's mighty spirit, released from its body — a little bottle — had swelled like the genie of fable. The smoke was tinted rose-hue from the flames, and perhaps the unutterable midnights of the universe will have no power to daunt the color of this soul.

A NORTHERN VIGIL.[1]

By BLISS CARMAN.

(From "Low Tide on Grand Pré.")

[BLISS CARMAN, Canadian poet, is a native of Fredericton, New Brunswick, where he was born April 15, 1861. He graduated with honors at the University of New Brunswick in 1881, and spent several years in private reading and study at Edinburgh and Harvard, occasionally contributing verse to American magazines. He assisted in starting the *Chap Book*; has been editorially connected with the New York *Independent* and *Atlantic Monthly*; and is now engaged in literary work in New York city. His chief publications are: "Low Tide on Grand Pré," "A Seamark," "Songs from Vagabondia," "Behind the Arras," and "Ballads of Lost Haven."]

HERE by the gray north sea,
 In the wintry heart of the wild,

[1] By permission of the author and Lamson, Wolffe & Co.

Comes the old dream of thee,
  Guendolen, mistress and child.

The heart of the forest grieves
  In the drift against my door;
A voice is under the eaves,
  A footfall on the floor.

Threshold, mirror, and hall,
  Vacant and strangely aware,
Wait for their soul's recall
  With the dumb expectant air.

Here when the smoldering west
  Burns down into the sea,
I take no heed of rest
  And keep the watch for thee.

I sit by the fire and hear
  The restless wind go by,
On the long dirge and drear,
  Under the low bleak sky.

When day puts out to sea
  And night makes in for land,
There is no lock for thee,
  Each door awaits thy hand!

When night goes over the hill
  And dawn comes down the dale,
It's O for the wild sweet will
  That shall no more prevail!

When the zenith moon is round,
  And snow wraiths gather and run,
And there is set no bound
  To love beneath the sun,

O wayward will, come near
  The old mad willful way,
The soft mouth at my ear
  With words too sweet to say!

Come, for the night is cold,
  The ghostly moonlight fills
Hollow and rift and fold
  Of the eerie Ardise hills!

The windows of my room
  Are dark with bitter frost,
The stillness aches with doom
  Of something loved and lost.

Outside, the great blue star
  Burns in the ghostland pale,
Where giant Algebar
  Holds on the endless trail.

Come, for the years are long,
  And silence keeps the door,
Where shapes with the shadows throng
  The firelit chamber floor.

Come, for thy kiss was warm,
  With the red embers' glare
Across thy folding arm
  And dark tumultuous hair!

And though thy coming rouse
  The sleep cry of no bird,
The keepers of the house
  Shall tremble at thy word.

Come, for the soul is free!
  In all the vast dreamland
There is no lock for thee,
  Each door awaits thy hand.

Ah, not in dreams at all,
  Fleering, perishing, dim,
But thy old self, supple and tall,
  Mistress and child of whim!

The proud imperious guise,
  Impetuous and serene,
The sad mysterious eyes,
  And dignity of mien!

Yea, wilt thou not return,
  When the late hill winds veer,
And the bright hill flowers burn
  With the reviving year?

When April comes, and the sea
 Sparkles as if it smiled,
Will they restore to me
 My dark Love, empress and child?

The curtains seem to part;
 A sound is on the stair,
As if at the last . . . I start;
 Only the wind is there.

Lo, now far on the hills
 The crimson fumes encurled,
Where the caldron mantles and spills
 Another dawn on the world!

WOODCUTTING.[1]

By ANDRÉ THEURIET.

(From "Rustic Life in France": translated by Helen B. Dole.)

[André Theuriet: A French writer; born at Marly-le-Roi, October 8, 1833. He was educated at Bar-le-Duc, studied law in Paris, and was subsequently employed in the treasury department. His first literary work consisted of poems and stories contributed to periodical literature. His writings include the poems, "In Memoriam" (1857), "The Road through the Woods" (1867), "The Peasant of D'Argonne, 1792" (1871), "The Blue and the Black" (1873); and "Our Birds" (1886); the dramas, "Jean-Marie" (1871), "The House of the Two Barbeaux" (1885), and "Raymonde" (1887). He has also published "Jules Bastien-Lepage, the Man and the Artist" (1885).]

The forest resembles human society in more than one respect, — it has an aristocracy, a middle class, and the common, unknown people; trees of noble growth which every one knows, by name at least, and the more humble species which hardly any one notices. The great lords of the forest are the fir tree, the oak, the beech, and the chestnut; but besides these princely races, there are the people of trees and shrubs, the appearance of which is as original, although not so well known.

Curious monographs might be written on these secondary

[1] Copyright, 1896, by T. Y. Crowell & Co. Used by permission.

species abounding in our woods, all of which have very different habits and usages. The enumeration alone of these various species is not enough. We must note in passing, and with a characteristic word, the appearance and manner of living belonging to each individual. There is the hornbeam, with its light foliage, its elegant nodosity, and its graceful, spreading branches; the ash, with its hard wood, slender trunk, and pinnated leaves, around which buzz the Spanish flies; the aspen and the birch, with their smooth, satinlike bark, nervous foliage, continually in motion; the maple and the sycamore, two first cousins, with lobed leaves, bark which decays easily, and wood valuable for carpentry; the linden, loved by the bees, with its supple bark, fragrant flowers, and leaves as sweet as honey; the alder and the willow growing near running water; the hazel tree, with its healthful, bushy shade; the lote tree, beloved by thrushes; the service tree, preferred by bullfinches and blackbirds; the holly and the boxwood, hard, resisting, and ever green; the wild cherry, or wood of Sainte-Lucie, with its fragrant branches.

All these varieties are well known to foresters, who take great account of their qualities and different characters when they are considering the cultivation or felling of trees.

According to the rules of forestry, woods should be felled as the trees reach their maturity. This maturity is announced by exterior signs, which the trained eye of the forester promptly recognizes. When the annual shoots are strong and lengthened out, when the foliage is abundant and large, the bark unbroken, the young branches supple, it is evident that the tree is still growing in size and height; but when the shoots do not lengthen the branches more than the length of the bud, there will be no more growth, either in height or diameter, and the wood has reached its natural maturity. The inclination of the branches towards the horizon furnishes as well very sure indications in the case of isolated trees. They indicate, for example, that a tree is in its full vigor when its branches describe an angle of from forty to fifty degrees, and that it is on the decline when the angles fall to seventy degrees. Besides, the age or maturity of forest trees, especially of the oak, is recognized by an especial and exceptional fertility: *In senecta*, said Pliny, *fertillissimæ glandiferæ*. When all these indications are found together, it can be assured that the tree will grow no more, and that it is ripe for felling.

The most favorable season for cutting trees is the beginning of winter; that is to say, the time when the sap seems to be dormant. On this point science and tradition agree; the ancient rules of forestry forbade the felling contractors to cut any wood in the forests "while the sap was circulating; namely, from the middle of May until the middle of September." At the present time the contracts for woodcutting are made the last of September, and the felling of the sections awarded generally begins with winter.

When the contracts have been made, each contractor takes the most expeditious means to cut the section or felling which has been assigned to him. As soon as he has recruited the necessary workmen for clearing the woods, — the pruners, cutters, fagot makers, — as soon as he has commissioned the woodcutter's agent appointed to oversee the work, the felling begins. The woodcutters, divided into gangs, arrive on the spot, and prepare to cut down the trees marked for felling.

The woodcutter's first work — when the canton where the work is to be done is too far from any village, and the workmen cannot go home every evening — consists in building a hut to shelter the men and their tools. This hut or cabin, the site of which is chosen by the *administration forestière*, generally assumes a conical shape; it is built with stakes and branches intertwined, the whole is covered on the outside with sods of grassy earth, over which the rain is carried off, and which protect the sleepers from the wind and dampness. Inside, two field beds, raised above the ground, and covered with moss, straw, and brakes, serve as a sleeping place for the woodcutters; between these two litters is left an empty space opposite to the entrance, and in these narrow limits the workmen cook and eat their food.

The day for building the hut is a festal day. They celebrate it by swallowing a great many bumpers of wine, and especially brandy; so that when night comes the whole crowd is quite exhilarated, and the men, half intoxicated, stretch themselves out on the very ground where the felling is to be made. But the next day the work begins in earnest. The overseer is no joker; they must set about their task, and work hard, although their tongues are thick, their backs bent, and their limbs stiff. The woodcutter's work is rough. According to the rules of forestry, the trees must be cut with the ax, and as close to the ground as possible; the use of the billhook or saw is strictly prohibited; the stocks or stumps must be cut level with the ground, smooth, and slightly sloping, in order to prevent the rain water from standing on them and causing them to decay.

When large trees are to be felled, the task demands vigorous muscular strength, an accurate eye, and, above all, long experience. A master woodcutter, understanding his business, should cut the tree from twelve to eighteen inches from the foot, and lay it on the ground "as if it had been given a single cut with a razor."

Nothing is more dramatic and affecting than the fall of a lofty beech tree or oak. The repeated blows of the ax leave the great tree at first immovable and haughty; the woodcutters redouble their efforts, and at times the trunk trembles and quivers from the base to the summit like a living personality. Then one understands all the energetic truth of Sophocles' comparison when he said, Ægisthus and Clytemnestra killed Agamemnon "like woodcutters felling an oak." The steel of the ax makes the bark, sapwood, and the heart of the wood fly in showers; but the tree recovers its impassibility, and stoically submits to the assault of the cutters. To see it still straight and proud in the air, it seems as if it would never fall. Suddenly the woodcutters draw back; there is a moment of waiting which is terribly solemn, then suddenly the enormous trunk sways, and falls to the ground with a tragic crash of broken branches. A sound like a lamentation runs through the hazy forest; then all becomes silent again, and the woodcutters, with unconscious emotion, contemplate the giant lying on the ground.

Then begins the work of lopping the branches. The principal branches, when sawed off, are destined for carpentry or fuel, according to their size and state of health; the small twigs serve for making fagots. Sometimes, when it is desirable to obtain the branches whole, unharmed by the fall, they are taken off while the tree is still standing. A workman with sharp spurs on his feet, carrying a rope with a slip noose in his hand, climbs the tree, with the help of the spurs which he plunges into the bark, leather kneecaps worn on the legs, and the rope which he fastens to the branches as he mounts. While climbing, he supports himself with a knot, hangs from his rope, and cuts off the branches with a billhook. It is a dangerous employment, full of risks. To perform it requires the agility of a squirrel, and the ability to crawl around the trunks with the dexterity of a woodpecker; above all, it requires a steady hand. When the branch cutter has hoisted himself to the top of the tree, in order to deprive it of its last branches, the least breeze rocks him on the summit, now flexible and cracking. Above him he sees the clouds passing by; beneath he sees, as far as his eye can reach, the undulating sea of green or yellowing foliage of the forest. If dizziness seizes him, or if a branch which he thinks solid breaks beneath his feet, it is all over with him; and he is precipitated, bleeding, on the ground. Such accidents happen sometimes; but in spite of the difficulties and risks of the profession, the branch cutters love this adventurous occupation, and are glad to pass in this way a good part of their life between heaven and earth.

When the felling is over, the wood that has been cut is divided into two categories, — that which is intended for timberwork and carpentry, and that reserved for burning. The latter, in round or split sticks, is piled and measured on the ground of the clearing; the smaller branches intended for charcoal are piled separately, as well as the fagots made up by the fagot makers. The wood for timbers with the bark still on is transported whole by means of trucks, underneath the axles of which the enormous trunks of beech, fir, or oak are fastened by chains or cables. Often the large pieces are sawed up on the spot, and in this case the sawyers establish their wood yard in the clearing. When the forest is traversed by watercourses, the sawing is done by machinery, and permanent sawmills lift their wooden buildings above the streams, and their shafts are turned by a wheel, over which the running water is scattered like rain.

Nothing is more picturesque than these rustic sawmills, astride the brooks, shaded by the edge of the forest, and sending afar the bubbling water, the strident sound of the saw, the aromatic odor of freshly cut boards.

When the forests have no very abrupt slopes, when they are penetrated by good roads, transporting the wood away from the clearing is easily effected in carts. But in the mountains, the cantons where the felling is done are frequently situated on slopes too steep for any conveyance to reach. In such cases the wood is sent to the bottom of the valley through almost perpendicular slides, called *couloires*, where it descends rapidly. It is a very primitive mode, in use principally in the

Alps and the Pyrenees. But in more ingenious countries they make from the woods to the winding road at the bottom of the valley tracks on a very inclined plane, formed by logs fastened to crossbeams. Trains loaded with piles of wood slide slowly over these primitive tramways, conducted by a single man, who regulates the speed of the train by leaning his back against it and bracing himself against the logs of the track as it descends the slope. This is the method of the *schlitteurs*, very much in vogue in the Vosges and in Alsace.

There is still another mode of transportation which I ought to mention here; but this is not looked upon with favor by the forest administration, because it is employed principally by the gatherers of dead wood, and trespassers. I mean the carrying of wood on a man's back.

Among the people on the borders, it has always been admitted that the forest ought to support the village. Indeed, under the feudal system it frequently happened that the seigneurs generously ceded to the commune, or transferred in exchange for certain services, numerous rights in the forests belonging to them, — the right to cut wood for fuel and for wheelwright's use; the right to gather acorns, and for common pasturage; the right to burn charcoal, and to gather the forest fruits, dead wood, and dead leaves. When after the promulgation of the forest laws the administration took in hand the management of the forests, it began by severely revising all these privileges, and by reducing them as strictly as possible.

Among the privileges taken from the communes by the forest regulations, none was felt more by the peasants living on the borders of the forest than the gathering of dead wood. This was a resource to poor creatures who counted on this windfall to keep themselves warm in the winter season. So, in spite of the law and the guards, this gathering is made every day. The administration itself is indulgent on this point, and shuts its eyes; it is implacable only when the green wood is concerned. So, as soon as fall comes, in the paths of the woods one meets more than one old man or woman bent over beneath a load of dead branches on the back, and walking towards the nearest village. The gatherers of dead wood are to the woodcutters what the gleaners are to the harvesters. They wander through the forest, every corner of which is familiar to them. They appear especially after stormy days or nights, when the high winds of October have covered the ground of the forest with *débris*. Sometimes, it must be admitted, they help to change the green wood to dead wood. A stroke with the billhook is very quickly made in a tuft of shoots; the green wood thus cut off is left to dry in the underbrush, then a week or two later they pass by, and without the least remorse pick up the branch, now useless.

Other rovers, still less scrupulous, have no hesitation in cutting a green bough of good size, and slipping it into their bundle, where it disappears among the dead branches. But the foresters have their eyes open. Just as the delinquent is slyly leaving the forest, a guard suddenly falls on him, forces him to untie his bundle of fagots, detects the presence of the green wood, and enters a complaint against him, after confiscating the *corpus delicti*, in spite of the fagot maker's lamentations.

Culprits of this sort are very numerous, but the foolish little thefts which they commit do not harm the forest to any extent. The greatest source of trouble to the guard is the habitual offender, who makes the illicit removal of wood a business and a trade. This forest ravager practices his profession boldly by night. He pulls up the young shoots by hundreds to sell; he cuts the finest branches from the cornel tree, the holly, and the wild medlar tree, to make whip handles; he breaks down the young trees unmercifully, and does not even respect the very old ones. In addition to this he has several occupations, and to the profession of trespasser joins that of poacher. His familiarity with the woods makes him acquainted with all the haunts where game is to be found, all the paths where it goes.

He hunts small and large game, feathers and fur alike, but not with the gun, which would too easily put the guards on his track, but with good snares of horsehair or wire. I knew one who made his traps so ingeniously that he caught deer in his snares, and one day a horse wandering through the woods was completely strangled in a master slip noose of wire stretched by this desperate poacher. The foresters had entered mountains of complaints against him, but he laughed at them and their documents. The court condemned him; but as he had no seizable property, and lived in the woods, he did not care. Sometimes the officers would catch him: he would sleep in prison for two months, and then quickly return to take up his vagabond life again. One winter's day he was found dead in a valley where he had spread his snares. He had been intoxicated the day before, had been overcome by the cold, and congestion had stiffened him out in the depths of the forest.

ROSES.[1]

BY LOUISE CHANDLER MOULTON.

(1835–.)

ROSES, that briefly live,
  Joy is your dower —
Blest be the Fates that give
  One perfect hour: —

And, though, too soon you die,
  In your dust glows
Something the passer-by
  Knows *was* a Rose.

AT TINTERN ABBEY.[2]

BY LOUISE CHANDLER MOULTON.

THE gray day's ending followed the gray day, —
  All gray together, ruin and air and sky, —
  And a lone wind of memory whispered by,
And told dark secrets on its wandering way.
Through the blank windows' space, like ghosts astray,
  Sad crowds of black-winged jackdaws came and went.
  Were they dead monks on some strange penance sent,
Who used within these walls to preach and pray?

Do they return, from the far, starry sphere,
  To their old haunt within these ruins old,
    To celebrate, perchance, some mystic rite,
Some yearning soul's outcry of pain to hear —
  And, when the awful story has been told,
    Will priest and sinner vanish on the night?

[1] By permission of the author and of the publishers, Little, Brown & Co., Boston.

[2] By permission of the author.

THE WASHERWOMEN.[1]

BY BLANCHE WILLIS HOWARD.

(From "Guenn.")

[BLANCHE WILLIS HOWARD: American author, was born in Bangor, Me., July 21, 1847. She now resides in Stuttgart, Germany, having in 1890 married Baron von Teuffel, a physician of that city. Among her popular novels are: "One Summer," "One Year Abroad," "Aunt Serena," "Guenn," "The Open Door."]

SOME days after the great sardine catch, Guenn Rodellec went to the river. Going to the river was an event which took place three or four times a week in Plouvenec, but its frequency made it none the less delightful to Guenn. How could she fail to enjoy it? All the women clustered on the bank, kneeling and washing their linen, and spreading it out to dry on the clean grass, reeds, brambles, and tufts of heather and brake; and everything, positively everything that had happened in Plouvenec since the last time, — with much, indeed, that had not, — related in stirring style by practiced tongues.

Guenn had gone to the river earlier than most girls, and was rather proud of being one of the regular members of this great sisterhood, that bleached clothes diligently, but never by any chance whitened a reputation. Girls who had mothers rarely went to the river very young. Even here, where childhood was so unguarded, there was a tacit understanding that it was in a certain sense a decided step in a girl's life, a crisis, when she first went to the river. She was old enough now for anything. It was an event of as much importance as the first ball of a girl in the great world.

But Guenn, having no mother, began in her ninth year to represent her family in the washing conclave, and to look forward to its chronique scandaleuse with as much eagerness as a fashionable young lady awaits the next installment of a sensational novel. She could now hold her own, in racy anecdote and piquant repartee, with the most virulent old fishwife among them. It was always dull, or worse, at home. Nannic was never there; for all day long he was hanging about the wharves,

[1] Copyright, 1883, by James R. Osgood & Co. Published by permission of Houghton, Mifflin & Co.

listening to the sailors' talk, or begging sous and lumps of sugar of strangers at the inns, — trading cleverly upon their pity for his misshapen little person, or opposing his uncanny slyness to the brute force of the other boys. . . .

Rodellec's house was on a lonely road, somewhat remote from the village. Guenn, this morning, arrived late at the assembly of her peers. The women were in full force, already hard at work, — kneeling in their boxes, which rested on smooth flat stones fairly in the water, soaping, dipping their linen, and pounding it on the stones with heavy little wooden paddles, — all chattering at once, and exchanging volleys of what elsewhere would be termed insult and vituperation, but which, in Plouvenec, seemed to represent a certain form of the amenities of life.

Guenn came springing down the bank. She observed with delight that old Mother Nives and other veterans were present, a sure indication of a lively morning. Jeanne Ronan too, whom Guenn liked, was there.

"There's Guenn!" cried some of the younger girls.

"Oh, you're a nice lot, you are!" was Mademoiselle Rodellec's courteous morning salutation, her hands on her hips, a light smile of conscious power, like that of a famed gladiator entering the arena, playing about her mouth. "You couldn't any of you take a little more room, could you, or a few more of the best places at once? Modest, you are! Move your things over, Marie, and be quick about it too. I'm coming there by Jeanne."

Marie grumbled that people who came late better take what was left, upon which Guenn unceremoniously pushed the girl's basket aside, tossed her box and loose clothes in various directions, and coolly usurped the desired position.

Having made this triumphant entrance, she plunged into her work, saying in an undertone: "What's in the wind? Anything new?"

"Mother Nives' rheumatism has left her. She's got five weeks' cooped-up hatefulness to let out."

"I thought I smelt fire and brimstone," laughed Guenn.

"Are you two little fools gabbling about me?" called an ugly old woman in a dark-red petticoat, from the opposite side of the pool.

"Oh, no, Madame Nives," Jeanne answered blandly, "I was only asking Guenn why she's so lazy to-day."

Mother Nives glared suspiciously at the two roguish faces.

"Ah, mon dieu, que la vie est amère!"

sang Guenn, beating time vigorously with her paddle on the stones, and smiling audaciously at the enemy.

"H'm!" sneered Mother Nives. "Your life is likely to be bitter enough. Just keep on with your monkey tricks, and I can tell you where they'll lead you, Guenn Rodellec!"

"Madame Nives knows, because she's been there herself," interposed Mother Quaper's strident tones, advancing to the fray, not in the least on Guenn's account, but because she never declined the pleasure of a little round with Mother Nives, with whom, however, she was by no means on bad terms, as Plouvenec neighbors go.

"Been where, Madame Quaper?" demanded the old woman, with dangerous suavity. "I've been about my own business, which is where you never were yet, Madame Quaper. You wash your clothes and I will wash mine, Madame Quaper, or one of us will be missed by the river for several to-morrows, Madame Quaper."

This was considered by the listeners one of Mother Nives' best efforts, the veiled suggestion of personal violence being particularly admired. But Mother Quaper, upon whom all eyes were now turned, was equal to the occasion.

"Madame Nives means that the judge of the peace is going to lock her up in good earnest, this time, as a public nuisance," she exclaimed. The repartee, based on historical fact, caused laughter and cries of delight.

"Ah, mon dieu, que la vie est amère!" . . .

"Now this young gentleman," and Mother Quaper held up a shirt to general inspection, gazing at it meditatively, with an "Alas, poor Yorick" air, "this poor little dear Monsieur Staunton," — she looked as if she were beholding Staunton in person, instead of his innocent garment, — "a good-looking gars, to be sure, and the finest of linen. Rich as a duke, most likely; gave my Kadoc ten sous yesterday. Well, as I was saying, my neighbors sold him some old sails for his studio, — the Lord above knows what he wants of them, seeing as he can't sail his studio on the bay —— "

"Window curtains, and such," called out Jeanne Ronan, instructively.

"Curtains or fiddlesticks, for all o' me, but they made him pay twice as much as the very best brand-new ones are worth. I heard it all. How I laughed! If they hadn't been neighbors, you know, and old friends, I'd have given him a wink. Such a good-looking gars as he is, ce cher petit Staunton!" Down went Mr. Staunton's shirt in the water with eclat.

"Well, now, nobody can tell anything about messieurs les artistes," and little Jeanne raised her voice with conviction. She was a model, and knew what she was talking about. "Perhaps he wasn't cheated, after all. If the sails looked old and rusty and faded and dirty and patched and stained — why, he liked them better than new ones. He wanted to pay more for them. Here is my kerchief. It was a beauty once," — glancing down at it regretfully. "You remember, Guenn? I bought it at the Beûzec Pardon." Guenn nodded assent. "The spots were bright blue, and the stripes were bright red, and the crisscross lines were green and yellow. Now, what do you think? Mr. Staunton wouldn't paint it; — wouldn't so much as look at it, until the colors had all run together and it was dirty. He said it made his eyes ache. He called it hard."

"A cotton kerchief hard!" screamed the women, in derision.

"That's what he said; and now, when I don't like it any more, and put on my new one, he sends me home every time I come without it. There was a yellow cashmere baby blanket little Hélène had. All the artists called it a *glory*. They hung it in the sun and they hung it in the shadow, and upside down and wrong side out. It had a big darn, but it was a glory all the same."

"A glory, a glory!" laughed the chorus. "Oh, mon dieu, a glory!"

"And so I say you can't tell anything about them, because they are different," concluded Jeanne, philosophically.

"Because they are idiots!" was Mother Nives' acrid amendment. "And as for your pretty gars, with his fine linen, he owes his carpenter's bill, let me tell you that. Who knows but he's only *show* rich?"

"And this much I can say," began the heavy peasant girl Marie, several times pushed aside as of no importance, and glad now to swim with the current, "since Nona Hévin has been posing for him, she hasn't a decent word in her mouth for anybody. My grandmother says it doesn't bode much good to girls when they get their heads turned by the artists. They are no better than they should be, the most of 'em. What happened to Yvonne, and whose fault was it but an artist's? Though my grandmother does say she was always a silly, vain thing, herself. And as for Nona Hévin, with her airs," — shaking her head significantly, — "we shall see!"

Jeanne looked up angrily; but Guenn sprang to her feet, and with uncompromising directness exclaimed hotly: "And why didn't you say all that when Nona was here? Because you did not dare, Marie Brenn! And it's a great deal you know about models and painters! Only you know very well nobody wants to paint your ugly frog face, and that makes you say mean things about the pretty girls. Nona is as good a girl as there is in Plouvenec, and Jeanne is the very best one. You'd better not say anything more about models!"

"The blessed Virgin forbid that I should be one," persisted Marie, piously; "and whether Jeanne likes it or not, my grandmother says, in Paris, models don't wear clothes. So there, Guenn Rodellec!"

Ejaculations of unspeakable astonishment followed this statement. Guenn's own amazement was boundless, but she would have died rather than betray it, or let it be even faintly surmised that Marie Brenn could give her the least information upon any point whatever.

"Well, who doesn't know that!" she retorted, staring haughtily at Marie, without the quiver of an eyelash. "Perhaps you and your grandma had better set up a school to teach the rest of us our A B C's. Doesn't everybody know there are black, heathen people in Africa and Italy, and such out-of-the-way places? They don't wear clothes, because" — hesitating a perceptible instant, then, with laudable aplomb, concluding — "they haven't got any to wear. They wear skins of animals, and such things. They climb trees and eat roots," she added, in a superior but somewhat vague manner. Descending from these heights of knowledge to her own territory, she advanced with splendid rapidity. "But I'll tell you what, Marie Brenn, — even if heathen don't know much, they can't be worse than you, saying behind a girl's back what you don't dare say to her face, and giving a dead girl a mean hit, too! As if it wasn't enough for poor Yvonne to drown herself and die, and her soul on a wave beating against the cliff every night!"

Guenn and all the women gave an involuntary glance at the towering crag, and crossed themselves. Marie, crushed by the weight of so much learning, after a little pause retorted sullenly: "Well, you never posed yourself, Guenn Rodellec!"

"Well, I never did," Guenn said mockingly.

"But they all want her," cried Jeanne, eagerly. "Monsieur Staunton, Monsieur Douglas, the French painters, the new one, — everybody wants Guenn, everybody! Only she won't come."

Guenn tossed her pretty head. "Why should I stand still, with a water jug in my hand, eight mortal hours, like you, Jeanne? I should throw the jug at the idiot and run away. But if it amuses you!" — she shrugged her shoulders and laughed.

"Oh, I like it well enough," Jeanne admitted cheerily. "I must say, it's better fun than the usine. They let you rest. But they are a queer set, and no mistake. Monsieur Douglas painted old Josèphe with her distaff in the wrong hand. I went into fits of laughter every time I saw it. He was at it six weeks. All the painters stood in front of it and told him how beautiful it was, and cackled like so many geese. One morning he said: 'Jeanne, you will tell me how you like my picture;'" wickedly imitating Mr. Douglas' solemn British-French. "'Oh,' said I, 'if it pleases monsieur — Josèphe's nose is shorter, and her eyes are squinter, but so ugly as the picture she never was; and O monsieur, — the distaff is in the wrong hand!'"

"But what made Josephe hold her distaff wrong?" demanded half a dozen voices in amazement.

"As if Josèphe cares!" began Guenn, contemptuously. "These painters are all mad, you know. Jeanne's Monsieur Staunton kneels down and says his prayers to a mud puddle, with a bit of light shining in it. Monsieur Douglas picks up a fish head on the road, and looks at it as if he was the curé reading his breviary. If they had told Josèphe to coiffer her distaff, and wear her sabots on her head, she'd have done it all the same. Oh, many's the time I've watched Jeanne through the gate, and Monsieur Douglas standing so," — giving a dramatic representation of Mr. Douglas' manner and attitude. "'Raise your left eyebrow, Jeanne. Draw your foot back. Breathe quite easily. Head to the right. Eyes to the left. Ah, charming! Now we will begin.' Then, after a couple of hours, 'Rest. Begin — Rest.' And so on all day. — 'Here is your money. Come to-morrow at eight.' — Allons donc, do you suppose I'd put up with that? Am I a stick or a stone, or a trained poodle at the fair? 'Give your paw, Guenn. Sit up and beg, Guenn.' No — no — no!" And raising her arms high above her head, with a swing of her lithe body expressive of the joys of savage freedom, Guenn resumed her duties as independent washerwoman, with a clear and sweet —

"Ah, mon dieu, que la vie est amère!"

Jeanne laughed merrily with the others.

"Oh yes, Guenn is hoity-toity enough," sneered Mother Nives. "But the young fellow who saw all her hair loose may see it again. Sainte Anne d'Auray! Wasn't the girl a sight, when milord the painter was looking at her?"

"Who cares about him!" Guenn exclaimed quickly, with heightened color.

"I saw him coming," the old woman went on, giving a mysterious leer. "In the candle I saw a stranger, the night before he came. I named three bits of straw, for you and Jeanne and Nona; when I blew, Jeanne and Nona flew over, but you fell into the flame."

Guenn, with a defiant toss of her head and a deeper flush, retorted: "Keep your candle fortunes for yourself, Madame Nives;" but she was uneasy nevertheless. Had not she herself, the very day she saw him on the sands, heard — alone at home — a loud noise three times repeated, as if the old armoire was trying to speak? Everybody knows that means misfortune. And did not a little gray bird fly more than once in her path as she came through the woods, quite fearless, though she was so near, and looking at her strangely with its little round eyes? She knew well what soul had returned in the form of a bird, to warn her of impending evil. Then, when madame, at the Voyageurs, asked her to pour out a glass of wine in the kitchen, she had spilled it on a white napkin. More misfortune!

All that in a couple of hours. Guenn had felt oppressed by these evil signs, but had put them out of her mind as soon as possible. Now old Mother Nives reminded her of her forebodings. Well, was it not misfortune enough to stand there with her hair hanging down, before a man, and to have them play her such a mean trick? She never believed more than half of anything the Nives said; still ——

That amiable person, observing that she had accidentally said something which disturbed the young girl, continued venomously: "You mark my words, you'll be posing like a lamb before long. He didn't lose much time with your father that night. He's a cool one. He can put out firebrands."

Again Guenn was lost in uneasy thought. She remembered, against her will, every feature of the stranger's face, as he calmly looked on her sorry plight, and as calmly afterwards restrained her father's drunken fury. Jeanne anxiously pulled her friend's sleeve. What could be the matter? Guenn, whose tongue never failed her, was surely not going to be beaten publicly by the Nives.

But Guenn rallied. "If he ever comes to me," she said impudently, "I'll send him to paint you and Loïc."

Now Madame Nives and her son Loïc were, even according to the unexacting Plouvenec standard, the ugliest people in existence; moreover Loïc, like many another young man, sighed in vain for Guenn Rodellec.

The mercurial chorus shouted with glee.

"You minx!" cried Mother Nives, in a fine rage. "But I dare you to swear you won't be his model. You will, I know you will."

"Well, now, I don't intend to be driven by anybody," Guenn returned stoutly. "I won't say yes to please him, or no to please you."

"What's the man's name, anyway?" demanded Mother Nives.

"Hamor," replied several women, who frequented the Voyageurs kitchen.

"Madame, at the Voyageurs, has him in tow?" . . .

"Who's to have his wash?" continued Mother Nives.

"Madame Quaper, if you are sure you don't mind at all," answered Guenn, wickedly.

"Is it your doing?" the old woman said with an oath.

"Never you mind her nasty temper, Guenn," roared Mother Quaper.

"My temper ain't so nasty as my fist, Madame Quaper, and don't you forget that!" . . .

"There's Morot's boat!" Guenn sprang eagerly up, shading her eyes with her hand.

"And what if it is?" grumbled Mother Nives. "Is that anything new? Isn't he always sailing and sailing, while we are scrubbing and scrubbing. What did he ever do in his life, but eat and drink and sail and amuse himself?" snarled the bitter old fishwife, accompanied by murmurs of mingled sympathy and dissent. "Lazy puppy, and his father before him, —and his grandfather, that hanged himself in the granary." She crossed herself furtively. Every other woman did the same. "Some folks sail, some folks scrub; that's life. As for me, I wouldn't turn my head a quarter of an inch to see Louis Morot's boat, unless it was to see it sink!" The old woman glared straight before her at a pair of blue socks, which she wrung in a vindictive manner.

Guenn retorted angrily: "What's the use of lying all the time, Madame Nives? Why don't you stop and rest once in a while? Answer me," she said imperiously, addressing each and all. "Who is the best sailor in Plouvenec? Monsieur Louis. Whose boat goes out in storms that send all the rest of them howling into port? Monsieur Louis. And isn't it his own boat? Then who has a better right to sail it, I should like to know. Who gives smiles and francs, and one as free as the other? Monsieur Louis. And how many of our men has he saved at the risk of his life, and he only a young fellow too! And who looked after Loïc Nives when he was down with a broken leg? Monsieur Louis! So I don't think I'd hit him behind his back, even if I was you, Madame Nives!"

"That's true, Guenn," cried the mobile chorus. "She'd better keep still about Monsieur Louis! She'd better hush up!"

"And what is he doing now?" Guenn waxed more impassioned with every word. "He is bringing over the Recteur of the Lannions." Her strong gaze searched the boat. "I know, because I see. That's what he's doing, good Monsieur Louis! And he couldn't do anything better, unless he should bring us an angel from heaven; for where the Recteur goes, comes a blessing and a joy, as everybody knows who isn't a knave or a fool or both. And Monsieur Louis will take him back with his supplies, and he's always looking out for him. And that's the kind of man Monsieur Louis Morot is, and shame on anybody who says he isn't, and she's got something still to hear from Guenn Rodellec, and here I am!" The girl stood with folded arms, her flaming eyes challenging them all.

"I say he isn't." Mother Nives' arms were akimbo, her face was venomous. "I say he's a dandy and a do-nothing, and if he swamps his cursed boat some day, and the precious pair drown together, I'll stand by and grin. I hate the father. I hate the son. As for your priest, there are too many priests, — too many priests. He'd better drown," — and she laughed her croaking laugh. "Oh, you can't frighten me with your big eyes, Guenn Rodellec, — shoot fire out of them as you will. What if he did cure Nannic's fever? Do you think anybody but you thanked him for that? Ugly, crooked little brat — always in the way!"

"Oh, come now, come now!" expostulated the women. Even the brutality of Plouvenec had its limits.

All the brightness faded from Guenn's face, and the little figure — so lightly poised, as she had gallantly defended Morot, and followed every movement of his boat — grew rigid with passion.

"You old devil!" Ugly lines gathered about the young mouth as it spoke the ugly words. "You say another word about Thymert, or about my brother Nannic," — she spoke slowly, with great pauses — "you understand, one word about the Recteur or my Nannic ——"

"Bo-o-o!" cried a shrill voice. "Here I am!" and the wizened face of a humpbacked child, with large eyes like Guenn's, and a sly, unpleasant smile, peered from the bushes on the wall.

The women crossed themselves. By oaks and running water, *nains* and *korrigans* might at any time appear. With many another old Druid superstition, this was a part of every Plouvenec woman's secret belief.

The boy came halfway down the bank and seated himself, resting his pale face on his hands, his long elbows on his knees, — motionless, watchful, uncanny.

"Who called Nannic? I was miles away, and I came." He made this preposterous statement solemnly, and as if he were chanting. His keen eyes searched the group. Madame Nives, with a guilty air, was busily washing. In spite of her boasts, she much preferred giving to receiving curses, and had a wholesome dread of the evil eye. The other women were all staring up at him. "Madame Nives," called the cripple, "it was you who said Nannic. I came. I will come to you again sometime at the stroke of midnight, when every corpse stirs and opens its eyes!"

The color crept back to Guenn's cheeks. The ugly lines

left her mouth, and the rigid extended arm fell by her side. With a beautiful smile she looked at Nannic; then out on the bay, where Morot's boat was just rounding the point. Her face grew tender, her great blue eyes bluer.

"Gamin," she said with inexpressible affection, "wait for me."

"I am waiting for Jeanne," answered the boy, perversely.

Guenn laughed. "Même chose," she said brightly.

Spreading out what remained of her linen, she gathered together her belongings, and, with Jeanne and Nannic, walked along the beach.

"Ah, mon dieu, que la vie est amère,"

sang their fresh laughing voices.

SPINNING.[1]

BY HELEN HUNT JACKSON.

(1831-1885.)

LIKE a blind spinner in the sun
I tread my days;
I know that all the threads will run
Appointed ways;
I know each day will bring its task,
And being blind, no more I ask.

I do not know the use or name
Of that I spin;
I only know that some one came,
And laid within
My hand the thread, and said, "Since you
Are blind, but one thing you can do."

Sometimes the threads so rough and fast
And tangled fly,
I know wild storms are sweeping past,
And fear that I
Shall fall; but dare not try to find
A safer place, since I am blind.

[1] By permission of Little, Brown & Co.

HELEN HUNT JACKSON

I know not why, but I am sure
    That tint and place
In some great fabric to endure
    Past time and race
My threads will have; so from the first,
Though blind, I never felt accurst.

I think, perhaps, this trust has sprung
    From one short word
Said over me when I was young,—
    So young, I heard
It, knowing not that God's name signed
My brow, and sealed me his, though blind.

But whether this be seal or sign
    Within, without,
It matters not. The bond divine
    I never doubt.
I know He set me here, and still,
And glad, and blind, I wait His will;

But listen, listen, day by day,
    To hear their tread
Who bear the finished web away,
    And cut the thread,
And bring God's message in the sun,
"Thou poor blind spinner, work is done."

THE ROMANCE OF CERTAIN OLD CLOTHES.[1]

By HENRY JAMES.

[HENRY JAMES: An American novelist; born in New York city, April 15, 1843. He traveled abroad 1855–1859; attended Harvard Law School for a time, and in 1865 began to contribute sketches to periodicals. His novels in almost every case treat of the distinction between the manners, customs, and people of the Old and New Worlds. He has resided abroad since 1869, with only occasional visits to his native country. Among his books are: "Roderick Watson" (1875), "Transatlantic Sketches" (1875), "A Passionate Pilgrim, and Other Stories" (1875), "The American" (1878), "Daisy Miller" (1878), "An International Episode" (1878), "The Europeans" (1878), "Confidence" (1879), "Washington Square" (1880), "A Bundle of Letters" and "Diary of

[1] Copyright, 1875, by James R. Osgood & Co. Used by permission of Houghton, Mifflin & Co.

a Man of Fifty" (1880), "The Portrait of a Lady" (1881), "The Siege of London" (1883), "Portraits of Places," "A Little Tour in France," and "A Tale of Three Cities" (1884), "The Author of Beltraffio" (1885), "The Bostonians" and "Princess Casamassima" (1886).]

TOWARD the middle of the eighteenth century there lived in the Province of Massachusetts a widowed gentlewoman, the mother of three children. Her name is of little account: I shall take the liberty of calling her Mrs. Willoughby,—a name, like her own, of a highly respectable sound. She had been left a widow after some six years of marriage, and had devoted herself to the care of her progeny. These young persons grew up in a manner to reward her zeal and to gratify her fondest hopes. The firstborn was a son, whom she had called Bernard, after his father. The others were daughters,—born at an interval of three years apart. Good looks were traditional in the family, and this youthful trio were not likely to allow the tradition to perish. The boy was of that fair and ruddy complexion and of that athletic mold which in those days (as in these) were the sign of genuine English blood,—a frank, affectionate young fellow, a deferential son, a patronizing brother, and a steadfast friend. Clever, however, he was not; the wit of the family had been apportioned chiefly to his sisters. Mr. Willoughby had been a great reader of Shakespeare, at a time when this pursuit implied more liberality of taste than at the present day, and in a community where it required much courage to patronize the drama even in the closet; and he had wished to record his admiration of the great poet by calling his daughters out of his favorite plays. Upon the elder he had bestowed the romantic name of Viola; and upon the younger, the more serious one of Perdita, in memory of a little girl born between them, who had lived but a few weeks.

When Bernard Willoughby came to his sixteenth year, his mother put a brave face upon it, and prepared to execute her husband's last request. This had been an earnest entreaty that, at the proper age, his son should be sent out to England, to complete his education at the University of Oxford, which had been the seat of his own studies. Mrs. Willoughby fancied that the lad's equal was not to be found in the two hemispheres, but she had the antique wifely submissiveness. She swallowed her sobs, and made up her boy's trunk and his simple provincial outfit, and sent him on his way across the seas. Bernard was entered at his father's college, and spent five years in England, without great honor, indeed, but with a vast deal of pleasure and no discredit. On leaving the University he made the journey to France. In his twenty-third year he took ship for home, prepared to find poor little New England (New England was very small in those days) an utterly intolerable place of abode. But there had been changes at home, as well as in Mr. Bernard's opinions. He found his mother's house quite habitable, and his sisters grown into two very charming young ladies, with all the accomplishments and graces of the young women of Britain, and a certain native-grown gentle *brusquerie* and wildness, which, if it was not an accomplishment, was certainly a grace the more. Bernard privately assured his mother that his sisters were fully a match for the most genteel young women in England; whereupon poor Mrs. Willoughby, you may be sure, bade them hold up their heads. Such was Bernard's opinion, and such, in a tenfold higher degree, was the opinion of Mr. Arthur Lloyd. This gentleman, I hasten to add, was a college mate of Mr. Bernard, a young man of reputable family, of a good person and a handsome inheritance; which latter appurtenance he proposed to invest in trade in this country. He and Bernard were warm friends; they had crossed the ocean together, and the young American had lost no time in presenting him at his mother's house, where he had made quite as good an impression as that which he had received, and of which I have just given a hint.

The two sisters were at this time in all the freshness of their youthful bloom; each wearing, of course, this natural brilliancy in the manner that became her best. They were equally dissimilar in appearance and character. Viola, the elder,—now in her twenty-second year,—was tall and fair, with calm gray eyes and auburn tresses; a very faint likeness to the Viola of Shakespeare's comedy, whom I imagine as a brunette (if you will), but a slender, airy creature, full of the softest and finest emotions. Miss Willoughby, with her candid complexion, her fine arms, her majestic height, and her slow utterance, was not cut out for adventures. She would never have put on a man's jacket and hose; and, indeed, being a very plump beauty, it is perhaps as well that she would not. Perdita, too, might very well have exchanged the sweet melancholy of her name against something more in consonance with her aspect and disposition. She was a positive brunette, short of stature, light of foot, with a vivid dark brown eye. She had been from her childhood a creature of smiles and gayety; and so far from making you wait for an answer to your speech, as her handsome sister was wont to do (while she gazed at you with her somewhat cold gray eyes), she had given you the choice of half a dozen, suggested by the successive clauses of your proposition, before you had got to the end of it.

The young girls were very glad to see their brother once more; but they found themselves quite able to maintain a reserve of good will for their brother's friend. Among the young men their friends and neighbors, the *belle jeunesse* of the Colony, there were many excellent fellows, several devoted swains, and some two or three who enjoyed the reputation of universal charmers and conquerors. But the home-bred arts and the somewhat boisterous gallantry of those honest young colonists were completely eclipsed by the good looks, the fine clothes, the punctilious courtesy, the perfect elegance, the immense information, of Mr. Arthur Lloyd. He was in reality no paragon; he was an honest, resolute, intelligent young man, rich in pounds sterling, in his health and comfortable hopes, and his little capital of uninvested affections. But he was a gentleman; he had a handsome face, he had studied and traveled; he spoke French, he played on the flute, and he read verses aloud with very great taste. There were a dozen reasons why Miss Willoughby and her sister should forthwith have been rendered fastidious in the choice of their male acquaintance. The imagination of woman is especially adapted to the various small conventions and mysteries of polite society. Mr. Lloyd's talk told our little New England maidens a vast deal more of the ways and means of people of fashion in European capitals than he had any idea of doing. It was delightful to sit by and hear him and Bernard discourse upon the fine people and fine things they had seen. They would all gather round the fire after tea, in the little wainscoted parlor,— quite innocent then of any intention of being picturesque or of being anything else, indeed, than economical, and saving an outlay in stamped papers and tapestries,— and the two young men would remind each other, across the rug, of this, that, and the other adventure. Viola and Perdita would often have given their ears to know exactly what adventure it was, and where it happened, and who was there, and what the ladies had on; but in those days a well-bred young woman was not expected to break into the conversation of her own movement or to ask too many questions; and the poor girls used therefore to sit fluttering behind the more languid — or more discreet — curiosity of their mother.

That they were both very fine girls Arthur Lloyd was not slow to discover; but it took him some time to satisfy himself as to the apportionment of their charms. He had a strong presentiment — an emotion of a nature entirely too cheerful to be called a foreboding — that he was destined to marry one of them; yet he was unable to arrive at a preference, and for such a consummation a preference was certainly indispensable, inasmuch as Lloyd was quite too gallant a fellow to make a choice by lot and be cheated of the heavenly delight of falling in love. He resolved to take things easily, and to let his heart speak. Meanwhile, he was on a very pleasant footing. Mrs. Willoughby showed a dignified indifference to his "intentions," equally remote from a carelessness of her daughters' honor and from that odious alacrity to make him commit himself which, in his quality of a young man of property, he had but too often encountered in the venerable dames of his native islands. As for Bernard, all that he asked was that his friend should take his sisters as his own; and as for the poor girls themselves, however each may have secretly longed for the monopoly of Mr. Lloyd's attentions, they observed a very decent and modest and contented demeanor.

Towards each other, however, they were somewhat more on the offensive. They were good sisterly friends, betwixt whom it would take more than a day for the seeds of jealousy to sprout and bear fruit; but the young girls felt that the seeds had been sown on the day that Mr. Lloyd came into the house. Each made up her mind that, if she should be slighted, she would bear her grief in silence, and that no one should be any the wiser; for if they had a great deal of love, they had also a great deal of pride. But each prayed in secret, nevertheless, that upon *her* the glory might fall. They had need of a vast deal of patience, of self-control, and of dissimulation. In those days a young girl of decent breeding could make no advances whatever, and barely respond, indeed, to those that were made. She was expected to sit still in her chair with her eyes on the carpet, watching the spot where the mystic handkerchief should fall. Poor Arthur Lloyd was obliged to undertake his wooing in the little wainscoted parlor, before the eyes of Mrs. Willoughby, her son, and his prospective sister-in-law. But youth and love are so cunning that a hundred signs and tokens might travel to and fro, and not one of these three pairs of eyes detect them in their passage. The young girls had but one chamber and one bed between them, and for long hours together they were under each other's direct inspection. That each knew that she was being watched, however, made not a grain of difference in those little offices which they mutually rendered, or in the various household tasks which they performed in common. Neither flinched nor fluttered beneath the silent batteries of her sister's eyes. The only apparent change in their habits was that they had less to say to each other. It was impossible to talk about Mr. Lloyd, and it was ridiculous to talk about anything else. By tacit agreement they began to wear all their choice finery, and to devise such little implements of coquetry, in the way of ribbons and topknots and furbelows, as were sanctioned by indubitable modesty. They executed in the same inarticulate fashion an agreement of sincerity on these delicate matters. "Is it better so?" Viola would ask, tying a bunch of ribbons on her bosom, and turning about from her glass to her sister. Perdita would look up gravely from her work and examine the decoration. "I think you had better give it another loop," she would say, with great solemnity, looking hard at her sister with eyes that added, "upon my honor!" So they were forever stitching and trimming their petticoats, and pressing out their muslins, and contriving washes and ointments and cosmetics, like the ladies in the household of the Vicar of Wakefield. Some three or four months went by; it grew to be midwinter, and as yet Viola knew that if Perdita had nothing more to boast of than she, there was not much to be feared from her rivalry. But Perdita by this time, the charming Perdita, felt that her secret had grown to be tenfold more precious than her sister's.

One afternoon Miss Willoughby sat alone before her toilet glass, combing out her long hair. It was getting too dark to see; she lit the two candles in their sockets on the frame of her mirror, and then went to the window to draw her curtains. It was a gray December evening; the landscape was bare and bleak, and the sky heavy with snow clouds. At the end of the long garden into which her window looked was a wall with a little postern door, opening into a lane. The door stood ajar, as she could vaguely see in the gathering darkness, and moved slowly to and fro, as if some one were swaying it from the lane without. It was doubtless a servant maid. But as she was

HENRY JAMES' HOUSE AT RYE

about to drop her curtain, Viola saw her sister step within the garden, and hurry along the path toward the house. She dropped the curtain, all save a little crevice for her eyes. As Perdita came up the path, she seemed to be examining something in her hand, holding it close to her eyes. When she reached the house she stopped a moment, looked intently at the object, and pressed it to her lips.

Poor Viola slowly came back to her chair, and sat down before her glass, where, if she had looked at it less abstractedly, she would have seen her handsome features sadly disfigured by jealousy. A moment afterwards the door opened behind her, and her sister came into the room, out of breath, and her cheeks aglow with the chilly air.

Perdita started. "Ah," said she, "I thought you were with our mother." The ladies were to go to a tea party, and on such occasions it was the habit of one of the young girls to help their mother to dress. Instead of coming in, Perdita lingered at the door.

"Come in, come in," said Viola. "We've more than an hour yet. I should like you very much to give a few strokes to my hair." She knew that her sister wished to retreat, and that she could see in the glass all her movements in the room. "Nay, just help me with my hair," she said, "and I'll go to mamma."

Perdita came reluctantly, and took the brush. She saw her sister's eyes, in the glass, fastened hard upon her hands. She had not made three passes, when Viola clapped her own right hand upon her sister's left, and started out of her chair. "Whose ring is that?" she cried passionately, drawing her towards the light.

On the young girl's third finger glistened a little gold ring, adorned with a couple of small rubies. Perdita felt that she need no longer keep her secret, yet that she must put a bold face on her avowal. "It's mine," she said proudly.

"Who gave it to you?" cried the other.

Perdita hesitated a moment. "Mr. Lloyd."

"Mr. Lloyd is generous, all of a sudden."

"Ah no," cried Perdita, with spirit, "not all of a sudden. He offered it to me a month ago."

"And you needed a month's begging to take it?" said Viola, looking at the little trinket; which indeed was not especially elegant, although it was the best that the jeweler of the Province could furnish. "I shouldn't have taken it in less than two."

"It isn't the ring," said Perdita, "it's what it means!"

"It means that you're not a modest girl," cried Viola. "Pray does your mother know of your conduct? does Bernard?"

"My mother has approved my 'conduct,' as you call it. Mr. Lloyd has asked my hand, and mamma has given it. Would you have had him apply to you, sister?"

Viola gave her sister a long look, full of passionate envy and sorrow. Then she dropped her lashes on her pale cheeks and turned away. Perdita felt that it had not been a pretty scene; but it was her sister's fault. But the elder girl rapidly called back her pride, and turned herself about again. "You have my very best wishes," she said, with a low courtesy. "I wish you every happiness, and a very long life."

Perdita gave a bitter laugh. "Don't speak in that tone," she cried. "I'd rather you cursed me outright. Come, sister," she added, "he couldn't marry both of us."

"I wish you very great joy," Viola repeated mechanically, sitting down to her glass again, "and a very long life, and plenty of children."

There was something in the sound of these words not at all to Perdita's taste. "Will you give me a year, at least?" she said. "In a year I can have one little boy,—or one little girl at least. If you'll give me your brush again, I'll do your hair."

"Thank you," said Viola. "You had better go to mamma. It isn't becoming that a young lady with a promised husband should wait on a girl with none."

"Nay," said Perdita, good-humoredly, "I have Arthur to wait upon me. You need my service more than I need yours."

But her sister motioned her away, and she left the room. When she had gone poor Viola fell on her knees before her dressing table, buried her head in her arms, and poured out a flood of tears and sobs. She felt very much the better for this effusion of sorrow. When her sister came back, she insisted upon helping her to dress, and upon her wearing her prettiest things. She forced upon her acceptance a bit of lace of her own, and declared that now she was to be married she should do her best to appear worthy of her lover's choice. She discharged these offices in stern silence; but, such as they were, they had to do duty as an apology and an atonement; she never made any other.

Now that Lloyd was received by the family as an accepted suitor, nothing remained but to fix the wedding day. It was appointed for the following April, and in the interval preparations were diligently made for the marriage. Lloyd, on his side, was busy with his commercial arrangements, and with establishing a correspondence with the great mercantile house to which he had attached himself in England. He was therefore not so frequent a visitor at Mrs. Willoughby's as during the months of his diffidence and irresolution, and poor Viola had less to suffer than she had feared from the sight of the mutual endearments of the young lovers. Touching his future sister-in-law, Lloyd had a perfectly clear conscience. There had not been a particle of sentiment uttered between them, and he had not the slightest suspicion that she coveted anything more than his fraternal regard. He was quite at his ease; life promised so well, both domestically and financially. The lurid clouds of revolution were as yet twenty years beneath the horizon, and that his connubial felicity should take a tragic turn it was absurd, it was blasphemous, to apprehend. Meanwhile at Mrs. Willoughby's there was a greater rustling of silks, a more rapid clicking of scissors and flying of needles, than ever. Mrs. Willoughby had determined that her daughter should carry from home the most elegant outfit that her money could buy, or that the country could furnish. All the sage women in the county were convened, and their united taste was brought to bear on Perdita's wardrobe. Viola's situation, at this moment, was assuredly not to be envied. The poor girl had an inordinate love of dress, and the very best taste in the world, as her sister perfectly well knew. Viola was tall, she was stately and sweeping, she was made to carry stiff brocade and masses of heavy lace, such as belong to the toilet of a rich man's wife. But Viola sat aloof, with her beautiful arms folded and her head averted, while her mother and sister and the venerable women aforesaid worried and wondered over their materials, oppressed by the multitude of their resources. One day there came in a beautiful piece of white silk, brocaded with celestial blue and silver, sent by the bridegroom himself,—it not being thought amiss in those days that the husband elect should contribute to the bride's trousseau. Perdita was quite at loss to imagine a fashion which should do sufficient honor to the splendor of the material.

"Blue's your color, sister, more than mine," she said, with

appealing eyes. "It's a pity it's not for you. You'd know what to do with it."

Viola got up from her place and looked at the great shining fabric as it lay spread over the back of a chair. Then she took it up in her hands and felt it,—lovingly, as Perdita could see,—and turned about toward the mirror with it. She let it roll down to her feet, and flung the other end over her shoulder, gathering it in about her waist with her white arm bare to the elbow. She threw back her head, and looked at her image, and a hanging tress of her auburn hair fell upon the gorgeous surface of the silk. It made a dazzling picture. The women standing about uttered a little "Ah!" of admiration. "Yes, indeed," said Viola, quietly, "blue is my color." But Perdita could see that her fancy had been stirred, and that she would now fall to work and solve all their silken riddles. And indeed she behaved very well, as Perdita, knowing her insatiable love of millinery, was quite ready to declare. Innumerable yards of lustrous silk and satin, of muslin, velvet, and lace, passed through her cunning hands, without a word of envy coming from her lips. Thanks to her industry, when the wedding day came Perdita was prepared to espouse more of the vanities of life than any fluttering young bride who had yet challenged the sacramental blessing of a New England divine.

It had been arranged that the young couple should go out and spend the first days of their wedded life at the country house of an English gentleman,—a man of rank and a very kind friend to Lloyd. He was an unmarried man; he professed himself delighted to withdraw and leave them for a week to their billing and cooing. After the ceremony at church,—it had been performed by an English parson,—young Mrs. Lloyd hastened back to her mother's house to change her wedding gear for a riding dress. Viola helped her to effect the change, in the little old room in which they had been fond sisters together. Perdita then hurried off to bid farewell to her mother, leaving Viola to follow. The parting was short; the horses were at the door and Arthur impatient to start. But Viola had not followed, and Perdita hastened back to her room, opening the door abruptly. Viola, as usual, was before the glass, but in a position which caused the other to stand still, amazed. She had dressed herself in Perdita's cast-off wedding veil and wreath, and on her neck she had hung the heavy string of pearls which the young girl had received from her husband as a wedding gift. These things had been hastily laid aside, to await their possessor's disposal on her return from the country. Bedizened in this unnatural garb, Viola stood at the mirror, plunging a long look into its depths, and reading Heaven knows what audacious visions. Perdita was horrified. It was a hideous image of their old rivalry come to life again. She made a step toward her sister, as if to pull off the veil and the flowers. But catching her eyes in the glass, she stopped.

"Farewell, Viola," she said. "You might at least have waited till I had got out of the house." And she hurried away from the room.

Mr. Lloyd had purchased in Boston a house which, in the taste of those days, was considered a marvel of elegance and comfort; and here he very soon established himself with his young wife. He was thus separated by a distance of twenty miles from the residence of his mother-in-law. Twenty miles, in that primitive era of roads and conveyances, were as serious a matter as a hundred at the present day, and Mrs. Willoughby saw but little of her daughter during the first twelvemonth of her marriage. She suffered in no small degree from her absence; and her affliction was not diminished by the fact that Viola had fallen into terribly low spirits and was not to be roused or cheered but by change of air and circumstances. The real cause of the young girl's dejection the reader will not be slow to suspect. Mrs. Willoughby and her gossips, however, deemed her complaint a purely physical one, and doubted not that she would obtain relief from the remedy just mentioned. Her mother accordingly proposed on her behalf a visit to certain relatives on the paternal side, established in New York, who had long complained that they were able to see so little of their New England cousins. Viola was dispatched to these good people, under a suitable escort, and remained with them for several months. In the interval her brother Bernard, who had begun the practice of the law, made up his mind to take a wife. Viola came home to the wedding, apparently cured of her heart-ache, with honest roses and lilies in her face, and a proud smile on her lips. Arthur Lloyd came over from Boston to see his brother-in-law married, but without his wife, who was expecting shortly to present him with an heir. It was nearly a year since Viola had seen him. She was glad — she hardly knew why — that Perdita had stayed at home. Arthur looked happy, but he was more grave and solemn than before his marriage.

She thought he looked "interesting,"—for although the word in its modern sense was not then invented, we may be sure that the idea was. The truth is, he was simply preoccupied with his wife's condition. Nevertheless, he by no means failed to observe Viola's beauty and splendor, and how she quite effaced the poor little bride. The allowance that Perdita had enjoyed for her dress had now been transferred to her sister, who turned it to prodigious account. On the morning after the wedding, he had a lady's saddle put on the horse of the servant who had come with him from town, and went out with the young girl for a ride. It was a keen, clear morning in January; the ground was bare and hard, and the horses in good condition,—to say nothing of Viola, who was charming in her hat and plume, and her dark blue riding coat, trimmed with fur. They rode all the morning, they lost their way, and were obliged to stop for dinner at a farmhouse. The early winter dusk had fallen when they got home. Mrs. Willoughby met them with a long face. A messenger had arrived at noon from Mrs. Lloyd; she was beginning to be ill, and desired her husband's immediate return. The young man, at the thought that he had lost several hours, and that by hard riding he might already have been with his wife, uttered a passionate oath. He barely consented to stop for a mouthful of supper, but mounted the messenger's horse and started off at a gallop.

He reached home at midnight. His wife had been delivered of a little girl. "Ah, why weren't you with me?" she said, as he came to her bedside.

"I was out of the house when the man came. I was with Viola," said Lloyd, innocently.

Mrs. Lloyd made a little moan, and turned about. But she continued to do very well, and for a week her improvement was uninterrupted. Finally, however, through some indiscretion in the way of diet or of exposure, it was checked, and the poor lady grew rapidly worse. Lloyd was in despair. It very soon became evident that she was breathing her last. Mrs. Lloyd came to a sense of her approaching end, and declared that she was reconciled with death. On the third evening after the change took place she told her husband that she felt she would not outlast the night. She dismissed her servants, and also requested her mother to withdraw,—Mrs. Willoughby having arrived on the preceding day. She had had her infant placed on the bed beside her, and she lay on her side, with the child against her breast, holding her husband's hands. The night lamp was hidden behind the heavy curtains of the bed, but the room was illumined with a red glow from the immense fire of logs on the hearth.

"It seems strange to die by such a fire as that," the young woman said, feebly trying to smile. "If I had but a little of such fire in my veins! But I've given it all to this little spark of mortality." And she dropped her eyes on her child. Then raising them she looked at her husband with a long penetrating gaze. The last feeling which lingered in her heart was one of mistrust. She had not recovered from the shock which Arthur had given her by telling her that in the hour of her agony he had been with Viola. She trusted her husband very nearly as well as she loved him; but now that she was called away forever, she felt a cold horror of her sister. She felt in her soul that Viola had never ceased to envy her good fortune; and a year of happy security had not effaced the young girl's image, dressed in her wedding garments, and smiling with coveted triumph. Now that Arthur was to be alone, what might not Viola do? She was beautiful, she was engaging; what arts might she not use, what impression might she not make upon the young man's melancholy heart? Mrs. Lloyd looked at her husband in silence. It seemed hard, after all, to doubt of his constancy. His fine eyes were filled with tears; his face was convulsed with weeping; the clasp of his hands was warm and passionate. How noble he looked, how tender, how faithful and devoted! "Nay," thought Perdita, "he's not for such as Viola. He'll never forget me. Nor does Viola truly care for him; she cares only for vanities and finery and jewels." And she dropped her eyes on her white hands, which her husband's liberality had covered with rings, and on the lace ruffles which trimmed the edge of her nightdress. "She covets my rings and my laces more than she covets my husband."

At this moment the thought of her sister's rapacity seemed to cast a dark shadow between her and the helpless figure of her little girl. "Arthur," she said, "you must take off my rings. I shall not be buried in them. One of these days my daughter shall wear them,—my rings and my laces and silks. I had them all brought out and shown me to-day. It's a great wardrobe,—there's not such another in the Province; I can say it without vanity now that I've done with it. It will be a great inheritance for my daughter, when she grows into a young woman. There are things there that a man never buys twice, and if they're lost you'll never again see the like. So you'll watch them well. Some dozen things I've left to Viola; I've named them to my mother. I've given her that blue and silver; it was meant for her; I wore it only once, I looked ill in it. But the rest are to be sacredly kept for this little innocent. It's such a providence that she should be my color; she can wear my gowns; she has her mother's eyes. You know the same fashions come back every twenty years. She can wear my gowns as they are. They'll lie there quietly waiting till she grows into them,—wrapped in camphor and rose leaves, and keeping their colors in the sweet-scented darkness. She shall have black hair, she shall wear my carnation satin. Do you promise me, Arthur?"

"Promise you what, dearest?"

"Promise me to keep your poor little wife's old gowns."

"Are you afraid I'll sell them?"

"No, but that they may get scattered. My mother will have them properly wrapped up, and you shall lay them away under a double lock. Do you know the great chest in the attic, with the iron bands? There's no end to what it will hold. You can lay them all there. My mother and the housekeeper will do it, and give you the key. And you'll keep the key in your secretary, and never give it to any one but your child. Do you promise me?"

"Ah, yes, I promise you," said Lloyd, puzzled at the intensity with which his wife appeared to cling to this idea.

"Will you swear?" repeated Perdita.

"Yes, I swear."

"Well—I trust you—I trust you," said the poor lady, looking into his eyes with eyes in which, if he had suspected her vague apprehensions, he might have read an appeal quite as much as an assurance.

Lloyd bore his bereavement soberly and manfully. A month after his wife's death, in the course of commerce, circumstances arose which offered him an opportunity of going to England. He embraced it as a diversion from gloomy thoughts. He was absent nearly a year, during which his little girl was tenderly nursed and cherished by her grandmother. On his return he had his house again thrown open, and announced his intention of keeping the same state as during his wife's lifetime. It very soon came to be predicted that he would marry again, and there were at least a dozen young women of whom one may say that it was by no fault of theirs that, for six months after his return, the prediction did not come true. During this interval he still left his little daughter in Mrs. Willoughby's hands, the latter assuring him that a change of residence at so tender an age was perilous to her health. Finally, however, he declared that his heart longed for his daughter's presence, and that she must be brought up to town. He sent his coach and his housekeeper to fetch her home. Mrs. Willoughby was in terror lest something should befall her on the road; and, in accordance with this feeling, Viola offered to ride along with her. She could return the next day. So she went up to town with her little niece, and Mr. Lloyd met her on the threshold of his house, overcome with her kindness and with gratitude. Instead of returning the next day, Viola stayed out the week; and when at last she reappeared, she had only come for her clothes. Arthur would not hear of her coming home, nor would the baby. She cried and moaned if Viola left her; and at the sight of her grief Arthur lost his wits, and swore that she was going to die. In fine, nothing would suit them but that Viola should remain until the poor child had grown used to strange faces.

It took two months to bring this consummation about; for it was not until this period had elapsed that Viola took leave of her brother-in-law. Mrs. Willoughby had shaken her head over her daughter's absence; she had declared that it was not becoming, and that it was the talk of the town. She had reconciled herself to it only because, during the young girl's visit, the household enjoyed an unwonted term of peace. Bernard Willoughby had brought his wife home to live, between whom and her sister-in-law there existed a bitter hostility. Viola was perhaps no angel; but in the daily practice of life she was a sufficiently good-natured girl, and if she quarreled with Mrs. Bernard, it was not without provocation. Quarrel, however, she did, to the great annoyance not only of her antagonist, but of the two spectators of these constant altercations. Her stay in the household of her brother-in-law, therefore, would have been delightful, if only because it removed her from contact with the object of her antipathy at home. It was doubly — it was ten times — delightful, in that it kept her near the object of her old passion. Mrs. Lloyd's poignant mistrust had fallen very far short of the truth. Viola's sentiment had been a passion at first, and a passion it remained,—a passion of whose radiant heat, tempered to the delicate state of his feelings, Mr. Lloyd very soon felt the influence. Lloyd, as I have hinted, was not a modern Petrarch; it was not in his nature to practice an ideal constancy. He had not been many days in the house with his sister-in-law before he began to assure himself that she was, in the language of that day, a devilish fine woman. Whether Viola really practiced those insidious arts that her sister had been tempted to impute to her it is needless to inquire. It is enough to say that she found means to appear to the very best advantage. She used to seat herself every morning before the great fireplace in the dining room, at work upon a piece of tapestry, with her little niece disporting herself on the carpet at her feet, or on the train of her dress, and playing with her woolen balls. Lloyd would have been a very stupid fellow if he had remained insensible to the rich suggestions of this charming picture. He was prodigiously fond of his little girl, and was never weary of taking her in his arms and tossing her up and down, and making her crow with delight. Very often, however, he would venture upon greater liberties than the young lady was yet prepared to allow, and she would suddenly vociferate her displeasure. Viola would then drop her tapestry, and put out her handsome hands with the serious smile of the young girl whose virgin fancy has revealed to her all a mother's healing arts. Lloyd would give up the child, their eyes would meet, their hands would touch, and Viola would extinguish the little girl's sobs upon the snowy folds of the kerchief that crossed her bosom. Her dignity was perfect, and nothing could be more discreet than the manner in which she accepted her brother-in-law's hospitality. It may be almost said, perhaps, that there was something harsh in her reserve. Lloyd had a provoking feeling that she was in the house, and yet that she was unapproachable. Half an hour after supper, at the very outset of the long winter evenings, she would light her candle, and make the young man a most respectful courtesy, and march off to bed. If these were arts, Viola was a great artist. But their effect was so gentle, so gradual, they were calculated to work upon the young widower's fancy with such a finely shaded *crescendo*, that, as the reader has seen, several weeks elapsed before Viola began to feel sure that her return would cover her outlay. When this became morally certain, she packed up her trunk, and returned to her mother's house.

HENRY JAMES IN HIS STUDY

For three days she waited; on the fourth Mr. Lloyd made his appearance,—a respectful but ardent suitor. Viola heard him out with great humility, and accepted him with infinite modesty. It is hard to imagine that Mrs. Lloyd should have forgiven her husband; but if anything might have disarmed her resentment, it would have been the ceremonious continence of this interview. Viola imposed upon her lover but a short probation. They were married, as was becoming, with great privacy,—almost with secrecy,—in the hope perhaps, as was waggishly remarked at the time, that the late Mrs. Lloyd wouldn't hear of it.

The marriage was to all appearance a happy one, and each party obtained what each had desired—Lloyd "a devilish fine woman," and Viola—but Viola's desires, as the reader will have observed, have remained a good deal of a mystery. There were, indeed, two blots upon their felicity; but time would, perhaps, efface them. During the first three years of her marriage Mrs. Lloyd failed to become a mother, and her husband on his side suffered heavy losses of money. This latter circumstance compelled a material retrenchment in his expenditure, and Viola was perforce less of a great lady than her sister had been. She contrived, however, to sustain with unbroken consistency the part of an elegant woman, although it must be confessed that it required the exercise of more ingenuity than belongs to your real aristocratic repose. She had long since ascertained that her sister's immense wardrobe had been sequestrated for the benefit of her daughter, and that it lay languishing in thankless gloom in the dusty attic. It was a revolting thought that these exquisite fabrics should await the commands of a little girl who sat in a high chair and ate bread and milk with a wooden spoon. Viola had the good taste, however, to say nothing about the matter until several months had expired. Then, at last, she timidly broached it to her husband. Was it not a pity that so much finery should be lost?—for lost it would be, what with colors fading, and moths eating it up, and the change of fashions. But Lloyd gave so abrupt and peremptory a negative to her inquiry, that she saw that for the present her attempt was vain. Six months went by, however, and brought with them new needs and new fancies. Viola's thoughts hovered lovingly about her sister's relics. She went up and looked at the chest in which they lay imprisoned. There was a sullen defiance in its three great padlocks and its iron bands which only quickened her desires. There was something exasperating in its incorruptible immobility. It was like a grim and grizzled old household servant, who locks his jaws over a family secret. And then there was a look of capacity in its vast extent, and a sound as of dense fullness, when Viola knocked its side with the toe of her little slipper, which caused her to flush with baffled longing. "It's absurd," she cried; "it's improper, it's wicked;" and she forthwith resolved upon another attack upon her husband. On the following day, after dinner, when he had had his wine, she bravely began it. But he cut her short with great sternness.

"Once for all, Viola," said he, "it's out of the question. I shall be gravely displeased if you return to the matter."

"Very good," said Viola. "I'm glad to learn the value at which I'm held. Great Heaven!" she cried, "I'm a happy woman. It's an agreeable thing to feel one's self sacrificed to a caprice!" And her eyes filled with tears of anger and disappointment.

Lloyd had a good-natured man's horror of a woman's sobs, and he attempted — I may say he condescended — to explain. "It's not a caprice, dear, it's a promise," he said, — "an oath."

"An oath? It's a pretty matter for oaths! and to whom, pray?"

"To Perdita," said the young man, raising his eyes for an instant, but immediately dropping them.

"Perdita, — ah, Perdita!" and Viola's tears broke forth. Her bosom heaved with stormy sobs, — sobs which were the long-deferred counterpart of the violent fit of weeping in which she had indulged herself on the night when she discovered her sister's betrothal. She had hoped, in her better moments, that she had done with her jealousy; but her temper, on that occasion, had taken an ineffaceable fold. "And pray, what right," she cried, "had Perdita to dispose of my future? What right had she to bind you to meanness and cruelty? Ah, I occupy a dignified place, and I make a very fine figure! I'm welcome to what Perdita has left! And what has she left? I never knew till now how little! Nothing, nothing, nothing."

This was very poor logic, but it was very good passion. Lloyd put his arm around his wife's waist and tried to kiss her, but she shook him off with magnificent scorn. Poor fellow! he had coveted a "devilish fine woman," and he had got one. Her scorn was intolerable. He walked away with his ears tingling,—irresolute, distracted. Before him was his secretary, and in it the sacred key which with his own hand he had turned in the triple lock. He marched up and opened it, and took the key from a secret drawer, wrapped in a little packet which he had sealed with his own honest bit of blazonry. *Teneo*, said the motto,—"I hold." But he was ashamed to put it back. He flung it upon the table beside his wife.

"Keep it!" she cried. "I want it not. I hate it!"

"I wash my hands of it," cried her husband. "God forgive me!"

Mrs. Lloyd gave an indignant shrug of her shoulders, and swept out of the room, while the young man retreated by another door. Ten minutes later Mrs. Lloyd returned, and found the room occupied by her little stepdaughter and the nursery maid. The key was not on the table. She glanced at the child. The child was perched on a chair with the packet in her hands. She had broken the seal with her own little fingers. Mrs. Lloyd hastily took possession of the key.

At the habitual supper hour Arthur Lloyd came back from his countingroom. It was the month of June, and supper was served by daylight. The meal was placed on the table, but Mrs. Lloyd failed to make her appearance. The servant whom his master sent to call her came back with the assurance that her room was empty, and that the women informed him that she had not been seen since dinner. They had in truth observed her to have been in tears, and, supposing her to be shut up in her chamber, had not disturbed her. Her husband called her name in various parts of the house, but without response. At last it occurred to him that he might find her by taking the way to the attic. The thought gave him a strange feeling of discomfort, and he bade his servants remain behind, wishing no witness in his quest. He reached the foot of the staircase leading to the topmost flat, and stood with his hand on the banisters, pronouncing his wife's name. His voice trembled. He called again, louder and more firmly. The only sound which disturbed the absolute silence was a faint echo of his own tones, repeating his question under the great eaves. He nevertheless felt irresistibly moved to ascend the staircase. It opened upon a wide hall, lined with wooden closets, and terminating in a window which looked westward, and admitted the last rays of the sun. Before the window stood the great chest. Before the chest, on her knees, the young man saw with amazement and horror the figure of his wife. In an instant he crossed the interval between them, bereft of utterance. The lid of the chest stood open, exposing, amid their perfumed napkins, its treasure of stuffs and jewels. Viola had fallen backward from a kneeling posture, with one hand supporting her on the floor and the other pressed to her heart. On her limbs was the stiffness of death, and on her face, in the fading light of the sun, the terror of something more than death. Her lips were parted in entreaty, in dismay, in agony; and on her bloodless brow and cheeks there glowed the marks of ten hideous wounds from two vengeful ghostly hands.

EVENING PRIMROSES.[1]

BY HELEN GRAY CONE.

(1859-.)

WHILE gray was the summer evening,
  Hast never a small sprite seen
Lighting the fragrant torches
  For the feast of the Fairy Queen?

The buds on the primrose bushes
  Upspring into yellow light
But ever the wee deft spirit
  Escapes my bewildered sight.

Yet oft, through the dusky garden,
  A dainty white moth will fly,
Or, pink as a pink rose petal,
  One lightly will waver by.

Perhaps 'tis the shape he comes in,
  Perhaps it is he indeed,
Sir Moth, or the merry Cobweb,
  Or the whimsical Mustard Seed!

[1] Copyright by Houghton, Mifflin & Co. Used by permissic.

THE PUPPY: A PORTRAIT.[1]

By LOUISE IMOGEN GUINEY

(From "Patrins.")

[Louise Imogen Guiney: An American poet and essayist; born in Boston, Mass., January 17, 1861. She was educated at the Convent of the Sacred Heart, Providence, R.I., and began her literary career as a contributor to current periodicals. Her published volumes include: "Songs at the Start" (1884), "Goosequill Papers" (1885), "The White Sail" (1887), "Brownies and Bogies" (1888), "Monsieur Henri" (1892), "A Roadside Harp" (1893), "A Little English Gallery," "Lovers' Saint Ruths," and "Patrins" (1897).]

He is the sixty-sixth in direct descent, and his coat is like amber damask, and his blue eyes are the most winning that you ever saw. They seem to proclaim him as much too good for the vulgar world, and worthy of such zeal and devotion as you, only you, could give to his helpless infancy. And, with a blessing upon the Abbot of Clairvaux, who is popularly supposed to have invented his species, you carry him home from the Bench show, and in the morning, when you are told that he has eaten a yard and a quarter of the new stair carpet, you look into those dreamy eyes again: no reproach shall reach him, you swear, because you stand forevermore between. And he grows great in girth, and in character the very chronicle and log book of his noble ancestry; he may be erratic, but he puts charm and distinction into everything he does. Your devotedness to his welfare keeps him healthful and honest, and absurdly partial to the squeak of your boots, or the imperceptible aroma which, as it would seem, you dispense, a mile away. The thing which pleases you most is his ingenuous childishness. It is a fresh little soul in the rogue's body: —

> Him Nature giveth for defense,
> His formidable innocence.

You see him touch pitch every day, associating with the sewer-building Italians, with their strange oaths; with affected and cynical "sales ladies" in shops (she of the grape stall being clearly his too-seldom-relenting goddess); and with the bony Thomas cat down street, who is an acknowledged anarchist, and

[1] Copyright, 1897, by Copeland & Day. Used by permission.

whose infrequent suppers have made him sour-complexioned towards society, and "thereby disallowed him," as dear Walton would say, "to be a competent judge." But Pup loses nothing of his sweet congenital absent-mindedness; your bringing up sits firmly upon him and keeps him young. He expands into a giant, and such as meet him on a lonely road have religion until he has passed. Seven, nine, ten months go over his white-hooded head; and behold, he is nigh a year old, and still Uranian. He begins to accumulate facts, for his observation of late has not been unscientific; but he cannot generalize, and on every first occasion he puts his foot in it. A music box transfixes him; the English language, proceeding from a parrot in a cage, shakes his reason for days. A rocking-horse on a piazza draws from him the only bad word he knows. He sees no obligation to respect persons with mumps, or with very red beards, or with tools and dinner pails; in the last instance, he acts advisedly against honest labor, as he perceives that most overalls have kicks in them. Following Plato, he would reserve his haughty demeanor for slaves and servants. Moreover, before the undemonstrated he comes hourly to a pause. If a wheelbarrow, unknown hitherto among vehicles, approach him from his suburban hill, he is aware of the supernatural; but he will not flinch, as he was wont to do once; rather will he stand four-square, with eyebrows and crinkled ears vocal with wonder and horror. Then the man back of the moving bulk speaks over his truck to you, in the clear April evening: "Begorra, 'tis his furrust barry!" and you love the man for his accurate, affectionate sense of the situation. When Pup is too open-mouthed and curious, when he dilates, in fact, with the wrong emotion, it reflects upon you, and reveals the flaws in your educational system. He blurts out dire things before fine ladies. If he hear one of them declaiming, with Delsarte gestures, in a drawing-room, he appears in the doorway, undergoing symptoms of acutest distress, and singing her down, professedly for her own sake; and afterward he pities her so, and is so chivalrously drawn toward her in her apparent aberration, that he lies for hours on the flounce of her gown, eying you, and calumniating you somewhat by his vicarious groans and sighs. But ever after, Pup admits the recitation of tragic selections as one human folly more.

He is so big and so unsophisticated, that you daily feel the incongruity, and wish, in a vague sort of way, that there was a street boarding school in your town, where he could rough it away from an adoring family, and learn to be responsible and self-opinionated, like other dogs. He has a maternal uncle, on the estate across the field: a double-chinned tawny ogre, good-natured as a baby, and utterly rash and improvident, whose society you cannot covet for your tender charge. One fine day, Pup is low with the distemper, and evidence is forthcoming that he has visited, under his uncle's guidance, the much-deceased lobster thrown into hotel tubs. After weeks of anxious nursing, rubbings in oil, and steamings with vinegar, during which time he coughs and wheezes in a heartbreaking imitation of advanced consumption, he is left alone a moment on his warm rug, with the thermometer in his special apartment steady at seventy-eight degrees, and plunges out into the winter blast. Hours later, he returns; and the vision of his vagabond uncle, slinking around the house, announces to you in what companionship he has been. Plastered to the skull in mud and icicles, wet to the bone, jaded, guilty, and doomed now, of course, to die, Pup retires behind the kitchen table. The next morning he is well. The moral, to him at least, is that our uncle is an astute and unappreciated person, and a genuine man of the world.

Yet our uncle, with all his laxity, has an honorable heart, and practices the *maxima reverentia puero*. It is not from him that Pup shall learn his little share of iniquity. Meanwhile, illumination is nearing him in the shape of a little old white bull terrier of uncertain parentage, with one ear, and a scar on his neck, and depravity in the very lift of his stumped tail. This active imp, recently come to live in the neighborhood, fills you with forebodings. You know that Pup must grow up sometime, must take his chances, must fight and be fooled, must err and repent, must exhaust the dangerous knowledge of the great university for which his age at last befits him. The ordeal will harm neither him nor you: and yet you cannot help an anxious look at him, full four feet tall from crown to toe, and with a leg like an obelisk, preserving unseasonably his ambiguous early air of exaggerated goodness. One day he follows you from the station, and meets the small Mephisto on the homeward path. They dig a bone together, and converse behind trees; and when you call Pup, he snorts his initial defiance, and dances away in the tempter's wake. Finally, your whistle compels him, and he comes soberly forward. By this time the ringleader terrier is departing, with a diabolical wink. You remember that, a moment before, he stood on a mound, whispering in your innocent's beautiful dangling ear, and you glance sharply at Pup. Yes, it has happened! He will never seem quite the same again, with

— the contagion of the world's slow stain

beginning in his candid eyes. He is a dog now. He knows.

GEORGE BORROW AND THE PUBLISHER.[1]

(From "Lavengro.")

[George Borrow, philologist, was born at East Dereham, Norfolk, England, in 1803, and was educated chiefly in Edinburgh, Scotland. He published "Faustus" (translated from German, 1825), "Romantic Ballads" (translated from Danish, 1826), "Targum" (1835), "The Zincali; or, an Account of the Gypsies in Spain" (2 vols., 1841), "The Bible in Spain" (3 vols., 1843), "Lavengro" (1851), "The Romany Rye" (1857), "The Sleeping Bird" (translated from Cambrian-British, 1860), "Wild Wales" (2 vols., 1862), and "Romano Lavo-Lil" (1874). He died at Oulton, Norfolk, England, July 30, 1881.]

There were two individuals in the room in which I now found myself; it was a small study, surrounded with bookcases, the window looking out upon the square. Of these individuals he who appeared to be the principal stood with his back to the fireplace. He was a tall stout man, about sixty, dressed in a loose morning gown. The expression of his countenance would have been bluff but for a certain sinister glance, and his complexion might have been called rubicund but for a considerable tinge of bilious yellow. He eyed me askance as I entered. The other, a pale, shriveled-looking person, sat at a table apparently engaged with an account book; he took no manner of notice of me, never once lifting his eyes from the page before him.

"Well, sir, what is your pleasure?" said the big man, in a rough tone, as I stood there, looking at him wistfully — as well I might — for upon that man, at the time of which I am speaking, my principal, I may say my only, hopes rested.

"Sir," said I, "my name is so-and-so, and I am the bearer of a letter to you from Mr. so-and-so, an old friend and correspondent of yours."

[1] By permission of Mr. Murray. (Price 2*s.* 6*d.*)

The countenance of the big man instantly lost the suspicious and lowering expression which it had hitherto exhibited; he strode forward, and, seizing me by the hand, gave me a violent squeeze.

"My dear sir," said he, "I am rejoiced to see you in London. I have been long anxious for the pleasure — we are old friends, though we have never before met. Taggart," said he to the man who sat at the desk, "this is our excellent correspondent, the friend and pupil of our other excellent correspondent."

The pale, shriveled-looking man slowly and deliberately raised his head from the account book, and surveyed me for a moment or two; not the slightest emotion was observable in his countenance. It appeared to me, however, that I could detect a droll twinkle in his eye: his curiosity, if he had any, was soon gratified; he made me a kind of bow, pulled out a snuffbox, took a pinch of snuff, and again bent his head over the page.

"And now, my dear sir," said the big man, "pray sit down, and tell me the cause of your visit. I hope you intend to remain here a day or two."

"More than that," said I; "I am come to take up my abode in London."

"Glad to hear it; and what have you been about of late? got anything which will suit me? Sir, I admire your style of writing, and your manner of thinking; and I am much obliged to my good friend and correspondent for sending me some of your productions. I inserted them all, and wished there had been more of them — quite original, sir, quite: took with the public, especially the essay about the non-existence of anything. I don't exactly agree with you though; I have my own peculiar ideas about matter — as you know, of course, from the book I have published. Nevertheless, a very pretty piece of speculative philosophy — no such thing as matter — impossible that there should be — *ex nihilo* — what is the Greek? I have forgot — very pretty indeed; very original."

"I am afraid, sir, it was very wrong to write such trash, and yet more to allow it to be published."

"Trash! not at all; a very pretty piece of speculative philosophy; of course you were wrong in saying there is no world. The world must exist, to have the shape of a pear; and that the world is shaped like a pear, and not like an apple, as the fools of Oxford say, I have satisfactorily proved in my book.

Now, if there were no world, what would become of my system? But what do you propose to do in London?"

"Here is the letter, sir," said I, "of our good friend, which I have not yet given to you; I believe it will explain to you the circumstances under which I come."

He took the letter, and perused it with attention. "Hem!" said he, with a somewhat altered manner, "my friend tells me that you are come up to London with the view of turning your literary talents to account, and desires me to assist you in my capacity of publisher in bringing forth two or three works which you have prepared. My good friend is perhaps not aware that for some time past I have given up publishing — was obliged to do so — had many severe losses — do nothing at present in that line, save sending out the Magazine once a month; and, between ourselves, am thinking of disposing of that — wish to retire — high time at my age — so you see ——"

"I am very sorry, sir, to hear that you cannot assist me" (and I remember that I felt very nervous); "I had hoped ——"

"A losing trade, I assure you, sir; literature is a drug. Taggart, what o'clock is it?"

"Well, sir!" said I, rising, "as you cannot assist me, I will now take my leave; I thank you sincerely for your kind reception, and will trouble you no longer."

"Oh, don't go. I wish to have some further conversation with you; and perhaps I may hit upon some plan to benefit you. I honor merit, and always make a point to encourage it when I can; but — Taggart, go to the bank, and tell them to dishonor the bill twelve months after date for thirty pounds which becomes due to-morrow. I am dissatisfied with that fellow who wrote the fairy tales, and intend to give him all the trouble in my power. Make haste."

Taggart did not appear to be in any particular haste. First of all, he took a pinch of snuff, then, rising from his chair, slowly and deliberately drew his wig, for he wore a wig of a brown color, rather more over his forehead than it had previously been, buttoned his coat, and, taking his hat, and an umbrella which stood in a corner, made me a low bow, and quitted the room.

"Well, sir, where were we? Oh, I remember, we were talking about merit. Sir, I always wish to encourage merit, especially when it comes so highly recommended as in the present instance. Sir, my good friend and correspondent speaks of you in the highest terms. Sir, I honor my good friend, and have the highest respect for his opinion in all matters connected with literature — rather eccentric though. Sir, my good friend has done my periodical more good and more harm than all the rest of my correspondents. Sir, I shall never forget the sensation caused by the appearance of his article about a certain personage whom he proved — and I think satisfactorily — to have been a legionary soldier — rather startling, was it not? The S—— of the world a common soldier, in a marching regiment — original, but startling; sir, I honor my good friend."

"So you have renounced publishing, sir," said I, "with the exception of the Magazine?"

"Why, yes; except now and then, under the rose; the old coachman, you know, likes to hear the whip. Indeed, at the present moment, I am thinking of starting a Review on an entirely new and original principle; and it just struck me that you might be of high utility in the undertaking — what do you think of the matter?"

"I should be happy, sir, to render you any assistance, but I am afraid the employment you propose requires other qualifications than I possess; however, I can make the essay. My chief intention in coming to London was to lay before the world what I had prepared; and I had hoped by your assistance ——"

"Ah! I see, ambition! Ambition is a very pretty thing; but, sir, we must walk before we run, according to the old saying — what is that you have got under your arm?"

"One of the works to which I was alluding; the one, indeed, which I am most anxious to lay before the world, as I hope to derive from it both profit and reputation."

"Indeed! what do you call it?"

"Ancient songs of Denmark, heroic and romantic, translated by myself; with notes philological, critical, and historical."

"Then, sir, I assure you that your time and labor have been entirely flung away; nobody would read your ballads, if you were to give them to the world to-morrow."

"I am sure, sir, that you would say otherwise if you would permit me to read one to you;" and, without waiting for the answer of the big man, nor indeed so much as looking at him, to see whether he was inclined or not to hear me, I undid my manuscript, and, with a voice trembling with eagerness, I read to the following effect: —

"Buckshank bold and Elfinstone,
And more than I can mention here,
They caused to be built so stout a ship,
And unto Iceland they would steer.

"They launched the ship upon the main,
Which bellowed like a wrathful bear;
Down to the bottom the vessel sank,
A laidly Trold has dragged it there.

"Down to the bottom sank young Roland,
And round about he groped awhile;
Until he found the path which led
Unto the bower of Ellenlyle."

"Stop!" said the publisher; "very pretty indeed, and very original; beats Scott hollow, and Percy too: but, sir, the day for these things is gone by; nobody at present cares for Percy, nor for Scott either, save as a novelist; sorry to discourage merit, sir, but what can I do! What else have you got?"

"The songs of Ab Gwilym, the Welsh bard, also translated by myself, with notes critical, philological, and historical."

"Pass on — what else?"

"Nothing else," said I, folding up my manuscript with a sigh, "unless it be a romance in the German style; on which, I confess, I set very little value."

"Wild?"

"Yes, sir, very wild."

"Like the Miller of the Black Valley?"

"Yes, sir, very much like the Miller of the Black Valley."

"Well, that's better," said the publisher; "and yet, I don't know, I question whether any one at present cares for the miller himself. No, sir, the time for those things is also gone by; German, at present, is a drug; and, between ourselves, nobody has contributed to make it so more than my good friend and correspondent; — but, sir, I see you are a young gentleman of infinite merit, and I always wish to encourage merit. Don't you think you could write a series of evangelical tales?"

"Evangelical tales, sir?"

"Yes, sir, evangelical novels."

"Something in the style of Herder?"

"Herder is a drug, sir; nobody cares for Herder — thanks to my good friend. Sir, I have in yon drawer a hundred pages about Herder, which I dare not insert in my periodical; it would sink it, sir. No, sir, something in the style of the 'Dairyman's Daughter.'"

"I never heard of the work till the present moment."

"Then, sir, procure it by all means. Sir, I could afford as much as ten pounds for a well-written tale in the style of the 'Dairyman's Daughter'; that is the kind of literature, sir, that sells at the present day! It is not the Miller of the Black Valley — no, sir, nor Herder either, that will suit the present taste; the evangelical body is becoming very strong, sir; the canting scoundrels ——"

"But, sir, surely you would not pander to a scoundrelly taste?"

"Then, sir, I must give up business altogether. Sir, I have a great respect for the goddess Reason — an infinite respect, sir; indeed, in my time, I have made a great many sacrifices for her; but, sir, I cannot altogether ruin myself for the goddess Reason. Sir, I am a friend to Liberty, as is well known; but I must also be a friend to my own family. It is with the view of providing for a son of mine that I am about to start the Review of which I was speaking. He has taken into his head to marry, sir, and I must do something for him, for he can do but little for himself. Well, sir, I am a friend to Liberty, as I said before, and likewise a friend to Reason; but I tell you frankly that the Review which I intend to get up under the rose, and present him with when it is established, will be conducted on Oxford principles."

"Orthodox principles, I suppose you mean, sir?"

"I do, sir; I am no linguist, but I believe the words are synonymous."

Much more conversation passed between us, and it was agreed that I should become a contributor to the Oxford Review. I stipulated, however, that, as I knew little of politics, and cared less, no other articles should be required from me than such as were connected with belles-lettres and philology; to this the big man readily assented. "Nothing will be required from you," said he, "but what you mention; and now and then, perhaps, a paper on metaphysics. You understand German, and perhaps it would be desirable that you should review Kant; and in a review of Kant, sir, you could introduce to advantage your peculiar notions about *ex nihilo.*" He then reverted to the subject of the "Dairyman's Daughter," which I promised to take into consideration. As I was going away, he invited me to dine with him on the ensuing Sunday.

"That's a strange man!" said I to myself, after I had left the house; "he is evidently very clever; but I cannot say that I like him much, with his Oxford Reviews and Dairyman's Daughters. But what can I do? I am almost without a friend in the world. I wish I could find some one who would publish my ballads, or my songs of Ab Gwilym. In spite of what the big man says, I am convinced that, once published, they would bring me much fame and profit. But how is this?—what a beautiful sun!—the porter was right in saying that the day would clear up—I will now go to my dingy lodging, lock up my manuscripts, and then take a stroll about the big city." . . .

On the Sunday I was punctual to my appointment to dine with the publisher. As I hurried along the square in which his house stood, my thoughts were fixed so intently on the great man that I passed by him without seeing him. He had observed me, however, and joined me just as I was about to knock at the door. "Let us take a turn in the square," said he, "we shall not dine for half an hour."

"Well," said he, as we were walking in the square, "what have you been doing since I last saw you?"

"I have been looking about London," said I, "and I have bought the 'Dairyman's Daughter'; here it is."

"Pray put it up," said the publisher; "I don't want to look at such trash. Well, do you think you could write anything like it?"

"I do not," said I.

"How is that?" said the publisher, looking at me.

"Because," said I, "the man who wrote it seems to be perfectly well acquainted with his subject; and, moreover, to write from the heart."

"By the subject you mean ——"

"Religion."

"And ain't you acquainted with religion?"

"Very little."

"I am sorry for that," said the publisher, seriously, "for he who sets up for an author ought to be acquainted not only with religion, but religions, and indeed with all subjects, like my good friend in the country. It is well that I have changed my mind about the 'Dairyman's Daughter,' or I really don't know whom I could apply to on the subject at the present moment, unless to himself; and after all I question whether his style is exactly suited for an evangelical novel."

"Then you do not wish for an imitation of the 'Dairyman's Daughter'?"

"I do not, sir; I have changed my mind, as I told you before; I wish to employ you in another line, but will communicate to you my intentions after dinner."

At dinner, beside the publisher and myself, were present his wife and son with his newly married bride; the wife appeared a quiet respectable woman, and the young people looked very happy and good-natured; not so the publisher, who occasionally eyed both with contempt and dislike. Connected with this dinner there was one thing remarkable: the publisher took no animal food, but contented himself with feeding voraciously on rice and vegetables prepared in various ways.

"You eat no animal food, sir?" said I.

"I do not, sir," said he; "I have forsworn it upwards of twenty years. In one respect, sir, I am a Brahmin. I abhor taking away life—the brutes have as much right to live as ourselves."

"But," said I, "if the brutes were not killed, there would be such a superabundance of them that the land would be overrun with them."

"I do not think so, sir; few are killed in India, and yet there is plenty of room."

"But," said I, "Nature intended that they should be destroyed, and the brutes themselves prey upon one another, and it is well for themselves and the world that they do so. What would be the state of things if every insect, bird, and worm were left to perish of old age?"

"We will change the subject," said the publisher; "I have never been a friend of unprofitable discussions."

I looked at the publisher with some surprise; I had not been accustomed to be spoken to so magisterially; his countenance was dressed in a portentous frown, and his eye looked more sinister than ever; at that moment he put me in mind of some of those despots of whom I had read in the history of Morocco, whose word was law. He merely wants power, thought I to myself, to be a regular Muley Mehemet; and then I sighed, for I remembered how very much I was in the power of that man.

The dinner over, the publisher nodded to his wife, who departed, followed by her daughter-in-law. The son looked as if he would willingly have attended them; he, however, remained seated; and, a small decanter of wine being placed on the table, the publisher filled two glasses, one of which he handed to myself, and the other to his son, saying, "Suppose you two drink to the success of the Review. I would join you," said he, addressing himself to me, "but I drink no wine; if I am a Brahmin with respect to meat, I am a Mahometan with respect to wine."

So the son and I drank success to the Review, and then the young man asked me various questions; for example—How I liked London?—Whether I did not think it a very fine place?—Whether I was at the play the night before?—and whether I was in the park that afternoon? He seemed preparing to ask me some more questions; but, receiving a furious look from his father, he became silent, filled himself a glass of wine, drank it off, looked at the table for about a minute, then got up, pushed back his chair, made me a bow, and left the room.

"Is that young gentleman, sir," said I, "well versed in the principles of criticism?"

"He is not, sir," said the publisher; "and, if I place him at the head of the Review ostensibly, I do it merely in the hope of procuring him a maintenance; of the principle of a thing he knows nothing, except that the principle of bread is wheat, and that the principle of that wine is grape. Will you take another glass?"

I looked at the decanter; but, not feeling altogether so sure as the publisher's son with respect to the principle of what it contained, I declined taking any more.

"No, sir," said the publisher, adjusting himself in his chair, "he knows nothing about criticism, and will have nothing more to do with the reviewals than carrying about the books to those who have to review them; the real conductor of the Review will be a widely different person, to whom I will, when convenient, introduce you. And now we will talk of the matter which we touched upon before dinner: I told you then that I had changed my mind with respect to you; I have been considering the state of the market, sir, the book market, and I have come to the conclusion that, though you might be profitably employed upon evangelical novels, you could earn more money for me, sir, and consequently for yourself, by a compilation of Newgate lives and trials."

"Newgate lives and trials!"

"Yes, sir," said the publisher, "Newgate lives and trials; and now, sir, I will briefly state to you the services which I expect you to perform, and the terms which I am willing to grant. I expect you, sir, to compile six volumes of Newgate lives and trials, each volume to contain by no manner of means less than one thousand pages; the remuneration which you will receive when the work is completed will be fifty pounds, which is likewise intended to cover any expenses you may incur in procuring books, papers, and manuscripts necessary for the compilation. Such will be one of your employments, sir, — such the terms. In the second place, you will be expected to make yourself useful in the Review — generally useful, sir — doing whatever is required of you; for it is not customary, at least with me, to permit writers, especially young writers, to choose their subjects. In these two departments, sir, namely compilation and reviewing, I had yesterday, after due consideration, determined upon employing you. I had intended to employ you no farther, sir — at least for the present; but, sir, this morning I received a letter from my valued friend in the country, in which he speaks in terms of strong admiration (I don't overstate) of your German acquirements. Sir, he says that it would be a thousand pities if your knowledge of the German language should be lost to the world, or even permitted to sleep, and he entreats me to think of some plan by which it may be turned to account. Sir, I am at all times willing, if possible, to oblige my worthy friend, and likewise to encourage merit and talent; I have, therefore, determined to employ you in German."

"Sir," said I, rubbing my hands, "you are very kind, and so is our mutual friend; I shall be happy to make myself useful in German; and if you think a good translation from Goethe — his 'Sorrows' for example, or more particularly his 'Faust' ——"

"Sir," said the publisher, "Goethe is a drug; his 'Sorrows' are a drug, so is his 'Faustus,' more especially the last, since that fool —— rendered him into English. No, sir, I do not want you to translate Goethe or anything belonging to him; nor do I want you to translate anything from the German; what I want you to do is to translate into German. I am willing to encourage merit, sir; and, as my good friend in his last letter has spoken very highly of your German acquirements, I have determined that you shall translate my book of philosophy into German."

"Your book of philosophy into German, sir?"

"Yes, sir; my book of philosophy into German. I am not a drug, sir, in Germany as Goethe is here, no more is my book. I intend to print the translation at Leipsic, sir; and if it turns out a profitable speculation, as I make no doubt it will, provided the translation be well executed, I will make you some remuneration. Sir, your remuneration will be determined by the success of your translation."

"But, sir —— "

"Sir," said the publisher, interrupting me, "you have heard my intentions; I consider that you ought to feel yourself highly gratified by my intentions towards you; it is not frequently that I deal with a writer, especially a young writer, as I have done with you. And now, sir, permit me to inform you that I wish to be alone. This is Sunday afternoon, sir; I never go to church, but I am in the habit of spending part of every Sunday afternoon alone — profitably I hope, sir — in musing on the magnificence of nature and the moral dignity of man."

A BALLAD OF LONDON.[1]

By RICHARD LE GALLIENNE.

(1864-.)

Ah, London! London! our delight,
Great flower that opens but at night,
Great City of the Midnight Sun,
Whose day begins when day is done.

Lamp after lamp against the sky
Opens a sudden beaming eye,
Leaping alight on either hand
The iron lilies of the Strand.

[1] By permission of Mr. John Lane.

Like dragon flies, the hansoms hover,
With jeweled eyes, to catch the lover;
The streets are full of lights and loves,
Soft gowns, and flutter of nocturnal doves.

The human moths about the light
Dash and cling close in dazed delight,
And burn and laugh, the world and wife,
For this is London, this is life!

Upon thy petals butterflies,
But at thy root, some say, there lies
A world of weeping trodden things,
Poor worms that have not eyes or wings.

From out corruption of their woe
Springs this bright flower that charms us so;
Men die and rot deep out of sight
To keep this jungle flower bright.

Paris and London, World Flowers twain
Wherewith the World Tree blooms again,
Since time hath gathered Babylon,
And withered Rome still withers on.

Sidon and Tyre were such as ye—
How bright they shone upon the Tree!
But Time hath gathered, both are gone,
And no man sails to Babylon.

Ah, London! London! our delight,
For thee, too, eternal night;
And Circe Paris hath no charm
To stay Time's unrelenting arm.

Time and his moths shall eat up all;
Your chiming towers, proud and tall,
He shall most utterly abase,
And set a desert in their place.

A MAN OF GREAT PROJECTS.[1]

By IVAN SERGYEVICH TURGENIEFF.

(From "Rudin": translated by Constance Garnet.)

[IVAN SERGYEVICH TURGENIEFF, one of the most celebrated of modern Russian novelists, was born at Orel, Russia, November 9, 1818. Educated at Moscow, St. Petersburg, and Berlin, he entered the civil service, and established his reputation as an author with "Sketches from the Diary of a Sportsman" (1845–1847). In 1852 some remarks on Russian officialism, made in an obituary letter on Gogol, led to his being imprisoned and afterwards banished for several years to the interior of Russia. He subsequently lived in Baden-Baden, and after the Franco-Prussian War removed to Paris, where he mainly resided until his death, September 3, 1883, at Bougival. Among his chief novels are: "Dmitri Rudin," "A Nest of Nobles," "Helene" (translated as "On the Eve"), "Fathers and Sons," "Smoke," and "Virgin Soil." They have been translated into many languages, — into French largely by the author himself.]

SEVEN o'clock struck, and they were all assembled again in the drawing-room.

"He is not coming, clearly," said Darya Mihaïlovna.

But, behold, the rumble of a carriage was heard: a small tarantas drove into the court, and a few instants later a footman entered the drawing-room and gave Darya Mihaïlovna a note on a silver salver. She glanced through it, and turning to the footman asked: —

"But where is the gentleman who brought this letter?"

"He is sitting in the carriage. Shall I ask him to come up?"

"Ask him to do so."

The man went out.

"Fancy, how vexatious!" continued Darya Mihaïlovna, "the baron has received a summons to return at once to Petersburg. He has sent me his essay by a certain Mr. Rudin, a friend of his. The baron wanted to introduce him to me — he speaks very highly of him. But how vexatious it is! I had hoped the baron would stay here for some time."

"Dmitri Nikolaitch Rudin," announced the servant.

A man of about thirty-five entered, of a tall, somewhat stooping figure, with crisp curly hair and swarthy complexion, an irregular but expressive and intelligent face, a flickering brilliance in his quick, dark gray eyes, a straight bread nose, and well-curved lips. His clothes were not new, and were somewhat small, as though he had outgrown them.

[1] By permission of Mr. Wm. Heinemann. (Fcap. 8vo. Price 3s.)

He walked quickly up to Darya Mihaïlovna and with a slight bow told her that he had long wished to have the honor of an introduction to her, and that his friend the baron greatly regretted that he could not take leave of her in person.

The thin sound of Rudin's voice seemed out of keeping with his tall figure and broad chest.

"Pray be seated . . . very delighted," murmured Darya Mihaïlovna, and, after introducing him to the rest of the company, she asked him whether he belonged to those parts or was a visitor.

"My estate is in the T—— district," replied Rudin, holding his hat on his knees. "I have not been here long. I came on business and stayed for a while in your district town."

"With whom?"

"With the doctor. He was an old chum of mine at the university."

"Ah! the doctor. He is highly spoken of. He is skillful in his work, they say. But have you known the baron long?"

"I met him last winter in Moscow, and I have just been spending about a week with him."

"He is a very clever man, the baron."

"Yes."

Darya Mihaïlovna sniffed at her little crushed-up handkerchief steeped in *eau de cologne*.

"Are you in the government service?" she asked.

"Who? I?"

"Yes."

"No. I have retired."

There followed a brief pause. The general conversation was resumed.

"If you will allow me to be inquisitive," began Pigasof, turning to Rudin, "do you know the contents of the essay which his excellency the baron has sent?"

"Yes, I do."

"This essay deals with the relations to commerce — or no, of manufactures to commerce in our country. . . . That was your expression, I think, Darya Mihaïlovna?"

"Yes, it deals with" . . . began Darya Mihaïlovna, pressing her hand to her forehead.

"I am, of course, a poor judge of such matters," continued

Pigasof, "but I must confess that to me even the title of the essay seems excessively (how could I put it delicately?) — excessively obscure and complicated."

"Why does it seem so to you?"

Pigasof smiled and looked across at Darya Mihaïlovna.

"Why, is it clear to you?" he said, turning his foxy face again towards Rudin.

"To me? yes."

"H'm. No doubt you must know better."

"Does your head ache?" Alexandra Pavlovna inquired of Darya Mihaïlovna.

"No. It is only my — *c'est nerveux.*"

"Allow me to inquire," Pigasof was beginning again in his nasal tones, "your friend his excellency, Baron Muffel — I think that's his name?"

"Precisely."

"Does his excellency, Baron Muffel, make a special study of political economy, or does he only devote to that interesting subject the hours of leisure left over from his social amusements and his official duties?"

Rudin looked steadily at Pigasof.

"The baron is an amateur on this subject," he replied, growing rather red, "but in his essay there is much that is curious and valuable."

"I am not able to dispute it with you; I have not read the essay. But I venture to ask — the work of your friend Baron Muffel is no doubt founded more upon general propositions than upon facts?"

"It contains both facts and propositions founded upon the facts."

"Yes, yes. I must tell you that, in my opinion — and I've a right to give my opinion, on occasion; I spent three years at Dorpat . . . all these so-called general propositions, hypotheses, these systems — excuse me, I am a provincial, I speak the truth bluntly — are absolutely worthless. All that's only theorizing — only good for misleading people. Give us facts, sir, and that's enough!"

"Really!" retorted Rudin, "why, but ought not one to give the significance of the facts?"

"General propositions," continued Pigasof, "they're my abomination, these general propositions, theories, conclusions. All that's based on so-called convictions; every one is talking about his convictions, and attaches importance to them, prides himself on them. Ah!"

And Pigasof shook his fist in the air. Pandalevsky laughed.

"Capital!" put in Rudin, "it follows that there is no such thing as conviction according to you?"

"No, it doesn't exist."

"Is that your conviction?"

"Yes."

"How do you say that there are none then? Here you have one at the very first turn."

All in the room smiled and looked at one another.

"One minute, one minute, but ——" Pigasof was beginning.

But Darya Mihaïlovna clapped her hands, crying, "Bravo, bravo, Pigasof's beaten!" and she gently took Rudin's hat from his hand.

"Defer your delight a little, madam; there's plenty of time!" Pigasof began with annoyance. "It's not sufficient to say a witty word, with an appearance of aptness; you must prove, refute. We had wandered from the subject of our discussion."

"With your permission," remarked Rudin, coolly, "the matter is very simple. You do not believe in the value of general propositions — you do not believe in convictions?"

"I don't believe in them, I don't believe in them a bit!"

"Very good. You are a skeptic."

"I see no necessity for using such a learned word. However ——"

"Don't interrupt!" interposed Darya Mihaïlovna.

"At him, good dog!" Pandalevsky said to himself at the same instant, and smiled all over.

"That word expresses my meaning," pursued Rudin. "You understand it; why not make use of it? You don't believe in anything. Why do you believe in facts?"

"Why? That's good! Facts are matters of experience, every one knows what facts are. I judge of them by experience, by my own senses."

"But may not your senses deceive you?" Your senses tell you that the sun goes round the earth, . . . but perhaps you don't agree with Copernicus? You don't even believe in him?"

Again a smile passed over every one's face, and all eyes

were fastened on Rudin. "He's by no means a fool," every one was thinking.

"You are pleased to keep on joking," said Pigasof. "Of course that's very original, but it's not to the point."

"In what I have said hitherto," rejoined Rudin, "there is, unfortunately, too little that's original. All that has been well known a very long time, and has been said a thousand times. That is not the pith of the matter."

"What is then?" asked Pigasof, not without insolence.

In discussions he always first bantered his opponent, then grew cross, and finally sulked and was silent.

"Here it is," continued Rudin. "I cannot help, I own, feeling sincere regret when I hear sensible people attack——"

"Systems?" interposed Pigasof.

"Yes, with your leave, even systems. What frightens you so much in that word? Every system is founded on a knowledge of fundamental laws, the principles of life——"

"But there is no knowing them, no discovering them."

"One minute. Doubtless they are not easy for every one to get at, and to make mistakes is natural to man. However, you will certainly agree with me that Newton, for example, discovered some at least of these fundamental laws? He was a genius, we grant you; but the grandeur of the discoveries of genius is that they become the heritage of all. The effort to discover universal principles in the multiplicity of phenomena is one of the radical characteristics of human thought, and all our civilization——"

"That's what you're driving at!" Pigasof broke in in a drawling tone. "I am a practical man and all these metaphysical subtleties I don't enter into and don't want to enter into."

"Very good! That's as you prefer. But take note that your very desire to be exclusively a practical man is itself your sort of system—your theory."

"Civilization you talk about!" blurted in Pigasof; "that's another admirable notion of yours! Much use in it, this vaunted civilization! I would not give a brass farthing for your civilization!"

"But what a poor sort of argument, African Semenitch!" observed Darya Mihaïlovna, inwardly much pleased by the calmness and perfect good breeding of her new acquaintance. "*C'est un homme comme il faut*," she thought, looking with well-disposed scrutiny at Rudin; "we must be nice to him."

Those last words she mentally pronounced in Russian.

"I will not champion civilization," continued Rudin after a short pause; "it does not need my championship. You don't like it; every one to his own taste. Besides, that would take us too far. Allow me only to remind you of the old saying, 'Jupiter, you are angry; therefore you are in the wrong.' I meant to say that all those onslaughts upon systems — general propositions — are especially distressing, because together with these systems men repudiate knowledge in general, and all science and faith in it, and consequently also faith in themselves, in their own powers. But this faith is essential to men; they cannot exist by their sensations alone, they are wrong to fear ideas and not to trust in them. Skepticism is always characterized by barrenness and impotence."

"That's all words!" muttered Pigasof.

"Perhaps so. But allow me to point out to you that when we say 'that's all words!' we often wish ourselves to avoid the necessity of saying anything more substantial than mere words."

"What?" said Pigasof, winking his eyes.

"You understood what I meant," retorted Rudin, with involuntary but instantly repressed impatience. "I repeat, if man has no steady principle in which he trusts, no ground on which he can take a firm stand, how can he form a just estimate of the needs, the tendencies, and the future of his country? How can he know what he ought to do, if —— "

"I leave you the field," ejaculated Pigasof, abruptly, and with a bow he turned away without looking at any one.

Rudin stared at him, and smiled slightly, saying nothing.

"Aha! he has taken to flight!" said Darya Mihaïlovna. "Never mind, Dmitri. . . . I beg your pardon," she added with a cordial smile, "what is your paternal name?"

"Nikolaitch."

"Never mind, my dear Dmitri Nikolaitch, he did not deceive any of us. He wants to make a show of not *wishing* to argue any more. He is conscious that he *cannot* argue with you. But you had better sit nearer to us and let us have a little talk."

Rudin moved his chair up.

"How is it we have not met till now?" was Darya Mihaïlovna's question. That is what surprises me. Have you read this book? *C'est de Tocqueville, vous savez?*"

And Darya Mihaïlovna held out the French pamphlet to Rudin.

Rudin took the thin volume in his hand, turned over a few pages of it, and laying it down on the table replied that he had not read that particular work of M. de Tocqueville, but that he had often reflected on the question treated by him. The conversation became general again. Rudin seemed reticent at first, and not disposed to give his opinions; his words did not come readily, but at last he grew warm and began to speak. In a quarter of an hour his voice was the only sound in the room. All were crowding in a circle round him.

Only Pigasof remained aloof, in a corner by the fireplace. Rudin spoke with intelligence, with fire, and with judgment; he showed much learning, wide reading. No one had expected to find in him a remarkable man. His clothes were so shabby, so little was known of him. Every one felt it strange and incomprehensible that such a clever man should have suddenly made his appearance in the country. He seemed all the more wonderful and, one may even say, fascinating to all of them, beginning with Darya Mihaïlovna. She was pluming herself on having discovered him, and already at this early date was dreaming of how she would introduce Rudin into the world. In her quickness to receive impressions there was much that was almost childish, in spite of her years. Alexandra Pavlovna, to tell the truth, understood little of all that Rudin said, but was full of wonder and delight; her brother too was admiring him. Pandalevsky was watching Darya Mihaïlovna and was filled with envy. Pigasof thought, "If I have to give five hundred roubles I will get a nightingale to sing better than that!" But the most impressed of all the party were Bassistof and Natalya. Scarcely a breath escaped Bassistof; he sat the whole time with open mouth and round eyes and listened — listened as he had never listened to any one in his life — while Natalya's face was suffused by a crimson flush, and her eyes, fastened unwaveringly on Rudin, were both dimmed and shining.

"What splendid eyes he has!" Volintsef whispered to her.

"Yes, they are."

"It's only a pity his hands are so big and red."

Natalya made no reply.

Tea was brought in. The conversation became more general, but still by the sudden unanimity with which every one was silent, directly Rudin opened his mouth, one could judge of the strength of the impression he had produced. Darya Mihaïlovna suddenly felt inclined to tease Pigasof. She went up to him and said in an undertone, "Why don't you speak instead of doing nothing but smile sarcastically? Make an effort, challenge him again," and without waiting for him to answer, she beckoned to Rudin.

"There's one thing more you don't know about him," she said to him, with a gesture towards Pigasof,—"he is a terrible hater of women, he is always attacking them; pray, show him the true path."

Rudin involuntarily looked down upon Pigasof; he was a head and shoulders taller. Pigasof almost withered up with fury, and his sour face grew pale.

"Darya Mihaïlovna is mistaken," he said in an unsteady voice, "I do not only attack women; I am not a great admirer of the whole human species."

"What can have given you such a poor opinion of them?" inquired Rudin.

Pigasof looked him straight in the face.

"The study of my own heart, no doubt, in which I find every day more and more that is base. I judge of others by myself. Possibly this too is erroneous, and I am far worse than others; but what am I to do? it's a habit!"

"I understand you and sympathize with you," was Rudin's rejoinder. "What generous soul has not experienced a yearning for self-humiliation? But one ought not to remain in that condition from which there is no outlet beyond."

"I am deeply indebted for the certificate of generosity you confer on my soul," retorted Pigasof. "As for my condition, there's not much amiss with it, so that even if there were an outlet from it, it might go to the deuce, I shouldn't look for it!"

"But that means—pardon the expression—to prefer the gratification of your own pride to the desire to be and live in the truth."

"Undoubtedly," cried Pigasof, "pride—that I understand, and you, I expect, understand, and every one understands; but truth, what is truth? Where is it, this truth?"

"You are repeating yourself, let me warn you," remarked Darya Mihaïlovna.

Pigasof shrugged his shoulders.

"Well, where's the harm if I do? I ask: where is truth? Even the philosophers don't know what it is. Kant says it is one thing; but Hegel—no, you're wrong, it's something else."

"And do you know what Hegel says of it?" asked Rudin, without raising his voice.

"I repeat," continued Pigasof, flying into a passion, "that I cannot understand what truth means. According to my idea, it doesn't exist at all in the world, that is to say, the word exists but not the thing itself."

"Fie, fie!" cried Darya Mihaïlovna, "I wonder you're not ashamed to say so, you old sinner! No truth? What is there to live for in the world after that?"

"Well, I go so far as to think, Darya Mihaïlovna," retorted Pigasof, in a tone of annoyance, "that it would be much easier for you, in any case, to live without truth than without your cook, Stepan, who is such a master hand at soups! And what do you want with truth, kindly tell me? you can't trim a bonnet with it!"

"A joke is not an argument," observed Darya Mihaïlovna, "especially when you descend to personal insult."

"I don't know about truth, but I see speaking it does not answer," muttered Pigasof, and he turned angrily away.

And Rudin began to speak of pride, and he spoke well. He showed that man without pride is worthless, that pride is the lever by which the earth can be moved from its foundations, but that at the same time he alone deserves the name of man who knows how to control his pride, as the rider does his horse, who offers up his own personality as a sacrifice to the general good.

"Egoism," so he ended, "is suicide. The egoist withers like a solitary barren tree; but pride, ambition, as the active effort after perfection, is the source of all that is great. . . . Yes! a man must prune away the exuberant egoism of his personality, to give it the right of self-expression."

"Can you lend me a pencil?" Pigasof asked Bassistof.

Bassistof did not at once understand what Pigasof had asked him.

"What do you want a pencil for?" he said at last.

"I want to write down Mr. Rudin's last sentence. If one doesn't write it down, one might forget it, I'm afraid! But you will own, a sentence like that is such a handful of trumps."

"There are things which it is a shame to laugh at and make fun of, African Semenitch!" said Bassistof, warmly, turning away from Pigasof.

Meanwhile Rudin had approached Natalya. She got up;

her face expressed her confusion. Volintsef, who was sitting near her, got up too.

"I see a piano," began Rudin, with the gentle courtesy of a traveling prince; "don't you play on it?"

"Yes, I play," replied Natalya, "but not very well. Here is Konstantin Diomiditch plays much better than I do."

Pandalevsky put himself forward with a simper.

"You don't say that seriously, Natalya Alexyevena; your playing is not at all inferior to mine."

"Do you know Schubert's 'Erlkönig'?" asked Rudin.

"He knows it, he knows it!" interposed Darya Mihaïlovna. "Sit down, Konstantin. You are fond of music, Dmitri Nikolaitch?"

Rudin only made a slight motion of the head and ran his hand through his hair, as if disposing himself to listen. Pandalevsky began to play.

Natalya was standing near the piano, directly facing Rudin. At the first sound his face was transfigured. His dark gray eyes moved slowly about, from time to time resting upon Natalya. Pandalevsky finished playing.

Rudin said nothing and walked up to the open window. A fragrant mist lay like a soft shroud over the garden; a drowsy scent breathed from the trees near. The stars shed a mild radiance. The summer night was soft — and softened all. Rudin gazed into the dark garden, and looked round.

"That music and this night," he began, "reminded me of my student days in Germany; our meetings, our serenades."

"You have been in Germany, then?" said Darya Mihaïlovna.

"I spent a year at Heidelberg, and nearly a year at Berlin."

"And did you dress as a student? They say they wear a special dress there."

"At Heidelberg I wore high boots with spurs, and a hussar's jacket with braid on it, and I let my hair grow to my shoulders. In Berlin the students dress like everybody else."

"Tell us something of your student life," said Alexandra Pavlovna.

Rudin complied. He was not altogether successful in narrative. There was a lack of color in his descriptions. He did not know how to be humorous. However, from relating his own adventures abroad, Rudin soon passed to general themes, the special value of education and science, universities, and university life generally. He sketched in a large and comprehensive picture in broad and striking lines. All listened to him with profound attention. His eloquence was masterly and attractive, not altogether clear, but even this want of clearness added a special charm to his words.

The exuberance of his thought hindered Rudin from expressing himself definitely and exactly. Images followed upon images; comparisons started up one after another — now startlingly bold, now strikingly true. It was not the complacent effort of the practiced speaker, but the very breath of inspiration that was felt in his impatient improvising. He did not seek out his words; they came obediently and spontaneously to his lips, and each word seemed to flow straight from his soul, and was burning with all the fire of conviction. Rudin was the master of almost the greatest secret — the music of eloquence. He knew how in striking one chord of the heart to set all the others vaguely quivering and resounding. Many of his listeners, perhaps, did not understand very precisely what his eloquence was about; but their bosoms heaved, it seemed as though veils were lifted before their eyes, something radiant, glorious, seemed shimmering in the distance.

All Rudin's thoughts seemed centered on the future; this lent him something of the impetuous dash of youth. . . . Standing at the window, not looking at any one in special, he spoke, and inspired by the general sympathy and attention, the presence of young women, the beauty of the night, carried along by the tide of his own emotions, he rose to the height of eloquence, of poetry. . . . The very sound of his voice, intense and soft, increased the fascination; it seemed as though some higher power were speaking through his lips, startling even to himself. . . . Rudin spoke of what lends eternal significance to the fleeting life of man.

"I remember a Scandinavian legend," thus he concluded, "a king is sitting with his warriors round the fire in a long dark barn. It was night and winter. Suddenly a little bird flew in at the open door and flew out again at the other. The king spoke and said that this bird is like man in the world; it flew in from darkness and out again into darkness, and was not long in the warmth and light. . . . 'King,' replies the oldest of the warriors, 'even in the dark the bird is not lost, but finds her nest.' Even so our life is short and worthless; but all that is great is accomplished through men. The consciousness of being the instrument of these higher powers ought to outweigh all other joys for man; even in death he finds his life, his nest."

Rudin stopped and dropped his eyes with a smile of involuntary embarrassment.

"*Vous êtes un poète,*" was Darya Mihaïlovna's comment in an undertone.

And all were inwardly agreeing with her — all except Pigasof. Without waiting for the end of Rudin's long speech, he quietly took his hat and as he went out whispered viciously to Pandalevsky, who was standing near the door: —

"No! Fools are more to my taste."

No one, however, tried to detain him or even noticed his absence.

The servants brought in supper, and half an hour later, all had taken leave and separated. Darya Mihaïlovna begged Rudin to remain the night. Alexandra Pavlovna, as she went home in the carriage with her brother, several times fell to exclaiming and marveling at the extraordinary cleverness of Rudin. Volintsef agreed with her, though he observed that he sometimes expressed himself somewhat obscurely — that is to say, not altogether intelligibly, he added, — wishing, no doubt, to make his own thought clear; but his face was gloomy, and his eyes, fixed on a corner of the carriage, seemed even more melancholy than usual.

Pandalevsky went to bed, and as he took off his daintily embroidered braces, he said aloud, "A very smart fellow!" and suddenly, looking harshly at his page, ordered him out of the room. Bassistof did not sleep the whole night and did not undress — he was writing till morning a letter to a comrade of his in Moscow; and Natalya, too, though she undressed and lay down in her bed, had not an instant's sleep and never closed her eyes. With her head propped on her arm, she gazed fixedly into the darkness; her veins were throbbing feverishly and her bosom often heaved with a deep sigh.

TO-MORROW.[1]

By PHILIP BOURKE MARSTON.

[1850-1887.]

I SAID "To-morrow!" one bleak, winter day,
"To-morrow I will live my life anew"—
And still "To-morrow!" while the winter grew
To spring, and yet I dallied by the way,
And sweet, dear Sins still held me in their sway.
"To-morrow!" I said, while summer days wore through;
"To-morrow!" while chill autumn round me drew;
And so my soul remained the sweet Sins' prey.
So pass the years, and, still, perpetually,
I cry, "To-morrow will I flee each while—
To-morrow, surely, shall my soul stand free
Safe from the siren voices that beguile!"
But Death waits by me, with a mocking smile,
And whispers, "Yea! To-morrow, verily!"

DEATH OF BARNIER.

By E. AND J. DE GONCOURT.

(From "Sister Philomène": translated by Laura Ensor.)

[EDMOND and JULES HUOT DE GONCOURT: French artists and men of letters. Edmond was born at Nancy, May 26, 1822; died July 16, 1896; Jules was born at Paris, December 17, 1830; died June 20, 1870. They began active life as artists, and in 1850 commenced a literary partnership. A series of monographs on art and the stage first gave them repute in 1851-1852. They wrote always in collaboration, kept a journal together, and lived almost as one man until Jules' death; after which Edmond continued to publish novels of the same high degree of excellence as those written with his brother. Among their works, historical and fictitious, are: "Gavarni" (1873), "L'Art au XVIIIe Siècle" (1874), "Watteau" (1876), "Prud'hon" (1877), "Les Hommes de Lettres" (1860), "Sœur Philomène" (1861), "Renée Mauperin" (1864), "Germinie Lacerteux" (1865), "Manette Salomon" (1867), and "Madame Gervaisais" (1869). Jules wrote "La Fille Élisa" (1878), "La Faustin" (1882), and "Idées et Sensations" (1866). The "Journal des Goncourt" was published in six volumes, 1888-1892.]

WHEN in the hospital the patient—man or woman—is not a brutish creature, a kind of animal whom poverty has hard-

[1] From "A Last Harvest, Lyrics and Sonnets from the Book of Love." By permission of C. Elkin Mathews. (Post 8vo. Price 5s. net.)

EDMUND DE GONCOURT IN HIS STUDY

ened and filled with enmity; when he shows some of the feelings of human nature, and under the hand that tends him reveals some moral sentiments; when his heart has received even the slightest education, he at once finds the doctors and students full of kindly attention.

The Sisters, too, obey the irresistible law of sympathy. They are involuntarily attracted where their tenderness will meet with the best reward, and where also they may hope, in their pious zeal, to find the greatest facility in propagating their religious ideas, and sowing thoughts of God in a soul.

This affection for grateful and favorite patients sustained Sister Philomène's courage; it made her strong and patient. Often she reproached herself for it; she fancied, in her hours of stern self-examination, that her preferences were unjust; but as she felt no remorse, she concluded that God did not demand this sacrifice of her.

Was not her whole life made up of those affections created by her self-devotion, formed by the bedside of the patients, and too often broken by death — abrupt separations that made her so sad? Was it not all her consolation, her love for these women whom she saw, after many long days and much suffering, start off one morning with the joyousness of renewed health, turn the handle of the door, and disappear, leaving with her a feeling of intense happiness, but also the pang of parting?

Amongst her patients Sister Philomène had a young woman whom they had at first hoped to cure, and whose life was now despaired of. In her speech and attitude this woman — entered on the books as a seamstress, and who never spoke of her past — betrayed early traces of education, of fortune, and of a once happy life. A catastrophe could be suspected — one of those misfortunes that oblige unaccustomed hands to work. The emotion of her thanks, her deep and subdued despair, and her resignation had interested every one, the surgeon, the students, and the other patients. Every day — taking advantage of the permission granted to the patients' sons and daughters, a little boy, whom they soon found out lived in a common lodging house in the Rue de l'Hôtel-de-Ville, came and sat by the poor woman's bedside, and called her mother. He was dressed in the old clothes of a better class, which he seemed to have grown up in, and grown out of. He sat on a tall chair, dangling his legs, with the unhappy expression of a child longing to cry, looking at his mother, who, too weak to talk to him, devoured him with her eyes for a full hour, and then dismissed him.

Sister Philomène took a fancy to the child; every day she had some fruit or tidbit put aside for him as a surprise. She led him by the hand to her little room, and there talked to him, showed him religious picture books, or gave him a pencil and, seating him at her desk, let him scribble on blank tickets. Sometimes she would wash his face, part his hair, and bring him back clean and tidily combed to the sick bed of his mother, who blessed her with a look such as she would have bestowed on the Holy Virgin if she had appeared to her holding her son's hand.

The woman was fading away. One day the child was seated by her side on a chair. He gazed at her almost terrified, seeking in vain his mother in the face he no longer recognized. The Sister tried in vain to amuse and coax him. At the foot of the bed Barnier was putting mustard plasters on the patient's legs. And the woman, turned toward the Sister, was saying in the slow, low, penetrating voice of one about to die:

"No, Sister, it is not . . . dying . . . that frightens me. . . . I am ready . . . if it were only I . . . but he, my Sister." And she glanced at the child. "When I shall be no longer there . . . so young a child . . . what will become of him?"

"Come, come," said Sister Philomène, "you are going to recover . . . we shall cure you, shall we not, Monsieur Barnier?"

"Certainly . . . we shall cure you, . . ." replied the house surgeon, slowly and with difficulty bringing out his words.

"Oh!" said the sick woman, with a broken-hearted smile, and half-closed eyes. "You cannot understand, Sister, . . . a poor child left all alone in the world. . . . He had but me. . . ."

"As a Christian, you cannot doubt God's goodness and mercy. . . . He will not abandon your child. . . ."

And from Sister Philomène's lips rose an exhortation, which became a prayer, and seemed to lift up and stretch wings out to God, over the bed of the dying woman and the poor little unhappy orphan.

When the Sister had finished, the patient remained silent for a time, and then she sighed: —

"Yes, Sister, I know . . . but to leave him . . . without knowing; . . . if I were only sure he would have food . . .

bread even . . . if I only were certain he would have bread every day!" And the tears streamed from her eyes half dimmed by death.

Barnier, after putting on the mustard plasters, had remained motionless at the bedside, turning his back on the woman; his hands behind him played nervously with the iron post of the bedstead, when suddenly, carried away by one of those impulses that sometimes seize hold of the strongest, he turned round, and in a short, abrupt voice said to the dying woman:—

"Well, if that is all you want, you may make your mind easy. . . . I have a kind old mother who lives in the country. . . . She says the house seems too big now I have left. . . . It is an easy matter; your boy will keep her company. . . . And I can answer for it, she does not make children unhappy."

"Oh!" said the woman, who seemed to revive for a moment. "God will reward you!"

And she drew the child toward her in an ardent embrace, as though she wished, before giving him up to another woman, to fill his memory with his mother's last kiss.

"Yes," repeated the Sister, looking at the surgeon—"yes, indeed, God will reward you."

Sometimes the surgeon was in a teasing mood. On such days he amused himself by tormenting Sister Philomène on religion. He would argue, philosophize, dispute with mischievous persistency, but yet handle his subject with as light a touch as that with which a well-mannered man makes fun of the tastes of a young girl he honors, or the convictions of a woman he respects. He would press the Sister, worry her by jesting in order to make her speak and reply to him. He would have liked to make her impatient; but the Sister understood his maneuvers and guessed his intention from the smile that he could not conceal. She would allow him to talk, look at him, and then laugh. The surgeon, with his most serious air, would renew his arguments, seeking for those that might most embarrass the Sister; trying, for example, to prove to her by scientific reasons the impossibility of such and such a miracle. The Sister, undisturbed, replied by evading the question with a jest, a sally of natural mother wit and honest common sense, by one of those simple and happy phrases that faith puts into the mouths of the ignorant and the simple. One day, pushed to the far end, Barnier said to her:—

"After all, Sister, suppose heaven does not exist: you will be famously sold."

"Yes," replied Sister Philomène, laughing, "but if it does, you will be much more sold than I."

The next morning the whole hospital knew that Barnier, having scratched his hand on the previous day while dissecting a body in a state of purulent infection, was dying in terrible agonies.

When at four o'clock Malivoire, quitting for a few moments the bedside of his friend, came to replace him in the service, the Sister went up to him. She followed from bed to bed, dogging his steps, without, however, accosting him, without speaking, watching him intently, with her eyes fixed on his. As he was leaving the ward:—

"Well?" she asked, in the brief tone with which women stop the doctor on his last visit at the threshold of the room.

"No hope," said Malivoire, with a gesture of despair, "there is nothing to be done. It began at his right ankle, went up the leg and thigh, and has attacked all the articulations. Such agonies, poor fellow; it will be a mercy when it's over."

"Will he be dead before night?" asked the Sister, calmly.

"Oh, no! He will live through the night. It is the same case as that of Raguideau three years ago; and Raguideau lasted forty-eight hours."

That evening, at ten o'clock, Sister Philomène might be seen entering the church of Notre-Dame-des-Victoires.

The lamps were being lowered, the lighted tapers were being put out one by one with a long-handled extinguisher. The priest had just left the vestry.

The Sister inquired where he lived, and was told that his house was a couple of steps from the church in the Rue de la Banque.

The priest was just going into the house when she entered behind, pushing open the door he was closing.

"Come in, Sister," he said, unfurling his wet umbrella and placing it on the tiled floor in the anteroom. And he turned toward her. She was on her knees. "What are you doing, Sister?" he said, astonished at her attitude. "Get up, my child. This is not a fit place. Come, get up."

"You will save him, will you not?" and Philomene caught hold of the priest's hands as he stretched them out to help her to rise. "Why do you object to my remaining on my knees?"

"Come, come, my child, do not be so excited. It is God alone, remember, who can save. I can but pray."

"Ah! you can only pray," she said, in a disappointed tone. "Yes, that is true."

And her eyes sank to the ground. After a moment's pause the priest went on:—

"Come, Sister, sit down there. You are calmer now, are you not? Tell me, what is it you want?"

"He is dying," said Philomène, rising as she spoke. "He will probably not live through the night," and she began to cry. "It is for a young man of twenty-seven years of age; he has never performed any of his religious duties, never been near a church, never prayed to God since his first Communion. He will refuse to listen to anything. He no longer knows a prayer even. He will listen neither to priest nor any one. And, I tell you, it is all over with him, he is dying. Then I remembered your Confraternity of Notre-Dame-des-Victoires, since it is devoted to those who do not believe. Come, you must save him!"

"My daughter . . ."

". . . And perhaps he is dying at this very moment. Oh! promise me you will do all at once, all that is in the Confraternity book; the prayers, everything in short. You will have him prayed for at once, won't you?"

"But, my poor child, it is Friday, to-day, and the Confraternity only meets on Thursday."

"Thursday only; why? It will be too late Thursday. He will never live till Thursday. Come, you must save him; you have saved many another."

Sister Philomène looked at the priest with wide-opened eyes, in which, through her tears, rose a glance of revolt, impatience, and command. For one instant in that room there was no longer a Sister standing before a priest, but a woman face to face with an old man.

The priest resumed:—

"All I can do at present for that young man, my dear daughter, is to apply to his benefit all the prayers and good works that are being carried on by the Confraternity, and I will offer them up to the Blessed and Immaculate Heart of Mary to obtain his conversion. I will pray for him to-morrow at Mass, and again on Saturday and Sunday."

"Oh! I am so thankful," said Philomène, who felt tears

rise gently to her eyes as the priest spoke to her. "Now I am full of hope; he will be converted, he will have pity on himself. Give me your blessing for him."

"But, Sister, I only bless from the altar, in the pulpit, or in the confessional. There only am I the minister of God. Here, my Sister, here I am but a weak man, a miserable sinner."

"That does not signify; you are always God's minister, and you cannot, you would not, refuse me; he is at the point of death."

She fell on her knees as she spoke. The priest blessed her, and added, —

"It is nearly eleven o'clock, Sister; you have nearly three miles to get home, all Paris to cross at this late hour."

"Oh! I am not afraid," replied Philomène, with a smile; "God knows why I am in the street. Moreover, I will tell my beads on the way. The Blessed Virgin will be with me."

The same evening Barnier, rousing himself from a silence that had lasted the whole day, said to Malivoire: "You will write to my mother. You will tell her that this often happens in our profession."

"But you are not yet as bad as all that, my dear fellow," replied Malivoire, bending over the bed. "I am sure I shall save you."

"No, I chose my man too well for that. How well I took you in, my poor Malivoire!" and he smiled almost. "You understand, I could not kill myself. I did not wish to be the death of my old mother. But an accident — that settles everything. You will take all my books, do you hear, and my case of instruments also. I wish you to have all. "You wonder why I have killed myself, don't you? Come nearer. It is on account of that woman. I never loved but her in all my life. They did not give her enough chloroform; I told them so. Ah! if you had heard her scream when she awoke — before it was over! That scream still reëchoes in my ears! However," he continued, after a nervous spasm, "if I had to begin again, I would choose some other way of dying, some way in which I should not suffer so much. Then, you know, she died, and I fancied I had killed her. She is ever before me, . . . covered with blood. . . . And then I took to drinking. I drank because I loved her still. . . . That's all!"

Barnier relapsed into silence. After a long pause, he again spoke and said to Malivoire, —

"You will tell my mother to take care of the little lad."

After another pause, the following words escaped him,—

"The Sister would have said a prayer."

Shortly after, he asked,—

"What o'clock is it?"

"Eleven."

"Time is not up yet, . . . I have still some hours to live. . . . I shall last till to-morrow."

A little later he again inquired the time, and crossing his hands on his breast, in a faint voice he called Malivoire and tried to speak to him. But Malivoire could not catch the words he muttered.

Then the death rattle began and lasted till morn.

A candle lighted up the room.

It burned slowly, it lighted up the four white walls on which the coarse ocher paint of the door and of the two cupboards cut a sharp contrast. One of the open cupboards displayed books crowded and piled up on its shelves; on the other was an earthen jug and basin. Over the chimney, painted to imitate black marble, a petrified *Gorgone* leaf hung in the middle of the empty panel. In one corner, where the paint was worn by scratching matches, was a little glass framed in gilt paper, a souvenir of some excursion in the neighborhood of Paris. The curtainless window revealed a roof and blank darkness beyond. It was the counterpart of a room of some inn in the suburb of a great city.

On the iron bedstead, with its dimity curtains, a sheet lay thrown over a motionless body, molding the form as wet linen might do, indicating with the inflexibility of an immutable line the rigidity, from the tip of the toes to the sharp outline of the face, of what it covered.

Near a white, wooden table Malivoire, seated in a large, wicker armchair, watched and dozed, half slumbering and yet not quite asleep.

In the silence of the room nothing could be heard but the ticking of the dead man's watch.

From behind the door something seemed gently to move and advance, the key turned in the lock, and Sister Philomène stood beside the bed. Without looking at Malivoire, without seeing him, she knelt down and prayed in the attitude of a kneeling marble statue; and the folds of her gown were as motionless as the sheet that covered the dead man.

At the end of a quarter of an hour she rose, walked away without once looking round, and disappeared.

The next day, awaking at the hollow sound of the coffin knocking against the narrow stairs, Malivoire vaguely recalled the night's apparition, and wondered if he had dreamed it; and, going mechanically up to the table by the bedside, he sought for the lock of hair he had cut off for Barnier's mother — the lock of hair had vanished.

FORGOTTEN AIRS.

By PAUL VERLAINE.

I.

'Tis ecstasy languishing,
Amorous fatigue,
Of woods all the shudderings
Embraced by the breeze,
'Tis the choir of small voices
Towards the gray trees.

Oh, the frail and fresh murmuring!
The twitter and buzz,
The soft cry resembling
That's expired by the grass . . .
Oh, the roll of the pebbles
'Neath waters that pass!

Oh, this soul that is groaning
In sleepy complaint!
In us is it moaning?
In me and in you?
Low anthem exhaling
While soft falls the dew.

II.

In the unending
Dullness of this land,
Uncertain the snow
Is gleaming like sand.

No kind of brightness
In copper-hued sky,
The moon you might see
Now live and now die.

Gray float the oak trees —
Cloudlike they seem —
Of neighboring forests,
The mists in between.

Wolves hungry and lean,
And famishing crow,
What happens to you
When acid winds blow?

In the unending
Dullness of this land,
Uncertain the snow
Is gleaming like sand.

THE BOWDEN REUNION.[1]

By SARAH O. JEWETT.

[SARAH ORNE JEWETT: An American author; born in South Berwick, Me., September 3, 1849. She was educated in the Berwick Academy and traveled extensively through Europe and America. Her stories are distinctly New England in style, the scenes being laid chiefly in her native state. She has published: "Deephaven" (1877), "Playdays" (1878), "Old Friends and New" (1880), "Country Byways" (1881), "The Mate of the Daylight" (1883), "A Country Doctor" (1884), "A Marsh Island" (1885), "A White Heron" (1886) and "The Story of the Mormons" (1887).]

It is very rare in country life, where high days and holidays are few, that any occasion of general interest proves to be less than great. Such is the hidden fire of enthusiasm in the New England nature that, once given an outlet, it shines forth with almost volcanic light and heat. In quiet neighborhoods such inward force does not waste itself upon those petty excitements of every day that belong to cities, but when, at long intervals, the altars to patriotism, to friendship, to the ties of kindred,

[1] Copyright, 1896, by Sarah Orne Jewett. Used by permission of Houghton, Mifflin & Co.

are reared in our familiar fields, then the fires glow, the flames come up as if from the inexhaustible burning heart of the earth; the primal fires break through the granite dust in which our souls are set. Each heart is warm and every face shines with the ancient light. Such a day as this has transfiguring powers, and easily makes friends of those who have been cold-hearted, and gives to those who are dumb their chance to speak, and lends some beauty to the plainest face.

"Oh, I expect I shall meet friends to-day that I haven't seen in a long while," said Mrs. Blackett, with deep satisfaction. "'Twill bring out a good many of the old folks, 'tis such a lovely day. I'm always glad not to have them disappointed."

"I guess likely the best of 'em'll be there," answered Mrs. Todd, with gentle humor, stealing a glance at me. "There's one thing certain: there's nothing takes in this whole neighborhood like anything related to the Bowdens. Yes, I do feel that when you call upon the Bowdens you may expect most families to rise up between the Landing and the far end of the Back Cove. Those that aren't kin by blood are kin by marriage."

"There used to be an old story goin' about when I was a girl," said Mrs. Blackett, with much amusement. "There was a great many more Bowdens then than there are now, and the folks was all setting in meeting a dreadful hot Sunday afternoon, and a scatter-witted little bound girl came running to the meetin'house door all out o' breath from somewheres in the neighborhood. 'Mis' Bowden, Mis' Bowden!' says she, 'your baby's in a fit!' They used to tell that the whole congregation was up on its feet in a minute and right out into the aisles. All the Mis' Bowdens was setting right out for home; the minister stood there in the pulpit tryin' to keep sober, an' all at once he burst right out laughin'. He was a very nice man, they said, and he said he'd better give 'em the benediction, and they could hear the sermon next Sunday; so he kept it over. My mother was there, and she thought certain 'twas me."

"None of our family was ever subject to fits," interrupted Mrs. Todd, severely. "No, we never had fits, none of us, and 'twas lucky we didn't 'way out there to Green Island. Now these folks right in front: dear sakes knows the bunches o' soothing catnip an' yarrow I've had to favor old Mis' Evins with dryin'! You can see it right in their expressions, all them Evins folks. There, just you look up to the crossroads, mother," she suddenly exclaimed. "See all the teams ahead of us. And, oh, look down on the bay; yes, look down on the bay! See what a sight o' boats, all headin' for the Bowden place cove!"

"Oh, ain't it beautiful!" said Mrs. Blackett, with all the delight of a girl. She stood up in the high wagon to see everything, and when she sat down again she took fast hold of my hand.

"Hadn't you better urge the horse a little, Almiry?" she asked. "He's had it easy as we came along, and he can rest when we get there. The others are some little ways ahead, and I don't want to lose a minute."

We watched the boats drop their sails one by one in the cove as we drove along the high land. The old Bowden house stood, low-storied and broad-roofed, in its green fields as if it were a motherly brown hen waiting for the flock that came straying toward it from every direction. The first Bowden settler had made his home there, and it was still the Bowden farm; five generations of sailors and farmers and soldiers had been its children. And presently Mrs. Blackett showed me the stone-walled burying ground that stood like a little fort on a knoll overlooking the bay, but, as she said, there were plenty of scattered Bowdens who were not laid there, — some lost at sea, and some out West, and some who died in the war: most of the home graves were those of women.

We could see now that there were different footpaths from along shore and across country. In all these there were straggling processions walking in single file, like old illustrations of the "Pilgrim's Progress." There was a crowd about the house as if huge bees were swarming in the lilac bushes. Beyond the fields and cove a higher point of land ran out into the bay, covered with woods which must have kept away much of the northwest wind in winter. Now there was a pleasant look of shade and shelter there for the great family meeting.

We hurried on our way, beginning to feel as if we were very late, and it was a great satisfaction at last to turn out of the stony highroad into a green lane shaded with old apple trees. Mrs. Todd encouraged the horse until he fairly pranced with gayety as we drove round to the front of the house on the soft turf. There was an instant cry of rejoicing, and two or three persons ran toward us from the busy group.

"Why, dear Mis' Blackett! — here's Mis' Blackett!" I heard them say, as if it were pleasure enough for one day to have a sight of her. Mrs. Todd turned to me with a lovely look of triumph and self-forgetfulness. An elderly man who wore the look of a prosperous sea captain put up both arms and lifted Mrs. Blackett down from the high wagon like a child, and kissed her with hearty affection. "I was master afraid she wouldn't be here," he said, looking at Mrs. Todd with a face like a happy, sunburnt schoolboy, while everybody crowded round to give their welcome.

"Mother's always the queen," said Mrs. Todd. "Yes, they'll all make everything of mother; she'll have a lovely time to-day. I wouldn't have had her miss it, and there won't be a thing she'll ever regret, except to mourn because William wa'n't here."

Mrs. Blackett having been properly escorted to the house, Mrs. Todd received her own full share of honor, and some of the men, with a simple kindness that was the soul of chivalry, waited upon us and our baskets and led away the white horse. I already knew some of Mrs. Todd's friends and kindred, and felt like an adopted Bowden in this happy moment. It seemed to be enough for any one to have arrived by the same conveyance as Mrs. Blackett, who presently had her court inside the house, while Mrs. Todd, large, hospitable, and preëminent, was the center of a rapidly increasing crowd about the lilac bushes. Small companies were continually coming up the long, green slope from the water, and nearly all the boats had come to shore. I counted three or four that were baffled by the light breeze, but before long all the Bowdens, small and great, seemed to have assembled, and we started to go up to the grove across the field.

Out of the chattering crowd of noisy children, and large-waisted women whose best black dresses fell straight to the ground in generous folds, and sunburnt men who looked as serious as if it were town-meeting day, there suddenly came silence and order. I saw the straight, soldierly little figure of a man who bore a fine resemblance to Mrs. Blackett, and who appeared to marshal us with perfect ease. He was imperative enough, but with a grand military sort of courtesy, and bore himself with solemn dignity of importance. We were sorted out according to some clear design of his own, and stood as speechless as a troop to await his orders. Even the children were ready to march together, a pretty flock, and at the last moment Mrs. Blackett and a few distinguished companions, the ministers and those who were very old, came out of the house together and took their places. We ranked by fours, and even then we made a long procession.

There was a wide path mowed for us across the field, and, as we moved along, the birds flew up out of the thick second crop of clover, and the bees hummed as if it still were June. There was a flashing of white gulls over the water where the fleet of boats rode the low waves together in the cove, swaying their small masts as if they kept time to our steps. The plash of the water could be heard faintly, yet still be heard; we might have been a company of ancient Greeks going to celebrate a victory, or to worship the god of harvests in the grove above. It was strangely moving to see this and to make part of it. The sky, the sea, have watched poor humanity at its rites so long; we were no more a New England family, celebrating its own existence and simple progress: we carried the tokens and inheritance of all such households from which this had descended, and were only the latest of our line. We possessed the instincts of a far, forgotten childhood; I found myself thinking that we ought to be carrying green branches and singing as we went. So we came to the thick-shaded grove still silent, and were set in our places by the straight trees that swayed together and let sunshine through here and there like a single golden leaf that flickered down, vanishing in the cool shade.

The grove was so large that the great family looked far smaller than it had in the open field; there was a thick growth of dark pines and firs, with an occasional maple or oak that gave a gleam of color like a bright window in the great roof. On three sides we could see the water shining behind the tree trunks, and feel the cool salt breeze that began to come up with the tide just as the day reached its highest point of heat. We could see the green, sunlit field we had just crossed as if we looked out at it from a dark room, and the old house and its lilacs standing placidly in the sun, and the great barn with a stockade of carriages from which two or three care-taking men who had lingered were coming across the field together. Mrs. Todd had taken off her warm gloves and looked the picture of content.

"There!" she exclaimed. "I've always meant to have you

see this place, but I never looked for such a beautiful opportunity — weather an' occasion both made to match. Yes, it suits me: I don't ask no more. I want to know if you saw mother walkin' at the head! It choked me right up to see mother at the head, walkin' with the ministers," and Mrs. Todd turned away to hide the feelings she could not instantly control.

"Who was the marshal?" I hastened to ask. "Was he an old soldier?"

"Don't he do well?" answered Mrs. Todd, with satisfaction.

"He don't often have such a chance to show off his gifts," said Mrs. Caplin, a friend from the Landing, who had joined us. "That's Sant Bowden; he always takes the lead, such days. Good for nothing else most o' his time; trouble is, he ——"

I turned with interest to hear the worst. Mrs. Caplin's tone was both zealous and impressive.

"Stim'lates," she explained scornfully.

"No, Santin never was in the war," said Mrs. Todd, with lofty indifference. "It was a cause of real distress to him. He kep' enlistin', and traveled far an' wide about here, an' even took the bo't and went to Boston to volunteer; but he ain't a sound man, an' they wouldn't have him. They say he knows all their tactics, an' can tell all about the battle o' Waterloo well's he can Bunker Hill. I told him once the country'd lost a great general, an' I meant it, too."

"I expect you're near right," said Mrs. Caplin, a little crestfallen and apologetic.

"I be right," insisted Mrs. Todd, with much amiability. "'Twas most too bad to cramp him down to his peaceful trade, but he's a most excellent shoemaker at his best, an' he always says it's a trade that gives him time to think an' plan his maneuvers. Over to the Port they always invite him to march Decoration Day, same as the rest, an' he does look noble; he comes of soldier stock."

I had been noticing with great interest the curiously French type of face which prevailed in this rustic company. I had said to myself before that Mrs. Blackett was plainly of French descent, in both her appearance and her charming gifts, but this is not surprising when one has learned how large a proportion of the early settlers on this northern coast of New England were of Huguenot blood, and that it is the Norman

Englishman, not the Saxon, who goes adventuring to a new world.

"They used to say in old times," said Mrs. Todd, modestly, "that our family came of very high folks in France, and, one of 'em was a great general in some o' the old wars. I sometimes think that Santin's ability has come 'way down from then. 'Tain't nothin' he's ever acquired; 'twas born in him. I don't know's he ever saw a fine parade, or met with those that studied up such things. He's figured it all out an' got his papers, so he knows how to aim a cannon right for William's fishhouse five miles out on Green Island, or up there on Burnt Island where the signal is. He had it all over to me one day, an' I tried hard to appear interested. His life's all in it, but he will have those poor gloomy spells come over him now an' then, an' then he has to drink."

Mrs. Caplin gave a heavy sigh.

"There's a great many such strayaway folks, just as there is plants," continued Mrs. Todd, who was nothing if not botanical. "I know of just one sprig of laurel that grows over back here in a wild spot, an' I never could hear of no other on this coast. I had a large bunch brought me once from Massachusetts way, so I know it. This piece grows in an open spot where you'd think 'twould do well, but it's sort o' poor lookin'. I've visited it time an' again, just to notice its poor blooms. 'Tis a real Sant Bowden, out of its own place."

Mrs. Caplin looked bewildered and blank. "Well, all I know is last year he worked out some kind of a plan so's to parade the county conference in platoons, and got 'em all flustered up tryin' to sense his ideas of a holler square," she burst forth. "They was holler enough anyway after ridin' 'way down from up country into the salt air, and they'd been treated to a sermon on faith an' works from old Fayther Harlow that never knows when to cease. 'Twa'n't no time for tactics then, — they wa'n't athinkin' of the church military. Sant, he couldn't do nothin' with 'em. All he thinks of when he sees a crowd is how to march 'em. 'Tis all very well when he don't 'tempt too much. He never did act like other folks."

"Ain't I just been maintainin' that he ain't like 'em?" urged Mrs. Todd, decidedly. "Strange folks has got to have strange ways, for what I see."

"Somebody observed once that you could pick out the likeness of 'most every sort of a foreigner when you looked about you in our parish," said Sister Caplin, her face brightening with sudden illumination. "I didn't see the bearin' of it then quite so plain. I always did think Mari' Harris resembled a Chinee."

"Mari' Harris was pretty as a child, I remember," said the pleasant voice of Mrs. Blackett, who, after receiving the affectionate greetings of nearly the whole company, came to join us, — to see, as she insisted, that we were out of mischief.

"Yes, Mari' was one o' them pretty little lambs that make dreadful homely old sheep," replied Mrs. Todd, with energy. "Cap'n Littlepage never'd look so disconsolate if she was any sort of a proper person to direct things. She might divert him; yes, she might divert the old gentleman, an' let him think he had his own way, 'stead o' arguing everything down to the bare bone. 'Twouldn't hurt her to sit down an' hear his great stories once in a while."

"The stories are very interesting," I ventured to say.

"Yes, you always catch yourself athinkin' what if they was all true, and he had the right of it," answered Mrs. Todd. "He's a good sight better company, though dreamy, than such sordid creatur's as Mari' Harris."

"Live and let live," said dear old Mrs. Blackett, gently. "I haven't seen the captain for a good while, now that I ain't so constant to meetin'," she added wistfully. "We always have known each other."

"Why, if it is a good, pleasant day to-morrow, I'll get William to call an' invite the capt'in to dinner. William'll be in early so's to pass up the street without meetin' anybody."

"There, they're callin' out it's time to set the tables," said Mrs. Caplin, with great excitement.

"Here's Cousin Sarah Jane Blackett! Well, I am pleased, certain!" exclaimed Mrs. Todd, with unaffected delight; and these kindred spirits met and parted with the promise of a good talk later on. After this there was no more time for conversation until we were seated in order at the long tables.

"I'm one that always dreads seeing some o' the folks that I don't like, at such a time as this," announced Mrs. Todd, privately, to me, after a season of reflection. We were just waiting for the feast to begin. "You wouldn't think such a great creatur' 's I be could feel all over pins an' needles. I remember, the day I promised to Nathan, how it come over me, just's I was feelin' happy's I could, that I'd got to have an own cousin o' his for my near relation all the rest o' my life, an' it seemed as if die I should. Poor Nathan saw somethin' had crossed me, — he had very nice feelings, — and when he asked me what 'twas, I told him. 'I never could like her myself,' said he. 'You sha'n't be bothered, dear,' he says; an' 'twas one o' the things that made me set a good deal by Nathan, he didn't make a habit of always opposin', like some men. 'Yes,' says I, 'but think o' Thanksgivin' times an' funerals; she's our relation, an' we've got to own her.' Young folks don't think o' those things. There she goes now, do let's pray her by!" said Mrs. Todd, with an alarming transition from general opinions to particular animosities. "I hate her just the same as I always did; but she's got on a real pretty dress. I do try to remember that she's Nathan's cousin. Oh dear, well; she's gone by after all, an' ain't seen me. I expected she'd come pleasantin' round just to show off an' say afterwards she was acquainted."

This was so different from Mrs. Todd's usual largeness of mind that I had a moment's uneasiness; but the cloud passed quickly over her spirit and was gone with the offender.

There never was a more generous out-of-door feast along the coast than the Bowden family set forth that day. To call it a picnic would make it seem trivial. The great tables were edged with pretty oak-leaf trimming, which the boys and girls made. We brought flowers from the fence thickets of the great field; and out of the disorder of flowers and provisions suddenly appeared as orderly a scheme for the feast as the marshal had shaped for the procession. I began to respect the Bowdens for their inheritance of good taste and skill and a certain pleasing gift of formality. Something made them do all these things in a finer way than most country people would have done them. As I looked up and down the tables there was a good cheer, a grave soberness that shone with pleasure, a humble dignity of bearing. There were some who should have sat below the salt for lack of this good breeding; but they were not many. So, I said to myself, their ancestors may have sat in the great hall of some old French house in the Middle Ages, when battles and sieges and processions and feasts were familiar things. The ministers and Mrs. Blackett, with a few of their rank and age, were put in places of honor, and for once that I looked any other way I looked twice at Mrs.

Blackett's face, serene and mindful of privilege and responsibility, the mistress by simple fitness of this great day.

Mrs. Todd looked up at the roof of green trees, and then carefully surveyed the company. "I see 'em better now they're all settin' down," she said with satisfaction. "There's old Mr. Gilbraith and his sister. I wish they were settin' with us; they're not among folks they can parley with, an' they look disappointed."

As the feast went on, the spirits of my companion steadily rose. The excitement of an unexpectedly great occasion was a subtle stimulant to her disposition, and I could see that sometimes when Mrs. Todd had seemed limited and heavily domestic, she had simply grown sluggish for lack of proper surroundings. She was not so much reminiscent now as expectant, and as alert and gay as a girl. We who were her neighbors were full of gayety, which was but the reflected light from her beaming countenance. It was not the first time that I was full of wonder at the waste of human ability in this world, as a botanist wonders at the wastefulness of nature, the thousand seeds that die, the unused provisions of every sort. The reserve force of society grows more and more amazing to one's thought. More than one face among the Bowdens showed that only opportunity and stimulus were lacking, — a narrow set of circumstances had caged a fine, able character and held it captive. One sees exactly the same types in a country gathering as in the most brilliant city company. You are safe to be understood if the spirit of your speech is the same for one neighbor as for the other.

The feast was a noble feast, as has already been said. There was an elegant ingenuity displayed in the form of pies which delighted my heart. Once acknowledge that an American pie is far to be preferred to its humble ancestor, the English tart, and it is joyful to be reassured at a Bowden reunion that invention has not yet failed. Besides a delightful variety of material, the decorations went beyond all my former experience; dates and names were wrought in lines of pastry and frosting on the tops. There was even more elaborate reading matter on an excellent early apple pie which we began to share and eat, precept upon precept. Mrs. Todd helped me generously to the whole word *Bowden*, and consumed *Reunion* herself, save an undecipherable fragment; but the most renowned essay in cookery on the tables was a model of the old Bowden house made of durable gingerbread, with all the windows and doors in the right places, and sprigs of genuine lilac set at the front. It must have been baked in sections, in one of the last of the great brick ovens, and fastened together on the morning of the day. There was a general sigh when this fell into ruin at the feast's end, and it was shared by a great part of the assembly, not without seriousness, and as if it were a pledge and token of loyalty. I met the maker of the gingerbread house, which had called up lively remembrances of a childish story. She had the gleaming eye of an enthusiast and a look of high ideals.

"I could just as well have made it all of frosted cake," she said, "but 'twouldn't have been the right shade; the old house, as you observe, was never painted, and I concluded that plain gingerbread would represent it best. It wasn't all I expected it would be," she said sadly, as many an artist had said before her of his work.

There were speeches by the ministers; and there proved to be a historian among the Bowdens, who gave some fine anecdotes of the family history; and then appeared a poetess, whom Mrs. Todd regarded with wistful compassion and indulgence, and when the long, faded garland of verses came to an appealing end, she turned to me with words of praise.

"Sounded pretty," said the generous listener. "Yes, I thought she did very well. We went to school together, an' Mary Anna had a very hard time; trouble was, her mother thought she'd given birth to a genius, an' Mary Anna's come to believe it herself. There, I don't know what we should have done without her; there ain't nobody else that can write poetry between here and 'way up towards Rockland; it adds a great deal at such a time. When she speaks o' those that are gone, she feels it all, and so does everybody else, but she harps too much. I'd laid half of that away for next time, if I was Mary Anna. There comes mother to speak to her, an' old Mr. Gilbraith's sister; now she'll be heartened right up. Mother'll say just the right thing."

The leavetakings were as affecting as the meetings of these old friends had been. There were enough young persons at the reunion, but it is the old who really value such opportunities; as for the young, it is the habit of every day to meet their comrades, — the time of separation has not come. To see the joy with which these elder kinsfolk and acquaintances had looked in one another's faces, and the lingering touch of their friendly hands; to see these affectionate meetings and then the reluctant partings, gave one a new idea of the isolation in which it was possible to live in that after all thinly settled region. They did not expect to see one another again very soon; the steady, hard work on the farms, the difficulty of getting from place to place, especially in winter when boats were laid up, gave double value to any occasion which could bring a large number of families together. Even funerals in this country of the pointed firs were not without their social advantages and satisfactions. I heard the words "next summer" repeated many times, though summer was still ours and all the leaves were green.

PRESCIENCE.[1]

By THOMAS BAILEY ALDRICH.

THE new moon hung in the sky, the sun was low in the west,
And my betrothed and I in the churchyard paused to rest:
Happy maid and lover, dreaming the old dream over:
The light winds wandered by, and robins chirped from the nest.

And lo! in the meadow sweet was the grave of a little child,
With a crumbling stone at the feet, and the ivy running wild:
Tangled ivy and clover folding it over and over:
Close to my sweetheart's feet was the little mound uppiled.

Stricken with nameless fears, she shrank and clung to me,
And her eyes were filled with tears for a sorrow I did not see:
Lightly the winds were blowing, softly her tears were flowing —
Tears for the unknown years and a sorrow that was to be!

[1] Used by permission of Houghton, Mifflin & Co.

THE ADVENTURES OF A FOURTH.[1]

BY THOMAS BAILEY ALDRICH.

(From "The Story of a Bad Boy.")

[THOMAS BAILEY ALDRICH, American poet and novelist, was born in Portsmouth, N.H., November 11, 1836, and during the early part of his career was clerk in a mercantile house. The success of his first contributions to periodicals induced him to adopt literature as a profession, and after a few years' experience as proof reader and "reader" for a publishing firm, he became a frequent contributor to the New York *Evening Mirror and Home Journal*, conducted *Every Saturday* in Boston (1870–1874), and was editor of the *Atlantic Monthly* (1881–1890). "The Story of a Bad Boy," "Marjorie Daw," "The Stillwater Tragedy," and "From Ponkapog to Pesth" are his principal prose publications. Among his poetical works may be mentioned: "Ballad of Baby Bell," "Flower and Thorn," "Lyrics and Sonnets," "Wyndham Towers," "Judith and Holofernes," and "The Sisters' Tragedy."]

THE sun cast a broad column of quivering gold across the river at the foot of our street, just as I reached the doorstep of the Nutter House. Kitty Collins, with her dress tucked about her so that she looked as if she had on a pair of calico trousers, was washing off the sidewalk.

"Arrah, you bad boy!" cried Kitty, leaning on the mop-handle, "the Capen has jist been askin' for you. He's gone up town, now. It's a nate thing you done with my clothesline, and it's me you may thank for gettin' it out of the way before the Capen come down."

The kind creature had hauled in the rope, and my escapade had not been discovered by the family; but I knew very well that the burning of the stagecoach and the arrest of the boys concerned in the mischief were sure to reach my grandfather's ears sooner or later.

"Well, Thomas," said the old gentleman, an hour or so afterwards, beaming upon me benevolently across the breakfast table, "you didn't wait to be called this morning."

"No, sir," I replied, growing very warm, "I took a little run up town to see what was going on."

I didn't say anything about the little run I took home again!

"They had quite a time on the Square last night," remarked

[1] Copyright, 1869 and 1877, by Thomas Bailey Aldrich; 1897, by Houghton, Mifflin & Co. Used by permission.

Captain Nutter, looking up from the *Rivermouth Barnacle*, which was always placed beside his coffee cup at breakfast.

I felt that my hair was preparing to stand on end.

"Quite a time," continued my grandfather. "Some boys broke into Ezra Wingate's barn and carried off the old stage-coach. The young rascals! I do believe they'd burn up the whole town if they had their way."

With this he resumed the paper. After a long silence he exclaimed, "Halloo!" — upon which I nearly fell off the chair.

"'Miscreants unknown,'" read my grandfather, following the paragraph with his forefinger; "'escaped from the bridewell, leaving no clue to their identity, except the letter H, cut on one of the benches.' 'Five dollars reward offered for the apprehension of the perpetrators.' Sho! I hope Wingate will catch them."

I don't see how I continued to live, for on hearing this the breath went entirely out of my body. I beat a retreat from the room as soon as I could, and flew to the stable with a misty intention of mounting Gypsy and escaping from the place. I was pondering what steps to take, when Jack Harris and Charley Marden entered the yard.

"I say," said Harris, as blithe as a lark, "has old Wingate been here?"

"Been here?" I cried, "I should hope not!"

"The whole thing's out, you know," said Harris, pulling Gypsy's forelock over her eyes and blowing playfully into her nostrils.

"You don't mean it!" I gasped.

"Yes, I do, and we are to pay Wingate three dollars apiece. He'll make rather a good spec out of it."

"But how did he discover that we were the — the miscreants?" I asked, quoting mechanically from the *Rivermouth Barnacle*.

"Why, he saw us take the old ark, confound him! He's been trying to sell it any time these ten years. Now he has sold it to us. When he found that we had slipped out of the Meat Market, he went right off and wrote the advertisement offering five dollars reward, though he knew well enough who had taken the coach, for he came round to my father's house before the paper was printed to talk the matter over. Wasn't the governor mad, though! But it's all settled, I tell you. We're to pay Wingate fifteen dollars for the old gocart, which

THOMAS BAILEY ALDRICH

he wanted to sell the other day for seventy-five cents, and couldn't. It's a downright swindle. But the funny part of it is to come."

"O, there's a funny part to it, is there?" I remarked bitterly.

"Yes. The moment Bill Conway saw the advertisement, he knew it was Harry Blake who cut that letter H on the bench; so off he rushes up to Wingate—kind of him, wasn't it?—and claims the reward. 'Too late, young man,' says old Wingate, 'the culprits has been discovered.' You see Slyboots hadn't any intention of paying that five dollars."

Jack Harris' statement lifted a weight from my bosom. The article in the *Rivermouth Barnacle* had placed the affair before me in a new light. I had thoughtlessly committed a grave offense. Though the property in question was valueless, we were clearly wrong in destroying it. At the same time Mr. Wingate *had* tacitly sanctioned the act by not preventing it when he might easily have done so. He had allowed his property to be destroyed in order that he might realize a large profit.

Without waiting to hear more, I went straight to Captain Nutter, and, laying my remaining three dollars on his knee, confessed my share in the previous night's transaction.

The Captain heard me through in profound silence, pocketed the bank notes, and walked off without speaking a word. He had punished me in his own whimsical fashion at the breakfast table, for, at the very moment he was harrowing up my soul by reading the extracts from the *Rivermouth Barnacle*, he not only knew all about the bonfire, but had paid Ezra Wingate his three dollars. Such was the duplicity of that aged impostor!

I think Captain Nutter was justified in retaining my pocket money, as additional punishment, though the possession of it later in the day would have got me out of a difficult position, as the reader will see further on.

I returned with a light heart and a large piece of punk to my friends in the stable yard, where we celebrated the termination of our trouble by setting off two packs of firecrackers in an empty wine cask. They made a prodigious racket, but failed somehow to fully express my feelings. The little brass pistol in my bedroom suddenly occurred to me. It had been loaded I don't know how many months, long before I left New

Orleans, and now was the time, if ever, to fire it off. Muskets, blunderbusses, and pistols were banging away lively all over town, and the smell of gunpowder, floating on the air, set me wild to add something respectable to the universal din.

When the pistol was produced, Jack Harris examined the rusty cap and prophesied that it would not explode.

"Never mind," said I, "let's try it."

I had fired the pistol once, secretly, in New Orleans, and, remembering the noise it gave birth to on that occasion, I shut both eyes tight as I pulled the trigger. The hammer clicked on the cap with a dull, dead sound. Then Harris tried it; then Charley Marden; then I took it again, and after three or four trials was on the point of giving it up as a bad job, when the obstinate thing went off with a tremendous explosion, nearly jerking my arm from the socket. The smoke cleared away, and there I stood with the stock of the pistol clutched convulsively in my hand,—the barrel, lock, trigger, and ramrod having vanished into thin air.

"Are you hurt?" cried the boys, in one breath.

"N—no," I replied dubiously, for the concussion had bewildered me a little.

When I realized the nature of the calamity, my grief was excessive. I can't imagine what led me to do so ridiculous a thing, but I gravely buried the remains of my beloved pistol in our back garden, and erected over the mound a slate tablet to the effect that "Mr. Barker, formerly of new orleans, was Killed accidentally on the Fourth of july, 18— in the 2nd year of his Age." Binny Wallace, arriving on the spot just after the disaster, and Charley Marden (who enjoyed the obsequies immensely) acted with me as chief mourners. I, for my part, was a very sincere one.

As I turned away in a disconsolate mood from the garden, Charley Marden remarked that he shouldn't be surprised if the pistol butt took root and grew into a mahogany tree or something. He said he once planted an old musket stock, and shortly afterwards a lot of *shoots* sprang up! Jack Harris laughed; but neither I nor Binny Wallace saw Charley's wicked joke.

We were now joined by Pepper Whitcomb, Fred Langdon, and several other desperate characters on their way to the Square, which was always a busy place when public festivities were going on. Feeling that I was still in disgrace with the

Captain, I thought it politic to ask his consent before accompanying the boys.

He gave it with some hesitation, advising me to be careful not to get in front of the firearms. Once he put his fingers mechanically into his vest pocket and half drew forth some dollar bills, then slowly thrust them back again as his sense of justice overcame his genial disposition. I guess it cut the old gentleman to the heart to be obliged to keep me out of my pocket money. I know it did me. However, as I was passing through the hall, Miss Abigail, with a very severe cast of countenance, slipped a brand-new quarter into my hand. We had silver currency in those days, thank Heaven!

Great were the bustle and confusion on the Square. By the way, I don't know why they called this large, open space a square, unless because it was an oval,—an oval formed by the confluence of half a dozen streets, now thronged by crowds of smartly dressed townspeople and country folks; for Rivermouth on the Fourth was the center of attraction to the inhabitants of the neighboring villages.

On one side of the Square were twenty or thirty booths arranged in a semicircle, gay with little flags and seductive with lemonade, ginger beer, and seedcakes. Here and there were tables at which could be purchased the smaller sort of fireworks, such as pin wheels, serpents, double headers, and punk warranted not to go out. Many of the adjacent houses made a pretty display of bunting, and across each of the streets opening on the Square was an arch of spruce and evergreen, blossoming all over with patriotic mottoes and paper roses.

It was a noisy, merry, bewildering scene as we came upon the ground. The incessant rattle of small arms, the booming of the twelve-pounder firing on the Mill Dam, and the silvery clangor of the church bells ringing simultaneously — not to mention an ambitious brass band that was blowing itself to pieces on a balcony — were enough to drive one distracted. We amused ourselves for an hour or two, darting in and out among the crowd and setting off our crackers. At one o'clock the Hon. Hezekiah Elkins mounted a platform in the middle of the Square and delivered an oration, to which his "feller-citizens" didn't pay much attention, having all they could do to dodge the squibs that were set loose upon them by mischievous boys stationed on the surrounding house tops.

Our little party, which had picked up recruits here and there, not being swayed by eloquence, withdrew to a booth on the outskirts of the crowd, where we regaled ourselves with root beer at two cents a glass. I recollect being much struck by the placard surmounting this tent: —

ROOT BEER SOLD HERE.

It seemed to me the perfection of pith and poetry. What could be more terse? Not a word to spare, and yet everything fully expressed. Rhyme and rhythm faultless. It was a delightful poet who made those verses. As for the beer itself, — that, I think, must have been made from the root of all evil! A single glass of it insured an uninterrupted pain for twenty-four hours.

The influence of my liberality working on Charley Marden, — for it was I who paid for the beer, — he presently invited us all to take an ice cream with him at Pettingil's saloon. Pettingil was the Delmonico of Rivermouth. He furnished ices and confectionery for aristocratic balls and parties, and didn't disdain to officiate as leader of the orchestra at the same; for Pettingil played on the violin, as Pepper Whitcomb described it, "like Old Scratch."

Pettingil's confectionery store was on the corner of Willow and High streets. The saloon, separated from the shop by a flight of three steps leading to a door hung with faded red drapery, had about it an air of mystery and seclusion quite delightful. Four windows, also draped, faced the side street, affording an unobstructed view of Marm Hatch's back yard, where a number of inexplicable garments on a clothesline were always to be seen careering in the wind.

There was a lull just then in the ice-cream business, it being dinner time, and we found the saloon unoccupied. When we had seated ourselves around the largest marble-topped table, Charley Marden in a manly voice ordered twelve six-penny ice creams, "strawberry and verneller mixed."

It was a magnificent sight, those twelve chilly glasses entering the room on a waiter, the red and white custard rising from each glass like a church steeple, and the spoon handle shooting up from the apex like a spire. I doubt if a person of the nicest palate could have distinguished, with his eyes shut, which was the vanilla and which the strawberry; but if I could at this moment obtain a cream tasting as that did, I would give five dollars for a very small quantity.

We fell to with a will, and so evenly balanced were our capabilities that we finished our creams together, the spoons clinking in the glasses like one spoon.

"Let's have some more!" cried Charley Marden, with the air of Aladdin ordering up a fresh hogshead of pearls and rubies. "Tom Bailey, tell Pettingil to send in another round."

Could I credit my ears? I looked at him to see if he were in earnest. He meant it. In a moment more I was leaning over the counter giving directions for a second supply. Thinking it would make no difference to such a gorgeous young sybarite as Marden, I took the liberty of ordering ninepenny creams this time.

On returning to the saloon, what was my horror at finding it empty!

There were the twelve cloudy glasses, standing in a circle on the sticky marble slab, and not a boy to be seen. A pair of hands letting go their hold on the window sill outside explained matters. I had been made a victim.

I couldn't stay and face Pettingil, whose peppery temper was well known among the boys. I hadn't a cent in the world to appease him. What should I do? I heard the clink of approaching glasses, — the ninepenny creams. I rushed to the nearest window. It was only five feet to the ground. I threw myself out as if I had been an old hat.

Landing on my feet, I fled breathlessly down High Street, through Willow, and was turning into Brierwood Place, when the sound of several voices, calling to me in distress, stopped my progress.

"Look out, you fool! the mine! the mine!" yelled the warning voices.

Several men and boys were standing at the head of the street, making insane gestures to me to avoid something. But I saw no mine, only in the middle of the road in front of me was a common flour barrel, which, as I gazed at it, suddenly rose into the air with a terrific explosion. I felt myself thrown violently off my feet. I remember nothing else, excepting that as I went up, I caught a momentary glimpse of Ezra Wingate leering through his shop window like an avenging spirit.

The mine that had wrought me woe was not properly a mine at all, but merely a few ounces of powder placed under an empty keg or barrel and fired with a slow match. Boys who didn't happen to have pistols or cannon generally burnt their powder in this fashion.

For an account of what followed I am indebted to hearsay, for I was insensible when the people picked me up and carried me home on a shutter borrowed from the proprietor of Pettingil's saloon. I was supposed to be killed, but happily (happily for me at least) I was merely stunned. I lay in a semiunconscious state until eight o'clock that night, when I attempted to speak. Miss Abigail, who watched by the bedside, put her ear down to my lips and was saluted with these remarkable words: —

"Strawberry and verneller mixed!"

"Mercy on us! what is the boy saying?" cried Miss Abigail.

"ROOTBEERSOLDHERE!"

BABY BELL.[1]

By THOMAS BAILEY ALDRICH.

I.

HAVE you not heard the poets tell
How came the dainty Baby Bell
Into this world of ours?
The gates of heaven were left ajar:
With folded hands and dreamy eyes,
Wandering out of Paradise,
She saw this planet, like a star,
Hung in the glistening depths of even —
Its bridges, running to and fro,
O'er which the white-winged Angels go,
Bearing the holy Dead to heaven.
She touched a bridge of flowers — those feet,

[1] Used by permission of Houghton, Mifflin & Co.

So light they did not bend the bells
Of the celestial asphodels,
They fell like dew upon the flowers:
Then all the air grew strangely sweet.
And thus came dainty Baby Bell
Into this world of ours.

II.

She came and brought delicious May;
The swallows built beneath the eaves;
Like sunlight, in and out the leaves
The robins went, the livelong day;
The lily swung its noiseless bell;
And on the porch the slender vine
Held out its cups of fairy wine.
How tenderly the twilights fell!
Oh, earth was full of singing birds
And opening springtide flowers,
When the dainty Baby Bell
Came to this world of ours.

III.

O Baby, dainty Baby Bell,
How fair she grew from day to day!
What woman nature filled her eyes,
What poetry within them lay —
Those deep and tender twilight eyes,
So full of meaning, pure and bright
As if she yet stood in the light
Of those oped gates of Paradise.
And so we loved her more and more:
Ah, never in our hearts before
Was love so lovely born.
We felt we had a link between
This real world and that unseen —
The land beyond the morn;
And for the love of those dear eyes,
For love of her whom God led forth,
(The mother's being ceased on earth
When Baby came from Paradise,) —
For love of Him who smote our lives,
And woke the chords of joy and pain,
We said, *Dear Christ!* — our hearts bowed down
Like violets after rain.

IV.

And now the orchards, which were white
And pink with blossoms when she came,
Were rich in autumn's mellow prime;
The clustered apples burnt like flame,
The folded chestnut burst its shell,
The grapes hung purpling, range on range:
And time wrought just as rich a change
In little Baby Bell.
Her lissom form more perfect grew,
And in her features we could trace,
In softened curves, her mother's face.
Her angel nature ripened too:
We thought her lovely when she came,
But she was holy, saintly now. . . .
Around her pale, angelic brow
We saw a slender ring of flame.

V.

God's hand had taken away the seal
That held the portals of her speech;
And oft she said a few strange words
Whose meaning lay beyond our reach.
She never was a child to us,
We never held her being's key;
We could not teach her holy things
Who was Christ's self in purity.

VI.

It came upon us by degrees,
We saw its shadow ere it fell—
The knowledge that our God had sent
His messenger for Baby Bell.
We shuddered with unlanguaged pain,
And all our hopes were changed to fears,
And all our thoughts ran into tears
Like sunshine into rain.
We cried aloud in our belief,
"Oh, smite us gently, gently, God!
Teach us to bend and kiss the rod,
And perfect grow through grief."
Ah! how we loved her, God can tell;
Her heart was folded deep in ours.
Our hearts are broken, Baby Bell!

VII.

At last he came, the messenger,
The messenger from unseen lands:
And what did dainty Baby Bell?
She only crossed her little hands,
She only looked more meek and fair!
We parted back her silken hair,
We wove the roses round her brow —
White buds, the summer's drifted snow—
Wrapt her from head to foot in flowers . . .
And thus went dainty Baby Bell
Out of this world of ours.

MONSIEUR VIPLE'S BROTHER.[1]

By PAUL BOURGET.

(From "Pastels of Men": translated by Katharine Prescott Wormeley.)

[Paul Bourget: A French novelist; born at Amiens, September 2, 1852. He studied at the Lycée of Clermont, and at the Collège de Sainte-Barbe at Paris. He began his literary life as a journalist, and in 1872 became a collaborator on the *Renaissance*. He is best known as a novelist, though probably equally able as a critic. He was made an officer of the Legion of Honor in 1886. His published works include: "La Vie Inquiète" (1874), "Les Aveux" (1882), "Ernest Renan" (1883), "Essais de la Psychologie Contemporaine" (1883), "L'Irréparable," "Deuxième Amour," "Profils Perdus" (1884), "Une Cruelle Énigme" (1885), "Un Crime d'Amour" (1886), "Nouveaux Essais de Psychologie Contemporaine" (1886), "Mensonges" (1888), "Études et Portraits," (2 vols., "Un Cœur de Femme" (1890), "Le Disciple" (1890), "Nouveaux Pastels" 1889), (1891), "Sensations d'Italie" (1891), "La Terre Promise" (1892), "Un Saint" (1894), "Outre-mer: Notes sur l'Amérique" (2 vols., 1895), "Un Idilio Trágico" (translated, 1896), and "Voyageuses" (1897.)]

One of the most exciting impressions of my childhood was the sojourn of the Austrian soldiers made prisoners during the campaign of 1859 in the provincial town where I grew up.

I recall this sojourn of the prisoners with strange uniforms (which was in fact very brief), because another recollection is attached to it, — that of an incident which long remained mysterious to my boyish mind, and on which I still reflect with passionate interest whenever I hear a discussion on the nature

[1] Copyright, 1891, by Roberts Brothers. Used by permission of Little, Brown & Co.

of children. I must add that the person who told it to me lives in my memory as one of the most original types which I knew in this old provincial town, where my ferreting eyes were already opening to every peculiarity of countenance and to the slightest oddity of behavior. He was an old friend of my family, once actively connected with the university and now retired with the function of inspector, who answered to the somewhat fantastic name of Monsieur Optat Viple, the man being as fantastic as the name. I see him now across the vanished years, as though he were coming from the cemetery to take his accustomed walk along the Cours Sablon in the sunshine, — very tall, very lean, his hat in his hand, with a pointed, bald head, spectacles on an endless nose, his overcoat buttoned tightly round his elongated waist, in summer as in winter, in winter as in summer, his feet incased in double-soled boots, which he never changed, even in the house, for fear of taking cold. He had kindly offered to teach me the rudiments of Latin and Greek for the pleasure of testing a method of his own, and I went every day at nine o'clock to take my lesson in his study before his dinner, which he invariably ate at ten o'clock, that he might sup (as they call it in those parts) at half-past five.

I remember, as though it were but yesterday, the morning when my old friend related to me the incident to which I just now made allusion. As the weather seemed uncertain, we had started for the Bughes, a sort of square planted with trees quite near the town and reached through the faubourg Saint-Allyre. We were just about to meet on the Poterne terrace a group of Austrian prisoners in their white uniforms, when Monsieur Viple, as if to avoid them, pulled me abruptly down the side street which leads to Notre Dame du Port, an old Roman basilica with a dark crypt. He was silent for some minutes. I looked into his furrowed face, on which the rounded point of his shirt collar was pressing, and I said to him suddenly, —

"Monsieur Viple, don't you want to look at those Austrians a little nearer?"

"No, my child," he said, with a look I had never yet seen on his face, — full, it seemed to me, of the shadow of some dark memory, — "the last time I saw their uniform was too dreadful."

"When was that?" I persisted.

PAUL BOURGET IN HIS STUDY

"At the time of the invasion," he replied. Then, as if making a calculation in his head, he added, "About forty-five years ago."

"Did they get as far as Issoire?" I asked, knowing that he came from that town.

"Yes, as far as Issoire," he answered slowly. Presently, as we were going down the road which leads to the station, he added, pointing to another parallel road, which is called the route to Issoire: "First they reached Clermont; then they came direct to us. Ah! our house was very near being burned at that time — yes, yes, even so. We did not expect them. We knew very well that the Emperor had been defeated, but we could not believe it was all over with him, — that devil of a man had won the game so often. And then, we loved him; my father loved him; he had seen him once reviewing his troops in the Carrousel after the campaign of Austerlitz. How often he told us of that wonderful blue eye which forced you to cry 'Vive l'Empereur!' by merely looking at you. And mind you, my boy, that Emperor was not like this present one. *He* was a man of the Revolution, a jacobin at heart, who wasn't afraid of *hommes noirs*. Enough, enough!"

"But why did the Austrians want to burn your house?" I asked with the persistency of a small boy who perceives a story and does not mean to let it escape him.

"The invaders arrived one evening," continued the old man, as if he had forgotten me, and was following the visions which crowded on his memory. "They were not very numerous, — a single detachment of cavalry, commanded by a tall officer, very young, with an insolent face and a long, fair mustache which almost floated in the wind. We had spent that day in horrible anxiety. We knew the enemy were at Clermont. Would they come to us, or would they not come? How ought we to receive them? A council was held at my father's house, for he was then mayor of the village. If he hadn't been so sick he was the man to put himself at the head of a determined troop and barricade the streets. Who knows whether, if all the towns and villages had done that, the allies might not have met the fate of our grumblers in Spain. There is but one policy for an invaded people, — guerrilla warfare and sharpshooting, the taking off of the enemy head by head. Yes, we might have defended ourselves. We had provisions, and all the peasantry round about had guns hanging to a nail in their chimneys. But my poor, dear father was in bed shaking with chills and fever, which he caught in the marshes of Courpières while snaring birds. So wiser counsels prevailed. Suddenly a burst of trumpets; the enemy were upon us! Ah, boy, may you never know what it is to hear the clarions sound a foreign march like that. Such superb disdain was in that blast, — disdain and hatred! How well I remember listening to it in my father's bedchamber, my forehead against the window panes as I watched the officer caracoling at the head of his troop; and when I turned away I saw the old man weeping."

"Then you ought to be pleased, Monsieur Viple, to see those very soldiers prisoners now," I said.

"Pleased? pleased! I have no confidence in this Emperor. But enough, enough!"

This was the customary exclamation of the old jacobin, when he did not wish to say anything I might repeat to the displeasure of my family. He continued his tale: —

"The Austrians had not been fifteen minutes in the town before they knocked violently at our door. The handsome officer with the long mustache chose to install himself in the mayor's house in company with two others, and I was ordered to move out of my room. I can see myself still, inveighing against them and hiding a pistol which I had loaded for the defense in a sort of cupboard, which served me for a poke-away. I was furious at having to leave my room, which was the prettiest in the house: it looked out upon a terrace where I played constantly, from which a flight of stone steps covered with mosses led down into the garden. Beneath it was the billiard room, and above a sort of attic to which I was relegated during the time the Austrian officers were in the house. They immediately ordered dinner; and as they were tired with their day's march, every one had to put his or her hand to the business of getting their meal ready at once. These three officers and six persons with them made nine, and that was a good many to provide for suddenly. However, we managed to get up a repast which my mother was anxious to make succulent. 'We must mollify them,' said the poor woman, as she sent me to the fish pond to catch some trout, — those beautiful fresh trout I was so fond of feeling slip through my fingers as I caught them. I was also sent to the cellar for champagne,

—four bottles of which my father used formerly to uncork for each of the great Emperor's victories. The supply was almost exhausted. I can't tell you my distress in having to prepare such a feast for these men with our own provisions in our own house, by this time noisy with their boisterous gayety, —the racket increasing and still increasing with laughter and the clinking of glasses as the meal went on. They drank toasts given in a language I had never heard. I listened to the noise from the kitchen, where it was decreed that we should take our own meals in the chimney corner. What were they toasting? Our defeat, no doubt, and the death of our poor Emperor. I was only twelve years old at the time, but I swear to you no one ever suffered more from anger and indignation than I did sitting on my little chair opposite to my mother. As a good housewife her mind dwelt chiefly on the breakage of the plates and glasses. 'I hope they have all they want,' she said anxiously to the servant. 'They want this, and they want that,' answered our good Michel; and this and that were accordingly sent in to them until the moment when Michel came into the kitchen with a troubled face. 'They want coffee!' he said."

"Coffee was easy enough to supply," I remarked, interrupting Monsieur Viple.

"Do you think so?" he replied. "You don't know, child, what rarities coffee and sugar were in those days. You have been told how the Emperor had the idea of a great continental blockade for the purpose of preventing all commerce between England and the European nations. Yes, it was an idea, and a great idea, though it came to nothing. However, it had the immediate result to us of the lesser bourgeoisie of diminishing and even stopping altogether the sale of certain foreign products. So, when the servant came in with this fresh demand, my mother was aghast. 'Coffee!' she cried; 'but we haven't an atom of it in the house. Go and tell them so.' Two minutes later Michel returned. 'They are drunk, madame,' he said; 'and they declare they will either have the coffee or smash everything.' 'Good God!' cried my mother, clasping her hands; 'and I have left my Sèvres set on the sideboard!'

"The racket in the dining room increased. The officers were rapping on the floor with their sabers and shouting till the window panes rattled. That good Michel of ours tried three several times to make them listen to reason, and three times he returned to us fairly routed by a shower of abuse.

They shouted: 'Coffee! coffee!' and the mere words, pronounced in the German way, seemed a hoarse growl of savagery. At last the uproar became so loud that the sound of it reached my father's room, and presently the kitchen door opened and his tall figure, wrapped in a brown dressing gown, with a foulard round the head, appeared, his eyes gleaming. 'What is all this?' he said, and I saw his lips tremble as he asked the question; with fever was it, or anger? They explained the matter to him. 'I will speak to them,' he said, and he went into the dining room. I followed him. I shall see that scene throughout my whole life,—the Austrian officers in their white uniforms, their faces flushed with drink, broken plates and bottles flung here and there upon the floor, the soiled cloth, and the smoke of their tobacco curling about the heads of our insolent conquerors. Yes, all my life I shall hear my father saying: 'Gentlemen, I give you my word of honor that I do not possess what you ask; I have risen from a sick bed to come here and ask you to respect the hearth on which I have received you as my guests.' He was hardly allowed to finish before the man with the long mustache, whose blue eyes gleamed with an evil look, rose and came up to him with a goblet of champagne in his hand. 'Very well!' he said in a tolerably pure accent, which showed him to be a man of superior education to his fellows, 'we will believe you if you will do us the pleasure of drinking to our august master, who has come here to save your country. Gentlemen, we will all drink to the health of our Emperor.'

"I looked at my father in terror, and, knowing him as I did, I saw that he was in a paroxysm of anger. He took the glass; then lifting it towards the portrait of Napoleon, which the brutes had not observed, he said in a ringing voice: 'Yes, gentlemen, long live the Emperor!' The officer with the long mustache followed the direction of my father's eyes. He saw the portrait,—an ordinary engraving. Breaking the glass and frame into fragments with one blow of his saber and refilling the glass my father had emptied, he cried brutally: 'Come, shout, "Long live the Emperor of Austria!" and make haste about it.'

"My father took the glass, raised it again, and said, 'Long live the Emperor!' 'Ha! you French scoundrel!' shouted the officer, and catching up a chair he struck my sick father a violent blow in the chest, flinging him backward with his head against the angle of a door, while my mother and the servants and I uttered cries of horror."

"Was he dead?" I asked, interrupting the old man.

"We thought he was," answered Monsieur Viple; "for we saw the blood reddening the white handkerchief about his head. But he lived, though it took him six months to recover from the shock of that blow."

"What did you do, Monsieur Viple?" I asked.

"I?" he said, hesitating, "nothing, absolutely nothing; but my brother——"

"Your brother? you never told me about him."

"No, he died young. We were nearly of an age; he was scarcely a year older than I. After he had gone to bed in his garret (for we had the same bedroom, and both of us were exiled to the attic), he began to think—think—think. Little boys in those days, you must know, were trained to be soldiers; they heard so much of fights and dangers and cannon balls and musquetry that there was very little they were afraid of. So after he went to bed he could think of nothing but the troubles of that miserable day, the arrival of the enemy, their entrance into the house, the preparations for dinner, the assault upon his father, the insults to the Emperor. He imagined the officer asleep in his own bed,—his, and he the son of that old man basely injured. Suddenly an idea of vengeance began to grow, to grow, in his little head. He knew the old house as you know yours, in every corner of it. It was built at various times, and the skylight of the attic room to which the boy was now consigned opened upon a gently sloping roof, with a ledge or coping some seven feet below it. By walking along that ledge one could reach an ivied wall; in the wall were iron spikes which made a sort of ladder by which to reach a chimney in one direction, and in the other a second ledge from which it was possible to get down upon the terrace which I mentioned to you. The room in which the officer slept opened upon this terrace; and so, you see, my brother got out of bed, dressed in haste, crept like a cat down the slope of the roof to the coping, then along the coping down the iron spikes to the terrace, and so to the window of his old room. 'Twas a warm summer's night. The officer had closed the blinds, but not the window. My brother made sure of this by passing his little hand through the heart-shaped hole in the shutter. He stretched out his arm and felt no glass. Close to the hole was a bit of twine which served to open the shutters from within. He was brave enough to pull it. 'The worst that can happen to me,' thought he, 'is to be caught. Well, if I am, I shall say that I had forgotten something in my room and came to get it.' A foolish excuse; but the boy was possessed by an idea. The shutter creaked as it opened, but no one stirred. The officer was sleeping soundly, — stupefied no doubt by wines and liquors. His snores echoed from the room in regular cadence. With all the precautions of a thief my brother glided along the floor till he reached the cupboard where he had seen me hide that pistol. He took it out. You can fancy how his heart beat. He stayed there perfectly still a quarter of an hour perhaps, crouching on the floor, hugging his weapon, without really knowing what he meant to do with it. The moonbeams entering through the window fell athwart the room, lighting it just enough to show a vague outline of the various objects. The officer slept on; still the same calm, unbroken sleep, proclaimed by the monotonous snore. An image of his father entered the child's mind. He saw the scene of the evening; that old man raising his glass towards the portrait; the chair flung upon him, then his fall, and the flowing blood. The boy half rose and crept to the bed. He could almost distinguish the features of the sleeper. He cocked the pistol — how tremendous such little sounds as that can seem in moments like these! He pointed the pistol to the corner of the man's ear, there, just there below the hair, and he fired ——"

"What then?" I exclaimed as he paused.

"Then," continued the old man, "he ran to the window, jumped the balustrade of the terrace, crept along the coping of one roof, climbed the iron spikes of the wall, and along the coping and slope of the other roof till he gained his room. Once there he closed the skylight, hid the pistol beneath his pillow and went to bed again, pretending to sleep, while a sudden uproar filled the house, showing that the pistol shot had wakened the household, who were doubtless searching for the murderer."

"Did they find him?"

"Never. Threats and search all failed. The Austrians wanted to burn the house down; they arrested our servants one by one, but each could show an alibi, fortunately, — my brother, too. But who would think of suspecting a child? Moreover, the dead man was hated by his soldiers and also by his superior officers."

"Ha! then he was really dead, was he? It served him right!" I cried.

"Yes, did it not? You think it was right, don't you?" asked the old inspector, his eyes glittering with a feverish recollection of a long past yet ever present memory.

"And your brother?" I persisted, "what became of him?"

"I have told you already that he died young," he replied.

Passing through Issoire a few years ago, I met, at the house of a distant relative of mine, an old lady over eighty years of age, who was a sort of cousin of my early friend the inspector. We talked of him a great deal, and, in the course of conversation, I chanced to say, —

"Did you know his brother?"

"What brother?" she asked.

"The one who died young."

"You are mistaken," she replied; "Optat never had a brother; he was an only son, — as I know very well, for I was brought up with him."

I then understood why it was that Monsieur Viple did not choose to cross the market place where the Austrian prisoners were assembled. He himself was the child who had avenged his outraged father, — he, the old university professor, who since that day had probably never touched a weapon. What strange mysteries are sometimes hidden in the depths of a peaceful and humble destiny!

ON HELL-FER-SARTAIN CREEK.[1]

By JOHN FOX, Jr.

(From "Hell fer Sartain.")

[John Fox, Jr.: An American author; born about 1860. He was graduated from Harvard in 1883, and was connected with New York newspapers for two or three years. He then went South for the benefit of his health, and there made a study of the mountaineers of the Cumberland Range. His first published work appeared in the *Century* in 1892, under the title "A Mountain

[1] Copyright, 1897, by Harper Brothers. Used by permission.

Europa," a novelette. His subsequent works are: "A Cumberland Vendetta and Other Stories" (1896), "Hell fer Sartain" (1897), and "The Kentuckians" (1898).]

THAR was a dancin' party Christmas night on "Hell fer Sartain." Jes tu'n up the fust crick beyond the bend thar, an' climb onto a stump, an' holler about *once*, an' you'll see how the name come. Stranger, hit's *hell* fer sartain! Well, Rich Harp was thar from the head waters, an' Harve Hall toted Nance Osborn clean across the Cumberlan'. Fust one ud swing Nance, an' then t'other. Then they'd take a pull out'n the same bottle o' moonshine, an' — fust one an' then t'other — they'd swing her agin. An' Abe Shivers asettin' thar by the fire abitin' his thumbs!

Well, things was sorter whoopin', when somebody ups an' tells Harve that Rich had said somep'n' agin Nance an' him, an' somebody ups an' tells Rich that Harve had said somep'n' agin Nance an' *him*. In a minute, stranger, hit was like two wild cats in thar. Folks got 'em parted, though, but thar was no more aswingin' of Nance that night. Harve toted her back over the Cumberlan', an' Rich's kinsfolks tuk him up "Hell fer Sartain"; but Rich got loose, an' lit out lickety-split fer Nance Osborn's. He knowed Harve lived too fer over Black Mountain to go home that night, an' he rid right across the river an' up to Nance's house, an' hollered fer Harve. Harve poked his head out'n the loft — he knowed whut was wanted — an' Harve says: "Uh, come in hyeh an' go to bed. Hit's too late!" An' Rich seed him agapin' like a chicken, an' in he walked, stumblin' might' nigh agin the bed whar Nance was alayin', listenin' an' not sayin' a word.

Stranger, them two fellers slept together plum frien'ly, an' they et together plum frien'ly next mornin', an' they sa'ntered down to the grocery plum frien'ly. An' Rich says, "Harve," says he, "let's have a drink." "All right, Rich," says Harve. An' Rich says, "Harve," says he, "you go out'n that door an' I'll go out'n this door." "All right, Rich," says Harve, an' out they walked, steady, an' thar was two shoots shot, an' Rich an' Harve both drapped, an' in ten minutes they was stretched out on Nance's bed an' Nance was alopin' away fer the yarb doctor.

The gal nussed 'em both, plum faithful. Rich didn't hev much to say, an' Harve didn't hev much to say. Nance was sorter quiet, an' Nance's mammy, ole Nance, jes grinned.

Folks come in to ax atter 'em right peart. Abe Shivers come cl'ar 'cross the river — powerful frien'ly — an' ever' time Nance ud walk out to the fence with him. One time she didn't come back, an' ole Nance fotched the boys thar dinner, an' ole Nance fotched thar supper, an' then Rich he axed whut was the matter with young Nance. An' ole Nance jes snorted. Atter a while Rich says: "Harve," says he, "who tol' you that I said that word agin you an' Nance?" "Abe Shivers," says Harve. "An' who tol' you," says Harve, "that I said that word agin Nance an' *you?*" "Abe Shivers," says Rich. An' both says, "Well, damn me!" An' Rich tu'ned right over an' begun pullin' straws out'n the bed. He got two out, an' he bit one off, an' he says: "Harve," says he, "I reckon we better draw fer him. The shortes' gits him." An' they drawed. Well, nobody ever knowed which got the shortes' straw, stranger, but ——

Thar'll be a dancin' party comin' Christmas night on "Hell fer Sartain." Rich Harp'll be thar from the head waters. Harve Hall's agoin' to tote the Widder Shivers clean across the Cumberlan'. Fust one'll swing Nance, an' then t'other. Then they'll take a pull out'n the same bottle o' moonshine, an' fust one an' then t'other — they'll swing her agin, jes the same. *Abe* won't be thar. He's asettin' by a bigger fire, I reckon (ef he ain't in it), abitin' his thumbs!

STORIES OF UNCLE REMUS.[1]

BY JOEL CHANDLER HARRIS.

(From "Nights with Uncle Remus.")

[JOEL CHANDLER HARRIS, American writer, was born at Eatonton, Ga., December 8, 1848, and has been successively printer, lawyer, and journalist. In 1890 he became editor of the Atlanta *Constitution*. He is best known as the author of books on negro folklore: "Uncle Remus: his Songs and his Sayings" (1880), "Nights with Uncle Remus," "Mingo, and Other Sketches," "Daddy Jake, the Runaway," etc. A "Life of Henry W. Grady," his predecessor on the *Constitution*, appeared in 1890.]

[1] Copyright, 1881, by the Century Co., and 1883 by Joel Chandler Harris. Published by permission of Houghton, Mifflin & Co.

Mr. Fox and Miss Goose.

It had been raining all day, so that Uncle Remus found it impossible to go out. The storm had begun, the old man declared, just as the chickens were crowing for day, and it had continued almost without intermission. The dark gray clouds had blotted out the sun, and the leafless limbs of the tall oaks surrendered themselves drearily to the fantastic gusts that drove the drizzle fitfully before them. The lady to whom Uncle Remus belonged had been thoughtful of the old man, and 'Tildy, the house girl, had been commissioned to carry him his meals. This arrangement came to the knowledge of the little boy at supper time, and he lost no time in obtaining permission to accompany 'Tildy.

Uncle Remus made a great demonstration over the thoughtful kindness of his "Miss Sally."

"Ef she aint one blessid w'ite 'oman," he said in his simple, fervent way, "den dey aint none un um 'roun' in deze parts."

With that he addressed himself to the supper, while the little boy sat by and eyed him with that familiar curiosity common to children. Finally the youngster disturbed the old man with an inquiry, —

"Uncle Remus, do geese stand on one leg all night, or do they sit down to sleep?"

"Tooby sho' dey does, honey; dey sets down same ez you does. Co'se, dey don't cross der legs," he added cautiously, "kase dey sets down right flat-footed."

"Well, I saw one the other day, and he was standing on one foot, and I watched him and watched him, and he kept on standing there."

"Ez ter dat," responded Uncle Remus, "dey mought stan' on one foot an drap off ter sleep en fergit deyse'f. Deze yer gooses," he continued, wiping the crumbs from his beard with his coat tail, "is mighty kuse fowls; deyer mighty kuse. In ole times dey wuz 'mongs de big bugs, en in dem days, w'en ole Miss Goose gun adinin' all de quality wuz dere. Likewise, en needer wuz dey stuckup, kase wid all der kyar'n's on, Miss Goose wer'n't too proud fer ter take in washin' fer de neighborhoods, en she make money, en get slick en fat lak Sis Tempy.

"Dis de way marters stan' w'en one day Brer Fox en Brer Rabbit, dey wuz settin' up at de cotton patch, one on one side de fence, en t'er one on t'er side, gwine on wid one er n'er, w'en fus' news dey know, dey year sump'n — *blim, blim, blim!*

"Brer Fox, he ax w'at dat fuss is, en Brer Rabbit, he up'n 'spon' dat it's ole Miss Goose down at de spring. Den Brer Fox, he up'n ax w'at she doin', en Brer Rabbit, he say, sezee, dat she battlin' cloze."

"Battling clothes, Uncle Remus?" said the little boy.

"Dat w'at dey call it dem days, honey. Deze times, dey rubs cloze on deze yer bodes w'at got furrers in um, but dem days dey des tuck'n tuck de cloze en lay um out on a bench, en ketch holt er de battlin' stick en natally paddle de fillin' outen um.

"W'en Brer Fox year dat ole Miss Goose wuz down dar dabblin' in soapsuds en washin' cloze, he sorter lick he chops, en 'low dat some er dese odd come shorts he gwine ter call en pay he 'specks. De minnit he say dat, Brer Rabbit, he know sump'n 'uz up, en he 'low ter hisse'f dat he 'speck he better whirl in en have some fun w'iles it gwine on. Bimeby Brer Fox up'n say ter Brer Rabbit, dat he bleedzd ter be movin' 'long todes home, en wid dat dey bofe say good-by.

"Brer Fox, he put out to whar his fambly wuz, but Brer Rabbit, he slip 'roun', he did, en call on ole Miss Goose. Ole Miss Goose she wuz down at de spring, washin', en b'ilin', en battlin' cloze; but Brer Rabbit he march up en ax her howdy, en den she tuck'n ax Brer Rabbit howdy.

"'I'd shake han's 'long wid you, Brer Rabbit,' sez she, 'but dey er all full er suds,' sez she.

"'No marter 'bout dat, Miss Goose,' sez Brer Rabbit, sezee, 'so long ez yo' will's good,' sezee."

"A goose with hands, Uncle Remus!" the little boy exclaimed.

"How you know goose aint got han's?" Uncle Remus inquired, with a frown. "Is you been sleepin' longer ole man Know-All? Little mo' en you'll up'n stan' me down dat snakes aint got no foots, and yit you take en lay a snake down yer 'fo' de fier, en his foots'll come out right 'fo' yo' eyes."

Uncle Remus paused here, but presently continued: —

"Atter ole Miss Goose en Brer Rabbit done pass de time er day wid one er n'er, Brer Rabbit, he ax 'er, he did, how she come on deze days, en Miss Goose say, mighty po'ly.

"'I'm gittin' stiff en I'm gittin' clumpsy,' sez she, 'en mo'n dat I'm gittin' bline,' sez she. 'Des 'fo' you happen 'long, Brer Rabbit, I drap my specks in de tub yer, en ef you'd 'a' come 'long 'bout dat time,' sez ole Miss Goose, sez she, 'I lay I'd er tuck you for dat nasty, owdashus Brer Fox, en it ud er bin a born blessin' ef I hadn't er scald you wid er pan er b'ilin suds,' sez she. 'I'm dat glad I foun' my specks I dunner w'at ter do,' sez ole Miss Goose,' sez she.

"Den Brer Rabbit, he up'n say dat bein's how Sis Goose done fotch up Brer Fox name, he got sump'n fer ter tell 'er, en den he let out 'bout Brer Fox gwine ter call on 'er.

"'He comin',' sez Brer Rabbit, sezee; 'he comin' sho', en w'en he come hit'll be des 'fo' day,' sezee.

"Wid dat, ole Miss Goose wipe 'er han's on 'er apun, en put 'er specks up on 'er forrerd, en look lak she done got trouble in 'er mine.

"'Laws a massy!' sez she, 'spozen he come, Brer Rabbit! W'at I gwine do? En dey aint a man 'bout de house, n'er,' sez she.

"Den Brer Rabbit, he shot one eye, en he say, sezee: —

"'Sis Goose, de time done come w'en you bleedzd ter roos' high. You look lak you got de dropsy,' sezee, 'but don't mine dat, kase ef you don't roos' high, youer goner,' sezee.

"Den ole Miss Goose ax Brer Rabbit w'at she gwine do, en Brer Rabbit he up'n tell Miss Goose dat she mus' go home en tie up a bundle er de w'ite folks cloze, en put um on de bed, en den she mus' fly up on a rafter, en let Brer Fox grab de cloze en run off wid um.

"Ole Miss Goose say she much 'blige, en she tuck'n tuck her things en waddle off home, en dat night she do lak Brer Rabbit say wid de bundle er cloze, en den she sont wud ter Mr. Dog, en Mr. Dog he come down, en say he'd sorter set up wid 'er.

"Des' fo' day, yer come Brer Fox creepin' up, en he went en push on de do' easy, en de do' open, en he see sump'n w'ite on de bed w'ich he took fer Miss Goose, en he grab it en run. 'Bout dat time Mr. Dog sail out fum und' de house, he did, en ef Brer Fox hadn't er drapt de cloze, he'd er got kotch. Fum dat, wud went 'roun' dat Brer Fox bin tryin' ter steal Miss Goose cloze, en he come mighty nigh losin' his stannin' at Miss Meadows. Down ter dis day," Uncle Remus continued, preparing to fill his pipe, "Brer Fox b'leeve dat Brer Rabbit wuz de 'casion er Mr. Dog bein' in de neighborhoods at dat time er night, en Brer Rabbit aint 'spute it. De bad feelin' 'twix' Brer Fox en Mr. Dog start right dar, en hits bin agwine on twel now dey aint git in smellin' distuns er one er n'er widout deys a row."

The Pimmerly Plum.

One night, when the little boy had grown tired of waiting for a story, he looked at Uncle Remus, and said, —

"I wonder what ever became of old Brother Tarrypin."

Uncle Remus gave a sudden start, glanced all around the cabin, and then broke into a laugh that ended in a yell like a view halloo.

"Well, well, well! How de name er goodness come you ter know wa'at runnin' on in my min', honey? Mon, you skeer'd me; you sho'ly did; en w'en I git skeer'd I bleedz ter holler. Let 'lone dat, ef I keep on gittin' skeerder en skeerder, you better gimme room, kaze ef I can't git 'way fum dar somebody gwine ter git hurted, en deyer gwine ter git hurted bad. I tell you dat right pine blank.

"Ole Brer Tarrypin!" continued Uncle Remus, in a tone of exultation. "Ole Brer Tarrypin! Now, who bin year tell er de beat er dat? Dar you sets studyin' 'bout ole Brer Tarrypin, en yer I sets studyin' 'bout ole Brer Tarrypin. Hit make me feel so kuse dat little mo' en I'd a draw'd my Rabbit foot en shuck it at you."

The little boy was delighted when Uncle Remus went off into these rhapsodies. However nonsensical they might seem to others, to the child they were positively thrilling, and he listened with rapt attention, scarcely daring to stir.

"Ole Brer Tarrypin? Well, well, well! —

"W'en in he prime
He tuck he time!

"Dat w'at make he hol' he age so good. Dey tells me dat somebody 'cross dar in Jasper County, tuck'n kotch a Tarrypin w'ich he got marks cut in he back dat 'uz put dar fo' our folks went fer ter git revengeance in de Moccasin war. Dar whar yo' Unk' Jeems bin," Uncle Remus explained, noticing the little boy's look of astonishment.

"Oh!" exclaimed the child, "that was the Mexican war."

"Well," responded Uncle Remus, closing his eyes with a sigh, "I aint one er deze yer kinder folks w'at choke deyse'f wid names. One name aint got none de 'vantage er no yuther name. En ef de Tarrypin got de marks on 'im hit don't make

31

no diffunce whe'er yo' Unk' Jeems Abercrombie git his revengeance out'n de Moccasin folks, er whe'er he got it out'n de Mackersons."

"Mexicans, Uncle Remus."

"Tooby sho', honey; let it go at dat. But don't less pester ole Brer Tarrypin wid it, kaze he done b'long ter a tribe all by he own 'lone se'f. — I 'clar' ter gracious," exclaimed the old man, after a pause, "ef hit don't seem periently lak 'twuz yistiddy!"

"What, Uncle Remus?"

"Oh, des ole Brer Tarrypin, honey; des ole Brer Tarrypin en a tale w'at I year 'bout 'im, how he done tuck'n do Brer Fox."

"Did he scare him, Uncle Remus?" the little boy asked, as the old man paused.

"No, my goodness! Wuss'n dat!"

"Did he hurt him?"

"No, my goodness! Wuss'n dat!"

"Did he kill him?"

"No, my goodness! Lots wuss'n dat!"

"Now, Uncle Remus, what *did* he do to Brother Fox?"

"Honey!" — here the old man lowered his voice as if about to describe a great outrage — "Honey! he tuck'n make a fool out'n 'im!"

The child laughed, but it was plain that he failed to appreciate the situation, and this fact caused Uncle Remus to brighten up and go on with the story.

"One time w'en de sun shine down mighty hot, ole Brer Tarrypin wuz gwine 'long down de road. He 'uz gwine 'long down, en he feel mighty tired; he puff, en he blow, en he pant. He breff come lak he got de azmy 'way down in he win'pipe; but, nummine! he de same ole Creep-um-crawl-um Have-some-fun-um. He 'uz gwine 'long down de big road, ole Brer Tarrypin wuz, en bimeby he come ter de branch. He tuck'n crawl in, he did, en got 'im a drink er water, en den he crawl out on t'er side en set down und' de shade un a tree. Atter he sorter ketch he win', he look up at de sun fer ter see w'at time er day is it, en lo en beholes! he tuck'n skivver dat he settin' in de shade er de sycamo' tree. No sooner is he skivver dis dan he sing de ole song: —

"'Good luck ter dem w'at come and go,
W'at set in de shade er de sycamo'.'

"Brer Tarrypin he feel so good in de shade so cool, dat twa'n't long fo' he got ter noddin', en bimeby he drapt off en went soun' asleep. Co'se, Brer Tarrypin kyar he house wid 'im eve'ywhar he go, en w'en he fix fer ter go ter sleep, he des shet de do' en pull too de winder shetters, en dar he is des ez snug ez de ole black cat und' de barn.

"Brer Tarrypin lay dar, he did, en sleep, en sleep. He dunner how long he sleep, but bimeby he feel somebody foolin' 'long wid 'im. He keep de do' shet, en he lay dar en lissen. He feel somebody tu'nin' he house 'roun' en 'roun'. Dis sorter skeer Brer Tarrypin, kaze he know dat ef dey tu'n he house upside down, he 'ull have all sorts er times gittin' back. Wid dat he open de do' little ways, en he see Brer Fox projickin' wid 'im. He open de do' little furder, he did, en he break out in a great big hoss laff, en holler: —

"'Well! well, well! Who'd a thunk it! Ole Brer Fox, cuter dan de common run, is done come en kotch me. En he come at sech a time, too! I feels dat full twel I can't see straight skacely. Ef dey wuz any jealousness proned inter me, I'd des lay yer en pout kaze Brer Fox done fine out whar I gits my Pimmerly Plum.'

"In dem days," continued Uncle Remus, speaking to the child's look of inquiry, "de Pimmerly Plum wuz monst'us skace. Leavin' out Brer Rabbit en Brer Tarrypin dey wa'n't none er de yuther creeturs dat yuvver got a glimp' un it, let 'lone a tas'e. So den w'en Brer Fox year talk er de Pimmerly Plum, bless gracious! he h'ist up he head en let Brer Tarrypin 'lone. Brer Tarrypin keep on laffin' en Brer Fox 'low: —

"'Hush, Brer Tarrypin! you makes my mouf water! Whar'bouts de Pimmerly Plum?'

"Brer Tarrypin, he sorter cle'r up de ho'seness in he throat, en sing: —

> "'Poun' er sugar, en a pint er rum,
> Aint nigh so sweet ez de Pimmerly Plum!'

"Brer Fox, he lif' up he han's, he did, en holler: —

"'Oh, hush, Brer Tarrypin! you makes me dribble! Whar'bouts dat Pimmerly Plum?'

"'You stannin' right und' de tree, Brer Fox!'

"'Brer Tarrypin, sho'ly not!'

"'Yit dar you stan's, Brer Fox!'

"Brer Fox look up in de tree dar, en he wuz 'stonish'."

"What did he see in the sycamore tree, Uncle Remus?" inquired the little boy.

There was a look of genuine disappointment on the old man's face, as he replied: —

"De gracious en de goodness, honey! Aint you nev' is see dem ar little bit er balls w'at grow on de sycamo' tree?"

The little boy laughed. There was a huge sycamore tree in the center of the circle made by the carriage way in front of the "big house," and there were sycamore trees of various sizes all over the placc. The little balls alluded to by Uncle Remus are very hard at certain stages of their growth, and cling to the tree with wonderful tenacity. Uncle Remus continued: —

"Well, den, w'en ole Brer Tarrypin vouch dat dem ar sycamo' balls wuz de ginnywine Pimmerly Plum, ole Brer Fox, he feel mighty good, yit he dunner how he gwine git at um. Push 'im clos't, en maybe he mought beat Brer Tarrypin clammin' a tree, but dish yer sycamo' tree wuz too big fer Brer Fox fer ter git he arms 'roun'. Den he up'n low, —

"'I sees um hangin' dar, Brer Tarrypin, but how I gwine git um?'

"Brer Tarrypin open he do' little ways en holler out: —

"'Ah yi! Dar whar ole Slickum Slow-come got de 'vantage! Youer mighty peart, Brer Fox, yit somehow er nudder you aint bin akeepin' up wid ole Slickum Slow-come.'

"'Brer Tarrypin, how de name er goodness does you git um?'

"'Don't do no good fer ter tell you, Brer Fox. Nimble heel make restless min'. You aint got time fer ter wait en git um, Brer Fox.'

"'Brer Tarrypin, I got all de week befo' me.'

"'Ef I tells you, you'll go en tell all de te'er creeturs, en den dat'll be de las' er de Pimmerly Plum, Brer Fox.'

"'Brer Tarrypin, dat I won't. Des try me one time en see.'

"Brer Tarrypin shet he eye lak he studyin', en den he 'low:

"'I tell you how I does, Brer Fox. W'en I wants a bait er de Pimmerly Plum right bad, I des takes my foot in my han' en comes down yer ter dish yer tree. I comes en I takes my stan'. I gits right und' de tree, en I r'ars my head back en opens my mouf. I opens my mouf, en w'en de Pimmerly Plum draps, I boun' you she draps right spang in dar. All you got ter do is ter set en wait, Brer Fox.'

"Brer Fox aint sayin' nothin'. He des sot down und' de tree, he did, en r'ar'd he head back, en open he mouf, en I wish ter goodness you mought er bin had er chance fer ter see 'im settin' dar. He look scan'lous, dat's de long en de short un it; he des look scan'lous."

"Did he get the Pimmerly Plum, Uncle Remus?" asked the little boy.

"*Shoo!* How he gwine git plum whar dey aint no plum?"

"Well, what did he do?"

"He sot dar wid he mouf wide open, en eve'y time Brer Tarrypin look at 'im, much ez he kin do fer ter keep from bustin' aloose en laffin'. But bimeby he make he way todes home, Brer Tarrypin did, chucklin' en laffin', en 'twa'n't long 'fo' he meet Brer Rabbit tippin' 'long down de road. Brer Rabbit, he hail 'im.

"'W'at 'muze you so mighty well, Brer Tarrypin?'

"Brer Tarrypin kotch he breff atter so long a time, en he 'low: —

"'Brer Rabbit, I'm dat tickle' twel I can't shuffle 'long, skacely, en I'm fear'd ef I up'n tell you de 'casion un it, I'll be tooken wid one er my spells whar folks hatter set up wid me kaze I laugh so loud en laugh so long.'

"Yit atter so long a time, Brer Tarrypin up'n tell Brer Rabbit, en dey sot dar en chaw'd terbacker en kyar'd on des lak sho' nuff folks. Dat dey did!"

Uncle Remus paused; but the little boy wanted to know what became of Brer Fox.

"Hit's mighty kuse," said the old man, stirring around in the ashes as if in search of a potato, "but endurin' er all my days I aint nev' year nobody tell 'bout how long Brer Fox sot dar waitin' fer de Pimmerly Plum."

TO PEPA.[1]

By ALFRED DE MUSSET.

(Translated by Toru Dutt.)

[Louis Charles Alfred de Musset, French poet and dramatist, was born in Paris, November 11, 1810. Hesitating in the choice of a profession, he successively tried and abandoned law, medicine, and painting, and ultimately,

[1] From "A Sheaf gleaned in French Fields." By permission of Kegan Paul, Trench, Trübner & Co.

under the influence of the so-called romantic movement, applied himself to literature, making his début as an author with "Contes d'Espagne et d'Italie" (1830). In 1833 he went to Italy with George Sand; but, after an extended trip, fell out with her at Venice, and returned to France alone. He was librarian to the Department of the Interior under Louis Philippe, and in 1852 was received at the French Academy. Irregular and dissolute living undermined his health, and he died at Paris, May 1, 1857. Among his noteworthy works are: the poem "Namouna"; "The Confession of a Child of the Century"; and the plays "Fantasio," "Barberine," "Lorenzaccio," "On ne badine pas avec l'Amour" ("One does not play with Love"), etc.]

PÉPA! when the night has come,
And Mamma has bid Good Night,
By thy light, half clad and dumb,
As thou kneelest out of sight,—

Laid by cap and sweeping vest
Ere thou sinkest to repose,
At the hour when half at rest
Folds thy soul as folds a rose,—

When sweet Sleep, the sovereign mild,
Peace to all the house has brought,
Pépita! my charming child!
What, O what is then thy thought?

Who knows? Haply dreamest thou
Of some lady doomed to sigh,
All that Hope a truth deems now,
All that Truth shall prove a lie.

Haply of those mountains grand
That produce — alas! but mice;
Castles in Spain; a Prince's hand;
Bonbons, lovers, or cream ice.

Haply of soft whispers breathed
'Mid the mazes of a ball;
Robes, or flowers, or hair enwreathed
Me; — or nothing, Dear! at all.

WHAT THE SWALLOWS SAY.[1]

By THÉOPHILE GAUTIER.

[1811-1872.]

(Translated by Toru Dutt.)

Leaves, not green but red and gold,
  Fall and dot the yellow grass;
Morn and eve the wind is cold:
  Sunny days are gone, alas!

Showers lift bubbles on the pool;
  Peasants harvest work dispatch;
Winter comes apace to rule;
  Swallows cluster on the thatch.

Hundreds, hundreds of the race
  Gathered, hold a high debate,
One says — "Athens is my place:
  Thither shall I emigrate.

"Every year I go and build
  On the famous Parthenon:
Thus the cornice hole is filled, —
  Mark of an insulting gun!"

"Smyrna suits my humbler needs," —
  Says a second, twittering gay:
"Hadjis there count amber beads,
  Sitting in the sun's bright ray.

"In a café's little room,
  Where chibouks a vapor raise,
Floating 'mid the strange perfume,
  Turbans shall I, skimming, graze."

"Balbec! triglyph that I love!
  Thee again," — says one, "I seek;
There shall I hang soon above
  Little ones with open beak."

One cries out, — "Lo, my address!
  Rhodes, the palace of the Knights;
Year by year my nest I tress
  On the black stone pillar heights."

[1] From "A Sheaf gleaned in French Fields." By permission of Kegan Paul, Trench, Trübner & Co.

Says a fifth — "Old age, you see,
  Weighs me down, I scarce can fly;
Malta's terraced rock for me!
  Azure wave and azure sky."

And the sixth, — "In Cairo fair,
  On a lofty minaret,
Mud headquarters lined with hair,
  Make me winter quite forget."

"At the Second Cataract,"
  Says the last, — "'mid beauties brown,
Is my nest; the place exact
  Is a granite monarch's crown."

All, — "To-morrow many miles,
  File by file, we shall have gone;
Peaks of snow and plains and isles
  Vanish far — yet on! — still on!"

Twinkling bright their eyes of jet,
  Clapping wings in brotherhood,
Twitter thus the swallows met,
  When the rust is on the wood.

All they say I understand:
  For the poet is a bird,
Captive, broken-winged, and banned,
  Struggling still, though oft unheard.

O for wings! for wings! for wings!
  As sings Rückert in his song:
To fly with the birds and Springs
  Wheresoever the sun shines long.

5
5957
10/8/90